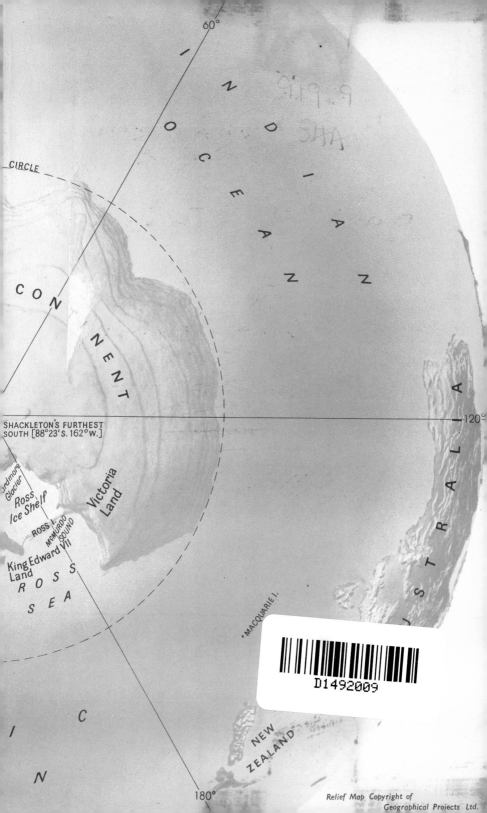

CIRCLE

INDIAN OCEAN

CONTINENT

60°

SHACKLETON'S FURTHEST
SOUTH [88°23'S. 162°W.]

120°

Beardmore Glacier
Ross Ice Shelf
ROSS I.
MCMURDO SOUND
Victoria Land
King Edward VII Land
R O S S
S E A

MACQUARIE I.

AUSTRALIA

C
I
N

NEW ZEALAND

180°

SHACKLETON

MARGERY AND
JAMES FISHER

SHACKLETON

DRAWINGS BY W. E. HOW
WHO SERVED WITH THE
ENDURANCE EXPEDITION

BARRIE

JAMES BARRIE BOOKS LTD
3-4 St. Clement's Inn, London, W.C.2

Made and printed in Great Britain by
WILLIAM CLOWES AND SONS, LIMITED, LONDON AND BECCLES

BLOCKS BY EROS ENGRAVING LTD.

TO GRUFFY

CONTENTS

List of Illustrations

PLATES

MAPS AND LINE ILLUSTRATIONS

Authors' Preface

IT is not easy to find the truth about any character who is in the process of passing into history, especially when the character is as complex as that of Ernest Shackleton. Shackleton died in 1922. About half the men who explored with him are still alive and well. Indeed, this book has been written under the eyes of Shackleton's own generation by two people of the next generation who neither saw nor heard him. When the writers of this biography were children Shackleton was a living hero. Few of those who knew him can speak or write of him without emotion. At least the writers were able to start their task dispassionately and impersonally, and would like to think that they have finished it so. This is for others to judge.

In the preparation of this biography, the writers have had full access to the principal repositories of documents concerning Ernest Shackleton. Prime among these is the collection which is the property of Shackleton's only daughter, Miss Cecily Shackleton. Nearly all the personal diaries and memoranda of Ernest Shackleton are in this collection,* as are (probably all) his letters to his wife. All documents quoted in this book, incidentally, are quoted with the original literal mistakes and punctuation. It emerges from this faithful transcription, as the reader will see, that Ernest Shackleton's punctuation was eccentric but consistent.

Miss Cecily Shackleton made the Shackleton papers available to the writers without any conditions or reservations (as far as this book is concerned). We are specially grateful to her and to Mr. Edward Shackleton for many hours of help. While expressing disagreement with us on occasions at no time did they attempt to influence the scope or direction of our investigations. The facts and conclusions in this book are the entire responsibility of the authors, and in so far as they may err the reader may blame nobody but them. In the following acknowledgements is a complete list of those whom we wish to thank for information. We apologise to them for any mistakes or misjudgments we may have made in the use of it. As well as the Shackleton family, practically all those whom we sought have opened their hearts or their files to us without any sort of reservation. These include the Royal Geographical Society, the Royal Scottish Geographical Society and the Scott Polar Research

* These papers have been designated S.F.P. (Shackleton family papers) throughout this book, for convenience, although they are the property of Miss Cecily Shackleton.

Institute. Some have not only contributed much time in tape-recorded interviews, and much unpublished information, including personal diaries, but have also responded to our request to read all or part of the book in manuscript or in proof. In thanking Sir Jameson Boyd Adams, Commander A. E. Harbord, Dr. L. D. A. Hussey, Dr. A. H. Macklin, Dr. J. W. S. Marr, Sir Raymond Priestley, Mr. R. W. Richards and Sir James Wordie, most particularly, we would reiterate that none bears any responsibility for the final form of this book.

This book has been planned and written by Margery Fisher. James Fisher's chief rôle has been the collection of information, often armed with the biographer's new ally, the tape-recorder. These tape-recorded interviews, some of which lasted many hours, were faithfully transcribed and the transcript submitted to the person interviewed for a final control and checking, and no quotations or deviations have been made from such interviews without the express permission of the person interviewed.

Possibly the next generation may be able to reach a fuller objectivity about one of the greatest explorers the world has known. It is not easy to write of someone so close to many who survive. Yet, though Shackleton is so close to many survivors of his own generation and his children's generation, he seems a surprisingly vague figure already to the next one.

During their investigations the writers circulated a questionnaire to the boys of three famous public schools and two famous grammar schools. Only a few boys remembered anything about the wreck of the *Endurance*, and one or two of them thought that Shackleton had died in the ice on that expedition. Often his achievements were identified with those of Robert Falcon Scott—indeed, a few believed that he had actually reached the South Pole. It is true that a few had heard of his remarkable journey across South Georgia, but as many thought that he had tried for the North Pole or for the North-West Passage. He was confused not only with Scott but with Greely, Franklin and Amundsen. Some thought that he was lost when flying over the North Pole, others that he was lost when climbing Everest, others that he was set adrift in a boat in the Arctic by mutineers and died of exposure.

Shackleton's true life was an inspiration to the fathers of these muddled boys. It is thirty years since his biography was written. We are sure that it will have to be written again some years from now, when the cool judgments of history replace the warmer judgments of his contemporaries. We offer this book, therefore, as an interim study of a great man.

M.F.

J.F.

Ashton, Northampton, July 1957

Acknowledgements

The list of organisations and persons who have helped this book is a long one, including as it does many surviving relations and friends of Ernest Shackleton, and nearly all the known survivors of the expeditions which he led. Some have endured many hours of questioning for tape recordings; all have contributed at least one fact not gleaned by us from any other source. We are deeply grateful to them for their time, in libraries, in correspondence, or in interviews.

The *Admiralty* (J. M. M. McKay and R. A. Davey, Record Office), the *American Geographical Society* (Charles B. Hitchcock, Director), the *Australian External Affairs Office*.

The *Berkshire Record Office* (Peter Walne, Archivist), the *Bond Street Association* (Alan Whitworth), the *British Film Institute* (Ernest Lindgren, Curator National Film Archive), the *British Museum* (Bloomsbury and Colindale).

The *Chilean Foreign Office*, Santiago (José Miguel Barros), the *Colonial Office* (B. Cheeseman, Librarian).

The *Daily Mail* (Editorial Department).

The *Eton College Library*, the *Explorers' Club, New York* (Serge Korff, President).

Wm. Heinemann, publishers (Allen Hill), *His Master's Voice* (record division), *Housewife* (Hulton Press—especially Miss Caroline Mackinlay).

Lloyd's (especially Wilfrid Hatch), *Lloyd's Bank* (Lombard Street branch), the *London Library*.

News Chronicle (correspondence department), the *Northampton County Library* (especially Miss S. Brothers).

Permutit Ltd. (R. T. Pemberton), the *Public Record Office* (H. Noel Blakiston, Director of the Public Search Rooms).

The *Royal Geographical Society* (L. P. Kirwan, Director and Secretary, and G. R. Crone, Librarian and Map Curator), the *Royal Scottish Geographical Society* (Squadron-Leader B. K. D. Robertson, Secretary), the *Royal Society* (Dr. D. C. Martin, Secretary).

The *Scott Polar Research Institute* (Dr. G. C. L. Bertram, Director, Dr. B. B. Roberts, Senior Research Fellow, Dr. T. E. Armstrong, Research Fellow, H. G. R. King, Librarian and Information Officer, Miss A. M. Savours, Assistant Librarian and Information Officer), *Her Majesty's Stationery Office*.

The *Ministry of Transport* (Percy Faulkner), the *Treasury* (D. J. D. Clark, Information Division), the *Alexander Turnbull Library, Wellington, N.Z.* (especially Mrs. Margaret Broadbent).

The *War Office* (Under Secretary of State's Department), *Wintle and Co.* (R. A. Williams).

The *Zoological Society of London* (G. B. Stratton, Librarian).
Commander Sir Jameson Adams, R.N.R. (retd.), Miss J. Atkinson.
William L. Bakewell, Captain Michael Barne, R.N. (retd.), Captain
Thomas Barlow, R.N., James Barrie, George Barry, Stanley Bell,
Alfred Berry, Major-General Sir Wilfred Beveridge, A. F. Birch-Jones,
Sir Harry Brittain, Lieutenant-Colonel Sir Philip Brocklehurst, Bart.,
Miss Barbara Bruce, J. McL. Buckley, Mr. and Mrs. Richard Buckley,
John M. Bunting.
Colonel H. M. Cadell, Air Marshal Sir Roderick Carr, Duncan
Carse, Mrs. B. C. Cass, M. C. Christison, Miss M. Clayton, G.
Constantinescu, Miss A. Conway, Miss Mildred Crosby.
W. E. Dance, Mrs. E. C. Davies, Captain Lionel Dawson, R.N.,
Prof. Frank Debenham, J. W. Dell, Mrs. Stella Donald, Prof. G.
Vibert Douglas.
Miss Norah Enderby, Mrs. Rupert England, H. E. J. Evans, Mrs.
Richard Eyre.
Dr. R. A. Falla, Mrs. Freda Fee, E. B. Fisher, K. N. Fisher, Charles
Ford, Lieutenant-Commander M. J. N. Foster, R.N.
Miss Valerie Gould, Mrs. Pamela Gow, C. J. Green, Commander
Lionel Greenstreet, R.N.R. (retd.).
Commander A. E. Harbord, R.N. (retd.), C. H. Hare, Humphrey
Hare, Mrs. Ruth Hatch, Dudley S. Heesom, F. L. Horton, W. E. How,
B. C. Howell, Captain J. Frank Hurley, Dr. L. D. A. Hussey.
Dr. L. Jacobs, Prof. R. W. James, Mrs. E. S. Jutsum.
A. Keith Jack, A. Keve, Major Maxwell Knight.
Sir Shane Leslie, Bart., Mrs. Henrietta Lomas, Dr. T. G. Longstaff,
Mrs. M. C. Lovell.
D. J. Macaulay, A. B. MacDuff, Dr. J. A. McIlroy, Dr. A. H.
Macklin, Lieutenant-Commander J. W. S. Marr, R.N.V.R., Dr. Eric
S. Marshall, Prof. Sir Douglas Mawson, Malcolm Miller, H. J. Mills.
Christopher Naisbitt, Martin Nettleton.
Lieutenant-Colonel T. Orde-Lees.
Thomas Peers, Ernest M. Perris, A. W. Phillips, Mrs. George
Pitcairn, Frank Plumley, Mrs. I. H. Powell-Edwards, Sir John Pratt,
Sir Raymond Priestley.
L. A. Quartermain.
R. W. Richards, Captain E. Ritchie, R.N., Mrs. J. Q. Rowett.
Miss Alice Saunders, Mrs. Edward Saunders, Theodore Savory,
Peter M. Scott, Miss Shackleton (Dublin), Miss Cecily Shackleton,
Edward Shackleton, Miss Eleanor Shackleton, Miss Gladys Shackleton,
Miss Kathleen Shackleton, Raymond Shackleton, Gilbert Simons,
Mrs. L. Sims.
Mrs. E. Thomson, James Thomson, K. Graham Thomson, Mrs. V.
Thomson, Mrs. E. G. Thornton, Mrs. M. E. Tindall, L. O. H. Tripp,
Sir Henry Turner.
Sir Hubert Wilkins, A. E. Wilson, Mrs. Peter Wood, Sir James
Wordie, Mrs. Frank Worsley.

Chapter I

ERNEST SHACKLETON was a great explorer who discovered his true bent almost by chance. There was no tradition in his family to send him in the direction of the Antarctic: no tradition of seafaring or adventuring. The Shackletons were teachers, landowners, cultivated folk; his father was a doctor practising in a London suburb. Other men—Amundsen, for instance, or Byrd—spent their youth in a devoted apprenticeship to polar work. Ernest Shackleton first entered upon it as a way to fame and fortune. Fortune eluded him: fame came to him but did not satisfy him. He found something better in the Antarctic—a challenge to every talent he possessed, a challenge which he never resisted.

Shackleton was a fighter. If the circumstances of his life had not led him, at a certain time, to join an Antarctic expedition, he might have become a great general, a great headmaster, a great politician. He could not have led an ordinary life. His energy, his combative temperament, his vision of something unknown, would have pushed him to the forefront, in whatever sphere he entered. He could not rest on his achievements. The mere fact of being alive was to him an invitation to action: the power that was in him would not let him rest. He is famous now not as a man who was a brilliant success but as a man who was a splendid failure—who fought against enormous odds and never gave in. If his great failures had been successes, they could not have satisfied him. It was the fight that he wanted, not the result or the prize. It has often been said that this combative side of Shackleton came from his north-country forebears. This is little more than a convenient shorthand. Shackleton's courage and belligerence were not 'north country' any more than his charm or his love of poetry were 'Irish'. A study of his family can only supply a background for him; it cannot explain him.

Ernest Henry Shackleton was born on 15 February 1874, the second child and elder son of Henry Shackleton of Kilkea, County Kildare. Henry Shackleton came of Yorkshire stock, but his family had lived in Ireland for four generations.

The name came from the village of Shackleton, near Heptonstall, in the West Riding. The family is known to have settled in Keighley towards the end of the fifteenth century and to have resided in Bingley in 1591. Ernest Shackleton could trace his line back to John Shackleton, who left Shackleton House to his son Roger in 1654; the property went to Roger's son Richard in 1675.

I

Richard Shackleton at some time in his life became a Quaker, and for a century the family lived in this discipline. It was Richard Shackleton's younger son Abraham who migrated to Ireland. Born in 1696, a delicate and backward child, he was orphaned before he was ten. His gift for learning and teaching was strong, and he so successfully worked to educate himself that he was invited by some Quaker friends to go to Ireland as a private tutor. Later, with his wife, who was also of Yorkshire stock, he opened a boarding school for boys at Ballitore, in County Kildare.

This school was to become known as the Eton of Ireland. Abraham's son Richard carried it on from 1756. Richard had studied at Trinity College, Dublin, the first Quaker to do so. He had married first an Irish wife (Elizabeth Fuller of Ballitore) who gave him a son, Abraham; next, Elizabeth Carleton, whose daughter Mary afterwards became a celebrated Irish writer.

Richard Shackleton in his turn handed Ballitore school to his son Abraham in 1779, and this second Abraham continued in the civilised tradition of the place. He was a man noted for his good conversation, a lover of good literature and a keen student of the natural sciences.

In 1779 Abraham Shackleton married Lydia Mellor, whose father was a citizen of Manchester and whose mother was descended from Quaker stock. He was the first of his family to try to learn its history, and from a cousin living in London he obtained a copy of the coat of arms of Richard Shackleton. These arms were confirmed to him by the Heralds' Office in Dublin, to be used by the Irish branch of the family, and three gold buckles on a red ground were emblazoned on the crest to distinguish it from that of the Yorkshire branch, with which the Irish branch shared the device of the poplar tree. The motto assigned to the Irish branch*—*Fortitudine Vincimus*, By endurance we conquer—was as inspiring as it was appropriate to Ernest Shackleton.

Ebenezer, son of Abraham and Lydia Shackleton, born in 1784, did not take on the school at Ballitore but acquired flour mills at Moone, in the same county, which he administered himself. He was married twice, his second wife being of Quaker stock. He brought his children up in the Church of England doctrines, having left the Quakers because he considered they had become lax.

Henry Shackleton belonged to the second family. He was sent to school in England, to Wellington, his mother hoping to make him a soldier; but illness interfered with this ambition, and he returned to Ireland to school, afterwards graduating in Arts, in 1868, at Trinity College, Dublin.

Henry Shackleton began his married life as a landowner, having bought a small property at Kildare which he farmed himself. Here six children were born—Gertrude Alice, Ernest Henry, Aimée Vibert, Ethel Rose, Eleanor Hope and Clara Lilian. His wife, Henrietta Letitia Sophia Gavan, was Irish, gay, charming and with a quick sense of humour. Her paternal grandfather was Rector of Wallstown in County Cork; her father, Henry John Gavan, qualified as a doctor but afterwards applied for a commission in the Royal Irish Constabulary. In her ancestry there were tough fighting elements as well as a love of civilised pursuits. She emerges from the recollections of her children and grand-children as an energetic and amusing woman, and one who was well equipped, as was her husband, to create an atmosphere of security for the large family of which Ernest Shackleton was a happy member.

The importance of this security and affection can hardly be exaggerated. It was the foundation of that buoyancy of temperament so noticeable in the explorer. As a child he knew only an atmosphere of approval and goodwill. He learned, in this large family, to approach people cheerfully and with genuine interest; in social life he always had the courage of complete confidence. All through his life he took people at their face value. Sometimes this led him into trouble, but as a general rule his cheerful approach to his fellow men pleased and interested them.

His mother's optimistic and happy nature was something he took for granted as a child but which he must have copied without knowing it. His father, a man of tolerant, affectionate, but strong, character, had much to give his children. He communicated to them his love of poetry; he supported them in their ambitions; he set his face against mean or shoddy actions.

At Kilkea, then, Ernest wandered through his childhood, wrapped round with the cheerful love of a large family, dreamily trailing behind on family walks to pick leaves and examine holes in the ground; nicknamed Mr. Lag by his nurse, happy, enquiring, and in no way remarkable.

He was not to wander long in the lanes of Kilkea, for when he was six his father made a decision which must have exercised the mind of the father of a family. The agricultural depression in Ireland in the late 'seventies no doubt had much to do with Henry Shackleton's resolve to leave Kilkea and move his home to Dublin, where he could train for a new profession.

In 1880 he returned to his old college as a medical student, establishing his family at 35 Marlborough Road, Dublin. Here Ernest Shackleton lived for four years, indulging in the amusements proper to small boys. He is reputed to have had a passion for funerals, which he often followed in the street; he tried to dig his way to Australia in the back garden; he staged the first of many practical jokes when he planted a ruby ring of his mother's in the garden and persuaded a maid to help him to dig for buried treasure.

He took part, too, in one of the favourite activities of the Shackleton family—capping quotations. In 1901 the geographer Dr. Hugh Robert Mill, a passenger on the *Discovery* for some of its journey to the Antarctic, was surprised to find a young officer on the bridge who could equal him—outdo him, even, at times—in this game. He was to become firm friends with this young officer, Ernest Shackleton, and to discover that in his youth he had joined with his sisters in answering his father's searching questions or listening to him reciting Tennyson, his favourite, and many other English poets. Ernest Shackleton's memory for poetry, and his genius for producing the right quotation for every occasion, became celebrated in many spheres of his life.

Henry Shackleton moved across to England in 1884. He was now a qualified doctor, having taken his medical degree with distinction at Trinity College, Dublin, and having also passed as a member of the Royal College of Surgeons of England.

Ernest's first home in England was at South Croydon; but his father found it difficult to build up a practice there and moved to Aberdeen House, 12 West Hill, Sydenham. He now had ten children. Three more daughters had been born since the family left Kilkea—Helen, Kathleen and Gladys—and a son, Frank.

In the pleasant and peaceful setting of Victorian Sydenham the Shackleton children grew and flourished. Stories of their games and jaunts remind one of the families in E. Nesbit's books. There is the same air of jollity and family affection, the same inspired improvisation of games, the same tolerance and mutual understanding, the same family jokes.

Ernest now emerges as a typical prep-school boy—boasting of his prowess at football, playing noisy games of whist, sitting aloof on the garden wall with his friend Maurice Sale-Barker, surrounded by ginger-beer bottles, watching from this elevation his three youngest sisters being taken for a walk by their nurse. At his first English school—Fir Lodge Preparatory School, not far from his home—he is said to have had the reputation of a fighter. He acquired the nickname of Mick and had to live down various comments on his brogue.

It was perhaps at this time that he began reading about Polar exploration. None of his sisters can remember that he had any books on the subject, but he is reported to have said in an interview later in his life that he was tremendously keen on this kind of reading. Certainly he revelled in the serials of Jules Verne in the *Boy's Own Paper*, and in particular the character of the mysterious Captain of *Twenty Thousand Leagues under the Sea* seems to have impressed him. Like hundreds of other boys he responded to that lonely figure outlawed from the world. It was a conception that appealed to him now and again in his adult life, in moments of uncertainty. He used Jules Verne's character in a letter[1] to Emily Dorman during their courtship, to indicate his feeling of inadequacy: ' . . . I have nothing to offer you: I am poor: I am not clever. It is as wicked of me to want you to keep caring for me when my name is "Nemo" as it is to make or do other wrongs.' In 1902, when he contributed to the *South Polar Times*, the magazine of the *Discovery* expedition, he chose the pseudonym NEMO.

But if he dreamed of himself occasionally as a Captain Nemo, he was a boy with many outside interests. It was the external, the concrete world which stirred him. In spite of his natural love of poetry and his varied vocabulary, he never shone in the academic side of school life. Reports from his years at Dulwich College—which school he entered as a day boarder in the summer of 1887—have a steady sequence of 'Could do better', phrased in different ways. It is clear from the reports, and from the memories of one or two of his masters as communicated to Dr. Mill, that he was not suffering from lack of brain but rather from lack of incentive. An inspired teacher of geography or natural history might have changed his school life completely. As it was, Dulwich could give him cricket and football, at which he was a fair performer, boxing and gym, at which he excelled. From one school-fellow, who had many relations abroad, he begged foreign stamps, prizing them, apparently, for their association with distant lands. It was in fact a life of action he wanted, even then, not a life of books. In 1909 he returned to his old school as its most celebrated pupil, to give away the prizes, and here he brought out the familiar gambit, exclaiming that he had never been so near to a Dulwich College prize before. He could afford to joke about it then, for he had just been within 100 miles of the South Pole. But we can be sure that while he was at school he did not let his lack of academic distinction worry him.

Certainly he was drawn to the sea at this time, though not conspicuously more than numbers of other small boys. His sisters remember that he enjoyed reading sea stories, and many of his games centred round a nautical life. He and three schoolfellows spent many happy days creating in their games the more romantic aspects of life under sail. In a strip of private wood adjoining the railway on days when they should have been at school, the boys played, ate smuggled food and smoked smuggled cigarettes. Mick read sea stories aloud, and they all determined on a life at sea.

On one occasion they escaped to London Bridge and got into a queue of applicants for jobs under the chief steward of a big steamer. The steward packed them off home, and they were forced for a little longer to forgo the glories of shipboard life for the routine of school. Perhaps Shackleton thought of this incident when he had to talk to a young stowaway who had taken this unconventional way of joining his expedition. Perhaps, too, this anecdote or something like it set off the train of stories of 'How Shackleton ran away to sea', the most romantic version of which can be found in a memoir of 1922.

A journalist, Harold Begbie, made Shackleton's acquaintance in London just before he sailed on his last expedition. It must be supposed that the conversations they had (if indeed they were authentically reported) were in the nature of a joke as far as Shackleton was concerned, for many of the anecdotes are apocryphal. According to Begbie,[2] Shackleton described the 'rough spirits' for whom the school system is chafing. 'I was one of those' said Shackleton. 'I realised it, and stuffing a Browning into my pocket, and taking all my savings with me, a matter of £8 or £9, off I went one fine day to Liverpool, and shipped on a sailing vessel at a shilling a month.'

This story suited so well the popular idea of Ernest Shackleton as a dashing character that it was repeated more than once in books on polar exploration.

But Ernest Shackleton did not run away to sea, though he was quite capable of having done so. His wish for a career at sea was seriously discussed at home. The Navy was ruled out as the family means did not seem adequate, and a formula had to be found by which he could get a suitable trial trip in the Mercantile Marine.

Here Henry Shackleton's cousin, the Rev. G. W. Woosnam (at that time Superintendent of the Mersey Mission to Seamen) was able to help. He arranged with the North-Western Shipping Company that Ernest should make a voyage on probation. He would have the status of Boy but would receive the treatment, uniform and accommodation of an Apprentice. It was a sensible arrangement, and the boy's own appreciation of it was marked by a great improvement in his school reports once it had been settled that he was to leave school. He left at the end of the Lent Term of 1890. The first purposeful stage of his life had begun.

Chapter II

WHEN Ernest Shackleton joined the *Hoghton Tower* at Liverpool, on 30 April 1890, he exchanged the comfortable, civilised atmosphere of Aberdeen House for the crowded quarters of a sailing ship in cargo. The life he had led up to his sixteenth year had perhaps not entirely fitted him for this.

It cannot have been altogether an advantage to the new Boy that he was in the habit of reading, and reciting poetry, quite naturally; that he was an ardent member of the Band of Hope; that he had been brought up to read a piece in the Bible every night. If his addiction to poetry was laughed at, he managed to live it down and most of his shipmates regarded this habit with friendly admiration; on none of his voyages was he without one or other of the great poets, and his sisters remember especially a Dante in translation, with Doré engravings, being unpacked from his trunk. As for his teetotalism, it is hard to say how serious he had been about it at the time when he and his youngest sisters paraded the streets of Sydenham, enjoying the banners and show; but it is obvious that up till now his life had hardly brought him in touch with drunkenness, and from his letters home it seems that he found it hard to accept.

His religious habits he had felt nervous about, but he wrote in a letter home[1] that 'the first night I took out my Bible to read they all stopped talking and laughing, and now every one of them reads theirs excepting a Roman Catholic, and he reads his prayer-book'. Shackleton's behaviour does not seem to have been dictated by a missionary fervour. Probably he was merely acting out of habit, with a strong feeling that he was not going to change his ways.

His keen interest in the external world was probably his biggest asset. After three days of sea-sickness he began to learn his work, to grasp the principles of sail, to accept drudgery and enquire into everything. He was helped, too, in that Captain Partridge, who commanded the *Hoghton Tower*, was a kindly man, who entertained his apprentices to dinner now and then, and saw that they were well instructed. This ship was bound for Valparaiso, and the journey passed first in fine weather—with a pleasant night off St. Paul's Rocks, where on 30 May Neptune came aboard and Shackleton, among others, was solemnly tarred, shaved and ducked while crossing the Line; afterwards in gales off Cape Horn, which gave him his first taste of danger, for spars were smashed and several members of the crew injured. At Valparaiso there was a chance to rest, but on 1 October the ship left for Iquique, where a cargo of hay was discharged and a cargo of nitrates taken on board. It was not until 1 December that the *Hoghton Tower* turned towards England, and as it was diverted to Hamburg after a brief call at Falmouth, Shackleton was not discharged until 22 April 1891.

The Captain got a chance to have a word with Archdeacon Woosnam about him, and reported him[2] 'the most pig-headed obstinate boy I have ever come across'. However, he assured the Archdeacon that he had no real fault to find, and he was willing to take him again.

What the boy had been pig-headed and obstinate about cannot now be discovered; but there can be little doubt that the Captain, used to assessing the characters of young people, had sensed in this cheerful sixteen-year-old with the square chin the unwillingness to be checked, the impatience with routine, that characterised Shackleton all his life.

In June 1891 Ernest Shackleton was formally indentured by his father as an apprentice to the North-Western Shipping Company, and he sailed again on the *Hoghton Tower* on 25 June, this time from Cardiff, bound for Iquique.

Now he knew what to expect, and provided himself with such home comforts as could be enjoyed on board. With no novelty now to console him, and with a sterner captain (Captain Robert Robinson), Shackleton seems to have felt increasingly homesick. Life in a day school had not prepared him for the complete dislocation of home life which a boy learns by easy stages at boarding school. He consoled himself to some extent with books—poetry, a few books of 'readings', Scott's novels, and *Vanity Fair*; also with letters. He wrote home often, and begged his family to send him as many letters as they could. To his three youngest sisters he would send competitions for drawings; they remember that he always tactfully gave first, second and third prizes.

The temporary loss of his secure and affectionate home must have seemed still harder when the ship reached the Horn and encountered severe weather. Many of the crew were injured and Shackleton himself suffered severely from lumbago. Arrived at Iquique, in October, he had dysentery, and he must have been relieved when this trying second voyage was over and he reached home again on 16 May 1892.

His sisters had perhaps missed him more on this occasion, as he had certainly missed them, for they had hung flags, silk sashes and painted greetings out of the nursery window, and people passing had asked the coachman if there was to be a wedding. 'Oh dear me, no,' he had told them; 'the eldest son is coming home from sea.' The eldest son professed himself to be displeased with these conspicuous signs of rejoicing, and made his sisters promise not to do it again, but he was always apt to laugh off an affecting moment, and it seems that the ceremony was repeated on other occasions.

Perhaps it was during this shore period, too, that the sea-going brother, turning over his sisters' bedside book—*Little Pillows*, by Frances Ridley Havergal—solemnly told them that he had a companion volume on board which had been specially produced for sailors, called *Little Bolsters*. It was some years before they realised that their hope of seeing this book could never be realised, as no such book existed except as their elder brother's teasing invention. -

There were still two years of apprenticeship to go, and it was now decided that the apprentice was to serve his last two years in the *Hoghton Tower*, although he was not very willing to ship in her again. The new voyage, which started on 27 June for India, followed the same pattern as the previous two, fair weather followed by disastrous storms. This time the worst gale struck the ship near the Cape of Good Hope while Shackleton was at the wheel, and he had a chance to show his mettle. He spent the time in India chiefly in working cargo. He was bored and depressed. There was an especially hard period at False Point in the Bay of Bengal, where the crew loaded rice for Mauritius, bag after bag by hand. In Mauritius fever hit the crew and Shackleton was particularly ill; but time spent in Newcastle, New South Wales, in April 1893, cheered and recovered him.

From Australia the ship sailed across the Pacific to Chile, and Shackleton did not reach home until 3 July. His years of learning had been hard ones, but they had strengthened his determination to make himself into a good sailor. On his second voyage, the second mate had spoken to him about the future and had stimulated his ambition. A shipmate on the *Hoghton Tower* on these two voyages, Mr. Thomas Peers,* remembers[5] that 'the other lads used to say "Old Shack's busy with his books". When he wasn't on duty on the deck he was stowed away in his cabin, studying. He was full of poetry and could quote it by the yard.' But there was the other side of the picture too. Mr. Peers remembers him as a very normal young fellow, hail-fellow-well-met with everyone, cheerful and cheeky, running to the galley with concoctions of salt beef and chopped biscuit and trying to persuade the cook to stoke the fire and heat them up for him. For all the apprentice's application to his books, he was no pale scholar but a broad-shouldered lad with a voice that made itself heard above the others when they were pulling on a rope.

Now that Shackleton's indentures were completed he discovered a

---

* Mr. Peers, just two years older than Shackleton, joined the *Hoghton Tower* as an A.B. in 1892. In 1909 he was Master of the Birkenhead Ferry boat and took Shackleton over to the *Conway*, where he was to distribute prizes. On the return journey he accosted Shackleton, who remembered him as a shipmate and settled on the top deck to chat with him with real pleasure about the old days.

nautical school in London, and was coached for his first Board of
Trade examination by the principal, Captain J. Netherclift Jutsum. He
passed the examination for second mate on 4 October 1894.*

Shackleton had now reached a new phase in his career as a sailor—
still at this time the only career which had presented itself to him and,
apparently, one with which he was well content. At this date it was
customary, after an apprenticeship in sail, for a young man to fill in
time in tramp steamers while he was qualifying as master. Accordingly
he left London River, on 15 November 1894, as Third Mate of the
Monmouthshire, a tramp steamer of the Welsh Shire Line bound for
the Far East. He owed the job to the good offices of an old schoolfellow,
Mr. Owen Burne, who had taken him to see the manager. It seems,
however, that the post originally offered was Fourth Mate. Shackleton,
on seeing the quarters assigned to him, had announced that he did not
approve of them but that he would go as Third Officer—an offer which
was accepted because as the managing partner said, 'I rather liked the
chap.' If the story is true—and there seems no reason to disbelieve it—
it is the first time we hear of Shackleton playing the *enfant terrible*
outside his family. It was a rôle he played with considerable success
through his life, and the chief reason for this success was the simple
fact that people did 'rather like' him. If we wanted to, no doubt we
could call this attribute simply 'Irish charm'.

He was now settling down to his at-sea character, a somewhat
contradictory one. In one aspect he was the sociable fellow, the good
mixer; men who remembered him at this phase of his life and spoke of
him after his death nearly always used the word 'cheerful'. Yet he spent
much time in his cabin while his brother officers were enjoying themselves—sometimes reading, sometimes studying for his next examination,
sometimes writing poetry of his own.

The ship's course through the Mediterranean and through the Indian
seas to China was distinctly more romantic and poetical than the stormy
sailing passages round Cape Horn had been, and roused in him feelings
which were expressed in a long poem of quest and endeavour called
A Tale of the Sea (pp. 496–98).

Shackleton was the officer responsible for checking cargo in the
various ports of China, North America and Europe which the ship
visited, and he seems to have done this with the quick accuracy which
was later useful to him as an expedition leader. When he came home,

* When Captain Jutsum started the Cardiff Nautical Academy, Shackleton
was pleased to be able to help his old teacher, and his picture appears, in
sledging dress, in a prospectus of (presumably) 1910, together with extracts
from a letter, written by him to Captain Jutsum on 6 July 1910, in which he had
spoken of his 'untiring patience' and asserted 'I feel that I owe you a great
deal for the conscientious, painstaking and successful manner in which you
prepared me for my examinations.'

late in July, he brought three baby alligators from Florida, Faith, Hope
and Charity, as they were christened, appealed more to his sisters than
to the family servants, or to his father; but Henry Shackleton—a
keen member of the Royal Horticultural Society and Vice-President
of the National Rose Society—allowed Ernest to keep the alligators
in a pond in the garden, until it was conveniently arranged that they
should go to the Zoo.

His second voyage in the *Monmouthshire*, between August 1895 and
April 1896, he used once more as an opportunity for study as well as
for acquiring experience on the Eastern run; and during his leave of
April–June 1896 he passed his Board of Trade examination for First
Mate.

On 19 June 1896, at the age of twenty-two, Ernest Shackleton
signed on the *Flintshire* as Second Mate, at a salary of £8 per month.
The *Flintshire*, a larger ship than the *Monmouthshire*, was at that time
under the command of Captain J. Dwyer, and under him Shackleton
made no less than six voyages of varying lengths. The first took him to
Penang, Singapore, Hongkong, Yokohama and San Francisco, and he
was discharged on 27 January 1897. On 26 February he was off again
for Saigon and Singapore, returning on 29 June.

It was during this spell ashore that he first met Emily Dorman, a
tall, quizzical beauty who had, while he was away at sea, become very
friendly with his sister Ethel. With his usual *sans-gêne*, he stood leaning
over a chair in the drawing-room, looking at her, and lost no time in
making it clear that he wanted to see more of her.

Emily Dorman was at this time a beautiful woman of twenty-eight
who, although she had had many proposals, had not so far found it
worth her while to change a very comfortable single state for the duties
of marriage. Like Ernest Shackleton, she was the child of a happy
marriage and one of a large family. Her father, Charles Dorman, was a
wealthy man, partner in the family business—Kingsford Dorman,
solicitors. His home farm in Kent was well run, and he was one of
the first private orchid-growers in England. His wife, Janie Swinford,
had been born and brought up at Minster Abbey, in the Isle of
Thanet, Kent, in a strict but comfortable and secure home. To these
well-to-do and amiable parents were born six children. Two sons,
Herbert and Frank, entered the family business; the third, Arthur,
went into the church. Julia, the eldest daughter, remained unmarried
until she was over forty. She was much exercised by the love affairs
of her two gay young sisters, Emily and Daisy, who were always refusing one young man or agonising over another. But she perhaps
realised that marriage was not altogether or instantly attractive to girls
who had travelled abroad, who had lived in an atmosphere of gaiety
and music and good living as a matter of course. There was always

something to do, and in this kind of atmosphere the more young men the merrier.

When Emily Dorman met Ernest Shackleton for the first time she was unhappy. Reading between the lines of a letter she wrote to him later, we can guess that she was unhappily in love, perhaps thought her love unrequited. At first, the young officer must have presented himself to her simply as her friend's brother—attractive, well spoken, and pleasant to talk with. There was not time to find out much more, for on 17 July the *Flintshire* left England again, for a long voyage by Singapore, Hongkong, Nagasaki, Hiogo, Yokohama to Portland, Oregon and then on to Marseilles in February of the next year (1898). It was not till the 20th of that month that Ernest Shackleton was discharged.

He had only a fortnight to pursue Miss Dorman's acquaintance before the ship sailed again, but he knew his mind, and on their visits to the British Museum and the National Gallery they talked more intimately than before. Like most people attracted to each other they exchanged favourite poets. Shackleton was immersed in Swinburne at this time—the rolling rhythms and sonorous words gave him great pleasure. He told Emily Dorman, whose favourite poet was Browning, that he did not much care for that poet. She at once gave him a pocket volume of selections and a biography. Shackleton was quickly converted.[*] Men who met him at all stages of his life recall his habit of quoting Browning on every occasion; some remember that he could recite long passages from *Paracelsus*, most obscure of poems, and that he was quite capable of filling in the blanks with his own words if his memory failed him. Most important of all, the poem *Prospice*, with the courage and love expressed so strongly in it, became for them a watchword, and in telegrams and letters they used the word 'Prospice' as a symbol of devotion and hope.

But in 1898 all this was to come. They gave each other Browning birthday books and parted with the delightful feeling of having a taste in common. Shackleton went off to sea once more.

On this next voyage (a short one, from 11 March to 29 June 1898) he was once more signed on as Second Mate. He spent much of his time working at his books and was rewarded by the award of his Master's Certificate at a Naval Court in Singapore on 28 April.

His period of shore leave, again not very long, advanced him further into Emily Dorman's attention and probably into her heart as well. Certainly she was pleased to have a personable young man in whom to

---

[*] Lady Shackleton told[6] Dr. Mill, when he was writing his *Life*, that Canon Woosnam said he had seen the boy on to his first ship and noticed a volume of Browning 'sticking out of his pocket'. She did not know whether his memory was to be relied on, but she was still sure that she had first touched off the enthusiasm for Browning which became so much a part of Ernest Shackleton.

confide her sorrows, and both of them were, in a youthful way, enjoying these sorrows considerably. When Ernest left England, again on the *Flintshire*, on 27 July, they were at the analytical stage of their relationship, and although Ernest Shackleton was desperately uncertain of the degree of Emily's interest in him, it is clear that he need not have been, for already she was writing long letters, and then notes to contradict what she had said in them.

'You say I must not think of you as unhappy', he writes [7]: 'after what you said to me that day I must believe there is something wrong: you say it is your temperament: why, it is always that: it makes me what I am: a man longing for the good of life which he sees shining ahead but unreachable, at least now: and the future so uncertain that I dare hardly shape a hope. . . .'

She has told him he has 'won' unworthily; he hints that he is having to hold himself back because of some feeling she has for someone else. She has apologised for winning his sympathy; he asserts 'You know I wish you happy.' But at the end of this delicious welter of tentative feelings there comes a pertinent remark from him. He had recalled a ride they had had together, and then, remembering Browning's poem, he thinks too of that poet's romantic marriage.

'How happy that woman must have been who wrote those lines [he has quoted one of Elizabeth Barrett Browning's sonnets] and when she married she was thirty-seven years old; that was not too old for fifteen years of bliss and life; and he was three years younger than she. . . .'

They had evidently spoken of marriage, and Shackleton, having determined to win Emily against any challenger, was not likely now to stay in the *Flintshire* without making a bid for something more ambitious. His fifth voyage on this ship ended on 5 December, when she returned to England from Rangoon and Penang; then he signed on again on 25 December, again as Second Mate at the old salary, for a coastal voyage in the United Kingdom. A visit to Middlesbrough was followed by an accident when the ship ran ashore off Redcar. In this crisis Shackleton was said by his shipmates to have been most firm and resolute.

He was discharged once more on 7 January, and at once wrote to the Welsh Shire Line to resign his position. There was no reason yet, however, for him to look further than the Merchant Service; and so he enlisted the help of his friend Owen Burne once more. His new run was to be England to Cape Town, and at the end of March he left on the *Tantallon Castle*, as Fourth Officer. This, in a liner of 3,000 tons, with interesting passengers, comfort and variety of employment, was regarded as promotion.

In this ship he made three voyages during 1899, and then, in

December, was transferred to the *Tintagel Castle*. The South African War had made troop-carrying ships essential and important, and Ernest Shackleton, Third Officer now with a salary of £7 a week, was in his element. Among the 1,200 troops on board there were many individuals whose company he could enjoy; and his practical jokes (the state visit of King Neptune, which he largely organised, being the most elaborate) exactly fitted the occasion.

Someone, perhaps Shackleton himself, had the good idea of writing a *souvenir de voyage*. The two trips on the *Tintagel Castle* (14 December 1899 to 25 February 1900, and 8 March 1900 to 31 May 1900) were commemorated in a small, board-covered volume: the title page bears the explanatory title *O.H.M.S.: An Illustrated Record of the Voyage of S.S. "Tintagel Castle", conveying Twelve Hundred Soldiers from Southampton to Cape Town, March 1900*; but the cover has a freer (and more Shackletonian) title: *O.H.M.S. or How 1200 Soldiers went to Table Bay*.

This is not a work which can be discussed critically as Shackleton's, for it was really a work of editing rather than of writing. It was written in collaboration with Dr. W. McLean, the ship's surgeon, but we do not know if the doctor did any of the writing, or if, as has been said, he simply contributed the photographs.

Various portions of the book are by other hands. There is a patriotic poem by W. J. Heley; a short piece on 'a day in the life of a subaltern' by A. F. Howe, presumably the subaltern in question; an article on the Maxim machine-gun lent to his regiment, by A. Lupton; another on the ship's concert by E. Fletcher and on a sports meeting by the same hand, assisted by C. A. Barron. But the general impression made by the book, the engaging mixture of factual detail and uproarious humour, is so typical of Shackleton that we may safely guess that he dictated the editorial policy. He was to produce the same mixture most successfully, when he edited the first number of the *South Polar Times*, the first of the celebrated 'school magazine' volumes to come from the Antarctic expeditions of the twentieth century.

We may, too, identify as Ernest Shackleton the 'vision in white and gold' who appeared above the deck before the sports meeting[3] and 'in a few terse words described its [the Book's] aims and objects'.

Those aims and objects were frankly sentimental ones. Here in this liner were soldiers, full of the uninhibited patriotism of their day, wanting something by which to remember the voyage, and no doubt something to convince them that they would get back home safely to do their remembering in peace and quiet. As the writer of the log says[4]:

'. . . in a day or two our friends and companions for the last three weeks will be scattered. But the doings of all on board, and the things we have seen, will be recorded in this book faithfully and truly for us all to look back upon when we return to the dear old country.'

It is, indeed, a splendid little book, and worth every penny of the 2s. 6d. it cost. In the compass of sixty small folio pages it gives a detailed description of the ship, some menus, brief biographical sketches of some of the officers (marine and army), accounts of festivities such as the sports and the highly dramatic visit of Neptune. There are some humorous items, including *Tommy's Tintagel Trials*, an alliterative patter of considerable wit which could be by Shackleton; some well-observed descriptions of ports of call; a clear account of the formation of the Lovat Scouts (one of the regiments represented on board); the roll of every regiment thus represented; finally (and this might well have been Shackleton's idea) a list of the peace-time occupations of every man among the troops, a list which is a social study in itself.

With this variety of subjects well arranged, neatly and succinctly handled (except for Neptune's visit, where we suspect Shackleton spread himself), with the excellent choice of photographs and the effective captions, the book was a souvenir worthy of a cargo of heroes, and the heroes showed they realised it by subscribing freely. Before Shackleton returned to London he had got more than 2,000 names on his list, and the book, privately printed and distributed by the co-authors, was sold out during the summer and even made a small profit. Two copies were particularly important to Shackleton. One, specially bound, was presented to Queen Victoria; the other was inscribed 'E. to E. July 1900. "The First Fruits".'

No doubt this was meant to indicate that he intended to offer Emily Dorman much more than this. Certainly he had plans already for what it would be. During this year he had been elected a Fellow of the Royal Geographical Society, and he became keenly interested in the National Antarctic Expedition which was being planned by a committee made up from the Royal Geographical Society and the Royal Society.

Through all his years in sailing and steam ships, Shackleton had been finding his powers, very slowly—surprisingly slowly, when we think of the speed with which he later won a world-wide reputation. But all this time he had been growing up. Now he was ready to strike out into a totally different world, made confident by his experiences of the sea, and by the fact that Emily—still hesitant, still splitting emotional hairs—had decided that she loved him and was willing to wait for him. He began to enquire whether this Antarctic expedition would have room for him, and refusals did not daunt him. He began, too, to make enquiries about applying for a commission in the Royal Naval Reserve; but this too went slowly at first.

His career as a ship's officer was not quite over. On 4 October 1900, he joined the Union Castle liner *Gaika*, as Third Officer, at a salary of £8 per week, and sailed with her to the Cape, returning to England on 16 December. He signed on again for the same ship on 27 December, but was discharged two days later and appears, on 5 January 1901, as Third Officer of the *Carisbrooke Castle*, a ship of the same company. He served in her for two months, on another Cape voyage, being discharged on 13 March. He closed his career as a ship's officer, at the age of twenty-seven, by leaving the ship with the lowest pay-off of anybody—£1 16s. 3d.

Henrietta Letitia Sophia Shackleton   Dr. Henry Shackleton

Fir Lodge Preparatory School, Sydenham, *c.* 1885. Ernest Henry
Shackleton is the boy in the window

Ernest Henry Shackleton, aged 16, in uniform of White Star Line

Ernest Henry Shackleton, aged 11

Chapter III

'THERE is a perfect run on the Antarctic.' In this jocular vein began an article in the *Sphere* on 30 March 1901[1] on the forthcoming expeditions of Scott, Drygalski and Nordenskjöld. The writer had caught the right note to interest his public. Antarctic expeditions, at the turn of the century, were news to many of his readers : they were to remain news for the next fifty years and more.

In November, 1893, Sir John Murray addressed the Royal Geographical Society on 'The Renewal of Antarctic Exploration'. Twenty years before, as an unknown oceanographer, he had crossed the Antarctic Circle, one of a group of scientists on H.M.S. *Challenger*. The *Challenger*, captained by George Nares, R.N., had been equipped by the Admiralty, as had the whole expedition, which was designed to study the depth of all the oceans in the world and the living creatures in them. The scientific value of this expedition was great and lasting; it was one of the most notable of the many contributions the British Navy had made, and was to make, to the cause of science. One of the achievements of the *Challenger* most interesting to Murray was the collection, early in 1874, of circumstantial evidence—consisting mainly of soundings and bottom samples—that a great continent lay to the south of them. Here was one starting point, Murray stressed, and another was provided by the voyage of Sir James Ross between 1839 and 1843, during which he had located the South Magnetic Pole, seen and named Victoria Land, discovered and wondered at the Great Ice Barrier (which we now must call the Ross Ice Shelf), christened the two volcanic mountains, Erebus and Terror, under the shadow of which Ernest Shackleton was to make his name, and conjectured the existence of more land which he was not able to prove.

Ross's naval voyage, with the ships *Erebus* and *Terror*, the approach of the *Challenger* to the Antarctic continent—these things, Sir John Murray felt, had for too long been forgotten.

He might have gone further back in Britain's record of exploration, for she had been foremost in the Antarctic since this last great mysterious continent was first challenged. It was an Englishman, James Cook, who first crossed the Antarctic Circle—in 1773 (though he did not, as Markham believed he did, ever see the Antarctic continent). It was an Englishman, who sighted the first outpost—William Smith, who in February 1819 saw the South Shetland Islands. An Englishman, Edward Bransfield, shares the honour with a Russian, Thaddeus von

Bellingshausen, of being the first to sight the mainland in 1820: there were no more than two days between the Russian's sight of 'an icefield strewn with hummocks', which was very probably what is now Dronning Maud Land, and Bransfield's certain sight of what he called Trinity Land, now part of Graham Land.

Britain continued to lead the siege of this frozen land and of its innermost citadel, the South Pole. In the roll of Antarctic explorers, the names of James Weddell, John Biscoe and John Balleny are emblazoned with their great successor, James Clark Ross.

But it was now long since Ross's remarkable voyage, long since the *Challenger*'s sortie. Each of these important steps in the campaign had been taken after a long interval of inaction. Shackleton came upon the scene of the fight just when it was about to begin with fresh vigour, partly because of the stirring call of Sir John Murray. 'Is the last great piece of maritime exploration on the surface of our Earth,' he asked, 'to be undertaken by Britons, or is it to be left to those who may be destined to succeed or supplant us on the Ocean?' The Royal Geographical Society, roused by his call, undertook to dispatch an expedition, and in 1895 appealed to the Admiralty for help. As the President, Sir Clements Markham,[2] put it, in his Anniversary Address, in June 1897, '. . . it must be borne in mind that hitherto, alike in the days of Cook as in the days of Ross, Antarctic work has always been undertaken by the Government, and is strictly naval work'.

The Admiralty did not respond, but Sir John Murray's disciples did not give up hope. In particular, Sir Clements Markham kept pressing for an expedition. It was his dream that the Antarctic should be conquered by the Senior Service, and he urged the advantage of such adventures. He pointed out that officers and men would be given opportunities for distinguishing themselves. 'Work requiring special care and coolness of judgment, work needing an accurate decision to be formed and acted upon on the instant, work presenting novel situations and suggesting new ideas, all these kinds of work strengthen and form a sailor's character, widen his perceptions, and increase his self-reliance.' All these lessons were to be found, he was sure, in an Antarctic expedition.

Another learned body was alive to the call of the new continent also. On 24 February 1898 the Royal Society held a special Antarctic meeting to discuss the scientific advantages of an expedition to the South. Murray's 1893 address was summarised. His many suggestions about research—about meteorology, glaciology, coastal surveying, biological and geological investigation, soundings and the like—were vigorously discussed by a body of men including Nansen, Sir Joseph Hooker, Dr. Neumayer, and Sir Clements Markham.

It was clear after this meeting, if it had not been clear before, that the movement towards exploring the South, the unknown continent, was vigorous not only in Britain. In January 1899, Markham[3] in his presidential address, announced that Dr. Neumayer was arranging for a scientific expedition to leave in 1900 under Drygalski, and that he was hoping for British co-operation, especially in the field of magnetic research.

It was a matter not of international rivalry but of national honour that Sir Clements Markham put before the Fellows. He deplored the fact that our Government would not act: he sympathised with the Royal Society, who, keenly interested as they were in the research, had no funds available. The Royal Geographical Society, however, he was able to announce, would put up £5,000 for a private expedition, for Britain must not 'resign its proud old position in the van of discovery and exploration'. If the Admiralty would not act quickly, the navy must forfeit its right to this new sphere of action to the general public. It was, as he saw it,[4] Britain's last chance to acquit herself well.

'Let it, therefore, be clearly understood', he ended, 'that if we are unable to do our bounden duty, and to take our place by the side of the German antarctic explorers, if we are obliged to hold back, our credit as a nation is gone. We must, for the first time in our history, disgracefully take a back place. Worst of all, it will not be from poverty of means, but from poverty of patriotic feeling amongst those who possess the means. But we cannot believe this, and we therefore confidently make an appeal for funds to equip an Antarctic Expedition.'

On 27 March he was able to announce that a Fellow of the Society, Mr. W. L. Longstaff, had contributed £25,000 to the fund. The President of the Royal Society, Lord Lister, commented dryly[5] that the Government was evidently not to be expected to come to the aid of science, but 'so long as we have such donations from private individuals, science will get on very well'.

Encouraged by the healthy state of the expedition fund, the Royal Geographical Society and the Royal Society together sent a deputation to the Government to explain their aims and stress the importance of a magnetic survey. The Government allowed a grant of £45,000 on condition that an equal sum was raised by public subscription. It was largely through the efforts of Sir Clements Markham that this was achieved.

Altogether £100,000 was budgeted for a three-year expedition, which was to be planned to support that of Neumayer. It was agreed between the German and British expedition committees that the Antarctic should be divided into four quadrants—Victoria, Ross, Weddell and Enderby. The British expedition was to work in the Ross and Victoria quadrants, and their plans included a coastal survey of the

land previously viewed by Ross, between Cape Adare and McMurdo
Sound, and along what was then called the Great Ice Barrier, and one
sledging expedition which would be directed due south. In none of the
plans, published and otherwise, was the South Pole mentioned. At this
stage of exploration, a high south latitude was all that could be expected:
it was enough that the Union flag should be planted on whatever surface
the unknown continent should be found to possess. For all the scientific
equipment—the balloons for meteorological work, the nets for
dredging, and the taxidermists' apparatus—this was, first and foremost, a patriotic venture.

We can trace this in the diaries of Scott and Wilson, of Shackleton
and Royds. We can see it in the celebrations for the King's Birthday.
We can trace it in a poem which appeared in the expedition magazine[6]
during its second winter,* which begins:

'A ship is gliding out of port borne on the evening tide.
She sails in Britain's name and entrusted with her pride.
Her crew are Britons to a man, her name 'Discovery',
That England still shall set the pace as Mistress of the Sea.'

"DISCOVERY"

The same note is sounded in an essay on 'Seafaring', sent in for a
competition in the magazine, in which sailors see 'their country's
flag proudly waving in every quarter of the globe both on land and sea'.†

There is patriotism, too, in an ingenious piece of foolery contributed
to an earlier number of the magazine by an A.B. called Frank Wild, an
'ancient document' supposedly found in 2198 A.D. during excavations
on the site of Ancient London:

* August 1903. This poem was signed 'Matutinus', which Captain Barne
recalls was the pseudonym of Arthur Quartley, leading stoker.

† Signed 'Egat Imra', an anagram of Armitage, Second in Command of the
expedition. The essay was never used in the magazine but survives among the
Shackleton family papers.

'Now Edward the King was a great and wise sovereign, and a popular ruler over his vast dominions, which did extend to the uttermost ends of the earth, but did not cover the whole world. . . . And there lived at this time in the land many wise and learned men, and these were encouraged in their pursuit of further knowledge by the King. And it came to pass that certain of these wise men did hear news of a vast country far to the south of any of the Great King's possessions, and that it did contain many wonderful birds and beasts, also useful plants and herbs, and vast quantities of gold and precious stones. And . . . they did gather themselves together and commune amongst each other, saying, Lo, this country of which we do hear, is indeed a rich country; let us therefore collect money, to build unto ourselves a ship, and some of our brethren shall travel thence, and not only shall we become rich above all men, but will also add greatly to the dominions of the Great King, and thereby shall we gain more favour in his sight.'

Frank Wild, a remarkable man who was to become important in the life of Ernest Shackleton, probably shared with him the engaging mixture of go-getting and idealism reflected in the above passage. Not that anybody thought seriously that the expedition was likely to find gold or precious stones in the Antarctic snows, although Shackleton never quite got the idea out of his head. At any rate, to Wild, as to Shackleton, this was a chance to make good, to make a name, to make a stir, even (possibly) to make some money.

To Ernest Shackleton this was of very great importance, as can be seen in the following letter which he wrote on 3 August 1901 to Emily Dorman's father.

My dear Mr. Dorman,

I must thank you very much for all your good wishes for the coming voyage. I would like to tell you in this letter that it is mainly for one reason that I am going, is to get on so that when I come back or later when I have made money, I might with your permission marry Emily if she still cares for me then as I feel she does now: It is needless to say to you that I care for her more than anyone else in the world, but I fully see the difficulties in the way as regards my not having money but time will overcome that and you will not object if I have sufficient to keep her as you would wish. I can see well how you must look at my wanting always to be with Emmie knowing that my circumstances are not rosy, and I can only thank you for your goodness in allowing me to see so much of her: If she cares for me later and you can see that I may honestly marry her, I would be ever happy: I have of course spoken to her all these years: but only lately has she I think really cared altogether for me: However, she will talk to you: As for me, my fortune is all to make but I intend making it quickly: I would have spoken to you myself before only Emily had not given me a full answer, now I feel it is all right so am asking you, not now, but when I have made money or position and money to marry her.

Yours very sincerely,
ERNEST H. SHACKLETON.

It is a simple manly letter, and its directness evidently pleased Charles Dorman, who wrote with cordial good wishes for the voyage, and assured the young lieutenant that when he returned, if he and Emily were still of the same mind, his consent would not be wanting.

But the National Antarctic Expedition, besides offering the ambitious young man his first real chance to get on and make a name for himself— and, characteristically, he wanted to 'do this quickly'—offered something else that he needed by temperament. All through his life Ernest Shackleton was happiest when he was active, or inaugurating future action. His enormous physical vitality, his mental inquisitiveness, had been satisfied by the work for his master's ticket; but once that was achieved, once promotion had become merely a matter of good behaviour, steady work and seniority, the charm had gone. The restlessness which people noticed in him during his period with the Castle ships was not only due to his slowly proceeding love affair; more than this, it was due to his desire for change, not for its own sake, but to bring him into a new field of action. This prospective expedition, these plans for a small new ship going to a vast unknown country, appealed to the romantic in him, and set spinning in his head ideas of immensity and effort, the type of ideas with which he was apt to recharge his energy. It was his chance, and with every aspect of his being—as the devoted lover, the ambitious sailor, the aspiring poet, and the cheerful companion—he welcomed it.

It had not been easy, though, for Ernest Shackleton to get on to the expedition list. All along the line it had been Sir Clements Markham's intention that this should be a naval expedition, even if it were not organised by the Admiralty. Early on in its history (in June 1900) he had succeeded in getting appointed as leader a young naval lieutenant, Robert Falcon Scott, who was promoted Commander for the occasion. He had also recommended his own nephew, Charles William Rawson Royds, another naval lieutenant, who became Scott's Number One.

Scott had promptly set about acquiring as large a body of naval men as he could. Two of his shipmates in the *Majestic*—a young lieutenant, Michael Barne, and a senior engineer, Reginald Skelton—were released for the expedition. For the crew, once the Admiralty had given permission for naval men to serve in the expedition ship, he had asked friends in the Channel fleet to select suitable men from among the many volunteers. The Admiralty was generous. The final list showed that only two men were civilians. There were two officers from the Merchant Navy and eight of the crew; the rest of the personnel came from the regular Navy.

The expedition's second in command, Albert Armitage, had trained in the *Worcester* and had worked in the P. and O. Company. In 1894 he had been given leave to go on the Jackson-Harmsworth expedition to Franz Josef Land, and his four years in the Arctic gave him experience which he was now to use in the *Discovery*, as navigator and as counsellor. A man with his experience of polar lands was clearly going to be an asset to the expedition. The claims of Ernest Shackleton, the second of the Merchant Service officers, were less obvious.

His first application, made in the summer of 1900, was turned down. But he had made friends with a fellow member of the Royal Geographical Society, a young man, Cedric Longstaff, who had travelled on one of the Castle ships to the Cape. It was his father who had been so generous to the expedition fund. Mr. Longstaff approached Sir Clements Markham and begged for a place on the expedition for Shackleton. Armitage was asked by Scott to vet him, and found[7] that everyone spoke well of him.

'The Marine Superintendent and his Captain in the U.C. Line both told me that he was more intelligent than the average officer. His brother officers considered him to be a very good fellow, always quoting poetry and full of erratic ideas.'

Markham regularised Shackleton's position by getting him a commission in the Royal Naval Reserve, and he was seconded to H.M.S. *President* for service with the expedition. It was intended (so his biographer Mill would have it) that Shackleton's experience in sail should be put to good use, for the other naval men had trained in steam-ships, except for Royds, and the *Discovery* was to make use of her sails on the southward journey, to save coal. This qualification, however, is not mentioned[8] in the 'Final List of Officers and Crew of the *Discovery* who entered the Ice':

'5. Third Lieutenant—ERNEST SHACKLETON, born November 4,* 1874. He entered the Merchant Service in 1890, and served in sailing ships in the Pacific, afterwards in the *Castle* line. *Sub-Lieut.*, R.N.R. F.R.G.S. In charge of sea-water analysis. Wardroom caterer. In charge of the holds, stores, and provisions, and arranges and serves out provisions. He also arranges the entertainments.'

There was nothing particularly noticeable about the Third Lieutenant when he joined the *Discovery* in the London Docks in July of

---

* This is in fact incorrect. Shackleton was born on *15 February* 1874.

1901. He was young, cheerful, and energetic; but so were his colleagues Charles Royds and Michael Barne, and the geologist, Hartley Ferrar, who sailed a scant month after he had taken his finals at Cambridge.* He was hard-working and painstaking, but so were the warrant officers, in particular Mr. Thomas Feather, the boatswain, of whom Scott said that he never lost so much as a length of rope. He had risen the hard way in his profession; but so had Thomas Hodgson, the marine biologist, who had studied in his spare time while uncongenially employed in business. He had knocked around the world a bit; but so had Albert Armitage, so had Koettlitz, the senior doctor, who had also been on the Jackson-Harmsworth Expedition, and so had Bernacchi, who under Borchgrevink on the *Southern Cross* had wintered in the Antarctic, on Cape Adare, in 1898–99. He was of a thoughtful and literary turn of mind; but so was Edward Wilson, doctor and naturalist, and official artist to the expedition.

No, there was nothing special about Ernest Shackleton then, and though he was popular with his shipmates, none of them could honestly have said otherwise. Nor was there anything in itself overwhelmingly important about his contribution to the work of the expedition. The list of his duties is not a particularly impressive one. On the voyage to the south, he acted as one of the three watch-keeping officers, with Royds and Barne, but it is clear that Royds, who had been in the *Conway*, was a good mast-and-yard seaman, and well able to organise the *Discovery's* canvas. In winter quarters Shackleton had very many duties; but for only one of them—the testing of salinities—did he need any special scientific training. He owed his position as store-keeper to the fact that by the naval system no branch of the ship's activities could be carried on without a supervising officer. Certainly his experience in the Merchant Service helped him to organise the stores efficiently, but when (as we shall see later) he had to be replaced, it was possible for Michael Barne, the Second Officer, and Charles Ford, the ship's clerk, to take over with very little trouble.

With such unspecialised duties, Shackleton had time to be of considerable help to the biologist during the winter and to take a keen, later an important interest, in sledging techniques. His comparative freedom may have roused feelings of envy in Royds, who as First Officer and meteorologist was much tied to the ship. But Shackleton could have seen in this very freedom an indication that he could easily be replaced.

Sir Clements Markham had got his way. The *Discovery* expedition

---

* Youth, in fact, was the keynote of the expedition. Royds wrote in his diary on 29 November 1901, when the *Discovery* lay in Lyttelton Harbour: 'The papers have got the *Daily Mail*'s account where it talks about the youth on board, and as the ship is entirely wood, they call us the "Babes in the Wood".'

was emphatically a naval one. It was planned that the ship should remain in the Antarctic during one or more winters, provided a suitable place could be found. Markham made detailed recommendations about the ship's route, and suggested either McMurdo Sound or Wood Bay, both in the Ross Quadrant, as suitable winter quarters. The final choice was left to Scott, but it was certain that if it was humanly possible he would keep the ship as his base. The portable wooden hut which was taken south was to be used as an emergency shelter for sledging parties, if they were for any reason cut off from the ship, and possibly for some branches of research; but the ship would remain the centre of everything. Once frozen in, it was to be run as a shore station, with naval formalities and under naval discipline.

Technically, however, the *Discovery* did not come under the Naval Discipline Act. Legally, she was a merchant vessel flying the blue ensign by special warrant from the Admiralty, and registered in Scott's name in the Royal Harwich Yacht Club. She had been specially built for the expedition. Her stout wooden frame showed her to be intended for ice work, and her many up-to-date instruments marked her out from the ordinary naval vessel.

The discipline and organisation of the ship, in fact, were based on what Scott himself called a 'pleasing fiction'. The men, as well as the officers, were well aware of this, and there were occasional difficulties, especially when the ship called at foreign ports. The naval personnel were informed by their shipmates from the Merchant Service that they could not be punished, and from time to time they took advantage of this. There were one or two complaints to the First Lieutenant, from the lower deck, about the mixing of the two services.

Shackleton, however, could well appreciate the need for some firm disciplinary plan. Naval routine provided a known background for the events of two years which were to be novel to everybody. If some of the formalities seemed irksome to him, he could find in the broad outlines of naval organisation something not unlike the system he had himself lived by as a professional sailor. All the same, it was to be important later that he was a Merchant Service officer working with Naval officers.

At the time when he joined the *Discovery* his position did not cause him any uneasiness. Of all the enthusiastic young men who joined the party, none was more triumphantly interested than Ernest Shackleton, as he took instruction in the new technique of ballooning, practised firing detonators (which might be needed in the ice), organised the stowing of the ship's stores and made his own last-minute dispositions.

It was on 31 July 1901 that the *Discovery*, free at last from harbour regulations, the disagreements of committees and the complexities of loading, left the East India Dock and made her way down the Thames for Spithead. Shackleton had managed to discourage his large family from any farewell ceremony; only his three youngest sisters were on the dock to wave to him. He had been instructing them in the art of semaphoring and had provided each with a large handkerchief; as the *Discovery* moved down the river he signalled good-bye to them by this means, in strict nursery order of precedence: Good-bye Kathleen, Good-bye Helen, Good-bye Gladys.

Crowds had gathered to see the ship go down the river; cameras were clicking in every direction, and every vessel in the river sounded off whatever form of siren or hooter she possessed. The loud and hearty farewell from the training ship *Worcester* set the seal on the naval expedition.

It was to be some days, however, before the ship left England. First, she had to lie off Spithead while the ship was swung and the compasses corrected, and when this was completed, on 5 August, they were ordered to Cowes. Here, just before noon, King Edward and Queen Alexandra visited the vessel. Mementoes were given to the expedition; the King conferred the Royal Victorian Order on the Commander and pronounced a formal but cordial farewell message. It was a scene which was to be repeated for Ernest Shackleton six years later; but as they steamed towards the Needles Channel on 6 August 1901, he had to put his mind to the duties of an executive officer.

Apart from these, he had still to take some specialist instruction. Dr. Hugh Robert Mill, noted as an oceanographer and meteorologist, had undertaken to sail in the *Discovery* as far as Madeira to help the scientists in preparing their programmes, and to Ernest Shackleton he gave lessons in the determination of the density and salinity of sea-water.

Mill recorded[13], twenty-two years later, when he wrote the biography of the great explorer Sir Ernest Shackleton, that the young officer 'found the minute accuracy required rather irksome, and was long in grasping the importance of writing down one reading of an instrument before making the next. But his inexhaustible good humour made correction easy, and his determination to excel served him here as in other tasks'.

The comment was shrewd, as were most of Mill's pronouncements about the man he came to know so well. Ernest Shackleton, for all the quickness and orderliness of his mind, was not the kind of man ever to make a pure scientist. He required to see a result too quickly. He could put forward his massive energies for some definite end, but for the patient accumulation of facts whose application he himself might never see—for that he had no taste. Throughout his life he regarded scientists with a certain respect tempered with scorn: respect based perhaps on a latent feeling of inferiority, scorn because he sometimes found that scientists were unpractical men.

In the *Discovery*, however, he conducted his experiments and made his records as efficiently as he did everything else, and that Scott was well pleased with the result can be seen from a letter he wrote[14] to Dr. Mill from the *Discovery*, after the former had returned to England :

'Shackleton keeps going at the water samples but has transferred most of the work to his cabin. He is always anxious lest he has been unmindful of some little precaution or made some error in calculation. His ambition is to have as perfect a record as circumstances will permit, and to keep two hydrometers unbroken.

I am certain the business could not be in better hands and I dont forget that you suggested its allocation and gave the necessary tuition.'

Mill's tuition indeed sweetened the work for Shackleton. Hugh Robert Mill was a man of scholarly temperament and dry humour, but he concealed, not always very deeply, a romantic soul. It was not long before he discovered that the burly young officer whom he had been set to instruct was as well versed in the English poets as he was. This discovery was made early on the voyage; and by the time Mill left the ship at Madeira the two men were fast friends. Shackleton kept an abiding impression of a kind and interesting companion; Mill remembered, and afterwards sought out, a man whose physical strength he could vicariously enjoy. Gradually, through Shackleton's complex and exciting career, the friendship became closer; and it is clear that Mill came to depend on Shackleton in a way that only a frail and delicate man can depend on a strong one. Mill had a brave and ardent spirit in a small, inadequate body; through books, and through the actions of his friend, he could carry out the explorations which his physique made impossible in fact.

Shackleton, like everyone else on board, regretted Dr. Mill's departure from the *Discovery*, a departure which Mill himself signalised by presenting the ship's company with an elaborate pepper mill, a nice example of his humour. But for Shackleton there were to be plenty more friendships. On that long voyage of ninety-one days, before the ship was safely tied up to a jetty in Lyttelton Harbour, he made himself popular with everybody, and in particular endeared himself to Edward Wilson, the spare, not too strong, dedicated scientist, the most cultivated and probably the most intelligent man in the ship.

Shackleton expressed his liking for Wilson early in the voyage by giving him the benefit of his experience. At Funchal he took him to visit some friends and, with Barne, they took horses up the mountain road to see the beauties of the island. In Madeira Shackleton invested in some matting so that Wilson could lie cool in the tropical heat. 'He has quite taken me in his charge,' Wilson wrote in his diary[9] on 19 August, 'and puts me up to endless tips and does no end of things for me.' In return for this practical help, Wilson now and then saved Shackleton from getting into trouble. For instance, when the sail-cloth bath was fixed on the deck, the good-natured Hodgson was thrown in by Shackleton, because, as he said, his pyjamas looked as if they needed a wash. Wilson regarded the scene with amusement; but when Hodgson and Shackleton proposed trying the same remedy with the somewhat dignified Dr. Koettlitz, he advised against it, and his advice was taken.

Wilson and Shackleton shared a liking for horseplay, but they were drawn together too by mutual literary tastes. Wilson often visited the bridge during Shackleton's watch, and Shackleton would recite Browning to him, or read Swinburne. Sometimes when the Third Officer's time was his own, the two of them retired to the poop deck to read and doze in the sun until tea and macaroons called them at 3.30. It became the custom for Shackleton to rouse Wilson in the early hours of the morning to see a particularly spectacular sunrise (other colleagues, when roused, muttered a temporising phrase and went to sleep again).

On one occasion (26 October) Wilson recorded what he called a soirée in his cabin, with Barne and Armitage disposed as comfortably as possible, together with two of the dogs, while the host painted the woodwork or at least what he could see of it, and Shackleton read aloud from 'The Day's Work'. The afternoon, redolent with the fumes of paint and tobacco, was a great success.

Though it was not in Shackleton to apply himself assiduously and continuously to scientific research, he became interested in Wilson's subject; he would note birds for him, and on one occasion at least, on the voyage out, became an enthusiastic collector. This was at South Trinidad, a lonely, inhospitable island which the ship visited on 13 September. Shackleton went with the scientists and one or two fellow-officers on a trip ashore, the general orders being to bring in everything of natural history interest.

> 'We were all strung up like Christmas trees' Wilson remarks[9], 'with bags & satchels & boxes & bottles. . . . Shackles found grasshoppers—Cockroaches—ants—also a Gannet's nest made of sticks on one of the dead trees, & adorned with a green trailer which carried pods as big as our broad beans. He also found the black Petrels breeding on shelves of rock—and the white terns . . .'

Years later Shackleton planned to visit the island again (pp. 456-7) —this time not as a collector of natural history specimens but as a treasure seeker. In 1901, however, friendship, activity and new scenes were more precious to him than tangible treasure.

The voyage of the *Discovery* was broken when on 3 October she took on coal in Table Bay and then proceeded to the naval station in Simon's

Bay, Cape Town. Here she lay for nearly a fortnight, while the magnetic instruments, of such importance to the success of the expedition's survey, were checked with the permanent instruments at the Cape's magnetic station. The South African War was not yet over, and Shackleton must have felt strongly the contrast between his present status and his position as Third Officer in the *Carisbrooke Castle* on his last visit to Cape Town. From the round of dinner parties and entertainments the members of the expedition were taken into a very different atmosphere. A month after leaving Simon's Bay quite a few of them were having their first sight of ice as they entered the pack in the Southern Ocean on the 60th Parallel; and Shackleton, who had last seen ice on a journey in the North Atlantic as a boy of seventeen, was to have a foretaste of the sailing conditions he was to know so well.

The *Discovery* was taken to within 200 miles of Adélie Land before she turned north, and on 22 November they sighted Macquarie Island, where there was a landing in the afternoon. From this landing came another first experience.[10]

'On Sunday, November 24, a penguin stew was prepared, and Armitage wanted to cook it in Worcester sauce, a glass of Madeira, and a glass of port. But Shackleton and Wilson, the mess and wine-caterers, declared that the stores would not stand such waste, and the penguin had to be cooked without that epicurean sauce. Shackleton pronounced it to be all right, and that it had the merit of being fresh, but he would not ride a mile to eat it. Royds highly approved of scrambled penguins' eggs for breakfast, and thought the roast penguin at dinner very good. The men had it boiled. Some liked it and some did not. Captain Scott had anticipated considerable prejudice on the part of the men to this form of diet, which it will so often be necessary to enforce, and he was agreeably surprised to find that they were by no means averse to it. Many pronounced it excellent, and all appreciated the necessity of cultivating a taste for it.'

Not long after they had crossed the line an emergency arose in Shackleton's province as storekeeper, when it was discovered that the ship was leaking and that some of the provisions had been damaged by water. To the restowing which he had to superintend then was added a far more considerable task when they reached New Zealand. Here the expedition spent nearly a month, between 29 November and 24 December. Most of that time the ship was lying in Lyttelton Harbour, and while the scientists were free to take train through the tussocky hills to the English-looking city of Christchurch, the officers were kept much by the vessel, while the sails were overhauled, and the ship docked for repairs. The entire contents of the holds were taken out and re-stowed, and there was added to them a considerable bulk of replacement stores, both dry goods and fresh food. Last of the consumable goods, a flock of forty-five sheep (a present from the New Zealand farmers), was driven on board. Shackleton, directing the stowing, had plenty of scope for his marked organising ability.

In Christchurch, meanwhile, Wilson and the other scientists were working at the Museum. The last of their number now joined the ship, Louis Bernacchi the physicist,* a rotund, cheerful man who was to become a most acceptable member of the expedition and who was to write[12] a frank and pertinent description of Shackleton as he was at that time,

> 'Shackleton's character was a queer combination of elements, difficult to understand. He was a buccaneer in some of his ways, dominating, truculent and challenging. He could be very unpleasant if he were attacked. But he knew his failings, and never concealed his faults. He was essentially a fighter, afraid of nothing and of nobody, but, withal, he was human, overflowing with kindness and generosity, affectionate and loyal to all his friends.'

* Bernacchi had remained in England to collect some belated instruments, and had travelled to New Zealand by fast steamer. He had been appointed physicist to the expedition at short notice, to replace W. Shackleton, who had been appointed early in the year and had then resigned the post. It was assumed by Dr. Mill, and by others after him, that this name was in some way a mistake and that *Ernest* Shackleton was intended. In fact they were two distinct persons, and their pictures appear in the same issue of the *Sphere*[11] on the opposite sides of a page.

Chapter IV

THE next phase of the journey now began. After a short service held by the Bishop of Christchurch on the mess-deck, the *Discovery* left Lyttelton on 21 December, coaled at Port Chalmers and saw the last of New Zealand on Christmas Eve. She proceeded quickly towards the south, for the Captain wanted to make as extensive a coastal survey as possible before the Antarctic winter set in. Christmas Day was celebrated on 5 January in the pack ice, two days after they had crossed the Antarctic Circle: on the eighth the coast of Victoria Land was sighted: and the following day, on shore at Cape Adare, Bernacchi was showing his interested comrades the hut where he, with Borchgrevink's *Southern Cross* expedition, had spent the winter of 1896–97, the first winter which anybody had spent on the Antarctic continent.

The locality was still so little known that it had been left to the expedition leader to decide whether he could over-winter with his ship in 1902 or whether he must return to England. Scott had arranged with his committee that he would leave messages at various suitable places so that if a relief ship should be sent down in the winter of 1903 it would be able to find the party. The first of these messages was left in the hut of the *Southern Cross* expedition, the second off Cape Wadworth (Coulman Island) three days later. On 18 January they reached Wood Bay, suggested by Sir Clements Markham as a possible wintering place; but the bay was found to be full of fast-frozen pack-ice, and they pushed on.

They had long passed the furthest point of Ross's explorations of 1841–42, and were seeing land which he had only observed from a great distance. Everything was new and stimulating. On 20 January a natural harbour, afterwards named Granite Harbour from the rock formations there, strongly tempted Scott, for it offered shelter and food supply in the form of seals. He was afterwards glad that he had moved on to look for a base further south, for Granite Harbour, backed by mountains and with constantly shifting sea-ice outside, would have much restricted the movement of sledging parties.

Arrived at the entrance of McMurdo Sound, Scott thought he had found what he wanted. This piece of water, sometimes open, sometimes full of pack-ice, sometimes frozen over, was to become a testing ground for many captains after Scott. It is an enclosed bay running south, forty miles across at its entrance, thirty miles across at its head, with considerable slopes on both sides. On the west side, snow slopes rise fairly gently to the mountains of Victoria Land. On the east side lies Ross Island, surrounded partly by the Barrier ice and partly by the sea, much crevassed and broken up, and rising more steeply, with the two volcanic mountains, Erebus and Terror, as landmarks. On Ross Island, at Cape Armitage, Cape Royds and Cape Evans, stand three wooden huts, weather-beaten, littered with the débris of successive visiting parties, but still to this day bearing witness to the tenacity and enterprise of man the explorer.

The sound and the island, so rich now in history and tradition, were as yet only names to Scott and to his Third Officer. Scott took his ship some way south in the sound and was satisfied that he could find in this area a sheltered place to winter in—perhaps even a route to the Pole. Then he turned eastwards for a further coastal survey.

On 22 January another record was left at Cape Crozier, beneath the shadow of the mountain Terror, and the ship then began a cruise along the Great Ice Barrier, the spectacular apron of thick continental ice, ending in a sea-cliff of varying height, which Ross had sighted from far off, and which was to remain the wonder of every newcomer to the Antarctic scene. Towards the eastern end of the Barrier Ross had sighted what he thought was land, but he had not been able to confirm this, and it was the privilege of the National Antarctic Expedition to sight, on 30 January, the cliffs of the land afterwards named King Edward VII Land.

The discovery of this land was one of the principal achievements of the expedition, but there was no time now to explore it, nor did Scott feel that they were justified in entering upon a prolonged land journey while they were still completely inexperienced sledgers. The ship was turned once more towards the west and towards the sound where he intended to establish winter quarters.

On 3 February they reached a deep bight in the Barrier which they had noted on the way east, and here the ship was halted. Armitage and Bernacchi, with four men and light sledge equipment, set off towards the south for a brief reconnaissance trip, while other members of the party, in the poor light of the evening, tumbled about on the ice on skis—to most of them an entirely new instrument of travelling.

The next day they experimented with something even more new and exciting—ballooning, a method of observing the extent and nature of Barrier ice which had been suggested by Sir Joseph Hooker. Scott made the first ascent and in spite of some absent-mindedness about the ballast he managed the craft successfully and made detailed observations of the surrounding country. Then he sent Shackleton up with a camera. Others had been promised an ascent in the afternoon but the balloon was found to be leaking and they had to forgo this 'novel sensation'. It was found then, and only then, as Wilson[1] remarked, 'that had

Royal Naval Reserve, 1904

Third Officer of *Carisbrooke Castle*, 1901

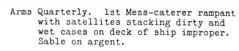

ARMS AND THE MAN.

Arms Quarterly. 1st Mess-caterer rampant with satellites stacking dirty and wet cases on deck of ship improper. Sable on argent.

2nd Hydrometer in cylinder of sea water suspended supported by burette and pipette crossed proper sable on or.

3rd Typewriter restant proper attendant for S.P.T. and other Antarctic papers sable on vert.

4th Caput poetatis with long hair lisant with benign expression inspired by Browning gules on azure.

Crest Homo posterior half performing with seven balls gules, in cold climates.

Motto FACILE PRINCEPS.

E. H. SHACKLETON.

One of a series of mock-heraldic pieces by Wilson and Shackleton (June 1902)

'The Parsenger'. Caricature by Michael Barne (May 1902)

Silhouette of Ernest Shackleton by E. A. Wilson

The above three pictures show Shackleton as seen by his messmates on the National Antarctic Expedition (July 1902): from the *South Polar Times*. (See pp. 41–6.)

anyone used the valve in the morning when the balloon was up it would
not have closed properly & nothing could have prevented the whole
show from dropping to earth like a stone!' Ballooning seemed to him an
'exceedingly dangerous amusement'. He thought the training had been
wholly inadequate,* and felt that 'if some of these experts don't come to
grief over it out here, it will only be because God has pity on the foolish'.

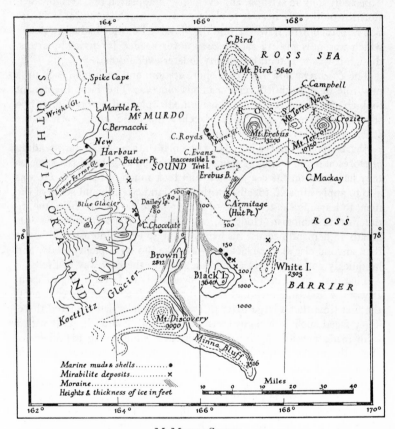

McMURDO SOUND.
(slightly modified from Debenham[17], by courtesy of the Royal Geographical Society)

The ship now proceeded directly for McMurdo Sound. On 8
February they reached a long cape on Ross Island in the south-east
corner of the sound, afterwards called Cape Armitage. Scott hoped that

* The balloon section consisted of Skelton and Shackleton as officers, Lashly,
Leading Seaman Kennar and Heald, A.B. They had been on a short course with
the R.E. Balloon section at Aldershot under Colonel Templar.

they might find an open strait beyond the cape that would lead on to the south; they found instead the westernmost edge of the Barrier. The ship lay for the night in a small bay off the north side of the cape, and on the following day Scott found a bay on the south side which seemed a suitable sheltered place for wintering. Here the *Discovery* was anchored, to wait until she could be frozen in. The ice proved unexpectedly long in settling, and even after it appeared to be established, storms would carry it away to within a very short distance of the ship. She remained firm, however, and the portable hut they had taken down, which was now put up ashore, was never needed for living quarters, though it was to extend hospitality to later expeditions.

The *Discovery* now became a shore station, and each man took up a new rôle or a modified version of his old one. The First Lieutenant took charge of regular and extensive meteorological observations: two small huts were erected for Bernacchi's magnetic work: each of the scientists laid his individual plans.

Shackleton was never idle. His two chief duties—the superintending of stores and the taking of salinities—remained in general the same as they had been on the sea journey, and took much of his time. He was also to apply himself, together with Barne and Skelton and some of the men, to learning the technique of sledging. He gave much help, too, to the marine biologist, Hodgson, with his fish traps (finding he was greatly in demand because his hands stood up to the intense cold better than anyone else's). Shackleton always liked to have plenty to do, and he quickly and effectively adapted himself to the new way of life.

That first winter in the Antarctic, everybody had everything to learn. It was the first time men had sledged into the interior of the continent, the first time that a large party of men of all ranks had wintered there. They faced such dangers as crevasses and scurvy and blizzards with a calm made possible by lack of experience, while being apprehensive about the melancholy effect of a long Polar winter—effects which, in this cheerful and well-organised party, were never felt at all.

If the National Antarctic Expedition was pioneering, it was doing so, to be sure, with some weight of experience behind it, the experience of the great British naval expeditions in the Arctic in the previous century. This was particularly the case with the provisioning.

Dr. Koettlitz, who had drawn up the original lists of provisions for the expedition, had learnt much from his period with the Jackson–Harmsworth expedition, on which he was able to profit from the experience and knowledge of Nansen. Koettlitz had two points chiefly in mind—to provide food nourishing and sufficient for work in low temperatures, and to prevent scurvy. He had also to cater for two types of stores—those for meals at the base, and those needed for the sledging journeys, which had to be highly compressed to save weight and space.

The diet worked out by Scott and Koettlitz satisfied the first point: it was nourishing and sustaining, with its preponderance of tinned meat and fruit pies. As for the sledging ration, it can only be described as a starvation diet, but this applied also to many subsequent Antarctic expeditions where small parties had to haul their provisions for long distances. Nor was the diet at the base as satisfactory as it seemed. Plum-duff and tinned meat stew might satisfy the bluejacket but such dishes could not prevent scurvy.

It is now well known that scurvy is caused by a deficiency of vitamin C. When the National Antarctic Expedition set out, current theories of its cause and prevention were in a chaotic state.

As early as the thirteenth century it had been recognised that the disease was connected with a lack of fresh fruit and vegetables. At the end of the sixteenth century Sir Richard Hawkins had noticed oranges and lemons to be particularly valuable for long sea voyages, and in 1601 Sir James Lancaster had introduced the regular use of these fruits into the ships of the East India Company.[2] The investigations of a naval surgeon, James Lind, in the middle of the eighteenth century, were so conclusive that in 1803 lemon juice was made compulsory in the Royal Navy, and scurvy was practically wiped out. Unfortunately during the nineteenth century West Indian limes were substituted for Mediterranean lemons. The West Indian fruit being far less rich in vitamin C, scurvy again became prevalent in the Navy, and there was a tendency to discredit fruit as an antiscorbutic.

At the time when Scott was preparing his provisions, it was widely believed that the disease was due to the toxic properties of tinned food or fresh meat that was not in prime condition. Consequently, the doctors examined every tin that was opened throughout the voyage and the first winter, rejecting any that was at all suspicious; they did not realise the inadequacy of the tins that did pass muster. In fact, during the winter of 1902, the men were not getting enough vitamin C. The fruit, which the bottling process had robbed of some of its value, lost more when it was cooked again in pies: the tinned vegetables were mostly of disappointing quality: the tinned Danish butter, though good, was less valuable against scurvy than the small amount of fresh butter bought in New Zealand.

New Zealand had provided them also, as we have seen, with a small flock of sheep. When the ship reached the ice, these were slaughtered and hung in the rigging. With the Antarctic as a deep freeze, the company was able to enjoy roast mutton for Sunday dinner all through the first winter. The experience of Armitage and Koettlitz in the Arctic had made them well aware of the power of fresh meat to counteract scurvy or at least help on recovery from it. On the way south the larder was replenished with seal meat at several points, and seal hunting became a regular sport in winter quarters. Armitage, however, always felt that his leader had allowed his humane instincts to prevent him from building up a large enough store of this valuable food. Moreover, seal meat was only put on the menus two or three times a week, with tinned meat on the intervening days.* Even these days of fresh meat were less beneficial than they might have been, for the cook, who was dirty and inefficient, served seal-meat customarily in an unappetising stew, so that there was soon a strong prejudice against any part of the animal except the heart and liver.

Shackleton, as caterer, did all that he could in the circumstances. That he was alive to the enormous importance of expedition diet can be seen in his diary.[3]

'Spent most of the day checking over the stores & making up books. I am rather worried about some of our food for instead of being in good condition for the winter the vegetables got from Germany have turned out to be in a wretched state, so that will shorten a great deal of that sort of food, and I specially wanted the crew and ourselves to have plenty of those sort of things. After the sun goes on the 23rd of this month we will have the New Zealand mutton that I have had frozen and kept. every Sunday. and seal for all hands every second day. so there ought to be no chance of scurvy with all this food fresh. Then I am allowing all through the winter a double supply of fruit. So really we ought all to do well. (*April* 2.)'

The entry is particularly interesting because it shows that Shackleton, like Armitage and Koettlitz, laid stress first of all on the need for fresh food as a preventive, whereas Scott's history of the expedition makes it clear that he and Wilson were preoccupied with the theory of the toxic cause of scurvy. This winter of 1902 was to make them think again. If they did not entirely abandon the theory, at least Scott was sufficiently convinced of the importance of fresh meat to alter the menus drastically for the second winter. To none of them was the lesson brought home more forcibly than to Shackleton.

In 1902 the expedition had much to find out, too, about Polar transport. Sledges had never been used before in the Antarctic for extended journeys. 'We were forced to assume,' Scott wrote,[4] 'that southern conditions were more or less similar to those of the north, and in so far as they proved different our sledging outfit ran the risk of failure.' For the actual construction of his sledges and their equipment, for advice on sledge cookers, tents, sleeping bags, travelling clothes, and the multifarious details of ice and snow travel, Scott had consulted Nansen and had visited the factories at Christiania (Oslo). Scott valued Nansen's advice very highly, but he could not accept

* In his book[4], Scott refers to 'seal meat three times a week' on p. 248, but on p. 407 he says it was served twice a week.

his views on dog-teams. To Scott, as to most members of this expedition, dogs were pets rather than draught animals, and the discipline which Nansen advised Scott to use with them seemed to him to be cruelty. Entirely inexperienced in dog-driving, he was disappointed by the poor way the animals worked, their shrinking from snow, their habit of fighting and becoming tangled in their harness. In an article on 'Sledging at 40° Below', in the May number of the *South Polar Times*[5] in 1902, he recalled sadly 'those well-known Arctic pictures in which a sledge is gliding swiftly along behind a group of galloping quadrupeds with erect curly tails'. The sailors felt a similar disappointment. 'I was under the impression from books Etc that I had read', Rhossilly wrote wistfully in a letter to the Editor in the June number, 'that a sledge journey was quite a sporting affair, and all one had to do was to walk alongside the sledges, and the dogs done the pulling part of the business, but I was quickly undeceived . . .'.*

The truth of the matter was that none of the would-be sledgers had the least idea of how to handle a dog-team, but went off in happy-go-lucky fashion, learning as they went along, and at first not managing too well. It was the same with all aspects of sledging. Bernacchi commented afterwards[6] that

> 'competitions in making camp, including all the multifarious duties to be performed in a tiny tent before toggling down for the night, might advantageously have taken the place of moonlight football matches during the comparative idleness of the winter, and competitions in dog-driving would have taken the keen edge off our ignorance of that most important accomplishment'.

Impatient with the dogs, the men made the fatal mistake of helping them out by pulling in harness with them, in spite of warnings from Armitage, who knew very well that dogs would not work together with men and needed a special discipline.

But inexperience was not the whole trouble. There was a deeper psychological factor. From the classic naval journeys in the Arctic, notably those of Parry and McClintock, there had descended to Sir Clements Markham and thence to Scott a stubborn, sentimental, wholly understandable but regrettably unpractical devotion to the cause of man-hauling. Scott[4] summed up his view thus:

> 'In my mind no journey ever made with dogs can approach the height of that fine conception which is realised when a party of men

---

* This passage, which was not printed in the *South Polar Times*, is taken from the original MS., which survives exactly as it was handed to Shackleton, as editor of the magazine, in the winter of 1902. Rhossilly was the pseudonym of Edgar Evans, the burly seaman who went with Scott on the *Terra Nova*, and died on the tragic Southern Journey of 1911–12.

go forth to face hardships, dangers, and difficulties with their own unaided efforts, and by days and weeks of hard physical labour succeed in solving some problem of the great unknown. Surely in this case the conquest is more nobly and splendidly won.'

This idealism, which if carried to its logical conclusion must have robbed the expedition of many external aids, undoubtedly stood in the way of real efficiency in respect of the dogs. Heroism is apt to prove a wasteful virtue, and never more so than in the splendid days of man-hauling.

The first sledging trips, in the autumn of 1902, were completely experimental, and Shackleton was among the first to discover the difficulties of travel in the Antarctic—the rough surface, the sudden blizzards, the incredibly low temperatures. On 19 February he led Wilson and Ferrar on a reconnaissance trip to White Island, having tossed a coin for the privilege with Barne. The ship was now anchored in her final position for the winter, but the ice was still unstable in the vicinity; and as well as dragging a sledge the party was given orders to take a pram (a light boat) and not to cross extensive stretches of sea-ice without it.

The three men set out gaily, man-hauling the sledge, with sledge flags flying, and marched for twelve hours. For much of this time they were wasting their strength against a blizzard, a form of weather then unproved by them, and one which Shackleton did not propose to allow to defeat him. However, at 11.30 p.m. they were forced to give in, and with some difficulty they pitched a tent, had some food and got what rest they could. Wilson had a bad attack of cramp and he comments on the kindness with which Shackleton and Ferrar dressed him first and then sat on him while they dressed themselves. At 3.30 the following morning they turned out, since the wind had dropped, and set off towards the island. Having been deceived by the light, they found the journey far longer than they had expected, but once there they found plenty to occupy them. They took detailed observations and surveyed the Barrier from a height of 2,730 feet which they had some difficulty in reaching. Their explorations lasted for three days. They sighted a new range of mountains running south and made the first short journey on the Barrier ice. We can guess that these were days of sheer delight to Shackleton, in spite of the physical discomfort, for the romantic side of his nature reacted now, as always, to a new scene. 'It is a unique sort of feeling to look on lands that have never been seen by human eyes before,' he had written in his diary a month before, and he had occasion to feel this many times before his first year in the Antarctic was over.

By 22 February Shackleton and his companions judged that they had done what they had been sent[7] to do—namely, to 'proceed to the left hand extremity of the Island or Peninsular [*sic*] which bears S by

W (true) from the ship', to investigate this land and the corner of the bay in which it is situated, and in particular 'the snow slope which appears to run out from the Western Extremity of the Island or Peninsular to the Eastward of that to which you are going and endeavour to obtain information as to the nature of the country to the Southward of this slope'.

They returned to the ship, by a slightly different route, getting in at 10.30 p.m. Wilson[1] recorded 'Sardine supper & Cocoa the things I think we all enjoy most as a treat, were ready for us, & then we slept the sleep of the just.' The results of their journeying[8] were presented to the Captain in 'a very tidy official budget' containing a map which Shackleton and Wilson had made together from the angles and bearings Shackleton had taken, some sketches done by Wilson, and a geological report from Ferrar. Just as valuable to the expedition was the confused and tumbled account of the hardships of the journey with which the travellers regaled the stay-at-homes as they drank their cocoa. 'It is strange now,' Scott wrote[4] retrospectively, 'to look back on these first essays at sledging, and to see how terribly hampered we were by want of experience.' The discussions after a journey were exceptionally valuable in the first year, and Scott always made a point of them.

The stay-at-homes were not always entirely appreciative. On this particular occasion Skelton[9] remarked on the return of the sledge party and the way 'Shackleton immediately started in with tremendous accounts,—& hardly stopped talking until everybody had turned in'; he added, '—I will do him the credit to say, that he talks sense, & not blooming nonsense like at least one of our members, if not two, or three.'

Shackleton's part in the next sledging trip was somewhat different. In his capacity as officer-in-charge of stores it fell to him to prepare sledges for two teams, under Royds and Skelton, who were to visit Cape Crozier, at the north-east point of Ross Island, to reconnoitre and to leave messages for the relief ship. To Wilson,[1] who helped Shackleton, the job seemed a long and tedious one—'weighing out pounds & ounces of tea, sugar, cocoa, butter & pemmican &c. & putting them all in separate canvas bags one bag for each day for three men in a tent— and all numbered & labelled. It means a lot of work, & much depends on it, but there is little kudos attached.'

The party set out on 4 March, and it was not until a week had passed that it was learned at the base that this time inexperience had led to tragedy. The party had separated after going some way, because of bad weather. Royds pushed on to Cape Crozier with one party and Barne led the rest of the men back towards the base. Barne's party had been split up in the fog, and some of the men, supposing themselves near the ship, suddenly found themselves close to the edge of a cliff and slipping down it towards the sea. One sailor, Vince, slid over the precipice before he could be stopped, another disappeared as they were climbing out of danger, and the leader was unable to get his party together because of the thick weather. Now, on the evening of 11 March, four men turned up at the ship, exhausted and excited, under the self-assumed leadership of Frank Wild.

Scott had injured his leg, so when the story had been extracted from Wild, the only one capable of telling it coherently, Armitage was despatched with a search party, and shortly afterwards Shackleton was sent out with a crew of six men to take a whaler by sea to the scene of the accident, in case either of the missing men had tried to escape along the ice-foot.

Wilson[1] only heard about this relief party the next day.

'I think they had about the worst part of all the searching [he commented in his diary on 12 March]. There was a regular sea on, & the drift was racing down the slopes & the ice-foot, burying the boat in freezing drift & spray, every drop freezing where it fell—and the boat continually drifting to leeward notwithstanding the efforts of the heaviest crew our ship could provide. They all worked like bricks —it must have been a very trying business, as they all knew that they were prepared for emergencies, for three weeks' provision had been put in the boat at the start, and indeed there was but small prospect of this boat getting back to the ship that night—and every prospect of its getting drifted right out to the mouth of the bay—or at least to the other side—where they would have had to build a snow hut & camp until the wind dropped. However this didn't happen, & although they saw no sign of anyone, nor indeed of anything else in such thick drift, they succeeded in getting back to the ship the same night.'

Wilson himself took out another search party on the 12th, bringing back a sledge and two of the four dogs which had been attached to it, and on the 13th the youngest member of the expedition—Charles Hare, a lad of eighteen—appeared at the ship. The story of how he had slept buried in the snow, existing in severe weather conditions for forty hours without food, is one of the most remarkable tales of this expedition, and one of the oddest, for he was quite unconscious of the passage of time, and was surprised, when he reached the ship, to find so much fuss being made about him.

Vince's body was never found, and his death was a severe shock to the other members of the Cape Crozier party when they returned a few days later.

Greater precautions were now taken in travelling anywhere away from the ship. Guiding lines were fixed along the regular route from ship to huts. Scott determined to organise one more autumn journey,

partly to improve sledging technique, partly to leave a depôt of food
on the track which would afterwards be taken by the southern party.
For this journey to the south was to be the most important feature of
the work of the coming summer, more important than the westward
journey in which Armitage was to push inland in search of a way to
the South Magnetic Pole, or that of Royds towards the glacier afterwards
named after the geologist Ferrar.

Scott had discussed these journeys with Wilson while the ship was
cruising along the Barrier at the beginning of the year. Perhaps at this
early date the Southern Journey had not captured their imagination in
the way it did later. The magic phrase South Pole does not seem to
have been used yet; it was dropped first by Wilson, quite casually,
in an entry in his diary on 12 June. But by the end of March, when
the depôt party was being arranged, the journey was beginning to be
interesting to everybody, for although it was now known that Scott
would lead it himself, it was not yet decided who would go with him.

The last sledging party of the autumn was delayed for some days,
for the old ice had by now completely moved out of the bay where the
Discovery lay, and the new ice, shifted by changeable weather, was not
yet safe for travelling. Shackleton worked hard at preparations for this
journey. He spent what time he could spare with the dogs, trying to get
them in some kind of shape for sledging. He was not much impressed,
by their performance. 'Few of them seem to be used to pulling,' he
thought,[3] 'though their leader Nigger is a splendid animal.' On 31
March he walked out with Koettlitz to see the large depôt party start,
and took some photographs of them. He noted that the dogs did not
seem over-anxious to work, and when the party returned three days
later, defeated by the low temperatures, he was amused to see that they
were now pulling well 'for they knew they were homeward bound'.

The day after the departure of the depôt party Shackleton began to
clear out L Store, in the hold of the ship, as an office for his new
venture—for he was now to become a magazine editor.

The *South Polar Times*, the first periodical to be produced[5] in the
Antarctic, owed its origin to a meeting in the ward-room of the
Discovery at the beginning of the winter, when, as Armitage[10] explained :

'. . . it was decided to bring out a monthly paper something like a
London magazine. Each of us wrote on a piece of paper what we
thought the best title for this Southern publication . . . Shackleton
was appointed editor, and Wilson principal Artist. It was to be
published on the 1st of each month; and every member of the ship's
company was invited to contribute towards it making it the most
amusing, instructive, up-to-date journal, with *the* largest circulation
of any periodical within the Antarctic Circle. It was to combine all
the best qualities of all the penny and halfpenny London dailies,

together with those of the superior comic papers, as well as of the fourpenny-halfpenny and half-crown monthly magazines. Notwithstanding this super-excellence, the *South Polar Times* was to be issued free to all the population of our small colony, the cost of production being more than covered by the grateful feelings of the recipients, to say nothing of the advertisers. . . . A carved box was placed outside the office for the receipt of contributions, but would-be authors much preferred a personal audience; so our editor, in self-defence, removed his office fittings to a storeroom in the bowels of the ship, where the wicked ceased from troubling, and his poetical nerves were at rest.'

Scott in his account of the magazine,[4] says that at this meeting it was resolved 'that each number should contain, besides the editorial, a summary of the events and meteorological conditions of the past month, certain scientifically instructive articles dealing with our work and our surroundings, and certain others written in a lighter vein'.

The mingling of grave and gay, scholarly and facetious, in the pages of this fascinating Polar periodical may have been decided in committee, but we may be sure that Shackleton's voice was not silent; for this was exactly the mixture that best suited his own temperament, and he had already edited one volume, *O.H.M.S.*, in the same vein. He threw himself into the work with all the enthusiasm he was apt to display for something new.

He and his crony, the artist, lost no time in establishing themselves in their office, where they arranged cases for seats and for a table to hold Shackleton's typewriter. 'The place is most comfortable,' Wilson[1] wrote, 'not cold or stuffy, & lit by candle-lamps. There are cases of chocolate & raisins here which we keep an eye on to see that they don't get spoilt by the damp.' Shackleton[3] phrased this somewhat differently. The chocolate and raisins were for the artist 'who has a weakness for sweets . . . he says he only tries them to be sure that they are not getting damp'.

The phrasing, and the situation which each man describes, irresistibly brings to mind the cosy, stuffy study of a boys' public school, just as the warm relationship between Shackleton and Wilson at this time, based on a mutual admiration for courage, poetry and horse-play, is reminiscent of the classic friendships of schoolboys, none the less important because they are possible only in youth. The atmosphere of the *Discovery* was in many ways like that engendered by the active presence of a pack of schoolboys, and this can be seen most clearly in the animated pages of the *South Polar Times*, stuffed as it is with topical jokes and casual erudition.

Shackleton was a good editor. He ran the magazine for five issues, keeping to the plan of mixing humour and serious writing, running regular features to sustain interest and introducing new elements with a judicious hand. Thus Scott's excellent acrostics, appearing each month, were turned into a competition (won jointly by Skelton and Wild); a series called 'Arms and the Man', with mock-heraldic devices and mottoes adapted by Shackleton and Wilson from an idea in *Punch*, gave endless opportunity for wit at the expense of others; and a series under the heading 'Told at one bell', consisting of conversations of the Amos-and-Andy type, in rich sailor idiom, gave scope for similar jokes from the forecastle.*

Regular features, too, appeared among the illustrations—a series of silhouettes, another of caricatures by Barne, with titles as amusing as the drawings, and pages of sledging flags which, beside being of considerable topical interest, are also highly decorative. (see illus. opp. page 33).

Shackleton was the first to admit that the high quality of the *South Polar Times* was largely due to Wilson's illustrations. There can be few magazines with such beautiful and dignified tail-pieces, such meticulous and attractive line-drawings. Wilson's own scientific articles on seals, penguins and Antarctic birds owe much of their value to drawings that make identification a joy as well as an education; and throughout the paper, under Shackleton's editorship and later, many articles of only moderate merit were enhanced by drawings over which he took no less trouble.

Remarkable though Wilson's talents were, it would not be true to say that all else in the magazine seemed mediocre beside his contributions. Scott, whose serious articles were well written, showed also a talent for facetious writing, in a vein very much of his period. Barne had a gift for occasional verse, and one of his poems, 'Ode to a Penguin', would go well in the Oxford Book of Light Verse. Frank Wild, under the psuedonym of Shellback, showed his quality in the first number with an ingenious bit of foolery, 'Some of my Messmates' and his mock-Biblical narrative 'An Old Document', stands comparison with the ward-room entries.

Shackleton did a good deal of talent-hunting and kept his eyes open for suitable subjects for the paper. Thus on 6 April, attracted by a commotion in the evening, he went out to find that two crabeater seals had come out of Hodgson's fish-trap hole near the ship and had strayed among the dogs. After the seals had been tied up, to be killed the next day, he asked Petty Officer Cross to write 'a little account of the event

---

* These were written by T. Kennar, one of the Petty Officers, under the name of Jacker. The original entries are extant among the Shackleton family papers, and also copies in Scott's writing, punctuated (which the originals are not!) but otherwise almost unaltered, the supposition being that Scott was called in to help either editor or author. It must be noted that Scott was most anxious that the mess-deck should join in the magazine.

for the paper'. The little account duly appeared in the first number as
'A Seal Chase' by Jumper, and very vivid it is too. On 26 April,
enjoying with the rest the first meeting of the Debating Club, Shackleton
asked Bernacchi to write a report on it for the May number. Thinly
disguised as Veritas, the cheerful physicist took the chance of penning
a character sketch of the editor, representing him as 'a gentleman with
a blatant voice, & rubicund countenance & a never-to-be-eradicated
brogue', who contributed to the discussion on whether the Great
Barrier was movable or fixed a succession of epigrammatic remarks,
ending with the solemn statement that the barrier 'is adhering to the
bottom of the sea in the form of a huge icy sticking-plaster'—at which,
the reporter comments 'you could have heard a mangle drop'.

Another time-honoured editorial device was used in the June
number, when Shackleton answered a letter from Koettlitz complaining
of the inaccurate heraldry of 'Arms and the Man' in a neat rejoinder
under the signature Chrononhotonthologos, Secretary to the College of
Heralds. The joke was a good one, filled three pages of the magazine,
and had doubtless been concocted between the two of them in the
editorial office. Another scheme for getting material was less successful.
In the May number the editor announced that there would be a prize
for the best essay on Seafaring, which would be printed, but though he
tried again in June to whip up enthusiasm, only one essay, by Armitage,
was sent in. Somehow Shackleton got out of using it (it was very dull)
and the idea was dropped.

At the beginning of the paper's career the beautiful carved box provided was stuffed to overflowing with contributions. A few days after
the office had been opened, Shackleton[3] remarked 'Articles coming in
freely. A bit awkward to discriminate and arrange them but they are
doing very well.' The spirit of the mess-deck may be fairly represented
in a note which Duckridge, A.B., attached to his contribution :*

> 'Dear Sir, If you think (as I do) that the enclosed MSS. is too
> insipid for publication please don't hesitate to throw in the waste
> paper basket. I am sending it in, simply to show that, though the
> spirit is willing the flesh is weak.'

Shackleton must have had just the right manner for encouraging
budding and bashful authors. No doubt a good deal of unofficial
preliminary editing went on in the office. The floor of this room was
so well insulated by the magazines stored there that the temperature
was several degrees higher than in the rest of the ship. Indeed, the
atmosphere of the office was so attractive that there was a danger that
it might turn into a club-room, and Shackleton attached a piece of

---

* This contribution, which survives among the Shackleton family papers,
was not in fact used.

string to the door-hook so that nobody could get in until he had released the door.

It is clear from the magazine which ultimately emerged from the hold that Shackleton had been diplomatic as well as energetic. The standard was high: more than that, it remained high throughout the five numbers which he brought out in that first winter. His actual editing seems to have been light; his literary taste was excellent, and he knew when to touch up and when to leave alone.* The only contributor Shackleton dealt severely with was himself. His editorials are slashed and slashed again, and there are no less than eight different versions of the very simple paragraph announcing the appearance of *The Blizzard*.

The Blizzard represented Shackleton's final gesture of tact towards his contributors. It was 'a sort of safety valve for the *South Polar Times* . . . for anxious contributors whose things would not do for our paper'.[3] One version of the advertisement for this supplementary journal, written in a flamboyant style very typical of Shackleton in a certain mood, ran as follows:

'Owing to the large number of contributions of a humorous type, and of fleeting local interest, which would be lost ere another number of the *Times* appeared; and which, if appearing in the current month, would upset the balance of grave and gay we strive to maintain; it has been decided to publish, as early as possible next month, a paper which is to be called 'The Blizzard'. Opportunity will thus be given to all contributors to make their ideas and opinions public, and the editor of The Blizzard will be glad to insert any advertisements of lost goods and so forth. The poet is invited to awaken his muse; the essayist to let his pen run free: the Artist to send in any sketch he may have made of his fellow men or unique surroundings. And the dramatist the plot that has been only awaiting a chance to arouse the enthusiasm of the theatre going public: failing a play it would be most useful in view of the coming season: if any suggestion that has any local colouring that might be introduced into a piece should be sent in. One of the main points of value about the Blizzard will be the fact that every citizen of this colony can obtain a copy as often as it is published.'

In this ten-page paper the poet certainly awakened his muse, but her utterances were predominantly scurrilous, and the tone was set by the title-page, which represented a figure wreathed in snow-flakes, holding a bottle for consolation, with the caption 'Never mind the blizzard, I'm all right.' Besides verses contributed by the men, Barne produced, in 'The Blizzard's Gallery of Famous People', three lively caricatures of members of the crew, with ribald explanations attached.

* A number of MSS. survive among the Shackleton family papers, chiefly entries for the first two numbers and a few odd entries for the other three.

The one and only number of *The Blizzard* appeared on 1 May, a copy being made for each member of the expedition; the paper then died a natural death. Meanwhile a routine had been established for the *South Polar Times*. Because of the large number of drawings and paintings, it was impossible to produce more than one copy of each number. This was typed out by Ford, and Shackleton and Wilson gummed the pages into a book with the leaves cut out. Barne made a cover for it, and it was, as the proud editor said, 'a nice little volume', though the illustrator was afraid 'its chic and artistic appearance' would 'soon be hidden under a sufficiency of dirty finger marks'. The Captain had first go at it and could be heard laughing in his cubicle. Then it went to the ward-room, where Royds read out the best pieces, and after-wards to the mess-deck. Wilson felt his work to be well worth while for the sake of general morale. The book had amused people and had recorded 'a heap of little odd things that would otherwise be forgotten & lost'.

Shackleton, he said,[1] had had the drudgery of its production, and also the thankless task of rejecting certain of the contributions; but he had stuck to his original idea that the magazine 'should not be made use of for personal spite or as a perpetrator of any feelings that are not up to its high standard as a pioneer paper in the far South'.

There can be no doubt that Shackleton enjoyed editing far more than he enjoyed taking salinities or weighing out sledging rations: it was a more sociable occupation. He was an insatiable talker and a good mixer, and curious about his fellow men. Sometimes they exasperated him, sometimes they amused him; he probably never took a negative attitude towards anyone. It is easy to imagine him dealing confidently with the learned, the aspiring and the illiterate, in that office in the hold.

His relations with the lower deck hands seem always to have been cordial. 'He was a very nice gentleman, always ready to have a yarn with us' one of them[1] remembers. In one case Shackleton took a closer interest in a member of the lower deck than was strictly orthodox on a naval expedition. In singling out Frank Wild for his friendship, Shackleton did one of the most useful actions of his lifetime.

The son of a clergyman, Wild had been first a pupil-teacher, but he and his profession did not agree and he went into the Merchant Service, making one voyage also in Lord Brassey's yacht. Leaving the service at the end of the century, he went into the Navy as a rating, and almost at once applied to go on the National Antarctic Expedition. Spare in figure, amazingly strong, apparently impervious to fatigue, cold or danger, quick-witted but cool in judgment, warm-hearted towards his comrades, and above all incurably adventurous—such was Frank Wild when Shackleton got to know him on the *Discovery*, a man after his own heart.

On this expedition Wild distinguished himself in many spheres, frivolous and serious. He was a popular winner of the Shove Ha'penny Tournament of the first winter, and he beat Edgar Evans unmercifully in a draughts contest, their final game being depicted in the *South Polar Times* as a fight between David and Goliath. In the autumn of 1902, as we have seen, he had revealed himself as a natural leader on the sledging party which ended in Vince's death. Later he made one of a sledging combination (Royds, Quartly, Lashly and Wild) which became known as the Guarantee Party, because it would guarantee to go anywhere and do anything.

During the winter, as well as winning tournaments, Wild spent a good deal of time studying so as to improve his position in the Navy. In particular he wanted to study navigation, and Shackleton lent him books and gave him personal help. Scott perhaps did not approve of this alliance, but he does not seem to have stood in its way.*

In later life, when Shackleton's rivalry with Scott became obvious to the outside world, much was made of the difference between the Merchant Service and the Navy. It was often suggested that Shackleton had been frustrated by naval restrictions and hampered by service jealousy on this, his first expedition. *Discovery* men who still remember those days give varying opinions on this point. Mr. Charles Hare thinks that Shackleton's breaking of the unwritten law that officers and men of the lower deck did not fraternise 'did cause some feeling amongst a few of the ward-room staff—but not the scientists with whom he was most popular'. To James Dell,[13] who as butcher and sailmaker worked directly under Shackleton and whose memories of 1901–03 are most vivid, the Third Officer seemed oppressed by the naval atmosphere. But this impression is at least partly based on a conversation he had with Shackleton many years after the National Antarctic Expedition, as they stood together on the bridge of the *Quest* not far from South Georgia, when Shackleton was looking back from the vantage point of his own two expeditions and recalling certain aspects of naval discipline which now seemed to him out of place in the Antarctic. Certainly Mr. Dell recalls that Shackleton got on very well with his brother officers. Charles Ford,[14] ship's clerk and steward, also worked in close contact with Shackleton and was in a position to observe closely the atmosphere in the ward-room. Mr. Ford's opinion is now emphatic:

'I did not ever feel that in the *Discovery* there was the slightest difference between the personnel who belonged to the Royal Navy

* We are indebted for much of this information to Mr. Charles Hare,[12] ward-room assistant and Captain's steward on the *Discovery*, and a messmate of Frank Wild.

or to the Merchant Navy, at least as far as the officers were concerned. There was the greatest good feeling throughout and as far as I am aware, the question of Royal and Merchant Navy never arose in the *Discovery*.'*

Captain Michael Barne,[15] who remembers well the period when he was brother officer to Shackleton, is equally of the opinion that the difference between the Services 'counted for nothing'.

There is no doubt that the naval men must have been more at ease in each other's company, sharing as they did a strong tradition and a particular habit of work and outlook, and it is possible that they were occasionally critical of the manner Shackleton had with everybody, lower deck included, which was certainly more free and easy than their own. Bernacchi,[6] as a scientist, thought the naval formality was of great benefit to the expedition, but he also sympathised with Shackleton's ebullience, and was amused when on one occasion in the ward-room the young officer was fined by the President of the evening 'five times during one meal, for offering to bet that someone was wrong'. The abiding impression of that first winter, in fact, is of a cheerful group of men working hard and amusing themselves hard; and in that group none was more instrumental in warding off the dreaded 'cafard polaire' than Ernest Shackleton.

Early in the winter he developed one habit which helped to break the monotony. He shared with Wilson a passion for fresh air and exercise. For Wilson, who had recovered from tuberculosis, this was a matter of medical necessity as well as of habit: with Shackleton it was equally a matter of necessity, for he was a robust young man with an outsize share of physical energy. As the winter set in, he and Wilson started the custom of walking out together over the hills near the ship to the top of Ski Slope, or to the Gap, or to Crater Hill.

They turned this custom to practical use by setting up a high-level observatory on Crater Hill, where they could record temperatures and study air-currents. Their observations were made consistently and were added to those taken at the outside screen near the ship, which were under Royds's control. On these more or less daily walks, too, the two men were often able to spot a seal in the distance which might otherwise have safely reached its native element.

More important than this, in the walks abroad a warm friendship was built up as they watched together the spectacular sunsets of the Antarctic and pointed out to each other the telltale signs of frostbite. There was an almost cosy atmosphere in this regular walk past landmarks which became as familiar as the village church or the railway station at home. Lest the parochial aspect be stressed too much, here

* Mr. Ford confesses that in conversation with Armitage, some years after the expedition, he was surprised at his bitterness on this point.

is the magnificently vivid description of what the walk to Crater Hill was really like, from Wilson's diary[1]:

'We know every step of the way—which is a great advantage as it is sometimes so dark that one can see nothing at all of the ground. Often in this light we step down two, three or four feet off a wind furrow—thinking we are on flat snow—& everyone knows what it is to miss a step on a staircase, it nearly shakes your head off to miss four at once on hard snow—and it is no help to sit on the lantern. Well, to begin with you put on your woollen socks—two pair of thick hair socks—a pair of fur boots—reindeer finneskoe—tied on with a length of lamp wick—and crampons—a sort of metal hoof with five steel spikes in each for the snow slopes. These are tied on with thongs. Then you put on a pair of Burberry overall trousers & a blouse & a balaclava helmet knitted—with a Burberry cover— showing only your eyes & nose & mouth—& then with a belt & a pair of wolf skin fur gloves which you hang round your neck you are ready. We leave the ship by a sloping gangway to the floe—cross a few hundred yards of smooth floe ice & over the tide crack to get on the land ice—then a gradual ascent till one reaches a steep snow slope of a quarter of a mile—which is known as the ski slope. Down this—even in the deadest calm there is always a cold breeze of air which nips your nose & cheeks sometimes in a cruel way. It is the natural outlet for the air which has cooled on the snow plateau to which it leads above. We go up this ski slope—stumbling not a little over the furrows made in the hard driven snow by the last blizzard. Ruts & grooves & ridges are cut everywhere by the blast of wind— often a foot or two or three deep. We get to the top & find smooth snow again hard & flat, & climb a sort of snow rampart formed by the lee drift under a patch of dark rock, the remains of an old volcanic core. Once over this we have Mt. Erebus full in sight, & we are looking at it across an extensive snow plateau of hard flat snow & ice. Part of this we cross and after half a mile of it we come to a slope upon which are the crevasses I mentioned a few days back. They run in all directions & cross one another at right angles chiefly, & the depth is 40 feet to a snow bottom. We pass over this area & get on to a steeper slope of smooth ice and snow—gradually leading to the foot of the old crater—known to us as Crater Hill. Then we have a very steep piece of hard icy snow slope which is hardly manageable in Finnesko without Crampons; we used to try it—but several times slid the whole way down which is risky & uncomfortable as you get up a tremendous pace, can't stop by any means, & have all your work cut out to keep right side up. However we now manage easily in crampons. & at the top you find yourself at the lip of a very big old crater half full of snow—the crater being oval in shape & about as big as Montpelier Gardens. From this spot—which is just 1000 ft. above sea level we have a fine view of Mount Erebus—& Terror— & the Ice barrier surface stretching East & South of them a dead level snow plain as far as the eye can see. Northward we look out

4

into Ross Sea away at the entrance of MacMurdo Strait—all frozen over—and our little hopeful sunrise at midday every morning on the far northern horizon. Westward we look back & down in the bay a mile or two below us lies the ship & the huts & a lantern glint here & there on the floe—& across the strait, some 60 miles away is a gigantic range of snowy alps with the volcanic mound Mt. Discovery—our new one. Again to the South we see this range ends in a bluff and this bluff is where our Depot camp is to be placed for our journey to the far South. It is separated by a narrow strait—permanently frozen over—from the island we first visited on our little sledging trip last March. Beyond this—all barrier ice & the unknown. As soon as the light comes back I hope to get a series of sketches from this point all round—because one sees everything from here . . . The way home from Crater Hill is all down hill—the same way as a rule though one can vary it to one's heart's content. In the dark however we always stick to the same & simplest route . . . the walk takes about 2 hours—one can do it in less. . . .'

There was now a very cogent reason why Wilson and Shackleton should keep fit. On 12 June Scott called Wilson in to his cubicle for a talk about the summer season's sledge parties. He said that he had not yet decided whether the Southern Journey party would consist of two men or three but that he definitely wanted Wilson to go with him. Wilson felt very strongly[1] that three men should go.

'. . . the weights are not proportionately increased as the tent & cooker & dogs food & sledges are the same for three as for two—only his food is extra & yet there is an extra man to work at the job. Then if one gets ill, all *could* get back if there were three. So eventually it was decided that the party should consist of three—who then was to be the third? He said; so I told him it wasn't for me to suggest anyone. He then said, he need hardly have asked me because he knew who I would say, & added that as a matter of fact he was the man he would have chosen himself. So then I knew it was Shackleton, & I told him it was Shackleton's one ambition to go on the Southern journey. So it was settled—and we three are to go.'

Shackleton was informed the next day in confidence, and was told that there would be a careful medical examination.

Lord Mountevans[16] wrote of Shackleton that 'His striking personality, admirable humour, and inexhaustible energy won for him his place in the Southern Sledge Journey . . .', and though Scott never put on record his reasons for choosing Shackleton, there can be no doubt that he had these qualities in mind. Besides, as well as being energetic Shackleton was capable, as a man of his training was bound to be. James Dell[13] put it bluntly: 'We of the seaman branch, we understood quite well that the naval officer in a position such as that misses the rattle of feet, and the merchant officer as a rule is far more resourceful than the naval man is.' Certainly from the point of view of physique Shackleton seemed to have everything to commend him. He always gave the impression of immense physical power; it is significant that, although he was in fact only five foot ten in height, people nearly always thought of him as being very tall. His shoulders were immensely broad, and the bright eye, firm mouth and square chin enhanced the impression given by the man himself, that he would stand out against wind and weather much as he could stand out against his fellows if he was opposed in anything he badly wanted.

So Shackleton went into training for the first really big chance of his life. It was now obvious to everybody that a high south latitude, and if possible the South Pole itself, was the aim of the journey, and this was a large and concrete ambition of a kind to suit him.

Scott had decided to use all the dogs for this journey, leaving the other sledging parties to rely on man-hauling, so that as soon as the sun returned Shackleton had to work hard to try to produce good working teams. He worked also on the packing of the sledging rations and equipment, making such improvements as had been suggested by the experiences of the autumn journeys. Wilson had many conferences with Scott about the daily ration for men and dogs. Scott did not like the prospect of killing off the dogs one by one and feeding them on each other, but he realised it was the only way to manage the hauling of provisions for a sledging trip of three months. Shackleton spent many hours below decks superintending Dell, who besides being butcher and bosun's yeoman, worked the antiquated sewing machine with which he made the food bags for the sledging parties. Dell's sailmaking skill was also employed on the furs purchased in Norway. These had been made into fur suits to be used at night instead of sleeping bags, but the autumn sledging had shown these to be useless, as they soon froze hard and were impossible to get into. Accordingly they were adapted, with the addition of unused skins, to make large sleeping bags, in which, theoretically, three men could be comfortable while keeping each other warm. Later these were again changed for the single bags of which only a few had previously been made, for it was felt that the privacy of a single bag was highly important, even though the weight on the sledges was necessarily increased.

The sail-maker was disposed to get on well with the Third Officer from the start because of their mutual liking for sail rather than steam. Dell had been disappointed, when he joined the Navy, to find he would be serving in steam, and when he was lent to the *Discovery* (he had just left the *Pembroke*) he was pleased to find an officer who shared his views and who would talk of his experiences in the Merchant Navy as a youth. In a sense James Dell's whole life has been shaped by those

days working under Shackleton, and he speaks of him as warmly now
and as vividly as though he had just left off talking to him.

He speaks with amusement of Shackleton's most original contribution to the technique of Polar travel—a vehicle which, as Scott[4] put it,
'was to burst suddenly on our awestruck world, to carry immediate
conviction as it trundled easily over the floe, . . . and once and for all
to wipe the obsolete sledge from off the surface of the snow'. It was
'the queerest sort of arrangement, consisting of two rum-barrels placed
one in front of the other and acting as wheels to a framework on which
the load was intended to be placed.' Wilson[1] called it 'Shackleton's new
go cart' and described it as 'exactly like the carriages in Reid's Pre-
historic peeps!' The general opinion of the expedition was expressed
by the unknown person who, in Shackleton's absence, chalked on the
contraption the words 'The Rum Idea'. He persuaded Barne to spend
a whole morning with him trying to rig up a sail, but it was not a
success, and the machine was abandoned. Scott[4] remarks that the
inventor must be given the credit for noticing that the ice surface was
at times suitable for wheeled vehicles; and no doubt when Shackleton
was experimenting with motor transport on the Barrier, five years later,
he spared a thought for 'the first wheeled vehicle the Antarctic has
ever seen.'[3]

As in most of Shackleton's practical jokes, there was a germ of sense
somewhere. But he was to have less time for the development of
fantastic schemes, for with the first days of September the spring
depôt-laying trips were to begin. While Armitage took out a party to
recover the depôt which had been left near the ship in the previous
autumn, Scott led a reconnaissance party northwards, principally to
test dog harness and practise dog-driving.

There were two tents, with Scott, Wilson and Shackleton in one,
and Skelton, Ferrar and Feather (the Bosun) in the other. Four small
sledges were taken, each with three or four dogs. '. . . the sledge
Shackles and I took,' Wilson wrote[1] on 2 September, 'was a heavy one
with 4 dogs—two pullers & two "sooners" as they are called; Why?
because they'd sooner do anything than pull.' The drivers *did* improve
in their handling of dogs, though they decided to reject a new harness
they had had made of very supple steel rope, because they found that
it chafed the animals and that hemp rope would be better.

Shackleton's telegraphic entries in his diary about this trip show his
usual lively interest in a new experience. On 3 September 'Photo shows
place full crevasses' he notes, 'pitch tent badly. move it. just by crack.
What-O if it opened. no fear.' One night it is 'fitful sleep. I had
weather corner. no catch': on another 'in middle of bag tonight all
right': and he makes a memo. 'D [*i.e.* describe] three man bag.'
He was 'glad to get in and have bath' but he did not at first find

it easy to settle into the tempo of the ship, where everything seemed hot and stuffy. 'I suppose the correct thing to do,' he wrote,[3] playing down his sense of wonder at this Antarctic scenery 'is to make a glowing description of everything that one sees; and then it will strike people more at home than any amount of straightforward talk'. But there were other moments, when in the intervals between his work he let his poetic feelings have full expression:

'How splendid the Western Mountains looked today. Tongue or pen or pencil would sadly fail were they to attempt to describe the magic of the colouring and later on the afternoon the very clouds light and fleecy were of rainbow hue. iridescent and opaline in their many tints. Days like these stand out amongst the grey ones that are so common here. The sunset was a poem. The change of twilight into night, which was lighted by the crescent moon was weirdly beautiful for the cliffs of white gave no part of their colour away. and the rocks beside them did not part with their blackness so it was a curious effect of the deepening shadow over these contrasts.'

Time now seemed to him to be going at once too fast and too slowly. He was trying to finish the fifth number of the *South Polar Times* and straighten out his routine work before his next sledging assignment, but all the time the real journey was uppermost in his mind. 'I hope that there will be nothing to throw me back from that,' he wrote on 10 September, 'for I have been look [*sic*] forward to it all the winter. but one always gets a bit anxious if one wants anything much . . . The winter has gone and half the things one desired to do have remained undone. yet have we never been idle. I do hope that the time will go quickly on our journeys and so before we can realize it the relief ship will be down here with our letters and little presents from home. I wonder if people at home can imagine what a large part "Relief Ship" plays in our vocabulary.'

Most members of the expedition were now drawn into the spring sledging. Shackleton commented that when the Bluff party had left, there would only be four left in the ward-room. On 10 September Royds and Koettlitz left with a party of four for Cape Crozier, and on the following day Armitage and five others left on a journey to the west, pulling sledges on ski. On 17 September Scott, with Shackleton and Barne, set out on a reconnaissance trip southwards towards Minna Bluff, with thirteen dogs divided into two teams. This was to be a full dress rehearsal for the great Southern Journey, and there had been much discussion of arrangements. Too much, indeed, for Skelton,[9] who complained 'While they are preparing, the ward-room becomes a simple nursery,—Shackleton "gassing" & "eye-serving" the whole time,—ponderous jokes flying through the air,—articles being weighed to a hundredth of a pound.—instructions being given not to beeswax the thread, or to go easy with brass eyelets,—on account of the extra weight,—well the whole thing makes one "feel tired". . . .'

Through the diaries of Royds and Skelton we catch glimpses of a Shackleton wise-cracking, exuberant, noisy and egotistical—a Shackleton behaving, in fact, as a young man of his open temperament would behave when he saw ahead a wonderful chance to prove himself: while the crustiness of his brother officers is equally natural in men whose duties would keep them, for much of the summer, tied to the ship.

When Scott's reconnaissance party set out it was with the goodwill of those left behind, who hoped they would learn something about the prospects ahead. Their trip was full of accidents. On their first night out one side of the tent, insufficiently weighted with snow, came adrift, and Scott woke to find that he had rolled outside and was lying in the thick of a blizzard. For most of the next day the three men spent a miserable time holding down the sides of the tent with fingers rapidly becoming frostbitten. Twice they were able to get to the sledges and bring in some cold food. On 19 September they returned to the ship, to get dry and warm, and set out again five days later, knowing a little more about the behaviour of blizzards and the need for what might otherwise have seemed exaggerated caution over the pitching of tents.

This time Barne, whose fingers had suffered the previous autumn and were now again badly frostbitten, was replaced by Thomas Feather. This journey taught the travellers much about the variable surface of the ice to the south and about the disadvantages of using dogs on the rough hills and dales they encountered. The boatswain had the first experience of falling down a crevasse, and rather later a sledge went down. After this the party went roped together, with Shackleton travelling in the rear to check everything.

Scott had hoped to find land beyond the Bluff where they could leave a depôt easy to pick up on the Southern Journey. The impressive scene they saw, on reaching the point, was of an immense, continuous stretch of white, on which it seemed impossible ever to pick up a small dump of stores. However, Shackleton suggested that a small crater on the end of the Bluff should be brought into line with the cone of Mount Discovery, and a depôt left at the point where the junction was made. On the morning of 1 October they left six weeks' provision for men and 150 lb. of dog food, and marked the spot with a large black flag before they turned homeward.

Scott was well satisfied with the trip as a reconnaissance, though he wondered what they would feel when they were marching over that illimitable expanse of white. Wilson[1] was very definite about it. 'We shall probably do a most monotonous three months on barrier surface— our prospects of finding land due South are not by any means bright—

still he is bent on going a long journey in that direction—and I shall say nothing against it.'

Shackleton's attitude was simpler and more optimistic, though he was quite as deeply impressed by the Barrier as either of his companions. '. . . as far as we could see to the South,' he wrote in his diary on 1 October, 'there is a level plain and a plain stretches away to the West till it comes to a range of mountains. . . . I do hope that we will be able to do a good journey to the South.'

If Scott was pleased with the result of the trip, he was gravely disconcerted by the report he received from Armitage when he got back to the ship. Armitage, as we have described, had left the ship on 11 September with a party, to sledge towards the west; his companion officer was Ferrar, the geologist, and four sailors—Cross, Scott, Walker and Heald—went with them. They met severe weather, and Armitage was inclined to blame this for the fact that, when they had been out about ten days, the men were seen to be tiring easily, and suffering unduly from minor sprains and bruises. The condition of the party deteriorated quickly, and by the time they got back to the ship, on 25 September, they were in a bad state. Wilson examined them and diagnosed scurvy, bad in Ferrar, Heald and Cross, present in a milder form in the others. The Captain being absent, Armitage[10] consulted with Wilson and Royds, and at once took drastic steps to overcome the disease.

' Mr. Ford (the chief steward) was ordered to give all hands fresh seal-meat for dinner every day; to place lime-juice on the mess tables at dinner; to give all hands oatmeal porridge as well as meat for breakfast each morning; to see that their jam supply was liberal, and to serve out an extra ration of bottled fruits. I made the cook thoroughly understand that there were a variety of ways of cooking and serving up the seal-meat and the dried potatoes and vegetables, and that I quite intended to have them placed before us in a palatable form. Royds commenced a thorough cleansing of the holds, which were far from being sweet, the mess-deck and the living-quarters were kept well ventilated, and dry, and all clothing and bedding was aired. A regular system of outdoor exercise, too, was promoted; and before the Captain's return the symptoms of scurvy, that bugbear of Polar explorers, were already disappearing.'

Scott approved all that Armitage had done, and reinforced his measures by ordering that no tinned meat of any kind was to be issued. The spring-cleaning of the holds was made Shackleton's responsibility, with four hands under him to get everything thoroughly cleaned and dried out—for the doctors thought the dampness on the ship might be affecting the general health. The work took ten days and was vigorously done. On 7 October, fumbling in the bilges of the main hold, Shackleton

discovered that some of the provisions had gone bad, and these had to
be thrown overboard. In stirring up the bilges, he may have succeeded
in stirring up a germ, harboured since the ship last touched land, for
on 8 October he had a bad throat, which sent him early to bed the next
night. 'Coughing all night kept me awake', he wrote in his diary,
'gargling Condy's fluid of permanganate of Potash'; and the entry ends,
characteristically, 'What an egotistical production a diary is.'

This outbreak of scurvy made it necessary for Koettlitz, as senior
doctor, to examine the whole of the ship's company. He found signs of
scurvy in most of the men. The outbreak, unpleasant though it was,
was useful in that it forced a radical change in the diet, which greatly
improved the general health. When Armitage left the ship on 29
November, to lead a large party towards the western mountains, he
had been warned by Koettlitz that the men still had the taint of scurvy
in their systems, but there was no illness on the journey except in
Macfarlane, who seems to have suffered from altitude sickness, and
there were no more reports of scurvy symptoms on sledging trips or at
the base.

Inevitably, from the state of knowledge at that time, Scott[4] concluded that scurvy had been beaten; and he was still sure that the cause
of it lay in the food they had eaten, the 'tinned meats which were to
all appearances of the best quality, and apparently fresh mutton taken
in small quantity. . . . Beyond this it seems impossible to go, and
consequently, as far as the investigation of the disease is concerned, we
are left in an unsatisfactory position of doubt.'

It was not possible on this expedition to take the next step, and
conclude that the cause was not in the food they had eaten but in the
food they had *not* eaten. But, doing the right thing for the wrong
reason, they had succeeded in building up a substantial resistance to
scurvy in all but two of the men who now set out on a sledging journey.
These two—Scott and Shackleton—had had only a month in which to
benefit by the improved diet at the base, and this was not long enough
for their systems to become saturated with the essential vitamin C
before their three-month journey began.

Scott, then, had no worries about health when they set out. Wilson[1]
was not wholly confident that the trouble was over.

> 'We are taking a certain amount of fresh seal meat [he wrote on
> 15 October] in case we find ourselves attacked by scurvy. "L'homme
> propose, mais le bon Dieu dispose"' is never out of my mind in all
> these preparations. I rather think that things will turn out very
> different to what is being arranged.'

Shackleton, his work on the stores over for the moment, was not
worrying about health or diet. He prepared for the Southern Journey

in a spirit of ardent curiosity, and with a cheerful courage[3] that was soon
to be severely tested.

'. . . danger is rife and I say it without wishing to unduly exaggerate
these sort of things. one of our number has lost his life and more
than once the escapes have been a narrow margin from here. it is on
one before a word can be uttered. and of course it is all part of the
game. we did not expect a feather bed down here. and so de rien.'

Chapter V

In planning his attack on the unknown South, Scott had decided to take a supporting party of twelve men for a couple of weeks, to carry stores additional to those carried by the Southern Party. Scott and his two companions were to take five sledges and all the dogs (nineteen in number) and were to pull 1,850 lb., comprising food for men and dogs, tent, extra clothes, sleeping bags, cooker, oil and miscellaneous tools and equipment. This weight only allowed them food for nine weeks, but it was hoped that, adding the stores carried to a certain point for them by the supporting party, they could stay out for thirteen. Although Scott's first Southern Journey was always afterwards referred to as one of geographical exploration and not as a dash for the Pole, his diary and Shackleton's leave no doubt that the high latitude was paramount for them. Wilson alone was intent upon discovering and describing the coast line to the south, so much so that he was actually relieved when the 'dash' had to be given up.

The men on the *Discovery* had become greatly excited by this major journey. On 30 October, when the supporting party set out, they were given a holiday, and many of them went eagerly along for a time to help with the sledges.

It was a cheerful party that went off under Barne's command, the sledges flying various flags and pennants. One of these bore the device 'No dogs need apply'. After they had gone, Shackleton took the despised dogs out on a short trip with the sledge-runners and found them so wild to work that they carried away the central trace to which each was fastened, and galloped some distance before they were caught and brought back.

The next day the three men of the Southern Party sorted their private possessions and wrote their farewell letters. Wilson, writing to Oriana, to whom he had been married a short time before he left England, was brooding over the departure from the ship, their only contact with the past. 'Can anyone I wonder', he wrote in his diary[1] on 31 October, 'realize exactly what it is, leaving the ship & all one's companions, except two, for three months in this desolate region—to walk down into the absolutely unknown South where as far as one can see nothing awaits one but an icy desert and one literally carries one's little all on a sledge. It's a funny game because one has got so very attached to the ship as a home and the whole bay here & hut as a sort of estate. One's cabin moreover is full of one's home associations, a small sanctuary for happy recollections, lamp soot and general comfort.'

Shackleton's letter[2] to the woman he was waiting to marry was candid and full of feeling. Dated 1 November 1902, it was marked to be read only if he failed to return.

Beloved I hope you may never have to read this, but darling loved one if it comes to you. you will know that your lover left this world with all his heart yours my last thoughts will be of you my own dear Heart, Child I am carrying your little photo with me South and so your face will be with me to the last : Child remember that I am your true lover, that you and you alone have been in my heart and mind all this time. Beloved do not grieve for me for it has been a man's work and I have helped my little mite towards the increase of knowledge : child there are millions in this world who have not had this chance. You will always remember me my own true woman and little girl. I cannot say more my heart is so full of love and longing for you and words will not avail, they are so poor in such a case. Child we may meet again in another world, and I believe in God, that is all I can say, but it covers all things : I have tried to do my best as a man the rest I leave to Him. And if there is another world and he wills it we shall find each other. I feel that there must be. this cannot be the end, but I do not know, I only believe from something in me. Yet again I cannot tell if there is, I hope. Child you will comfort those at home. Know once more that I love you truly and purely and as dearly as a woman can be loved. And now my true love goodnight.

Your lover
ERNEST

Child keep the little things I send you and take what you want from home.

God bless you and keep you safe forever.

Give my love to Jué and Daisy and tell them I often thought of them.

This adventure now beginning was as significant for him as his sailing on the *Hoghton Tower* twelve years before. He was the junior member of the party, with no responsibility either for leading or for geographical research. He was free to appreciate with all his energy the discovery of new places; and if there is something of apprehension in his letter, that is all part of the atmosphere, romantic and exciting, which he was building up in his mind, the climate of the explorer.

At 10.0 on the morning of 2 November the Southern Party set off, cheered on by the whole of the ship's company gathered on the floe. Like the supporting party, they carried sledging flags attached to their ski-poles, and according to custom they were photographed in all their glory before they went off in a magnificent burst of speed. The dogs pulled so vigorously that for the first two miles two of the men had to sit on the sledges to check them. A couple of hours later, when

Koettlitz, Skelton and others who had accompanied them turned back, the explorers were still almost running to keep up with the animals. During the afternoon, in fact, they caught up the supporting party by White Island (but these men had lost some time in their tents during bad weather).

For the next few days the two parties passed and repassed each other, and the dogs still maintained a good pace in spite of a variable surface, sometimes of deep snow which tired the men. At night in the tent Scott and his two companions took it in turns to read aloud from Darwin's *Origin of Species*, a practice they continued with enjoyment for some time.

Their splendid start, however, was not long maintained. They had to contend with blizzards which more than once kept them inside, and Wilson, two days out, confesses[1] to being troubled by a bad cold in the head and aching pains in the joints. This he passed on to Shackleton, who on 6 November 'started a most persistent & annoying cough in the tent' which remained troublesome for at least four days.

Then, too, the dogs began to flag. Scott noticed that they seemed to pull only when they saw men ahead. He had not anticipated that the animals would get bored with the white expanse in front of them; but for the time being the supporting party, when it was visible in front, solved the problem.

Shackleton was impatient at the delay forced on them by bad weather, and far less philosophical than Wilson, who was able to occupy himself in his sleeping bag, reading, sewing and sleeping, without any urge to push on quickly. But while Shackleton wanted to get south, he was not indifferent to the feeling of loneliness which grew on them as the familiar landmarks disappeared one by one. The appearance of a snow-petrel, when they were nine days out, called forth the observation[3] that 'right out on the barrier as we are with our old friend Erebus growing dim in the distance—it seemed to bring back the days of last summer before the birds left us'.

On 13 November half the supporting party turned back, in charge of Dailey the carpenter; the rest of the party stayed on for another two days. Wilson went the round of the tents before Dailey left. The men were cheerful because they had beaten Borchgrevink's furthest south record (they were now nearly up to latitude 79° S.), and he found them 'sound and free from any trace of scurvy'. The farewell to Barne and his men was equally cheerful and carefree when they turned back to the ship, carrying news of land ahead, trending south and consisting apparently of many lofty mountains.

Scott, Wilson and Shackleton were in excellent spirits as they struck off in the afternoon of 15 November, now entirely on their own; but evening saw them in a very different frame of mind. The dogs for the

first time on the day before had appeared to be 'done'. Now they were
not pulling well. In his diary Scott[4] suggests as possible reasons for this
the soft surface, the additional weight they had taken over from the
supporting party, the absence of men in front to cheer them on, or the
rise in temperature to something around +20°F. The next day when
the time came to start, the dogs could not break the loads and 'looked
round with the most pathetic expression as much as to say we were
really expecting too much of them'.

There was only one way to get on—by relaying. They began the
heart-breaking task of dividing the sledges, taking on three on the first
journey, and then returning over the same ground for the rest of the
load. They could have accepted this more cheerfully, as Scott said[4], 'had
the dogs showed their former vigour; but now, for some reason which
we could not fathom, they seemed to be losing all their spirit, and they
made as much fuss over drawing the half-load as a few days before they
had done over the whole one'.

This miserable situation lasted for 31 days, during which time the
dogs grew steadily less useful and the men exhausted themselves in
work which they had never expected to do. Not only were they covering
extra miles but they were also forced to help the dogs in pulling, a
procedure which did no good to man or beast. In the week after they
said good-bye to the supporting party they averaged only just over four
miles a day for hours of back-breaking and heart-breaking work. They
were forced to spend time in the tents which they could have spent in
marching if they had been without the dogs. Their transport, far from
helping to advance them, was actually holding them back.

Shackleton was desperately impatient and frustrated as he realised
that any idea of a dash to the Pole would have to be forgotten, but he
was fascinated by the new country they were opening up, and the
strong romantic side of his character was deeply satisfied by the feeling
of mingled power and awe in penetrating the unknown. 'Ah well we
will plod on and on till we find out all we can in the time allowed us.
it is an unique experience', he wrote in his diary on 20 November, and
again, 'Slowly but surely we are finding out the secret of this wonderful
place.'

The Barrier was indeed a wonderful place, and a mysterious one.
The three men were travelling on what could be called neither land nor
sea. The vast stretch of ice which they knew as the Barrier might be
resting on sea or it might be a huge sheet over low-lying land. The
problem, which has not yet been completely solved, was one which they
could not tackle. Their observations suggested that the Barrier lay over
the sea and thus they spoke of the slopes that rose to the south-west, as
they travelled, as 'coast'. They thought of themselves as moving a
certain distance out from 'the land'. They knew that the latitude of the

South Pole was beyond those slopes, and beyond the mountains that
rose behind them. They thought it must be on a plateau of some kind
rather than in a mountain range. Scott planned to sledge on the
comparatively flat surface of the Barrier until he could find a break
in the 'coast-line' through which they could strike directly for the
Pole.

The Barrier surface varied from day to day and now snow crystals
were holding up the smooth progress of the sledges. All the same, they
realised that this could not be the sole cause of the dogs' poor performance. Pretty soon they came to the conclusion that the trouble lay
in the food (Norwegian torsk or dried codfish); this may have
deteriorated in the tropics and was now upsetting the dogs, who were
suffering from dysentery and growing perceptibly weaker.

Because this undoubted fault in the dog diet was easy to see, it was
natural that Scott and his companions should overlook the fact that the
animals were also being slowly starved. Nor were the men getting the
food they needed, although for the moment they felt moderately
satisfied by their meals. Wilson[1] enumerates them thus:

> 'Our meals now consist of Bacon for breakfast—chopped in small
> pieces & fried with pounded biscuit, about a breakfast cup full each
> of this. With this, two large cups of tea and a dry biscuit or two. For
> lunch we have dry biscuit and two cups of hot Bovril chocolate with
> sugar and Somatose. For supper we have a thick soup of pemmican—
> Red ration (pea meal & bacon powder) Pounded biscuit—a soup
> square (Lazenbys) some powdered cheese boiled up in water with
> pepper & salt making each of us two pannikins—ie about two large
> cups full. After this we each have a cup full of sweet hot cocoa boiled
> with plasmon, & some dry biscuit. These are days of full meals—
> we are eating just about as much as we want, and cooking three times
> a day.'

Even when they were admitting that the dogs seemed to be suffering
from 'a species of scurvy', they had no conception of what lay ahead for
themselves. Not that they were unaware of the danger of scurvy; but
Wilson found no trace of it when he examined them all thoroughly on
4 December, and they had no reason to fear ill-health. They arranged
the work so that one man drove the team, with more or less continuous
shouting that left him as hoarse at the end of the day as the others were
tired with hauling. There was no time or opportunity for conversation
on the march.

On 24 November they altered their routine, leaving one man with
the first load, to prepare lunch or supper, while the other two took the
dogs back, harnessed to an empty sledge, to fetch the rest of the load.
Later, when their progress became even slower, they saved time and
fuel by eating a cold lunch while on the relaying march. There were a

few moments which compensated for their efforts. On 25 November
they crossed the 80th Parallel and felt their efforts had been worth
while. The distant mountains were splendid and uplifting, and there
were changing effects in the sky, displays of colour and light which
left them at a loss for words.

Throughout December, conditions on the march became steadily
worse. On 9 December one of the dogs, Snatcher, died, and Shackleton
had the job of cutting him up for the others to eat. '. . . they went for
it good oh' he remarks. The dogs were now killed one by one as they
became too weak to travel, and the remainder of the team showed
occasional signs of improvement after the fresh food. On 14 December,
too, they were able to lighten the load by leaving a depôt of dog food,
and on the following day, at what they called Depôt B, they discarded
a great deal more weight. They were near enough to the mountains
to be able to fix a bearing for this depôt, but it was also marked by a
large flag made by Wilson out of Burberry material. They were now
able to go ahead without relaying, taking provisions for just over four
weeks, a little dog food and their camp equipment; with this load they
would push on as far as possible before they had to turn.

They were on very short rations now and were all of them thinking
constantly about food—dreaming about it, too, dreams of deprivation
which increased their hunger. Wilson dreamed that he was shouting at
waiters who refused to bring him anything, or that he was brought a
plate of beef that turned to ashes in front of him. Scott had the
advantage that in his dreams he was able to enjoy the illusory taste of
food, and this seemed to the other two an unfair advantage, added to
the fact that Scott was a smoker and they were not. Shackleton headed
a whole page in his diary 'Desire', and wrote:

> 'Duck crisp fried bread with salt and pepper
> Thick bread soaked in golden syrup
> Porter House steak and onions with plenty gravy
> Huge salad of fruit. and also green stuff.
> Sirloin of beef with brown crisp fat. soak bread in the gravy.
> Pastry 3 cornered tarts fresh hot crisp. jam hot inside. a pile of
>   these with a bowl of cream
> jam sandwich crisp but heavy pastry & jam between.
> The end of a porridge pot providing there is plenty of stuff'.

It was Shackleton who at this time hit on a device which made the
division of food scrupulously fair. On such short rations they could
hardly be blamed for having uncharitable thoughts about each other
when these were doled out. Scott described how 'after the division was
made one of us shut his eyes, another pointed to a portion and said

"Who's is that?" This ingenious game of "Shut-eye" was practised at each meal and avoided all necessity of attempting to persuade your neighbour to take the largest share'.*

The simple and effective trick became customary on polar expeditions for many years—in fact, until improved methods of transport and of compressing food made it possible for expeditions to travel with something more than starvation rations. The travellers were at this time doing hard labour on about a pound and a half of food a day.

Hunger now ruled their distance. The dogs were doing practically no pulling, and the men were pulling less well than before, with a load of about 170 pounds each. 'Either the surface is extraordinarily bad', Scott[4] wrote in his diary, 'or we are growing weak.'

A new problem was now added to that of hunger. Scurvy had been developing even as they discussed it in relation to the dogs, and on this day Wilson told Scott that on his previous Sunday examination he had found Shackleton's gums looking angry and that they were getting worse. The following Sunday, Christmas Eve, the doctor reported that both Scott and Shackleton had this symptom, 'though hardly enough to swear to scurvy in them.' They all agreed that it was not yet time to decide to turn back. With a course slightly east by south they were all the time opening up new mountains; Wilson regularly sketched the new contours, risking frostbite as he took off his outer fur mitts and having much difficulty in holding his pencil.

Christmas Day had been in their minds for some time, and they had been saving biscuit so that for one day they would be able to have enough to eat. It was a glorious day of blazing sunshine, and in spite of the scurvy (for they all gave their new enemy a name now) they contrived to enjoy themselves. Shackleton described[3] the day in his diary:

'The warmest day we have yet had. yet we made our best march doing over ten miles. though we did all the pulling practically for the dogs were done up with the heat. got up at 8.30 a.m. and B was cook. Breakfast a panikin of seal's liver and bacon with biscuit topped up with spoonful of blackberry jam each. then I set camera and took 2 photos of party connecting piece of rope to camera lever. then did 4 hours march. lunch I cook. Bov Choc. Plasmon biscuit 2 spoons jam each. very good. hot lunch. then 2½ hour march camp for night. I cook and in 35 min. cooked 6 pan of N.A.O.R & biscuit for Hoosh Boiled plum pudding and made cocoa. then we had jam to finish up so were really full for once. It is settled for our furthest South to be on 28th then we go[t] into the land. Medical examtn. shews

* This description comes from a fine article, 'The Southern Sledge Journey 1902–1903', which he contributed to the *South Polar Times*[5] and which was put in the June number (page 10).

Sledging on the National Antarctic Expedition, 1902

Furthest South Party with sledge-flags, 1902

Emily Mary Shackleton in 1909

Capt & I to be inclined to scurvy so we will not be going on further as we are so far from our base. we hope to cross 82° S in 2 days anyhow. What a Christmas baking hot. it must have been so different at home.'

High spot of the day was the pudding, which Shackleton had carried in the toe of a spare sock, in secret, together with a piece of artificial holly. It was heated up in the cocoa and served (without 'whose-ing' this time) from the cooker lid, and it set the seal of difference on this most unusual Christmas.

Just then they were passing a coastal peak nearly 7,000 feet high and about 18 miles away from them. They marked the day by christening it Christmas Mountain. Now, in the unusually clear weather, another peak appeared far to the south, a lofty mountain rising out of snow-slopes which they decided to name Mount Longstaff, for the principal benefactor of the expedition.

They were moving towards a long spur of land which prevented them from judging what kind of road lay ahead of them. To their right, a high undulating snow-cap led to a steep irregular coastline emergent from the ice; behind this again rose cliffs of alternate red and black colour.

Scott decided that after making their last camp on 28 December they would push forward on skis, without the sledges, to establish their Furthest South and to try to get a closer sight of the mountainous land they had only been able to glimpse ahead of them. They got far enough to see the broad, deep inlet, sheltered by the spur of land, which ran to the south-west, bounded by cliffs. Somewhere along this impressive coast a gateway might be found to lead them to their goal.

'I do hope', Shackleton wrote[3] on 28 December 'that the photos will be a success so that the most Southerly land in the world may be seen. How strange & wild it is to be out here so many miles away from all people!' To Wilson[1] the sight of the new mountain ranges was worth infinitely more than their long journey due south on a plain 'for so many hundred miles & back again' and indeed they were all taken out of themselves by the majesty of the scene.

But 'We have almost shot our bolt' Scott admitted on that day. The following day they were forced to keep to their tents because of a blizzard, and by evening the coastline was hidden in a thick fog. As this still hung about on 30 December, they could not leave their goods behind for fear of losing them, and carried them on, camping at midday after having gone about four miles.

This was their furthest south, at latitude 82° 15' S. Scott and Wilson pushed on in the afternoon on ski for a mile or more, hoping to see more of the inlet, which they agreed should be named after their companion. Visibility was so poor that they soon had to retrace their

steps to the camp, and on the last day of the month they turned their
back on Shackleton Inlet.

They were now following a course to take them nearer to the coast,
and after lunch on 31 December they again started out on ski, hoping to
reach the rocks that fringed the coast and get specimens for the geologist.
The Barrier surface here was rough and crevassed, and they roped
together. It soon became clear that they would not be able to reach
the land, for they saw before them an enormous chasm which they
could not cross.

The entries for this day, the last on which they could attempt any
true exploration, were typical of the three men. Scott laid out a long
and meticulously detailed description of the scene, with his theories of
the origin of the chasm; the whole account is clearly intended to help
future explorers. Wilson's description is poetic and vivid. Shackleton
wrote[3] laconically :

> 'Last day of the old year and today we turned back after a blowy
> night. the dogs are awful not pulling at all. Clarence gave up the
> ghost today. camped 2 pm went on ski to try and land full of
> crevasses no go wonderful sight.'

The plan now was to make for Depôt B. The signs of scurvy had
lessened, but the New Year of 1903 did not open very propitiously, for
the remaining dogs proved of little use. The situation became ludicrous.
On this first day of the year Spud was actually dragged on the sledge,
tucked inside the canvas tank, before he was fed to his comrades in the
evening. The following day they abandoned one of the three sledges
they had taken on from Depôt B, and were able to set a sail in the
afternoon to help themselves along. On 6 January, after some days of
slow and painful effort, the dogs were all hitched behind the sledges—
'a very striking example of the cart before the horse', as Scott put it.[4]
Without the incentive of new land to make for, and with a shockingly
tight ration, the journey became a nightmare; but Shackleton remained
cheerful in his attitude to the work, which he still felt to be an adventure,
and on 11 January he wrote at the end of his day's entry 'Tennyson's
Ulysses keeps running through my head'.

The dogs were now unhitched and allowed to run beside the men,
who painfully hauled the sledges on step by step. They found steering
difficult when the weather was bad. On 10 January they could only see
twenty or thirty yards ahead, and eventually Shackleton was sent to
walk on ahead, Scott steering a course by observing[4] 'the manner in
which the snow was drifting against his back'.

On this day they were all terribly exhausted and the leader was not
happy about Shackleton's condition. Once more scurvy was beginning
to get a hold on them all. Matters improved a little when they reached

Depôt B on 13 January. Inspired by the feeling of having had almost enough to eat, Shackleton once more listed his wants in his diary. He wanted bread, and also '6 jam puffs 3 cornered 2 raspberry, 2 Blackberry. 2 greengage with 2 tins of Viking milk as a cream. puffs hot and flaky.'

Wilson's examination on 14 January, while they were re-packing the depôt, was far from satisfactory. Shackleton, besides having the angry-looking gums typical of a scurvy subject, was suffering from shortness of breath and had coughing fits, in which he occasionally spat blood. Scott and Wilson also had signs of scurvy in their gums, and Scott had a stiffness in his heel, but they felt fit and well.

Scott had hoped to take time off to steer inwards towards the coast once more but this idea now had to be abandoned. Wilson had expressed grave fears about Shackleton's condition, and the leader had to plan with this in mind. He foresaw that it would be difficult to keep Shackleton, 'with his restless, energetic temperament', idle in camp. He gave him orders that he was to do no cooking or tent work and that on the march he was to walk beside the sledges. He spoke very seriously of the folly of pretending to be stronger than he was, and told him that it was essential to nurse himself.[4] Shackleton's comment on this day was simply 'Am afraid we all are scurvy tainted. I am especially so. de rien we shall soon be back.'

Wilson took the last two dogs a little way from the camp and despatched them, as they were quite useless. They cut down the remaining stores and redistributed the weights. The next few days were days of mental disturbance and shocking effort for Shackleton. Though there is little sign of this in his diary, it is clear from those of Scott and Wilson, and from what Scott wrote afterwards, that he was seriously ill. It is impossible to say whether he was suffering simply from an aggravated form of scurvy, or whether this was complicated by something else. So far as we can discover, Wilson never suggested that there was any weakness of heart or lungs; this must have been revealed by the routine examinations during the winter and by Wilson's examinations during the Southern Journey.* Shackleton was heavier in build than the other two and may have been harder hit by the low ration. It is possible that the cough he had developed at the beginning of the journey had a tendency to recur. The physical strain of coughing while in a low state would be enough to account for the burst blood vessel which produced such alarming symptoms.

* In his diary, 4 January 1901, Wilson states that Shackleton and Bernacchi were not examined at the outset of the expedition as the other members of the party were: but this remark was made in the early stages of making up the party, and it is not clear whether he meant E. Shackleton or W. Shackleton, who had not resigned at this time.

Whatever Shackleton's illness really was, the effect on him can be guessed at. Here was a man in the full flush of life, virile, energetic and ambitious. He had been singled out for an important journey, and he must have thought the choice at least in part due to his physique. He was the junior member of the party and so was bound to give of his best, to make every effort to justify his place. Now he had broken down. He could not help to pull the sledges or to do camp work. The precautions Scott ordered him to take, sensible and inevitable as they were, must have been bitterly mortifying to Shackleton. To the physical effort of getting along was added the even greater effort of keeping calm, of controlling his pride, of not making a fuss, of obeying orders without argument.

At one point Wilson did not expect him to last to the end of the journey. Shackleton—or so the story goes—overheard a conversation outside the tent in which Wilson gave him about twenty-four hours; Shackleton told them both firmly that he would outlive them.* Whether this dramatic scene took place or not does not matter. The diaries make it clear that the doctor was prepared for Shackleton to die on the march, and that Shackleton was determined not to die. It was the first (but not the last) time in his life when he was to turn a failure into a triumph.

At the time he did not see it this way. Pride forbade him to make much of his illness in his diary, which becomes brief and detached in the latter part of the journey. Pride and courage inextricably mingled kept him going. After the visit to the depôt the party was on full rations for a time. Wilson, noting the improvement in the health of all three of them, felt this to be a confirmation that the bacon (for which seal-meat was now substituted) had been the cause of their scurvy.

Shackleton's condition was only momentarily improved, and the congestion in his chest was little relieved in the next days. However, on 19 January he said in his diary that he was 'nearly well', and on the next day he was able to cook the supper while Scott took a round of angles and Wilson sketched (the sky having suddenly cleared). The following day Shackleton wrote:

> 'Strong following wind all day. had sledge sail up but the sledges overran us. I sat on for an hour and put brake on then Billy went astern and Captain ahead and steered. I walked astern. not being allowed to help, as my chest was dicky. In afternoon I went on ski and the others with sledges. We must have done about 12′ today . . . splendid day but for my trouble which weighs on my mind for I would like to be doing more than just going along.'

* The story was told to Dr. Hussey later in Shackleton's life, and it appears in Harold Begbie's book.[6] Shackleton was so sensitive on the subject of his breakdown on the Southern Journey that it seems possible that he dramatised the situation a little. To Hussey he used to observe that 'ten years later, within a mile of the same spot, Wilson and Scott were both dead and I was still alive'.

Wilson's entry for the same day likewise explains Shackleton's ride on the sledge.

'Had breakfast, struck camp & were away with floor cloth sail set to the fair wind at a great rate. Shackle at first was walking in harness but we made him sit on the after sledge & break its pace with a ski pole as the sledges were going too fast for us. This worked for an hour or two but not well so we made him walk behind at his own pace while the Captn hauled back on the port side of the front sledge and I on the starbd side of the after sledge & so we guided them & went gaily along.'

Scott's account[4] of the day was somewhat differently phrased.

'. . . we have had a brisk southerly breeze, and, setting on sail, got along at a fine rate. For a time Shackleton was carried on the sledges, but for most of the march he walked along independently, taking things as easily as possible. Our sail did most of the pulling.'

It was unfortunate for Shackleton that it was Scott's account that was referred to for most future published accounts of the journey. Inevitably it was believed that Shackleton at this stage had been completely helpless, whereas it is clear that in fact, in the fight against his illness, he never let up for a moment. Few men have lived up to their family mottoes as Shackleton lived up to his—By endurance we conquer.*

* Scott himself freely admitted this in a letter in the *Daily Mail*, dated 7 November 1904. The letter was written to correct a false impression given in a report of Scott's Albert Hall lecture on the expedition; whether the correction was written at the desire of Shackleton or someone else is not clear.
About this newspaper report, Scott wrote:

'. . . The inference is that after Mr. Shackleton broke down on our southern sledge journey he had to be carried on the sledge for 150 miles.
The facts were that though Mr. Shackleton was extremely ill, and caused us great anxiety, he displayed the most (*sic*) extraordinary pluck and endurance, and managed to struggle on beside the sledge without adding his weight to our burden.
The struggle over those wearisome miles was bad enough for Dr. Wilson and myself, but it was infinitely worse for a sick man who under ordinary conditions would have been sent straight to bed.
I assume you will see the reason why in remembering the courage and spirit shown by Mr. Shackleton, I am anxious to correct the statement made in the report.

R. F. Scott'

If it was Shackleton who objected to the newspaper inference, he had every right to do so, but it was unfortunate that he evidently wished to forget that he had in fact ridden on the sledges twice. There is no doubt that the latter part of the journey was, for him, a desperate affront to his pride, and when he rewrote his diary, which may have been soon afterwards, he omitted any reference to the incident, although he laid greater stress on his obligation to his comrades.

The next few days were hard ones for Scott and Wilson, for the surface was increasingly heavy and the hauling of the sledge was exhausting work. On 23 and 24 January the weather was overcast and Shackleton was sent ahead on ski, partly so that he could maintain his own pace, which was necessarily slow, and partly so that he could steer by compass and give them a course. He was a great deal better, but the least exertion made him breathless. Wilson had to admit that his left knee had felt strained at the back for some days, and Scott wondered whether their seal-meat had been tainted by the warm weather, for their symptoms of scurvy remained much the same.

It was in fact a depressing ending to a journey which had been begun with such hopes, and so when on 26 January they came up to the tracks of Barne's western survey party, they were all disproportionately excited, and tried to deduce the whole history of the party from them. The familiar landmarks, the Bluff and the two volcanic mountains, now reappeared. 'Cleared old Terror' Shackleton wrote on 27 January, 'it looks quite homely'. The next day they reached the last of their depôts, where to the cheer of food (luxuries as well as necessities) was added the delight of letters and notes containing the news of the rest of the expedition.

There was still trouble to come. A heavy blizzard on 29 January brought a renewed and painful attack of asthma to Shackleton; after a disastrously bad night he was 'livid and speechless, and his spirits were very low'.[4] Wilson had advised Scott that the thick weather was probably the chief cause of Shackleton's relapse, and that at all costs they must push on to the ship. Shackleton was helped out of the tent (he found bending to get out most difficult) and put upon ski, and with a great effort and with many halts he set out upon his way. Scott and Wilson caught him up before long and he rode on a sledge[4] for the rest of the morning until lunch-time*; after lunch, though still very weak and breathless, he continued the march (five hours) on ski. After a good night he seemed much improved and Scott remarked on his wonderful recuperative powers, though a fainting fit on the evening of 1 February

It is not clear if the second version of his diary, which survives in typescript, was intended for anyone but his wife to see; it is superscribed to her. In fact Shackleton wrote very little about the National Antarctic Expedition, and in his articles he gave all the credit for his survival to Scott and Wilson. Scott's diary of the journey, published in 1905,[4] gave his version unaltered, with its somewhat unfortunate phrasing, and this cannot have made matters easier for Shackleton when the two men met, though there is no evidence that he addressed any objection to Scott. Had Wilson's diary been quoted, the matter might have been far clearer.

* This was stated in Scott's diary: Wilson does not mention the incident. Shackleton's sledging diary stops on 27 January; the typed version is made up to 3 February.

alarmed them. The last entry in Scott's sledging diary[4] for 3 February
gives the background to this time very clearly.

'We are as near spent as three persons can well be. If Shackleton
has shown a temporary improvement, we know by experience how
little confidence we can place in it, and how near he has been and
still is to a total collapse. As for Wilson and myself, we have scarcely
liked to own how "done" we are, and how greatly the last week or
two has tried us. We have known that our scurvy has been advancing
again with rapid strides, but as we could do nothing more to prevent
it, we have not looked beyond the signs that have made themselves
obvious. Wilson has suffered from lameness for many a day; the
cause was plain, and we knew it must increase. Each morning he has
vainly attempted to disguise a limp, and his set face has shown me
that there is much to be gone through before the first stiffness wears
off. As for myself, for some time I have hurried through the task of
changing my footgear in an attempt to forget that my ankles are
considerably swollen. One and all we want rest and peace, and, all
being well, tomorrow, thank Heaven, we shall get them.'

Rest and peace were not far off. After a march of two or three hours
on 3 February, they saw figures hurrying towards them on ski, and just
six miles from the ship they were met by Skelton and Bernacchi ('clean
tidy looking people they were', Wilson remarks), who gave them the
news that a relief ship, the *Morning*, had arrived, and letters from home
were waiting for them. They had their lunch and then, their two
heralds pulling the sledges, they marched in towards the ship with flags
flying. As they got nearer more people came to meet them, and 'as we
turned Cape Armitage we saw the ship decorated from top to toe with
flags & all the ship's company up the rigging round the gangway ready
to cheer us which they did most lustily as we came on board. They
were all most enthusiastic & everyone shook us by the hand all round,
it was a most delightful welcome.'[1]

Chapter VI

ALL three members of the Southern Party now entered upon a period of recuperation. Wilson's knee kept him in his bunk for a fortnight, during which he put on weight rapidly, as did the other two. Shackleton was also advised to go to bed. He found that, in spite of his determination not to be ill, he was still having fits of breathlessness and coughing after the least exertion. Scott, though fitter than the other two, was immeasurably tired, and the swollen legs and gums characteristic of scurvy took some time to right themselves.

For all of them the good-humoured atmosphere of the ward-room was most cheering, though they could not take it for long at a time. There was, as well, the new company from the *Morning*, and the hospitable exchanges between the two ships in the way of dinners and evening entertainments were a welcome change from the privations of their journey.

The *Morning* had been sent out to support the *Discovery* and supply her needs, either in the way of an escort, or, if Scott should decide on a second winter in the Antarctic, with fresh stores. Sir Clements Markham had made himself responsible for raising the money needed to finance a relief expedition and he had engaged a Norwegian whaler with its commander, Captain William Colbeck, an R.N.R. officer who had been at Cape Adare with Borchgrevink.* The Admiralty, though not directly concerned with this relief expedition, did lend two naval officers, one of whom was to be of some importance in Shackleton's life.

Captain Colbeck had tracked the *Discovery* to her winter quarters, but McMurdo Sound was not yet completely open and his ship was held up a few miles away. When the Southern Party returned they found that the ice between the two ships had become a regular thoroughfare for the inquisitive and the sociable. Scott, before the lassitude of his extreme exertions and his illness had passed, had to make a decision as regards the approaching winter. He had hoped to find the ice gone out from their winter bay and the *Discovery* once more afloat, and he had left orders that the ship was to be prepared for sea in his absence.

---

* When the *Morning* went south again in 1904, accompanied by the *Terra Nova*, *The Field*[1] while warmly commending Captain Colbeck's work in the previous years, expressed some disappointment that 'blue jackets are not going to the rescue of blue jackets held fast in the clutches of the Antarctic ice'. The tradition of the naval expedition was very strong.

Now it became clear to him that the ice at the south-east end of the Sound was unlikely to go out so late in the season, and that the *Discovery* would therefore have to be turned into a shore station once more. He had already made provisional plans for a second winter. Though another journey towards the Pole was impossible without dogs, there was much to be discovered and surveyed in the western mountains and on the Barrier, and much could be done by man-hauling. Accordingly he set plans in motion for transferring supplies of food and coal from the *Morning*, while letters and messages went back from the expedition ship to her relief.

On 24 February Scott had a talk to the men. By now he was more or less certain of his plans for the future, and he was anxious to have an entirely loyal and co-operative company for the second winter, which, because of its lack of novelty, might be more trying than the first. He put it to the men that anyone who wished to go home could be taken on the *Morning*, without prejudice, and the eight sailors who asked to leave were those he would most have wished to lose. It is clear from the diaries of Royds and Wilson that they were all Merchant Service men, and no doubt they had to some extent hung together during the first season. One of them, Macfarlane, had been put on the sick list by Dr. Koettlitz, who advised Scott that he had not stood the winter well and that he ought not to stay for another.

Scott had requested Koettlitz, in a note of 19 February,[2] to report on 'the ability of the various individuals aboard this ship to withstand the rigours of another season'. He had stated clearly the terms in which this report was to be conceived. 'I wish you to consider . . . the work which the various individuals have to perform and the different degrees of exposure which their duties may require them to face. For instance the work of the scientific officers can be carried on, greatly to the advantage of the expedition, without the necessity of those officers leaving the ship for a protracted period, but the executive officers should in my opinion enjoy such health that they can at any moment be called on to undergo hardships and exposure. . . .'

Koettlitz's report[2] stressed the fact that he believed scurvy could now be avoided 'with proper attention to regular consumption of fresh seal-meat'. He advised that Clarke, the cook,* should be given greater opportunities for fresh air and exercise, and noted that he could not take the responsibility of advising Hodgson to remain for a second winter.† He was not prepared to be so categorical in the case of Shackleton.

---

* Clarke had been cook's mate during the first winter and was promoted when the unsatisfactory cook elected to go back on the *Morning*.

† Hodgson, whose chest was apparently weak, decided to remain—so far as can be discovered, with no detriment to his health.

'Mr. Shackleton's breakdown during the southern sledge journey (he wrote) was undoubtedly, in Dr. Wilson's opinion, due in great part to scurvy taint, I certainly agree with him, he has now practically recovered from it; but referring to your memorandum as to the duties of an executive officer, I cannot say that he would be fit to undergo hardships and exposure in this climate.'

Wilson evidently advised Scott that Shackleton should not stay; he commented in his diary[3] that the decision 'had upset him a great deal as he was very keen indeed to stop & see the thing through. It is certainly wise for him to go home though'.

The fact that a naval officer, Sub-Lieutenant Mulock, replaced Shackleton from the *Morning*, gave rise afterwards (and possibly also at the time) to the idea that Shackleton had been sent away because he belonged to the Merchant Navy.

There is no doubt that Scott was more at his ease with a naval complement, as also was his First Lieutenant; but they can hardly be blamed for this, after a lifetime of training in a highly specialised environment. At the same time, Scott had himself chosen Shackleton and had expressed approval of the qualities of resourcefulness and adaptability which might be considered to be characteristic of the Merchant Service. The idea of a Service rift certainly came in part from Armitage, second in command of the expedition and an old P. and O. man, and it is therefore necessary to examine what he said on the subject and try to suggest something of the background of his statements.

Armitage had originally been approached by Sir Clements Markham and asked to lead the National Antarctic Expedition, before the Societies which were sponsoring it were sure of Admiralty support. Afterwards, when Markham realised that the expedition would in fact be a naval one, he had asked Armitage to go as second in command, to add his most valuable experience to the party. Armitage had agreed under pressure and on certain conditions (which he afterwards said were not kept) concerning the apportioning of the sledging and surveying journeys.

In his book on the expedition, *Two Years in the Antarctic*, published in 1905, Armitage[4] did not allow any hint of bitterness to creep in, but his grievance grew as time went on. In New Zealand, in later years, he talked freely to Charles Ford about the fact that he had not led the sledging journey he had been promised, and he said he felt that he had suffered because he was a Merchant Service officer. In an autobiography, published in 1925, he puts his case[5] very plainly:

'When the *Morning* came down to us, Shackleton, the only other Merchant Service officer, and all but one or two of the men, cook and dog-attendant, who were not R.N. ratings, were returned with

her. Scott asked me to go with her because—so he said—of my wife
and child, although I would be a great loss to the expedition and
himself. Fortunately my appointment was independent of him. I
absolutely refused, and thus quite unconsciously spoilt Sir Clements
Markham's dream—the idea of years . . . another "Great Royal
Naval Polar Expedition".'

This bitterness pervades Armitage's account of the invaliding home
of Shackleton. He makes it clear that in his opinion Shackleton need
not have gone, and states that the senior doctor, Koettlitz, had been of
the same mind.

In a confidential memorandum which he sent to Dr. Mill in May
1922, when Mill was writing *The Life of Sir Ernest Shackleton*,
Armitage[6] was still more outspoken. He alleged that there had been
a dispute between Shackleton and Wilson on one side and Scott on
the other, on the Southern Journey, and that this had led to bad feeling
between Shackleton and his leader. This quarrel, Armitage said, had
given Scott a strong additional reason for not wanting to keep Shackleton
for a second winter. Those who knew Armitage remember him as a
sound and honest man, but from the way his views about the *Discovery*
expedition develop, in his two books and in this memorandum, it is
obvious that time intensified his rancour. He cannot therefore be
regarded as a completely unprejudiced witness. Apart from his statements, there is no direct evidence that Shackleton was sent home for
personal reasons, although some people believe this to be so.*

It seems likely that Armitage projected his own sense of grievance
into Shackleton's case, and to some extent identified himself (perhaps
not actively at the time) with the disappointed young officer. Probably
his evidence contains the mixture of truth, exaggeration and misunderstanding which is natural in a situation such as this.

It is certainly not impossible that there was some issue between
Scott and Shackleton on that great journey. Hardship is not always
ennobling: if it produces self-sacrifice, it can equally well produce
irritation and hostility. The enforced physical proximity of the three
men, while they were pushing themselves to the uttermost, must have
had an effect on their behaviour to each other. There are hints in
Wilson's diary that he, the most charitable of men, was now and then
exacerbated by having to live cheek and jowl with his friends. Any
latent antagonism or rivalry between two strong characters could hardly
be concealed all the time. Scott and Shackleton took each other's
measure on that journey, and who is to say whether the measuring up
was exclusively friendly. It can only be said that at the end of the

* Professor Frank Debenham, who went on Scott's second expedition and
who knew all three men who went on the Southern Journey of 1902–03, concluded
from conversations with Wilson that there had been some disagreement.

journey Wilson and Scott had become closer to each other, Scott and Shackleton probably less in sympathy than before.

There is still no reason to suppose that Scott's primary motive in sending Shackleton home was a desire to get rid of a possibly disloyal element. He need have had no conscious motive other than the simple one, that he did not consider Shackleton fit enough for a second winter. It is hardly reasonable to expect a leader to be at ease about a man who had burst a blood vessel from his exertions and whose frame had been racked by severe coughing. There was no guarantee that the illness would not recur: there was not even any certainty as to what that illness had been. Scurvy had seized upon Shackleton in a far more extreme form than it had upon the other two men, and there was no means of telling why this was so. All things considered, Scott would have been rash if he had allowed Shackleton to stay on, in spite of his quick recovery.

Shackleton's reaction to his invaliding home would seem to have been at first a simple one. At least there is no indication in his diary that he felt any resentment at the time or thought that he had been victimised. Later his attitude changed, and we must attribute this partly to the friends who encouraged him to nurse a grievance. But on the first day of March 1903, when he went over to the *Morning* with his luggage, he must have been thinking chiefly of the cheerful dinner the night before on the *Discovery*, designed as a farewell for him, and of what that side of the expedition had meant to him. His mood was expressed in his diary[8] more strongly than usual with him:

> 'A beautiful day, but a sad one indeed for me: for today I left my home and all those who are chums as much as I ever will have any one for chums. I cannot write much about it, but it touched me more than I can say when the men came up on deck and gave me 3 parting cheers. Ah. it is hard to have to leave before the work is over and especially to leave those who will have to stay down here in the cold dark days for there seems to my mind but little chance of the old ship going out: Michael and Ferrar came along with me and I went slowly for I had only been twice out of the ship since I came back from the Southern journey. We had a very pleasant evening on the "Morning" and with songs and one thing and another it was 3 am before we went to bed:'

and again on the following day:

> 'Today we left our comrades today we steamed away and on the edge of the obdurate ice which holds the "Discovery" in an iron grasp we left them: Ah me it was a sad parting. I took the photos of all our chaps before starting so that our people at home may have the last glimpse of their faces should we not succeed in getting out or they succeed. I mean.'*

* Shackleton dates his moving to the *Morning*, 28 February, and the sailing of that ship 1 March. He may be wrong in his dating, for both Scott and Wilson

The rather dramatic note in the entries (part of the journalistic side of Shackleton and a note which he was apt to play when he had plenty of time to write his diary) does not do more than underline the real feeling of loss with which he left McMurdo Sound. It was indeed a 'sad parting' for Shackleton and a sad day as he watched the familiar landmarks falling behind; and that night, as he tried to read in his cabin, he found his thoughts returning to his 'home' on the ice.

He missed his old comrades all through the voyage to New Zealand, but consoled himself with the thought that there was much he could do for the expedition when he reached England. He found the ship's pace through the ice very slow, but the officers were congenial and he got on well with them. He took a good many photographs, and watched with interest the tow-netting which the chief officer, Rupert England, was managing. There were birds to identify, a concert to attend and letters to write, and so the time passed until, towards the end of March, the *Morning* reached Lyttelton.*

In Christchurch he had to wait for a passage home, and was occupied in arranging for stores for the *Morning*, for she would be returning to McMurdo Sound as a relief ship in the following year. It was during this time that Shackleton met a Miss Tripp who invited him to go with her family to their place at Orari Gorge, and here he got to know the Tripp brothers, Leonard and Bernard; the friendship with Leonard in particular was to last all his life and to be a most important one for him.

On 9 May he sailed on the *Oratava* from Auckland, bound for San Francisco. His first impressions of the passengers, no doubt coloured by his mood of homesickness for the South, were hardly favourable.

'there are a fair number of passengers on board but they seem to me to be a pretty dull and uninteresting crowd. There is one individual or rather two that I have made up my mind not to sit next to: for coming up in the train they did nothing but growl and talk about themselves "More! More! About yourself!!!" You know the type a very fussy reddish grey beard man and a fat unwieldy woman they instinctively repell one even before you say a word to them and I do not intend to: There is the usual assortment Yankees seem to predominate. The old Scotch Chap sat down beside me in the smoking room after dinner and was an unmitigated bore telling me about his various journeys and his health. We have a number of bejewelled beringed persons with loud voices and louder manners who drink

give 1 March as the date when he moved to the ship and 2 March as the date when the *Morning* sailed. These entries of Shackleton's and a few others are among some loose papers, and represent the only entries we have of any date later than the last entry in his sledging diary. Mill, in his biography,[7] accepts Shackleton's dates.

* Possibly not 19 March, as Mill[7] states, for a diary entry[8] of 18 March says 'hope to see Lyttelton within a week'.

largely and at the same time growl exceedingly at the cost of the
whisky. I expect as a character study. Some of these persons will
repay watching. How glad I am to be on the road at last for there
was a feeling of far awayness in the time I was in Ch.Ch. but now
[9 May] I am really going home. . . .'

He recorded with glee the next day that the fussy man and his fat
wife had been 'told by the purser that they have done enough growling'.
He began to expand a little, however, and enjoyed the company of the
manager of a pianola firm who sat in the deck-chair next to him. His
energy so far asserted itself that he was put on the Sports Committee
and found himself getting up a concert 'which was fairly done indeed
I think people were generally pleased with it'. From San Francisco he
proceeded to New York and so home, arriving sunburnt and in
conspicuously good health.

He was still clinging to memories of the *Discovery* and was anxious
to keep in touch with the expedition, from however great a distance.
In this he was helped by Sir Clements Markham,[9] who on 4 June wrote
expressing his warm admiration of Shackleton's work in the south and
of his pluck on the Southern Journey. 'Every one speaks with admira-
of it and of their sincere friendship for you, both officers and men.'

Markham realised how keen Shackleton's disappointment was, but
assured him that in England he could be still very useful to the expedition, arranging what should be sent out by the next relief ship,
and settling various other matters. He was to assist in making arrangements for an Antarctic meeting of the Royal Geographical Society in a
week or two; funds were still short and Markham wanted to keep public
interest in the expedition alive and active.

Meanwhile, the Admiralty had decided to send out a second relief
ship under their own direction, and Shackleton was engaged to work
in Dundee, helping to equip the sealer *Terra Nova*. His services were
also enlisted in equipping the *Uruguay*, sent out by the Argentine
Government to rescue the Nordenskjiöld expedition, which had spent
a terrible two years in the Weddell Sea and had finally lost its ship.

In September, too, at the British Association meeting at Southport,
Shackleton gave a running commentary on lantern slides made on the
National Antarctic Expedition. It was a fine lecture, not least because
of the free and easy manner in which it was delivered, and Mill wrote
to Scott praising the way the young officer had selected his material so
as to whet the public appetite without spoiling any of the effect that
Scott would want to make when he lectured on his return.

There were opportunities, too, for writing about the expedition. On
27 June and 4 July the *Illustrated London News* carried a supplement
with an account of the expedition's first year written by Shackleton. It
is a good, straightforward piece of reporting, and remarkably modest.

The writer says little of himself, but he defends the expedition against public criticism of extravagance, and he gives conspicuous praise to his companions on the Southern Journey.

'On January 15 I broke down owing to overstrain, and hæmorrhage started, which was naturally a rather serious matter, as the party was a hundred and seventy miles from the ship. I was, however, able to march the nine or ten miles a day that the party made . . . Captain Scott and Dr. Wilson could not have done more for me than they did. They were bearing the brunt of the work, and throughout the difficulties and anxieties of such a time showed ever cheery faces.

We may suppose that Shackleton was not permitted to interfere with the caption under a picture of the Southern Journey camp 80 miles from the ship, which reads: 'Lieut. Shackleton broke a blood vessel, was five times laid down to die' or with the pictures framing one page of text, which include an unmistakable polar bear.

About this time, too, Shackleton wrote a similar article for *Pearson's Magazine*, and handed over the proceeds to the *Discovery* Relief Fund, which particularly pleased its organiser.

This kind of work, soothing as it must have been to his pride, was not going to provide Shackleton with a living, and since he wanted to get married as soon as possible, he had to find a reasonably well-paid post and hoped to find a congenial one. The Navy seemed to him to hold out good prospects, and in July 1903 he applied for an appointment as Supplementary Lieutenant. He was handsomely supported by the two Societies who had sponsored the National Antarctic Expedition, and on 28 June the following letter[29] was sent to the Admiralty:

Sir,

We have the honour to request that you will bring the valuable work of Sub-Lieutenant Shackleton, R.N.R., during his service in the Ant-Arctic Expedition, to the notice of the Lords Commissioners of the Admiralty.

Captain Scott speaks of Mr. Shackleton as a 'marvel of intelligent energy'. Besides keeping watch, he had charge of the holds, of the issue and management of provisions, fixing the dietary, and keeping all the books.

He also undertook the examination of sea-water with hydrometer and titration, and obtained a thorough practical grasp of the scientific observations entrusted to him.

He was never tired, always cheerful, and is exceedingly popular with everyone.

Mr. Shackleton retained Captain Scott's confidence and warm approval for his diligence and usefulness, throughout the voyage, and he accompanied his Commander on the memorable sledge journey to the South.

The severe work led to his breaking a blood vessel, and to his life being in danger; and it was due to his indomitable pluck, while in that condition, that he and his companions were enabled to reach the ship.

It was necessary to send this valuable officer home invalided.

Any compliance with his wishes would afford great pleasure to your obedient servants,

(*signed*) WILLIAM HUGGINS

President of the Royal Society

CLEMENTS MARKHAM

President of the Royal Geographical Society

The naval list being closed at this time as full, his application could not be entertained. It was suggested, however, that he be promoted Lieutenant R.N.R. 'on his obtaining a test certificate for drill as a special case'. This suggestion was passed on from the Admiralty to the two Presidents on 24 July. There is no record available of how Shackleton reacted to it; no record, in fact, until 26 February 1904, when he wrote to the Admiralty resigning his commission in the Royal Naval Reserve for the reason that he had taken an appointment on shore.*

By this time he had tried one shore job and had settled down in another. Each was to be the perfect solution to his problem, and each was approached with the lively enthusiasm and optimism which for the time being masked, for him and for others, the fact that he was really a square peg in a round hole.

So it was, for instance, when in the autumn of 1903 he became sub-editor of the *Royal Magazine*, one of Sir Arthur Pearson's papers. Armitage[6] wrote to Mill later, of the *Discovery* period, that 'Shackleton had leanings towards journalism and told me that he had thought seriously of trying it'. But though Shackleton was observant, quick and ready with words, as a journalist should be, he was less well suited to office work although he applied himself to it with vigour. Some years later the Editor of the *Royal Magazine* published[27] his impressions of his former colleague:

'You may wonder why exactly I gave him this appointment on the *Royal*. He had had no practical experience of journalism—I remember his coming to me and asking how to correct a proof!—and he was the first to admit, with that big laugh of his which one never forgets, that office work was out of his line altogether.

But I am convinced that if he had gone to a stock-broker, a butcher,

---

* The Navy List (1903) shows Shackleton as Sub-Lieut., R.N.R., with seniority of 4 June 1901. The last list he appears in is March 1904, which list is correct to 18 February.

Sounding round a stranded berg

Landing stores from the boat

Both taken in McMurdo Sound, 1908

The hut at Cape Royds, 1908

a carpenter, or a theatrical manager and asked for a job, he would have got it. There was something about him that compelled confidence. And none of these good folk would have regretted taking him on. Though stock-broking and acting may have been as little in his line as journalism, he would have made his mark in them somehow or other.

. . . I was very sorry when he left us. He was brimming over with original, unconventional, racy ideas, which, whether practical or not, were always stimulating and suggestive.

He worked well. Though sitting at a desk the best part of the day must have gone sorely against the grain, he sat at the desk—sat tight —and tackled manuscripts, proofs, and callers with the same ardour that he brought to the exploration of the Antarctic wilderness.

. . . He was the most friendly "hail-fellow-well-met" man I have ever come across . . . There was not an ounce of "side" in him. He loved telling of his adventures in all parts of the world, but never for the purpose of self-glorification; he talked from the sailor's zest for spinning a yarn.

I remember well neglecting my work for the best part of a day, in company with two other Editors and several juniors, to sit in a circle round Shackleton while he related some particularly dangerous exploit. And no man told a story better. Whether it was the rich, husky voice and compelling gesture or the Irishman's natural gift for expression, he made us see the things he spoke of, and held us all spell-bound.'

Shackleton certainly gave much to his job—not least the warm encouragement that was always ready for the young men whose writings came before him; but the work must always have seemed to him less than he wanted. It was not long before something else offered with better prospects.

In November he had been invited to lecture in Dundee and Aberdeen for the Royal Scottish Geographical Society, an old-established organisation with a reputation for helping geographical research. Shackleton, as a member of the Royal Geographical Society, was well aware of the high standing of the Scottish body and of its sponsorship, in particular, of the great *Challenger* Commission. When he learnt that a paid secretarial post was open, because of the retirement of Colonel Bailey, he decided to apply. The salary offered was no more than he was getting at Pearson's but the post carried more prestige; perhaps he had realised that he was not going to make his mark very quickly in Fleet Street.

Then, too, his ambition was stimulated by his forthcoming marriage in the spring. He became concerned about the milieu in which he and his wife would live. A post on a magazine in London carried with it no special social advantages, and although he might meet many interesting people, his particular niche must be carved out in some other way.

6

At this time he did not belong anywhere in particular. He would not want to settle in the leafy backwater of Sydenham nor yet to hang on to the coat-tails of his in-laws. He wanted a position—not only in the worldly sense of the word, in 'society', though this was attractive; but he wanted to live somewhere where he would be someone. From what he had seen and heard of Edinburgh and its Geographical Society, the post seemed to offer what he needed. 'I should think that I would do all right here,' he wrote[10] to his fiancée from Pearson's, 'but the other job has the best position I think.'

His formal application to the Royal Scottish Geographical Society was sent in on 4 December. He had armed himself with a four-page, printed document[30], which, together with his own succinct statement of his capabilities, contained recommendations from many men important in the geographical world.

The letter which Sir William Huggins and Sir Clements Markham had sent to the Admiralty was quoted, and each man also provided a more direct expression of their desire to see him elected. The President of the Royal Society stated that he felt Shackleton would be suitable 'alike from the literary and from the social side; and also from his enthusiasm for geographical exploration, for which indeed during his recent Antarctic experiences he paid so dearly': while Sir Clements Markham, praising his energy and powers of organisation, felt that he would be 'invaluable in the work of increasing the number of members, and widening a knowledge of the work and objects of the Society'. Admiral Aldrich, under whom Shackleton had worked on preparing the *Terra Nova*, spoke of his energy and unstinted willingness in that work.

Dr. Mill's testimonial mentions the same qualities and stresses the fact that Shackleton 'was keen in taking up a new train of thought or line of work, and persevering in carrying it out'. His recommendation, which is warm beyond the requirements of such a document, bore witness to Shackleton's courage as an explorer, his tact as an editor, his experience of varied countries and people and his capacity for efficient and painstaking work, and made the point that 'His own personality is singularly attractive'. It is a testimonial that shows not only the extent of Mill's goodwill towards Shackleton but also his thorough knowledge of his character and attainments at this time; and the brief letter from J. Scott Keltie (then Secretary of the Royal Geographical Society) is equally discerning. 'I have no doubt,' he wrote, 'you would be able to fill the post of Secretary, and of critic if required, with complete efficiency; and I think the Society would be fortunate in obtaining your services.' Keltie was well aware that the Royal Scottish Geographical Society had fallen into somewhat slow and over-orthodox ways since its foundation, and both he and Mill realised not only that

Shackleton was the kind of person needed to stir things up but also that this would not be entirely easy to do.

Shackleton, once he had decided to apply for the job, could think of little else. Even anticipation of his marriage was sometimes less evident in his letters than his anxiety about the committee's decision. Dr. Mill became his chief confidant. On 15 December Shackleton wrote to him indignantly that the selection committee had found two grammatical mistakes in his letter of application. He was too deeply concerned to see any humour in this. 'I have heard,' he wrote[11] to his friend, 'that there are many men with splendid qualifications against me so I suppose that I am found somewhat lacking. I will not give up heart though. I feel that if I had the job they would not regret appointing me.'

Dr. Mill bore with his impatience. When he sent the testimonial Shackleton had asked for, he accompanied it[28] with one of the most sympathetic and delightful letters ever written to an ambitious young man by one older and wiser who is waiting for that young man to fulfil himself.

My dear Shackleton

I hereby declare that if you are not appointed Secretary of the R.S.G.S. I will resign my membership of that Society and take no more interest in its affairs to the end of time.

I also declare that if you are appointed you will have a deal to put up with as the Council is a large, heterogeneous and opinionative body. You and Miss Dorman don't in the least realize how young you are & how wholesome is the discipline of waiting! It is a thing we have all experienced & none of us has ever thought the advice of older people better than wet blankets and cold water.

I have seen a statement of the claims of your competitors and I flatter myself that I am something of a judge of the capabilities of men and if the Council prefers any of them to you I think that the collective wisdom of the said council is inferior to the spark of common sense I flatter myself I possess. Whatever other people may think I know you are the best man for the job and a great deal too good for it too.

When I look back on the "hopes and fears, beliefs and disbelievings" I have come through I don't think you have any reason to despair now or henceforth, and my advice to you is to keep up your heart and if they give that appointment to another be sure that there is something better waiting for you.

I know how I looked upon similar sentiments in my time so I don't expect you will see the point of them at present.

Yours ever

HUGH ROBERT MILL

As things turned out, Mill's gesture of resignation was not to be required of him, but Shackleton had a long time to wait before he could be certain of this. At a meeting of the Council on 24 December opinions were found to be equally divided between Shackleton and a certain Mr. Johnstone. Dr. J. G. Bartholomew, the cartographer, who as foundation Honorary Secretary had always wanted the Society to move with the times, was very much in favour of Shackleton. He let him know that he had been instrumental in moving a postponement of the decision, because he had realised that if a vote had been taken at this particular meeting Shackleton must have lost the day, as some of the members who favoured him were away for Christmas. Shackleton had been very much troubled by the postponement, before he realised the reason for it, and had written[11] forcibly to Mill that he supposed Johnstone was strenuously canvassing while his rival was out of the way in London. 'I cannot understand Johnstone getting so many on his side when they say that he will not give all his time to the work.'

The news from Bartholomew about the postponement made things a little more hopeful, and Shackleton specially requested Dr. Mill to get hold of Richardson, a member of the Committee who was coming through London on his way from Berlin to Scotland, and who would be a valuable ally if he could be won over. This manoeuvring for position perhaps had the desired effect. At all events, on 11 January Shackleton was unanimously elected Secretary and Treasurer, to work under the two Honorary Secretaries and the two Honorary Treasurers. His employer at Pearson's was, as he told[12] Miss Dorman, 'resigned to my final leaving though I am going on with writing for him'. On 10 January Shackleton had delivered one of the Scottish Society's Christmas lectures, at which the audience 'quite fell in with all the jokes', and a few days later he began his work.

The ensuing few months were so busy and happy that Shackleton was able to forget his disappointment and mortification over the *Discovery* expedition. Just how much Miss Dorman had done to assuage this disappointment will never be known, but one can guess that it was very much. Shackleton was still in some ways immature, and not by any means as sure of himself as he wished to appear. The fact that a beautiful woman, older than himself and with brilliant prospects, had been sufficiently interested in him to allow herself to be waited for (to put it no more strongly) for seven years must have contributed enormously to his development as a person. Armitage[6] wrote to Mill that he had thought him, on the *Discovery*, very boyish:

'He was greatly influenced by the romance of his engagement and marriage, and Lady Shackleton, for whom I have a very great admiration, was, no doubt, mainly responsible, together with the love of the open spaces, in raising him from a rather dreamy ambitious boy with no settled ideas to a man of strong character, one who, although always keenly sensitive to the opinions of others, placed the work which he had set out to do before everything else.'

The letters which Ernest Shackleton wrote to Emily Dorman at this time are full of pride and energy, devotion and ambition. He addresses her very often as 'child', an appellation which shows very clearly the attitude he had taken up in his own mind. He was always to be the dominant partner in the marriage. But he did not realise how much this domination was a conscious, an intended thing on his part. Emily Shackleton, all through their life together, deferred to her husband, quoted his opinions, did what he wanted and subordinated her life and personality to his: but, all through their life together, he was in fact completely dependent on her. Even in the last years, when they were sometimes at variance, she was always the audience of one to whom he addressed his hopes and wishes and ambitions, the source of refreshment at which he replenished his flagging strength as the world made more and more demands on him.

But now, in Edinburgh, he took the lead, emphatically and cheerfully. He now had two new jobs, each occupying his mind simultaneously and exercising all his powers. He was buoyantly wading into the fight against what seemed to him to be the reactionary methods and prejudices of the Society, and in his off-time he was seeing to the furnishing of the 'little house' at 14 South Learmonth Gardens, on the outskirts of Edinburgh, where he was to take his bride.

It is pleasant to see the organising ability which had been so well employed in the Antarctic being turned now to a smaller domestic sphere. Shackleton had found the house himself, with the help of his new friends in the city, and on 10 February he wrote enthusiastically about it to Emily Dorman, who was to come up for a weekend to inspect wallpapers and decide on electric fittings. There was plenty of space, he told her[13] proudly: 'the cupboards in the spare room are not very good but in our rooms they are large enough': the landlord had to do the fittings and was said to be generous. The visit was a happy and a profitable one. Miss Dorman approved of the house, and on 18 February Shackleton wrote that he had been to see a lawyer and had the lease drawn up. No detail was too trivial for the ebullient young man.

He took 'a great fancy to have a radiator in the hall' and was persuaded that this would be very economical; he sent a batch of advertising leaflets for his fiancée to see. Letters went back and forth about details in which he took the lead but in which he always sought her opinion—about candles for the dining-room, about friezes, about getting a woman to come in until they could engage servants, about staining the boards of the bedrooms because they seemed rather shabby, about whether to have felt or carpet for his dressing-room.

One letter at this time contained a budget (opposite) which shows the standard of living to which he aspired.

Through all the letters he wrote to Emily Dorman at this time there runs, besides the note of passion and longing which is that of all lovers, a note of protectiveness which is very revealing. The tenderness in Shackleton's nature was seldom very obvious, and many people would have denied its existence altogether. To the outside world he presented a front that was forceful and at times aggressive. Loving a fight, expecting no quarter for himself, he was not always willing to make concessions for other people. But those who really knew him, and above all those who followed him to the Antarctic, knew the depths and strength of his affections, even if he did not always find it easy to express them.

If his marriage was an achievement for which he had worked, his new job was a fight, and one which he would make every effort to win. So keen was he to make a success of it that he persuaded his fiancée, clearly against her will, to postpone their honeymoon. His arguments, in a letter of 3 February,[13] are somewhat disingenuous.

'Dearest I want to do what you want but really my heart I think we would be happier in our own little home than out there and after all dearest we would spend money and we could not help it. Child there is sunshine here too and there will be sunshine in our lives, and I know we would be happier on the spot. Beloved when I make a little more I will take you anywhere you like for a holiday, but I feel this a little. I would love to have you enjoy yourself and I suppose I could easily take a fortnight Still dear one you know how I feel. It would be such a rush there really and here we would be so quiet and I could take you away for a month in Sept or August or whenever you like. Dearest do you really set your heart on going there?'

Faced with his implicit wish Emily Dorman agreed not to remove him from Edinburgh at this crucial time.

The situation at the Society headquarters was one which appealed to Shackleton's sense of humour as well as to his youthful, belligerent desire to change everything quickly.

'I will tell you the principal changes (he wrote[14] to Mill on 3 February). The books are dusted, the place behind where the maps were lying all adrift is clear(ed) up, I am in a nice light room upstairs where you must visit me when you come up. There is a typewriter in the office and there is a telephone!! You should have seen the faces of some of the old chaps when it started to ring today. They had, after a great discussion decided that I could have it in, and said "Well, it will take six months to get in but that was four days ago

	£	s	d
Food washing. Extras a year.	260	0	0
Food 15/= per head per week = £3			
Washing " " £1			
Extras " " £1			
Wages for 2 servants per year	42	0	0
Cook at £24 } Both trained			
Housemaid £18			
Coals and light per year £34	34	0	0
Kitchen and 3 fires all the year £18			
But it would be about £14 without			
3 fires all year.			
Electric light at 1½d per hour per point			
for 10 points for 6 hours each light 16 candle power			
# 1/3d per day = roughly £20			
Wine and entertaining for 1st year	25	0	0
Clothes and personal for Me	50	0	0
" " " " " darling	150	0	0
Doctor perhaps	10	0	0
Rent	125	0	0
Taxes between ⅕ + ⅙ =	25	0	0
	711	0	0

and by worrying I got it in and working today. I had said nothing and you would have laughed had you seen their faces when the jangle of the telephone disturbed them in a discussion as to whether the younger of the two lads in the office should continue to spend one week a month addressing wrappers or should we be up to date and save time badly needed for looking after the library and get the wrappers finished and printed at Constable's. Thank goodness the progressives carried it. I want to see the Society do all in its power to promote geography and unless we have a system and go at the thing thoroughly, not stepping aside for politics or sport or our other little interests, we can do nothing of use.'

He reports cheerfully on the attitude of Council to him. One or two members are still sitting on the fence: one or two are hostile: one particularly depressing member is alluded to as the 'Ancient Druid': Dr. Bartholomew, happily, 'loves the taste of the millennium on his tongue' and 'hails any new idea with applause'.[14]

There was a dangerous moment when Shackleton undid a packet in the presence of one of the most reactionary of his employers, and the contents turned out to be a copy of a society rag, *The Smart Set*; the owner had sent it to Shackleton (as an ex-journalist) for inclusion in the Society's Reading Room. Shackleton[14] put on an air of righteous indignation 'at the thought of them sending such a rag to a scientific society', and the awkward moment passed.

One of the features of the Society on which Shackleton decided to concentrate was the lecture list, and in this, naturally, the Antarctic preponderated. On 25 February, while he was still taking the measure of the Council, he gave a lecture himself on 'Farthest South' at the Synod Hall in Edinburgh. He felt the responsibility of this, his first important public appearance since his appointment. At the same time he was not willing to let himself be intimidated by the occasion. To an eminent member who told him that there would be 'a very full gathering of Council to support me to the platform' he replied[14] 'that as long as I happened to be on the spot it did not matter about the rest. I said I thought I could struggle along without support'. Ernest Shackleton, who could make charming remarks when his heart warmed towards someone, was never willing to be conciliatory for purely social reasons, and no doubt this particular die-hard thought his reply was unbecoming.

All the same, Shackleton got a lot of fun out of this lecture, or rather out of the large audience, the female section of which produced some remarkably silly remarks. One lady (he felt she ought to have known better, as she had geographical connections) asked him the usual question, whether it was not very hot at the South Pole, and another delivered a battery of even more foolish queries 'Where did you get such a charmingly delicious map?' 'What pretty little ships you have on it'. 'Oh, I am so fond of all geography'—which Shackleton quoted[14] gleefully to Mill. 'I had to stand like a fool', he commented, 'while she poured out that drivel, and two or three other people looking at the map at the same time. How would you have answered her? With your infinite tact and being always equal to the occasion, I'm sure you would have been all right, but I was out of soundings entirely.'

A mixture of insouciance and toughness carried Shackleton through a busy season, during which he increased the membership of the Society from 1,430 to 1,832, the bank balance from £50 to £347, and the attendance at lectures from about 250 to about 1,630 at each meeting. He was also able to arrange a greater number of lectures than usual in the four centres of the Society—Edinburgh, Glasgow, Dundee and Aberdeen. He enlisted his wife's help to get members in England and went after more advertisements for the Society's magazine, improving its finances considerably.

It is a wonder, indeed, that he had time for his wedding. But this day, for which he had served as faithfully as ever Jacob did, was one which transcended all others. On 9 April 1904, at Christ Church, Westminster, he and Emily Dorman were married, and returned to their Edinburgh home with the good wishes of all their friends; and if they had no honeymoon, there can be no doubt that they were as happy as they could be. For him, after his absences in London on the Society's business, there was the joy of homecoming which made him feel at once secure and free. On Emily's first birthday after their marriage, when he had to be away, he wrote[16]:

My darling Sweeteyes and Wife

Just a bunch of roses from your husband and lover Sweetheart your boy sends you his love all all his love for ever and ever I can see you darling reading this in bed today and am longing to be beside you in my own place I am coming back quickly to you dear heart; so do not be sad; I will be wanting you sorely today dearest. I hope the roses will be sweet The lovingliest birthday wishes to my darling from her husband.

Their world was a far more distinguished and lively one than they would have fallen into in London at this time. Dr. Mill,[7] in his *Life of Sir Ernest Shackleton*, recaptures its atmosphere very clearly. Edinburgh was, he says:

'in the opening years of the twentieth century warm with kindliness, bright with cultured intelligence, glowing with humour and flashing with wit, retaining still much that was best in the Edinburgh which was to Sir Walter Scott "mine own romantic town". Here Shackleton was in a new world which gratified him as he pleased it, and he made new friends who held the keys to many locks. He had opportunities of familiar conversation with statesman like Lord Rosebery, men of science and culture like Professor Crum Brown, leaders of the business world like Mr. William Beardmore, guardians of the social charm of bygone days like Mrs. W. Y. Sellar, and luminaries of the Bench, the Bar, and the University, who were deep in all the movements of the time. Rarely has so dazzling a transformation befallen the third mate of a steamer in the course of three short years.'*

If it was a transformation, it was one that suited Shackleton. Those who remember him in those early days of his married life remember his liveliness, his ready wit and sparkling conversation; they remember him as becoming the centre of every gathering he went to, without making any effort to be so; they remember that he and his wife, without any ostentation, entertained delightfully those people whose company they liked.

Shackleton's position led also to many interesting acquaintances outside Edinburgh. He represented the Society on many occasions in London, and most successfully. During the summer of 1904 memories of the previous year were revived when, calling on Sir Clements Markham at the Royal Geographical Society, he read all the letters which had come from the *Discovery*, now safely in New Zealand after the second season in the Antarctic. On this same occasion, as he told his wife, he saw 'the great Bruce' riding in a cab with a girl; he met him later in somewhat more dignified circumstances when, in July, he had to arrange a reception in Edinburgh for the man who had returned from two profitable summers of scientific research in the Weddell Sea.

During the summer, too, Shackleton was able to take his wife for a belated honeymoon. They stayed at Dornoch, where they played a good deal of golf. It was a game they both continued to enjoy, though Emily Shackleton was always better than her husband.

In September the *Discovery* returned to England, and the members of the expedition were fêted by the many people who had been inspired to an interest in the South by the news of their success. Shackleton went up to London and attended the lunch given on the deck of the ship at the East India Dock, and the ceremonial dinner given the same evening by the Royal Geographical Society at the Criterion Restaurant. He was also at the more informal welcome home dinner given by the Savage Club on Guy Fawkes Night, when a large collection of old *Disovery* members listened to a poem about themselves, written by Sir Clements Markham and set to music by Herbert Schart—its title, Intrepid Souls.

In company with his old comrades, Shackleton received the Polar Medal, the King's award for distinguished service in the field of Polar

---

* Mill, in spite of his admiration for Shackleton, never lost the slightly patronising attitude of patron to protégé.

exploration, and a silver replica of the special gold medal which the Royal Geographical Society had presented to Scott.

The trimphant return of Scott and Bruce from their journeys was turned to good account by Shackleton. In the prospectus he drew up of the Royal Scottish Geographical Society's activities during the winter of 1904–05, there appear announcements of lectures by both men in Edinburgh, Glasgow and Dundee. Two pages of the prospectus carry photographs of these notable explorers, and of the medals they had received—an idea which makes something special of a perfectly ordinary Society programme. On 12 November the Scottish Society held its Twentieth Anniversary Banquet, with Scott, Bruce and Markham as the principal guests. Markham stayed with the Shackletons on this occasion, and in a letter to his hostess[15] he took the opportunity of giving her a word of warning. 'I hope Ernest will not overtax his strength', he wrote, 'for he is, I am afraid, doing much more than the work of one man.' Far from taking things more easily, however, Shackleton soon began to look out for more work.

His position at the Society was perhaps not perfectly clear to him, for his predecessor had held a lectureship at the University, and had not attended regularly at the office. Shackleton had put in a great many hours on the Society's business, but he saw no reason to sit at his desk when there was nothing to do, and he saw no harm in doing two things at once. At this period of his life he was trying out a number of ideas through which he hoped to find prosperity and fulfilment. It is notice-able that his innate quality of leadership was trying to show itself even now. Each of the jobs he applied for between 1903 and 1906 involved the organisation of a large concern and the overseeing of a number of people. The future expedition leader now turned his mind to a sphere which demanded intelligence and force in the handling of people. He decided to enter the world of politics.

In October Shackleton, on a flying visit to London, wrote[16] to his wife 'I went to the Lecture Agency and made final arrangements with them and then to Liberal Unionist Council and had a long talk with Boraston, he is going to wake them up in Dundee'. As to the agency, no further information is available than that he was sure that such a business, under his name, would make big money; but nothing came of the idea. The suggestion that he should stand as Liberal-Unionist candidate for Dundee was a firmer proposition altogether.

The great happiness Shackleton was enjoying in his married life had not damped his ardour for personal success. Although the first keenness of his disappointment over the *Discovery* expedition was blunted, it may be doubted whether he forgot for long that, in his own view, he had made a failure of his own part in it. He had always been ambitious, and since his first meeting with Emily Dorman the desire to win fame and fortune for her had become steadily stronger. Moreover, his job at the Scottish Society, though it was interesting, was no longer new. It was an essential part of his character that he should enjoy the preliminaries of a fight, and the fight itself, far better than the aftermath of victory. The opposition of some members of the Council had been just enough to convince him that this post was what he wanted above all things: and when Shackleton wanted something, his desires were strong, overwhelming and immediate. He had put all his energies into defeating his rivals in the field, and over-riding, cajoling or diverting the doubts of some of his employers. A new broom, he had enjoyed sweeping the Society with a vigour that had sent some of the older members scurrying from the dust-storm. But this period was now over, and his innate dislike of routine was at work in him, urging him to look out for something else, not necessarily as an alternative but at least as an exciting addition to his present work.

Consequently, when he was approached by the Liberal-Unionists*, he eagerly agreed to contest a ward in Dundee. He had never taken an active interest in politics before, and it may be doubted whether he was better informed than any other intelligent man of his day in his own circle. But the Party officials wanted a fighter, and it was primarily because he was so obviously a fighter that they approached Ernest Shackleton.

During the winter he was summoned to Dundee to meet members of the party, and he was adopted as their candidate for the next general election, which appeared to be imminent. The Dundee seats were regarded as safe for the Liberals, but it was thought that Shackleton had a sporting chance of undermining one of them. He could not have resisted such a challenge.

Complications now arose. Unfortunately the Dundee committee let it be known publicly that they had adopted Shackleton as their candidate before he had been accepted by the General Committee of the party, and before he had time to prepare his case fully for the Society which at present employed him. He realised that this body must be carefully handled, and he had set out to do just that—but, it seemed, too late. He explained the situation fully in a letter[17] to Mill:

> 'Now as to the details of this episode, the following are the facts. When I was approached by a prominent member of the Government who asked would I come forward and stand for Dundee in the Liberal Unionist interest, I was startled, to say the least of it. I had only expressed my views privately to another man, who had passed them on, with the result above mentioned. I asked for time to think it

---

* In 1886 the Liberal Party had split over Home Rule for Ireland. The 'Liberal-Unionists', led by Joseph Chamberlain, had moved into alliance with the Conservatives and opposition to the Liberal Party.

over and then I said that if it could be managed with(out) stopping my work in the Society in any way, I would do so. I saw clearly that Dundee was a hard fight, but that did not matter. I knew that I had influence there, having been associated in more ways than one with the people, and I had got on well with them and as a sailor in the Merchant Service it would be a point in my favour. Altogether I saw there was an opportunity of helping my party so I decided to go in for it. But before going any further in the matter I thought it best to ask the opinion of the leading members of Council as to what they thought of it, and from all I asked—they numbered about twelve— the idea was received with approbation, though some were not politically on my side. I asked Geekie [*sic*], the President, and he said "Go in". I found that it would not take up my time in the Society, as having worked from 9 a.m. till 12 a.m. for a month, I had everything in good order. Bartholomew and Richardson, the Honorary Secretaries, were quite agreeable, so I went to Dundee and saw the small committee there and they accepted me and they let the papers get wind of the fact. . . . An old member of Council, who is about 85 and has to have his letters written for him and never attends a meeting, wrote to Geekie, asking if it was true and saying that it would harm the Society. Geekie called a Recommendations Committee and there was a vote taken as to whether it was all right for the Society. In the meeting there were only two who voted against it, but as the vote was not unanimous the affair would have to go to Council, and I was not going to have that, as it would make a split, and was not the right thing that I should be subjected to this . . . I have decided to let the matter slide, and I will not at any rate do anything now in the matter. . . . The General Committee in Dundee not having accepted me leaves the matter easier, but I want you to understand that we are not going to make a formal statement that I am not going to come forward, just let it died down, and when they get another man the talk will be diverted to him.'

The letter shows clearly that Shackleton, on the defensive, and as always in such a case protesting a little too much, wanted to leave himself a loophole to consider politics again, and yet was most anxious to justify himself to the man he respected most of all his friends. Mill, whose political opinions were not Shackleton's, and who in any case thought that an officer of a learned society should not have any, had evidently written frankly and forcibly. Among other points, he had put it to Shackleton that he was courting newspaper publicity in a most undesirable way, and this Shackleton strongly denied. 'I want to get on' he wrote frankly 'and I want to get on in any line I take up, but I feel that in doing so I am perfectly honest and it is not from any idea of newspaper publicity I became connected with politics, but as the result of careful thought on my part and a conviction that what I uphold is right.'

No doubt he wrote this in all sincerity, but the real source of his ambition may be found in the same letter. Shackleton was never good at hiding his feelings. He preferred to be absolutely honest, and his letters were written, for the most part, with an unusual absence of guile. It is the true Shackleton, the man who wanted to achieve, and to achieve grandly, who speaks out to Mill.

'I want to do a little in the world to help it and no honest endeavour can be without its result. With life before me, and strength and hope, all these things which time will whittle down, I may achieve something before the period at which life grows stale and strength wanes and hope flies, or if it does not fly, assume the dignified attitude of resignation.'

He was at this time twenty-nine years old.

He could not endure the ambiguous situation for long. Early in January 1905, he handed in his resignation to the Society, feeling that he should not continue to serve it if his actions were not approved by the whole of Council. A Recommendations Committee met on 9 March to discuss the position and after some argument 'The Committee while deeply regretting Mr. Shackleton's standing as a Parliamentary Candidate, resolved to recommend that the Council take no immediate action on his letter of 16th January last'.[18] The Committee were not unanimous, the President in particular having changed his opinion since the previous year. This recommendation was brought forward by Mr. Bartholomew at a Council meeting on 14 March, and after some discussion Shackleton's resignation was again shelved.

The situation could not go on like this, of course. Everybody in geographical circles had heard rumours, if not facts, and early in January Scott had written a letter of friendly warning to Shackleton, having heard gossip about the secretary having neglected his work for outside interests. Shackleton[19] answered firmly with an outline of what he had done for the Society, and made it clear that although his resignation had not yet been accepted, he intended to leave. 'I quite know that I do owe a great deal to those who helped me to get into the Society and will leave everything shipshape.'

His resignation took effect in July, and Major C. A. Forbes of the Indian Army was elected in his place. Now that the uncomfortable situation had been resolved, everyone who had worked with Shackleton felt able to look at the credit side of his work. At a Council Meeting of 20 July, Dr. George Smith[18] moved:

'That this Council, as representing the Society, thanks Mr. Shackleton for his services as secretary which have substantially increased the membership of the Society and have also placed the Society's magazine in a more satisfactory financial position. The motion was carried unanimously.'

Shackleton's future was still unsettled, and this now became increasingly important since on 2 February his eldest son Raymond had been born. His letters at this time show that he felt entirely confident of making a success of his life, but it was not clear whether this was to be done by means of business, politics, speculation, or by an independent Antarctic expedition. All these possibilities presented themselves, more or less strongly, during 1905.

In the spring of that year Shackleton had had much talk about his future with William Beardmore, a wealthy Clydeside ship builder with numerous interests. Beardmore (afterwards Lord Invernairn) was an old Dulwich boy whom Shackleton had met in Edinburgh, and who had been attracted, like so many others, by Shackleton's drive and directness. He made it clear that he could find him something to do in one of his companies, although it was not yet clear what that something would be. In April Shackleton went to Parkhead, Beardmore's extensive works in Glasgow, and wrote[20] optimistically to his wife from there:

'He tells me definitely that there are four separate things I can go into and showed me the lines on which I am to work if I go to Parkhead; he tells me I can only begin at £300 but that the beginning is nothing if I do what he wishes and show that I can work then I am sure to get on. He is the sort of man who would raise me another £300 if he thinks I am doing well and I would rather start on a low basis than feel that he was giving more just because he knew me.'

William Beardmore had just taken over the Arroll-Johnston motor works, and at this time was inclined to think that Shackleton could be useful to him here. Beardmore's wife, however, anxious that her husband should spare his health, perhaps tended to give Shackleton the impression that he might become a confidential right-hand man to Beardmore. It seems unlikely that this was ever intended by William Beardmore himself, but there is no doubt that he was willing to guarantee Shackleton a job if he did not get into Parliament by August, and Shackleton was well satisfied.

Nevertheless, he was not prepared to let other possibilities go. The attraction of making a lot of money quickly was always very strong, and among the many people he had met during this year, there were some who seemed able to help him to do this. He wanted money partly for his family, and partly for the expedition which, at this time, was never far from his thoughts. Hopefully entering the business world, certain that his energy would lead to success, he wasted much time in projects which were, each one in turn, totally alluring to him.

Late in 1904, for instance, he had formed a company called Tabard Cigarettes, with a shop and office in Jermyn Street. For the next few years he took every opportunity of advertising the company. It appeared in the pages of the Royal Scottish Geographical Society's magazine.

Such friends of his as had money to spare invested in it. The cigarettes were prominent in his own expedition of 1907–08, and his connection with the company was pushed whenever possible. It flourished for a time, but it never became the spectacular success for which he had hoped.

Part of the summer of 1905 was spent at St. Andrews, where Shackleton took a house, and where he and his wife assiduously practised the congenial game of golf. During this time Dr. Charles Sarolea, Belgian Consul in Edinburgh and Professor of French at the University, became engaged to Emily Shackleton's elder sister Julia. Sarolea, a brilliant, versatile man, was as violent in his enthusiasms as Shackleton himself, and together they visited the Continent with the idea of establishing an international news agency which should be larger, more truthful and more profitable than any other. This scheme, like the others, came to nothing.

For the rest of this year Shackleton had no regular employment. During the autumn he was working hard in the effort to raise money for an Antarctic expedition, which was more and more strongly presenting itself as the essential and ideal direction of his life. But he was not able to find enough support, and no doubt it was a relief when the Unionist Government resigned in December and he began to work for the forthcoming election—for he had some time before been accepted as prospective candidate by the General Committee of the Party. For the next few weeks he was hectically and continuously busy, in the way he best liked to be, throwing himself vigorously into the campaign, rushing from one meeting to another, on one occasion even chartering a special train to be in time for a meeting (it is not recorded who paid for this).

His political views were for the most part the conventional views of his party, and no doubt much of what he said was said under instruction. He stood out as an individual, because he canvassed as a working man, a man who had in fact worked with his hands, even in the ship-yards of Dundee, and who could therefore appreciate the particular needs of some of the Dundee populace. He made himself immensely popular by his cheerfulness, his blunt and free approach to all his prospective constituents, his ready wit when he was heckled, and his dogged fighting spirit.

The letters he wrote to his wife at this time show how much he enjoyed the fight. 'Sir G.B. says that he considers I have a good chance' he wrote on one occasion.[21] That was a good day. He had addressed six meetings, over 2,000 people, and had had what he described as a 'splendid vote'. 'They threw our photos on the screen tonight Mine was loudly cheered and Smith clapped, Wilkie cheered, R & R silence!!!'

All the same, it was one of the R's thus received in silence who topped the poll on 16 January 1906, while Shackleton's name stood

above only one candidate—the Conservative Smith, whose canvassing
had been easy-going and who had tried at one time to exploit Shackleton's energy in a joint meeting.

It cannot be regretted now that Shackleton was not elected to a seat
in Dundee. A Parliamentary career would have masked from him, for
a time at least, the true nature of his gifts. He was certainly not suited
by temperament to the political life. An interesting article in a French
history of exploration[22] puts this point neatly:

> 'Son dégôut des feintes et des hâbleries, son impétuosité et sa
> juvénile aggressivité l'auraient certainement exposé a de serieux
> déboires dans le monde parlementaire; il en acquérait une domination
> sur ses hommes quand il etait chef incontesté, mais il en eût été peu
> avantagé dans le dédale d'obscurs compromis et de transactions peu
> loyales de la carrière politique.'

As always, it was the fight that had absorbed Shackleton; the victory
could not have satisfied him.

He did not approach William Beardmore for work straight away.
Instead, February saw him in London following the dancing light of a
prospective fortune across a marsh of speculation. He had become one
of the principal shareholders in a company, and in this month[23] he
wrote from Sydenham to his wife:

> 'I hardly like to look forward but there is a chance of our little
> steam boat company doing a big deal in a few days, and getting the
> contract to take 40,000 Russian troops back to Russia from the Far
> East; Prince Alexieff has cabled us that he will give £12 per head for
> the soldiers and £40 for each officer, so that would cost £450,000
> and we would clear £100,000 but there is a lot to pay for: the Chair-
> man and the Russian attaché go to St. Petersburg on Saturday, and
> we ought to get a cable on Wednesday night to say if the contract is
> on or off: it would mean £10,000 to me, but I cannot go into details
> now: and I don't want to raise hopes . . . It is awfully exciting, we
> have got the option of 11 large steamers so there is a lot of work if
> it does come off. Dont say anything darling to a soul: for it is dead
> secret.'

It cannot be discovered who Shackleton's associates were in this
enterprise, nor what grounds they had for supposing the contract would
come through. Shackleton seems to have plunged into the affair
headlong, and before any news could be hoped for, he was calculating
enormous profits and making wonderful plans for the future. The
company's shares would go up as soon as the contract was through, he
said, and he would be personally responsible for the organising and
fitting of the ships; but his wife must not be disappointed if they did
not get it. On 5 February he had a busy day seeing to the underwriting

7

of the steamers 'if we get the contract', the afternoon working on details
of fitting, and the evening seeing the Russian agents off to St. Petersburg. 'Cheer Oh and don't be down; things will be all right' he wrote[23]
on 9 February, still in London. 'We got cables tonight fixing up 10
steamers so we are practically sure of the contract, I think we have
checkmated our opponents this time.' On 14 February[24] he was able
to give her more definite information.

> '6,500 troops have been signed for by contract which will receive
> official rectification tomorrow, and then we send out the stores etc.,
> but we will not hear for some time as to whether we are going to get
> the full 40,000 men or not, one of our men arrives on Saturday
> morning and we will get full news from him he says in a letter or wire
> rather that if we initiate this 1st lot well we will get more. but it is
> not very satisfactory though I shall make at least £1000 out of this
> small deal. now that the contract is signed one feels more at ease but
> not really till we get a cable saying it has the official ratification and
> that will come tomorrow. We have orders to hold 9 more vessels in
> readiness so I hope we will get the other orders in the course of a
> week.'

But nothing came of the Russian contract after all. The dreams of
spectacular profits were far less real than the dreams of spectacular
distances in the Antarctic with which they probably alternated.
Shackleton always conceived his plans on a large scale, and his disappointments were correspondingly bitter.

However much he regretted the loss of this chimerical fortune, he
wrote[25] about it very cheerfully to his wife. 'About the Russian business,
there still is a chance of the whole thing coming off all right but it
looks very dicky at present and the contract will have to be sold if they
do not carry it through.' He had made up his mind to cut his losses,
and by the end of February he was in the employment of William
Beardmore.

Of this change Dr. Mill[7] says dryly 'It was a wholesome corrective
to the excitement of visionary news agencies, and the hunt for contracts
to yield fabulous profits'. But there was something of the same
atmosphere about this new job, as Shackleton saw it. The very vagueness
of his terms of reference was attractive. Writing from William Beardmore's library,[25] he told his wife on the first day:

> 'Will has given me a room right opposite his own so I am to be in
> close touch with him all the time and he told me that I will get on
> all right if I only work and the future depends on myself so I mean
> to do my very best in this matter as he says his trouble is with men
> not having initiative enough that he has to keep stirring them up
> the whole time.'

At this time no salary had been settled, but this did not deter Shackleton from seeing himself as a director of the company in two or three years—and (at the moment when he wrote) really wanting above all things to be one. In this he was only following the pattern of hundreds of thousands of ambitious young men who found it easier to run in fancy than to walk in fact. The important point was that Beardmore recognised that he was not really cut to this pattern at all. While giving Shackleton work to tide him over a difficult time (and making him work hard, too), he was shrewd enough to realise that this particular young man was not yet in his proper sphere.

So Shackleton once more became an office worker, travelling from Edinburgh to Glasgow every day, correctly dressed in city clothes, and lunching at the works. The work he did there has been explained most clearly[26] by Mr. A. B. MacDuff, who was personal secretary to Beardmore at that time.*

'First, Shackleton was made secretary of a committee he was forming to look into a new design of gas engine. The Chairman of the committee was the late Archibald Barr of the Royal Technical College Glasgow; it was formed of important gas experts, and functioned for about 18 months. Shackleton would attend the meetings of this committee and make full notes. Then he would come to me and read them over, and I would fill in the bare patches and take it down in shorthand and send it to the typists' room to get it typed out, and then give it to Shackleton again.'

Mr. MacDuff makes it abundantly clear that he was willing to have his time taken up by Shackleton, because of his personality. 'He was such a charming fellow, when he came into my room, even if I was in the thick of things, I'd give them up to do what he wanted, I'd such a liking for the fellow.'

In this amicable way Shackleton's duties as committee secretary were carried out. Besides this, he held what Mr. MacDuff describes as a 'roving commission' for his employer, which took him much to London. One can guess it was work in which his personality was most of all in demand. Much of his time was spent in interviewing prospective clients, both in London and at Parkhead, entertaining the Company's business friends, sometimes receiving important visitors in Beardmore's absence. 'Looking back', Mr. MacDuff said, 'I can see him as a fine fellow, but it wasn't in any way a really important job in connection with the business.'

Mr. MacDuff noticed that Shackleton's charm, which he felt was

* Mr. MacDuff was Mr. Beardmore's personal secretary from 1899 until his death in 1936, and then looked after his widow's interests until her death in 1955; he was thus associated with the family for 56 years, and he and his employer used to take much pleasure in talking of Shackleton together.

spontaneous as well as effective, did not mean that he was easily deluded by people. On the contrary, he was aware that Shackleton became very cold towards anyone who 'came along and tried to impose on him or behave ostentatiously towards him.' He noticed, too, towards the end of 1906 that Shackleton was getting restless and fidgety, and when he asked him if he wanted to get away, Shackleton replied 'Yes, I want to go on a further expedition soon. This time I want to command it myself.'

Chapter VII

IN 1907 the South Pole had something of the emotional value that Everest has had in our own time. If it was not constantly in the minds of the general public, at least they were willing to be excited by the thought of a man setting out to reach this mysterious spot, which no doubt some of them visualised as a post stuck in a waste of snows. Unfortunately, although people were willing to respond to headlines in the daily papers, they were less willing to give money to help to turn desire into fact. They liked to think of exploration as something dangerous and splendid; they preferred to ignore the fact that it was expensive.

So when Shackleton, early in 1906, tried to raise money for an expedition, he found himself without backers. It is possible that his illness on the *Discovery* expedition counted against him with the business men he approached, even though they may have been impressed by his ardent way of stating his case. The name of Shackleton was unknown to the general public, except for the small section of it in Dundee who, from recent experience, could have testified to his fighting qualities; so public subscription offered no promise. It was not likely that the Government would sponsor an expedition with a comparatively unknown leader, and the learned societies which had supported Scott were not now inclined—or indeed able—to find any more money.

For more than a year now Shackleton had followed every path that seemed likely to lead towards the South, but to no avail. When a determined effort now failed to raise money, he 'put a black mark' as he told Mill later, against the names of seventy-odd rich men who had declined to help him, and, in the course of time, settled down at Parkhead Mills to make himself useful to William Beardmore. But perhaps it would be more accurate to say 'seemed to settle down'.

In fact his plan had been an extraordinarily interesting one. He had outlined it in a printed document, presumably intended to help in finding backers.*

---

* This document, a copy of which survives in SFP, is not dated, but internal evidence suggests that it must have been drawn up early in 1906. Sir Philip Brocklehurst remembers that when he first met Shackleton during 1906 he was very critical of the use of dogs for transport and intended to rely mostly on ponies: in this document, obviously, the dogs are to be the chief haulers. The four-sheet pamphlet has the title 'Plans for an Antarctic Expedition to proceed to the Ross Quadrant of the Antarctic with a view to reaching the Geographical South Pole and the South Magnetic Pole'.

The chief purpose of the expedition was to be to reach the South Pole and the South Magnetic Pole. In addition, there would be other inland sledge journeys (not specified) and there would also be continuous scientific work, to appeal to 'the purely scientific world and the general public.' Shackleton proposed to make use of the *Discovery* hut—that is to say, he intended to go to McMurdo Sound.

The most interesting feature of this document is the plan for transport.

'The main features for facilitating Sledge Travelling in order to reach the South Pole would be the use of dogs, ponies, and a specially designed motor car. In the opinion of experts, notably the late President of the Automobile Club, the third of these means is quite feasible; and the Chief Engineer of the *Discovery*, who has studied the matter carefully, informs me that, in his opinion, it is quite feasible to use a motor car over the ice we may expect on the way to the South Pole. I am informed that two or three of the largest motor firms would be only too ready to give a car specially designed, if only as an excellent advertisement to them. But though I propose taking a motor, I would not rely entirely upon this, as, with sixty dogs and a couple of ponies, I am quite certain the South Pole could be reached.'

At this time Shackleton's attitude to dogs was evidently more sensible than it was in the final making of his plans. He pointed out that it was only 'an insufficient number of dogs, and consequently a great overstrain and lack of food, that made us turn back on our Southern Journey.' He commented that 'dogs were only taken as a sort of stand-by on the remote chance of their being useful. If we had had sixty dogs I believe we should have reached the South Pole.'

His plan was to proceed towards the South Pole with the motor drawing ten sledges. One of these would be dropped every 100 miles, to form depôts. If the car should break down, the dogs and ponies could take over the loads. In fact Shackleton seems at this time to have put an inordinate amount of faith in the car. He estimated that he might be able to travel from 30 to 50 miles a day with it, and that he might therefore have time 'to go beyond the South Pole, and branch off East and West on the way home, so as to discover as much as possible of this great unknown land.'

The Magnetic Pole party would not use a car, because of the mountains that would have to be climbed; but Shackleton seems to imply that they would have the assistance of dogs and ponies.*

---

* 'The journey to the Magnetic South Pole would be done by another party travelling in the same way, except that they would not use a motor, as they must climb a height of 9,000 feet in order to reach the inland ice sheet.' In fact, as will be seen (p. 228), the Magnetic Pole party had to rely entirely on man-hauling.

The financial estimate for this early project is also interesting. It is prudently headed Rough Estimate of the Cost of the Expedition:

Vessel fully equipped	£7,000
Provisions for three years—Clothing—Salaries for staff—Scientific equipment—Oil—Sledge equipment, dogs and ponies—Carriage of dogs, ponies, and passages—General expenses	£10,000
Total	£17,000

He explained that this represented his estimate of the outside cost, and that he thought he could reduce the figure. He must have spent almost £50,000 when he did at last get his expedition.

He proposed at this stage of his planning to have a boat specially built, fitted with a motor capable of doing five knots. This he proposed to winter in the Antarctic. 'After landing the stores at the hut built by the *Discovery* Expedition, which will be in good condition, I would take the vessel nine miles out and let her be frozen in under the lee of an island, where the ice always breaks up in the summer time, and so obviate any risk of the vessel being frozen in for two consecutive seasons.'

There was to be no separate ship's crew. The expedition would consist of ten men, 'five of whom, besides being scientific observers, would also be sailors; three would have knowledge of working the engine, and all would be trained to help generally. I shall have no difficulty in getting suitable men, as some of the *Discovery* people are quite ready to go with me. There will be on the Expedition one commander, five scientific men, who would represent Magnetic Work, Geology, Biology, Zoology, and Meteorology; two other sailors, one Cook, and one General Help.'

Shackleton was sure that by the time the ship reached New Zealand every member of the expedition would be capable of ship work and that a large ship's crew was quite unnecessary for a schooner. He planned to leave New Zealand late enough in February for the Southern Ocean to be clear of ice 'and then we should have a clear run, assisted by our engine, right down to winter quarters.'

This early plan for what was afterwards to become the British Antarctic Expedition is extraordinarily appealing in its confidence and in the enthusiasm which is far less obvious in his later announcements. It has the special interest of any first draft, coming (as it must do) nearer in some ways to the original conception in the author's mind. In some ways it is a more practicable plan than the version Shackleton put forward a year or more later; and it is impossible not to feel that, with regard to his transport, he gave himself a better chance to get to the Pole, the goal of these years, the one strong desire in his mind.

Shackleton would have found it very difficult to arrange in order of importance his many reasons for wanting to get to the South Pole. There was his passionate wish to be worthy of his wife. He had waited many years to win Emily Dorman, and after she was won, his passionate feelings for her as a woman, no less than his gratitude to her as a mother and a home-maker, demanded some special expression. Nothing less would do than that he should lay the South Pole at her feet.

There was personal ambition too—the desire of an obscure but determined young man to make his mark on the world. One facet of this was his hope that he could make people forget his breakdown in 1903. There is no doubt that in the course of time Shackleton had come to exaggerate the importance of this. He was convinced, among other things, that Scott blamed him for the fact that the three of them had not reached a higher latitude. How much this was the product of his own self-doubt and how much it was due to remarks from malicious outsiders cannot now be discovered; but those who knew him on his first independent expedition, notably Sir Raymond Priestley and Sir Philip Brocklehurst, are certain that this motive was a strong one. From wounded pride, from a desire to restore his self-respect, and perhaps from some direct antagonism, Shackleton developed a strong feeling of rivalry towards Scott, which was expressed not in deeds or words but in the aspiration towards the Pole.

Dr. Mill regarded this motive as highly important, and wrote[1]:

> 'Mr. E. H. Shackleton, who had been sent home by Scott from the *Discovery*, had resolved at the time to prove that he was in no way unfit for polar service by going out again at the head of an expedition.'

The fact that Shackleton wanted to win a name for himself did not make him any less sincere in wanting to win a name for Britain too. The patriotic motive is never absent from an expedition of this kind, and it was no accident that Shackleton's was named the *British* Antarctic Expedition. There runs through his letters at this time a note of delight at scoring off 'the foreigners'. There is, too, the deeper note of genuine feeling for his country. In a letter he sent to his wife[2] after he had written the public announcement of his intentions he told her cheerfully, 'The Belgians have not announced nor the Norwegians but we don't know what they are up to anyhow we have capped them in our quarters.' But the letter ends with a postscript which perhaps only Shackleton could have written with complete sincerity—'I am representing 400 million British subjects.'

Another motive for Shackleton's efforts to raise an expedition was, quite simply, that he wanted to make money, and big money too. He lived at a time when fortunes were large and not eaten away by taxes, and he saw no reason why he should not join his many wealthy acquaintances on their particular eminence. He combined a strong liking for the good things of life with an equally strong feeling against the erosion of routine work. To make a fortune was the obvious way to get what he wanted, and if he could get to the South Pole a fortune could be made, for the world would be his oyster.

In the last analysis, however, explorers go on expeditions because they want to reach a particular point, or because they have an obsession with some objective.

> 'There is a vast attraction [Mill[3] wrote] in the struggle to attain an extreme latitude in polar exploration, and, although it is usual for explorers and almost invariable for critics to make little of this incitement to exploration, there must always be for the geographer a feeling that it is, after all, a very great thing to press towards the mark of latitude 90°. The tradition of inaccessibility is a challenge to humanity; and, whether it be the end of the Earth's axis or the summit of a snowy mountain which throws down this challenge, there will never be lacking a few to take it up and many to applaud the enterprise. More valuable scientific work and more lucrative commercial returns will accrue for a long time to come from easier and less fascinating adventures; but the desire to wipe out *terra incognita* appeals more deeply to certain instincts of human nature than either science or trade, and the rough-and-ready test of highest latitude is in one sense a gauge of human progress.'

Shackleton's sister Kathleen[4] remembers how she talked to him one night after his return from the Antarctic in 1909, and how she asked him 'did you want to get there first, or what?' His reply was 'I don't want to race anyone, but you can't think what it's like to walk over places where no one has been before.'

So idealism, ambition, competitiveness and devoted love combined in Shackleton and kept the flame of his desire burning. No matter how good his prospects with William Beardmore, no matter how happy his home life, he could not forget the Pole.

Nor would he have been able to forget it easily, for being a Fellow of the Royal Geographical Society as well as of the Scottish counterpart, he naturally heard all the geographical gossip which babbled through these two clearing houses for exploration plans. At the beginning of 1907 he was alarmed by rumours that the French explorer Charcot and the Belgian Arctowski were planning expeditions to the Antarctic. It was said that Arctowski had already raised the money and that he would be going to McMurdo Sound. This gave an additional spur to Shackleton's ambition. He tried once more to find patrons, and succeeded in getting promises for a good deal of money. At last he squared up to the difficult task of approaching his employer. 'I came to Beardmore a year ago' (Shackleton[5] told Scott) 'with the idea of working

with him and told him that I had given up the idea of the expedition.
He was very good the other day not reminding me of this fact more
than to say that he thought I had chucked up the idea.'

Shackleton's request to be released probably did not surprise William
Beardmore. He could not but have realised, as many people did, that
Shackleton lived energetically in the present. What he planned one year
might be quite inapplicable the next: you could only be sure that the
current plan would be supported by every ounce of Shackleton's drive
and determination. Beardmore agreed to guarantee a sum of money
at the bank, and with this and the other promises lately made to him,
Shackleton felt able to announce a forthcoming expedition.

He had heard that Arctowski was to be in London early in February
for a meeting with Amundsen, and thought this a good moment to
break the secrecy which had surrounded his plans. A partial secrecy
only, for his wife had been told of them not long after the birth of their
second child, Cecily, on 23 December 1906. Clearly Beardmore and
the other benefactors were in the secret, and so was Shackleton's
counsellor and friend Dr. Mill.

More than one of Shackleton's revelations to Mill were made in a
railway carriage. Early in 1907 Mill met his protégé by chance in the
corridor of a sleeping car at Euston, and remarked[6] to him that 'now
he would be content to leave the South Pole alone. Like the Ancient
Mariner, he held me with his glittering eye until he unfolded the scheme
of his new expedition. There was no more chance of getting to bed then
than there had been six years before from the bridge of the *Discovery*.'

A formal announcement of Shackleton's intentions was now needed
and this was made on 11 February, when Shackleton and Arctowski
were both guests of the Kosmos Dining Club of the Royal Geographical
Society. Each man outlined his plans, and next morning the newspapers
carried full details. Shackleton had done his duty in warning Arctowski
off the British preserves; but *The Times*[7] remained majestically neutral,
commenting that 'As similar expeditions are being organised by other
nations, what may be called an international attack upon the South
Polar regions will be made which will be followed by keen interest.'

Shackleton's new scheme[8] was essentially the same as his earlier one,
but the divergences are of great interest. It was published in March,
a few weeks after the first public announcement of the expedition.

The journeys to the South Pole and the South Magnetic Pole were
still the main objects, although he made provision for a larger party
so as to be better able to carry out scientific research. 'I do not intend'
he wrote, 'to sacrifice the scientific utility of the expedition to a mere
record-breaking journey, but say frankly, all the same, that one of my
great efforts will be to reach the southern geographical pole.'

There would now be a shore party of nine to twelve men, and this party would winter at the *Discovery* winter quarters, in a hut specially made for Shackleton. The ship, which he now proposed to buy rather than to have built, would return to New Zealand after landing the party, and would have a separate charter to return as a relief ship in the summer of 1909. This was a sensible economy measure, and it was perhaps unfortunate that Shackleton later decided to retain the ship through the winter to do oceanographical research off New Zealand and Australia—for in the end far less was done than he had intended.

The party which was to try to locate the South Magnetic Pole was not, at this stage, intended to winter with the rest. Shackleton proposed to try to land them at a suitable point in Victoria Land, where they could winter near their route, and where they could carry out continuous magnetic and meteorological observations. Similar observations would also be made by the main party, carrying on the work of Scott's expedition in McMurdo Sound. It was planned that the summer sledge journeys should include one across 'the new land known as King Edward the Seventh's Land', to follow the coast line and discover its trend.

Shackleton also planned, if he could get a whaling ship capable of withstanding ice, to cruise north of the Balleny Islands and then south at the close of the expedition, to trace the north-westerly coast of Wilkes Land. Finally, he hoped to detach a party during the winter (presumably to send it to Cape Crozier, though no particular place is mentioned) 'to try and watch the breeding and nesting of the emperor penguins.' This party would make use of a cinematograph camera and a phonograph for recording sounds.

The plan was well-conceived and thorough. Shackleton summarised his aims thus:

> ' By the southern and eastern sledge journey we may possibly solve the problem of the great ice-barrier; by the journey along Wilkes' Land we may lay down a definite coast-line; by the charting of new mountains and discovery of new lands in the far south we aid geographical science; by the magnetic work we help not only the academic side of magnetic science, but we may help the mercantile community in the way of better variation charts.'

Since his first sketch of the expedition, Shackleton had had second thoughts about transport. For what reason we cannot discover, he had become completely critical of dogs, and he now proposed to rely almost entirely on ponies and on a motor car. He was now full of enthusiasm for the strength, endurance and spirit of Siberian ponies. It is possible that his change of front may have had something to do with Armitage, who had seen ponies doing fine work in the Arctic and who may have spoken of them to Shackleton. He could, however, have heard their merits extolled far earlier, and presumably did so—when the subject of The Best Means of Travelling in the Antarctic was debated in the ward-room of the *Discovery* in the winter of 1902. Royds recorded[9] in his diary for 8 July:

> 'I think that the main or best method decided upon was by means of ponies and dogs combined. Ponies can carry or I should say drag 1800 lbs a piece, whilst they eat, or require food at the weight of 10 lbs a day. A dog can carry 100 lbs, & requires $1\frac{1}{2}$ lbs per day, & a man can drag 200 lbs & wants 2 lbs a day food. So there is not much doubt that a combination between ponies & dogs with a small party of three men is the very best method of travelling over this snowy surface, & should I now have the running of a show like this, I should at once say give me 4 ponies, & about 40 dogs, the difficulty would be getting the animals here, but once here they would do most valuable work. Motors, bicycles, & other mechanical modes of travelling were suggested, but as nothing yet has been made—although I don't say that it would not be possible to make—they could hardly come into the practical part of the debate.'

In planning to rely chiefly on ponies, Shackleton had made it necessary to make a new estimate of speed. He reckoned to travel 20 to 25 miles a day with this new transport arrangement, dropping depôts every 100 miles as he had planned before. He was confident that he would have enough time and hauling-power to reach the Pole. The mountains trending to the South, which he had seen five years before, might constitute a difficulty but he did not expect they would be an obstacle. 'Should they turn to the eastward,' he wrote, 'and we find it impossible to get over them with the ponies, we would pull the sledges ourselves up to the nearest available glacier.'

Unlike the earlier document, this one had no budget. Shackleton's ideas had grown, and he was not prepared now to offer any estimate of how much they would cost. Instead, all through the article there runs a recurring phrase—'if we have the funds'—a key phrase, of course, in the whole of his exploring life.

This was an expedition run on credit. The National Antarctic Expedition had been official, sponsored by two learned societies, approved by the Admiralty, and organised within the framework of naval discipline. Shackleton wanted to take out a band of picked men and to keep the entire responsibility himself. The expedition would have to be small and economical: he wanted it also to be up-to-date.

He set out to finance it on a speculative basis. In effect, he sold shares in the South Pole to friends, acquaintances and even strangers, anyone who would be prepared to put up a sum of money on the guarantee of one man's personality and ideas. They were to guarantee money which Shackleton proposed to pay back after his return to England, from the proceeds of the sale of a book, articles and illustrated lectures.

Shackleton was sure that he could settle his debts after his return. His optimism leaped over all petty calculations to the far-distant prospect of a fortune. On 14 August he wrote[10] to his wife:

'I have already made arrangements with Heinemann to publish the book on my return and it means £10,000 if we are successful: and that is quite apart from all newspaper news which we hope to fix up tomorrow. The newspaper news will be paid now and the other when we come back so it will leave me all the lectures etc free and the book can pay off guarantees if the people really want them but I am of the opinion that they will not ask for them if we are successful: I think it will be worth about £30,000 in the way of lectures alone judging by what the lecture Agency said today: Then Sweetheart we will settle down to a quiet life with our little ones.'

For all the confidence of this letter, Shackleton knew very well that if he failed to get to the Pole he would have to work hard to redeem the pledges he had given. He felt a strong duty to his backers, and this contributed to the complexity of a situation which came hard upon his announcement in *The Times*.

He had written to George Mulock, the naval officer who had replaced him in 1903, to ask if he would join his expedition. Similar letters had gone off to Michael Barne and to Wilson. Mulock[11] replied:

'. . . I wish you all good luck & would like to be coming with you but I have volunteered to go with Scott & if I qualify for Torpedo Lieutenant after a year's course I doubt if the Admiralty would let me go even should you be willing to take me.

I had no idea you contemplated one & congratulate you on keeping it so dark. I do not know when Scott intends going.'

Shackleton's surprise, indeed his consternation, can easily be guessed. No inkling of his old leader's intention had reached him, and it must have struck him at once that Scott would above all try to reach the Pole. This was not stated categorically in a letter from Scott which reached Shackleton a few days later. In fact, the correspondence which now followed, and which extended over several weeks, is interesting in that it shows the endless power of self-deception; for these two men, normally forthright, now unwilling to express their deepest desire, wrote with an elaborate care and circumlocution in order to conceal it.

Scott was at a disadvantage in that he was at this time on H.M.S. *Albemarle* in the Atlantic. He could not really be sure what was going on, and so he wrote with considerable agitation. In his first hasty letter to Shackleton he said that he had already announced his intention to lead another expedition to his old base, but only in confidence to the President and Secretary of the Royal Geographical Society. He did not want any publicity, he said, until he was sure of getting the necessary funds.

This was a point which Shackleton could appreciate, as it had been his motive for secrecy also. His apparent motive, however. For it is clear that both he and Scott really wanted, though perhaps being genuinely unaware of it, to steal a march on each other.

It is easy to say now, reading the whole collection of letters between them from a detached point of view, that the whole matter should have been settled in the light of reason.* Certainly both men realised the *need* for reason, and Wilson was quickly called in as a mediator. It was a situation that called for the most delicate adjustment of emotions, that roused the most irrational feelings—rivalry, loyalty, jealousy, and that intangible which men call honour. It was a situation which had never risen before between two men of the same country, though as a result of Shackleton's announcement, Arctowski and Charcot were now in much the same position.†

Scott felt strongly that he had a right to reserve McMurdo Sound for his own expedition. He appealed to Shackleton's sense of duty, addressing himself to the young officer he had known on the *Discovery*, whose commander he had been. He did not realise that Shackleton had grown up.

Shackleton, for his part, felt his conflicting obligations very deeply. On the one hand there was his strong feeling for his old comrades, which was still lively although his life had moved on different lines from theirs since the *Discovery* days. It was not only because he knew their efficiency that he wanted Wilson and Barne with him, but also because he could renew with them the atmosphere of comradeship he had valued so much.

On the other hand, he had a strong duty to his backers. He had assured them that his chance of reaching the Pole was a good one because he would be using a base he knew and the first part of the journey would be over familiar ground. Now that Scott wanted to reach a compromise, Shackleton thought he would be at a disadvantage. For at this time McMurdo Sound seemed the only suitable starting-point.

* When Shackleton's expedition was actually in progress, Mill[12] wrote to Mrs. Shackleton, on 22 June 1908:

It is in a way unfortunate that King Edward Land could not be reached; but I for one never saw the reasonableness of looking upon the Macmurdo Sound route as reserved for a possible future expedition which had not even been planned. It seems to me that when no expedition is actually in course of organization to a particular quarter that region is absolutely open and free to any one who has the courage, perseverance and good luck to reach it, and whether my friend Shackleton brings back the South Pole or not I am quite sure that he will bring back a splendid record—and much do I look forward to hearing him recount it!

† In August, Arctowski, who had had ideas of going to McMurdo Sound, announced to Charcot that he would not abide by the agreement they had made in the previous year by which the land between Graham Land and King Edward VII Land should be left to Charcot.

In this dilemma Shackleton showed a self-control and a dignity which might have surprised some of his comrades of 1903. In minor matters, if he did not get his way, he sometimes lost his temper. Now, recognising this as a real crisis, he did not write off impulsively to Scott but gave himself time to consider. He had heard by this time from Wilson that he would not be able to join the British Antarctic expedition or, as Shackleton had hoped, to collaborate with him in a book afterwards. Wilson was at this time employed by Lord Lovat on his Grouse Disease Survey, and although he would have been very happy to join Shackleton, he did not feel it would be right to leave the survey with two years to run. He thought Shackleton had a good chance of success and was disappointed to have to refuse the invitation. The warmth of his letters must have been comforting to Shackleton but his refusal was a real blow. For a short time he tried not to accept Wilson's decision; he even sent long telegrams to his old friend, and to his employer. But Wilson stood firm, and his amiable reproof[13] ('No time for more—but please take this as final—& don't waste more money in long telegrams') made it impossible for Shackleton to argue any longer.

Once this matter was settled, Shackleton appealed to Wilson for advice, as Scott had suggested he should do. He sent Wilson[14] a copy of his reply to Scott's first letter. 'I have merely stated the facts of the case', he told Wilson, 'and cannot at this early stage go into more details for though I realise Scott's points I must think of my own position and though he writes very nicely there are points in his letter that I do not agree with and which I cannot quite realise that he means'.

To Scott he wrote[15] firmly and somewhat impersonally, giving his reasons for keeping his plans secret for so long. He promised to give Scott's arguments his fullest attention and was anxious to hear his counter proposition 'for naturally I would like to fall in with your views as far as possible without creating a position that would be untenable to myself in view of the arrangements already made'.

A letter from Wilson[16] reached him just after he had written thus to Scott. Wilson was uncompromising when he saw his duty clear, and he told Shackleton firmly, though in a friendly spirit, that he thought Scott had a prior claim to the base.

His regard for Shackleton made him write freely and frankly:

'I think that if you go to McMurdo Sound & even reach the Pole—the gilt will be off the gingerbread because of the insinuation which will almost certainly appear in the minds of a good many, that you forestalled Scott who had a prior claim to the use of that base.'

He admitted that it was a difficult position, though he did not refer to the one point which made Scott's request at this time unreasonable—

namely, that he was not expecting to be able to take his expedition out for two years. Undoubtedly it was Wilson's advice to Shackleton to be 'quixotic' that made Shackleton accede to a request which was, in effect, that Scott should have the reversion of McMurdo Sound for three years ahead. In agreeing to this request from motives that were generous, Shackleton placed himself in the very position Wilson had predicted had he been ungenerous. As things turned out, the gilt *was* off the gingerbread, though not in the way Wilson meant.

But this is in the future. At the end of February Shackleton made up his mind to withdraw from the *Discovery* base, and on 4 March he cabled[17] to Scott 'Will meet your wishes regarding base please keep absolutely private at present as certain supporters must be brought round to the new position please await second letter'. This was followed by a restrained and serious letter[18] explaining more fully that his money depended upon the approval of certain men who had promised to help him largely because he would be attempting the Pole from known ground.

Shackleton also communicated[19] his decision to Scott Keltie, Secretary of the Royal Geographical Society, first in a wire, then in a private letter on 5 March, and finally in a formal announcement on 8 March, in which he stated that he would seek a base in King Edward VII Land or as far east as possible on the Barrier. Keltie's opinion, expressed in a private letter,[20] was that it would do Shackleton no harm. He would probably have the start of any other expedition in the field. 'Did you see the long telegram in yesterday's Globe about Arctowski. It says all Belgium means to support him: Antwerp will present him with a ship, & parliament will grant him a subsidy. *Nous verrons*'.

Shackleton also wrote to Barne,[21] who was now on half-pay and acting as Scott's agent. He and Shackleton at once saw that Arctowski might take advantage of any change of plan by Shackleton to go to McMurdo Sound himself, as he had originally intended. It was highly desirable that Scott should make an announcement, though Scott did not want to do this because, as he said, his plans could not possibly mature till 1908 and probably not till later. He agreed, however, that Arctowski must be prevented from 'trespassing', and he hoped that Keltie, on behalf of the geographical body which could handle such delicate matters, would be writing to the Belgian leader to make the British position perfectly clear.

The classic expression of insularity had already been made by Sir Clements Markham in a letter[22] to Shackleton from Mallorca on 26 February. 'I certainly should have been much annoyed if that fellow Arctowski had gone poaching down in our preserves; but I believe he has not got any funds. Foreigners never get much beyond the Antarctic Circle.'

Matters now seemed to be considerably easier, and Shackleton was able to get on with some of the arrangements for his expedition. The following letter which he wrote to William Beardmore[23] on 8 March shows how one of his outstanding difficulties was settled:

'In consideration of the guarantee of £7000 (seven thousand pounds) which you have signed on my behalf, the said £7000 to be used for the British South Polar Expedition, I agree that the first profits of the expedition shall be given to you up to an amount which will release the guarantee and also that you are to be cleared of this guarantee in three years from this date.

Also that the vessel I propose purchasing for the expedition is to be your property but that you are to lend me the same for the period of the expedition, and that the vessel is to be entirely under my control during that period.

Further, that you, as owner of the vessel, will place her either in the Royal Yacht Squadron as a yacht of yours or in any other yacht club you desire, but preferably the Royal Yacht Squadron, as since 1842 no Antarctic exploring vessel has flown the White Ensign.*

I also acknowledge the fact that you have signed the above mentioned guarantee on my behalf.

I am, sir, yours faithfully
E. H. SHACKLETON'†

Before Shackleton was able to begin negotiations for a ship, however, there were more details to settle with Scott. On 8 March Wilson wrote[24] advising Shackleton not to make any new plans until he had heard definitely from Scott 'what limit he puts to his rights. I have asked him to write to you as soon as possible to tell you his views as regards other possible bases. I don't want you to drop into more trouble with him, & I think you can avoid it by waiting until he write you on this matter'.

In the face of this hint that Scott might want to claim the whole Ross Sea area, Shackleton not unnaturally exploded. First to Wilson[25]:

'I do not agree with you, Billy, about holding up my plans until I hear what Scott considers his rights. There is no doubt in my mind that his rights end at the base he asked for, or within reasonable distance of that base. I will not consider that he has any right to King Edward the Seventh's Land, and only regard it as a direct

* William Beardmore was elected a member of the Royal Yacht Squadron, and thus the *Nimrod* was able to fly the White Ensign.

† The guarantee was dated 25 March 1907, and was cancelled in November 1909, the guarantee document being returned to Beardmore from the Clydesdale Bank on 26 November. The money was paid back by Shackleton in full. This information was recorded at the time by Mr. MacDuff in the course of his duties as Beardmore's secretary.

attempt to keep me out of the Ross quarter if he should even propose such a thing. I have given way to him in the greatest thing of all, and my limit has been reached.'

There is much more to the same effect. Now that the glow of generosity and retrospective loyalty had faded a little, Shackleton was beginning to wonder just what his promise would involve.

Meanwhile Scott had made a firm proposal, and Shackleton, who had had time to reflect, stated his own position frankly[26]:

'I have been ready, as you realise, to meet you as regards McMurdo Base. I realise myself what I have given up in regard to this matter. Concerning the 170 Meridian West as a line of demarkation, this matter will have to be discussed. I must tell you quite frankly that my agreement to this proposition might perhaps make a position untenable to me on my Southward journey and that I do not see my way, at the present moment, to accede to this. I also consider that the unknown land or the disputed land of Wilkes is free to anybody who wishes to explore that part, and as you know, my programme originally included the exploration of this quarter.

I am ready to discuss with you the whole matter but I want you to understand that I do not look upon either Wood Bay or the land to the West of Cape North as being within the Province of any particular previous expedition. As you write to me openly, I therefore answer you in the same manner.'

In April Shackleton went to Norway for a short time to buy sledges, skis and other equipment. There is now a gap in the correspondence with Scott. During this month Scott came to England, and the two men were able to discuss their plans face to face. This cleared the air, and was far more satisfactory than the letters which were beginning to create suspicion and misunderstanding. Agreement was evidently reached, and on 17 May Shackleton set down categorically[27] a promise which, as an explorer and a prospective expedition leader, he should never have made, and which Scott, with the same background, should never have demanded. The promise was to have far-reaching consequences for Shackleton, and to affect his character as well as his plans.

Shackleton had drawn up a scheme of work which 'will not make both Expeditions over-lap each other in the exploration of the Ross Quadrant'.

'I am leaving the McMurdo Sound base to you, and will land either at the place known as Barrier Inlet or at King Edward VII Land whichever is the most suitable, if I land at either of these places I will not work to the westward of 170 meridian W. and shall not make any sledge journey going W. of that meridian unless prevented when going to the South from keeping to the East of that meridian by the physical features of the country.

If I encounter mountains and it is possible to ascend them by the glaciers, I shall do so.

I do not, however, expect, and neither do you, that there will be any land or open sea that will necessitate my going to the west of 170 W.

I propose to make one journey to the South of King Edward VII Land, one journey to the East and one to the Northeast.

On leaving the ice, I shall take the ship north of the Balleny Islands leaving a record if possible at Cape Adare in order that you may know what work I have done.

I shall steam West from the Balleny Islands and go south about the 154 meridian E., follow the coast line along towards the west, taking soundings when possible, and shall cease this work when I find it prudent to go north to New Zealand.

I shall not touch the coast of Victoria land at all.

If I find it impracticable to land at King Edward VII Land or at Barrier Inlet or further to the N.E., I may possibly steam north, and then to westward and try and land to the west of Kaiser Wilhelm II Land, going down to the meridian that the "Challenger" made her furthest south. This meridian is about 80 E.

If I find a landing there I will travel south and also west by sledge journeys.

I think this outlines my plan, which I shall rigidly adhere to, and I hope that this letter meets you on the points that you desire.

Should your ship not winter in the Antarctic, I will send you down a chart of whatever exploration I may have made.'

To the copy of this letter among the Shackleton family papers is appended a note in Scott's handwriting:

My dear Shackleton. I return you this copy of your letter which is a very clear statement of the arrangement to which we came. If as you say you will rigidly adhere to it, I do(not) think our plans will clash and I shall feel on sure ground in developing my own

Yours very sincerely

R. F. SCOTT

Thus the Antarctic was neatly carved up between them; but, to use a favourite phrase of Wilson's, 'L'homme propose, le bon Dieu dispose'.

There was to be one more threat to Shackleton's peace of mind. In *Harper's Weekly* for 11 May he read an article by Dr. Cook, the American North Polar explorer, discussing the possibility of reaching the South Pole from Mounts Erebus or Terror, and stating that this was work that should be done by Americans. Shortly afterwards Shackleton saw a cable to the Royal Geographical Society stating that Cook was definitely to start from Erebus. Fearing for the safety of his own plans and Scott's, he rushed an announcement into the papers of his proposal to go to King Edward VII Land. At the same time he wired to Scott suggesting that he too should make an announcement about using McMurdo Sound. Scott assured Shackleton that Cook was a discredited man after his false claims about the North Pole and that he was unlikely to be able to raise the money for an expedition. Time proved him to be right, but there was an uncomfortable period of doubt for Shackleton. The first three months of preparation for his expedition must have been altogether a severe mental strain on him.

The months that followed were not entirely free from anxiety either. Shackleton could now go ahead without any of the frustration of private rivalry, but there was a recurrent frustration in the lack of funds. The advertising of his intentions had aroused public interest and money was coming in slowly; but it was not enough.

Lack of funds, for instance, affected Shackleton's choice of a ship. He had badly wanted to buy the *Bjorn*, a vessel belonging to Christiansen the sledge-maker. Like the *Discovery*, the *Bjorn* had been specially built for polar work, and he felt she would give him flexibility of action once he got down to the South. He had to admit, however, that this ship was too expensive, and when he got back to London he went into treaty for a sealer he had heard of which would shortly be returning to Newfoundland. A small wooden vessel of about 200 tons, the *Nimrod* seemed big enough to accommodate his party.

The ship whose name was to become famous in Antarctic history gave Shackleton a shock when he first saw her, in the Thames on 15 June. She was dilapidated, her masts needed renewing, her sails were inadequate for Shackleton's purpose, and she smelt strongly of seal-oil. He put the necessary repairs and alterations into the hands of R. and H. Green of Blackwall, and gradually the *Nimrod* began to smell sweeter and to look more efficient. Shackleton began to feel that after all she would do the expedition no discredit. 'Later still', he wrote,[28] 'I grew really proud of the sturdy little ship'. Though he needed a ship strong enough to withstand the ice, she need not in fact be very large, since she was not to be used as a shore-station.

At the same time, he was determined to leave nothing to chance. His natural impulse was to have everything of the best, and besides, he knew from experience[29] that 'makeshift appliances mean increased difficulty and added danger'. He had had plenty of time since the previous expedition to think over every detail of the equipment that had been used then, and by 1907 he knew how far he would copy this and how far depart from it.

On his visit to Norway he had found that Christiansen (who had made the sledges for Scott) was absent in the United States, and because he wanted close personal attention, he went to Messrs. L. H. Hagen and Co., from whom he ordered sledges of the Nansen pattern. These were to be of three sizes—ten 12-foot sledges for pony-hauling, eighteen a foot shorter which could also be drawn by men, and two 7-foot sledges for short journeys. Shackleton's keen personal interest in everything connected with his plans always attracted strangers to him, and on the voyage from Hull to Christiania he had established good relations with Captain Pepper, commodore captain of the Wilson Line. Captain Pepper was at this time making regular visits to Christiania (Oslo), and both he and other experienced Arctic travellers agreed to keep an eye on the sledge-building.

Shackleton's own experience in 1902–03 had given him a high opinion of reindeer-skin for sleeping-bags, and from W. C. Möller of Drammen he ordered what he could afford. Having decided that the privacy of a one-man bag was of overriding importance, he ordered only three of the three-man type, and twelve one-man bags. From this firm too he bought a good stock of finnesko, the reindeer fur boots which, if properly treated, were both comfortable and adaptable for Polar work. With his usual attention to detail, he sent specially to Lapland to try to get finnesko made of the legs of the reindeer, these being the best. But he could only get 12 pairs from the Lapps, and 80 pairs made from the skin of the head were added to the store. In Norway, too, he acquired the necessary skis, ski boots and mitts of wolf and dog skins.

All these goods arrived in London early in June and were collected at the office which Shackleton had now established at 9 Regent Street, Waterloo Place. This was under the management of Mr. Alfred Reid, who had worked with other polar expeditions. The British Antarctic Expedition, as it was officially named, now went ahead with the collection of supplies.

In deciding what food to take, Shackleton had to find a compromise between quality and economy. This he managed partly by interviewing personally the heads of all the firms with which he had decided to deal. Many of them allowed him special concessions and some (among them the well-known firms of Colman, Rowntree, Bird and Lipton) presented him with food-stuffs. Shackleton's illness in 1903 had given him an obsession about scurvy, and in his selection of food this was his chief consideration. In 1907 the research on vitamins was in progress which was to lead among other things to the correct assessment of the causes of this disease, but no results were available to the public yet. Shackleton worked on the assumption which he felt had been abundantly proved on the *Discovery*, that scurvy was due to improperly prepared or tainted tinned food. His choice was extremely careful and he succeeded in collecting a supply of meat and fish which was in fact richer in vitamin C, as well as far more varied, than Scott's had been.*

* In the second winter of the National Antarctic Expedition, 1903–04, Scott paid far more attention to the provision of fresh food at the base, and he continued to do this on his second expedition of 1910–13. The fact that

In this respect Shackleton's lack of funds proved to be an advantage, for he left certain gaps to be filled in New Zealand, where he hoped to be able to raise more money. That hospitable country presented him with a generous supply of Glaxo dried milk, butter and cheese, all richer in food value than their English equivalents; while the year's supply of food which the *Nimrod* was ordered to bring down in 1909, part of which was used on the return voyage and part left for future explorers, was also of fine quality.

Shackleton believed in variety in expedition diet, for psychological as well as medical reasons. He allowed a considerable margin for personal taste, and the men at Cape Royds thought themselves well-fed. They were also catered for in the matter of vitamins as well as was possible at that time. Later expeditions thought Shackleton's men had been fed like fighting-cocks, but they were glad to profit by his lavishness. Griffith Taylor[30] who went with Scott on his second expedition, was told that 'when any of Mawson's acquaintances at Adelaide University wanted chocolate, the explorer would take an ice-axe and break a lump off the huge block he had looted from Shackleton's Expedition! I felt that an expedition of this type had peculiar attractions for me, but, alas! our chocolate supply was never on such a prodigal scale.' Members of Scott's second expedition of 1910–12 visited Shackleton's hut often, and found many gastronomic treats, from the wholemeal biscuits that 'swelled like muffins on the red-hot stove' and which Griffith Taylor described as 'a dream', to the bottles of fruit that they found still serving as an inside wall, the boiled chicken, kidneys, mushrooms, ginger and Garibaldi biscuits appreciated by Cherry-Garrard[31], and the 'mock turtle soup, mutton cutlets, and unlimited candied peel' that made a meal for Taylor and Debenham on another occasion. The generous catering was justified. The British Antarctic Expedition had a record of health conspicuously better than that of any other previous polar expedition.

Shackleton, as we have seen, had been closely concerned with the packing, stowing and unpacking of the stores for the National Antarctic Expedition, and had thought out the problem of packing very logically, making it his chief object to save as much time and trouble as possible. Scott, for the most part, had used the cases sent to him by the various firms supplying goods, but he had also had made a certain number of packing cases of Venesta wood. This was a composite material, made of three layers of hard wood compressed with intermediate layers of water-

Shackleton's expedition of 1907–09 was entirely free from scurvy no doubt encouraged Scott in the far better provisioning of his second expedition; he modified his earlier view that only a very simple diet was required in the Antarctic. Shackleton's provisioning, however ,shows an imagination which is not found in anyone else of his time.

proof cement; it was light and strong, and of obvious convenience to an expedition. Shackleton decided to standardise his packing cases, and used Venesta wood throughout.

He exercised considerable personal supervision over the making of the cases, and also kept a strict eye on the hut for the base, which was made for him by Messrs. Humphreys of Knightsbridge and shipped in sections. It was designed for twelve men, the outside measurements being $33 \times 19 \times 8$; in the end fifteen men wintered in it, slightly short of space but warm and comfortable. Fir timbering was used for the hut, which was lined with match-boarding, and warmth and insulation were supplied not only by layers of roofing felt between the layers of boarding on the roof and sides, but also by a thick packing of granulated cork. The hut was to stand on wooden piles let into the ground, and guy-ropes hung from the roof to give additional protection against storms. The entrance was through two doors, connected by a porch, and the windows too were double, to keep out the wind. No furniture was taken. Shackleton decided to save money by using empty cases, and the result, though sometimes grotesque, was decidedly practical.

Profiting by the experience of Scott, he took acetylene gas for lighting,* and for cooking a Smith and Wellstood anthracite stove which was extremely efficient for warming as well. The sledge-cookers, tents and clothing were all similar to those which had been tried and tested in 1902–04.

Thus far Shackleton's innovations had been few and successful. As we have seen, his greatest break with tradition was in the matter of transport. At some stage after he published his plans in the *Geographical Journal* in March, he decided to take some dogs as a second string, and negotiated with a breeder of Stewart Island, New Zealand, whose dogs were descended from the Siberian stock used on the *Southern Cross* expedition. He wanted to take forty but was only able to buy nine, and though several pups born on the journey out and at the base were also trained, it cannot be said that his dog-teams were of very great value to him. Regarding the ponies, he had arranged through the Hongkong and Shanghai Bank for an experienced man to go to Tientsin and choose fifteen. These were shipped to New Zealand by way of Australia, and turned out on Quail Island, outside Lyttelton, until they were needed. Shackleton's confidence in ponies turned out to be partly misplaced. Certainly they could not stand the Antarctic temperatures as well as could the dogs, and consequently they delayed the start of the summer journeys. Their weight caused them to sink in any soft surface, so that their speed was far less than that of dogs would have been. They needed greater care all round and their food was heavy to transport. All the same,

* Scott changed to this method in the second winter of the National Antarctic Expedition, having used candle lamps in the first.

Shackleton made excellent use of his ponies, and with a little more luck he might have vindicated them by reaching the Pole with their aid. Certainly they did not deserve the phrase 'pathetic failure' which Bernacchi[32] applied to them or the equally scornful statement of J. Gordon Hayes[33] that Shackleton had had 'the whimsical notion of using ponies'.

The car Shackleton took on his expedition was presented to him by William Beardmore, and much of the rather small amount of publicity for the expedition was concerned with it. Thus *The Times*[34]:

'The motor car which is to be used by Lieutenant Shackleton's Antarctic expedition is now on view at the Arrol-Johnston London depot before being shipped to Christchurch, New Zealand. The steel work in the frame of the chassis has been specially treated to make it resist the influence of low temperatures. The front pair of wheels are shod with wood, and provision has been made for the attachment of a sleigh, while the back wheels, similarly shod, have steel projections fitted, in which holes have been drilled to receive spikes in order to obtain increased adhesive power. The engine is a 12 to 15 h.p. engine, air cooled, capable of giving about 16 miles per hour, and two systems of ignition are fitted. The exhaust is to be utilised for warming purposes, and is also connected with a snow melter, which will provide water. The two petrol tanks, one fed by gravity and the other by pressure, hold sufficient fuel for 300 miles.

It is difficult to think back to the experimental period when this machine represented the most modern workmanship and the use of it a violent and bold break with tradition. Perhaps the sense of period can best be recaptured in quotations from the diary of Raymond Priestley,[35] one of the two youngest members of the expedition, during the voyage down to the base.

'The motor car is being unpacked and put ready for work by Day and Dunlop . . . Day is quite the most important man here at present and he has been all day getting the motor ready for action. At present when we speak to him we take off our hats but someone suggested that in a few weeks if the motor car did not come up to expectations our attitude towards him will be changed so much that when we wish to attract his attention we shall throw a brick at him. . . . [29 Jan. 1908].

Day has evidently got the car on his nerves. He says that the water has got into the Magneto and the sparking plugs whatever they may be, and he has got to take the first to pieces, and dry the latter before he can make her go.'

In the following year, while Shackleton, at his base, was planning his attack on the Pole, the car was still good copy; and an article in the *Sphere*[36] on the expedition ended with the spirited challenge: 'Towards the South Pole the best on record is a point 460 miles away. At the other end of the world Peary has reached a spot that is as far from the Pole as Blackpool is from London. Any advance on these figures, motorists, submariners, bear-drivers, and aeronauts?'

Shackleton was always interested in mechanical aids to human effort, and within the limits of his funds he collected for his expedition as much up-to-date equipment as he could. In addition to the latest photographic and cinematographic apparatus, he also took a complete printing-press. This was presented to him by Messrs. Joseph Causton and Sons, and the firm undertook to give two members of the expedition, Frank Wild and Ernest Joyce, some instruction in the art of printing and type-setting. In planning to produce a magazine during the winter Shackleton was following Scott's example, but he was determined to go one better, and in fact he became editor in chief of the first volume ever to be published in the Antarctic.*

In the matter of scientific instruments he dared not economise. He tried to borrow from the Royal Society the Eschenhagen magnetic instruments which had been used by the National Antarctic Expedition, but these were already on loan. The Royal Geographical Society lent him three chronometer watches, and another was presented by three wardens of the Skinners' Company. He also sent a list of his requirements to the Admiralty, and was able to borrow charts, compasses, two sounding machines and other instruments, on condition that he defrayed carriage expenses and made good any loss or depreciation. The rest of the instruments were purchased from Messrs. Cary, Porter and Co., and made up an impressive adjunct to the scientific research that was being planned.

The room in Regent Street was small indeed for the purposes of office work, even though the typing could be farmed out to an agency conveniently situated on the same floor of the building. It was certainly not large enough to contain the stores and equipment which came in constantly from every quarter, to be transferred gradually to the expedition ship. It was filled to bursting point by a non-functional but useful addition—the general public. Shackleton well understood the uses of advertisement. With his breezy sailor manner he 'sold' his enterprise to the large numbers of people who came to the office where his equipment was officially on show. By sixpences and pounds the money went on coming in to fill the gaping crack between debit and credit in this shoestring expedition.

* Technically this description is incorrect, since the *Aurora Australis* was never actually offered for sale at a place of business in the Antarctic: it is however, an exceedingly interesting and rare volume, bibliographically.

Chapter VIII

SHACKLETON'S expedition of 1907–09—called formally The British Antarctic Expedition, historically often the *Nimrod* Expedition, and by one or two of his old comrades The Great Expedition—was a one-man show. Shackleton did not want to submit himself to the direction of a committee. He was far too quick and impatient to suffer any delays that were not of his making, or to waste any time arguing about policy. This is not to say that he was too proud to take advice, from his friend Dr. Mill and from some of his old comrades. His plans were laid before the Royal Geographical Society at a very early date, and both here and at the Admiralty specialist knowledge was available to him. Moreover, the *Discovery* expedition gave him a pattern on which to improve.

It was not only because Shackleton was impatient that he wanted to do everything himself. There was a more important and fundamental reason. All Shackleton's expeditions were conceived in a creative spirit, as a projection of his own personality. No doubt he could have led an expedition very efficiently under instruction from a committee; but it would have lacked the vivid guiding spirit of the three expeditions he planned and led himself.

At the time when Shackleton took the *Nimrod* down to the South he had not come to complete maturity. His personality was still in some ways fluid and undeveloped; he was still changing. But he now began to take up, as though under some compulsion, the position of a leader—not merely the leader of an expedition but a leader of men. If he was an interesting man to most people who met him in 1907, to one or two he was potentially a great one. Thus Charles Mackeller,[1] whose thoughts had all his life been centred on Polar exploration, wrote to Mrs. Shackleton of his first acquaintance with her husband:

'To some people a Leader of Men is a strong stern masterful iron-visaged relentless person—but even such a person has another side and can be—if only rarely—as gentle and sympathetic as a woman. But your husband never struck me like that; in all that stress of business in the office with telephone going, telegrams coming in and a thousand things to think of and arrange, he seemed to me so calm, resourceful, equal and amidst it all so perfectly courteous and pleasant. He may be 'excitable' as Scott says, but I do not know him well enough to have seen any of that; and I have no doubt when necessary he can be *forcible*—but he inspires faith, loyalty and liking and therefore he has the great qualities in him which produce these things.'

It was on this first independent expedition that Shackleton learned to lead men, on the *Endurance* that he earned once and for all the title which the men he led accorded to him—'the greatest leader that ever came on God's earth bar none[2]'.

This power of his had many aspects, but perhaps the most important was that he could make every member of his expedition see, to some degree, the conception he had had in his mind, the shape of the crusade he was leading against the unknown. At once a visionary and a tactician, Shackleton had gifts which only he could harness and use. Dr. Mill probably knew this better than anyone. In a brilliant analysis[3] of Shackleton as an explorer, written soon after the return of the British Antarctic Expedition, he wrote:

'A mind given to exhaustive foresight and the mechanical provision of routine wants is rarely attracted to dangerous enterprises, hence the usual arrangement of a learned society or a cautious committee to plan and equip an expedition, and a daring fellow to carry it out under the restraint of prudent instructions. The best explorer, however, is the man who can both "conceive and dare", who carries his organising committee with him on his own feet, and knows that there is none to blame for failure but himself. To such an explorer is due on his return the undivided praise for plan and execution.'

Shackleton's particular aims for this expedition can be seen very clearly in his choice of men to go with him. Formality was not congenial to him. Instead of the naval organisation of the *Discovery*, he planned something more flexible. In any case, he had not enough money for the type of expedition in which half the men are engaged in looking after the other half. There could be no stewards, no ward-room servants. Instead, each man would do his share of the daily chores as well as running his own special job. Thus a first requirement was that the members of the expedition should be adaptable and energetic. There was no room for a scientist who could or would work only at research. If an occasion arose (and it often did) when killing a seal, mending a roof or pulling a sledge was most important, then the specialist must be prepared to leave his instruments and turn his hand to the more immediate problem.

If the members of the expedition were to live together in a group, and not be sub-divided, they must be to some extent homogeneous—not necessarily in class, but in their attitude to life. In sorting out the 400-odd applications he received, Shackleton was looking for cheerful men, with a strong desire for adventure, men with strength of mind as well as of body to endure hardship and possible danger. Men, above all, of optimistic temper.

Lieutenant Jameson Boyd Adams, one of the first men to be selected, commended himself to Shackleton by his toughness and his experience.

Like Shackleton, he had passed from the Merchant Navy to the Royal Naval Reserve. He had knocked around the world a good deal. At the time of leaving England for the Antarctic he was twenty-seven. He had first met Shackleton in the summer of 1906, when as an officer on H.M.S. *Berwick* he was sent to call on him at his holiday cottage in the Firth of Forth. He had stayed on late that evening, listening to Shackleton's talk of future plans, and as he was leaving he remarked,[2] 'If you go again, will you take me with you?'

After that Adams forgot the conversation until the dramatic moment, nearly a year later, when he was simultaneously offered a permanent commission in the Royal Navy and a place in Shackleton's expedition (by telegram). He chose the less orthodox job and has never regretted it.

From the moment of his appointment to the British Antarctic Expedition, he worked with Shackleton on the collection of stores and was present at the interviewing of other candidates. He was to be responsible for the meteorological observations, and took a course of instruction from Dr. Mill and Professor Glazebrook. His attitude to scientific discovery was at that time a negative one; he wanted to join the expedition for romantic reasons.[2] 'I had an interest in trying to see that England got where she should get. . . . When there was a question of trying to get to the South Pole, I wanted to be the one chap, that's all.'

Sir Philip Brocklehurst had first met Shackleton in London in 1906. At this time the young baronet was distinguishing himself as a Cambridge lightweight boxer, and the two men shared a strong interest in this sport. At this stage Shackleton saw his expedition as an attack on the South Pole—just that; and he promised to include Brocklehurst in the party of six that was to carry out this attack.

In the years that followed, when the idea of the expedition was put aside for lack of funds, the fact that Sir Philip's mother had guaranteed to help was a substantial encouragement to Shackleton. Plans were taken up again, expanded and changed, but the dash to the Pole remained the central theme, and it was in this sporting event that Brocklehurst remained interested. He too was a romantic rather than a scientific explorer. Like the rest of the company, however, he had to play several parts, and he took a course in geological and survey work so that he could be of use to the scientists in those spheres. He also undertook to help with the ponies.

Sir Philip Brocklehurst, in his nineteenth year when he left England, was the youngest member of the expedition, but scarcely older was the geologist. Raymond Priestley was a student of twenty at what was then Bristol University College at the time when Shackleton was choosing his scientists. He had written for help to Sir John Murray, who in his turn had written to the Curator of the Bristol Museum to ask whether his assistant, who had been on the *Challenger* expedition, was free to go with Shackleton. The assistant in question did not want to go to the Antarctic again. As it happened, Raymond Priestley's elder brother was present at this interview, and the Curator casually suggested his junior as a geologist. Sir Raymond Priestley[4] remembers:

'. . . it so happened that on his way back to his laboratory Bert had to pass through the library, where I was sitting . . . beautiful day and I was feeling like nothing on earth . . . and he said to me as he passed through "How would you like to go to the Antarctic, Ray?" and I said "I'd go anywhere to get out of this damned place". The next thing was I had a telegram from Shackleton asking me to go up and see him. And of course once I realised I'd got a chance of going I didn't make any mistake about it. But I could never understand why Shackleton took me, because I had no degree, and I know there were twelve people with Honours degrees after the job.'

He thought his acceptance all the more odd because of his memory of the interview with Shackleton. 'He asked me if I could sing and I said I couldn't; and he asked me if I would know gold if I saw it, and again I said No! He must have asked me other questions but I remember these because they were bizarre.'

Shackleton's judgment was not at fault in choosing the young man without a degree as his geologist. Raymond Priestley, quiet and conscientious, was to be one of the best-liked, as well as one of the most useful, members of the expedition.

Shackleton's character, and his particular requirements, are seen too in his selection of George Marston as the expedition artist. The occasion was described by Shackleton[5] in an article long afterwards.

'Out of some thirty applications I had weeded the number down to three. Finally, one Friday afternoon I sent a telegram to each of the three, asking him to be present at my office on Saturday morning at a certain time.

On Saturday morning I received a note from one saying that he would come on Monday, as he was going out of town for the week-end. I received a telegram from the second, asking whether if he travelled up to town—four hours journey—he would be practically certain to be taken.

I received no communication from the third, but on the Saturday afternoon, just as I was leaving my office, in he walked, somewhat dishevelled and rain-soaked. He informed me that he had been on a walking tour in Cornwall; my telegram had been forwarded to him where he was putting up for the night; he had just caught a train, and after many changes had arrived in London.

I promptly engaged him. I thought that if a man could be as quick as that in order to get a position, he was the man for it; and, as it turned out, my opinion was more than justified.'

At the time of the expedition Marston, Polytechnic trained, was earning his living as an art teacher. It may be guessed that it was the call of the unknown which led him to the Antarctic, first in 1907 and again with Shackleton in 1914. 'Putty', as he was called almost at once, was a large, brawny man, good with his hands, and with a sense of the ridiculous and a love of practical jokes which undoubtedly appealed to Shackleton.

The artist's chief duty was to make a record of the expedition with paint and pencil, and this record was also to be helped by photography. Dr. Eric Marshall was to be largely responsible for this. He joined the expedition as senior surgeon, and was also given special training in survey work, as Shackleton intended that he should go on the journey to the Pole as surgeon and cartographer. Marshall was one of the older members of the expedition, being twenty-eight when they left England. He was a tall man of strong physique and strong, sometimes intransigent, character.

The second surgeon, Alistair Forbes Mackay, a year older than Marshall, had had a varied career, as a trooper in the South African War, as one of Baden-Powell's police, and as a naval surgeon. He had done biological work early in his life and was to assist in this as well as in the general medical duties of the expedition. As principal biologist Shackleton engaged James Murray, who had been strongly recommended by Sir John Murray, under whom he had worked on a biological survey of the Scottish Lakes. Murray was over forty when he set out on the expedition and he did not stand the Antarctic climate as well as the others, but he was a conscientious and able man and his branch of the scientific research was carried out with conspicuous success.

All these men fell into two groups. Adams, Marshall, and Brocklehurst had almost certainly been ear-marked for the journey to the Pole in the early stages of planning, and perhaps Marston was also considered as a possibility. Murray and Mackay, sharing medical and biological knowledge, belonged rather to the scientists' side of the affair, and so did Priestley as geologist. Two other men were engaged for their special knowledge. Bernard Day had been working with the new Arrol-Johnston Motor-Car Company, and Shackleton was glad to take him as driver and mechanic. William Roberts, who went as cook, was a hotel chef when he applied to go on the expedition, but he had carried on his trade in many parts of the world and in varying degrees of company.

He had not, however, had any experience of the Antarctic, nor had any of the men so far mentioned. However willing they all might be to adapt themselves to the particular conditions, they would have everything to learn about working in low temperatures. It was probably at an early stage of planning that Shackleton decided to enlist the help of some of the men who had served under Scott in 1901–03. As we have seen, he failed to get hold of any of his brother officers from the *Discovery*. He took, finally, two men whom he had known as A.B.'s on that ship.

Frank Wild and Ernest Joyce had both taken readily to life on a shore station in the Antarctic, and Wild in particular had impressed himself on Shackleton as a sailor of unusual attainments. The story of the selection of Joyce is a dramatic one. Early in 1907 Shackleton, looking out of his office window in Lower Regent Street, had recognised Joyce on top of a passing bus. His secretary was sent out at once and succeeded in finding him, and he was at once offered the job of looking after the stores and the dogs.[6] We do not know how Wild came to apply but it is clear that both sailors were keen to get on the expedition list. They had risen to the rank of Petty Officer (First Class) in the Navy but were ready to forgo this position. Joyce bought his release from the Navy in 1907 to join the *Nimrod*, and it seems likely that he was considered, as early as this, as a possible member of the party to go to the South Pole, by virtue of his sledging experience. In after years he took the view that this had been a definite promise, but there is no definite evidence one way or the other.

Wild's discharge from the Navy did not take effect until 1909, but it seems clear that both he and Joyce regarded the expedition as their big chance to make a fortune and a name for themselves. Because they had made a complete break with the past, they were in a different position from the other members of the expedition, who had jobs or the prospect of jobs to come back to.

Frank Wild, who eventually became very intimate with Shackleton on his expeditions, never suggested that his leader had any special obligation towards him, but Joyce was to assert later that Shackleton had promised to recompense him for losing his naval pension. Written evidence is lacking on this point, but there is no doubt that the sailors were risking their futures in a way which was bound to involve Shackleton later. He was taking a responsibility in engaging them, but the skill that he bought was invaluable to his expedition. Both Wild and Joyce were excellent practical seamen, experienced sledgers, and men of courage and initiative, and they were used to hard physical work. Wild was to manage the stores and Joyce, in addition to managing the dogs, was to be responsible for the care of all the sledging equipment.

Shackleton also intended that Mackay's experience should be used in the care of the ponies. He added to his party an Australian, Bertram Armytage, who had served in the South African War and who was to join the expedition in Australia.

The pattern of the expedition, then, was very different from that of the expedition which had given Shackleton his first taste of the Antarctic.

It was an adventure, and a venture, that he was planning now, with the journey to the South Pole as the primary aim, the object of romantic dreams and the object also of more mundane hopes of money and fame.

The expedition left England as a band of explorers. Shackleton, as all his old comrades agree, had no personal interest in scientific research, but he was well aware of its importance, and he hoped that the magnetic and oceanographical work he planned for the expedition would be of direct value to the civilised world.

In particular, although he looked upon the journey to the South Magnetic Pole as being secondary to his own great South Pole journey, he had no doubt in his mind of the importance of the Magnetic Pole in the whole study of geophysics.

The scientists, for their part, were satisfied with their status, and were ready to subordinate their interests to those of the expedition as a whole, if this should be required of them. That they were content was largely due to Shackleton's way of trusting the men he had chosen. He was always willing to delegate responsibility. Priestley, for one, was always grateful for the way in which he was given the necessary equipment and allowed to get on with the job. As we shall see, this whole aspect of the expedition was to be changed by the arrival of a scientist more experienced and more eminent than any previously engaged for the expedition, and Shackleton, realising the value of Professor David, gave him likewise a free hand to plan and to enlarge the scientific programme. Probably Shackleton could never have tolerated a colleague working on equal terms with him in his own sphere. A joint expedition would have been insufferable to him. But he could respect a man of stature equal to his own if they could work on parallel lines.

While preparations had been going forward for the scientific side of the expedition, the ship had been put in good order and her complement made up. Shackleton had put her under the command of Lieutenant Rupert England, whom he had met as First Officer of the *Morning* in 1903. The First Officer, John King Davis, was to become one of the best and most experienced of Antarctic navigators. The Second Officer, Æneas Mackintosh, had the same background as Shackleton, having been an officer in a P. and O. liner. The ship's surgeon was a Canadian, Dr. W. A. R. Michell, and the chief engineer an Irishman, H. T. L. Dunlop. Alfred Cheetham, Third Officer and boatswain, had served on the *Morning* and was to take part in other Antarctic expeditions.

The *Nimrod* had a slow journey ahead of her, round the Cape of Good Hope and across to New Zealand. The expedition would ultimately leave from Lyttelton. Murray and Mackay were to go on the ship to carry out a full programme of zoological observations, including oceanic dredging, on the journey over. Alfred Reid, as secretary to the expedition, went ahead by steamer to arrange for the accommodation of the ship in New Zealand and to order extra stores.

It was on 30 July that the *Nimrod* left the East India Docks, with Shackleton on board to see her on her way. The first night was spent at Greenhithe, and on the 31st the ship continued on her way to Torquay. A message, sent by Admiralty tug from Sheerness to catch the *Nimrod* off Ramsgate, requested Shackleton to proceed to Cowes. He stopped for an hour at Eastbourne on 1 August so that some of his supporters could pay the ship a farewell visit, and reached Cowes on Sunday, 4 August.

The Fleet was at this time drawn up for a Naval Review and *The Times*[7] made the most of the scene:

' ... the *Victoria and Albert*, steaming at slow speed, entered the Fleet, and passed up between the battleship line and that of the second cruisers and auxiliary vessels, the Ships' companies waving their hats and cheering most vigorously as his Majesty passed. ... The Swedish Squadron lying close under the Island shore were now visible; and as the eastward end of the line was reached the brightly-decorated yachts anchored off Cowes came into view, the roadstead being crowded, and amongst them was observed the auxiliary barquentine yacht *Nimrod*, Lieutenant Shackleton, about to start for the Antarctic, on a vessel the King and Queen are to visit.'

Shackleton wanted this honour not only because he wanted every advantage that Scott had had on his expedition, though to some extent this motive can be detected in many of his preparations. He had a

9

strong sense of occasion. Being comparatively unknown when the
Nimrod sailed, he was not in a position to obtain much press publicity.
A visit from the King would give a cachet to the expedition, and, duly
reported, would ensure that the *Nimrod* left England with the breath of
public approval in her sails.

The occasion was all that Shackleton could desire. A large party
came on board the ship. Besides King Edward VII and Queen Alexandra, there were the Prince of Wales, Princess Victoria, Prince Edward
and the Duke of Connaught, Admiral Sir Berkeley Milne, Lord Fisher
and other important Naval figures. Shackleton was invested with the
Victorian Order (4th Class) and the Queen presented the expedition
with a Union Flag to be hoisted at their Farthest South. The Queen in
particular was struck by the personality of the leader. She and King
Edward were to take a considerable personal interest in the career of
this man who, more than any other explorer in the twentieth century,
looked and acted the part. The *Nimrod* now proceeded on her way to
Torquay, where Shackleton's family was living for the summer and
where he left the ship. He still had a great deal of organising to do, and
in particular must still try to raise more money for the expedition.

Eight members of his expedition left Liverpool in October in the
White Star liner *Runic*, a one-class emigrant ship. To save money,
they were packed in one cabin; the price of each passage was £19.
Priestley, who was one of the eight, thus describes* the party and the
voyage:

'There was J. B. Adams in charge; Eric Marshall, doctor with the
build and arrogance of the class Rugger forward; Ernest Joyce and
Frank Wild, naval petty officers, veterans of Scott's *Discovery*
Expedition, and my self-appointed male nurses; George (Putty)
Marston, artist with the frame and face of a prize-fighter and the
disposition of a fallen angel; Bernard Day, motor mechanic, cynic,
and philosopher; last, but not least from the point of view of entertainment value, Roberts, our cook. . . . We spent the next six weeks
getting acquainted; we formed a solid block with esprit-de-corps
laid on with a trowel and expedition consciousness sticking out a mile,
and with deepest cleavages among ourselves which later developed to
advantage when sharing out the work and picking out the sledge
parties in the following year. Cubicle mates were chosen before even
we left the *Runic*. Friendships and rivalries made then persist until
today or have only been ironed out by death. They are still overlaid
by the greater loyalty to the leader and the expedition and the sense
of comradeship in a great and distinctive enterprise. Shackleton men
remain Shackleton men.'

* Sir Raymond Priestley has given us permission to quote this extract from
an essay written during the leisure incidental to a lecturing visit to the Scapa
Fleet at Scapa Flow in the winter of 1943.

Arrived in New Zealand, they were provided with free passes on the railways, and five of them enjoyed a visit to the attractive resort at Hanmer Springs. As the *Nimrod* was still re-fitting, they were adopted by various hospitable Christchurch citizens. Priestley found the artificial isolation of the explorers most interesting, and was to comment often, in later life, on its effects : for instance, in a lecture delivered to the Australian Institute of Philosophy and Psychology in 1935 :

'From the time that the small party of men have been picked, and, so to speak, set aside from their fellow men and dedicated to a great adventure, the psychological experiment begins. A well-advertised expedition—especially when, as in my exploring days, the objective was the Pole—was an object of interest and admiration to everyone around. Before they had had a chance to justify themselves the men were fêted, wined and dined, exposed to flattery and special attention, listened to with respect as authorities on subjects of which they often knew little enough. . . . It requires the nerves and temperament of a test match cricketer of the better sort to withstand the strain.'

From August to October Shackleton was fully occupied with last-minute preparations in England. In September he announced in the *Geographical Journal*[8] his change of plan for a base, without giving any reasons.

'King Edward VII Land has been selected in place of the winter quarters of the *Discovery* as the base of operations of the exploring party. A landing will, it is hoped, be effected by about the end of January of next year, in time to permit of the establishment of depôts to the south before the close of the Antarctic summer. The winter months are to be devoted to the pursuit of scientific investigations in the neighbourhood of the living hut, and with the return of spring in the latter half of 1908, exploring parties will be sent out southwards in the direction of the Pole, south-eastwards into the unknown region at the back of King Edward VII Land, and east-north-east along the coast in the direction of Alexander I Land and Graham Land. Nothing definite is known of the geographical conditions in any of these directions, and whether or not the polar contingent succeeds in covering the 700 or 800 geographical miles that will separate the winter quarters from the south pole, the combined explorations of the three parties may be expected to make interesting additions to knowledge of the distribution of land and sea in the Ross quadrant.'

Shackleton had been able to convince his financial backers that his change of plan was a sensible one, and they all appear to have continued to support him. There had been enough money to equip the expedition, but there was nothing in reserve for salaries and wages, nothing for extra stores that might be needed, nothing for the *Nimrod* during her waiting period in New Zealand. Then, too, Shackleton wanted to take more scientists but did not know how he was going to pay them.

The financial aspect of expeditions is not a pleasant one. Scott, Shackleton, Byrd, Bruce, Mawson, all had to exhaust themselves in the effort to raise money, and to waste time and energy which could have been better used in other ways. As a writer in *The Field*[9] put it; 'the primary qualification of the leader of a modern polar expedition is that he should be a good beggar. Before he starts he is worn out, not merely with seeing to the thousand and one details connected with the organisation of his expedition, but with the worry of securing just enough financial support to make it possible for him to start'. Byrd[10] described himself as starting one of his expeditions owing 'more money than I used to think existed'. The situation is not unknown today, but many expeditions, sponsored by a Government or an organisation, offer an enviable contrast.

One of the members[11] of the Australian Antarctic Expedition to Heard Island in 1947 commented on the efforts which Shackleton and others had to make to pay for their expeditions, and made the comparison with his own outfit, where 'members had been drawing award salaries since their appointments were made. We were enrolled as temporary public servants of the Commonwealth Government. As such, we became entitled to certain holiday and sick leave and to workers' compensation. In the event of the death of a member, the next-of-kin would receive £800'.

At least Shackleton's men were on a salary list. His own position, on the contrary, was precarious. Working harder than anybody, carrying the responsibility, he still had to deal with the entirely separate problem of providing for his family. It is true that the expedition was a speculation: he hoped to become rich. But this must not be allowed to obscure the fact that he was, to put it simply, trying to earn a living as an explorer. He was hiring out his brains, his experience and his personality for an unknown sum. In this respect the leader of any private expedition is in an uneasy position. He tries to assess honestly what the expenditure of brains and energy is worth to him: but if he is successful, and large financial benefits accrue, the public is only too likely to see him as a profiteer.

So it was with Shackleton in 1907. The financial arrangements he had made for his men meant that they might reasonably expect to add to their reputation and their bank balance by going with him, and might be sure that they would not lose by doing so. For himself, the matter was not so simple. Much of the money guaranteed was for the exclusive use of the expedition. Some that had been given by friends could be left to keep Mrs. Shackleton and the two children during Shackleton's absence. Her own money he steadfastly refused to touch. Though he had no intention of being careless with his life, his return could not be said to be a matter of complete certainty, and he intended that her money from her own family should be guarded at all costs so that if anything happened to him she would be secure. All he could do now was to deposit what money he could in the bank and to leave his brother-in-law, Herbert Dorman, who was acting as solicitor for the expedition, to collect various sums which had been promised and which could legitimately be used for the Shackleton family. He was deeply grateful to his wife for accepting calmly the unsatisfactory situation.

It was not easy, when the time came, for him to leave her. He knew perfectly well what he was asking of her. Throughout the summer, he had been too busy to see much of his family, and when the time came to go, it seemed to him that the only thing he really wanted was peace and quiet in his own home.

On the last day of October he boarded a Channel steamer at Dover, and some hours later, in the train on the way to Paris, he wrote a farewell letter to his wife[12] which shows, better than any analysis can, the mood in which he set out at last on the enterprise which he had planned and worried over for so long.

'My darling Wife,' he wrote, 'Your dear brave face is before me now and I can see you just as you stand on the wharf and are smiling at me my heart was too full to speak and I felt that I wanted just to come ashore and clasp you in my arms and love and care for you: Child honestly and truly it was the worst heart aching moment in my life. If I failed to get the Pole and was within 10 miles and had to turn back it would or will not mean so much sadness as was compressed into those few minutes: I never realized till we had parted all that it was going to mean to me but above all I was proud of your dear face so brave and the thought that you could be all that braced me up and made me really feel how wonderful you were: Child little wife I am thinking very much of you now and I want to tell you that in those last few moments you showed yourself to be a splendid glorious woman: and now for the brighter side of things darling: You have the two darlings—and they will be a great comfort and help to you whilst I am away and they are two of the sweetest and dearest in the world. You will be happy with them and will watch them during the time I am away even more lovingly if that is possible: And now child the time will go more quickly than you may think for you will be in touch with me till March and then again next March soon it will be 1908 and then you can say that next year I will be back: you will be just one year without hearing from me and I promise you that I will take every care and run no risks and this time there is no need to as the equipment is perfect the ship is really better than the "Discovery" though not so big and the men are all picked with the greatest care: and we have our experience with us this time of one thing I am certain I shall not run any risk for the sake of trying to get the "Pole" in the face of hard odds. I have not only myself but you and the children to consider and always remember that and also that you will be with me wherever I go in storm or calm and if inclined to do anything rash I will think of my promise to you and not do it. You must think that from this our (*sic*) you are with me and in the morning instead of being sad be proud that it is my chance to do a great work there are thousands who would give their eyes to go: and this Expedition owes nothing to the World at large and yet it may help the honour of the Country: if successful there will be ample money and instead of having to grind away at W.B's year in and out and only save a few hundreds a year there will be plenty for us to live our lives as we wish: I promise you darling that I will come back to you safe and well if God wishes it and also that I will not be sharp or hasty with my men You are a thousand times too good for me darling, and I see and know it in a hundred ways, but I can say no more than this that I will try and be worthy of the glory that is you. from early days you have been my light and my pride and in the everyday existence I may not have always realized it yet in the bottom of my heart I knew it. I will write again tomorrow the train is awfully jerky: My dear love to the children.

Your husband

Ernest.

Embarked on the *India*, he was glad of some last-minute paper work to dull the sharp pain of homesickness; but the image of his wife on Dover pier kept him awake on more than one hot night, as the ship crawled through the Red Sea. One night he wrote some verses to her— verses in no way remarkable but comforting to him because they helped him to express his feelings.

There were injunctions about money, too, in his letters. From Port Said he wrote[12] that he had arranged for her brother to pay her a monthly sum from the expedition funds, and that he was confident that he would be able to raise more money in Australia, to help her as well as the expedition. He had quickly become acquainted with his fellow-passengers and they had as quickly become interested in his plans. Inevitably his natural gregariousness was sometimes coloured by utilitarian needs.

'We are just at Port Said now' he wrote to his wife on 5 November, 'and I have been very busy with my papers and letters and have not been much on deck but there seem to be very nice people' and then he adds candidly: 'at least I mean useful people as there are some rich Australians on board and I hope before we get to Sydney I may manage to get something out of them:'

Other letters[12] show a simpler enjoyment of the voyage.

'I am sitting at the captains table at which there are some very jolly people:' he wrote on 16 November; and in the same letter: 'Everyone I have shown the photos of you and the children to are simply charmed with them and well they might be indeed.' He was still very homesick, and reiterated the promise that was to comfort him as well as his wife. 'Oh it is hard indeed to be away from it all and the only compensation that can be will be the doing of the work really and then the homecoming *never* never again for us to be separated it means so much out of one's life and life is so short yet we will have good times and happy times together again both in Edinburgh and in London and in any place that we and the children are it will be Home; sometimes to hear people sing some of the songs that take me back to ourselves I am filled with a great longing and desire to see you and hear your voice. . . .'

It gave Shackleton great pleasure, it is clear, to talk about his family and also his work; and when one of the passengers, Mr. Fry, secretly gave him £100 towards the Expedition, he had an access of confidence in his mission.

Travelling with Mr. Fry were his friends Mr. and Mrs. Gerald Lysaght, who also interested themselves in the expedition. Lysaght wrote a poem on it which he copied into a book of his verses which he gave to Shackleton, and he sent a copy home also, to be published on New Year's Day in *The Spectator*.[13]

Lysaght and Shackleton became close friends, for they had very much in common. Shackleton was particularly delighted when Lysaght introduced him to Meredith's poetry, and he wrote to his wife that he felt specially appropriate the lines from *Love in the Valley*:

'She whom I love is hard to catch and conquer,
Hard, but oh the glory of the winning were she won.'

Into this very long letter, written at sea to be posted in Colombo, Shackleton poured once more all his homesickness, his love and longing for his wife, and revealed very clearly his dependence on her as well as his determination to be worthy of her. 'I want the glory of the Conquest for ourselves and for the Country and I want to make this great in the golden world for you my Queen.' Once more he thought of her courage and generosity, and he signed the letter 'Your proud husband, Ernest'.

Then scrawled on the back of this long, loving letter a request—'Will you tell Kelly at Tabard that any orders from abroad are to be forwarded to Cook at once. I think Colombo will take thousands.'*

---

* Shackleton had controlling interests in the Tabard Cigarette Company, cf. p. 95.

Now the Expedition had to take first place again. Shackleton reached Melbourne at the beginning of December and on 3 December he gave a public lecture there which was enthusiastically received. This was nothing, however, to the audience he confronted on 6 December in Sydney, where he was escorted by Professor David, who after the lecture sent a cable[14] to Mrs. Shackleton. 'Sydney seventh December Brilliant lecture last night enthusiastic audience over four thousand sends you heartfelt wishes for your brave husbands success and safe return.'

Instead of using the money from these lectures for expedition expenses, Shackleton presented it on the spot to local charities. This gesture, which was repeated when he got to New Zealand and lectured in Wellington and Christchurch, was no calculated one. Shackleton always established a close and warm relationship with an appreciative audience, and was deeply stirred by the applause and the excitement which his lectures roused. He *could not* be impersonal, except with a room of unresponsive people, and this he seldom had to endure. But the warm feeling his audiences had for him roused in him a feeling equally warm but more expensive.

This time the gesture had a useful result. The Governments of Australia and New Zealand were inspired by his behaviour to vote him liberal grants, the Commonwealth of Australia £5,000 and the New Zealand Government £1,000.

Behind the grant from the Australian Government, as well, there lay much lobbying by Professor David, to whom Shackleton had appealed for help and advice. David's letter[15] to the Prime Minister, written on 10 December, is a cogent statement of the case. By the time Shackleton reached Australia he had only managed to raise £24,000 by private subscription and loans. A further £4,500, promised from the United States, had been withheld because of bank failures there. Money was urgently needed if the expedition was to carry on at all.

David stressed the particular importance of Antarctica to the Commonwealth of Australia, and in particular the value, to that country, of meteorological research. He hinted at possible mineral discoveries: he stressed that Australian scientists were going on the expedition and that collections would be given to Australian museums. He shrewdly remarked, too, that if Shackleton reached the Pole, all the countries that had helped him would gain in prestige thereby. The Leader of the Opposition, speaking to the proposal that the Government should make a grant, is reported[16] to have said 'If Professor David says he wants it, that ends it'.

The man who could thus sway a Parliamentary decision was at this time Professor of Geology at Sydney University. Shackleton had invited him, early in 1907, to accompany the expedition from Lyttelton to

King Edward VII Land and advise the geologists of the landing-party about their work there.[8] David was a Welshman who had spent much of his life in Australia. He had always been keenly interested in polar exploration, not only as it threw light on glaciation but also for the spirit of adventure that ran through its history. His presidential address to the Linnean Society of New South Wales, in 1895, had been on *Recent Research in the Arctic and Antarctic Regions*. He had taken a considerable interest in the published details of Shackleton's plans during 1907 and had readily agreed to go south on the *Nimrod*.

He was then a man of nearly fifty, wise and charming, with a lively sense of humour and a passionate devotion to his work. His physical fitness (he was slight and very spry) and his intellectual acuteness were alike remarkable.

When Shackleton had got his extra money from the Dominions, he was able to enlarge the shore party. He asked David's advice once more, and Douglas Mawson, a young lecturer in mineralogy and petrology at Adelaide University, was engaged as physicist. It was also arranged that Leo Cotton, another young Australian, should go down as far as the base to help in preliminary geological survey work and to act as computer for certain types of scientific observations.

When the expedition reached New Zealand there was a further change in personnel. A few days before the *Nimrod* sailed A. E. Harbord joined her as auxiliary Second Officer, on Captain England's recommendation, to replace Æneas Mackintosh, whom Shackleton had decided to include in the shore party. Harbord had a Square-rigged Extra Master's Certificate in the Merchant Service and therefore held the highest qualifications for both sailing vessels and steamers. He had spent about four years in sailing ships, and his experience was of great value to the *Nimrod*, which was at times under sail alone and therefore needed officers with this technical knowledge.

Shackleton was always happy in New Zealand, and his open, cheerful manner suited a country where men were taken at their own valuation, where enterprise was valued and affectation frowned upon. He spent three weeks of furious activity travelling between Lyttelton, Christchurch and Wellington and the colonial hospitality took up so much time that the phrase 'mad rush' which he used in letters to his wife was entirely justified.

There were the ponies to be inspected on Quail Island, where Mackay, with some help, was hastily breaking them in. There were stores to be collected, and some work to be done on the ship, where part of the after-hold was enclosed to make a very tight bunk space for the scientific staff.

Captain England was naturally in charge of the stowing of the ship, but Shackleton, without interfering, made it his business to see that everything was as he wanted. The stowing was a marvel of ingenious planning, for the *Nimrod* was far too small for all that she had to hold; and the Captain was anxious because he knew she was carrying weight up to her fullest capacity.

There were stalls on deck for the ponies; the car, strongly cased, was chained on the after-hatch; there were sledges on the deck, tins of carbide, cases of maize and some coal; scattered everywhere was the private luggage of the expedition members. When the ship left Lyttelton, there was only three feet six inches of freeboard.

This overloading presented one particular problem, for there was not room to take enough coal both for the voyage down and back and for the wintering party in the hut. Shackleton hit upon a solution that was both bold and simple. He arranged to have the *Nimrod* towed down as far as the Antarctic Circle by a steel-built steamer, the *Koonya*. This ship, under the command of Captain F. P. Evans, was chartered from the Union Steamship Co., and Sir James Mills, the chairman of the Company, offered to pay half the cost of the tow, the New Zealand Government finding the other half. It was a fine gesture, and the expedition would have been crippled without the help of the *Koonya*. The New Zealand Government also smoothed one other difficulty by printing special stamps for the expedition (see pl. between pp. 192, 193). This made the return of mails by the *Nimrod* much simpler, and besides, the stamps* might be expected to realise a considerable amount of money for the expedition—up to £10,000 according to Government estimates, as Shackleton[17] wrote to his wife.

During all this time dinners, lunches and parties were continuous. On 30 December Mr. James Kinsey,† who was acting for Shackleton in New Zealand as he had previously acted for Scott, gave a dinner in Christchurch for the whole expedition. At this dinner Raymond Priestley was handed a note from Shackleton[4] asking him to make a speech of acknowledgement on behalf of the expedition scientists, since Professor David was unable to be present. 'You will touch briefly',

---

* Shackleton was sworn in as postmaster before Sir Joseph Ward, then Prime Minister of New Zealand, and was authorised to open a post office in King Edward VII Land. As things turned out, it was in fact opened, instead, in the territorial waters of the Antarctic, just before the *Koonya* turned north on 15 January 1908. She took back to New Zealand the first batch of letters bearing the special stamp and postmark. Later a branch office was opened at Cape Royds, and another batch of letters was sent back on the *Nimrod* on 22 February 1908. The post office was closed on 4 March 1909, when the final mail was made up.[18]

Of the 24,000 stamps, the most interesting, though the most inaccessible, were left by Shackleton at his furthest south (see p. 218), in a brass cylinder which he and his comrades buried in the snow.

† Afterwards Sir James Kinsey.

the note said 'on the importance of geology, botany, marine biology, oceanography, meteorology, to the expedition; and in particular to New Zealand. You are on no account to be more than three minutes.' These were Priestley's first instructions from his leader!

The following night they were all entertained by Sir Wilmot and Lady Fawkes on board H.M.S. *Powerful*. As the Admiral commanding the ships of the Australian Squadron then lying in Lyttelton Harbour, Sir Wilmot Fawkes proposed the toast of 'Success to the Expedition' and the band played *Hearts of Oak*.

Shackleton sat up all night writing,[17] and early the next day concluded a long letter to his wife full of the familiar habitual mixture of advice about money and warm feeling.

'Sweetheart we will do our best to win and though we may not and I may be disappointed I will come back to the loving arms and soft embraces of you my wife and in the joy of seeing you and being with you and our children all will (be) forgotten: But dearest I dont think we will lose: Everything is perfect in food and equipment and the ponies are splendid. . . . ours is a big work and if we carry through it will be worth it. All the men loved the presents and gave 3 hearty cheers for you. I think they are all a hard crowd good strong men and full of the importance of their work: Oh Child I do want so much to have you with me now: Cheer Oh Beloved the time will soon (come) I am keeping the little note from Ray and Baby. Sweeteyes I am going (to) send this now and may write another line later: Prospice your word darling: Love of mine I am always thinking and caring I am coming back safely to you darling and will do nothing rash May God keep you and our little ones: give them long loving kisses and you my Heart it is one kiss though absent lasting always: You are twisted into my being I am thinking of you in all ways now. Keep safe little girl
Your husband
Ernest.

Chapter IX

NEW YEAR'S DAY, 1908, the day the *Nimrod* left Lyttelton, was one which none of the men would ever forget. Young Raymond Priestley,[1] writing in some discomfort on the rolling ship but determined that his parents should be able to visualise the scene, described it thus:

'There were about 50,000 people in Lyttelton on New Year's Day to see us off though we were only a partial attraction for on New Year's Day they always have a regatta at Lyttleton which in the ordinary course of events usually attracts from 20 to 30,000 people. The wharf we were attached to was crowded from early in the morning until the moment we cast off with sightseers so that we were unable to allow anyone on board to look over the Nimrod unless they were personally conducted by a member of the ship's company or the shore party; still in spite of this precaution we were pretty full up all day for a good many of our old Runic friends and Lyttelton acquaintances came down to have a look at us and the interest in the ship was of course increased by the presence of the dogs and ponies on board.'

Two people joined the ship somewhat unceremoniously not long before her departure.

'In getting aboard the Nimrod,' Professor David wrote[2] 'with both my arms full of breakable packages, I was gently impelled backwards over the naked gang plank by the steady pressure of a stout lady moving resolutely in the opposite direction; she was for the shore, let who would be for the Pole. Fortunately for me, but unfortunately for some of my fellow-men, I fell on to their heads on the deck of the Nimrod below. No one, however, was hurt. I had hope that my ignominious embarkation had escaped detection, but even before I had time to straighten myself up again, I was disillusioned by the mellow tones of Shackleton's voice from the bridge: "Professor, you nearly lost the number of your mess that time!"'

Even later was George McLean Buckley, a wealthy sheep-farmer of Ashburton and a keen yachtsman. Buckley had become friendly with Shackleton during the brief stay in New Zealand and had gone down to the *Nimrod* on New Year's Day to see the party off. The conversation about the Antarctic was too much for him. Suddenly he suggested to Shackleton that he should travel down as far as the ice in the expedition ship and return on the *Koonya*.

'It was 2 P.M. when the decision was made,' Shackleton wrote,[3] 'and the *Nimrod* was to sail at 4 P.M. He managed to catch a train to Christchurch, dashed into his club, gave his power of attorney to a friend, slung his tooth-brush and some under-clothing into a bag, struggled through one seething crowd at Christchurch Station and another at the wharf, and arrived on board the *Nimrod*, a few minutes before sailing time, equipped for the most rigorous weather in the world with only the summer suit he was wearing—surely a record in the way of joining a Polar expedition.'

At precisely 4 p.m. the *Nimrod*'s lines were cast off from the wharf and she began to move towards the harbour entrance, accompanied by two Union Company passenger boats (the *Manaka* and the *Waikare*), two tugs (the *Cygnet* and the *John Anderson*) and a flotilla of private yachts and fishing boats. The steamers, Priestley noted,[1] 'were so crowded with people, especially on the side towards the *Nimrod*, that they had a very decided list'. There were cheers from the U.S. magnetic survey ship *Galilee*, cheers from H.M.S. *Pyramus*, and a little later from *Pegasus* and *Pioneer*, lying just inside the Heads. Then:

' . . . we neared H.M.S. Powerful, and to the onlookers the Nimrod beside the Powerful must have looked like a mouse alongside of a lion. It seemed wonderful that the huge ship should deign to notice the little whilom Newfoundland sailing boat, and yet as we drew level with her bows, she seemed to suddenly start into life, all because of us. Hundreds upon hundreds of men could be seen rushing to her bows at the word of command, "All hands cheer ship", and the tremendous cheers rent the air. Her band played "Heart of Oak" and "Auld Lang Syne."[2]

Soon afterwards the friends who had seen this tremendous farewell were transferred to the tug-boat *Canterbury*, and the *Nimrod* picked up a tow-line from the *Koonya*. They were soon in the open sea. Water began to pour in through the *Nimrod*'s ports and scupper holes as she moved through a choppy sea: Shackleton compared her with a reluctant child being dragged to school.

For the next fortnight the strength of the two ships and the efficiency of their crews were to be severely tested by atrocious weather. The members of the shore party were hurled about in their cramped quarters. Those of the scientists were nicknamed 'Oyster Alley'.

'The so-called "Scientists' Quarters" Priestley[1] wrote in his diary, 'is a place that under ordinary circumstances I wouldn't put ten dogs in, much less 15 of a shore-party. It can be compared with no place on earth and is more like my idea of Hell than anything I have ever imagined before. To begin with it is big enough for only four men to live comfortably under circumstances of ordinary comfort. There are no portholes that will open, the ventilation is

pre-historic, and on two successive nights we have had to have all doors
shut owing to seas being continually taken fair over the weather side
of the stern. Every blanket in the place is wet through with salt water
and the swell is almost insufferable. The floor is two or three feet deep
in meteorological and other instrument cases, and in personal bag-
gage . . .' and so on, until he ends cheerfully 'I am afraid that if I
write any more about our quarters at present I shall become pessimistic so I will knock off.'

Shackleton allowed the scientists no time to brood over their discomfort. On the second day out he divided them into watches with
the ponies, whose safety much concerned him. A day or two later he
instituted watches at the hand-pumps also, for the wooden ship was
showing a certain number of leaks. By the time the steam pump had
been rigged, a series of meteorological observations had been planned.
These were attended to in rotation by Priestley and the three Australian
scientists, while the rest of the party continued two-hourly watches
with the ponies in the uncomfortable shelter which earned the name of
the Cavalry Club. Here George Buckley did magnificent work and won
the admiration of everyone who worked with him, while the rest of his
time was spent on the bridge, watching how the *Nimrod* stood out
against the huge seas that were oppressing her, and exclaiming at intervals: 'Splendid! Well done, old girl!'

The scientists were, on the whole, relieved at having something to
do. Shackleton and the Captain, as David commented dryly in one
of his newspaper articles,[2] had decided 'that work was the great
antidote to sea-sickness and incapacity'. And indeed: 'Half an hour's
work at the cold iron tail of the pump, or four hours of meteorological
watch on a cold, wet, slippery deck, between the hours of midnight
and 4 a.m., was distinctly bracing to the appetite.'

Shackleton had taken up his quarters in Captain England's cabin,
and there the carpenter made him a low plank bed. He did not use it
very much. On the second day out the *Nimrod* had to ask her towing
ship to slacken speed, and for the next three days the two ships fought a
gale. On the morning of 5 January Captain England, at Shackleton's
request, signalled to the *Koonya* to pour oil on the water; even so, on
the same evening *Nimrod* was rolling dangerously. The temperature
had dropped and during the day there were showers of sleet.

It was on this wild night that one of the ponies, Doctor, was pitched
on to his back; as no efforts could get him on his feet again, the next
morning Shackleton ordered him to be shot. The ponies were very
much on everyone's mind, but little could be done to help them. As
Mackay told Priestley, 'The poor devils are doing as hard work now,
balancing themselves to suit the motion of the ship, as if they were
pulling a sledge the whole day long': and Priestley[1] reflected in his

diary, 'if the ponies go my private opinion is that our chances of getting to the Pole at all will go with them'.

He shared with the boatswain the conviction that the tough little animals could take a party to the Pole if they could survive the voyage.

The storm reached hurricane force on 6 and 7 January. Water poured continuously into the ship and numerous objects were floated from place to place. Shackleton was cheered by seeing one of the crew collecting potatoes from a split sack and singing as he gathered them 'Here we go gathering nuts in May'. The seas washing over the ship were dangerous, and Shackleton gave orders that no one was to go forward without permission from the officer of the watch.

On 8 January the sea and wind became so high that the *Koonya* was signalled to heave to, and shortly afterwards there broke over the ship a wave so overwhelming that it smashed part of the starboard bulwarks and a small deck house. This and many other seas washed into the galley, putting out the fire and making it still more difficult for the ship's cook and for Roberts, who was helping him, to provide the tired and battered party with hot food.

It was not until 13 January that these disastrous conditions changed, and the party was cheered by a blue sky and warm sun. The general mood became lighter, and the Captain of the *Koonya* took the time, early in the evening, to signal to the *Nimrod* 'My compliments to the scientific staff and how do they enjoy the simple life'. He received his answer—'The scientific staff thank some like some do not like all are already seamen enough to appreciate your skilful nursing'.

Captain Evans closed this marine communication with the words 'Embarrassment prevents my answering'.[4] He might have been embarrassed by far stronger words of praise, for the civilians could appreciate the conduct of both the captains at this difficult time. During the whole period of the storm, Shackleton and Captain England had been on the bridge of the *Nimrod* almost without a break, and the captain of the *Koonya* likewise did without rest. Shackleton[5] wrote to his wife on 10 January that the storm had shown him that he had 'one of the finest little sea boats in the world I do not believe for a moment that any other ship of this size would have lived through such a hurricane with so little damage . . .'. For the two captains he had unstinted admiration. Captain England had a difficult job in handling the overloaded ship in high seas, and Shackleton's letters and diary show how highly he estimated his conscientiousness and his skill.

He gave high praise, too, to Captain Evans, and this was echoed by George Buckley, whose keen interest in the management of sailing boats gave him a clear understanding of what was involved. When he got back to New Zealand he told a reporter[6]:

'The *Nimrod* was nursed by the *Koonya* in a most admirable manner. It should be remembered that the tow rope and chain weighed about nine tons. The *Koonya* was kept in a position about 100 yards on the lee bow of the *Nimrod*, with a ton of rope hanging slack in the water, thus enabling the *Nimrod* to maintain practically an independent position, and ride out the storm "on her own". It must be evident to everyone who realises the position that, if the liberty of the *Nimrod* had been interfered with, and a strain put on the tow-line at any critical moment, it might have gone very hard with her. The whole position necessitated unceasing care and watchfulness, and the greatest skill and resourcefulness were displayed by Captain Evans. During the gale, those on board the *Nimrod* quite expected that the *Koonya* would find it necessary to cast off and abandon the tow. It is impossible to speak in too generous terms of recognition of the ability displayed by Captain Evans during the whole of that anxious and critical time. The two vessels were in the thick of one of the most terrific gales ever experienced at sea. From start to finish he kept the vessels in their relative positions which alone ensured their safety.'

In the momentary respite from bad weather the damp shore party came out on deck and made some attempt to dry the private possessions which had been slopping about Oyster Alley for so many days. The pale sunshine cheered everyone up and made them ready for the special seven-course dinner which was held that evening. It was true that the occasion was not altogether one for rejoicing, for the dinner was a farewell to George Buckley, who was to go back with the *Koonya* and who had made himself popular with everyone. None the less, it was a good moment for a celebration, and it was greatly enjoyed. Harbord[7] described the occasion in his diary:

'The table in the ward-room is set to seat 22 persons, it's marvellous how it is done, but it is done, and we're all seated comfortably round it. Old Buckley wonders what all the fuss is about, and he's soon enlightened. There's a menu (painted by our artist)—it has got Buckley at the side of it, and he's busy with the ponies, who are on the other side of it. There is also his watchmate getting the cocoa. At the top the "Nimrod" being towed by the "Koonya" is depicted, at the bottom there is a scroll which we embellished with our autographs. There is also a picture of the dogs, and from a beam there hangs the stable lamp. The centre of the whole thing is devoted to that most important item "tucker".

The dishes were worthy of the Hotel Cecil . . ., and be it said with truth, that no dinner could have been made more enjoyable. In good time came the speeches, and they were great. After every one somebody would yell out "Who saved Zulu?" and then we'd all yell "Buckley" at the top of our voices. His speech was like himself, he felt as we did; and when he spoke on discipline, his words did'nt fall on altogether barren ground. At midnight the dinner was over, and sleep claimed those who were not watch keepers.'

The next morning the first iceberg was sighted, with two more on the same afternoon. Shackleton signalled to the *Koonya* that continuous ice (her cue for departure) might be sighted at any moment. Captain Evans killed and skinned the sheep which had been presented to the expedition, to have them ready for transporting to the *Nimrod*.

On 15 January, at 9.0 in the morning, a stretch of ice was sighted to the southward. The *Koonya* on this day (15 January) made two records. She had towed *Nimrod* 1,510 miles, further than any other vessel not built for the purpose, and she was the first steel vessel to cross the Antarctic Circle.

About an hour after the ice had been sighted a whale-boat was lowered, and Captain England and Buckley were taken across to the *Koonya* with the mails. It had been intended that several boat journeys should be made between the two ships, to ferry the sheep, and also eight tons of coal and some fresh water. The state of the sea made this impossible, so on the return journey a thin line was brought over, and a heavier one followed which was hauled on board, with ten of the sheep lashed to it. These arrived safely on board, but the line carried away before the second batch could be hauled in. This operation, and the hauling in of the port towing cable, were made far more hazardous than they would normally have been by the rising wind and sea, and all hands worked at 'the beastly, antiquated "armstrong" patent windlass for eight hours'.[7] Just after noon Captain Evans cut the hawser, the last tie between the ships. The *Koonya* steamed round the *Nimrod* and then turned north.

George Buckley,[6] on deck to cheer and to be cheered, was struck by 'the appearance of my late companions on the *Nimrod*, who, in their unshaven, weather-beaten appearance as they leaned over her rail to bid us goodbye, gave their craft quite a piratical look'. He added that he had never met a finer lot of men, and that 'under (Lieutenant Shackleton's) discipline and magnetic influence every member of the expedition will put forth his heartiest efforts to attain for (the expedition) the most complete success.'

So the towing ship took away with her a good friend of the party. The second visitor was to have a longer stay than he had planned. A day or two before the *Koonya* left, Shackleton told Priestley that Professor David might be going to join the shore party. The young geologist realised that this would mean less credit for him in his work, but that the expedition would benefit enormously from David's knowledge and experience. His generous impulse on hearing this news persists to this day.[8] He has always believed that it was a stroke of genius on Shackleton's part to persuade David to stay in the Antarctic. David became chief of the scientific staff, and he converted the not very precise programme into a serious scientific operation.

Shackleton wrote enthusiastically[5] to his wife about the strengthening of the scientific side. 'Professor David is charming' he told her 'and will be a great influence for good amongst the younger men: All are as keen as possible to carry on the work and will render a good account of themselves.'

In order to retain David's services, Shackleton had to offer him a salary high enough to compensate him for the loss of money during his absence, and had to guarantee that if the shore party was not able to get back to New Zealand in 1909, his wife was to receive a further year's salary from the expedition agents. But for the man who, as Shackleton put it, 'could charm a bird off a bough', a man who would be the mainspring of the scientific work, the price was not too high.

At this time, though, scientific work was far ahead, and the immediate problem was to establish a base. Shackleton wrote to his wife on 10 January that he had 'decided to winter at the Barrier Inlet and land all the stores and hut at once and get the ship away and then we will only be 660 miles from the Pole'.

He sent a message by the *Koonya* to the London headquarters of the expedition giving them details of this plan and making it clear that if the *Nimrod* did not return in 1908, she might be presumed to be frozen in. No alarm was to be felt until she had failed to return the year after, when a search should first be made at Barrier Inlet.

Their first task was to get through the ice. On 16 January they were passing through an extraordinarily impressive landscape of tabular bergs, silent, cold, exquisitely coloured; and at about 3 o'clock in the afternoon they moved into the open Ross Sea, having avoided the pack-ice by Shackleton's choice of an easterly route. The next two days saw snowstorms and an increase of wind, and all the newcomers to the Antarctic lived in hourly expectation of catching their first glimpse of the Great Ice Barrier.

The Oyster Alley contingent had led far more comfortable lives since the gale abated on 14 January, and Shackleton had been able to establish a routine which made for comfort.

'Since our first clean up of the Scientists' Quarters' Priestley wrote[1] on 21 January, 'we have them brushed out and tidied up every day at about 9 o'clock, Adams is in charge of the job and the rest of us take it in turns to assist him (two at a time). After we have reported the Quarters as cleared to Adams one of us remain(s) on the ground to see that no one goes down and the others stay below ready to answer any questions and Adams in his turn reports to the Commander and he comes round and inspects Quarters. After inspection we are free to clear down there and sleep, read, write letters, and mend clothes, and now that the weather is getting colder, since we cannot get much exercise because of the impediments on the deck, we usually take advantage of the opportunity to spend most of the morning downstairs. . . .'

Though the ship was far from steady, the scientific staff could get some rest to brace them for the work to come. Not so the leader of the expedition, nor the Captain of the ship. Cramped and uncomfortable in the Captain's cabin, or on the bridge, the two men spent many hours working out navigational plans, assessing what time they could afford to spend on this or that proceeding.

Time was always a vital factor. The *Nimrod* must leave the Antarctic by about the first of March, if she was not to be frozen in for the winter. On the other hand, the shore party must be settled in an advantageous position with all their stores and equipment before the ship left. Captain and Leader each had a heavy responsibility, the one for his ship, the other for his expedition, and as time became shorter, it was increasingly hard to be calm about plans. The close proximity in the cabin and on the bridge must have been intensely irksome to both men, worried as they were with the problem of taking the ship safely through patches of ice and into a suitable inlet.

It was on 23 January that the Barrier was sighted and they began to cruise along it, to find the inlet where Scott and a party had landed to send up the balloons in 1902, and where it seemed likely that a secure and peaceful anchorage could be found. It was not to be so simple. A cable[9] despatched on Shackleton's behalf as soon as the *Nimrod* reached New Zealand told his wife of a change of plan.

'Have had to winter Macmurdo Sound barrier inlet gone edward land unapproachable all well best love prospice Ernest.'

The Royal Geographical Society, who heard of the change of plan at the same time, reported[10] simply:

'The ice-barrier was sighted on January 22, and the expedition then turned eastward to carry out Mr. Shackleton's intention to establish winter quarters on King Edward VII Land. Mr. Shackleton reports, however, that access to the land in this direction was barred by the ice. Repeated spells of bad weather were experienced, and at last he decided to make for McMurdo Sound, at the other end of the ice-barrier.'

What had actually happened may be seen from one of Shackleton's letters[11] to his wife, in which he really argues out the position with himself.*

* This very long letter was written in two sittings. The second part, which is here relevant, is headed 'Towards Mt. Erebus, 26th Jan.' It is written in pencil in a firm hand, and is clearly the result of close thinking and written with

'26 January, 1908. . . . What a difference a few short hours can make in one's life and work and destiny : Child o' mine I have been through a sort of Hell since the 23rd and I cannot even now realize that I am on my way back to McMurdo Sound and that all idea of wintering on the Barrier or at King Edward VII Land is at an end that I have had to break my word to Scott and go back to the old base, and that all my plans and ideas have now to be changed and changed by the overwhelming forces of Nature. I am feeling more now than I can say darling and wish that I were close to you telling it all to you instead of locking it up in my heart as I have to do to a great extent : and all the anxiety that I have been feeling coupled with the desire to really do the right thing has made me older than I can (n)ever say. Child I must now write my heart out and it is to you alone that I can do for I never never knew what it was to make such a decision (which) as the one I was forced to make last night. Well child you will have seen about it roughly and in bald facts in the papers and cables, so can understand what has happened but you I know can read between the lines and realize what it has been to me to stand up on the bridge in those snow squalls and decide whether to go on or turn back my whole heart crying out for me to go on and the feeling against of the lives and families of the 40 odd men on board : I swept away from my thoughts the question of the Pole of the success of the Expedition at that moment though in doing so I know now in my calmer moments that I was wrong to even to do that : that my money was (not) given for me to reach the Pole not to just play with according to my ideas of right and wrong, that I had a great public trust which I could not betray that in all ways my one line of action should have been the one I am taking now : but that was not what weighed with me then and I feel that you will understand me in it all. Well to tell the story as it came : after getting into the ice clear sea On Jan 23 just at noon we were off the Barrier. and went steaming along all the afternoon passing a deep cutting in the Barrier and about 9 pm we thought we must be near the bay known as Borch-revinks (*sic*) Bight but it was not till nearly midnight that we turned a sharp corner and there in front of us lay a long range of peaks and undulations which certainly looked like land though even now I will not call it so as I did not see any bare rock and facing this Place which I call the Bay of Whales because of the hundreds of whales blowing there : was a plain of flat long ice about 4 feet thick on which were several seals and some Emperor penguins we came up against the ice and saw that it would be impossible to journey over it with safety to reach the cliffs in the distance as the ice was rapidly breaking up

energetic, controlled concentration. As her husband had given her leave to show the letter to friends, to explain his action, Mrs. Shackleton tidied up the grammar here and there and cut a little to clarify the sense. Dr. Mill quoted only part of the letter in his *Life*,[12] being short of space. The second portion is now reproduced from the original, exactly as Shackleton wrote it from *Nimrod*, during one of the most unnerving and lonely days in his life.

long cracks were visible in it which meant that it was liable to go
out any moment: Now all to the Eastward of us lay immense masses
of packed up hummocky ice and beyond that the Barrier with several
bergs showing close to it to the North lay a great pack but a lane of
open water showed that we could get through so I turned the ship
North and after passing on the outer edge of this line of pack we
headed in for the Barrier again commencing our journey along but
no sign of Balloon Inlet met our eyes; we went on till about 6.30
on 24th we turned another sharp corner and ran down into the
Barrier again at the angle of this corner was a slope which was high
except in the extreme angle where it went down to 20 feet at 8 am
we stopped and lay alongside a piece of floe ice whilst England and
I went down to the room to discuss matters it was quite evident to
us that Balloon Inlet had disappeared that it had been broken off
from the Barrier and that there was now no chance of our wintering
there we were quite prepared to have done so and I am thankful
that it went before we arrived sometime during the last 6 years
otherwise I would have landed and the whole thing might have gone
this year. We got our position then and found from observation of
the sun that we were to the Eastward of the Inlet's position, the (*sic*)
we went up and started the ship along the Barrier towards the East
to try and reach King Edward VII Land which really starts at the
Longitude of Balloon Inlet: but even as we started at 9 am the
outlook was very black for all to the North of us lay a huge mass of
pressed up hummocky ice interspersed with great bergs and all this
mass seemed to be moving down on the Barrier by 10 am I saw it
was hopeless to try and advance further East along the Barrier for
the ice ahead was jammed hard up against the Barrier which we could
see rending to the Northwards and looking back and from the crow's
nest was the pack we had passed slowly moving in towards the
point where we had turned round earlier in the morning. We turned
at once and only just in time for we at 10.40 passed between the
pack and the point with a bare 50 yards to spare we would have been
jammed up against the Barrier the result of which I did not like to
contemplate and do not like to think of it now. We steamed on to the
S West through loose pack keeping within 100 yards of the Barrier
which was about 150–200 feet high just here. Thus we steamed
along noting each change of course until we reached the place
where Balloon Inlet ought to have been but no Balloon Inlet was
there instead, we were at the entrance to the shallow Bay we had
passed out of last night and we we(re) able this time to skirt close into
the ice face and right along the Bay ice : the cliffs of ice trended right
round at heights varying from 100 to 250 feet with ridges, and hills
of snow mounting but to nearly 1,000 feet; all along the point of the
cliffs were seals penguins and skua gulls, and dozens of killer whales
and large finned backed whale playing about: By this time it was
3.20 pm and we passed out of the Bay at 4.20 pm then kept close
in the Barrier. to the West all the time: I was baffled in my attempt

to find Balloon Inlet; it had gone. In my attempt to reach K. Edward VII Land along the Barrier I was also foiled though without doubt we had reached the junction of K E VII Land and the Barrier. To the North close in the offing lay the heavy pack and I saw no chance of going North and trying again from the Northward of the pack away to the East. my heart was heavy within me for here was a direct check to my plans: if I had not promised Scott that I would not use "his" place, I would then have gone on to MacMurdo Sound with a light heart but I had promised and I felt each mile that I went to the West was a horror to me I could see nothing for it but to go there for after the fact became apparent that Balloon Inlet had gone then obviously any idea of wintering on any other part or inlet of the Barrier would be suicidal and fraught with most serious danger not only to the success of the Expedition but also to the lives of all the men who I am responsible for; my private word of honour my promise given under pressure was the one thing that weighed in the balance against my going back at once and I gladly saw towards 6 p.m. another loosening of the pack to the Northward and after a long talk with England who put the seriousness of my position, frankly before me; by the attempt; the shortage of coal which even then was only sufficient to ensure the arrival of the ship at New Zealand: the strained condition of the vessel: the fact that even if we eventually arrived at King E VII Land I might not be able to find a safe place to discharge and would probably have to abandon it in view of the enormous masses of land ice and hummocked up pack that was breaking away which would make the ship's position untenable: my duty to the country and King since I was given the flag for the Pole and lastly but not least my duty to all who entrusted themselves to my keeping: I myself recognised the weight and truth of all he said and I knew at the same time that he was heart and soul with me and had no thought of his personal safety indeed neither of us as we stood on the bridge the same morning thought of that but of the safety of the laughing careless crowd of men who little thought or dreamt what our feelings were as the ice was closing in; to them it was merely an interesting episode and gave them an opportunity of a nearer view of seals and penguins just you imagine if you were in charge of a little skiff right under the white cliffs of Dover and saw bearing down on you going to crush you against those cliffs great masses like the Royal Exchange; or a piece the size of the N B R Hotel and Prince's Hotel, great pieces twice the height of the Dean Bridge above the Waters of Leith other pieces as big and as square as all Belgrave Terrace and Buckingham Terrace coming down on to you one piece the length of West Hill from the top to Walter's corner; just imagine this and think that besides the safety of all those men who were with me I had had the success from the world's point of view and the eyes of the world on us, then it will come home to you what those hours meant to me and England. He said at last what limit of time would I allow for the attempt to go

East via North and he thought that at the utmost stretch of safety 48 hours would be the most we could allow to go East, and if we did not get a clear run to the land within that time it would be folly and madness from every point of view to go on I knew even then that I was building up for myself a most formidable task if I was to reach the Pole but I was determined in my mind that if difficulties were increased then all that was to be done in these circumstances was to increase the labour so that a successful conclusion should attend our efforts I said to England that as regards the fuel question which was so urgent a one; that I was willing for him not only to burn all easily available woodwork on the ship but also to burn the deck-house cut away the mizzen mast burn it and the main topmast and anything at all that would further our object and gain time so that I could carry out my personal promise to Scott. this weighed with me even more than I ought to have allowed it to when I come to think of it in calmer moments now: but I felt that I could not turn back without trying from the Northward a bit so I told England that if I could not get East within 48 hours I would turn back for Mac-Murdo Sound as there was no other place I could go to and make the Expedition a success for I have only my word to Scott against my promised plans to the whole world and my 40 comrades. We went up on the bridge and now it was nearly 8 pm and turned the ship through the loosening pack towards the East again and from that hope rose in me to be alternately dashed with physical failure. All that night we steered through ice making for every open spot to the Eastward being again and again brought up by impenetrable pack and bergs and having to retrace our way till to the North again we found another clear space: and when I laid down at 6 a.m. on the 24th we were in apparently open water with a bright sun shining and a good prospect of getting East after all in spite of the fact that we were only then just abreast of the place where we escaped from the ice the morning before, but when I got up again during the forenoon we were close up again to the ice and found that during the morning we had run about 8 am into another Bay of pack and had to steer to the West again: All that afternoon we came up against the ice and towards 4 pm a new trouble presented itself. The glass was going down rapidly the sky became thick with snow and an W or Westerly wind sprang up soon becoming strong with squalls of hail and snow so thick that we had at time to stop the engines and our horizon was limited to less than 100 yards huge bergs and great masses of land ice sprang up out of the gloom and when once it cleared we saw that all round us except the way we came was the ice and with the wind the way we had come was rapidly narrowing soon it was possible that the floes might close around us and we would if the ship was not crushed, be locked in the pack with perhaps days and weeks before us ere we could hope for release and one can realize what that would mean with the ponies already tired out with standing during their long voyage and bad weather: with very little coal and with insufficient food to last all hands for a year in the event of the ship having to winter. I realized that to push further on then would be madness We could not lie where we were on the chance of it clearing up for it might be days and our precious stock of coal would dwindle away: the ship will not sail and must depend on coal alone: so with a heavy heart I gave orders for turning back. all that night from 8 pm when we turned till midnight we ran or rather thumped into a rising sea and had the pack to the North of us, and so has ended my hope of reaching K. E. VII Land. My conscience is clear but my heart is sore, and writing now I feel it as much but I have one comfort that I did my best; if I had gone back without risking and trying all I did and if eventually I got the Pole from MacMurdo Sound Base it would have been ever tarnished and as ashes to me but now I have done my best and if the whole world were to cry out at me which I am sure they would not even then I would not worry myself for I know in my own heart that I am right. Now going as we are to MacMurdo Sound there is only one thing to do and that is to do the best possible work there and much may be done there still: Indeed we may reach King E VII Land by the journey across the Barrier.* I think that darling I have now put down all that has been on my mind and I know you will know that I have done all that any man could have done under the circumstances if you would like to send an extract of this part of my letter you can write it from one asterisk at the beginning to the one on this page and send it to anyone you like in the family Herbert etc. but not to outside people and to no enemies Not that I think there will be really any except the Scott faction: I dont want you little girl to be worried in any way over this for to my mind it is now perfectly clear and though I regret it all (re my promise to Scott) my mind is at rest and it will not weigh with me any more and will not in the slightest affect my work in the future: You will rest better too, knowing that we are in an absolutely safe place and that the work to be done scientifically will be even more valuable than the Discovery's as the men we have are of a far higher scientific calibre than on the last Expedition indeed, Professor David has a world wide reputation: we will not trench on the Discovery's work but there is ample chance of amplifying it in all ways: I am Sweetheart not going now to go further into these matters and there will be but little time for me to write when I get into port as there is so much to do we may not be able to get close to Hut Point so will be working day and night to get the stores ashore and let the ship get away again: so I will just add a little to this before I close it up. There is no need to bother about the stamps not being of use for I closed the post when we were in the area of King E. VII Land and if they call in the Stamps unissued now it will make the others all the more valuable. I don't think they will do this anyhow: As regards the rest of the world you will remember that when my original intention to go to S. Victoria Land was announced everyone was pleased so I do not think that it matters much.'

This letter has been quoted in full because it is a key document. For one thing, it gives details and motives for an event which was to prove of great importance in Shackleton's life. Nobody with any understanding of the conditions could but admit that he had acted in the only possible way. The obligations he held to his men, to the expedition, and to his financial backers weighed far more heavily in the scale than the promise he had ill-advisedly made to Scott. Indeed, Scott himself, in a similar situation, must have acted in exactly the same way, and there is no evidence that he indulged in any recriminations about the affair to Shackleton.

At the same time Shackleton, with his determined character and blunt way of speaking, did make enemies; and he knew very well that among those who knew that he and Scott had been at odds over McMurdo Sound, there would be some who would support Scott's belief that he had the right to reserve his old base. He could expect hostility when he got home, if he broke his promise, and he would need all his moral courage to back up his common-sense and his seaman's knowledge as he made the decision.

It is significant that in the course of his letter he echoes a phrase about 'dust and ashes' which Wilson had used about the very situation that had now arisen. Shackleton *would* now have to use Scott's route to the Pole, and he would never quite be able to forget Wilson's words. In fact, it was a great sadness to him, although he spoke of it only to one or two close friends, that his action in going to McMurdo Sound did cost him Wilson's friendship. In Wilson's character there was an element of the self-sacrificial which would probably have led him, alone among explorers, had he been in the same position, to turn back or to allow himself to be frozen in—actions satisfying to the conscience but useless to the job in hand. On Shackleton's return to England Wilson made it clear that he regarded the breaking of the promise as inexcusable, and the two men seem to have had no further communication with each other.

Shackleton was a man of action. Intent on furthering the purpose of the expedition, with only one possibility of success, he could only take that way out; but he did not do this without a struggle. This long, self-justifying letter to his wife was, ultimately, addressed to himself. It represented a most searching examination into his motives. He could never be *quite* sure that he had not always, deep in his heart, hoped to go to McMurdo Sound. Though not openly expressed, the doubt is everywhere in the letter, and it is a doubt which any man as sensitive and forceful as Shackleton would be bound to feel in circumstances such as these. Consciously, once he had made up his mind, Shackleton put the whole unfortunate business of the promise aside; subconsciously, the doubt could not be smothered.

When he returned from this great expedition Shackleton seemed to
the outside world more confident and assured than before. He had also
come to a deeper knowledge of himself that made him, in a sense, less
sure of himself. In later years he was apt to become aggressive when
any of his plans were questioned, and once or twice the quick and voluble
defence he put up suggests that he was not as confident as he seemed.
The decision he had taken, to break his promise to Scott for the welfare
and safety of the expedition, was the first of several decisions he had to
take during the next two years, each of them calling for courage and for
psychological acuteness. He faced each difficulty squarely; but if his
character was developed, it was also hardened. He went south on the
Nimrod with much of the unreflective enthusiasm of his youth, but this
boyish attitude to life seldom appears again in his letters after this
period.

During the three days of manœuvring in the ice, before the *Nimrod*
was turned towards McMurdo Sound, Shackleton and Captain England
were in close consultation. In his anxiety to keep his promise, Shackleton
did not give the order to turn until the last possible moment. Captain
England[13] wrote to his fiancée, about that crucial day, 24 January, that
he 'talked very strongly and used all my powers to urge him (Shackleton)
to return to McMurdo instead, every moment was endangering the ship
and we should soon be embayed. He consented and we turned and ran
out, clearing the western edge of the Barrier by nearly fifty yards. It
was now that I felt the strain, for he was horribly distressed and upset
and I had all my impulses roused to go again and again (to) attack, but
I felt keenly the probable ending of the whole expedition and my
responsibility and we returned to again attack from the North.'

Shackleton had discussed his pressing problem not only with Captain
England but also with members of the shore party—with David in
particular. The Professor had begged Shackleton to make one more
attempt to find a base in King Edward VII's Land, when the ship first
turned away from the Barrier, but it was soon obvious to him that if
they did not find such a base at once, it would be dangerous to prolong
the search. He therefore encouraged Shackleton by emphasising the
splendid opportunities for research in the McMurdo Sound area.
Adams and Marshall also seem to have been asked for their opinion,
and Joyce too, who was frankly keen to go to the area he knew and to
attack the Pole from there.

Harbord[7] described these critical events in his diary for 24 and
25 January:

> 'Reluctantly we had to give up all hope of establishing the base at
> Balloon Inlet, since our prospective port had disappeared. After a
> brief consultation, Shackleton decided to try to get to the actual
> mainland of King Edward VII Land, which lay to the Eastward

about 100 miles. Here again we were blocked by impassable ice, so we steamed to the North, hoping to find some other means of getting to the Eastward, but our luck was out, and although we came many miles North, and often compelled to go very much to the Westward, owing to the heavy ice, we made no progress, in fact we were losing valuable time, and gaining no ground. From the crow's nest, as far as the eye could see in a W/N direction, the ice stretched. There were signs of a blizzard coming on, which meant a lot to us, tangled up as we were in the ice, so Shackleton addressed the Ward-room officers, saying that as time was getting very short, and no base had as yet been established, he thought it advisable to seek Winter Quarters in McMurdo Sound.

Everybody was most disappointed at being thwarted in the attempt to reach the planned base, but all realised how necessary it was to abandon it.

(25) . . . Once again in clear water, it was decided to have another smack at King Edward VII Land. The news was received with great joy, and the old ship's nose was once more turned in an Easterly direction. The glass went up again, and the blizzard we expected came not, and just as we were beginning to hope for success we received a rebuff in the shape of heavier ice than before. We headed off North again, but with no better luck, really it was disheartening. Sick at heart, and utterly disappointed, we turned West in search for a suitable place to land.

Words cannot describe Shackleton's disappointment, he felt it very keenly, but "Hope springs" etc., and we soon began to hope for better things.'

Looking back, Commander Harbord[14] feels now that 'Shackleton's seamanlike action was dictated by common sense in the demanding difficulties of ice pressure, shortage of coal, pressing time and the lack of any sure base nearer than McMurdo Sound. There is no doubt in my mind, as a seaman, that the decision to seek winter quarters in McMurdo Sound was right, and I don't think Scott would have wanted Shackleton, in those circumstances, to have gone anywhere but the most accessible place.'

Priestley's diary[1] shows that for several days the position had been fully discussed among the shore party, and their attitude seems fairly expressed in an entry he made in his diary on 6.30 on the evening of 25 January:

'The ice to the West and North has become so thick and the symptoms of a gale are so evident that Lieutenant Shackleton has had to give up the idea of King Edward VII's Land when we were within 30 miles and we are now heading back for MacMurdo Sound, the Discovery winter quarters. It is just as well for the geological part of the expedition for we shall be able to do much more valuable work scientifically at the old winter quarters than at King Edward

VII's Land although there is not the glamour of something entirely new. . . . Shackleton naturally is much disappointed but he has done all he could do and has had to give up through no fault of his own; we shall have to hope for better luck in the future for as yet we have had not too much luck. Still we have done something already. We have sailed further south than any other ship, we have sighted land that the Discovery missed, we first met the ice under conditions such as have never been experienced before, we have proved that ten miles have been removed from Balloon Bight by sailing right over the place where the ice flanks of the Bight formerly were, and we have seen everything there is to be seen except King Edward VII's Land, and we have tried to reach that so that we can now return to do good work at MacMurdo Sound feeling satisfied with ourselves and with a clear conscience. . . .'

At about 8 o'clock on the evening of 25 January the ship was turned to the westward, and after a short course southward on the 26th to get within sight of the Barrier, a direct course was set for Mount Erebus. Much time that could ill be spared had been spent in trying to reach King Edward VII's Land. Shackleton now had to give up the idea of charting the Barrier all the way to McMurdo Sound, and had also to pass Cape Crozier without stopping to leave a depôt there for a possible spring visit to the penguin rookery.

28 January was the Professor's birthday—his fiftieth—and spirits were raised by a pleasant musical evening. The ship meanwhile was approaching Cape Bird, the north-westerly corner of Ross Island.

At 5.30 on the morning of 29 January the *Nimrod* rounded Cape Bird and began steaming into McMurdo Sound. Tired by the long and difficult journey down, tired by over-anxious thought, Shackleton had to brace himself for the last of his immediate problems. Before the *Nimrod* turned back towards New Zealand, he must find a suitable place for winter quarters and must organise the landing, against time, of stores and equipment, a motor car, dogs and ponies, and a band of fourteen weary men who must be freshly inspired and encouraged for the year's work that lay ahead.

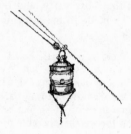

Chapter X

ON 23 January 1903, when the relief ship *Morning*, which took Shackleton home, reached McMurdo Sound, she was prevented from getting to Scott's Hut Point by the solid ice which stretched about twenty miles north of Scott's winter quarters down the Sound. The *Morning* lay for a month on the edge of the ice, and as it gradually broke up, she was able to creep to within five miles of the *Discovery*; but Scott's expedition ship remained frozen in for the whole of that year. In the following year the two relief ships, the *Terra Nova* and the *Morning*, arriving early in January, again found twenty miles of ice between them and Hut Point, but by 15 February the ice had broken away to the south of winter quarters and the *Discovery* was able to sail home in convoy.

Owing to the change in his plans, Shackleton was later arriving in the area than the ships of 1902 and 1903, and he hoped he might find the ice already so much broken up by the autumn gales that he would be able to reach Hut Point by ship and unload there. His hopes were not fulfilled. Just before noon, on this 29th day of January 1908, some twenty miles from Hut Point, the ship was stopped by ice so sludgy and decayed that it could not be cracked cleanly and there was no hope of forcing a passage through it. From the *Nimrod* Shackleton[1] could see the terrain he knew so well.

> 'To the south lay the Del(l)bridge Islands, and beyond appeared the sharp peak of Observation Hill under which lay the winter quarters of the last expedition. Castle Rock, towering about other local heights, seemed like an old friend, and White Island was dimly seen beneath the rising pall of cloud. To the south-west Black Island and Brown Island showed up distinctly, and behind the former we could trace the rounded lines of Mount Discovery. To the west were the gigantic peaks of the western mountains with their huge amphitheatres and immense glaciers. About seven miles to the eastward lay a dark mass of rock, Cape Royds, named after the first lieutenant of the *Discovery*. So familiar were they that it seemed as though it were only yesterday that I had looked on the scene, and yet six years had gone by.'

His problem now was one of time. He wanted to get to Hut Point, because he knew it was a suitable area for a base camp, and because he wanted this base camp to be as far south as possible, to shorten the distance of his dash to the South Pole. There was not time now to sledge the tremendous bulk of their stores across the ice for twenty

miles to Scott's hut; there was not time to wait very long for the ice
to break up.

Shackleton decided he could spare a few days and no more. The ice
was definitely in movement, and the ship could creep southwards if a
passage should open in time. He planned to spend the period of waiting
in bringing stores up from the holds, uncasing and preparing the car,
taking down part of the pony shelter—doing everything that could be
done on board, to save time when the moment for unloading should
come. It was particularly important to get the ponies ashore, since they
were badly bruised and skinned from the rolling of the ship; one of
them, Nimrod, was so bad that he had to be shot.*

To men less determined than these, the run of bad luck at this time
would have been daunting. The last day of January saw an unfortunate
accident to Mackintosh. He was working with others on deck, unloading
stores from the after-hold, when he was hit violently in the eye by a
hook which slipped from the lifting-tackle and swung across the deck.
Dr. Marshall examined him and decided that his eye must be removed.
He performed the operation successfully on the same day with the
help of Mackay and Michell. The accident meant that Mackintosh
would have to return in the *Nimrod* instead of joining the shore party.

He accepted the position sturdily. Marshall recorded in his diary
that when he came round from the anaesthetic his first thought was
about who would take his watch. There was not a man in the expedition by now who did not realise the value of Shackleton's optimism,
his power of recovery from ugly events. It is a tribute to his leadership
that this time of bad luck and delay did not upset morale.

Preliminary work on unloading stores went on all the time. Members
of the expedition went out after seal and penguin to add variety—and
fresh food—to their diet; and Dr. Marshall caught skuas from the ship,
which were much appreciated in the pot.

On 1 February history was made when the car was lowered on to the
ice. The engine was not started at once, but a party of about twenty
men dragged the vehicle nearly a mile from the ship. 'Here in comparative safety' Harbord wrote in his diary,[3] 'the car was put upon its own
merits, but alas, went a few feet, and then stopped dead, pulsating
violently until Day soothed it with a series of hammerings and screw-
ings. After a brief rest, the machinery was started again, and the
wheels in duty bound turned violently round in the snow, burying
themselves to such an extent that the car moved not an inch. This
sort of thing continued until three in the afternoon, when it was
decided to fit the proper wheels on to it, so we hauled the car on board.

* Shackleton[1] gives the name of this pony as Zulu; but both Marshall[2] and
Harbord[3] mention Nimrod by name in their diaries and this identification is
confirmed by an entry in the ship's log.[4]

This ended the day's excitement, which proved to us that the machinery was in good order, and that the fault, if fault there was, was in the wheels of the car.'

The old-fashioned method of travel proved more successful. On the same day Shackleton sent out Adams, Joyce and Wild with a sledge with orders to cover the sixteen miles which now lay between them and Hut Point, inspect the *Discovery* hut, and return to the ship on the following day. They did not in fact return until early on the morning of 3 February, having had a gruelling journey to the hut, which they found in good order and practically clear of snow. During their absence Shackleton and Captain England had gone southward on ski to look for cracks through which the *Nimrod* might be able to nose her way to Hut Point. But the ice was firm, and the leader decided to find another base without delay.

Accordingly, 3 February was spent sounding in the neighbourhood of Cape Royds and Cape Barne, about twenty miles north of Hut Point on the eastern (Ross Island) side of McMurdo Sound. About eight o'clock in the evening Shackleton, with Adams and Wild, went in a whale-boat towards the edge of the ice-foot, beyond which rose a snow slope and then the bare rock of Cape Royds. Sounding showed Cape Royds to be a suitable place for a base, with a depth* that should make it possible for the ship to discharge stores direct on to the ice-foot. By 10.0 that night she had come slowly in and was moored to the ice, ready for operations in the morning.

Shackleton could not rest yet. When the ship was safe, he went ashore with the Captain, the Professor, and the Chief Engineer. After prospecting they found a small valley which seemed a convenient sheltered site for the hut. It was time the expedition met with some good fortune to counterbalance the checks and frustrations of the past month.

The ensuing fortnight, however, turned out to be the most frustrating, as well as the most exhausting, period of the whole journey. To begin with, a fortnight was little enough time to land 180 tons of stores, and sledge them piece-meal across the ice-foot on to the shore. All this must be done in the quickest possible time, for if stores were dumped on the bay-ice, there was the constant danger of their being carried away if a piece of ice became detached.

There was no question of any set hours of work. The crew working the ship and the men ferrying the stores had to be ready to exploit every suitable moment. The weather was unsettled. From time to time shifting winds threatened to dash the ship against the ice-foot or

* An entry in the ship's log[4] on 3 February reads 'The water towards the land was found to shoal suddenly to 40 or 50 fathoms afterwards gradually to 5 fathoms at ice foot hard rocky bottom off the Northn End of Cape Royds.'

to pull away her ice-anchor and set her drifting in the loose ice. More than once the Captain had to steam away from the ice-foot and cut short the work of unloading until conditions improved. This meant that the members of the shore party, working for long periods under great pressure, had the additional strain of waiting about while the ship stood off, still on call and unable to take a real rest. They might have to wait on the ice for several hours : they might, as on 10 February, be discharging cargo from eight o'clock in the morning until midnight. The pattern of these days can be seen clearly in Harbord's diary,[3] from 6 to 9 February :

'8 a.m. Breakfast over, the work of discharging, and transporting stores was resumed, midst light variable airs and calm. Without warning, at 2 p.m. there came the treacherous SE. blizzard and again we had to make a run from the bay, this time leaving some of our men ashore to erect the hut, and attend to the horses and dogs. It took us no less than three and a half hours to get back to the fast ice, which had broken away considerably since we were there last. Midnight came with the blinding blizzard raging furiously.

February 7th.

The elements continue the same, and the ship is constantly breaking adrift. 10 pm. Commenced to snow.

February 8th.

At 4 am. there was a sudden lull, and the snowing ceased, there was a general look of improvement. Advantage was at once taken of it, the ice anchor was hoisted on board, and we were soon under way. But shortlived were our hopes, for we had not gone more than half a mile when the blizzard came down again with renewed violence, causing us to get back as quickly as possible.

Until 2 pm. we were busy re-anchoring the ship, as she kept breaking adrift in the blizzard.

Although we had quite made up our minds that this sort of thing was going to last for ever, it actually moderated suddenly, and at 4 pm. we were just going alongside the ice in Backdoor Bay. There had been a great change in the ice foot since we left it a couple of days ago.

After shifting about from floe to floe, we commenced work at the discharging and transporting of stores at six o'clock, and at midnight sought repose.

February 9th.

1–2 am. Fine snow accompanied the SSW. breeze that freshened towards noon.

Large quantities of ice are drifting down from the Southward, which means that the ice in McMurdo Sound is breaking up in good style.

6 am. Store work re-commenced. The weather is perfect, and today for the first time, the ponies are used for pulling the sledges. The work goes on fine. . . .'

And so it went on, the work stopping and starting, new hazards presenting themselves every day, sometimes every hour. The ice was constantly in movement, and on 10 February it became necessary to find a new place for discharging. From Front Door Bay, where some of the stores still lay on the ice just below the snow-slope, the scene of

WINTER QUARTERS
(from *The Heart of the Antarctic*, Heinemann, 1909)

activity moved to Derrick Point, a short way east along the bay, where the cliff beyond the ice-foot was higher, and where a boom and tackle had to be rigged to get stores ashore.

All this time the portable hut for the shore party, which had been taken ashore in sections, was being gradually pieced together. Tents had been set up as emergency dwellings on the occasions when the ship

11

had to move quickly without waiting for the men working on shore. They were used, too, by the men who looked after the ponies, now picketed in the valley, and the dogs, which were also ashore.

Derrick Point was not suitable for landing coal, and this was now taken round to Back Door Bay, a cove still further east with a very gentle slope from ice to rocks. The coal was transported by sledges hauled by ponies and this promised to be a most successful operation. Unfortunately the bay ice was now extremely insecure, and although bridges were improvised so that the ponies could cross the cracks between what were now ice-floes, there was an awkward moment, on 11 or 12 February, when Chinaman slipped while crossing from one moving piece of ice to another and was with great difficulty hauled out of the water and on to the ice again.

Most of the bay ice in the locality had moved away north and west by the afternoon, and the fast ice adjoining the land was now beginning to crack. There were still stores on the fast ice, and at six o'clock in the evening Shackleton, who was ashore, signalled a request that all hands should be sent at once to shift these from their precarious position. 'Everyone who could be possibly spared from the ship was bustled on shore', Harbord wrote. 'It was not before midnight, when all the stores were in safety, that a pause was made in the work. Shackleton was delighted to see everybody come right up to scratch in such an emergency.'

Shortly after midnight the party returned to the ship, and about half an hour later 'there was a loud crash, and the very piece of ice that the stores had been standing upon, fell into the sea with a mighty crash.' Shackleton's guess had been good.

The following day the swell made it impossible to land anything more in this area, so Shackleton sent Captain England some miles to the southward—the sea being now open in this direction—to land some stores at Glacier Tongue, a point which sledging parties would visit on journeys south and where a depôt would consequently be useful.

While the ship was absent, Shackleton remained on shore helping to improve on the temporary dwelling and cookhouse which was now being used by a considerable gang of navvies. Sheltered by walls of fodder, roofed with tarpaulin, with the efficient Frank Wild as chief cook, the party had settled down and provided for themselves a reasonable degree of comfort.

'. . . it was a sight to see us [Shackleton wrote[1] later], in the dim light that penetrated through the door of the fodder hut as we sat in a row on cases, each armed with a spoon manufactured out of tin and wood by the ever-inventive Day, awaiting with eagerness our bowl of steaming hoosh, or rich dark-coloured penguin breast, followed by biscuit, butter and jam—tea and smokes ended up the meal, and, as we lazily stretched ourselves out for the smoke, regardless of a temperature of 16 or 18 degrees of frost, we felt that things were not so bad.'

On 14 February the ship left Glacier Tongue and proceeded towards Cape Royds, but heavy ice kept her off and she drifted west again, to return the next day. At 8 a.m. on 15 February a boat was lowered and took soundings round the ice-foot, finding two fathoms deepening gradually to five, with a rocky bottom. At 9.0 a boat stood off to bring Shackleton on board.

He discussed with Captain England the possibility of trying once more to take the ship to Hut Point. Unloading was going on, and during the day Shackleton returned to the shore. At 5.0 a south-east swell made it necessary for the ship to stand off again. Captain England sent a boat ashore and 'received orders to remain in the offing till 8 a.m. the following morning',[4] for Shackleton realised that it had been necessary to move the ship out of danger.

This is perhaps the place to underline the relationship of an expedition leader and a ship's captain under his command. When an admiral or owner flies his flag, the captain of the vessel in which he does so remains master of it. Orders which the captain may receive must not be such as to take from him any of the responsibility for the management and safety of the ship, with which he is uniquely charged. We shall see that Shackleton, in his first expedition command, did not always remember to give his orders in a way that made it clear that he, the leader, fully understood the extent of the captain's responsibility and discretionary powers.* Shackleton and England had each served as an officer in a ship in the Antarctic (Captain England having made two full voyages to McMurdo Sound as a chief officer in the *Morning*): but neither had been faced with such hazards or such responsibility before. The assessment which each made of the situation the ship was in, depended upon the dictates of his own nature.

The ship was now driven northwards but got the opportunity to land some stores at an ice-foot north of Flagstaff Point. On 17 February they were back at Front Door Bay, landing stores from a whale boat, after which the shore party had to haul coal and provision cases up a fourteen-foot ice-face. In the afternoon this part of the bay was filled with floating ice, and the boat party had to move round to Back Door Bay, where the weary operation continued. The Professor, Mawson and others did a twelve-hour spell on this occasion, and their sleep, when they got it, was as prodigious as had been their toil.

All this time Captain England had been in considerable anxiety about his ship. Now that so many tons of stores had been discharged,

* A year later (p. 231) Shackleton showed more understanding.

her stability and awkward trim had made her much more difficult to manœuvre. It would have been possible to ballast her with stones, but the collecting and loading of these would have meant steaming some distance away. Already the moving of the ship to and from the ice-edge had used up much coal; the delay at the Barrier in January had accounted for more; what was left had to be shared between the ship and the shore party.

Shackleton and the Captain had had many consultations about the coal. Captain England had originally estimated that he would need 110 tons to give him a reasonable margin to take the *Nimrod* back to New Zealand. Shackleton, for his part, judged that the shore party would need a minimum of 30 tons for their hut. There was now not enough coal to meet both these requirements. Captain England wrote[5] to his fiancée:

> 'Soon the work of discharging begins and all must rush and let me away and now my coal is below 130 tons—and S. the other day said he would take none for the party but be without,—I refused absolutely and told him I would land it in spite of orders—how could I have them face the darkness and cold of an Antarctic night without coal. At whatever the cost I could not and would not—it is not a temptation to me—I shall absolutely refuse that.'

Shackleton knew as well as the Captain that the *Nimrod*, the lifeline of the expedition, must be equipped to reach New Zealand safely: there must be no doubt about that. In the end he and the Captain agreed that 92 tons should be taken as the minimum amount for the *Nimrod*; the remainder must be landed as and when possible for the use of the shore party.

It is possible that while this tricky calculation was being made, Shackleton was being submitted to a certain amount of pressure from some of his men. Certainly they were all well aware of the implications of this dividing up of the coal, and it must have been freely discussed among them. During this frustrating fortnight the shore party had certainly become critical of Captain England, and it may well be that, with no knowledge of the private conversations he had with Shackleton, they had come to think that the Captain was trying to take more coal for the ship than was strictly necessary.

We dwell upon the emotions of the shore party at this time because it is idle to pretend that brave men always behave logically in times of difficulty and danger. Some members of the shore party criticised the Captain: some certainly wanted to provoke Shackleton to criticism of him. They felt strongly that the Captain was being over-cautious and that he was moving the ship away from the ice-edge when this was not necessary, thus delaying the work at a time when it must go forward as quickly as possible.

They reached this assumption, of course, without full knowledge of the difficulty of working the ship, and very often without enough information about the wind, the ice or the depth of the water. For much of this time the civilians and some of the sailors were on the shore, and, as Commander Harbord has pointed out, it might often have seemed, from that vantage point, that Captain England was steaming away on very slight pretexts. Those on the ship, however, just as tired and overworked as those on shore, could see that manœuvring was inevitable, and the ship's log,[4] as well as Harbord's diary,[3] put it beyond question that Captain England was handling the ship properly in what were exceptionally severe conditions.

It was natural, of course, that the shore party should be impatient. They had been working for very long hours, and they knew that time was running short. While they waited at the ice-foot between one landing of stores and another, they discussed the situation, and discussion increased their excitement. Some seemed convinced that the Captain was suffering from strain and that his judgment was impaired. Eventually some of them challenged Shackleton, while he was on shore, and told him, that in 'giving in' to the Captain (for that was how they saw it) and accepting the intermittent moving of the ship, he was endangering the future of the expedition and losing the confidence of his men. Shackleton had already, on at least one occasion, severely reprimanded one of the shore party whom he had overheard criticising the handling of the ship.

He knew that if he continued to support the Captain he was himself courting criticism, while if he swung round to the attitude of certain members of the shore party he might gain in popularity. It was a situation where it would be very easy to make a false move.

Both Shackleton and his ship's captain had the same ultimate purpose. Captain England's duty was twofold. He had to manage his ship in such a way that the shore party was landed, with all necessary stores and equipment, while ice conditions still held. At the same time it was also his duty to keep his ship safe. This second duty was overriding, because the ship was the only form of communication the party had with the outside world. If it should now be lost, the survivors might perish before any relief expedition could find them. No news of the change of base had yet been sent home, and they would be looked for along the eastern part of the Barrier and not in McMurdo Sound. It began to look as though Captain England's two duties might conflict.

His long letter[5] to his fiancée makes it abundantly clear that his loyalty was to the expedition throughout this time of difficult decisions: but some of the men did not appreciate this, and looked upon his caution simply as a handicap to their work. On one occasion England took the ship to a place at the ice-edge from which the stores had to be dragged (Mackintosh said) a mile. Mackintosh[6] thought that the ship could easily have been brought to a place from which the drag was only a hundred yards. Shackleton appears to have thought the same—at least he was heard to ask England if it was not better to take the ship further in, or words to that effect. But the Captain said 'he was not going to take foolish risks'.

In times of crisis and anxiety, no individuals of a party, however brave and determined, have ever been able to watch the conflict of divided responsibilities without taking sides. Diverse loyalties will be aroused, and things will be said which in the cool light of reason are seen to be out of all proportion. The happiest and most successful expedition anywhere in the world cannot have been without some such hasty expressions of opinion.

The unfortunate thing about the difficulties on the *Nimrod* was that they got into the papers. Such harm as this may have done to the reputations of England and Shackleton was undeserved. Captain England proved that this was so when he was promoted to full Lieutenant in the R.N.R. after his return from the *Nimrod* voyage.* The effect on Shackleton's reputation was not perceived until much later (pp. 415–17, 420–22), and was probably more serious.

Mackintosh, who by temperament favoured Shackleton's drive rather than England's caution, reported that Shackleton was most patient with the Captain and accepted his decisions about the working of the ship while they were in the early stages of unloading. Mackintosh had been intended for the shore party and was completely devoted to his leader. Dunlop, the Chief Engineer, had been working on shore, helping to erect the hut, and had partly identified himself with the shore party. They were both passionately anxious for the unloading to proceed as quickly as possible, and their descriptions of the Captain's handling of the ship were thus heavily charged with emotion. Neither of the accounts they have left (the first in the letter to Mrs. Shackleton, the second in a letter to J. D. Morrison, a brother officer who had been on the *Morning* and knew both Shackleton and England) can be considered as giving an impartial view of the situation.

For this we must look principally in the ship's log[4] and in Harbord's diary.[3] Both these contain enough day to day details, written with no purpose except that of recording, to make it perfectly clear that caution was constantly necessary. Shackleton realised this very well, although he himself wanted to press on more quickly with the unloading and

* Captain England was married soon after his return, and left the sea to found his own business. He served in the Navy during the 1914–18 war and became first Lieutenant Commander and then Commander before he went back to civilian life.

believed that it was possible to do so. It is true that for much of the time he was on shore, and on one occasion, when he watched the ship steaming away in the middle of unloading, he pulled off his cap and jumped on it. This was interpreted by Dunlop as a direct criticism of the Captain. There is no reason to suppose that it was anything more than a vivid expression of impatience. But in their state of emotion, some of the men on shore took sides without their leader's wish or consent, and assumed that he also was taking sides.

It is perfectly clear that Captain England was anxious, and in this lies, perhaps, an explanation of why some of the men criticised him. Shackleton had in him a tremendous resilience. It had been a severe taxing of his energies to have to change his plans for a base, and with it so many of his plans for the whole expedition. But he was able to carry his cares unobtrusively. He was essentially a man of optimistic temper, and his invincible determination to achieve and to conquer buoyed him up at this time of ill-fortune. As Mackintosh put it,[6] 'he managed in a wonderful way to disguise the fact [that he was worried] for he was always to be seen with a cheery countenance; and some good joke to set us all laughing'.

This, then, was the difference between the two men. Shackleton was able to remain cheerful. Captain England, with as good reason to be worried as Shackleton, was not so well able to conceal his feelings. The rest of the company showed the usual human tendency to avoid an anxious and disturbed man and to side with a cheerful and confident one. Absorbing Shackleton's confidence, benefiting by it, they all, very likely, under-estimated the dangers to the *Nimrod* which were engaging the attention of their leader and the Captain alike. Moreover, Shackleton had an unusual intuition for danger, a power to take calculated risks, which had not yet been fully tested and which Captain England could hardly be expected to appreciate.

There came a day when the difference in temperament between the two men brought about a disagreement about the handling of the ship.*

Piecing together the fragments of information we have, we can reconstruct the scene. Shackleton had come on board and had joined Captain England on the bridge. It was getting very near the time when the ship must leave the south, and Shackleton was desperately anxious to complete the unloading. The Captain had stood off-shore and did not consider it safe or practicable to take the ship any nearer the ice-foot in the prevailing circumstances. Shackleton thought otherwise,

* This disagreement must have occurred on either 16, 17 or 18 February, but the ship's log[4] and Harbord's[3] diary are not enough to date it precisely. Mackintosh[6] and Dunlop[7] mention no date when discussing the incident, and Shackleton and Captain England did not mention it at all except, apparently, afterwards in the family circle.

and requested Captain England to take the ship closer inshore, as he was entitled to do. Captain England refused to comply with the request, saying that the risk was too great. It was soon known on the ship that there had been a disagreement between the two men, particularly as both left the bridge abruptly to continue their argument in the Captain's cabin. Inevitably reports were exaggerated. During the moments on the bridge Shackleton did put his hand on the telegraph to signal down 'Full speed ahead' and the Captain did put his hand over Shackleton's and give the order 'Full speed astern'. So much Captain England told his family in later years. This action was presumably seen by the man at the wheel, and it was easy for him to construe as the beginning of a real fight what was no more than an incautious gesture on Shackleton's part.

In fact, the disagreement was quickly and unobtrusively settled. The officer on watch on board during a great part of the period of landing stores was Harbord. His duties as officer of the watch kept him in close touch with events on and about the bridge. He says that he did not see or hear anything of the alleged 'incident' until he saw reports of it in the newspapers after the *Nimrod* had returned to New Zealand. He is able now, looking back on the past, to appreciate both sides of the situation, and his view of it has been most sane and helpful. He sums up :[8]

> 'England was a good seaman, but it must have been a big damper to him when the base had to be changed and there was a grave possibility of the stores not being landed in time. There was the stability of the ship, which must have given him a good deal of anxiety; and there was the pressing date for the ship's departure. Delay would probably have meant failure of the expedition. Where there are differences, of course, one man has to make up his mind, and that man is the leader of the expedition. Looking back on it, I can see that England had come through a harrowing time, and I think probably he was feeling the effects of strain, as he was entitled to do. He had a good deal of right on his side. But Shackleton, was leader, had the right to say 'I want the ship closer inshore' if he considered it safe and practicable, just as the Captain had the right (and indeed the duty) to refuse, if he considered that the ship might thereby be placed in jeopardy. Shackleton was an experienced seaman, and he had personally taken soundings at the ice-foot.
> After all, you don't expect things to go without differences of opinion in such circumstances. But I heard no hard words spoken. England must have been a very tired man; and one can assess that Shackleton, who had endured the hardship and strain and discomfort just as much, might well insist that the ship was brought close inshore to the ice-foot. It's one thing discussing it calmly here and another thing if you had to look at it as England had to.'

The key to the whole affair probably lies in the last sentence. It *is*, at this distance from the event, impossible to say categorically that one or other of the actors in the drama was wrong. Each made his decision according to his own temperament. The fact remains that Shackleton expected the Captain to abide by his decision, and that he considered he was acting against the best interests of the expedition in refusing to do so. Captain England, with his strong feeling of loyalty to the expedition, cannot have found it easy to oppose Shackleton.

But there was no time for the two men to discuss the situation before action was taken, and they were both so tired and overworked that there was no hope of retrieving the situation between them. During the next day or so they must have reached some compromise, and to some extent the blizzard which came down on the ship on 18 February solved the immediate problem for them. All we know is that Shackleton made up his mind, during the last days before the ship departed, that he could not allow Captain England to bring her south in the following year. According to Dunlop,[7] he felt that it would be unwise to tell the Captain of this decision. He therefore wrote a letter explaining his decision and another to Kinsey containing instructions. The Captain was to hand over his command after the ship reached New Zealand and was to retire as an invalid on full pay for a year, until Shackleton's own return. The *Nimrod* was to be brought down south in 1909 by Mackintosh, if the doctors considered him fit, otherwise by Captain Evans of the *Koonya*, or Captain Colbeck, or another suitable man.*

These dispositions were confided to Dunlop and Mackintosh, and Dunlop was instructed to deliver the letter to Captain England in Lyttelton. The contents were naturally shocking and distressing to the Captain, and it should be stated here that in private he refused to accept the formula that he had been ill, though he allowed it to be used in public. He told Mrs. Shackleton[9] that he had not in fact resigned from illness and had merely consented to this statement without comment. His attitude was expressed clearly and with dignity in a letter to Kinsey,[10] dated 20 March and written at Lyttelton:

'In accordance with my instructions from Mr. Shackleton, a copy of which I believe you hold, I beg to hand to you herewith my resignation as captain of S.Y. Nimrod. I also hand to you a statement of some of the repairs etc, which should be done before the Nimrod is, in my opinion, again ready for sea, and to inform you that she needs extensive overhauling and almost entire re-equipment.

You will, of course, understand that the limited time at my disposal if I am to complete this work in a fortnight makes it

---

* Presumably Mackintosh was not considered fit enough to take the ship down after his accident, for the *Nimrod* was put under the command of Captain Evans for the summer of 1909.

impossible for me to go into more details, and my instructions are that Mr. Dunlop will take charge of this matter, but I shall at all times be ready to assist you to the utmost of my ability. Should you consider that my knowledge can be of service to you or to those away, it is at your disposal.

I would also like you to feel assured that, in the event of any difficulty arising in the appointment of my successor, or in the work of repairs or equipment, causing thereby any anxiety as to the relief of those working in the South, or in any way tending to increase any risk to them, I am at your service to do anything that lies in my power at all times.

For your private information, since the question of my health in mind and body has been quoted as the reason for my resignation, I beg to inform you that I am perfectly sound both in body and mind, and that my resignation has been forced upon me, nor did I know of this, as you know, until I received my instructions from Mr. Shackleton at your hands. At present I do not wish this statement made public unless it becomes necessary in the interests of the Expedition.'

The letter ends with further details of outstanding business connected with the ship, and the captain particularly drew Kinsey's attention to certain arrangements Shackleton had made verbally with the ship's crew, regarding bonuses, which he now wished to confirm.

It is impossible not to feel that Shackleton would have handled the situation differently if he had had more time, and if he had had previous experience as an expedition leader. In fact, as will be seen, he did handle a somewhat similar situation very differently, only a year later, when he had had a chance, through the winter, to discover his own powers and to learn more about the behaviour of men in exceptional circumstances. In his dealings with Captain England he was perfectly within his rights, of course, in demanding loyalty. When he came up against a situation when Captain England exercised his discretionary powers in a way he did not approve, he seems to have wrongly concluded that the Captain was disloyal.

To Shackleton, loyalty was the essential quality in all his men. Throughout his life the few occasions when he was at variance with one of them will be seen to be occasions when, as he saw it, that man had failed in loyalty. He thought of himself as leader, and therefore thought of disloyalty to him as disloyalty, and possible danger, to the rest of his men. But there was also the personal aspect. Shackleton's relations with his men were always direct and personal. His temperament demanded co-operation and approval, and when a man's loyalty was in question, Shackleton reacted as a man no less than as a leader. It cannot be claimed that his behaviour in the difficult situation in McMurdo Sound was completely impartial; with no man, leading an expedition, could this have been so. When he made his decision he was influenced by pressure of circumstances, by fatigue, by emotion, by the expressed opinion of his men perhaps, and by cold hard judgment —in what proportions it is now impossible to say.

In this classic dilemma, Shackleton had arrived at what he believed to be the most suitable formula to meet the case. The formula was a simple one: Captain England's health had suffered. If it had been more than a formula, we may be sure that England would have been examined by the doctors—and he was not so examined. Neither Shackleton nor Captain England wanted any publicity. The good name of the expedition came first, and Shackleton evidently thought he had arranged matters so that there need be no public sensation.

Unfortunately his efforts were unsuccessful. When the *Nimrod* reached Lyttelton at the end of March and England's resignation was announced in the newspapers, the story was taken up with indecent enthusiasm. Not content with the simple formula of resignation, reporters descended on the ship and talked persuasively to the ship's crew. It was said afterwards that the sailors had been interviewed in the local pubs. Whether any inducements, liquid or pecuniary, were offered, the effect of the interviews was electrifying. While Captain England and his officers very properly declined to discuss his resignation, the Press concocted a startling story of harsh words, even of blows, between England and Shackleton.

The story broke on 10 March, in Christchurch and Lyttelton, and on the same day the London *Times*[11] carried the following paragraph:

> 'Captain England has announced his resignation of the *Nimrod* on the ground of ill-health. There are reports of serious dissension between Captain England and Lieutenant Shackleton.'

The story ran for over a fortnight, becoming daily more dramatic. The *Daily Mail*[12] on 11 March carried the headline 'Crew's Story of a Struggle on the Bridge', and asserted that Shackleton, in trying to get his way about the movement of the ship, had tried to interfere with the bridge telegraph and one of the combatants had been knocked down. In spite of firm denials from Captain England and Kinsey, the point was laboured, both in England and in New Zealand, and was even taken up again in Melbourne in the middle of April, when the man who had been at the wheel at the time, having just returned home from New Zealand, gave his version—a mild one, but also asserting that Shackleton had interfered with the telegraph.

There was one justification for the extraordinary persistence of the New Zealand press in printing the story. When the New Zealand Government had given the grant of £1,000, it had been understood that the money would help to enable the *Nimrod* to do magnetic survey work in the Indian Ocean during the period of waiting. This survey would have been of direct benefit to the Dominion. Now Captain England had resigned, the ship was in dock for extensive overhauling, and it seemed unlikely that this work could be carried out. The press certainly did not suppress the feeling aroused over this change of plan.

In fact, the idea of the magnetic survey was abandoned by Shackleton not because of the Captain's resignation but because of the state of the ship. Right back in January of 1908, while the *Nimrod* was still being towed down towards the Antarctic Circle, he had written[13] to his wife:

> 'We will be hard pressed for money as much has to be done to the ship when she gets back but I am not going to carry out the Magnetic Survey: the weather down here is too bad for the little ship and she will take a good time fixing up. . . . Don't be scared darling that the ship needs repairs; she will be quite safe but she is 40 years old and naturally the towing is a strain on her but she is quite seaworthy only the strain has made the deck over (and) the men's living quarters leak a bit; the actual hull and structure of the ship is as sound as can be.'*

On 24 April the *Lyttelton Times*[14] ran a long article on the subject, giving a résumé of the sensational rumours and concluding:

> 'The general public has absolutely no interest in the personal side of the incident, and it would be an impertinence for it to attempt to inquire into any little differences of opinion between members of the expedition until those differences reach a stage when they affect the whole operations of the expedition. It appears as if that stage had been reached. The Commonwealth of Australia voted a sum of £5000 to the expedition and New Zealand gave a further £1000 in cash and much in kind on the distinct understanding that the Nimrod, during the time the expedition was in the south, would return to Lyttelton and undertake exhaustive magnetic surveys of Australasian waters. These surveys would have been of more practical value to the Empire than even a successful dash for the pole, but they have not even been begun, and, it is understood, will not be undertaken at all. In the meantime the Nimrod is lying idly at Lyttelton, presumably awaiting the time when she will have to return to the Antarctic for the expedition. In view of these facts the public certainly have a right to ask whether the expedition intends to calmly appropriate £6000 and leave undone the greater part of the unwritten contract for which the money was donated. It is quite time that the whole position was cleared up and the country was put in full possession of the details and results of any question of divided authority that has arisen, and was informed of what bearing the developments that have occurred has upon the safety and scope of

---

* This was of course deliberate reassurance—for he well knew that the ship was too strained for the work entailed in the proposed magnetic survey.

the expedition. One local member of Parliament has already announced his intention of exploiting the matter when Parliament meets, but it is to be hoped that the position will be satisfactorily explained long before then.'

Righteous indignation of this kind is always appealing to the public and most difficult to dispel. The same newspaper published, on the following day, a statement from Kinsey that neither the Governments nor Shackleton recognised any special obligation attached to the grants. Shackleton's statement that the *Nimrod* was not in a fit state for an extended survey was fully and fairly quoted. All the same, the original article had done its work, and there was left in the public mind a faint unease with regard to Shackleton's handling of money which was most damaging to his reputation.

It must be admitted that this business of the magnetic survey was used as a moderately dignified excuse for repeating the story of the 'tiff' or 'fracas' or 'fight' once again. But the malicious way in which rumours were allowed to grow did inspire some disgust and disapproval. On 21 March Mr. William Coull[15] was reported as having written to the *Star*:

'It was with regret I read a statement made by a correspondent from Wanganui prejudicial to the character as a seaman and a gentleman of Lieutenant Shackleton. The sting was in the last sentence, in which it was said that "the men declared themselves perfectly willing to serve under Captain England, but did not relish the prospect of serving under Lieutenant Shackleton". I hold no brief for the latter, but, happening to have been a fellow-passenger of his in the *Maheno* when travelling from Sydney to Lyttelton, I noticed that the opinion among all was that Lieutenant Shackleton was most courteous and kind. I think all judgment should be suspended in relation to the unfortunate difference between himself and Captain England until the facts are fully known. Lieutenant Shackleton is now with his companions in the fastnesses of the ice in the Antarctic, with a long night before him, and he is deserving of all our sympathy, and, may I say, our prayers.'

Letters[16] as emphatic were sent to Mrs. Shackleton by the officers of the *Nimrod*, who felt this Press publicity very keenly. John King Davis, as Chief Officer, sent her on 23 April a letter signed by fourteen members of the ship's company which must have been some comfort to her.

'We all deeply regret to hear this morning for the first time of the false and malicious reports that have been circulating at home of which we had no idea, and emphatically deny that anything in the nature of a fracas took place on board the Nimrod between Lieut Shackleton and Captain England. During the whole of the time

Lieut Shackleton was on board he was most kind and courteous to all and we will spare no effort to bring him back safe and sound to give these would be mischief-makers the lie.'

Separate letters written by Davis and Harbord on the same day are equally whole-hearted and heartening. But the officers rightly thought it was undesirable to launch into a public defence, and the rumours, though repeatedly contradicted by Kinsey and Captain England, had their effect. Nothing is more susceptible to harm than the reputation of a prominent person, no body of people more avid for disgrace and calumny than the general public. The two or three weeks at Cape Royds when Shackleton and Captain England were fighting time, weather and fatigue had an effect on the expedition as a whole, but far greater was the delayed effect. The 'scene on the bridge' was widely believed in, and the disagreement was given an exaggerated importance. Indeed, it is more than likely that some people made deductions from it about Shackleton's character which he did not deserve.

Chapter XI

THE sturdy little *Nimrod* was to meet a more serious danger in the next few days than any she might meet on the homeward voyage. In the evening of 18 February a blizzard began to blow and the ship, with Shackleton on board, was forced to stand out into the Sound. The storm raged for four days and Shackleton, almost continuously on the bridge, had the double anxiety of observing the damage done to the *Nimrod* and of wondering how the shore party were managing in the unfinished hut. Worse than the heavy and erratic seas was the intense cold. The temperature was so low that the rudder-well was in continual danger of being choked with ice, and a sailor had to stand by with a long pole to keep it clear. On the fourth day of the storm, the water being frozen in ports and scupper holes, the seas that were shipped began to freeze on the deck, and the Chief and Second Officers, hanging precariously over the sides of the ship, took axes to the bulwarks in order to release the water.

It was not until early on the morning of 22 February that the *Nimrod* was able to steam back to Cape Royds. Shackleton, landing at Back Door Bay, walked over to the hut and found his men well, though greatly dissatisfied with the performance of the stove. The appearance of the land had been considerably changed by the storm. At the main landing-place the stores had been buried in frozen spray blown nearly a quarter of a mile inland.

The most pressing work was the landing of coal, and this went on all day, slowed up by the bad surface of the frozen snow. Shackleton spent part of the morning, with Priestley, in turning out the hut, airing sleeping bags, and putting things as far as possible in order. It was now clear that the ship must go north at once, and the shore-party must steal a few moments to write last-minute letters.

The leader of the expedition, tired and full of cares as he must have been, could have been forgiven for expressing some of his worries to his wife. But Shackleton did not do so. He was in the kind of situation that suited him. There were not at the moment any personal complications to be dealt with; what was needed now was hard, quick work and quick planning. He was thinking ahead, improvising plans, assessing the needs of the expedition in its present phase. His letter[1] to his wife, written on 18 February, is entirely characteristic of him :

Goodbye Darling wife

God keep you and our children. I think we will get the Pole. I cannot write more. My whole heart is with you.

Your husband
Ernest.

I am fit and well

In this brisk and optimistic fashion Shackleton signed off from civilisation for a year. At 10.0 on the night of 22 February the *Nimrod* turned to the north and moved away from Cape Royds with a fair wind. The shore-party retired to the hut and celebrated the true beginning of the expedition with their first cakes—'very creditable ones' which Roberts had made 'on a baking tin improvised from the tin top of one of Colman's flour boxes'.[2]

The week following was still given over to hard and incessant labour, as the various dumps of stores were attacked with picks and the cases sledged up to the hut. The surface, though rough, was suitable for the ponies, who worked as hard as the men. The day after the ship left some 129 penguins were slaughtered and buried in the snow. It was an unpleasant business, made more so by the dogs, who took every chance they could get to worry and mangle the birds. The weather was still uncertain, and stores were often hauled in snow and heavy wind. Meanwhile there was also the hut to organise. Partitions were put up to make cubicles; the doctor found, unpacked and sorted his medical stores; they started building a shelter for the ponies with stacked bales of fodder; and two of the bitches produced litters of pups.

Up till now they had not celebrated Sunday, the work being too pressing. On 1 March a restful and domestic atmosphere prevailed. In the morning hymn and prayer books were rummaged out and Shackleton read a shortened service. Wild leading them in his strong tenor voice, they all sang 'Onward, Christian Soldiers' and 'Oft in danger, oft in woe.'

The rest of the day was spent in what must have seemed to be mere pottering, after the events of the past fortnight. Wild and Joyce were at work in the storeroom; Adams was busy with meteorological instruments; Marshall stained a wall of the hut. Priestley spent most of the day sleeping or reading the 'Faerie Queen', since he was on night duty with the ponies. The woollen clothes were issued—for each man six pairs of mittens and gloves, six pairs of stockings and socks, three of bed socks, a pyjama suit of Jaeger wool, three singlets and three pants, three woollen outer shirts, two woollen caps, a scarf and a colic belt; there were added warm house-boots and Russian felt boots, each man fitting himself as best he could from the stock.

The hut was by now almost completed, and when, on 3 March, the

The Cape Royds hut in the winter of 1955–56, photographed on Operation Deepfreeze

M. J. N. Foster

The cubicle occupied by Professor David and Mawson: It was named 'The Pawn Shop'

Type-Case and Printing Press for the production of the *Aurora Australis* in Joyce's and Wild's cubicle, known as 'The Rogues' Retreat'

acetylene lamps were lighted for the first time, the explorers of 1908 felt the glow of pride and satisfaction that comes from using a modern invention.

Shackleton set great store by the comfort of his men. The ingenuity and thoughtfulness reflected in the whole plan of the hut may be attributed largely to him, even if the details were not always his own.

He had planned to divide the building into cubicles, so that his men could be convivial or peaceful, as they wished. None of the cubicles was more than 6 by 7 feet, and they were separated from each other only by sacking hung from wire, or by walls of boxes, but they were to all intents and purposes private.

Each reflected the personality of its owner. At No. 1 Park Lane, occupied by Adams and Marshall (called in Priestley's diary[2] 'The Surgery'), the shelves, well stocked with Napoleonic literature, were adorned with drawings and curtains of gauze, and on the curtains were life-sized drawings of Napoleon and Joan of Arc. At 'The Gables', Marston had provided a homelike atmosphere for himself and Day by painting on one curtain a fireplace with a fire burning in the grate and a vase of flowers on the mantelpiece. Armytage and Brocklehurst, in 'The Shruggery', lived in surroundings severely practical; and Mackay and Roberts concentrated their efforts largely on an elaborate bamboo bed, which proved to be collapsible in the wrong sense. The decorations in the 'Taproom',* where Priestley and Murray had their abode, were provided by a mixture of geological and biological tools and specimens. The artist had, however, been commissioned to decorate the 'Rogues' Retreat', home of Joyce and Wild, with a painting of two very tough characters drinking beer out of pint mugs.[3] Confusion reigned in the cubicle variously called the 'Pawn Shop' and 'The Old Curiosity Shop', where the Professor and Mawson accumulated a number of assorted objects; the Professor 'made a pile of glittering tins and coloured wrappers at one end of his bunk, and the heap looked like the nest of the Australian bower bird.'

The rest of the hut was taken up with Shackleton's cubicle (which housed most of the expedition library and a number of instruments), an efficient dark-room made by Mawson, and a pantry-cum-store-room lined with shelves. The stove stood in the centre of the hut's back wall, opposite the entrance; and in the narrow passage between, into which the cubicle-dwellers could erupt merely by lifting their canvas curtains, was a long dining table that could be slung up to the roof when it was not being used. It was an odd piece of furniture, made from the lids of venesta cases, and Priestley noted[4] with amusement 'in one place a legend informs the diner that the table contains a theodolite, some

---

* Priestley explained in his diary[2] that this was a 'somewhat indelicate reference' to a sub-dysentery which afflicted Murray during most of the winter.

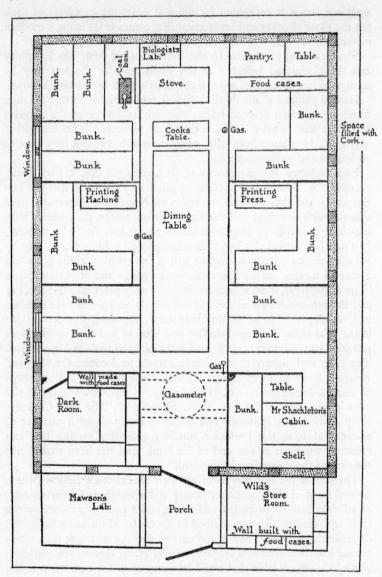

PLAN OF THE HUT AT WINTER QUARTERS
(from *The Heart of the Antarctic*, Heinemann, 1909)

ranging poles and other surveying apparatus, while another legend remarks that it is only "To be opened on Christmas Day", etc.'

Outside, the hut's simple rectangle was broken by a laboratory for the physicist and a store-room for Wild, on either side of the porch. The stables ran along one side.

This small, ingenious, well-insulated hut,* with its packing-case lockers, its quirks of decoration, its increasing sootiness, its adaptability, was exactly suited to the company within its walls. There was no need for any 'after' or 'fore' quarters, not only because the party was so small but also because class distinctions were not considered when it was designed. Not that these were not felt. The differences in the table manners of Petty Officers and scientists were duly noted—and laughed at. Once, a conversation about university education promised to become awkward—but didn't. The fact remained that, on this expedition, what counted was a man's proficiency. Some were proficient with their hands, some with their heads, some (notably Shackleton) with both. The scientific staff, taking their turn with domestic chores, acquired a few unwonted domestic skills. Priestley[4] supposed 'that nowhere else in the world is it a common sight to see two geologists and a meteorologist washing up dishes as if they had been used to nothing else'.

Adams has put on record his feelings about the atmosphere in the hut during the winter. He writes[19]:

'This amalgamation of (it must be admitted) somewhat strangely assorted men was made possible by Shackleton's particular form of control, based on his almost supernatural intuition for selecting men who believed in him implicitly and who were proud to have the honour of participating in this great adventure, no matter what part in it they were asked to play. The Antarctic winter, with its four months of complete darkness and its month of twilight at both ends was indeed a testing time. There were days on end during blizzards when no-one left the hut save for a natural purpose or to feed the ponies or take meteorological observations, but I never heard an angry word spoken during the whole of that period. Everyone was absorbed in his own particular function or engaged in preparing for the great journey ahead. Coarse language of any sort was automatically eschewed, and alcohol was not available. Shackleton did not insist on excessive formality towards himself; he was accepted as, and addressed as, The Boss. If a change in routine was suggested by any member of the party, or if an alteration in policy became necessary, it was quietly discussed with those who were affected. For instance, when we lost some of the ponies the situation was talked over with all hands and the leader's decision was accepted without any qualification. His exceptional powers of leadership were just as

* Shackleton gives a long and interesting description of the hut, its functions and its environs, in *The Heart of the Antarctic*, vol. 1, pp. 132—50.

much in evidence during the sometimes tiresome and intimate life
in the hut as they were on the sledging journey to the Pole.'

Shackleton's flexible discipline was far in advance of his own time.
It was based, in the last analysis, on two points—that Shackleton liked
to get on with people, and that he liked to get results.* On the whole
it seems to have been wonderfully successful. Allowing for inevitable
roughness of temper, that winter of 1908 at Cape Royds was a happy one.

During the days after the *Nimrod's* departure the weather had put
an end to Shackleton's plans for autumn sledging. He had hoped to be
able to make at least one journey to the south to lay a depôt for the
journey towards the Pole, but this could only be done if he could travel
on sea-ice, since the west side of Ross Island, sloping steeply from
Erebus and much crevassed, was impassable. But while the stores were
being collected, high winds had broken up the ice in the Sound and,
with it, the only sledge-road to the South. It was Dr. Mill's[5] opinion
that this early opening up of McMurdo Sound had practically destroyed
the chance of a successful Southern Journey.

Shackleton's other plan, to visit the Emperor penguin rookery at
Cape Crozier, was impossible for the same reason. Held off from Hut
Point first by too much ice and then by too little, he cast round for
something to employ the last days before the winter closed in.

The suggestion that Mount Erebus might be climbed seems to have
come first from Professor David. There was much to recommend an
expedition to Erebus. It was an adventure. The mountain had not been
climbed before, and Shackleton naturally liked the idea of bagging a
peak as well as a Pole. The journey would test the endurance of those
who made it. Then, too, it could be planned very quickly. Sledges could
be man-hauled as far as they could go, so the ponies would not be over-
strained; stores and equipment need not be excessive.

Most important of all, an expedition to Erebus would have great
scientific value. Observations at the summit would help to supply the
answers to outstanding questions. The whole climb would be interesting
and instructive to the geologists. The height of Erebus had so far only
been roughly estimated and it was important that previous figures
should be checked.†

* An interesting analysis by Captain John Giæver[6] of Polar leadership in our
own time enforces this point. Speaking of the party of fifteen men at Maudheim
in 1950–52, men from Finland, Sweden, Australia and Britain, he wrote:
'. . . the leader of such a wintering party, with its intellectual, and presumably
intelligent, individualists will not have an altogether simple task. . . . In such
a case one has to rely more on mutual respect than on discipline. Military
discipline is all too simple to maintain, but it would be hardly appropriate for
our community. We must rely upon the will to co-operate.'

† In 1841 Sir James Clark Ross had estimated the height of Erebus to be
12,367 feet, and on the National Antarctic Expedition two different heights had
been computed—13,120 and 12,922.

Finally, Erebus was an active volcano, and Shackleton, who had more than once in 1902 watched a glow in the sky above the mountain, must have felt the compulsion to discover more about this configuration just as strongly as the scientists whose special study it must be.

In the long run, however, the expedition was an adventure—the first challenging of the unknown. Professor David, who was to lead Mawson and Mackay as the main party, was no reserved or abstract scientist. On the many expeditions of his active life he had enjoyed his surroundings as well as discovering scientific facts. He had the same kind of poetic energy in exploration which characterised Shackleton. His description of the mountain, written for the expedition magazine[7], is a romantic one.

'If Ross Island be likened to a castle, flanking that wall at the World's End, The Great Ice Barrier, Erebus is the castle keep. Its flanks and foothills clothed with spotless snow, patched with the pale blue of glacier ice, its active crater crowned with a spreading smoke cloud, and overlooking the vast white plain of the Barrier to the East and South, the dark waters of Ross Sea and McMurdo Sound to the North and West, and still further West, the snowy summits of the extinct volcanoes of Victoria Land, Erebus not only commands a view of incomparable grandeur and interest, but is in itself one of the fairest and most majestic sights that Earth can show.'

It was on the evening of 2 March that the Professor talked over the plan with Shackleton, Adams and Marshall, and on 5 March a party set off, hurriedly but satisfactorily equipped. The three men were provisioned for ten days. With them went a supporting party of Adams (as leader), Marshall and Brocklehurst, carrying additional stores. They were themselves provisioned only for six days but they had permission to attack the summit if Adams thought it could be done. He thought it could and should. Shackleton, looking through Armytage's telescope on the fourth day, saw six small figures on the skyline near the summit.

During the days that followed the six men, armed with crampons and ice-axes but with no knowledge of the conditions they would meet, made a journey that would have been a considerable achievement for experienced mountain climbers but which was remarkable for amateurs.

After pulling the sledge with a load weighing 560 lb. over the lower slopes, carrying it over exposed areas of moraine, they decided, on 6 March at their second camp, to leave it at a depôt and push on with the essentials for four days.

'Dr. Marshall having photographed us,' David wrote, 'we filed off in a procession more bizarre than beautiful. Some of us with our sleeping bags hanging straight down our backs, with the foot of the bag curled upwards and outwards, resembled the scorpion men of the Assyrian sculptures: others marched with their household goods done up in the form of huge sausages; yet another presented Sindbad (*sic*), with the place of the 'Old Man of the Sea' taken by a huge brown bag, stuffed with all our cooking utensils; this bag had a knack of suddenly slipping off his shoulders, and bow-stringing him around his neck.'

Thus oddly strung about, the parties moved steadily upward over snow and ice. The weather at first was calm, though cold, and the view compensated for all the effort. Marshall's description[14], brief as it is, suggests the majesty of the scene.

'Very still. Never forget sunset. Sound freezing over with wonderful opal tints on open sea. W. mountains tipped with gold and base of Erebus with glaciers a sea of gold and purple. Sun dipped, whole scene changed to cold purple.'

The next day saw a heavy blizzard blowing, and the supporting party, forcibly kept in their tent, had only one biscuit and a cake of chocolate to eat during thirty-six hours. The weather remained intensely cold. When the party continued on 9 March, Brocklehurst was suffering from frost-bitten feet and Mackay was exhausted. Both were suffering from altitude sickness. The extinct crater was now reached and Brocklehurst was left in the three-man sleeping bag while the rest of the party made a thorough investigation of the place. On the following morning, 10 March, they pushed on and reached the edge of the active crater at about 10.0 in the morning. Again speedy but thorough observations were made, and the height of Erebus was subsequently calculated with an aneroid and hypsometer—13,370 feet above sea-level.*

The descent of the mountain, made in less than two days, was spectacular—a matter often of glissading, which certainly saved time but made heavy demands on clothes and courage. All the men fell about, and from time to time became separated on the snow slopes. At 11.0 on the morning of 11 March Shackleton, standing outside the hut, saw six figures coming over the ridge. The party staggered in, to be dosed with champagne and fed with enormous amounts of porridge, ham and bread and butter.

The attack on Erebus had been most valuable, as a piece of useful research and as a test of endurance. The height of the mountain had been established by direct observation. The position, height and character of the craters, extinct and active, had been carefully noted, and David had enough data to work on to produce interesting geological conclusions. The meteorological observations were various and of exceptional interest in connection with the weather conditions of Ross Island.

* The height generally adopted in 1957 was 13,200 feet.[8]

This was a magnificent record of scientific facts; but meteorology had impressed itself on the company not only in the abstract but through the direct and devastating effect of the weather. The expedition had shown the six men what they could do and what they were up against in travelling in the Antarctic.*

The combination of David, Mawson and Mackay had worked very well. They had proved themselves well able to exploit scientific opportunities, and Shackleton may have decided there and then to use the same party for the journey to the South Magnetic Pole in the summer. The supporting party had had a harder time of it, with their less adequate equipment, and the energy and resourcefulness of Adams, Marshall and Brocklehurst were now abundantly proved. It seems pretty certain that these three men had been in the original party of six Shackleton had planned for the Southern Journey, together with (probably) Wild and Joyce. Certainly Brocklehurst had been promised a place on that journey, and in the early part of the winter Adams and Marshall seemed reasonably certain that they were to go. Unfortunately the frostbite which had kept Brocklehurst from the summit of Erebus now ruled him out of the longer sledging journey. His foot was kept under observation, and by the end of March Marshall had decided that one or more of the toes would have to be amputated. He performed the operation on 6 April, with Mackay as anaesthetist. It was completely successful but the Antarctic temperatures made wounds very slow to heal, and Brocklehurst had to lie up for some time, being given Shackleton's cabin, while Shackleton moved in with Armytage. Bitterly disappointed, he accepted Shackleton's decision that he could not join in the dash for the Pole.

It seems likely that in the early part of the winter Shackleton was still thinking in terms of a six-man party, but another unfortunate circumstance now made it necessary to change his plan. When the party first landed, the ponies were picketed on a sandy beach some distance from the hut. While the Erebus party was away, one pony, Sandy, had died. When Marshall did a post-mortem he found the stomach full of volcanic sand, which the pony had been eating evidently as a substitute for salt. The remaining ponies were moved at once to the shelter on the leeside of the hut and given treatment, but it was too late. At midnight on 12 March Priestley found the pony Billy cast in his stable; they

---

* On Scott's second expedition of 1910–12, which followed the pattern of Shackleton's as closely as Shackleton had followed that of the National Antarctic Expedition, a party of six made an ascent of Erebus in December 1912, to make a more detailed survey of the craters. They found a route which allowed them to take a sledge up 3,000 feet higher than Shackleton's men had been able to, and thus they were able to spend longer on observations of the mountain.

could not get him on his feet again and he died the next day. On the
14th Mac was seen to be in distress, and on the next day he had to be
shot. His death was found to be due to corrosive poisoning, and they
conjectured that he had got hold of some shavings from one of the
chemical cases.

There remained four ponies as the mainstay of the Southern Journey,
and these were now watched over with the utmost care. Most members
of the expedition took turns in exercising them up and down the frozen
lake nearest to the hut (this smooth piece of ground was called,
nostalgically, Green Park) or down to Sandy Bay, where they could
enjoy a roll on the sand that had been so disastrous to them. Armytage
took charge of their stabling and feeding, and directed the amateurs,
who added horse-wrangling to their own special pursuits. It was not
until after midwinter, when the Southern Party was finally decided, that
the four men who were going each took over a pony as his special charge.

While the daylight lasted, too, Joyce was busy training the dogs,
young and old. Though his experience with dog-driving on Scott's
expedition had not perhaps been of much value, he set about his
job in a workmanlike way and produced a second form of transport
which was to be very useful in giving the Polar party a good start.
As in the old *Discovery* days, the dogs quickly became camp pets
and their particular temperaments were noted and discussed in detail.
Some men had their particular favourites, who went for walks with
them, and Priestley endeared himself to the puppies, so that in his
journeys down to the fish-trap he would be accompanied by a pack of
oddly assorted hounds. This did not prevent the party from getting
the dogs tolerably well disciplined to running in harness.

The car still remained a doubtful factor. It was tried on every
opportunity and with frequent changes of wheels, but in spite of its
advantages in horse-power over Quan, Grisi, Socks and Chinaman, it
was soon clear that because it could only operate on a hard, smooth
surface, its use could only be limited.

Everybody had a hand in these transport rehearsals and, indeed,
there was never a time when the expedition was not keyed to the great
journey towards the Pole. At the same time, Shackleton gave Professor
David full scope with the scientific work, and from this point of view
it was one of the most valuable winters ever spent in the Antarctic.

The terrain round the wintering hut gave plenty of opportunity for
the scientists. The Professor and Priestley used every hour of daylight
to collect geological specimens and to make surveys as far afield as
possible. Murray lowered a fish trap in Front Door Bay, and also
carried out investigations in the lakes near the hut. Mawson made
numerous experiments and observations on the character of the ice,
and with the help of an anemometer set up on a ridge, made regular

measurements of wind-forces. Adams established an extensive series of meteorological observations both inside and outside the hut.

The interested amateurs took a hand in all this. Because the meteorological record, to be useful, had to be unbroken, it was necessary to arrange for one period, between 10 p.m. and 6 a.m., when Adams could sleep, and the night watchman took over his duties with the various instruments. Meanwhile everyone kept a look-out for biological specimens for Murray: it was a party of amateurs who, one day, found some moss growing in a sheltered spot near Back Door Bay.

Assistance was not always as useful as it was intended to be. Sir Raymond Priestley recalls[2] how Marston, acting as porter to the Professor on one of his collecting walks, had the idea of taking a stone out of the bag when it was full and replacing it with a newer specimen. He said he did this to avoid disappointing the Professor, but his thoughtfulness set some geological problems in erratics for those who came afterwards.

Shackleton showed a keen and active interest in the scientific work, though it was not always expressed in an orthodox way. Priestley[2] described one incident in his diary for 1 April:

'Today after helping in the general work of getting ice I went with the Professor and Murray to dredge at the lake where we had sunk the trench. We took some plasmon biscuits, ginger nuts and chocolate as we did not intend turning up for lunch. The boring and dredging apparatus was tied on the 6 feet sledge and Armytage helped us to pull. We went round by the Blue and Green Lakes as they are almost connected with the trench lake and although the way is longer the sledging is much easier. When we arrived at the trench we found Shackleton already waiting for us, and were had by him in a very scientific way. He called our attention to the crackling of the ice and we were putting it down to the high tension produced by change of temperature and otherwise learnedly accounting for it, when he calmly took a shovel and removing the first layer of ice disclosed to view a lump of carbide which he had planted there and which was fizzing away merrily and making a most unholy smell. It was a fair do and well carried out.'

It was not in Shackleton's nature to waste an All Fools' Day. His attention to detail made it impossible for him to remain ignorant of anything that was going on. Besides, as a good leader and a good psychologist, he wanted to be satisfied that the men in his charge were contented and well occupied. For the two youngest members of the party, Priestley and Brocklehurst, he showed a special solicitude. He could not be sure at first how they would stand up to the peculiar conditions of life in the Antarctic, and unobtrusively kept a close watch on them until he was satisfied that they were settling down.

Not long after the winter set in, Murray had to be confined to the hut, for the cold had affected his health, and Priestley took over his dredging work. He would go out on most days, when the weather was at all possible, with a packed lunch in his pocket, and return home only at dark. On these occasions Shackleton would often pay him a visit. 'He used to come along and dig and yarn and sing and after a couple of hours he'd go away: he was the only chap who came down and helped normally, was Shackleton.'

It was entirely typical of Shackleton that he should take a hand with the digging, as he did also with the dog-driving and the horse-wrangling. While necessarily reserving to himself no particular job of work, he made it clear that he could take a hand in them all. His capability was always reassuring to his men; they came to know that he would never ask them to do anything that he could not do himself.

This energy and complicity with everything that was going on meant that Shackleton knew exactly what each man was doing and was able to assess his precise value to the expedition. He did not hesitate to let this value be known. To each man, whether he was physicist, dog-driver, or cook, he gave, not by direct words so much as by a constant encouragement and interest, the firm conviction that he was essential to the expedition. Sir Philip Brocklehurst[10] remembers 'He made us feel more important that we could have been.' This keen interest of Shackleton's was not entirely deliberate policy. It was also part of his temperament; to those who liked him, and showed that they liked him, his response was always warm and appreciative. He had, besides, the power to communicate his natural optimism to his comrades, so that when he asked them to do the impossible, they felt that this was within their power. Interest and inspiration combined to give him an exceptional hold over the men he led.

The warmth of his interest continued inside the hut, where a routine was soon established. There was plenty to do, during that winter— plenty of work and plenty of recreation.* Each man took his turn as messman and as night watchman. There were routine observations to be made all through the winter. There was work to be done on the sledges, on clothes, which must be both made and mended, and on the precision instruments. There was the constant improvement of the cubicles, on which at least some of the party lavished much artistic skill. There was an excellent general library, which was well used; and

---

* Shackleton and his companions at Cape Royds would have been amused by a paragraph contributed by C.T.V.M.[11] to the story of Byrd's second expedition.

'No doubt the strain of the winter night was more intense in the past, when exploring parties were smaller, comforts were scarcer, and there wasn't the opportunity to take up the slack by overhauling tractors and airplanes and preparing for half a dozen major journeys.'

if there was no scope for weekly lectures such as Scott inaugurated on his second expedition, there was very diverse and lively argument. There were impromptu theatricals, with Marston in a star part as a woman in butter muslin and a tow wig, and there was the gramophone, which carried memories of home through the warm clutter of the hut.

A good deal of credit for the harmony of the party must be given to the Professor, who was at his best in this kind of situation, constantly genial and helpful, amusing as well as intelligent in conversation, and with an obvious interest in his colleagues. He was, like Shackleton, a good mixer, and because the ultimate responsibility for the expedition was not his, he was able to preserve an equanimity which made him a dominant member of the party.

Shackleton was less equable, but his occasional bursts of temper, safety-valve for the worries inevitable for an expedition leader, were short-lived, and if anyone felt any resentment it was equally short-lived.

Any expedition leader becomes a scapegoat, and the unpopularity of an order or a change of routine is automatically shifted to the man who institutes it. In the nature of his position Shackleton could have called down upon himself much of criticism and disapproval. The ambitions of those who wanted to be on the Polar party, the recurring idea of the money to be made out of a success, the effect of necessary changes of routine—all these things produced strong feelings. Shackleton spent much time in his cubicle, writing, talking privately to people, and making plans to meet every contingency. With these necessary absences, Professor David might have taken to himself some of the loyalty due to his leader. He was a strong character and determined that Australia's representatives on the expedition should be fully appreciated. A man of his brilliance and wide interests, accustomed to influencing youth, would have found it easy to form a faction at the base without really intending to do so. That this did not happen was due partly to David's wisdom and common-sense, partly to the charm and vigilance of Shackleton. He was liked by his men: he was also respected, admired, and in a special way loved, for his weaknesses as well as for his strength.

If he did absent himself from the company from time to time, it was never for very long. He could seldom resist a joke, and a burst of laughter or the sound of an argument would always bring him out of his cubicle. He was always the life and soul of the party. The men who survive from that expedition well remember his tact and geniality and the way he took the lead in conversations at meal-times, discouraging gossip and dangerous personalities but always ready to promote, often even to provoke, an argument on a general subject.

Finally, the system by which each man took a turn with the domestic chores worked extremely well. Where there were no 'officers' and 'men', some coalescing in the party was bound to result. Friendships were broadened and strengthened in the knowledge that each man was pulling his weight. The job of night watchman, with its opportunities for brewing tea or cocoa, taking a bath or attending to personal laundry, was not unpopular. The duties of messman, if less agreeable, were done cheerfully, and inspired, incidentally, one of the best pieces of humorous writing that ever came out of the Antarctic.

Priestley's 'Trials of a Messman'⁴ was one of the pieces written under persuasion for use in the expedition magazine. Like the *South Polar Times*, this was to be at once a pastime and a memento of the expedition. With a party so very much smaller than Scott's, it was obvious that it could not be a periodical; and so Shackleton planned that the one volume should have at least technical advantages over its predecessor. It was to be a printed volume, and it was originally intended that it should be sold on their return to England. The *South Polar Times* had been printed by Smith, Elder & Co. in 1907* and had brought in some money for the funds of the National Antarctic Expedition; Shackleton wanted to do the same but with the expedition as publishers. However, some difficulty arose over the exact compensation to be given to the four people most concerned in the production of the book—Wild, Joyce, Marston and Day—and in the end, although a hundred copies were printed at Cape Royds, they were not sold.†　Presumably some were presented to benefactors of the expedition, and each member of the expedition received a copy. It is possible that some of the copies were never bound up.

Aurora Australis, which was at first to be called *Antarctic Ice-Flowers*, is a very different volume from the *South Polar Times*. Although it has its humorous items, there are none of the jokes or topical features of the *Discovery* production. It is an anthology rather than a magazine. That Shackleton took it very seriously may be seen in the two prefaces he wrote for it, each of which ends by apologising for the shortcomings of the book. He explains at some length that Wild and Joyce, instead

---

* This was a limited edition of 250 copies for private circulation; it was a facsimile of the original magazine.

† In 1909 Messrs. Heinemann brought out a limited edition of 300 copies of *The Antarctic Book*, as a third volume of the *de luxe* edition of *The Heart of the Antarctic*.¹² The two fore-titles, each headed 'The British Antarctic Expedition 1907', bear the signatures of the whole party. The book contains two of the contributions to the expedition magazine we are discussing, namely, Shackleton's poem 'Erebus' and Mawson's fantasy 'Bathybia'. There are five of Marston's drawings from the book, two of them illustrating 'Bathybia' and two showing aspects of Erebus; the last is a drawing of *Nimrod* on her journey south, which was perhaps Marston's best contribution to *Aurora Australis*. There are also five coloured lithographs, portraits of Shackleton, Adams, Marshall, Wild and Joyce. Decorative capital letters and the sign of the penguin are reproduced from the original book.

of serving an apprenticeship of seven years, had had to learn the art of printing and type-setting in three weeks, and that Marston had had to do the same with the process of lithography. He enlarges on the physical difficulties of producing the book—the size of the Rogues' Retreat, where the press was kept, and the fact that a candle had to be kept burning under the ink to keep it fluid.

His prefaces are most valuable, for *Aurora Australis* cannot be read like an ordinary book: it must be read with imagination. The reader must picture the various members of the party squaring up to their literary task in cubicles 6 × 7, with constant interruptions from work or idle friends, must picture the artist and the printers squaring up to *their* work in conditions still more adverse.

'It was winter' (wrote Marston later)[13] 'and dark, and cold. The work had to be done, in the intervals of more serious occupations, in a small room occupied by fifteen men, all of them following their own avocations, with whatever of noise, vibration and dirt might be incidental to these.

The inevitable state of such a hut, after doing all possible for cleanliness, can be imagined. Fifteen men shut up together, say during a blizzard which lasts a week. Nobody goes out unless on business; everybody who goes out brings in snow on his feet and clothes. Seal-blubber is burned, mixed with coal, for economy; the Blubber melts and runs out on the floor, the ordinary unsweepable soil of the place is a rich compost of all filth, cemented with blubber, more nearly resembling the soil of a whaling-station than anything else I know.

Dust from the stove fills the air and settles on the paper as it is being printed. If anything falls on the floor it is done for; if somebody jogs the compositor's elbow as he is setting up matter, and upsets the type into the mire, I can only leave the reader to imagine the result.'

Read like this, *Aurora Australis*, unique as an experiment in publishing, is seen also to be unique as a book. The *South Polar Times* expressed the mood of an expedition, intelligent and cheerful. *Aurora Australis* crystallises the temperaments of the writers.

There is the title-page, with Marston's lithograph of the Aurora, framed in an elaborate scroll, topped with two sailing ships. The workmanlike, pleasing design, the flamboyant colours are each characteristic of Marston. As an artist, he was not in the same class as Wilson, but his natural exuberance and his sense of wonder at the Antarctic scene come out in his paintings, just as his skill with his hands can be seen everywhere in the book, in the neat line-drawings and the good plain lay-out (see illustrations on p. 192 and opposite).

There is 'The Ascent of Mount Erebus', a flowing, romantic, forceful piece of writing as typical of Professor David as his fine despatches to the press written on the journey down. There is 'Trials of a Messman', a gay piece of irony in which the young geologist Priestley compensated himself for the dirt and discomfort of kitchen chores by describing the 'privileges' of the slave for the day; because of the keen eye of the writer, the piece gives a vivid picture of the interior of the hut and the organisation of the wintering party. There is 'A Pony Watch', in which Marston, under the name of Putty, gives an excitable, somewhat turgid impression of the storm on the journey down in the *Nimrod*, when Doctor had to be shot. There is 'Southward Bound', a nostalgic, patriotic poem by Marshall (under the name of Lapsus Linguae), again surveying the voyage to the South. There is 'An Interview with an Emperor', an odd little nightmare in Scottish idiom by the excitable Mackay; and 'Life under Difficulties', in which Murray dryly discussed the life-history of the Rotifer (a lowly, worm-like creature), his principal find in the biological world.

There is 'An Ancient Manuscript', in which Wild, calling himself Shellback, as he had done in the *South Polar Times*, described the beginnings of the expedition, and made some shrewd comments on his leader's exploring temperament. There is 'Bathybia', a curious and compelling fantasy beginning with an ordinary sledge journey into Victoria Land and eventually mixing the young Mawson's impressions of volcanic mountains, rotifers and the bare Antarctic plain into one extraordinary picture with a strange logic of its own.

And finally there are Shackleton's own contributions, signed with his pseudonym of *Discovery* days, Nemo. For his own Polar book, as for Scott's, he wrote a long descriptive poem. 'Erebus' (p. 502) is full of echoes of Swinburne and Longfellow, and full of the ardent resolve of the explorer. Very different was his second contribution, a piece of doggerel (p. 501) called 'Midwinter Night',* in which the night-watchman listens to the random mutterings of the sleepers and imagines their dreams. It is not distinguished poetry, but it reveals the rumbus-tious, joke-loving side of Shackleton's nature.

Just as the entries reflect the character of each writer, so the production of the book reflects the Antarctic scene. There is the neat trademark of the Penguins, executed in red and used at intervals through the book as a decoration. There are the board covers, made from Venesta packing cases, many with the legend 'British Antarctic Expedition' clearly to be read on the inside—covers which were thoroughly smoothed and sand-papered by Day, who also thonged the pages and made a thick leather spine to hold the covers. There is the title-page, with its amateurish but attractive type-setting, and the dedication to the Misses Dawson-Lambton, two generous benefactors. If this little volume provided occupation for many dark winter hours, it must since then

---

* Against this poem in the Contents list is the name *Nemo*, though it is signed *Veritas*. Marshall's Diary[14] makes it clear that the verses *were* Shackleton's.

have given pleasure and occupation to connoisseurs of the printed word.

Marston was officially editor, or editor in charge of *Aurora Australis*, but Shackleton, as editor-in-chief, no doubt did much to stimulate people to send in entries. He had many other devices with which to while away the time. He himself greatly enjoyed games of chess or poker, and like most Antarctic explorers before and after him, he seized every excuse for a party. There was Marston's birthday on 20 March, when they enjoyed turtle soup, blackcock and Christmas pudding, washed down with cider and beer; there was Marshall's on 23 May, when Roberts made a splendid cake; there was Day's, on 18 August, celebrated moderately, with a sing-song in the evening. There was Midwinter Day, too, traditional day of celebration in the Antarctic. For this occasion a four-page leaflet was printed, with a title-page, elegantly laid out, two drawings by Marston, and a menu both impressive and amusing.

After the feast, Shackleton distributed tins of toffee from Mrs. Shackleton, and numerous Christmas cards.

Throughout the winter of 1908, while gales shook the hut and the ponies rattled their chains outside, the party remained snug and cheerful; indeed Priestley[2] was surprised to find how surprisingly ordinary and comfortable it all was.

'The days pass very quickly and uneventfully [he wrote on 16 May]. None of us certainly have felt any ill effects from the darkness and occasional blizzards. Personally I feel as well as ever I did in my life, the only indisposition I suffer from, being indigestion after particularly rich dinners. . . . I have heard it said frequently on the way out here, that a well managed Expedition was nothing but a glorified picnic with a spice of danger, and our stay here has certainly upheld, so far, the truth of the remark for I never experienced as much pleasure and wild excitement when eating an outdoor meal under a notice "Trespassers will be prosecuted", as I have done here in living a very primitive life in a well equipped Expedition. We have now passed successfully through one month out of the four winter months, and I see no reason, given ordinary luck, why the next three should not be almost equally pleasant. Real hardships will resume their sway during the spring sledging Expeditions, which however, in the bliss of ignorance, we are all looking forward to. . . .'

After Midwinter Day, when they could begin to think once more of seeing the sun, the pace of the expedition began to quicken. Shackleton had spent much time, during the hours in his cubicle, in writing and reading, and much in planning. There had been conferences with Dr. Marshall, who was making a study of dietetics, about the food for the wintering party and about the vital sledging rations. Much time,

PUBLISHED AT THE
WINTER QUARTERS
OF THE BRITISH
ANTARCTIC EXPED
ITION, 1907, DURING
THE WINTER MON
THS OF APRIL, MAY,
JUNE, JULY, 1908.
ILLUSTRATED WITH
LITHOGRAPHS AND
ETCHINGS; BY
GEORGE MARSTON

PRINTED AT THE SIGN OF
'THE PENGUINS'; BY JOYCE
AND WILD.
LATITUDE 77° ·· 32' SOUTH
LONGITUDE 166° ·· 12' EAST
ANTARCTICA

TRADE MARK

The title-page of the magazine of the British Antarctic (Nimrod)
Expedition, designed by George Marston

RGS 48

One to be smoked on 1ˢᵗ of Each mouth!

	1ˢᵗ ᵧₛ	2ⁿᵈ
August	1	13
September	2	14
October	3	15
November	4	16
December	5	17
January	6	18
February	7	19
March	8	20
April	9	21
May	10	22
June	11	23
July	12	24

Emily Shackleton contrived this cigarette ration-box for her husband on the British Antarctic Expedition

24,000 New Zealand postage stamps were specially overprinted 'King Edward VII Land' in green for use by members of the expedition and a postmark inscribed 'BRIT. ANTARCTIC EXPED.' was used to cancel mail posted from the N.Z. base. Illustrated is a block of four stamps from the collection of Mr. H. E. J. Evans, Secretary of the Polar Postal History Society of Great Britain

One Thousand Feet below the active cone of Mount Erebus

The crater of Erebus, 900 feet deep and half a mile wide. Steam is seen rising on th
left. The photograph was taken from the lower part of the crater edge

too, was spent in planning for the Southern Journey and the subsidiary journeys which would be needed to help it along.

Shackleton's greatest gift as an organiser was his flexibility and his power to think quickly. His gift for improvisation had made it possible for him to turn his mind from the campaign planned from Balloon Inlet, and to work out very quickly an alternative plan for a base in McMurdo Sound, so that no time need be wasted. In this, it is true, he had been greatly helped by Professor David, who was well aware of the scientific opportunities at Scott's old base. However, the planning and replanning of the Southern Journey was Shackleton's own affair and this kept him occupied, and sometimes preoccupied, during the winter.

It was not for some time that he finally decided that the polar party must consist of four men and not six. Earlier in the winter, he had discussed plans for a party of six men in two three-man tents with Wild and Joyce, and they both expected to go. With only four ponies, the number must be cut down.

It was in July that Shackleton finally chose the three men to accompany him. He had to take various points into consideration. The journey to the South Magnetic Pole, most important branch of the scientific research, must be made by a scientific party. Professor David and Mawson were reserved for this, with Mackay to help with his strength and capability and to act as doctor to the party. Day's job was with the motor, which would be needed to shift stores forward whenever the surface was suitable. Priestley was to make a journey to the western mountains and carry out a sustained geological investigation. Murray, with his age and experience, was to remain in command at the base, a position which would assume increased responsibility when the time came for the ship and the different sledging parties to rendezvous.

The party of six men had fairly obviously been Adams, Marshall, Wild, Joyce, Brocklehurst and Shackleton. These six had taken every opportunity to gain sledging experience and each one had a claim to be included in the Southern party.

The final choice, which might have been difficult, was in fact made mainly on medical grounds. Brocklehurst, after the loss of his toe and the illness consequent on the operation, was not fit to make an extended journey. On 12 July, when Marshall examined the six men, he reported also that Joyce's physical condition was not perfect: his pulse was not strong and there was some weakness of the liver. Wild he found 'very sound'. Of Shackleton he recorded 'Pulm[onary] Systolic murmur still present' (he had examined him earlier, on 3 June). Throughout the great Southern Journey the doctor was to watch Shackleton closely for signs of weakness; he was to find, as Scott and Wilson had done some

13

years earlier, that it was not Shackleton's great strength of physique
that kept him going so much as his strength of will.

The short runs with ponies and dogs taken in the autumn had given
the novices little idea of what an extended journey could be like.
Consequently Shackleton resolved to begin spring sledging early in
August, sparing the dogs and ponies while the temperatures were still
very low and relying largely on man-hauling.

For the first journey he himself led David and Armytage, with one
sledge and provisions for a fortnight. They left Cape Royds on 12
August. The pony Quan pulled the sledge for an hour, but was sent
back before they got to Cape Barne, as the going was heavy. They
reached Glacier Tongue on the following day, and Hut Point on 14
August. Shackleton[3] was keenly interested to see the old scenes again.
'There was the place where, years before, when the *Discovery* was lying
fast in the ice close to the shore, we used to dig for the ice that was required for the supply of fresh water. The marks of the picks and shovels
were still to be seen. I noticed an old case bedded in the ice, and remembered the day when it had been thrown away.'

The *Discovery* hut had never had a very homely atmosphere and
now, with coal littering the floor, mixed with snow that had drifted in,
with cases of food lying about and a gap where the stove had been, it
had a neglected and unappealing look. Shackleton planned to use the
hut as a stores depôt, since it was twenty miles nearer to his objective
than Cape Royds, and besides, his own winter quarters would be cut
off from the south if the ice should break up in the Sound. The three
men began to make the hut habitable, piling up the cases to make a small
inner hut in which it would be warm enough to sleep. The next day
they pushed out on to the Barrier.

Here conditions were bad for travelling. The snow was soft and deep
over the ice, and the temperature fell in the early evening to −56° F.
At night it was even lower and they could not sleep but lay shivering
in the tent in their single sleeping bags. On the next day, 16 August,
Shackleton noticed signs of a blizzard coming up and they returned to
the *Discovery* hut just in time to escape it.

They were kept here for five days, during which time they put the
place in order and made it as comfortable as possible for the parties
Shackleton determined to send from Cape Royds each week with stores
for the Southern party. They got back to Cape Royds at 5 p.m. on
22 August, having made a valuable reconnaissance.

For the next month stores were steadily moved south to Hut Point.
Temperatures continued very low and every member of the party had
his share of discomfort.

On 14 September, the weather and the light now being improved,
Day unpacked the car engine from its winter case and reassembled the

machine. Numerous journeys were made, at first to test the various parts, to decide on the kind of wheel to be used, and so on; later, to haul stores. The surface was never entirely suitable, but across the bay-ice in the Sound, when the car hauled provisions for the party going to the western mountains, it did wonderful work. Day was particularly proud of its performance on 19 September, when it took a sledge and 750 lb. of stores to within a quarter of a mile of Glacier Tongue. The machine had done at least thirty miles at a speed ranging from three to fifteen miles an hour. 'The three men* left the winter quarters at 9.30 a.m. and arrived back at 6.45 p.m., having accomplished an amount of work that would have occupied six men for two or three days without the assistance of the car.'[3]

But Shackleton had regretfully to decide that he would not be able to take the car right along the Barrier, as he had hoped. He found the Barrier surface had changed considerably since 1902, and if he took the car with a supporting party on the first part of the Southern Journey it would be of little help and possibly even a hindrance. It was certainly no easy task to control it even on its straightforward journey and on the bay-ice. Priestley[2] described in his Diary on 3 October one dramatic journey towards the west.

'For several miles we went away at anything up to 15 miles an hour and over a fair surface and kept up an average pace of 7 or 8 miles an hour until an engine trouble necessitated a stoppage and the taking down of the carburettor as the inlet jet had got stopped up. Mackay who was officiating at the handle staved his wrist and as it was subsequently ascertained, broke one of the small bones. As he had considerable difficulty in swinging himself on to the back of the car after this, he was forced to ride on the sledge and this much increased the drag. After this stoppage the surface became consider-ably worse and the drifts thicker and more numerous and we had to hold ourselves ready to jump off the car at a moment's notice and shove her through the drifts and in the worst ones it was necessary to swing her out by catching hold of the spokes of the front wheel and rocking the car backwards and forwards, gradually increasing the swing until it was possible to heave the wheels out of the holes they had got into. A second accident was occasioned by the Professor catching hold of the spokes of the back wheel by mistake. When the engine was started the wheels raced, and the Professor's arms were unpleasantly strained. About 13 miles out from home in a more vigorous swing than usual I caught my fingers between the front wheel spokes and the brake mechanism, tearing skin and flesh off the third and fourth fingers of my right hand and crushing the nail of the little finger. The blood came out in streams and I was forced to borrow the Professor's handkerchief to bind them up.'

* Day, Brocklehurst and Adams.

The car had more tricks to play. Fifteen miles out, in a belt of pressure ice, there was more swinging and lifting, and they decided to turn. The Professor crushed a finger badly and bruised his thigh while they were pushing the car up a snow slope, and when they had reached the good ice and hoped to put on speed, they found the motor would only run on one cylinder at about two miles an hour. Mackay finally decided to walk back, and so missed the only good part of the journey, when the car reached, and maintained, a speed of twenty miles an hour. Now, however, the bulky loads on the sledges caused them to capsize when they were caught by the wind, and the journey ended with the professor lying on his stomach on the sleeping bags and Priestley running beside the sledge holding the load. 'We had . . . been out from 7 a.m. to 10 p.m.,' he comments, 'with only a plasmon lunch and some prunes between breakfast and supper, so we may be fairly said to have earned every inch we made.'

It was certainly by inches, as often as not, that the car moved. Shackleton had proved to future expeditions, at some expense to his own, that car wheels, whether rubber or wood, were not suited to Antarctic journeys. However, he had wisely not relied to any great extent on his most experimental form of transport. Man, as a beast of burden, was more predictable.

Using man-hauling parties, by mid-September he had at the *Discovery* hut the necessary stores and provisions for ninety-one days for the Southern Party, plus a ration of 10 lb. a day for each of the four ponies, made up of maize, Maujee ration and a little compressed fodder bought in Australia. The maize had to be ground ready for the journey, and each hauling party had to spend some hours at the grinding mill.

The bulkiness of the ponies' rations was a considerable disadvantage. For his one depôt journey Shackleton decided to take on as much pony food as could be managed to a point a hundred miles south of Hut Point. On the first stage of the Southern Journey, on the Barrier, he intended to steer much further out from the land (i.e., on to the Barrier ice) than Scott had done in 1902. He might therefore have no landmarks at all for a considerable distance, and a depôt in the expanse of snow, however marked, might be missed. He did not want to take this risk with rations for the men, which they would pull themselves.

On 22 September a party of six—Adams, Marshall, Wild, Joyce, Marston and Shackleton—left Cape Royds with two three-man tents and two three-man sleeping bags and a load of 170 lb. per man. The car, working at about six miles an hour, took the load as far as Inaccessible Island and then left the party to haul the sledges for the rest of the way. They spent the night at the *Discovery* hut, and pushed out on to the Barrier towards White Island. Here, on 25 September, they were halted for a day by a blizzard, and then slowed up by a badly crevassed surface. On 6 October they made Depôt A at 79·36° S., 120 miles from their own base; a gallon tin of oil and 167 lb. of pony maize were piled up, and marked with an upturned sledge and a black flag on a bamboo rod. The return journey was made in very severe weather and when they reached the *Discovery* hut on 13 October their food was finished, though they had not had to cut down their daily ration. From this point a day's journey brought them to Cape Royds. The car met them some way out and they drove home in comfort.

It was sometimes said afterwards that Shackleton would have been wise if he had made at least one more spring depôt-laying journey. Certainly a dump of provisions for the men, further south than Depôt A, would have greatly increased their margin of safety. Perhaps one reason why he did not send out another party was the lack of conspicuous landmarks; perhaps the severe and unpredictable weather, which had lengthened the depôt journey just described to over three weeks, made him fear that another party might not get back until it was time for him to start. At all events, he now relied on the help of a supporting party, as Scott had done, and on the ponies, which had responded magnificently to the careful training they were given.

Shackleton's original estimate[15] had been that the ponies would be able to drag up to 1,800 lb. weight and would be able to travel 20 to 25 miles a day. Later he made his calculations on the basis of 650 lb. per pony. He remained confident that they would travel fast enough to reach the Pole in the time at his disposal.

His calculations, and his optimistic manner of explaining them, certainly convinced the rest of the party. They could not tell what kind of country the party would meet after they had passed Scott's Furthest South, and one or two of them felt that the ration was a very tight one. All the same, nearly all of them thought Shackleton would 'get the Pole'.

The Northern (Magnetic Pole) Party, consisting of the Professor, Mawson and Mackay, had left Cape Royds on 5 October, during Shackleton's absence on the Barrier, and orders were given for Priestley, Armytage and Brocklehurst to leave at the beginning of December for the survey in the western mountains, on which journey they would take extra provisions for the returning Northern Party. It was planned that these two parties should join up, at the end of the Magnetic Pole journey, at a point to the west which they had named Butter Point. David was to take Mackay and Armytage back to Cape Royds, leaving a message at Glacier Tongue if open water should prevent him from reaching the hut. When he made contact with Cape Royds, either on foot or by ship, he was to load up with stores and return to Butter Point. Here he could continue with geological work at his discretion and was given permission to try to climb Mount Lister, provided he was sure of returning to Hut Point or to Glacier Tongue not later than 7 February 1909. Shackleton's instructions to David included a description of how, if the sun should be obscured, he could signal to Cape Royds with petrol and some of the fodder left at Glacier Tongue, and went into strict detail about whether or not this party should receive their letters from the ship when they reported to the Tongue. In these and all his orders, the leader left nothing to chance: those which survive show his meticulous and careful planning.*

Shackleton clearly intended to give the Professor every chance for geological research, whether or not he found the Southern Magnetic Pole; but there was something he considered as important in the western mountains. After the two parties joined up, Mawson, Brocklehurst and Priestley were to go to Dry Valley and to other points in the mountains of South Victoria Land. Here Priestley was to make geological observations, Brocklehurst to take photographs, and Mawson, with their assistance if necessary, was, quite simply, to look for 'minerals of economic value or precious stones'. It was natural that any expedition to an unknown country should entertain the idea of mineral wealth; but under the practical orders may be detected Shackleton's constant, romantic preoccupation with 'treasure'.

These instructions to David and Mawson, evidently written after Shackleton's return from his depôt journey, were to be taken by Armytage and his two companions to Butter Point and handed over. Further vital instructions relating to the Southern Party were given in writing to Murray, who, as we have seen, was officially put in charge at Cape Royds from the day of Shackleton's departure. In late December Day and Marston, using the car if possible, were to take a load of stores to the *Discovery* hut, and on 15 January 1909 Joyce was to take charge of a party, with Day and Marston, to lay a depôt at Minna Bluff, with enough provisions to take the Southern Party from there to Hut Point. They were to make their depôt 'about 8 miles off the Bluff with the end peak of the Bluff in line with the top of Mount Discovery'. They were to plant three depôt flags—'one at the depôt, one one mile inside and one 2 miles inside the depôt'. They were then to return to the hut, reload and proceed once more to the depôt. Here they were to wait for the Southern Party until 10 February, and if it had not appeared, were to return to Hut Point and from there to the ship, which would pick them up at whatever position it could then reach according to the state of the ice in the Sound. This depôt-laying party was to use the dogs 'if they are satisfactory'.

Shackleton's instructions both to Joyce and to Murray were designed

* Shackleton's own copies of these and other orders, in his own hand, survive among the family papers. There are letters to Adams, Marshall, Murray, Marston, Joyce, Mawson and David.[16]

to meet every contingency, and they bear witness to the extreme care
which he took for the safety of his men. The risks were exactly calculated,
and the time schedule worked out so that there was no chance of
anyone being away from Cape Royds at the time when the ship must
finally leave the South for New Zealand.

To Murray Shackleton also wrote instructions to be given to the
Master of the *Nimrod*, instructions first about picking up or, if
necessary, searching for the parties in the Western Mountains. Again,
allowance was made for every possible contingency, every possible
condition of the bay-ice.

With regard to his own party, Shackleton's orders again took into
account the fact that the ice might still be firm in the bay as far north
as Cape Royds or it might be broken out to any point up to Cape
Armitage. Signals, at the nearest possible point, were to be looked for
from the Southern Party until 25 February. If nothing had been heard
from them by then, Murray was to land at Cape Royds enough coal,
stores and extra clothing to support a party of seven men for one year.
He was then to ask for three volunteers for a relief party. ('If there are
no volunteers, which is highly improbable, you are to select three men
and order them to stay.') These men were to proceed south to the
168th meridian, with the dogs, and search as long as the weather
allowed, and thereafter to conduct a further search in the following
summer. Arrangement for the relief of such a search party by ship in
the summer of 1910 was provided in instructions to Messrs. Kingsford
Dorman, as agents for the expedition.

Shackleton intended to give himself every possible chance to reach
the Pole, and in talking over the vital question of dates with Murray,
was persuaded to take a chance with the ship.

'After reading the above instructions to you: you suggested that
it might be as well if latitude were given for you and the acting
master of the Nimrod to consult as to a further de(n)tention of the
ship beyond the 1st of March 1909. I therefore give you permission
to do so: but the ship must on the first of March steam to the
entrance of MacMurdo Sound to see the ice conditions and if there
is no heavy pack likely to hold her up she can return to Cape Royds
again: but I think that the utmost limit you should remain here is
the 10th of March 1909 as if we have not returned by then something
very serious must have happened.'

The letters to Murray also provided that if Shackleton perished on
the journey Adams would take command, and after him Marshall.
Shackleton realised very well the complications that might arise if he
should not get back. He made it perfectly clear that, in such circumstances, Marshall was to take over the lecturing (with exact provision
for the percentages he was to take at certain stages); Murray was to

remain in charge of working up the zoological collections, on a salary; David was to be in charge of the rest of the working up of the scientific results, with the financial compensation already arranged. Priestley was to be paid to work with him in Australia; and Joyce was to finish *Aurora Australis* and assist Kingsford Dorman to produce this in England, the proceeds to be divided between the four men concerned in its production.*

It is very clear from those of Shackleton's letters that survive that he felt deeply responsible for the future of the men whom he had thus removed for the best part of two years from their normal lives. To Joyce in particular he wrote that he had instructed Kingsford Dorman to help him to find work, and that he had also written to William Beardmore about him; and it is probable that a similar arrangement was made in the case of Wild, so that if Shackleton did not return, the two men who were, in a way, most dependent on him should not suffer. To each man he gave also written promises of equipment; in some cases they were to keep dogs if they wanted to. Marshall was to have a good deal of surveying and photographic equipment, Priestley geological tools, and so on.

Further, Shackleton intended that if they reached the Pole, everyone should share in the success. He had already, during the winter, spoken to most members of the party about an increase in salary; this became his typical way of expressing his appreciation of loyalty and good service. These prospective increases were now recorded in letters to each member of the expedition. In addition the men were promised bonuses, considerable sums of one, two and three thousand pounds according to their relative positions on the expedition. The members of the Southern Party were naturally promised larger sums. It was made perfectly clear that these bonuses would only be paid 'after the payment of all the liabilities I have incurred on behalf of the Expedition' and 'if the expedition is successful'.

The generosity is typical; so is the underlying conviction that the expedition *would* be successful. It was not Shackleton's fault that one or two members of the expedition made the natural psychological error of regarding the money as already theirs, but his optimism did, in fact, lead to some trouble for him.

Shackleton showed a robust realism in his attitude to his enterprise. He had always had every intention of making money out of the dash for the Pole, and he took it for granted that his men, like him, would find it possible to be at once romantic and practical about the matter. Unfortunately his talk of money, thoughtless as it sometimes was,

---

* It is not known what financial arrangements were made when the *Antarctic Book* was published in 1909; as we have seen, the copies of *Aurora Australis* printed in the Antarctic were not marketed.

hopeful as it always was, bred suspicion and distrust in one or two of his party. It might have been better for him if he had been less precise and careful in the arrangements he tried to make for the welfare of each of his men.

Some of his promises he was quite unable to fulfil, and this caused ill-feeling. But his responsible attitude, however dangerous to himself later, when the expedition returned in debt, is one which can only be applauded.

The whole buoyant, generous nature of the man towards those of his comrades who were completely loyal is seen best in a letter[16] to Murray, written from Cape Royds on 23 October.*

My dear Murray,

As you will only open this letter if I am dead I here express my opinion of all your services: You have never for one moment caused me the slightest anxiety in any way: I am most deeply indebted to you for the good quiet influence you have had on the Expedition: and also for the good sound advice you have given me. I know full well your retiring nature about accepting money and it is a pleasant thing indeed for me to feel that I could talk to you so freely: But Murray man must live and good work must be rewarded: so I have increased your salary from £250 p.a. to 350 p.a. to date from Jan 1st 1908. In event of you being in command your pay is to be £500 from date of taking command: If there are funds you are to be kept on at £400 p.a. till the work is all finished as you will have it all on your shoulders. If there are not funds you will understand and my instructions will enable you to know what to do. Messrs Kingsford Dorman are my executors and this letter is to be shown to them when you get home after my death and they will act on it: I think it sufficient in your case to write this to you and have not made a copy. I am not a good hand at saying things in praise but I hope you will know that your high character has been an incentive to me keeping up my heart in downward times: and I am

Yours most earnestly.

Ernest H. Shackleton,

Commander B.A.E.

P.S. You are to have all your biological equipment. Your pay of 350 p.a. is independent of my return.   E. H. Shackleton.

To his wife Shackleton wrote[17], less youthfully but just as candidly as he had done from the *Discovery*, a letter to be read only after his death and expressing his devotion to her. Implicit in the letter is the feeling that he may have done wrong thus to risk his life and leave his family, but that the work—the last and greatest piece of exploration—justified

* The letter was to be read in the case of Shackleton's death and otherwise to be returned to him unopened. It is preserved in S.F.P.

his action. The supporting party brought back a final note[17] he had scrawled just before he stepped out, with his three companions, on the final stage of the great journey.

My darling wife and children,

In case I do not come back from this journey. Remember that my last thoughts will be ever with you and that in the future life which I believe in we shall meet again and that you are my love my everything.

Your husband,

Ernest

All was now ready at Cape Royds. Shackleton's various letters, the result of much thought, were all written by 28 October, together with copies for the expedition agents. The sledge loads were expertly packed. Shackleton was satisfied with the equipment he was taking, and with the rations which he and Marshall had worked out together. He was allowing only one ounce a day more per man than Scott had allowed on the Southern Journey of 1902–03, but he placed great reliance on the quality of his pemmican (from the firm of Beauvais, in Copenhagen) and of his biscuits, which contained a high proportion of wholemeal. Everything had been done to make the journey a success and Shackleton intended that it should be so.

He was in an excited and determined mood, which is reflected in his diary[18] the next day:

'last night as we sat at dinner the evening sun entered through the ventilator and the circle of light rested (sic) shone full on the portrait of HM. slowly it moved across and found the portrait of Her Majesty: it seemed an omen of good luck for only on this day and at that particular time could this have happened and today we started to strive & plant Her flag on the last spot of the world that counts as worth the striving for though ungilded by aught but adventure.'

Chapter XII

EARLY in the morning of 29 October 1908, Shackleton's motor transport led off the great journey, taking the sledges on to the bay-ice; and at 9.30 the supporting party (Armytage, Brocklehurst, Day, Joyce, Marston and Priestley) set out with all the loads. The motor was running well and the car was soon out of sight. The Southern Party, leading the horses, left the hut at 10.0; only Murray and Roberts were left to see them go. 'A glorious day for our start', Shackleton wrote[1]: 'brilliant sunshine and a cloudless sky, a fair wind from the north; in fact everything that could conduce to an auspicious beginning.'

The first week of the journey, however, was to be full of setbacks. Shackleton and his three companions had not been travelling an hour when Socks went lame. This brought home to them sharply the dangerous position they were in, with only four ponies, and Shackleton realised at once that they would have to cut down their speed until the animal recovered. They had started their journey five days earlier in the year than the Southern Journey of 1902–03, and had expected to increase this advantage of time by the greater speed of the ponies. The cheerfulness of the party was not improved when, while they were halted for lunch, Grisi kicked Adams severely just below the knee, exposing the bone.

They pressed on to Glacier Tongue. Here the car had been halted by the soft snow, so Day took it back to the base, with Priestley and Brocklehurst to help him as his foot was weak from an accident. The rest of the party settled down by the crusher at the Glacier Tongue depôt to grind maize, and by eight o'clock in the evening had 600 lb. of pony-food prepared.

Lying in their camp that night, with Erebus steaming in the distance, and the noises of a seal rookery not far off, Shackleton confided to his diary, 'At last we are out on the long trail after 4 years thought and work. I pray that we may be successful for my Heart has been so much in this.'

The next few days were spent in preliminary work round the *Discovery* hut, which was their real starting place. The four members of the Southern Party left the Tongue for Hut Point on the morning of 30 October, taking all the ponies and three sledges. Socks went fairly well but could not pull. The supporting party remained behind to prepare some more maize. Shackleton's party reached the hut at 3.0 in the afternoon. They were determined to enjoy the comfort of a roof over their heads while they could. They allowed themselves all the luxuries they wanted in the way of food, including some liqueurs they had brought from Cape Royds. Wild killed a seal so that they would have plenty of fresh meat before going over to sledging rations. Physically they were in splendid shape and the good mixed diet they had enjoyed at the base was very much in their favour.

On the last day of the month Shackleton took Marshall and Armytage back to Glacier Tongue with the ponies, to bring on the remaining pony-food. Meanwhile the rest of the party repacked sledges and had a few hours geologising in the hills. At Glacier Tongue Shackleton found the car had not arrived (it should have brought a load of salt for the ponies and one or two pieces of equipment) so he walked on to Cape Royds, arriving there at 11.30 at night. He had done twenty-three miles in six hours and had no doubt worked off a good deal of impatience at the slow pace of these first days.

The next day he was taken on the car as far as Inaccessible Island, and the three men then took the sledges on to Hut Point. Shackleton decided they must take one more day off, to make sure of Socks. Although he wrote of the pony's lameness as 'almost a disaster for we want every pound of carrying power', he was well satisfied with the performance of the animals.

3 November saw the real start of the journey towards the Pole.* Some of the sledges had been taken out on to the Barrier the previous day, and at 9.30 a.m. the two parties left the hut, 'Quan pulling 660, Grisi 615, Socks 600, Chinaman 600. 5 men hauling 660: 153 being pony food for our party'.[1] The surface was very soft, the ponies at times sinking up to their bellies. Brocklehurst photographed the group, with sledge flags and the Queen's Union Flag flying, and they set off.

The Southern Party and supporting party took it in turns with the man-hauling, but even with this help it was obvious that the pace of the men could not equal that of the ponies, and Shackleton decided to send the supporting party back in two more days. The heat of the sun, as well as the soft surface, made travelling uncomfortable. Fretting at the delays, contemplating the next part of the journey over dangerously crevassed country, Shackleton for once let his feelings show. 'The skipper is rather irritable and excited', Wild wrote[3] that night: it was the first and last time that he made a note of any break in the leader's equanimity.

The weather continued fine, but on 4 November the sky was clouded, the light very bad and the going heavy, and on the following day snow obliterated most of the landmarks. Frozen furrows of ice under the soft snow made it easy for men and ponies to stumble. They were now near White Island and Shackleton was steering south-east to avoid

* See pp. 232–33 for a map of the long journey with positions of depôts.

crevasses, but the light was so bad that they had to rely on compasses and could not always hold the course.

In the afternoon they got into crevassed country and at 3.0 Shackleton decided to camp and wait for clearer weather, though their day's march had been only nine miles. He was sure the storm would have blown itself out by morning, but on 6 November a blizzard kept them encamped. They cut their lunch ration to two biscuits, to compensate for the wasted day. The food they had with them had been calculated to last for 91 days but Shackleton hoped with careful management to spin it out for 110; '. . . if we have not done the job in that time it is God's will', he wrote.*

The ponies were benefiting by the rest, standing tails to the weather and eating pretty well. The men, each lying in his own sleeping bag, reading and talking, hoped for better weather the next day. They were to be disappointed. Early in the morning they cleared the drifted snow from the sledges and by 8.30 were ready for the start. The supporting party, who were now to return to Hut Point, gave them three cheers as they set off into a dead white wall, the ponies pulling splendidly. But the march was abortive. The crevasses became so dangerous and the wind and snow so trying, that they camped again after doing only half a mile. Shackleton's diary at this time is full of remarks about the need for patience—a virtue which he had never had in excess but which he laboured to acquire.

They were forced to remain in camp until 9 November. They were now living in two tents, and Shackleton arranged that they were to change tent-partners each week, so that the party should not form into two groups. Psychologically this was a sound move, for Adams and Marshall had been close friends from the beginning of the expedition, and Wild tended to a rather belligerent loyalty to his leader. To a certain degree the Southern Party, at the outset, did fall into two parties of two; but it returned a weary but close group of four.

In the tents in these early November days they lay in their bags, each facing the delay in his own way. Shackleton was reading Shakespeare's comedies and Marshall the Bible. At this time Wild was cook with Marshall assisting, and the other two took meals in their tent, while attending to the pony work. They cut down once more on their rations, and on 8 November they had a cold lunch so as to use the cooker to make a hot mash for the ponies, who were not standing the storm very well.

9 November dawned fine and clear and, after digging out the sledges, the four men walked out to prospect a track through the crevasses

* In his diary on 13 November Shackleton[1] said they were going to try to make the rations last for 120 days.

which still lay all round them. These ran mostly south-east and north-west, but some curved to the south and some to the east. As Shackleton[1] said, 'There was nothing for it but to trust to Providence. We had to cross them somewhere'.

It was still early in the morning when they launched out into this dangerous country, and they expected to travel over it for some time. But in fact the only serious difficulty presented itself in the first quarter of a mile when Chinaman went down a crack about two feet wide. They got him out, but they found that two yards ahead of the spot the same crack widened to twenty feet, with no visible bottom. Although the ponies seemed very tired, the day's march was just over fourteen miles and they all felt more hopeful. The next few days also saw good distances, though the surface was very variable ('The Barrier is as wayward and as changeable as the sea', Shackleton commented[1]) and the light not always good. Shackleton, finding it difficult to prospect a way with snow-goggles on, took his off for a time and paid for it with an attack of snow blindness.

On 14 November, in their evening camp, he and Marshall were plotting their position on the chart when Wild, who had been outside to see to the ponies, shouted that he had spotted Depôt A, laid earlier in the spring. They were up to it by 9.20 on the following morning and spent some time redistributing weights and calculating what to leave here for the return journey. Reluctantly they deposited some spare gear which would only add to their weight, and a tin of sardines and a pot of blackcurrant jam that had been intended for Christmas Day. But it was more important to take on the extra food for the ponies, who were proving of such great value to the party, and who on the following day, 16 November, helped towards a record mileage of seventeen miles up to the 80th parallel, in spite of a crust of snow through which they sank heavily.

Shackleton, looking back, was well pleased with their progress during the past week. He was thinking and talking much about that other Southern Journey, and comparing their present mileage with the time when he 'was toiling along 5 miles a day over the same ground'. Their luck was not to be relied on, however, for the ensuing week was to be very hard for man and beast.

Each man had become attached to his own particular pony, and the temperaments of the animals provided a useful topic of conversation. Quan, the clown of the outfit, was a particularly knowing animal, who, Shackleton was sure, watched the men and provoked them by deliberately chewing his harness when they were looking. In one week he consumed 'the greater part of the inside of a horse cloth about a fathom of rope, several pieces of leather and other odds and ends such as nosebag buckle but his digestion is marvellous and he seems to thrive on it. He would rather eat a yard of creosoted rope than his maize and maujee indeed, he often in sheer wantonness throws it all over the snow'.[1]

The friendly ponies were all the better for being treated as pets and as individuals. It was obvious, however, that the surface they were now covering would have been far easier for a team of dogs. Chinaman, the oldest of them, was visibly flagging, and his fetlocks were badly chafed by the snow-crust. Shackleton decided that he must be shot when they had laid the next depôt.

The bad surface was a strain on the men too, and besides, they felt in these few days a nervous strain from the complete emptiness and immensity of the Barrier—for snowstorms were obliterating all traces of the distant land.

Both Marshall and Shackleton were deeply struck by the strangeness of the country, and the brief, practical entries in Wild's diary form an interesting contrast to their descriptions of it. With energy still to write at great length in his diary, Shackleton[1] tried to express the poetry of the place, and, implicitly, the inspiration that drew him back to the South.

'The whole place and condition seem so strange and unlike any-thing else in the world in our experience that one cannot describe them in fitting words: At one moment one thinks of Coleridge's A Mariner Alone alone. All all alone. Alone on a wide wide sea: and then when the mazy clouds spring silently from either hand and drift quickly across our zenith not followed by any wind it seems almost uncanny: Then comes a puff of wind from the N then from the S and anon from the E or W seeming to obey no law acting on erratic impulses It seems as though we were truly at the worlds end and were bursting in on the birthplace of the clouds and the nesting home of the four winds: and that we mortals were being watched with a jealous eye by these children of Nature To add to all this weird sort of impression that seems to grow on one in the seemingly limitless waste. the sun tonight was surround(ed) by mock suns and in the zenith was a bow turning away from the great vertical circle around the sun: all these circles and bows the colour of the rainbow. . . .'

The waste of snows might call forth poetic thoughts, but it was unprofitable for the travellers. So long as the land remained obliterated, they were obliged to steer by compass, with an occasional sun-sight. It was not until 22 November that the weather cleared and they were able to see what lay ahead and to their right, great snow-clad mountains rising beyond Mount Longstaff and to the north of Mount Markham. None of these peaks had been seen in 1902, when Scott's party had been much closer in to the foothills, and Shackleton and his companions were cheered to see that the coast trended south and east and therefore offered them a good prospect for their journey.

They were now working with three ponies, Chinaman having been shot on the previous evening. They had left a second depôt (B) at this spot, with enough stores and oil to see them back to Depôt A. The food that was left consisted chiefly of 50 lb. of meat from Chinaman. The rest of the horsemeat they enjoyed greatly, whether fried, or eaten raw, in strips dipped in fat. Wild especially was glad of it for he had been suffering from an upset stomach for three days and had not been able to eat any pemmican. He managed 'to lower quite a respectable amount' and thought it just like good beef.

At this time too Adams had some trouble with a tooth, and Marshall had two shots at it before he finally got it out. Otherwise the general health of the party was excellent and they were all in high spirits, particularly because of the new land which they could now see ahead of them—a range of mountains with sharp peaks running westward from Mount Markham, a table-topped mountain to the south between Mounts Longstaff and Markham, and a wide strait or inlet, with another lofty range south-east from Longstaff just coming into view.

As they pushed forward they could see that there seemed to be no straight coastline but a series of inlets and capes opening at all angles, with this lofty range continuing to the south. The Barrier remained 'level as a billiard table', and Shackleton was very conscious of the 'limitless solitude' in which they marched. They were pleased, however, with the distances they had so far been able to make. Wild wrote cautiously that he was beginning to think that they might get to the Pole, but he was not so sure about the return journey, and feared that at best they would be too late for the ship.

On 26 November they passed Scott's Furthest South, and made their night camp in latitude 82°.18½′, two miles beyond. They celebrated this by sipping from a four-ounce bottle of orange curaçao which Emily Shackleton had presented to the expedition. The weather was not clear enough for a 'souvenir picture' but the following day was fine and sunny and Shackleton took a photograph of their lunch camp, with Mount Longstaff in the background and their sledge-flags flying.

They were now a month ahead of the 1902–03 journey, in time, and although the three ponies were falling off in condition, Shackleton had good reason to be pleased with their averages. At the same time he was not altogether at ease about the mountains ahead, which were trending to the eastward so as to be directly in their path. His calculations had been made in the hope that they might not meet massive obstructions on their way to the Pole. Mountain-climbing would considerably upset these calculations. Besides, the Barrier itself was now showing signs of change. They noticed that they were moving over long undulations, the widest about a mile and a half from crest to crest, the rise about one in 500. The first indication they had of this came when the mound they

The old crater of Erebus, with an older crater in the background. Altitude 11,000 feet. The active cone is still higher

'The Boss', 1908

had built that morning disappeared before they had gone a quarter of a mile. Wild described this feature of the Barrier as being like 'a long and quiet deep sea swell'.

This same night Grisi was shot, for he had been growing weaker and had been suffering from snow-blindness. In place of the cairn of snow they had been putting up at each camp to mark the way home, they built up a depôt—Depôt C—containing provisions and oil for a week, to take them back to Depôt B; some horsemeat was again included. They repacked the sledges so as to take on a total weight of about 1,200 lb. (630 lb. to a sledge), which Shackleton hoped would keep them going for nine weeks.

He and Adams now pulled with Quan, Marshall and Wild with Socks. The surface was still very soft, and horses and men found the effort of lifting their feet out of the snow very exhausting. Hypsometer readings suggested they were now above sea level. They had done over 300 miles due south in less than a month, but it was obvious that the ponies would not last much longer. On 30 November they found Quan very shaky, and the men took turns hauling with him, while Socks forged ahead and stopped to rest. The surface was bad and they camped early with a day's march of only twelve miles. Shackleton was facing the fact that they *would* have to find a way through, or over, the mountains that were trending more and more easterly—'But, after all, we must not expect to find things cut and dried and (are) suited to us in such a place. . . .'

The first day of December again saw a short mileage of twelve miles, and in the afternoon Quan gave up completely, so that three men had to pull his sledge. He was shot that evening and cut up, providing less meat than the other two although he had been on full meals to the last. Hunger began to dominate their thoughts, as their diaries show.

'Ahead of us' (Shackleton wrote on this first day of December) 'we can see the land stretching away to the East with a long white line in front of it that looks like a giant Barrier and nearer a very crushed up appearance as though there were great pressure ridges in front (of) us. It seems as though the Barrier end had come and there is going to be a change in some gigantic way in keeping with the vastness of the whole place. We fervently trust it will not delay us in our march South. . . . At one moment our thoughts are in the grandeur of the scene the next on what we would have to eat if only we were let loose in a good restaurant, for we are very hungry these days and we know that we are likely to be for another three months.'

Socks, although he whinnied in camp for his dead comrades, was still willing to work, and soon fell into the routine of following with one sledge while the men hauled the other. Shackleton now decided to give

14

up any hope of finding a way round the formidable mountain range, and on 2 December they struck in due south across the Barrier towards the land, intending to climb a red granite hill about 3,000 feet high to prospect. They hoped they would be able to find a way up a glacier ahead of them on to the inland ice and so find a way to the Pole. 'It is an anxious thing for us', Shackleton wrote,[1] 'for time is precious and food more so, so we will be greatly relieved if we find a good route through the mountains. . . . If we can land tomorrow it will be the pioneer landing in the far South. . . .'

They got their pioneer landing. Soon after 5.30 on the morning of 3 December they left camp, taking a lunch of four biscuits, four lumps of sugar and two ounces of chocolate, and leaving plenty of food beside the pony. In a short time they got into very crevassed country and roped together. Before long they were held up by a chasm eighty feet wide and 300 feet deep. They found that it narrowed to their right, and by 12.30 they had passed the crevasses and were in an area of smooth blue ice, where they found water lying in the bare rock.

Half a mile further on they were at the base of the red granite hill they had marked out the day before, and after some food they began to climb the rock face, which was much weathered and split. However, early in the afternoon, they reached the summit, by way of rock, ice and snow, and were well rewarded for their efforts. What they saw from the summit of the hill—which they afterwards named Mount Hope—may be given in the words of Dr. Marshall[2]:

'. . . to the South a great glacier extended as far as the eye could reach, flanked on either side by rugged ice-covered mountains, until lost sight of 60 miles distant where the mountains on the East flank and the Cloudmaker on the West formed a "narrows" or waist, which forecast great ice disturbances as the glacier flowed from the distant plateau, which we now realised guarded the secrets of the Pole itself.'

The first sight of this gateway to the south was one which none of the men ever forgot, but in the ensuing weeks the inspiration they had felt when they saw the 'promised land' from the top of Mount Hope was often forgotten in efforts seemingly beyond the power of man to make.

On 4 December they set out on the new phase of their journey. Shackleton, Adams and Marshall went ahead with one sledge, prospecting a way for the pony, and by picking an easy gradient they got Socks safely over a pass flanked by great granite pillars on to the edge of the glacier. Shackleton[1] forgot the hazards of the journey in the grandeur of the place. 'It is all so interesting and everything is on such a vast scale that one cannot describe it well. We 4 are seeing these great designs and the play of Nature for the first time and possibly this may never be seen by man again.'

Once on the glacier they soon realised that their remaining pony must be considered as a source of food rather than a source of traction, for although they found one or two snow slopes up which he could pull a sledge, much of the surface was crevassed, and they had to lead him and take the sledges forward by relaying. The pony's behaviour was admirable, and Wild's handling of him little short of miraculous. Between the hard blue glacier ice and the granite of the mountain on the west side of the glacier, they found only occasional patches of snow on which they camped; boulders of all sizes perched precariously on the heights above them were not perhaps reassuring, but they could do nothing but trust in Providence, a concept very much present in the minds of all of them. After three days they had left another depôt (D), had climbed 1,700 feet on the glacier and could see down on to the Barrier, while ahead of them was that conspicuous isolated mountain with clouds always round its summit, the Cloudmaker.

The following day (7 December) was dramatic and disastrous. Wild[3] describes it thus:

'I was very nearly finished diary writing today. We started at 8 a.m. this morning, keeping rather close to the W. side of glacier, as the pressure ridges were not far away. The surface was dreadfully soft, we were sinking knee deep, and poor Socks was often in to his belly. Shortly after getting under way we got amongst crevasses again and made out towards the centre of the glacier. Several times Socks got his feet through the bridges, (all the crevasses here are snow bridged and difficult to see) and twice got his hind quarters in. S. A. and M. often walked over them without breaking them at all, but Socks being so much heavier, and having smaller feet went through, and I felt rather uneasy, as leading him I should stand a very good chance of going with him, especially as he required holding back all the time.

We camped at 1 p.m. for lunch, with a crevasse about 5 yards away on each side of us. After lunch, making for the centre of the glacier we got on a much better surface, and the sledges were running nicely; S. A. and M. were 10 yards ahead, when I suddenly stepped into space, felt a violent blow on my shoulder and a fearful rush of something past me, a vicious snatch at my right hand, and found myself hanging by my left arm only, in a horrible chasm, Socks gone, and the sledge with a broken bow very nearly following; I got out somehow, and the other three running back, we quickly got the sledge into safety. Socks must have been killed instantly, as we could hear no sound from below, and see nothing but an intense black depth.'

There are many *Ifs* attached to this great journey of 1908–09, but perhaps the most important one is 'If Socks had not been lost, they might have reached the Pole'. The remainder of the maujee ration, which they used in pemmican hooshes, was a poor exchange for the

horse-meat which they could ill afford to lose; and the pulling that
Socks had been able to do, intermittent though it was, had been a
valuable help to men who were finding the upward haul an increasing
strain on nerves and muscles. At the end of this seventh day of December
the prospect seemed black, but, as Wild commented, 'when things get
to their worst they must mend, so we are looking forward to better
times tomorrow'.

To the effort of dragging loads of 250 lb. per man uphill was added
the extra effort of relaying, for the glacier was still dangerously crevassed
and they could only take on one sledge at a time. Moreover, the ice
was so hard that the sledges slipped against the sharp edges of some of
the crevasses, and the bow of one of them eventually gave way.

The men were talking constantly about food, hoping constantly to
get off the glacier and on to the inland ice; but this moment was still
far ahead. Their mileage gradually dropped to three miles a day, for
nine hours or more of extreme labour. They were still able to afford a
good hoosh at night, but their meagre lunch-time ration of six biscuits
and two ounces of cheese or chocolate forced their thoughts more and
more to the subject of food.

Each night in camp all the visible peaks were plotted by theodolite
and the approximate height of their camp was calculated by hypsometer (boiling-point thermometer): from this a running-survey-map
emerged. The day's march up the glacier became a matter of calculated
risks, for the danger in delay was as great as the danger of falling into
a crevasse. Marshall[2] wrote afterwards:

> ' "Provy" became a personality and a dominant force in a world
> of our own, more than 2000 miles from civilization, which no other
> human eye had ever seen. "Luck"—there was no such thing, for
> luck comes to man whose foresight and planning can ensure
> perfection to the highest degree possible, and after that, what cannot
> be planned or foreseen is in the hands of "Provy". This was Shackle-
> ton's creed, and in the Antarctic wastes, under the shadow of the
> Pole, I learnt it. Risks must be taken, but they are part of the daily
> routine, and if you live and believe in your creed the word assumes
> its normal place in the vocabulary, and is meaningless.'

They were to need the help of Providence indeed during the rest of
this month. Not only were they doing the impossible physically, taxing
their strength up to and beyond the limit, but they were calling on
every reserve of determination and courage to face the changing dangers
and tasks before them. They had no idea of the height of the glacier
and they under-estimated it, so that every day they had to face the
disappointment of being still below the inland plateau that should lead
them to the Pole.

This straining of mind and body was, moreover, suffered by men

living on a straitened ration. Already at the beginning of the month
they were all talking about Christmas, when they were determined to
have full meals; and the cook for the week was putting by a small
portion of food each day to achieve this. On 10 December, while
Shackleton collected rock specimens on the moraine, the others,
imitating their remote ancestors, sat down to crush the pony maize into
flour between two stones. Much was wasted, but the flour they
managed to produce (one pannikin in half an hour) could be cooked
more easily and with less expenditure of fuel than the solid grain. They
did not adopt this costly method permanently, but they could not afford
to melt snow for water to soak the grain, and in the low temperature
the water froze round it almost at once. So they ate it in its hard
state, and, as Shackleton cheerfully put it, it swelled inside them
instead.

Fortunately the weather was always good enough for travelling,
though the intense cold was hard on men who were losing all their
body fat. Their bodies were misused, too, by the surface of the glacier
—ice pushed up into hard hummocks and ridges, frozen waves of
ice on which they stumbled and bruised themselves, and on which
they could find very little snow for their camp.

On the night of 11 December they had to make a level floor for the
tent, at the west side of the glacier, by chipping away the sharp pieces
of ice with their axes. The kind of work they were doing is best
described in Shackleton's own words[1]:

'Our distance 3 miles for the day expresses more readily than I
can write it the nature of the day's work. Started at 7.40 on the worst
surface possible sharp edged blue ice filled with chasm and crevasses,
rising into hills and descending in gullies : in fact a surface that
cannot be equal in any polar work for difficulty in travelling. Our
sledges are suffering greatly and it is a constant strain on us all both
to save the sledge from breaking or going down a crevasse and to
save ourselves as well: We are a mass of bruises where we have fallen
on the sharp ice; but thank God no one has even a sprain. It has been
relay work all day for we could only take on one sledge at a time
two of us taking turns pulling whilst the other steadied and
hauled on the sledge to keep it straight. Thus we advanced 1 mile
then returned over the crevasses and hauled up the other sledge.
Repeating this today for 3 miles gave us 9 miles marching over a
surface where many times a slip meant death. Still we have advanced
3 miles to the south. . . .'

The last sentence rings through Shackleton's diary at the end of
entry after entry about this gruelling effort. 'Difficulties are just things
to overcome after all', he wrote one evening, and the sentence is
typical of him. All the hazards of the climb were written down, for he

was keeping a diary for future explorers as much as for himself. But after the recital of each day's events would come an expression of confidence. Tomorrow the glacier would begin to flatten out, he believed, soon they would be on the plateau. 'S. is in the best of spirits', Wild wrote on 15 December, 'and I must say has been so all along, although several times things have looked rather gloomy'.[3]

The surface continued to be appalling, whether they were travelling over blue ice or over a patch of rotten old moraine. On 13 December, on the return journey of a relay, Shackleton fell on the ice and hurt his left knee; it gave him some pain in the following days but he was, as Wild remarked, 'pulling like the devil'.

On 15 December there were signs of a change. At their lunch halt they could see ahead of them what seemed to be a long wide plain, and though in their afternoon march they continued to rise, the surface of hard névé was an improvement on the sharp rippled ice they had been negotiating.

But though Shackleton was sure this was the plateau at last, they continued to climb and to meet frequent crevasses. On 17 December they made a depôt (E) by the rocks of an island in the ice, leaving all their clothes except what they were wearing, and four days' food at short ration, to get them down to the last depôt on the glacier.

They had now traversed nearly 100 miles of crevassed ice and risen 6,000 feet on what may be the largest glacier in the world. 'One more crevassed slope and we will be on the plateau, please God', Shackleton wrote in his diary.[1] 'We are all fit and well.'

They were carrying now only six weeks' full food, but they had cut the ration again, and were now saving two biscuits a day each, besides some pemmican and sugar. The ache of hunger was hardly assuaged by the hard pony maize, which they found increasingly difficult to digest.

They were now passing a quantity of rock exposed above the ice, and although Shackleton could not spare the time to examine it properly, he hoped to do so on the return journey. Wild, prospecting ahead of their camp on the evening of 17 December, had brought back a piece of rock from the mountainside which seemed more interesting than the surrounding sandstone: it turned out to be an inferior type of coal. But there was no time for geology. In spite of their hopes, they had not yet reached the plateau. They were climbing uphill, sometimes over ground so steep and broken that they had to cut steps and then haul sledges one by one by rope up the few yards they made.

On 20 December, when Marshall got a sun-sight in clear weather, they found they were at 85° 17' S., at a height of 8,000 feet, and still ahead of them the ground rose. Their ration was impossibly small. Breakfast consisted of one pannikin of hoosh and one biscuit; at lunch they had a little chocolate, tea with plasmon and four biscuits; and for dinner one pot of hoosh, a pannikin of cocoa and three biscuits.

On this ration they were averaging ten miles a day; but their body temperatures were falling well below normal. Their beards became a mass of frozen ice, and Shackleton commented that this was more like spring sledging than summer.

Still the plateau remained beyond their reach. On 22 December they saw ahead of them a smoother and flatter slope which quickened their hopes, but on the following day they were 8,820 feet up and still laboriously roping the sledges up rising ground. Often one or other of them would fall through the snow crust of a crevasse, to be hauled out by his sledge harness. They took these crevasses in their stride now, merely commenting on their good luck when they came to one with no covering to deceive them. The march on 23 December took them into a particularly dangerous series of crevassed ridges, and the strong wind cut their split lips and noses cruelly. Shackleton hoped that 'tomorrow will see the end of this bad travelling so that we can stretch out our legs for the Pole'.

Christmas Eve did in fact give them a better surface, and in the afternoon they were out of the crevassed area. They discarded one sledge at lunch time, keeping only the runners as spares, and this helped to increase their mileage.

The Christmas Day they had waited for was all that they had anticipated—a day of intense cold, intense wind, great effort and good eating. Wild,[3] who was feeling the strain not so much on his own account as on Shackleton's, wrote 'May none but my worst enemies ever spend their Christmas in such a dreary God-forsaken spot as this', but he was still optimistic. 'Here we are 9,500 ft. above sea level, farther away from civilisation than any human being has ever been since civilisation was, with half a gale blowing, and drift snow flying, and a temperature of 52° of frost, and yet we are not miserable.'

The day's march, starting after an extra allowance of pemmican at breakfast, took them over steeply rising ground. At noon a sight gave them a latitude of 85° 51'. They had extra cheese for lunch, with their usual four biscuits and tea, and Shackleton took a photograph of the other three at the camp, with the Queen's flag and their own sledge flags flying. Dinner was all that they had dreamed it would be. Shackleton as cook produced a hoosh made of pony ration boiled up with pemmican, Oxo and biscuits. A friend of Wild's had given him a small plum pudding, and this was boiled in the cocoa water and served with a drop of medical brandy. Cocoa, cigars and a spoonful of crème de menthe completed what Shackleton thought was a feast fit for Lucullus.

Sitting in one of the tents after this sumptuous meal the four men discussed a further cut in their food. They would make each week's food last for ten days, allowing only six biscuits each a day, and would leave behind everything they could do without. Shackleton wrote in his diary[1] 'It is the only thing to do for we must get the Pole, come what may,' and then—from caution, perhaps, or to remind himself of the limitations of man—crossed out the second part of the sentence. He ended the day's entry 'Marshall took our temperatures tonight. We are all 2° subnormal. But fit as can be. It is a fine open air life! and we are getting South,' and, as an afterthought, added the lines from Meredith which he had previously applied to his wife:

> 'Hard is our love. Hard to catch and conquer.
> Hard, but oh, the glory of the winning were it won.'

As they continued to toil upwards, hauling the sledge, pulling 150 lb. weight per man, Shackleton was planning to make a rush for the last sixty miles to the Pole, taking one tent and using the poles of the other for markers, and leaving all their food except the minimum needed to take them there and back. He hoped to reach the Pole on 12 January and then to get back to Hut Point in time for the ship.

The weather was against them. On the following day, a strong wind and a low temperature held them back, and on 30 December a blizzard forced them to camp after only four miles. They lay in their sleeping bags feeling the wind through the worn canvas and listening to the drift beating on the sides of the tents. The previous day the doctor had found their temperatures abnormally low, near the 94° mark, and advised Shackleton that they must return to their previous allowance of food. Adams, he noticed, was suffering very much from the cold, and Shackleton had been having severe headaches and fits of giddiness. They had all been short of breath on the march, and so tired that at intervals the leader called a halt and they lay flat on the snow for three minutes.

This delay as a result of the blizzard was the first they had had since the first week of their journey but they were now ill-equipped to stand disappointment, and although Shackleton had not given up hope, Wild commented on 30 December that he seemed 'a bit down'. Wild and Marshall had both by this time admitted in their diaries that they thought any hope of reaching the Pole had gone, but Shackleton still ended each day's entry with a hopeful remark. He may possibly have been suffering from altitude; at least his head troubled him all the time.

Travelling was still uphill, with a soft surface infinitely exhausting to them all, weakened with hunger as they were. The first day of the New Year saw them struggling through eleven miles of very soft snow, hardly able to enjoy the satisfaction of reaching latitude 87° 6½' and thus beating the Northern record. Shackleton, whose optimism could not make him lose his powers of reason, at last admitted that they might not be able to do what they had set out to do.

'God knows we are doing all we can' he wrote on 2 January 1909, 'but the outlook is serious if this surface continues and the rise. for we are not travelling fast enough to make our food spin out and get back to our depôt in time: I cannot think of failure yet I must look at the matter sensibly and the lives of those who are with me. I feel that if we go on too far it will be impossible to get back over this surface and then all the results will be lost to the world. We can now definitely locate the South Pole on the highest plateau in the world and our geological work and meteorology will be of great use to science: But all this is not the Pole and man can only do his best and we have arrayed against us the strongest forces of Nature.'

'I cannot think of failure.' Yet, weak and exhausted as he was, he set himself to do just that. His ambitions must be curbed, he must use his strength of mind to put first things first—the lives of the party before the most spectacular and satisfying success life had to offer.

They appeared now to have reached the plateau which he had anticipated nearly a month before, but this gave little satisfaction. To have climbed to the top of what they took to be the largest glacier in the world, to a height of over eleven thousand feet—the glow of this achievement could not prevail against the power of cold and bodily weakness.

Shackleton was helped on, as he said in his diary,[1] by 'the cheerfulness and regardlessness of self' of his comrades. All four men were working and thinking as one. They discussed the situation frankly, and on 4 January they agreed to take the risk of leaving a depôt (F) on the wide plateau, with only a mound and a bamboo pole with a bit of bag sewn on it to mark the provisions that must take them back to the depôt 150 miles down the glacier. The word 'trust' recurs in Shackleton's diary. He trusted that their footprints would remain clear in the snow, that no storm would arise to obliterate them; above all, he trusted his comrades. They would try to get within a hundred miles of the Pole: they could do no more.

It was now a matter of forced marches—some of the most astonishing marches ever achieved. On 5 January, with a head wind and drifting snow, a temperature of 50 degrees of frost, a soft surface through which they sank eight inches on to sharp ice-furrows, exhausted and hungry, the body temperatures of three of them now below the 94 mark, they did thirteen miles; and on the following day—their last with the sledge—twelve. They were in latitude 88° 5'. 'Tomorrow', Shackleton wrote,[1] 'we march South with the flag'.

But tomorrow, and the next day, found them lying in the tent, while a blizzard raged outside with a wind of up to 90 miles an hour. Through

the worn tent came an icy current of air, and, at times, even drifting
snow. They were so cold that they suffered from cramp, and their food
gave only a momentary warmth.

On 9 January they made their last effort, taking with them a small
supply of chocolate, biscuits and sugar. It was indeed a 'dash' for a
high latitude, for, strung up and determined as they were, they were
running much of the time, 'as hard as we could pelt over the snow',
as Wild[3] put it. It was the culmination of a series of calculated risks:
it is the considered opinion of Adams[4] that if they had gone on for an
hour longer than they did, they would not have got back alive.

Shackleton's diary[1] should tell the tale again. In one of his most
business-like entries he both hid and revealed the extent of his
disappointment.

'The last day out we have shot our bolt and the tale is 88. 23 S.
162 E. The wind eased down at 1 am At 2 am we were up had
breakfast and shortly after 4 am started south with the Union
Jacks and the brass Cylinder of Stamps. At 9 am hard quick marching
we were in 88. 23 and there hoisted H.M.'s flag took possession of
the Plateau in the name of H.M. and called it K. E. Plat. Rushed
back over a surface hardened somewhat by the recent wind and had
lunch took photo of camp Furthest South and then got away
marching till 5 pm dead tired Camped lovely night —19. Homeward Bound. Whatever regrets may be we have done our best.
Beaten the South Record by 366 miles the North by 77 miles.
Amen.'

In the tent that night they celebrated their distance with thick hoosh
and a drink of sloe gin, and Wild enjoyed a cigar which he had kept
specially for the occasion.

The decision* to return at this crucial moment was, up to a point,

---

* When he was on his way back to England Shackleton tried to think of a
way to convey the tension of this most critical time. A. B. Armitage[5], of the
Discovery, records how he met Shackleton, with Bertram Armytage and
Brocklehurst, on the *Isis* at Brindisi.

'He was cheery and full of vim as ever. The publisher of his book, "The
Heart of the Antarctic", . . . several reporters and Italian officials met him.
I took him to see my home, and then to our agency, where he composed a
number of telegrams. He wanted, so he said, a "catchword". He walked up
and down the room muttering several phrases to himself.

"I've got it at last", he cried. "Death lay ahead and food behind, so I had
to return."

He considered Brindisi to be a more desolate spot than the Antarctic, and
wondered how I could "live such a death". All on the jump, he thrust two
telegrams, which he had omitted to send, into my hand as the train moved
off. . . . A day or two later I received a copy of an interview with him from
my old friend Emmett, Reuter's agent. In it was the "catchword".'

The catchword is not a remarkable one and it certainly produces an effect too a matter for all four men. As in the case of the Southern Journey of 1902–03, the question of how long the party could afford to go on was fully and freely discussed. Shackleton did not impose a decision on the men he was leading. But even when he knew that it was impossible for them to reach the Pole and return alive, there was still the temptation, for a moment or two a strong one, to struggle on and let his comrades turn back if they would. Ultimately, the decision was his, and it showed a courage which the world was to recognise. It was this decision above anything else, for instance, that made Russell Owen[7] describe him as 'the greatest of all Antarctic leaders'.

J. Gordon Hayes[8] finds this point equally important.

'Shackleton had a remarkable gift for making correct and swift decisions that averted disaster, and his greatness as an explorer is largely attributable to this intuition. Success on his expeditions was very near his heart, but the safety and health of those who served under him came first; and the fact that he never lost a life may be regarded as the finest of all his feats and the greatest of all his triumphs.'

When Shackleton returned to England and his wife asked him how he had found the strength of mind to turn back, he made a joke of his answer, as he was apt to do in moments of deep emotion. 'I thought you'd rather have a live donkey than a dead lion,' he said. But more compelling than the thought of his wife and children at this moment was the thought of the three men who had followed him over the vast expanse of the Barrier and up the crevassed glacier, and for whom he was ultimately responsible.

In moments of stress, when he was worried or exasperated by minor setbacks, Shackleton had a rough, blunt, almost hectoring way of speaking to his men. In moments of extreme emergency, he battened down his temper. They observed that he became possessed of an extreme energy, an abiding cheerfulness, and a warm solicitude.

On this Southern Journey of 1908–09 Shackleton had drawn upon reserves of strength in his character as well as in his physique. The four men, in getting up the Beardmore Glacier, had time and again done the impossible. The three who followed Shackleton were themselves men of strong will, but none of them would have denied that Shackleton,

trivial for the immense issues of that January day of 1909, when the leader had to give up any hope of success; but it is significant that Shackleton should want a 'catchword'. This decision of his to turn back was one of the great dramatic moments of his life and he felt the need to crystallise it in some telling phrase. When he returned to England he prepared for reporters a more practical version, by repeating that 'with another 25 pounds of biscuits and 30 pounds of pemmican' they could have achieved the Pole.[6] This was perhaps consoling to his pride; it was certainly dramatic; and it was probably true.

without making any direct appeal, had drawn from them a reserve of strength they could scarcely believe. This was his supreme virtue as a leader, that he could inspire his men to follow him, and to do the impossible. To be a great leader it was not enough to be strong of will, it was not enough to set an example of extreme endurance. Ultimately it was Shackleton's power to *inspire* that made him the greatest leader in the whole history of Antarctic exploration.

The power he had over his men, developed and displayed on this tremendous Southern Journey, had its obligations. It meant that he must give his best, everything of his best, to his men. That was, in the last analysis, why he turned back at latitude 88° 23′ S., ninety-seven geographical miles from the South Pole, and that was why, whatever divergences appeared later in this party of four, they finished the Southern Journey not as four colleagues but as four brothers.

Chapter XIII

Iⁿ the journey up the glacier was all 'pulley-hauley', as Marshall[1] put it, the journey down was a free-for-all. On the way up they had learnt to deal briskly though carefully with crevasses; returning, when they were on the glacier, they were even at times glissading over them. Speed was essential, and must be their chief preoccupation. They now had fourteen days' short ration to take them to the depôt (E) at the top of the glacier, 180 geographical miles away, and for the next ten days they made what speed they could across the plateau. They were able to follow their outward tracks, which had frozen hard and stood out where fierce winds had cleared the loose surface snow from them; but these same winds had made in some places enormous sastrugi or ice waves which were difficult to negotiate with the sledge. On one or two days they were able to take advantage of the wind by setting the tent-cloth as a sail, but though this gave them a good average speed, it meant torture to their bruised and cracked feet as they veered with the sledge to steer it. Temperatures were consistently low and it was almost impossible for them to sleep at night.

On 14 January they had to cut down their biscuit ration, and they all felt an intense craving for cakes and doughy food. The effect of the short commons is expressed very forcibly in Marshall's diary[1] of 18 January: 'Never will I refuse a hungry man a feed and feed the hungry whenever possible!'

They reached depôt E on 20 January, after a day of shocking effort. Shackleton[2] described it thus:

> 'For two hours we were descending a snow slope, heavy sastrugi, then struck a patch of badly crevassed névé, about ½ mile, then on to blue slippery ice, where our finskoes had no hold. A gale was blowing, & often fierce gusts came along, sweeping the sledge sideways & knocking us off our feet. We all had many falls & I had two specially heavy ones which shook me up severely. When we reached steep slopes where we roped sledges up on our outward journey, we lowered sledge down by alpine rope using ice axe as a bollard to lower by. On several occasions one or more of us lost our footing & were swept by the wind down the ice slope, with great difficulty getting back to our sledge & companions. We arrived at our depôt at 12.30 with aching & sore bodies.'

Wild was watching Shackleton closely, his anxiety for him leading him into occasional uncharitable remarks about the performance of his two other companions. He had written the day before in his diary[3]: 'I don't know how S. stands it; both his heels are split in four or five places, his legs are bruised and chafed, and today he has a violent headache through falls, and yet he gets along as well as anyone.'

On the 20th he recorded that Shackleton, after many falls, was completely knocked up at the night camp.

Adams[4] remembers thinking all through the journey that Shackleton was doing too much, and the doctor advised him more than once that he should take things more quietly. Shackleton did not take the advice: it was not in his nature to do so in circumstances like these. Far from relaxing now that the climax of the journey had passed, he was taxing his reserves of strength more heavily than ever, and eventually he paid for it. On 21 January Wild wrote[3]:

'Poor S. has been very ill today, the heavy falls he had yesterday have shaken him up badly, and he has had to walk by the sledge. It is not surprising, as for a good six weeks he has been doing far more than his share of work. His stomach is out of order and he has very little appetite and cannot eat his pemmican, which is a serious matter here. I sincerely hope he will be better tomorrow.'

The doctor found his temperature a degree above normal and his pulse on the march thin and thready. On the next day, although still unable to eat very much, he was able to help guide the sledge, though not to pull it, and he continued to improve. At this time they were travelling downward over rippled ice where the need was for guiding and steadying as much as for hauling, but his frustration can well be imagined, although in his diary he made no comment on his health. 'The worst of it with him', Wild wrote on 23 January,[3] 'he worries so much because he thinks he is delaying us, but on this horrible ice we could not possibly go any faster, or we should break up both ourselves and sledge in very short time'.

Shackleton recovered in time to take his full share of the most exacting two days of the whole journey. Their mileage was small, because of the rough crevassed nature of the route, and after days of very short food they came to the morning of 26 January with all biscuits finished. Their previous day's allowance had been four biscuits, two ounces of cheese and one cup of pemmican, with a cup of tea for breakfast and another for lunch. With a battered sledge minus half a runner on one side, with bruised bodies and anxious minds, after breakfasting on the last of the maize in a hoosh, they set out over a cruelly rough and crevassed surface, to do the twelve miles or so to the next depôt (D). After travelling for five hours, they pitched camp. Their lunch consisted of tea with the last spoonful of sugar, and two ounces of chocolate each. In the afternoon they pushed on, averaging less than a mile an hour, and with a rest at 4.45 for some tea with plasmon. Then they marched until ten o'clock at night, stopped for a small pan of cocoa, and then continued for another four hours. Hauling was hard work in the soft snow, and they frequently broke through the crust to underlying crevasses.

Somewhere about 2.0 in the morning they were so played out that they were falling asleep in their tracks. They were only about three miles from the depôt but they had to put up the tent and get what sleep they could. They allowed themselves one cup of cocoa when they turned in, and another at 9.0 on the morning of 27 January, when they set out once more, pulling the sledge in bursts through very deep snow, with frequent halts to get their breath. At noon Adams fell in his tracks, but was able to go on after a few minutes; Wild had collapsed similarly on the night march. They pressed on until 1 p.m. and then camped within a mile of the depôt, while Marshall went ahead to bring back food. What he brought must at any other time have seemed very inadequate; now the small allowance of pemmican, horsemeat, biscuits, tea and sugar, was a feast, and the smoke afterwards complete luxury. They had been forty hours without solid food and had done sixteen miles over some of the worst country of the whole journey.

Time was still desperately short but they were weak after their forced march, and though they set out very early on the morning of 28 January to get down to the depôt, they allowed time to take photographs and collect some specimens of rock. At lunch time they had reached the pass by which they got on to the glacier on the way up, and by three o'clock in the afternoon they were once more on the Barrier.

The doctor[1] commented that Shackleton had stood the privation and hardship of the last few days wonderfully well, although he had celebrated what he himself described as a 'special sort of farewell to me from the glacier' by falling heavily into a hidden crevasse; the harness jerked up under his heart, shook him up badly, and brought on a fit of coughing.

On 29 January they ran into bad weather, and a blizzard forced them to camp after a short march of little more than two hours. They lay in their tents talking, patching what was left of their burberry suits, eating the little food they could allow themselves. They were able to travel on the next day, but conditions were very bad, with high winds and drifting snow, and pulling was hard work. They were anxious about finding the next depôt (C), which was more than forty miles away. They had done what they could to make it conspicuous, but with wind, snow and bad light, it would be dangerously easy to miss it.

There now came another setback. The pony meat from the last depôt affected their stomachs, perhaps because of some slight toxin, perhaps also because their stomachs had been disorganised by the constant changes in their starvation diet. On 30 January Wild was not well and on the next day, with bad dysentery, could only walk by the sledge, quite unable to eat either pemmican or horseflesh. The doctor had given him some medicine which made him so drowsy that he kept falling asleep on the march. It was impossible for him to have any extra biscuit, the allowance being so short; but Shackleton did what he could. That night Wild wrote in his diary[3]:

'S. privately forced upon me his one breakfast biscuit, and would have given me another tonight had I allowed him. I do not suppose that anyone else in the world can thoroughly realise how much generosity and sympathy was shown by this; I DO, and BY GOD I shall never forget it. Thousands of pounds would not have bought that one biscuit.'

The passage is underlined: the occasion was a momentous one. Wild, during the march out, had had reservations about Shackleton's planning; he thought they might reach the Pole but doubted whether, if they did, they could return safely. But now he was absolutely Shackleton's man. Their alliance could only be broken by death.

Dysentery now attacked all, which the food they picked up at Depôt C on 2 February did little to cure. On 4 February they were all so ill that they were unable to march at all. Marshall commented bluntly that the camp looked like a battlefield, that the day had cost him his pyjama trousers and shirt-tail. They had to cut down on horsemeat and were eating as much pony maize and biscuit as they felt they could spare.

The next day they were able to travel, but very slowly; the conversation was continuously about food, and about the meal each would choose in London to celebrate their Furthest South. They tried to eat meat again; Wild commented[3] that it 'will either buck us up a bit or kill us; pray God the former'. The horseflesh was not properly cooked because of shortage of fuel. Marshall and Adams suffered a relapse, and had to go back to pemmican and biscuits.

A stiff breeze on 7 February helped them along, and they were picking up the snow mounds left at their outward camps. Their mileage gradually crept up again, although they were so weak with hunger that they still could not move very fast. Their situation was desperate but they were so worn out that they had hardly the energy to be anxious; desire for food persisted and they talked of it all the time. Marshall on one occasion spilt his pannikin of cocoa at lunch and spooned it up carefully and meticulously off the floor-cloth. On 10 February Wild wrote: 'My greatest desire now seems to be to sit on the hearth-rug at Mother's feet and be petted, I feel *so* tired and hungry.'

The words, coming from a man of exceptional endurance, speak for themselves.

Two days later, from their evening camp, Adams sighted the B depôt

The Arrol-Johnston car, 1908

On the Southern Journey; looking south from the summit of Mount Hope (p. 210).
'D' Depôt was under the mountain casting a long shadow

Furthest South, 9 January 1909. Shackleton's photograph of (left to right):
Adams, Wild and Marshall

The Southern Party on the Nimrod. Left to right: Wild, Shackleton,
Marshall, Adams. 1 March 1909

flag, about seven miles ahead, and they allowed themselves an almost full allowance of pemmican and biscuit for supper. They reached the depôt at 11.30 the following morning, and that night they enjoyed a particularly good hoosh made from Chinaman's liver. The blood from the horse, which had congealed under the snow, gave them added nourishment.

They had now to reach Depôt A, about eighty-four miles north of them, and the meat gave them a little more energy to press on, though the craving for carbohydrates persisted. Shackleton's thirty-fifth birthday was celebrated, on 15 February, by a good thick pemmican hoosh, and with the present of a cigarette made by the other three from shreds of tobacco rolled in thick paper. In spite of a bad headache he was perfectly cheerful. All of them constantly remarked, with complete sincerity, on the goodness of Providence towards them.

They struggled on, inventing new dishes as they marched, and making the most of small encouragements, as when they sighted Mount Discovery in the distance, and two days later the familiar shape of Erebus. Their ration in the days between Depôt B and Depôt A was a bare cup and a half of meat and gravy a day with three spoonsful of pemmican, six biscuits, and half a spoonful of sugar in tea and cocoa. 'How is that,' Wild remarked in his diary,[3] 'for more than 50° of frost and a heavy sledge at 14 miles a day and underclad.'

20 February was a day to remember, for they sighted Depôt A soon after lunch and reached it at 4.0. Camping at once, they set to work to dig up the stores. Shackleton made a good fat hoosh and Marshall broke up biscuits and mixed them with a pound of jam to make a black currant pudding—'the best pudding I ever tasted,' Wild said. Their cocoa was nearly full strength; they had unlimited Tabard cigarettes and they turned in well content. They might now expect to reach Minna Bluff in four days, where Joyce should have left a substantial store of food. Their confidence in him was justified. On 22 February they picked up sledging tracks and later a deserted camping place. On 23 February, at eleven in the morning, Adams spotted the depôt flag, off their course and only visible because it was miraged up at exactly the right moment. It was one of several remarkable pieces of good luck which saved them from what must otherwise have been disaster.

They reached Joyce's depôt at 4.0 and enjoyed at last a varied diet— sausages for supper, eggs and porridge for breakfast the following morning. Shackleton had warned his companions to be careful not to overtax digestions which had already suffered so badly, but it was impossible to gauge just what they could stand in the way of real food, and after their shocking and persistent hunger, the power of reason was not invincible. The richer food affected Marshall with another attack of dysentery, and although he tried to keep on at the end of the day's

15

march on 27 February he was too ill to march any further. At the Bluff
Depôt Shackleton had found letters telling him that the *Nimrod* was
at Cape Royds, under the command of Captain Evans. It was impossible
to predict from the Barrier what was happening to the ice in McMurdo
Sound, or whether the ship would be able to wait till 28 February, the
date fixed for her departure. The only thing to do was to summon up
the energy for another forced march.

Marshall was left in the tent with Adams to look after him. Shackleton
and Wild, taking a light sledge and food for one day, would push on to
Hut Point to look for further messages. Shackleton had been suffering
much in the last few days from neuralgic headaches. His state of mind
is not difficult to imagine, as he and Wild forced themselves along. The
ice had gone out well to the south of Cape Armitage, so that they had
to make a détour of seven miles.

They reached the *Discovery* hut late on 28 February. Here they found
a note saying that the ship would wait for them at Glacier Tongue until
26 February. They could only guess at whether the Captain intended
to wait longer than this at Cape Royds. They sat up all night in the hut,
trying to keep warm, and early the next morning succeeded in firing
signals which were sighted by the ship. By 11.0 the next morning they
were on board and Shackleton took three hours' rest. He and Wild
enjoyed a meal of bacon and eggs—according to the Chief Officer's story
to the newspapers, the dish they had most hankered for ; with no more
rest, Shackleton then himself led a relief party of three men back to the
camp. Marshall was now very much better and the party made good time
from the camp to Hut Point, where the ship was signalled once more.*

Shackleton had walked over 90 miles in just over four days, with
very little rest since leaving the last camp. Few leaders would
have been capable of this last and greatest effort. But Shackleton had

---

* A nice example of the difference between what Gordon Hayes calls the
'heroic' and the 'mechanical' ages of exploration may be seen in a modern
account of this incident. In a popular history of Antarctic exploration, *The
Silent Continent* by William H. Kearns and Beverly Britton, we read[5] :

'Unless they got a message to the ship, they must spend the winter in
the Antarctic ice. The two men tried the radio in the thin hope that the ship
might not have departed on schedule. To their great relief, a response came
through—and before long, *Nimrod* itself hove into view.'

The signals after the Southern Journey of 1908–09 were, in fact, far more
primitive than this, for the ship had no radio. On 1 March Shackleton and Wild
got the *Discovery* magnetic hut burning as an urgent signal, and signalled
thereafter by heliograph. On 2 March, late at night, Shackleton and Adams
lighted a carbide flare : there being no liquid available for igniting the carbide,
they used their own natural water. So quickly have we become mechanised
since Shackleton's Great Expedition that it is a real effort to think back to the
climate of exploration fifty years ago.

determined to bring his men back safely, and he was going to do it himself.

Captain Evans, anxious about the *Nimrod*'s safety, had moved down the Sound, and in the dark night there seemed a chance that their signals would not be seen, and that by some disaster of the weather, they might even now be left behind. But Mackintosh, whose Celtic temperament was like that of his leader, felt a strong intuition that Shackleton had reached the hut, although at that time a blizzard was blowing which made travelling seem impossible. He climbed to the mast-head and at once saw the flare from the signal hill. The ship moved up the Sound, and by one o'clock in the morning Shackleton and Adams were on board, while men from the ship went out to fetch Marshall and Wild from the *Discovery* hut. 'Never was there such a return', Adams[6] wrote later, 'as when we climbed on the *Nimrod* again—we had been given up for 10 days past and killed in a hundred different ways.'

The four bearded, worn-looking men could now relax from an unremitting strain of four months. Their achievement was extraordinary. They had made[7] a journey of 1,613 geographical miles, more than half of it over new ground, in 126 days*; they had advanced 366 miles further south than any Antarctic travellers before them. They had withstood fifteen and a half weeks of dire hunger; they had endured blizzards and low temperatures at a high altitude. They had escaped danger countless times, sometimes by good fortune, more often by the planning of the leader.

Shackleton, for all his sailor's belief in Providence, believed also that God helps those who help themselves. Between his journey with Scott and the journey he led himself, he had read most of the polar literature then available, and he had discussed technical matters of diet and transport with anyone who might have useful advice to give him. He had studied his subject thoroughly; he forgot nothing and he wasted nothing he had learned. With this knowledge, theoretical as well as practical, he was able to assess a situation very quickly. His mind worked so efficiently in assembling facts to meet an emergency that his decisions often seemed to other people to be made on the spur of the moment. They were not. The risks he took were calculated as closely as they could be, but they *were* calculated. As one Antarctic historian[8] was to say later, 'He had the gift of backing his cold and considered judgment.' His power of quick thought, his remarkable intuition of danger gave him a power over circumstances which sometimes seemed like luck to the outside world: it was the 'luck' of a man who explored with his brain.

Shackleton's planning on his British Antarctic Expedition had been

* Shackleton gives the total distance including relay work and back marches, in statute miles: this was 1,725 miles 300 yards.

conspicuously successful. In spite of setbacks and difficulties he had done more than anyone could have believed possible. Moreover, he had brought all his men back from that unknown plateau. His care and forethought in the matter of diet meant that although they returned thin and worn with the hard work and inadequate food, they showed no signs of scurvy, nor had they done so at any stage of the journey.

To the public this great expedition will be always associated with the Southern Journey, but it was remarkable also for its scientific work. First and foremost among the other achievements of the summer of 1908–09 was the journey made by David, Mawson and Mackay to the South Magnetic Pole. They reached this point on the earth's surface on 16 January 1909, and formally claimed the area for the Crown. They too had made a formidable journey without any sickness, for under Shackleton's orders they had taken care to provide themselves with fresh seal-meat whenever possible. They had performed prodigies of strength and endurance, man-hauling for the whole of a journey of 1,260 miles (740 of them extended by relaying) over rough and some-times almost impossible country. Professor David's account of this journey* was modest and factual but the reader will have no difficulty in discerning the effort and danger behind his calm statements of fact.

Besides making plans for this long journey, during which observations of geological and meteorological, as well as magnetic, interest would be made, Shackleton had left orders that Priestley, assisted by Armytage and Brocklehurst, was to continue to make short useful journeys in the neighbourhood of the hut at Cape Royds so that the geology of the area should be studied as intensively as possible. Joyce had been given some instruction in taxidermy and was to prepare, under Murray's direction, a collection of zoological specimens. Murray's own biological observa-tions were to continue through the summer, and Marston was to devote most of his time to painting the Antarctic scene.

In December Priestley and his two companions left for a journey to the Western mountains to carry out investigations at Butter Point, Dry Valley and up the Ferrar Glacier. They were disappointed in finding very few fossils and no valuable minerals, but their investiga-tions of the geology of the neighbourhood were of great value.

Shackleton's orders had been conscientiously carried out. His own party and David's were late in returning. Joyce had laid a depôt at the Bluff as he had been instructed, and he stayed in the area until 17 Feb-ruary, when he was forced to lead his party north again. Meanwhile the *Nimrod*, following Shackleton's instructions, had begun to search for the overdue party from the South Magnetic Pole on 1 February.

* A full account of the journey, made from David's records and much of it quoted directly from them, can be found in Volume 2 of Shackleton's *The Heart of the Antarctic*.[7]

Captain Evans had reached Cape Royds on 16 January, after eighteen days of difficult manœuvring in pack-ice, and from that time he was moving the *Nimrod* from place to place in McMurdo Sound as the ice broke up and formed again. Stores were landed at Cape Royds, and on 4 January Armytage, Priestley and Brocklehurst were picked up at Butter Point.

On this day the ship's log[9] recorded 'Steaming through new ice.' Now the fast ice further south began to break up, and what was in fact an ice-pack of fragments drifted down to the north. Thus the search which the Captain conducted early in February for David's party was done in most difficult circumstances, the ship being driven through the loose ice and kept close enough to the shore for signals to be picked up. On 4 February a tent was sighted near Drygalski Barrier. David and his companions ran down thankfully to the ice-edge, to be taken back in safety to Cape Royds.

There now remained the task of picking up the Southern Party, and this, by Shackleton's instructions, was to be done with due attention to the safety of the ship. Although she had been provisioned adequately in case she had to remain for another winter, it was not Shackleton's intention that she should do so if it could be avoided. He had given precise orders to the Captain about the length of time he might search for the Southern Party.

From 11 February the *Nimrod* steamed up and down between Cape Royds and Hut Point, keeping a strict look-out. The temperature was falling and there were frequent blizzards during which the ship was in danger of drifting about in the loose ice. The Captain's policy is clear from entries in the log.[9] He was evading new ice, and retreating north-wards to Glacier Tongue whenever weather conditions seemed to hold any danger to the ship or whenever there seemed any likelihood of her being frozen in. On 15 February, after two days of driving snow, the entry against 8 p.m. reads, 'Moderate wind puffy fine drift water in Bay of Tongue quite smooth very sheltered position for ship.'

Everyone was now becoming anxious about the Southern Party. On 16 February Captain Evans took the ship to within two miles of Hut Point and fired detonators, but there was no answering signal. On 20 February, steaming through pack for part of the time, he returned to Hut Point from Glacier Tongue and took off the supporting party from the Bluff—Joyce, Day, Marston and Armytage—who had seen no sign of Shackleton. From now until the end of the month the weather was slightly improved, though there was still drifting snow and the ice continued in a state of movement. The ship remained at Glacier Tongue. It was at this point that dissension arose over two points—whether Shackleton and his comrades were to be assumed lost, and whether a relief party should be left behind to search for them, dead or alive.

Without Shackleton, the leader of the party, several men of dominant character found themselves temporarily at odds. In matters of navigation and in regard to the safety of the ship, Captain Evans took the lead. Murray had been appointed official leader of the expedition in Shackleton's absence. Joyce, a man of strong and outspoken character, was all for immediate action, and offered to lead a party back at once on his return from the Bluff, without rest. The Captain, however, did not feel it right, in the conditions which then obtained, to take the ship further south in order to land such a party. In a state of strong emotion, Mackay expressed in his diary[12] the conviction that not enough was being done to help the Southern Party—that the necessary relief was in fact being hindered.

Professor David probably acted with his usual diplomacy at this time, but the fact that he headed an Australian party produced an additional difficulty. Shackleton had instructed Murray to ask Mawson to lead the relief party, if such a party had to remain behind for another winter. The diaries of Priestley[4] and Mackay[12] indicate that there was strong feeling because the men chosen (from numerous volunteers) were all what was then called 'colonial'.*

Mackay led a deputation of protest to Captain Evans, urging particularly that Priestley should be allowed to stay, as he was very anxious to do so and as he was well equipped, by health and occupation, to get through another winter. There was some argument between the Captain and Mackay, and Mackay's diary at this time reflects strong excitement. The composition of the relief party was revised to include first Priestley and then Joyce.

Meanwhile the members of the shore party, in their state of anxiety, became critical of the Captain—Murray and Mackay forcibly and openly so. They seem genuinely to have believed that the Captain was deliberately hindering the immediate despatch of a relief party. The ship's log, as it stands, suggests that from the point of view of weather it would have been possible to go up and land a relief party at Hut Point at this time; but the state of the ice is not mentioned, and it cannot be considered that there is enough evidence to suggest that Captain Evans did not intend to land a party. The memories of those who survive from that time hold only an impression of tension and disagreement which lasted until a short time after Shackleton had been picked up. The ship was in fact at Glacier Tongue when, on 28 February, Shackleton and Wild reached the *Discovery* hut.

As soon as Shackleton had returned from his journey to bring in

---

* While the diaries leave no doubt as to the strong feeling over this, there is no indication as to which men were chosen to remain, nor whether they were picked by the Captain or by Murray. The only other Australian in the shore party was Armytage.

Adams and Marshall, he had to listen to the complaints and justifica-
tions of various members of the party. He had also to try to discover
why his orders for a relief party to be sent to Hut Point on 25 February
had not been carried out.

To return to an atmosphere of doubt and dispute must have been a
shock to him. Inevitably he must have recalled the details of his disagreement with Captain England. But the long winter and the long drag
of the Southern Journey had given him plenty of time to think about the
policy of a leader. These months had taught him, must have taught
him, more about the nature of men than he had learned in the rest of
his life. He had learned that he could dominate men: he had gained in
confidence as well as in wisdom. When he made his decision about
Captain England he had, we believe, allowed himself to be influenced
by his shore-party; he had been very conscious of their disapproval
and not altogether certain of his power to sway them. On this occasion,
when the issue between leader and ship's captain seemed to be arising
for a second time, he seems to have acted more wisely and more
firmly.

Unfortunately there is little written evidence to show what his
attitude was towards the actions of Captain Evans. He evidently
decided to accept the captain's assurances that he had acted according
to his leader's instructions and had paid due regard to the safety of the
ship. The attitude Shackleton took up was expressed in a letter of
thanks[13] which he wrote to Captain Evans from Christchurch on
27 March. It ended thus:

> 'It is the first rule of a master of a ship that he should exercise
> prudence, but under circumstances which attend Polar exploration,
> I realise he may be called upon to face contingencies which involve
> exceptional risk. Such circumstances arose in this particular case, and
> while you exercised the prudence, you never shirked the risks which
> you were called upon to face.'

We do not know whether Shackleton discussed this awkward
situation with anybody but the two people most concerned—the ship's
captain and Murray, the leader of the shore party. Certainly he was
wise to take more account of proven facts, such as the state of the
weather and of the ice, than of the allegations of disloyalty which were
made to him. When he came to describe this part of the expedition in
The Heart of the Antarctic, he implied that he had been satisfied with
Captain Evans's handling of the ship, and Murray believed that the
account was definitely unfair to him. He wrote to Shackleton, after
receiving a draft of this portion of the book, saying that he believed
that those who could read between the lines of the brief account would
be led to believe that he had been negligent in the matter of relief

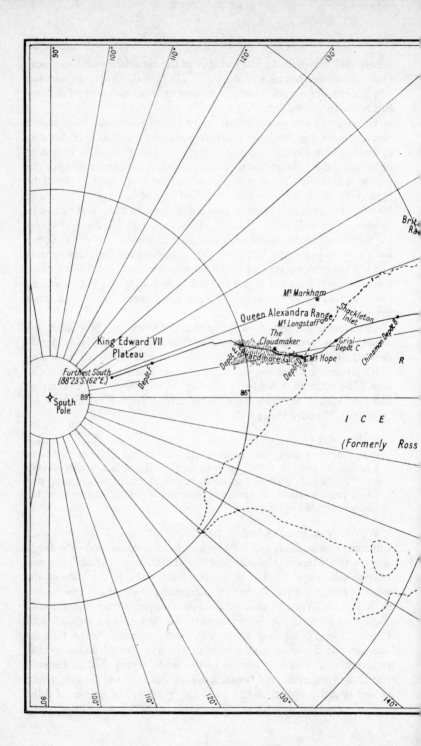

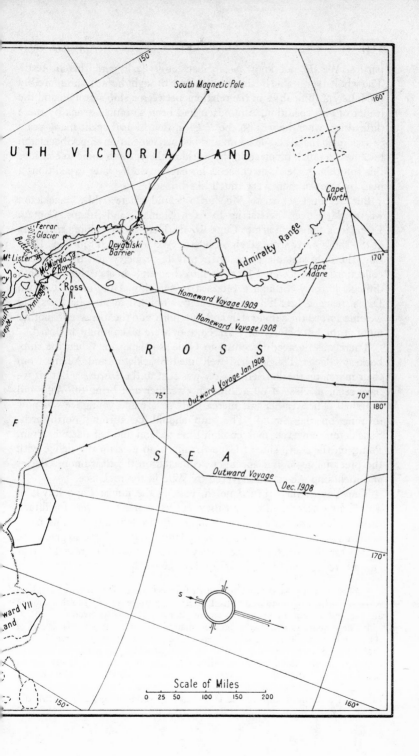

parties. We do not know how Shackleton dealt with this protest.*
The whole regrettable business must have brought home to him forcibly
the inherent difficulties in the relations between a ship's captain and the
leader of an expedition. Amundsen had been so much struck by these
difficulties, when he was on the *Belgica*, that he had spent many years
as a sailor so that he could command his own expedition ship. Shackleton
became too much involved in the world in the years to come to consider
this solution. Instead, he chose as his captain on his later expeditions a
man by temperament very much like himself.

But we must return to McMurdo Sound where, while Shackleton
was tracking over the Barrier to fetch Marshall and Adams, Captain
Evans took the ship back to Cape Royds. Here the remaining members
of the shore party were taken on board. At a low ice-cliff in Back Door
Bay, the only suitable place, their private property and the scientific
collections were lowered by rope into the ship's boats, which began a
difficult journey through a blizzard to the ship. One, under Captain
Davis, reached her. The other boat was obliged to turn back, as bad
weather forced the ship to stand off the shore, and the men spent another
night at the hut before, on 3 March, they were taken safely on board.

There was no need to return to Cape Royds again. When the ship,
back at Glacier Tongue, had welcomed Shackleton and Adams from
their march on the Barrier, a party was sent to the *Discovery* hut, as we
have seen, to close it up against the weather and bring off Wild and
Marshall. The weather was increasingly severe and young ice was now
forming on the Sound. The ship should be turning northwards.
Shackleton, however, took enough time to land another party at Pram
Point, on the south side of Cape Armitage, to pick up the sledge with
the precious geological specimens collected on the Beardmore Glacier
and including the coal discovered by Wild in the rock face.

The *Nimrod* then turned north, passing the hut at Cape Royds at
2 p.m. on 4 March. In the hut they had left stores for a year for fifteen
men, with a letter offering them to any future expeditions. The party
gathered on the deck to sing a verse of Auld Lang Syne and to give three
cheers for the quarters† where they had spent such a profitable year
and where they had found a unique comradeship.

---

* When news of the disaster to Scott's furthest south party reached England
in 1913, Murray wrote to Lady Shackleton[14] once more referring to that time of
anxiety and difficulty in 1909. No answer to his letter has survived.

† These quarters at Cape Royds had many, mostly happy returns. Many of
the members of Scott's second, great expedition of 1910–13 found the hut
useful for shelter, and had reason to bless Shackleton's generous ideas of
catering. On Shackleton's later expedition of 1914–17 it was used by his *Aurora*
party (p. 410), though this party was based mainly on Scott's hut at Cape Evans.

In 1955–56, during Operation Deepfreeze, parties were flown by helicopter
to Cape Royds from ships of the U.S. Navy operating in and near McMurdo

There was still time for a brief coastal survey. Shackleton was anxious to see what lay to the west of Cape Adare and Cape North, from which area pack-ice had previously barred ships. On 8 March, beyond Cape North, they saw a coast-line extending south and then west for forty-five miles. There was no time to go any closer. In his orders to Murray and Captain Evans, Shackleton had given 10 March as the last possible day on which the ship must stay in the south, and at about midnight on 9 March he gave orders for the course to be set for New Zealand. The ice closed in round the ship, but they found a lane through which they were able to move, and by the afternoon of 10 March they were free of the pack and in open water. Once more he had taken a risk, but he had thought the matter out carefully, and his boldness had been justified.

The members of the southern party began to recover some of their lost weight and to relax spirits strained to the utmost by their journey. Something of what it meant to them can be seen from a letter written by Adams,[6] dated on the day the ship finally evaded the pack.

> 'I have just been back a week from the journey and have already put on 12 lbs. of the 24 I lost. J.B.A. weighing $8\frac{1}{2}$ stone was a poor sight but I'm truly grateful to Providence at being able to get back at all. We all realized for the last 2 months of the journey that our own strength was down but as we were pulled out of difficulty after difficulty we at last got to believe we should get back somehow no

Sound. A British naval officer, Lieutenant-Commander M. J. N. Foster, accompanied the Americans as an observer, and he has commented[19] in detail on the state of the hut nearly fifty years after it was erected.

It was very weathered, and bleached almost white. The compressed fodder-bales used for the stable walls were crumbling, but still in their original shape. On the other (southern) side of the hut, tins and cases were lying about, including some unopened Venesta cases containing tinned food which was subsequently found to have kept quite well.

The main structure of the hut (pp. 176–79) had survived the years strongly. A north window was broken. On the west side the outer door was missing, though the porch survived. 'The inner door was jammed half open and there was a snow pile about three feet high in the doorway . . . The roof appeared as sound as the walls, and frapping lines, of wire about $\frac{1}{2}''$ to $\frac{3}{4}''$ in diameter, were still in position.'

Inside, the hut was in chaos. Only about eight bunks remained, and two canvas screens hanging from the ceiling were all that could be seen of the original partitions. On the shelves were instruments, test-tubes, some food. King Edward and Queen Alexandra (see illus. opp. page 176) still looked down from the south wall, upon various relics—reindeer-skin sleeping-bags, New Zealand newspapers, cook-pots, pony-harness, some emperor-penguin skins evidently left behind by Joyce in 1917, and a leg of meat 'hanging up on the north wall of Shackleton's cubicle, still wrapped in its muslin; this was a little soft'.

Tacked against the south wall, added Foster, 'was a statement signed by David Nutt, Commander U.S. Navy, who visited the hut from an American ice-breaker in 1948'.

matter what happened as we have done. It still seems too wonderful to be true. . . . No more exploring as no man would mount that plateau twice. . . . Do you know that we have come to the conclusion that none of us were ever known to laugh or smile, after we had been 13 days out on the journey and consequently now the poorest joke affords us great pleasure. . . .'

Before Shackleton left for the south he had made arrangements for guarding the news of the expedition, in which the *Daily Mail* had first exclusive rights. The *Nimrod* was to make her first landfall at Stewart Island, to the south of the South Island of New Zealand. The New Zealand Government thought it wisest not to use the telephone connection with the mainland, so a special operator and a Morse instructor were sent down on 10 March to wait until Shackleton should arrive. On 22 March the ship anchored on the south side of the island and waited, during a luxurious day of sunshine and greenery, until the pre-arranged time should arrive.* The next morning they moved into Half Moon Bay and Shackleton went ashore to the small office where the operator was waiting, avoiding the people gathered on the wharf.

From the office he sent to the *Daily Mail* first a coded message, at 9*s.* a word, and then a more detailed account of 2,500 words. It was the longest press cablegram ever transmitted from New Zealand and there was not a single mistake when it was printed. With the difference in time, the *Mail* offices in London got the message early in the morning; and so complete was the secrecy that New Zealand had the news not from the expedition members (who kept silent till they reached Lyttelton) but from the London newspapers. A full summarising telegram had been sent to the Queen, and her message of thanks and congratulations appeared in the same issue of the *Daily Mail* as Shackleton's long cable.

In England, Shackleton's brother-in-law Herbert Dorman, the expedition's representative, had arranged a telephone and telegram code with his sister in case he heard any news before it was officially published. The code he suggested was a simple one:

Hunter	= *Nimrod*
Rome	= New Zealand
Mike	= Ernest
Cardinal	= Pole
Words	= Miles
Daisy	= *Daily Mail*

---

* The luxury was not as carefree as it might have been. As they joyously sunbathed the men were badly bitten by sandflies, and Sir Raymond Priestley remembers that at all the social functions that followed you could pick out the members of the Expedition by their uneasy scratching!

'I think a telegram in my code would give nothing away,'[15] he told his sister, 'though it might give rise to a rumour that Daisy is in secret communication with the Pope.'
A telegram went to Mrs. Shackleton in Edinburgh, in fact, before the news was given to the public; it read:

'Cable from K. Hunter reached Rome. All well Daisy silent Say nothing. Herbert.'

Of all the messages and letters that poured in for her in the next five weeks—congratulations from friends, from explorers, from complete strangers—this one must have given her most pleasure; and next to it perhaps the cable that came a few days later, signed by Day, Joyce, Marston, Priestley, and Wild, and sending 'our heartiest congratulations on the success of your heroic husband and our brave Commander.'

The landing on the wharf at Lyttelton, on 25 March, was a wonderful moment for Shackleton, and he had his first taste of fame in the cheering throng waiting for him. His first reaction seems to have been one of genuine bewilderment. He told his wife[16] he was surprised that 'so much fuss is made of the little expedition'.

There was little time yet to enjoy the fruits of his success. He had plenty to do in New Zealand. From Christchurch he had to go to Wellington to give his formal thanks to the Government. He had to see satisfactory arrangements made for the *Nimrod*. The Lyttelton Harbour Board had put at his disposal, free of all charge, whatever port facilities he might require, as a way of expressing their appreciation of his achievements. The ship had now to be put in order, and Shackleton had to see this done and see her safely off to England, carrying most of the expedition. He had to spend some time with Edward Saunders, a journalist working on the *Lyttelton Times* who was to go home with him as secretary and help him with the book of the expedition, which should be ready by August. He had to accept invitations to innumerable functions, shake countless hands, make himself available to all comers. The people of New Zealand left him in no doubt of their feelings about him. From the solemn thanksgiving service in Christchurch Cathedral on the Sunday after their return to the last cheers as he left the country, there was an unending series of entertainments as exhausting as it was gratifying. In the midst of all this he must somehow find time to deal with a large mail, which included copies of all the newspaper articles which extolled his great expedition.

Shackleton might feel that he had failed, since he had not achieved the South Pole. Nobody else felt so. He could not have been more famous if he had indeed reached the Pole. Discerning geographers and explorers recognised, even before full details were known, what Shackleton had achieved.

ALMOST!

THIS CARTOON APPEARED IN THE NEW YORK HERALD ON THE 24TH MARCH 1909.

To the general public his great distance on the Southern Journey counted for much, but his personality for more. It was very soon clear to everybody that he was a remarkable man. Perhaps this was nowhere expressed more succinctly than in a long, jocular, somewhat laboured article in *The Winning Post*, a paper which was at this time running a series of articles entitled 'Celebrities in Glass Houses'. After discussing at some length Shackleton's life and work, and giving some account of the expedition, the article[17] ended:

'You had resources which Cook never dreamt of; you were equipped as no expedition was ever equipped before. You were served by the invaluable experiences of others as well as of yourself, and to this your success must in part be attributed. Yet let it be freely admitted that all would have been in vain if the leader had not risen to the occasion. In the long run all depends upon him and his capacity for getting the best work out of the best men. Hardships, toil, privation, pain must be expected by all who seek to pierce the secrets of the Poles. These you, sir, have faced twice, each time triumphantly, and you have helped others to do the same. He who can do that is a born leader of men, and as such you stand before the world today.'

One of Shackleton's most important attributes as a leader, his wish to give credit to his men, had at this time not much chance to show itself. Most of them had gone home, and it was with Brocklehurst and Armytage alone that he travelled from South Island to North and back again, enjoying the warmth of public appreciation. His formal farewell to the country took place on 14 April, when the Prime Minister, Sir Joseph Ward, and members of the Cabinet gave a luncheon for him at the Grand Hotel in Wellington. New Zealand's pride in having been able to contribute to the expedition, in money and in labour, was stressed in the Prime Minister's speech, and in reply Shackleton promised that when the time came for him to exercise his privilege of naming some of the new geographical features he had discovered, the Dominion would not be forgotten. His speech was typical of him— warmly grateful, full of quotations from his favourite poets, and conspicuously modest. The farewell was extended to a somewhat less formal occasion in the evening, when he joined a large gathering of the Wellington Club to dinner. The next day he sailed on the *Riverina*; the Prime Minister and a large number of friends gathered on the wharf to see him off, and the students of Victoria College suitably said goodbye with a Maori war cry.

His farewell to the people of New Zealand had taken the form of a public lecture at the Town Hall in Wellington, which earned him £300. This he handed over at once to local charities. The same expansive gesture was made in the great Australian cities where he now lectured to huge and enthusiastic audiences. He felt himself to be rich—rich in friends, rich in money, rich in a general goodwill as warm as the New Zealand sunshine. His letters to his wife are full of the usual exuberant calculations. It would be easy, he was sure, to pay off the expedition debts. The book would be ready for the Christmas market; the stamps would raise anything up to £20,000; the lecture agency was sure he would earn £10,000 in England alone. He was certain, from the reception he got everywhere, that the expedition would make as much money as if they had indeed got the Pole.

But this was not the greatest misconception in the loving, impatient letters he scribbled off to his wife between engagements.

'I just want to tell you now darling Heart' (he wrote[18] to her on 25 April) 'how much I love you how much I have missed you all this time and how I long to see you and our little ones again. Never again my beloved will there be such a separation as this has been never again will you and I have this long parting that takes so much out of our lives.'

At the time when he wrote this, and on many other occasions, he really meant what he said: he really believed that he would never return to the Antarctic. It was not because he discovered later that he was not to be a rich man that he changed his mind; it was not even because he was haunted by the unattained point of latitude 90°. It was because the whole of his nature—as poet, leader, ambitious family man, and comrade—could only be satisfied in the kind of life he was now leaving. To be with his men, leading them in a fight against the unknown, against long odds, against the impossible—it was this that he needed.

At this moment, however, there was no time for regret or longing. Sailing from Australia on the *India*, he spent the voyage working on his book with Edward Saunders.* At Port Said he transferred to the mail-boat *Isis* and went across to Brindisi and then on through France to England. He arrived in Dover on 12 June. He had arranged to spend two days quietly with his wife before the public was let loose on him, but there was, inevitably, a ceremony on the docks, when he was received by the Mayor and presented those members of the expedition who had travelled with him and those who had come to meet him. It was a friendly and warm-hearted scene, and reporters were amused by the slangy way he called his comrades up one by one. After a quiet two days, he took the train from Dover to Charing Cross on 14 June to make his delayed entry into London.

* But not the whole voyage. A girl in her teens, on her way to England, remembers[19] Shackleton, with his companions Mackintosh, Adams and Armytage, playing with the children, yarning with the ship's company and pacing the deck. 'In the dining-saloon his table was in a constant uproar from his Irish wit and inexhaustible supply of funny stories—stewards would clatter dishes and slop soup in futile attempts to preserve their dignified efficiency when overtaken by the giggles, until the Captain threatened them with ear-plugs.'

WELCOME HOME FROM THE FAR SOUTH: THE HERO OF THE MOMENT
IN DOVER AND IN LONDON.

From *The Illustrated London News*, 12 June 1909

Shackleton, Peary and Amundsen, New York, 1910

Drawing of Shackleton by E. T. Reeve, made at a London dinner on 3 May 1911

Thompson

Shackleton in October 1911

His train was due at 5.0 in the afternoon. It ran into a platform crowded with people, while outside the crowd was almost uncontrollable. Most of the prominent figures in the geographical world were there, and Shackleton had to make a speech of recognition on behalf of his colleagues, while his children impatiently waited to greet him. It was not for some time that he and his wife, with her sister Daisy, were able to make their way to the waiting carriage and pair. Shackleton had to stand up in the open carriage and show himself to the crowd which forced it to the slowest speed.

Legend has it that the people took the horses out of the shafts and formed into teams to draw the carriage. Press-reports make no mention of anything so dramatic, but it is significant that the story should have been told and should be believed even today. Shackleton had just returned from an heroic journey: the public were now in the process of making him a Hero.

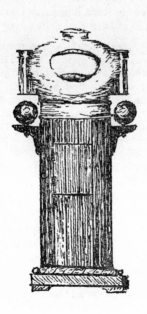

Chapter XIV

SHACKLETON was particularly suitable for elevation to public favour. His bluff sailor humour, his modesty, his direct way of telling his story, above all his power to establish instant warm contact with people—these were the right qualities. The public could recognise in him a man exceptional in strength and stature but still a man, not a super-human nor an unreal figure. He had the human touch.

But before we consider the evolution of Shackleton as a popular hero, we must see how his achievements were regarded and his ambitions treated in the inner circle of geographers and scientists whom, in some ways, those achievements and ambitions most closely concerned.

The British Antarctic Expedition, when it returned to civilisation, won the instant approval and admiration of explorers outside this country, and among the numerous letters of congratulation which Shackleton's wife sent out to reach him in the Dominions, the generous words of Nansen must have been especially satisfying.

'Please accept my most hearty congratulations', Nansen[1] had written to Mrs. Shackleton, 'upon his safe return and upon his unique expedition, which has been such a complete success in every respect. His remarkable deed, and important discoveries, and the excellent way in which he had led his men through all dangers speak for themselves, and are above any praise. . . . But may I ask you to convey to your husband my most hearty congratulation, tell him that I cannot express in words what I felt when I read the accounts which seemed to me like a fairy tale from another world. I only wish I could have pressed his hand and thanked him for what he has done. An excellent man he is.'

In a letter to J. Scott Keltie, Secretary of the Royal Geographical Society, Nansen[2] stressed the importance of the Magnetic Pole journey and the observations made on the nature of the inland ice in the Antarctic, and Nordenskjöld[3] also congratulated the Society on the way Shackleton had opened up 'a view of the central Antarctic regions'.

Amundsen's approval[4] was expressed even more emphatically:

'Now that the Shackleton expedition is a fact' (he wrote to Keltie) 'I must write and congratulate you and through you the Royal Geographical Society upon this wonderful achievement. When I first heard of it I thought it was some news brought out for sensation, especially coming from *Daily Mail*, but now that the expedition has reached port in safety, there is no more place for doubt. The English nation has by the deed of Shackleton won a victory in the Antarctic exploration which never can be surpassed.'

The Royal Geographical Society, who now received such congratulations as their due, had in fact played a comparatively small part in the preparations for Shackleton's expedition. Its officers had not been in a position to do more than lend him charts and instruments and to give a donation of £500 to the expedition fund: they had borne no responsibility for his plans. If Dr. Mill may be believed, this help had only been given in the face of some opposition from Sir Clements Markham, lately retired after a long term as President. For Markham the National Antarctic Expedition had been the crown of his long life as an active and a research geographer, and his strong personal regard for Scott had led him to feel that it should be left to him to achieve the South Pole.

Mill, whose knowledge of the counsels of the Society was intimate, admired Shackleton's independence but deplored the attitude to him. He wrote[5] on this point uncompromisingly, some years after Shackleton's death:

'Mr. E. H. Shackleton, who had been sent home by Scott from the *Discovery*, had resolved at the time to prove that he was in no way unfit for polar service by going out again at the head of an expedition. Markham considered ambition in a subordinate as little less than mutiny, and did not dissemble his opposition to Shackleton's plans; but the Society under Goldie gave them a hearing and afforded some slight support to his expedition in the Nimrod.'

There was some prejudice here, of course. In those exciting years when Scott and Shackleton were in direct rivalry to each other in the South Polar Stakes, the two distinguished geographers, Markham and Mill (the one precluded by old age, the other by ill health from active exploration) lurk in the background like two trainers, each exhorting and defending the champion of his choice. Each 'trainer', if we may use the term, allowed himself conveniently to forget the rights of the other side. Markham had been for so long the great power in the Society that he could hardly have helped imposing his attitude on some of his fellow members. But most of them had looked at the matter, in 1907, from a practical point of view too. The National Antarctic Expedition had been sent out under their patronage and guidance, and with their money (or money raised in their name) and their directive. It was quite another thing to contemplate allowing a comparatively unknown officer, invalided home from the Antarctic not many years before, to take the Society's money while keeping the entire control of the expedition in his own hands. This is what Shackleton would have wanted from the Society, and this they were not prepared to give. Consequently, although he had been aided by the specialist knowledge vested in the Society, its treasury had subscribed only in a small way.

The Society, then, was in no way responsible for Shackleton. It was, however, responsible for what it published about him, both before and after his return. The scientific and geographical results of his expedition, if they were given the seal of approval of the Society, would be accepted by the rest of the world. In Britain it was the final court of appeal in which the facts of geographical exploration—details of distance, position, natural features—were scrutinised, and either passed or rejected.

Shackleton's first communication to Scott Keltie from New Zealand was answered in a long letter which made the Society's attitude very clear. It is an interesting letter in its mixture of the personal and the official. Scott Keltie, judging from those of his letters which survive, was a man who liked to be involved in affairs, to be made the repository of secrets. He was given to making small calculated indiscretions of the kind that can be greatly flattering to the recipient. Before writing to Shackleton he had informed himself on every aspect of the expedition— geographical, personal, and financial. He had spoken to Heinemann about the contract for the book and to Gerald Christy the agent about a projected lecture tour for Shackleton. He had been looking up the possible shipping routes by which the explorer might reach home quickly. He had been gauging the temperature of Society meetings. His eager possessive delight in Shackleton's achievements was tempered by caution. If Shackleton had gone out to the Antarctic a dark horse, he was returning, unmistakably, a lion. In so far as the Society owed him an apology for their lack of enthusiasm in 1907, that apology is conveyed in Keltie's letter[6] in its praise, and in the tentative, respectful way in which he offers his advice (The formula 'I dare say you will have thought of this already' concludes nearly all his remarks). He is afraid the lion may roar a little too loudly in London; he does not quite know how to say so.

Keltie was responsible for planning the official announcement of Shackleton's results. He was anxious to have a summary of what Shackleton intended to say at his first meeting, when the Society was to present Shackleton to the world. He was also anxious to have maps. The Society had accepted at once Shackleton's own calculations, notably of his distances on the Southern Journey. Short quotations and points from the despatches from New Zealand were given in the *Geographical Journal* in April 1909,[7] including the following sentence:

'Carrying on the work so well begun by Captain Scott, and by the way opened by him, he has, by a bold dash south, pushed forward the farthest outpost of man's advance some 430 miles beyond the turning-point of his former leader, reaching a latitude never before attained in either hemisphere, and only turning when at a distance of little more than 100 miles [statute] from the South Pole.'

and a fuller account[8] given by Dr. Mill on 8 May congratulated Shackleton and his party 'on having set a new record of limit to human endurance'.

But among the points so tentatively and respectfully made by Scott Keltie[6] was the following:

'I do not know you said anything about the instruments you had with you, and of course the difficulty of taking any observations under the conditions must have been fearfully trying, but still, I have no doubt you established your latitude to your complete satisfaction.'

Shackleton's answer to this query is not extant, but a letter[9] he wrote to Mill shortly afterwards shows that he was well aware that in geographical circles his distance might be queried. The letter, too, shows that he knew his own strength. He was not going to play the young and unknown sailor now.

'Quite entre nous' (he wrote), 'K. is tumbling over himself at the present time as regards the Expedition. His first wire was a very guarded one, the second was the opposite. Even now he asks me if I can be sure of my latitude, as if I had not taken all possible means in my power to ascertain the exact position. I do not want any case of "Friend, come down lower" and in many things we have underestimated the results. You can rest assured that there is no confusion between true and magnetic as regards the winds, for we took our observations more carefully this time, guided by the experience obtained in connection with Scott's meteorology.'

The doubt about Shackleton's latitude may have been widespread in geographical circles; it was certainly felt strongly by Sir Clements Markham. As we have seen, he had so far adopted Scott as his protégé that he was convinced of his proprietary rights in the Ross Sea. For this reason Markham, who had bidden a cordial farewell to Shackleton in 1907, was not disposed to regard him in friendly fashion now that he had broken his promise to Scott about his base. To him there were no extenuating circumstances: it was a broken promise, and that was that. He did, it is true, keep his views for private circulation, so that the name of science and discovery should not be smirched in the public eye. When the news of Shackleton's change of base reached England, in 1908, he wrote[10] to Mrs. Shackleton explaining:

'I strongly advised Dr. Keltie not to put anything in the R.G.S. Journal about the reasons for giving up King Edward VII Land; and he has taken my advice. The reason is that an excuse would be implied; when the public are not aware that any excuse is needed.

It is a pity that Ernest worded his promise so strongly, and now the best thing is that nothing more should be heard of it.'

This was sensible advice, the advice of a man well accustomed to deal in geographical politics. Certainly many other people, including Shackleton himself, must have come to the same conclusion about that unfortunate promise. But Markham, even if he did help to confine any trouble within the walls of the Society, allowed his feelings to colour his attitude to Shackleton after the expedition.

Not, perhaps, at once. When the news of the great Southern Journey reached the Royal Geographical Society, Markham was on holiday in Portugal, and, being apprised of the news, hastened to link himself with the great event. He wrote[11] to Keltie:

'I have just seen the *Daily Mail* with the news about Shackleton. Please put me down at once as his proposer for the Patron's Medal. If the date is later than the rule directs an exception ought certainly to be made and I am the proper person to be his proposer. Everything seems to have turned out well and he has made as good a record as was possible. If the ponies turned out well I gave him 85 degrees. My proposal* is for reaching 88 degrees 23 minutes South and securing exceptionally valuable geographical results.

It seems to me that my theory of the Antarctic lands will turn out to be the correct one; for as far as I can understand it there is no bay. However, the telegram is not very intelligible.'

It is not clear why this attitude, so understandably possessive, should have hardened into suspicion and hostility; but so it did. Returned to England, Markham wrote[12] to Major Leonard Darwin, then President of the Royal Geographical Society:

'As I am responsible for having started all this Antarctic business, I think it right that I should send you a note of what I think of recent developments.

Shackleton's failure to reach the South Pole when it could have been done by another, and is really a matter of calculation, rather aggravates me. They will rouse ignorant admiration if the trumpets are blown loud enough, which they are sure to be. But I cannot quite accept the latitudes. For 88.20 they must have gone, dragging a sledge and on half rations, at the rate of 14 miles a day in a straight line, up a steep incline 9,000 feet above the sea, for 20 days. I do not believe it.

However, I have nothing more to do with it now. I am getting out of touch with new people, and deafness is beginning to come on, so I intend to retire from the Council next year. I shall then have served for 48 years continuously without a break, which is a fairly long service.'

---

* I.e. the formal proposal accompanying the Patron's Medal.

Just what Shackleton and his companions *had* done on that journey has already been described in these pages. In the face of a journey so incredible a man might be forgiven for allowing doubts to enter his mind, Markham went further. We do not know whether he asked privately to see Shackleton's records, but five months later we find him writing again to Darwin asserting that the Society had done wrong to accept the figures without close scrutiny. Clearly the whole business had been preying on his mind, and the jealousy which he felt on Scott's behalf (a jealousy which Scott himself would certainly not have felt or wished anyone else to feel) was infecting his judgment. To Darwin he made two astonishing remarks : first, that Shackleton had only got his Master's Certificate in an honorary form, without examination, as one of the officers on the *Discovery*, and secondly, that he had taken no observations on the Southern Journey of 1907–09 but had depended entirely on Dr. Marshall for records of distance.

Where so much of doubt and opinion is not now open to investigation, it is important to investigate matters of provable fact. As we have seen (p. 12), Shackleton already had his Master's Certificate when he joined the *Discovery*, having obtained it as the result of an examination in the normal way. Secondly, it is clear from the three diaries of the Southern Journey of 1908–09 which survive (the diaries of Shackleton, Wild and Marshall), as well as from the personal statement of Adams (except for Dr. Marshall, the only survivor of that journey), that all four men took independent observations and checked them with each other, although Marshall, as hydrographer, was responsible for surveying and making the map.

Markham's suspicions of Shackleton's accuracy in the matter of his distance may have been encouraged by another critic of Shackleton. Here the biographers are on difficult ground, for their statements depend at this point on hearsay and not upon documentary evidence. All the same, gossip is seldom *invented*, only distorted, and it is therefore necessary to believe that Shackleton had at least one critic who accused him of deliberate falsification. He was said to have added a small number of miles to the daily total, during the last days of the journey, between the last sun-sight on 3 January and the turning back on 9 January. The purpose of this imposture, it was suggested, was to break the last hundred miles.

Such an imposture would mean that Shackleton, day after day, when he was worn out with hunger and physical effort, deliberately imposed on his companions a falsification of the day's run. It would mean that he had to make a calculation each day, niggling a mile here and fiddling a mile there. It would mean that he had deliberately laid himself open to, at best, the distrust and disloyalty of his men, at worst to something more sinister. This implies in Shackleton and his companions a mean-mindedness and a foolishness which is simply not in character.

Shackleton had it in him to do wrong, as all of us have, and nobody can be dogmatic about honesty and dishonesty; but the petty falsification of a few miles for an insufficient gain was beyond the behaviour of this forceful man. Mean deceit of the kind we have described does not fit with what we know of him.

It has already been shown that all four men took observations, and there is no reason to suppose that they were not all concerned equally with the recording of the distances of those last seven days, from the sledge-meter. We have from Adams a categorical denial that any faking was even thought of.

This unpleasant allegation has been put on record for two reasons. First, it is still believed by one or two men in geographical circles that there may have been some falsification. Secondly, it is possible that this allegation, after Shackleton's return in 1909, helped to persuade Markham that the distance was incorrectly given. Certainly it seems to have been Markham who spread the rumour. 'For our own credit we cannot be too careful' he had warned the President;[2] and at some stage it appears that the Society did call in the maps and charts of the Southern Journey and, apparently, called upon Shackleton to defend his latitude. What happened then cannot be discovered. No records remain of any investigation at the Royal Geographical Society, and at some stage the maps and charts became 'mislaid'. Whatever steps Shackleton took to defend his calculations, the doubt seems to have persisted, and echoes of it sound down to the present day.

Shackleton dealt with the problem in an article in the *Geographical Journal*,[13] in which he explained:

'The latitude observations made on the Southern Journey were taken with the theodolite, as were all the bearings, angles, and azimuths. Variation was ascertained by means of a compass attached to the theodolite, and the steering compasses were checked accordingly. At noon each day the prismatic compasses were placed in the true meridian, and checked against the theodolite compass and the steering compasses. The last latitude observation on the outward journey was taken in 87° 22′ S. and the remainder of the distance towards the south was calculated by sledge meter and dead reckoning. The accuracy of the sledge meter had been proved by the fact that the daily record of distance travelled agreed roughly with the observations for position.* We took only one observation on the return

---

* Early on the outward journey Wild[33] entered in his diary: 'Sledgemeter records 30 yds. short in the mile.' This alleged error is so small as to be swallowed by the margin of accuracy of any observations they could have made to check it; and Shackleton's statement thus remains unexceptionable. If the sledge-meter really *did* record significantly short they probably got another mile or so nearer the Pole than they estimated.

journey, on 31 January, and then found that our position had been
accurately recorded by the sledge meter.'

At midday on 3 January 1909 they got their last sun-sight at 87° 22' S.
From here their sledge-meter gave exactly 47 geographical miles to
their blizzard-camp of 6 to 8 January. They logged this camp at 88° 7'
S., a straight distance of 45 geographical miles from the previous fix,
doubtless (and reasonably) allowing two miles for detours. On 9
January they left camp and sledge at 4 a.m. and marched, weighed
down with no more than a small camera and a small amount of food,
until 9 a.m., when they hoisted the Union Flag. They estimated that
in the five hours they had gone 16·5 geographical miles further, and
that they had reached Furthest South at 88° 23' S., 16 straight geographical miles south of their camp. On this last rush an average of 3·3
knots (geographical miles per hour) was not impossible to men who
were in a state of exalted determination. Sir Jameson Adams[14] recalls
that throughout those hours they were moving at a jog-trot much
of the time: Marshall's diary[15] says they 'marched hard'. The error here,
if any, was small.

We believe that the logging of the 61 last dead-reckoning miles was
scrupulous, and that the error in observation and estimation may not
have amounted to more than five per cent (plus or minus); and that the
party's claim to have planted the Union Flag within a hundred geographical miles of the South Pole was consequently proper.

Markham continued to make it quite clear that he thought Shackleton's
claims were exaggerated. In the autumn of 1912,[16] at the Dundee
meeting of the British Association, he read a paper on the exploration
of the Antarctic continent, in which he spoke extensively of Scott and
only cursorily mentioned Shackleton. In the discussion afterwards
Dr. Marshall rose to point out the great importance of the British
Antarctic Expedition, and to enumerate the several discoveries they had
made. In *The Lands of Silence*, published in 1921,[17] which Markham
called a history of Antarctic exploration, he made his partiality for
Scott still more emphatic. If any proof were needed of his prejudice
against Shackleton, it could be readily found in the difference in tone
between the chapters in which he writes glowingly of the achievements
of Scott and those in which he coldly and with notable omissions
describes Shackleton's expedition of 1907–09.

Whether or not Shackleton made any comment at any time on the
situation, it cannot but have had its effect upon him. He was always
acutely conscious of the opinion of other men, and an atmosphere of
doubt and distrust would be infinitely distressing to a man of his
temperament. Courageous and practical when faced with a concrete
problem, Shackleton, like many another man of action, had no mind

for dealing with intrigue, or with indirect criticism. He was blunt himself, and he expected other people to be blunt. If at any time he was faced with a direct question about his distance in 1909, we may be sure that he answered it directly: we can be equally sure that he would be troubled and confused by a whispering campaign of the kind which seems to have been carried on against him. His public manner may be said to have evolved rather in the same way as the caddis worm's outer covering. Gradually he had built round himself a protective layer of defiance and bluntness, and had exaggerated his natural openness of speech. The knowledge that he was regarded with distrust or at least with question made him speak aggressively, in a manner which antagonised those who did not know him. He had never wanted to become deeply involved in the affairs of the Royal Geographical Society, but he cannot have helped feeling, now, that the Society did not want to be involved with him.

Not that they allowed their doubts to prevent them from a due appreciation of his achievement. A cablegram had gone off to New Zealand on 25 March—'Council cordially invite for special meeting May or June please wire as to dates. Darwin President RGS'. Shackleton had evidently replied to this somewhat exuberantly, and had expressed a wish that they would take the Albert Hall and 'get the King'. To this Scott Keltie replied[6] 'It was not at all necessary for you to remind me about the Albert Hall and the King', and continued with some sound advice on the need for modesty in returning explorers.

In fact the Society did most handsomely by Shackleton. The great meeting was held on 28 June, prefaced by a dinner at the Royal Palace Hotel in Kensington given by the Geographical Club to Shackleton and the other members of the expedition. The King was unable to attend, but the Prince of Wales headed a distinguished company of guests. At the Albert Hall Shackleton was introduced by the President of the Society, whose congratulations on his great leap into the unknown were strongly and enthusiastically phrased—although he afterwards[18] made the kind of disclaimer which was expected of a scientific society:

> 'As to the latitude reached' (he said), 'it has been the policy of our Society neither to promote nor to reward either mere record breaking or any mere race to either pole, because there is no reason to suppose that any especial scientific interest attaches to that particular spot on the earth's surface. But it would be mere cant not to acknowledge that we are all proud of the fact that it is one of our own countrymen who at the present time has made the nearest approach to a pole of the Earth.'

Shackleton's address consisted of a condensed account of his expedition, with brief summaries of some of its results. His words were simple and straightforward, and were illustrated by slides made from

photographs taken by himself and by Marshall, and by the cinematograph films which Marshall had taken at the base.*

The climax of the evening came when the Prince of Wales, as Vice-
Patron of the Society, presented Shackleton with the special gold medal
which had been struck 'in recognition of his great and unique achieve-
ment of having reached a point within 100 miles of the South Pole.'
The Prince, in his short speech, alluded to himself as a brother sailor to
Shackleton, and sailor-like indeed was Shackleton's reply, which ended
'We feel awfully honoured, and I cannot make much of a speech about
it.'

There was nothing but generous appreciation in the presentation of
the medal, but the making of it had been attended with some ungenerous
impulses.[19] On 19 April a letter had gone from the Society to Cuthbert
Bayes the medal maker, stating 'We do not propose to make the Medal
so large as that which was awarded to Capt. Scott, and this I suppose
would make a difference in your estimate.' Then there were second
thoughts on the subject. On 11 May the Secretary wrote, 'I feel inclined
to try and induce the Council to let Mr. Shackleton have a Medal of the
same size', and another letter of 21 May shows that this he had succeeded in doing. It is an amusing indication of the climate of opinion
in certain quarters at the moment of Shackleton's triumph: but those
closely concerned in these confabulations cannot have regarded the
situation as particularly conducive to mirth.

When the moment came, however, enthusiasm prevailed over
caution. The vote of thanks to Shackleton was proposed warmly by
Scott, who had not allowed his private annoyance over the McMurdo
Sound business to spoil his public acclamation of Shackleton. Scott
made a graceful reference to Shackleton's presence on the expedition
of 1901–03 and to Markham's influence on the work of both expeditions,
and his final tribute was generous; 'We honour him', he said, 'for the
manner in which he organised and prepared his expedition, for the
very substantial addition he had made to human knowledge, but most
of all because he has shown us a glorious example of British pluck and
endurance.'

In fact, at this meeting, Scott played no small part in establishing
Shackleton in the eyes of the geographical world as a great explorer and
a great leader. At the same time, there could be no more genuine
friendship between the two men. They do not appear to have had any

* This was the equipment with which Shackleton lectured for the next
eighteen months. It had not been possible to take either the cinematograph
machine or the box camera on the Southern Journey because of their weight, but
both Shackleton and Marshall had pocket cameras, with which they took a
number of snapshots and some time exposures. Mawson also had a box camera
which he made good use of, particularly on the journey to the South Magnetic
Pole.

close contact with each other after this date, but to have communicated by letter when any matter for discussion arose between them. One small incident remained a mystery to Scott and his wife which could no doubt have been explained if he had asked Shackleton about it—which, apparently, he never did.

During 1908 or 1909 there reached Scott an envelope with one of the special King Edward VII Land stamps printed for the British Antarctic Expedition; it was addressed in Shackleton's hand. Inside there was a blank piece of paper. Scott and his wife thought this was a joke on Shackleton's part, but they were not amused by it. Evidently they spoke of it to A. E. W. Mason, with whom they were acquainted, for in 1912 he published a novel, *The Turnstile*, in which he used the incident.* The hero of the novel closely resembled Scott in many respects, in particular in receiving from a young explorer, who had once served with him, a letter with a 'Rexland' stamp containing a blank piece of paper. This he took to be neither a joke nor an insult, but a somewhat eccentric way of announcing that his former colleague's attack on the South Pole had failed.

Many years after Scott's death Professor Debenham,[20] as an old comrade of his, visited Lady Scott to receive some papers which she wished to give to the Scott Polar Institute. While he was with her she turned out the envelope with the blank piece of paper from a cupboard. She said impatiently 'Oh there's that silly thing Shackleton sent to Con' and made it clear that it had annoyed them both. She would not allow the envelope to be taken away, and it has now presumably been destroyed. Professor Debenham believes that this was one of the many 'letters' (that is, philatelic letters, or blanks) sent out by

---

* Two more Antarctic novels owe much to Shackleton's character and life.

(1) Hall Caine's *The Woman thou gavest me* (Heinemann, 1913) is a romantic account of Martin Conrad, who after a first expedition in a naval ship, takes his own men south on a voyage which owes most of its details to *The Heart of the Antarctic*. The book is a copious melodrama, in which Conrad leaves behind a devoted and tubercular mistress and an illegitimate child. His achievements in the Antarctic, inspired (at some removes) by Shackleton's expedition of 1907–09, include leading a party of men 'singing all the way' to the South Pole. If Shackleton read the book, it must have given him some amusement.

(2) W. B. Maxwell's *Spinster of this Parish* (Thornton Butterworth, May 1922) bore a note disclaiming any reference to Shackleton. Certainly the hero's lifelong attachment to the spinster, Emmeline Verinder (his wife being in an asylum), was pure novelists' invention, but the character of Anthony Dyke, a dashing, unconventional, insolvent and idealistic man, is clearly based on Shackleton, and the course of his exploration—the dash across the Antarctic continent, the disagreement with rivals, the attitude to scientists and numerous other details—showed that Maxwell was in fact taking liberties with a celebrated figure. It is a wry fact that Shackleton's death made the book a success: it had at least five impressions in 1922, a popular edition in the following year, and many subsequent impressions.

Shackleton and his comrades to friends and acquaintances, to give them the benefit of the special expedition stamps, which would in years to come be of considerable value. There was very little time for anyone to get mail ready before the *Nimrod* left for the north, and Shackleton had less time than anyone. In the circumstances, Professor Debenham suggests, he might well have availed himself of a widely recognised custom.*

Against this, it must be pointed out that Shackleton had written one letter to Scott already, to send back with the *Nimrod*, explaining his decision in regard to the change of base. Sir Philip Brocklehurst[21] remembers Shackleton writing this letter, and he himself thinks that the 'blank paper' episode could have been invented to discredit Shackleton. Whatever the truth of the matter, the story was widely believed at the time. One of the reviews of Mill's *Life of Shackleton*, dated May 1923,[22] revived the ancient piece of gossip as a fact. Writing of the McMurdo Sound affair, the reviewer said 'Shackleton simply broke his promise, landed at McMurdo Sound, and, we believe, announced it to Scott by simply sending him a blank piece of paper from the spot! What it meant Scott never knew and never asked.'

It is not likely that the truth of the matter will ever be established. What is significant is the fact that Scott was annoyed.

The rivalry of the two men was a very positive thing, rising out of their mutual determination to reach the South Pole; but it may be guessed that each man felt for the other also some uneasy combination of envy and disapproval. Their temperaments were in direct opposition. Scott was a man of great reserve, who found life on the whole a matter for effort. He had, as he himself said, a streak of indolence and softness which he had set himself to conquer. He had had to work hard to succeed in his profession, because his family depended on him. Shackleton, too, had worked hard to succeed: he too had retired to his cabin to work while his brother officers were merrymaking. But he had always been able to make the transition between solitude and conviviality. When his solitary work was over he could in a moment become the life and soul of the party; this was a phrase often to be applied to him throughout his life. Scott could not do this. In the company of his friends he could be gay, cheerful and charming, but the hard work and the determination had increased in him the habit of reserve. Shackleton's men, accustomed to their leader's flow of conversation, found Scott difficult to talk to if they met him at public gatherings. It may well be that Scott made Shackleton feel unpolished and uncontrolled: his

---

* Sir Raymond Priestley supports this theory. He himself has received empty envelopes from Antarctic bases during 1957, designed to give him the stamps and postmarks, and he believes Shackleton's 'blank piece of paper' must have been of the same philatelic kind.

comments on Shackleton's 'restless energy' in his reports from the *Discovery* may indicate impatience and possibly also a modicum of reluctant admiration. On that expedition the two men had taken each other's measure. Even then there was very likely a latent rivalry between them. Later, when their plans clashed, they must have recognised some clash of temperament as well.

When Shackleton returned in 1909, there were plenty of people in geographical and scientific circles, who would have enjoyed seeing a public quarrel between the two leaders. During the next two years there was much gossip—and a generous crop of apocryphal stories. The conspiracy to bring about a dramatic situation does not seem to have bothered Scott and Shackleton very much. Certainly they were critical about each other to their intimate friends, but they had no intention of demeaning themselves by any public hostility. Their behaviour, on the rare occasions when they met, seems to have been impeccable, though in their family circles an atmosphere of rivalry did develop. More than this, everyone interested in Antarctic matters sooner or later took sides. There were Shackleton men and Scott men: the division was a real one, so real that the ashes of the old controversy can still be fanned into verbal and epistolary flame at the time this book is being written.

But neither Scott nor Shackleton wanted to quarrel. They were too big to waste their time in pointless disagreement. Their few public meetings were conducted with complete propriety. If the Royal Geographical Society had been troubled by any reluctance in Scott to meet Shackleton on his return, they must have been reassured by a letter[23] he wrote to the President telling him that he did not intend 'the private feeling incurred by past incidents' to affect his judgment of what Shackleton had done in the Antarctic. All the same, the South Pole had still to be reached, and neither man had abandoned the ambition to reach it. Shackleton had been questioned by newspaper men about his plans as soon as he set foot in England. His replies were very guarded. It was clear, however, that he wanted to go back and reach the Pole and he had not been back two months before officers of the Society were discussing the possibility that Scott and Shackleton might decide to take out expeditions to the same spot at the same time.

If a delicate situation of this kind were to arise, the Society might have to step in. As the centre of all geographical activity, the Council was almost always informed of plans and intentions, and could do much, by personal contact, to avert the danger of a clash between explorers. It will be remembered that Scott Keltie had intervened between Arctowski and Shackleton in 1907, when such a clash seemed imminent.

The direct opposition of two Englishmen was unthinkable. Yet Scott was evidently thinking in terms of another attack on the Pole, and the newspapers were hinting that Shackleton would not long rest content with his near miss. On 19 June 1909, Admiral Sir Lewis Beaumont, Vice-President of the Royal Geographical Society, and one of its most important public figures, wrote at length[24] to the President, Major Darwin:

'I have thought carefully over what you told me of the Scott-Shackleton difficulty and I cannot think of any better way for the Geographical Society to deal with it—if it comes before it in the way you expect—than to reply as you said you thought of doing, that is, that the Society could not encourage or support an expedition merely intended to reach the Pole, but as individuals the members of Council could not help hoping it would be reached by an Englishman!

... The more I think of the difference between what Shackleton has done, and the mere act, difficult, almost unattainable, as that is, of standing at the position of the Pole itself—the less I think of it!— just now when Shackleton's exploit is still shrouded in mystery and only the nearness to a full accomplishment of a remarkable success is in the public mind—the bridging of that little distance seems to be very much worth doing, but later it will be considered in its truer light, and the final value of such a success could—I think— never be great.

Shackleton—if the money is forthcoming, will probably, most probably, try it, but I am quite clear in my own mind that Scott should not. Let him lead another Antarctic Expedition if he will . . . but let it be a scientific expedition primarily with exploration and the Pole as secondary objects—and so add to the good work and the fine reputation which he has already. He is looking at the thing now from too close individually and even nationally—for if Shackleton does it—this feat of standing at the Pole of the Earth—it will be to England's credit—and if he does it, which is *very* probable, then he, Scott, would still have a chance if he led a scientific expedition to new regions.

All this long story is to incline you to put Scott off from making what I think will be a great mistake—that is, competing with Shackleton and organising an expedition to go over the old route merely to do that 97 miles.'

Certainly, if Scott should appeal to the members of Council to support him in claiming priority in the Ross Sea area, it might put them in an awkward position. With the whole enormous unknown continent of Antarctica to be explored, it looked as though Scott and Shackleton were determined to restrict themselves to a small corner of it, a corner in which each had vested interests.

Admiral Beaumont's letter was sent on to Scott, who replied[25] at once to Major Darwin that there was no question of 'rivalry'. What worried him, he said, was that Shackleton spoke of plans in the Antarctic but would not define them. Scott left no doubt of his own strong desire to try for the Pole again. He had to know Shackleton's plans before he published his own: the ambitions of the two men had, in fact, come into direct conflict. In the end Scott wrote to Shackleton, a clear, careful and formal letter:[26]

Dear Shackleton

If, as I understand, it does not cut across any future plan of yours, I propose to organize the Expedition to the Ross Sea which, as you know, I have had so long in preparation so as to start next year.

My plan is to establish a base in King Edward Land and to push South and East. I cannot but think that late in the season with a heavier ship than the 'Nimrod' it will be possible to establish the base.

The prospect offers good geographical work as well as a chance of reaching a high latitude, and I am sure you will wish me success; but of course I should be glad to have your assurance that I am not disconcerting any plan of your own.

Shackleton replied[27] with equal formality:

Dear Captain Scott

. . . I understand that you have already your expedition in preparation, and it will not interfere with any plans of mine. If I do any further exploration it will not be until I have heard news of your expedition, presuming that you start next year. I may later on attempt the circumnavigation of the Antarctic Continent but my ideas as regards this are indefinite.

I wish you every success in your endeavour to penetrate the ice and to land on King Edward VII Land and to attain a high latitude from that base. I quite agree with you that good geographical work can be done from that quarter, and it will have a newer interest than McMurdo Sound.

If it is clear from this correspondence of July 1909 that the Pole was very much in Scott's mind, it is not quite clear just what it was that led Shackleton to abandon his idea of trying once more to reach that useless but desirable point of latitude; but perhaps there is a clue in the sentence about the circumnavigation of the continent. Perhaps some larger conception had turned his mind from the Polar plateau.

The officers of the Society, informed of the private agreement Scott and Shackleton had reached, were still undecided about their attitude to the difficult question of rival explorers. To Shackleton Major Darwin[28] put his own views:

'In my opinion, every explorer should in future be at liberty to go exactly where he likes, without, at all events, any liability to an accusation of breach of faith. This being adopted as a general principle, then in addition to this, it would be no doubt, very advantageous

if explorers would discuss how best to partition the work amongst
themselves so as to avoid overlapping as far as possible.

But the result of such negotiations should not involve more than
a statement of what each *intends* to adopt, but which each *can*
abandon *at any time* at will.

These are my views, which though uncalled for, by either party,
perhaps I may be permitted to mention.'

It was a sensible attitude, and the obvious one for the Society to
adopt. No doubt both Scott and Shackleton agreed with it in principle.
In practice, however, their opposition was not entirely at an end. Early
in 1910 Shackleton[29] communicated to Scott, to the Royal Society and
to the Royal Geographical Society, the outline of the expedition he
was contemplating at the time. The fullest statement of his intentions
went to Scott:

'I am preparing a purely Scientific Expedition to operate along the
coast of Antarctic commencing in 1911. The Easterly place is Cape
Adare and the farthest Gaussberg. It is intended to thoroughly
map in the coast between these two points by sledging journeys.
Work in all branches of Science will be prosecuted as thoroughly
as possible. I am particularly anxious not to clash with your Expedition, nor in any way to hinder your pecuniary activities.

With this object in view I have decided not to appeal for public
funds, either Government or for donations from Societies, as I am
being strongly supported by private individuals. I do not intend
to make any efforts towards reaching the South Geographical Pole,
and I do not intend to commence until about a year after you have
sailed for the South.

The Expedition is purely *Scientific*, and should your Expedition
be remaining in the Antarctic during any of the time that I shall be
there, I shall be very glad to co-operate with your Expedition and the
American in the same manner that you have already suggested with
the latter.

Dr. Mawson has gone very fully into the details of the Scientific
work remaining to be done in the area mentioned, and will undertake
direction of the same.'

It would appear that this expedition had in fact been originally
worked out by Mawson and discussed with Scott in February 1910,
when Mawson was in Europe. He had hoped that Scott would be
prepared to add the expedition as a subsidiary to his own, but Scott
had decided that his programme was already too full to make it practical
to include investigations in a region so far from the base and the work
he was planning. Shackleton, hearing of the plan from Mawson,[30] was
'warmly enthusiastic when the scheme was laid before him, and planned
to lead the undertaking himself.'

When Scott learned that Shackleton had adopted the plan, he wanted

17

to be quite clear about his intention. If the Ross Sea work was completed by the summer of 1911–12, Scott might want to extend his own area of investigation to the west of Cape North. He stated politely[31] that he would not feel obliged to modify his programme on account of any intention of Shackleton's, though he would welcome co-operation in this unknown area. To Major Darwin, whose advice he sought, he wrote[32] more openly:

> 'I think Shackleton wants the coast from Cape North to Gaussberg left alone to him in 1911—I have no objection to his going there but I don't want any objection from him to my going there. It is looking some way ahead for me but should the money last I have always wished to retreat round Cape North for a second season and possibly to establish meteorological stations on that coast. S. has not answered my last letter but I want it so settled before I leave that I am free to go where I please without the reproach that I am trespassing on his ground. Will you give the matter some thought from this point of view?'

Plainly the Antarctic was not big enough to hold both men. Although this time they did not in fact want exactly the same thing, and matters could obviously be adjusted, the note of rivalry was still strong. This did not upset their public relations. Shackleton, who was at this time doing a good deal of lecturing in the British Isles, took the opportunity to appeal for funds for Scott, and to speak of his forthcoming expedition with the greatest goodwill

On 15 June 1911, Scott left England at the head of an expedition which strikingly resembled that of Shackleton in 1907–09. His transport, his provisioning, his equipment, owed much to Shackleton's experiments: and, like Shackleton, he was to attack the South Pole. When Scott set out on his Southern Journey he had read and absorbed everything Shackleton had written of the Beardmore route to the plateau. At the base he had a copy of *The Heart of the Antarctic*, and on the journey he took with him a copy of Frank Wild's diary. Thus Shackleton and his comrades went before Scott as ghostly pacemakers. Day by day, as Scott wrote up his diary, he compared distances, times and observations. Beyond the practical usefulness of such comparisons there lay a deep personal feeling. It was a race, not with time, or to beat a record, but a race against Shackleton.

The story of Scott's epic journey, and of the tragedy that overtook his party on the Barrier on their way back, is universally known. Shackleton recognised Scott's greatness as clearly as anyone else, and was foremost in acknowledging it. But even before Scott left England Shackleton had put any clash between them out of question. For various reasons, one being his business affairs, he gave up the idea of leading the Gaussberg–Cape Adare expedition. It now became, with many modifications, the Australian Antarctic Expedition. During 1911, when Dr. Mawson and Captain Davis came to England to raise funds for it, Shackleton wrote on behalf of the expedition in the *Daily Mail*, where a campaign was now launched. It was not long before he was himself to appear before the public with a plan far more spectacular than any which he had hitherto entertained.

Chapter XV

WE have carried forward the story of Shackleton's Antarctic ambitions to a point nearly two years after his return to England. We must now return to Charing Cross Station on 14 June 1909, and see how the British public greeted its new hero.

In their eyes, certainly, he was already a great man before he actually appeared before them. His features, fixed almost always in a serious expression, were by now familiar to them from the newspapers. Reports of interviews from New Zealand had suggested that he was a simple, modest sailor, and they had been told enough of the achievements of the expedition to be sure that he was a brave one. Above all, the story of that great dash towards the Pole was so dramatic that the public was impressed as emphatically as if Shackleton had in fact reached it.

'The success of this great southern dash' (proclaimed a leader[1] in the *Lyttelton Times* in March) 'is even sensational. Not one fiftieth part of the effort expended on the exploration of the Arctic region has been given to the exploration of the Antarctic, and yet the history of the north has nothing to equal this story. For thorough organisation with scanty means, for careful planning and courageous execution, for endurance and determination, for all that we imply by the word grit, this dash for the South Pole stands by itself in the annals of polar exploration. The expedition makes an appeal to the imagination of the public because it has done work that the public can understand and appreciate.'

With his striking voice and appearance, his blunt and unaffected way of receiving reporters, his generous appreciation of material help, Shackleton endeared himself to New Zealanders at once. Though they had known comparatively little of him when he sailed from Lyttelton two years before, they now accepted him as completely familiar. He stepped into a niche that was waiting for a hero.

The spirit of the times in part explains this. After a long period of peace with foreign powers, Britain had begun to be conscious of distant thunder-clouds. Throughout the Empire could be heard the gloomy predictions which accompany the hint of war. Was England getting soft? Could she any longer breed heroic men? We have already seen that the *Discovery* left England with a breeze of strong patriotic fervour behind her. The same note of patriotism had always been strong in Shackleton's letters, and the public now welcomed his exploits as evidence of British heroism. In an inspiring sermon preached at the

Thanksgiving Service in Christchurch Cathedral on 28 March, Archbishop Julius[2] spoke out:

'I have no sympathy with the man who deprecates adventure unless, as we say, there is money in it. I have no sympathy with the men who tell us that we have no right to risk life and health in pursuit of that which may seem of little value to the world, as we think it. New Zealand has done well to give her Dreadnought to the Imperial service, and having given it I trust every one of us will know the measure of some sacrifice in that gift. But, my brethren, it is these men that are our Dreadnoughts. The Dreadnought that we build dreads naught because it knows naught. These men dread naught because there is in them, borne through the long ages, taken from their fathers, granted to them by the grace of God, a courage that can endure, a brave strength for service that can carry them through infinite dangers. And I say, brothers, that the heart of the whole nation is lifted up with thankfulness when they know that besides our ships we have the men that can stand by the country in her need, the men who will dare in her service and die if need be in the love of her and of her good.'

Most patriotic of the Dominions, New Zealand set a lofty note which was soon sounding in the English papers. In a leader on Shackleton's homecoming the *Daily Telegraph*[3] sounded it:

'. . . above all let us remember at this moment that in our age, filled with vain babbling about the decadence of the race, he has upheld the old fame of our breed; he has renewed its reputation for physical and mental and moral energy; he has shown that where it exerts itself under fit leadership it is still second to none . . . and at a critical time in the fortunes of all the Britains [*sic*] he has helped to breathe new inspiration and resolve into the British stock throughout the world. . . . That and nothing less is the praise Lieutenant SHACKLETON has earned and, to a character so sound in the fibre as his, the knowledge that he has enhanced the credit of his country, deserved honour wherever the flag flies, and secured the respect of all men, will be a higher reward than any formal testimony.'

A reporter in the *Sphere*[4] was confident that 'so long as Englishmen are prepared to do this kind of thing . . . we need not lie awake all night every night dreading the hostile advance of "the boys of the dachshund breed".'

Shackleton had always been a natural and unaffected patriot, and he was not now talking for effect when he spoke of his country. In his first great account of the expedition, given at the Royal Societies' Club at a luncheon on the day after his arrival at Charing Cross, he spoke enthusiastically of the call of the South, and remarked that although it was too soon to talk of it, he hoped that whatever expedition went next would be a British one.

Captain Scott echoed the sentiment a few days later, when he took the chair at a dinner given by the Savage Club to Shackleton and his men. The Pole must be discovered by an Englishman, he said, and Britain should speedily organise an expedition 'before another country stepped in'.

The public readily responded to such remarks as these when they were reported in the papers. But to have done a great thing for his country was not enough to make Shackleton for all time a popular hero. It was because he was a strong and interesting, often an unconventional personality that they admired and remembered him.

They appreciated his jokes, his breeziness, his impatience with formality. They appreciated the fact that when he spoke of that great journey he spoke simply and graphically, in words they could understand, and with no smear of sentiment or false heroics. Above all they appreciated his modesty. From the very start Shackleton had refused to be isolated on a public platform. He had taken every chance to introduce the members of the expedition, and to emphasise how they had all contributed equally to the success of the expedition.

There were occasions, indeed, when newspaper men wished that Shackleton was less retiring and reticent, 'even while they admired him for a quality that is far from common among people with much less to boast of'.[5]

This modesty was no publicity stunt. The feeling of comradeship was still warm and living among the members of the party who had lived through such an unusual two years together. To their leader the recollection of their energy, loyalty and goodwill was still entirely vivid. He realised very well how much he owed to them and wanted to say so.

His words at the Royal Societies' Club luncheon[6] were to be echoed and re-echoed in the months that followed:

'I notice it is "Mr. Ernest Shackleton" on the toast list. That should be Ernest Shackleton and his comrades—because they are here in this room at the present moment the men who have gone with me through thick and thin, through the stress and difficulty and the joys and sorrows of the last expedition. No fierce limelight of publicity beats down upon them, but I take this opportunity to say that the expedition would never have been such a success as it was if it had not been for the loyal co-operation, for the denial of self, and for the absolute interest in the objects of the expedition which was shown by the fourteen men whom I had the honour to have with me.

To get up at six o'clock in the morning and clean out stables does not look much as a dramatic performance, but it is that sort of work, cheerfully performed, that enabled the various journeys where horses and other means of progression were needed to be carried on in a way that helped forward the march which had added just one rung more

to the ladder of knowledge, and to which I hope other rungs will
continue to be added as the years go on.'

As Shackleton carried the story of the expedition to Scandinavia,
to the Continent, to America, remarks such as these became habitual,
but they did not become mechanical. That comradeship to which his
remarks bore witness was something which he had needed, which he
would always need. Although the trend of his life was now to be away
from his comrades, nothing he did altered the fact that he was most
completely himself as a leader of men, away from the civilised world.
He could not forget them.*

Yet there was much to turn his head and harden his character, in the
months that followed his return to England. Although he did not launch
into public lecturing at once, after his appearance at the Queen's Hall on
30 June, he was in demand everywhere. He went to his old school; he
received the freedom of the borough of Lewisham; he was the guest of
the Authors' Club, when he alluded ruefully to his own book.

Two honours in particular stand out in those early days. Two days
after his arrival in England he received a letter from the Secretary of
Trinity House.[7] The Court of this ancient and distinguished corporation
had decided to ask him if he would consent to be elected a Younger
Brother of the Corporation, in recognition of 'the very distinguished
services which you have rendered to the cause of science and Navigation
by your last successful voyage in the "Nimrod" to the Antarctic
regions'. This honour, so appropriate to Shackleton, had only been
given once before. On 12 July a still more gratifying invitation was
extended when Shackleton and his wife were commanded to Buckingham
Palace. Here he told to the King in person something of his adventures,
and here the King invested him as Commander of the Royal Victorian
Order.

These were honours worthy of his achievements, and he could accept
them without self-consciousness. The lionising of the leader and his
men was another matter. Because of what they had done, they had to
consent to be public spectacles. They were, as the *Daily Telegraph*
said,[3] 'as imminently threatened by hospitality now as by starvation
a few months ago, and on the whole there is less opportunity for

---

* Some years after the expedition Shackleton, who had kept up with many
of his old comrades, decided that it would be pleasant for them, and for other
polar veterans, to have a club in London where they could meet and revive the
spirit of those days. Thus the Penguin Club was formed. The club-room was on
the first floor of a restaurant in Greek Street, presided over by M. Gustave.
Shackleton took the chair at the inaugural dinner on 27 February 1913. Some of
the old *Nimrods* were present, and Harry Lauder looked in after dinner. The
room was decorated with a frieze depicting a party of polar men, with Shackleton
in the centre. The club flourished for some years, and Shackleton was the
honoured patron of it.

LIEUTENANT SHACKLETON'S ENGAGEMENTS.

Day	Date 1909	Host or Hostess	Place	Lunch, Dinner or Reception.	Time	Remarks.
Tuesday	20th July	Devine *Lady Crichett*	Claremore School	*Pangbourne Tables* Dinner –	*Afternoon 8. W.*	
Wednesday	21st July	Grocers' Company	Grocers' Hall, Prince's Street, Bank, E.	Dinner	7.15 for 7.30.	
Thursday *23rd*	22nd July	*Lunch Don Silver - Friday Italian Ambassador Lady Grey B. D. Intercaud -*	*Ritz* 20 Grosvenor Square	*tea - Dinner Victoria League Rinner -*	8.15. *11. ap.*	
Sunday Monday	27th. 26th July	*Browning settlement. Authors' Club Lady Clerk - Sea Line Lady Stracher. Lord Lord, Lady Grad -*	*H. J. Conino*	*Lunch Dinner Dinner Reception*	3.30 for 7 p.m.	
Tuesday	27th.					
Wednesday *Thursday 29th "*	28th July	Dulwich College *...*	*...*	Distribution of Prizes. *Dance –*	11. a.m. *10. p.a.*	

escape'. There were many luxurious and splendid entertainments—such as the At Home given by Mrs. Eckstein in Park Lane, where the expedition was entertained by Ysaye, Clara Butt, Tetrazzini and Kennerly Rumford, and presented to minor royalty and notabilities. It would have been easy to develop a taste for flattery and the plaudits of people who cared little for the fight against the unknown world of the South.

But before long the members of the expedition had gone off to their various avocations, taking with them the memory of a peculiar and artificial world, where they might be one hour drinking champagne in Mayfair and the next talking to a policeman on his beat, the friend of one of their number. Shackleton was left to accept fame and notoriety on their behalf.

It is exceedingly difficult to gauge the effect of sudden fame on him. Of course there was from the first an element of dramatisation in the Shackleton who faced the newspaper men and the lecture audiences. People wanted the bluff sailor and he was quite willing to be the bluff sailor. Any man who stands for long under the strong light of public attention must be prepared to present a certain aspect of himself to view. To some extent he has to put on an act. But Shackleton *was*, among other things, a bluff sailor. He liked to establish a warm relationship with people. He liked his friends and his audiences to be responsive and to laugh at his jokes (simple, facetious jokes which always went down well). The character which the press foisted on to him was a legitimate exaggeration of a character already his.

Indeed, if this had not been so, Shackleton's reputation would have been only ephemeral. As it was he won a place in the hearts of the people which he kept till the day of his death and after. This he did without the various aids of modern publicity. For Shackleton there were few of the advertising tricks of today—no television interviews, no news-reel cameras, no calculated revelations about his domestic life. The advertising of his lectures and public appearances was confined for the most part to the factual announcements that his agents thought necessary. Ernest Shackleton was built up before the public very largely by Ernest Shackleton, without any calculation on his part. From each lecture platform, from each school dais, from private dinner table and public rostrum, he projected his personality. He had something warm and living to give to each of his listeners, and they responded with a warmth of approval for this hearty, amusing, patriotic and thoughtful fellow who had such a good story to tell and who told it so well.

Besides making frequent journeys to this or that meeting or gathering, Shackleton was at this time working hard on the book of the expedition, upon whose sale so much depended. In his work on the book Shackleton was supported to a very great extent by the journalist, Edward Saunders, who had accompanied him to England and who now travelled with him, as his private secretary and friend. Saunders was a man of strong character and keen intelligence, whose outlook on life suited Shackleton very well. The two men became very close to one another, and Saunders felt the spirit of the Antarctic adventure so strongly and intuitively that he was able to draft portions of the book from Shackleton's own answers to his questions, as well as relieving him of the work of typing revisions.*

Publication was scheduled for November, and Shackleton had high hopes that the book would be a financial success. There was at this time a debt of some £20,000 to pay off on the expedition, representing guarantees made during 1907 and redeemable by July, 1910. Although he hoped that some of his benefactors, in view of the results of the expedition, would convert their loans into gifts, he had to try to raise the full amount. Even this sum represented less than half the money spent on the expedition. Much of the money had been given outright, in 1907, by friends and relatives, and much of what Shackleton then had of his own had gone into preliminary expenses. When he left England, as we have seen, he was still sending small sums back for the expedition fund. The deficit was, even so, a startling one.

In *The Heart of the Antarctic*[8] Shackleton published the only official account of his expedition expenses, amounting to a total of £44,380 14s. 9d. up to August 1909. This is nothing more than a general statement of the large items on which money had been spent. There is no means of telling how much of this money existed, in actual fact, in August 1909, how much was paid out in hard cash before the expedition started, and how much was subsequently owing. Letters from Herbert Dorman, acting solicitor to the expedition, to his sister, Mrs. Shackleton, make it clear that during 1908 there was something of a financial crisis. The New Zealand agent, James Kinsey, wrote that money was urgently needed out there to pay for the refitting and equipping of the *Nimrod* so that she could go down south as a relief ship in the summer of 1908–1909. Provisions, equipment, docking, repairs and men's wages made a formidable total.

'I want something like £7,000', wrote Herbert Dorman in June,[9] 'and Heaven only knows where it is to come from.' He urged his sister to live as economically as she could, and told her that he was writing to various people, including George Buckley, to see if they would help. He was considering also a possible appeal through the *Daily Mail*, and in November, 1908, got in touch with the newspaper about this. To his sister he wrote:

'. . . it surely cannot be very prejudicial to Ernest for it to become publicly known that after having raised something like £40,000 from

---

* A full account of Edward Saunders' work on Shackleton's books can be found in Appendix B on p. 49

private sources a small deficiency has to be raised through a public appeal. It can doubtless be explained in high quarters that when the assurance as to finances was given it was well founded but that further money is required, (*a*) Because of the heavy expenses in repairs and (*b*) Because a promised contribution of £4,000 has not been forthcoming.'*

A postscript to this letter tells her that the expedition secretary had come in with the news that the *Daily Mail* did not think an appeal would produce the desired effect. Herbert Dorman was at his wits' end. He had already appealed to the Government for help and 'now he sent a new memorandum to the Treasury. No help was forthcoming, however, and he set to work to scrape up the money as best he could. Much of it was contributed by the family—by himself and his brothers, and by the youngest Dorman sister, Daisy, whose loyalty to Shackleton was unswerving. It seems likely that Mrs. Shackleton was never allowed to draw on her own money, though her ardent wish to do so runs through all her letters to her brother. In January 1909 he wrote[9] firmly to her:

'I can't agree to your idea that the money which I am finding is to come out of your share of "the estate". If E. succeeds it should be repaid. If he can't repay you could not afford it . . . cheer up and don't look on the black side but be thankful that you have your family who *cheerfully* and ungrudgingly back you up in the time of suspense and anxiety.'

Somehow the necessary money was raised, and sent out to New Zealand, where Kinsey in his turn had been tapping such sources as he could think of. It was an awkward situation.

Shackleton returned, then, to a series of debts, the extent of which he may not even have known himself. Besides finding the money for the guarantees, he had also to provide for his own family. Then, too, the expedition was not yet over. The office must still be kept on. There were salaries to be paid for at least a year to the men who would now be working on the scientific results. There was money due to other members of the expedition whose wages and salaries had been guaranteed up to their return to England and which had not yet been drawn in full.

All the responsibility for these debts fell upon Shackleton at a time when he was heavily involved in other directions, writing, organising and administering. That he took these responsibilities seriously may be seen in his letters to his wife, in which several times he refers to the fact that he must 'settle' his men. Because he had lifted them right

---

* These two points were perfectly true, but judging from the way Shackleton wrote to his wife on the way out to New Zealand, the expedition had not been very secure financially even at the outset.

out of the world for two years, he owed a moral responsibility to them while they were adjusting themselves to a normal routine, and there can be no question that he realised this.

Unfortunately his attention to money matters was far from systematic. He had not the ready money to pay his men when he reached England, and after he had begun to earn money from lecturing, he had to be reminded of these debts.

The general feeling that he was irresponsible about money was increased by the circumstances of his life at the time. Those who saw him fêted, wined and dined in London were naturally quick to assume that fame was making him forget his old friends. That much of this social activity was useful, or that Shackleton hoped it would be useful, naturally made no difference to the critical attitude of some members of his expedition. As they saw it, Shackleton was having a good time and some of them had not been paid. They regarded this as dishonesty: it was apparently just lack of method. He was an impatient man; a brilliant organiser when action lay before him, a brilliant improviser in the centre of action, but less good at handling the aftermath, the winding up. It was with a great effort that he concentrated on the hard grind of paying off his debts, and while he was travelling, planning and writing, he completely failed to keep his finger on the threads of expedition finances. He does not seem even to have planned the order of paying off the debts. His natural inclination was to fork out money when it was asked for, from whatever money he had at the time, in whatever fund, and to let anything wait that was not immediately pressing. Although he employed secretaries and agents, he kept the control of expedition finances in his own hands. Nobody was in a position to regularise this unorganised business. His advisers, too, were hampered by impulses of generosity which diverted many of his profits to local charities. If he met an old comrade his first idea was to help him, whether he needed help or not: if he did not meet him, he was likely to forget that he owed him anything.

People more readily remembered his forgetfulness than his generosity. There grew up an atmosphere of suspicion and distrust, or at best of easy-going criticism, which was inevitable as Shackleton's life was thrown more and more into the limelight and his standard of living appeared to be rising. His domestic life, in fact, in spite of the glittering entertainments he and his wife were bidden to, seems to have been comparatively quiet, and was organised on the scale proper to a young couple of their class and standing at the time. But his few personal extravagances were, unfortunately, rather conspicuous. Had he decided to run a family carriage, even a car,* probably no one would have

---

* He did in fact own a car for a short time, in about 1910, and he employed a man to drive it, but he seems to have found taxis more convenient.

thought it out of the ordinary: but his habit of hiring a taxi for the day
and having it follow him from place to place became a point for gossip
which was not always kind. The impression that Shackleton was
feathering his own nest was due to the fact that there was not, so far as
can be discovered, any precise definition of the money Shackleton
himself could legitimately claim. He had richly earned what he did pay
himself; but because of his casualness, many people did not think so.
In short, the finances of the British Antarctic Expedition were a
glorious muddle.

He made something of an attempt to enlighten the public in an official
announcement to the Press in August 1909; but this did no more
than state the main sources of his money, and specify what guarantees
had to be paid back, how much money had been donated and what
sources of supply he hoped to tap. The announcement had been
inspired by Sir Henry Lucy, M.P., who had been greatly struck by
Shackleton when he met him, and who had written to the papers himself about the financial difficulties of the expedition.

One of the national newspapers described the situation fairly in a
leader[10]:

> 'Lieutenant Shackleton is quite right to say in his statement which
> we publish this morning that his famous Antarctic expedition, though
> begun as a private venture, has become of national interest. This
> being admitted, the question arises whether the Government, which
> has not been backward in recognising scientific research, should not
> relieve the explorer's mind by undertaking to clear off any deficit
> there may be in his balance-sheet. . . . We hope the Government will
> voluntarily do an act of justice, which would, we are convinced, be
> universally popular, by making some arrangement with Lieutenant
> Shackleton that will secure him against loss. It would be very un-
> gracious and very niggardly if we left the man whom we have hailed
> as a national hero to pay the expenses of his heroism out of his own
> not too well-filled purse.'

The point was well put, and the fact that the *Nimrod* was on her way
home roused public interest. A question was put down to be asked in
the House about a government grant, and Shackleton was invited to put
his case before the Prime Minister, Mr. Asquith. The Prime Minister's
formal letter[11] to him, dated 19 August, is as fine a citation as any for
Shackleton and for the expedition.

> 'With reference to the interviews which we have had on the subject
> of the liabilities incurred in connection with the British Antarctic
> Expedition commanded by yourself, I am pleased to be able to inform
> you that the Government have decided to recommend Parliament to
> make a grant of £20,000 to meet a portion of the expenditure.
> The Government have been induced to take this course as they

are much impressed both by the great value of the discoveries made in the course of your voyage, and by the efficient and economical manner in which your whole enterprise was conducted, as is shewn by the fortunate return of your entire party and by the comparatively small total outlay incurred.'

Shackleton had received a private intimation of the decision before this, and an excited letter[13] went off to his wife, who was away from home:

'My darling
    Isn't it splendid!! £20,000 will be paid in, in a few days and Asquith congratulated me on the Expedition and said the whole Cabinet was in favour of this grant. I am so glad darling. Just think of your Boy getting £20,000 from the Country: What Oh!!'*

The grant did not, of course, solve his own personal financial problem; nor did it solve the problem of the debts which would arise when the *Nimrod* returned, for wages and for the working up of the scientific results. These debts must be settled by lecturing, and a formidable programme was at this time being arranged for Shackleton by Gerald Christy. But at least the bank guarantees could be redeemed. More important than this, the expedition had received tangible recognition. Many people perceived the moral of the tale, and it was expressed widely in the press. A leader in the *Daily Mail* ended thus:

'It may be hoped that the grant will have the effect of a precedent. But without deducting from the value of the gift, we could wish for some precedent whereby Government assistance in great causes and on behalf of great pioneers, whether in exploration or science, were sometimes given before the event, not after. The search party for Franklin was a national duty. In another field assistance to the discovery of aniline dyes was a national duty. We lose as a nation because we recognise our pioneers too late and discourage enterprise. Perhaps this grant to Lieutenant Shackleton, given for an achievement not essentially utilitarian, may encourage for the future a wise expediture on behalf of other whole-hearted explorers into the unknown.'

The point was appreciated but the situation remained unchanged. Today explorers still leave our shores burdened by debt while the public,

* We are grateful to Mr. D. J. D. Clark,[12] of the Information Division of the Treasury, for the following note: 'In acknowledging this grant Shackleton (in a letter dated 19th August 1909) offered to submit the vouchers for his expedition, to the Treasury; but our papers show quite clearly that the offer was never taken up. The £20,000 was paid over in September 1909, a Supplementary Estimate being taken (Scientific Investigations etc. Vote) in the Spring of 1910. In acknowledging receipt of the money in September 1909, Shackleton states "I have acknowledged the Government grant in my forthcoming book, and have also put a balance sheet of expenditure, so that the public may have some idea of how the money has been spent".'

far more familiar with their features and their private lives than they were with those of Shackleton, are no more anxious to support them in the early stages than they were in 1907.

The *Nimrod* reached Torbay on 27 August and Shackleton went aboard with one of his sisters. There were new arrangements to be made. The ship reached the East India Dock two years and a month after she had left it. Unloading proceeded, and preparations began for an exhibition, which was put in the charge of Ernest Joyce. In the middle of September the ship was taken higher up the river to the Temple Pier, having been dismasted to get under the bridges, and on 28 September Shackleton paid a final visit to see that she was all ready for the public. Besides viewing the ship, people could go to the Examination Hall of the Royal College of Surgeons, a short distance away, and see an interesting collection of Antarctic equipment—a tableau made up of stuffed seals and penguins, a tent with a figure in sledging costume outside, sledges, instruments and so on, with numerous photographs on the walls.

The exhibition, opened by the Lord Mayor, was an imaginative one, and thousands of people visited it to see how the journey to the Antarctic could be made in London, as one newspaper put it. After preliminary expenses had been paid (and this was achieved in the first two days) the proceeds of the exhibition were given to various charities. Thus £100 went to the City and Metropolitan Police Orphanage, £50 to the Royal Aged Merchant Seamen's Institution, and the National Lifeboat Institution, £25 to the 'Fresh Air Fund' and the *Truth* Toy Fund, £66 12s. to a Cripples' Fund, and so on. By 25 October the exhibition had made over £2,000 from about 30,000 visitors.

The ship was now taken back to the East India Dock, and from there she proceeded on a tour of the principal ports of England, starting with Liverpool. She carried the exhibits, which were arranged at every stopping place under Joyce's supervision. Here, too, the receipts (smaller than in London) went to charity.

Shackleton's generous gesture with the money from the exhibition was also sound policy. He was not to appear before the public as a lecturer for some weeks and meanwhile his name must be kept before them. He was perfectly able to be realistic about such a matter while entertaining at the same time a genuine impulse to help people less fortunate than himself. Scott Keltie had advised him months before that he would be wise not to dissipate his energies and waste the public response on occasional appearances. One important exception was a lecture he gave before the King at Balmoral on 27 September. He enjoyed the occasion thoroughly. The King, he wrote to his wife, was 'very jolly', and busied himself personally over details of arrangements. The dinner beforehand was easy and pleasant; Shackleton[14] wrote,

'The King enjoys a joke very much. He asked me a lot about Cook and Peary and Scott: he seems to know everything that is going on'.

The atmosphere of ease and cordiality did not come only from gracious royalty. It was something called forth by Shackleton himself, by his spontaneous enjoyment of praise and attention; and the King and Queen seem to have felt a keener personal interest in him than was customary in those whose duty it was to appear interested in everything. It was not to be long before His Majesty was to make clear in a public manner the extent of his appreciation of Shackleton. On 1 November 1909 a note went out from 10 Downing Street to Shackleton telling him that his name would appear in the Honours List on the King's Birthday, and his knighthood was announced in the List on 9 November. The investiture was held on 14 December at Buckingham Palace. Afterwards Shackleton presented members of his expedition to the King, who gave them the Polar Medal—in silver for the shore party and in bronze for those who remained with the ship.

Shackleton could now afford to discard the title of Lieutenant, which he had continued to use in spite of criticism from naval men who pointed out that he was not entitled to do so. His new title would undoubtedly help him to turn his popularity into hard cash. But if Shackleton had now to concentrate on the material aspect of his reputation, it is certain that the honour received from the King was one he valued first of all as a loyal and patriotic subject. He had carried the Union Flag, given to him by the Queen, into a waste of snows: he had dared much and accomplished much for himself and for England.

Chapter XVI

Shackleton had established a public character. He had now to discover not only how it could be turned to practical account, but also how long he could maintain it. He had already had enough practice in handling audiences, humble and august, to approach his full-scale lecture tour with confidence. A tour of the Scandinavian capitals in October had been markedly successful. He had lectured to the Danish Geographical Society in Copenhagen on 10 October, to the Swedish society in Stockholm on 12 October, and then in Christiania and Gothenburg. He became the sixth man to be presented with honorary membership of the Swedish Royal Anthropological and Geographical Society: he received applause everywhere from the keenest and most discriminating of audiences. On 20 October he gave a lecture to the Royal Society of Brussels, his words being translated into French as he spoke by his fellow explorer de Gerlache. Back in England nine days later he spoke to the university at Cambridge. Replying to the vote of thanks, he remarked briefly, 'I will tell the other chaps of the reception which Cambridge has given me'.

Excellent advance publicity had been provided for his lecture tour by his book, *The Heart of the Antarctic*,[1] which was published on 4 November. It appeared simultaneously in seven languages. As well as an English and an American edition, there were others in French, German, Italian, Hungarian, Finnish and the Scandinavian languages. Review copies were well placed, and reviewers took full advantage of the dramatic and unusual nature of the subject-matter. On the day of publication the *Daily Mail* carried a long notice by Bernacchi which emphasised the interesting story the book had to tell but stressed other important points too. 'The book', he said, 'is a thoroughly human document, written by a strong, chivalrous, generous, ambitious personality: one claiming no pretence to impossibly perfect attributes, but understanding all the weakness of old human nature—and perhaps, too, all its subtle beauties, its tender and pathetic charms'. *The Times Literary Supplement*, while asserting that the volumes were 'entirely worthy of the great expedition whose exploits they record,' made particular reference to the warmth and humour of the book.

In fact this seems to have been the general reaction. Reviewers, bracing themselves for geographical exactitude, for accounts of sledging technique and changes of weather, found all this and more, for the book reflected all through, sometimes indirectly, sometimes straightforwardly, the writer's personality. Because of the modesty and humour in it ('Here is a record of good fellows having a good time' wrote the *Evening Standard*'s reviewer on 4 November), it reached and appealed to a great variety of readers. Book and lectures combined to make Shackleton the most popular of celebrities. The *Evening Standard*[2] gave an explanation for the heading of their review—'Shackleton's Book':

'There is a familiarity which rises higher than respect. London has seen much of Lieutenant Shackleton. It has heard many speeches from him. The Nimrod has been in the Thames, at close quarters with the Embankment. With few explorers has London become so intimate. He is fairly entitled to be docked, in the mouths of men or a newspaper headline, of his "Lieutenant" and "Mister".'

And, it may be said, of his 'Sir': for although his knighthood was announced in the first week of his tour, it was always as 'Shackleton' that he made his bow to an eager public.

His lecture tour was an impressive one. Beginning at the Queen's Hall in London on 1 November, he lectured in cities all over the British Isles for the next two months, returning to London for a final appearance on 30 December. Only once during that time did he pause more than three days—when he spent Christmas with his family in Edinburgh. On 13 November he and his wife paid a visit to Paris, where he lectured to the Société de Géographie at the British Chamber of Commerce. He was persuaded to have the lecture translated into French to help the *entente cordiale*. A British paper recorded his comment 'But you are asking me to make another record. . . . It will be your fault if I get lost'. The reporter continued 'So the lecture was given in French pronounced with an English accent, and Sir Ernest Shackleton disarmed all criticism by smiling boyishly whenever he got into trouble with a particularly difficult passage.'

Several points stand out in this first British tour of Shackleton's. One is his modesty, which reporters continued to find genuine and unaffected. In each city or town he visited he spoke not as an individual but as leader and representative of a group of men; and these men were brought before the audience as surely as if they had actually been on the platform.

If this gesture remained spontaneous, so did his lecturing style, which was always informal. A reporter,[3] writing up one of the last of his *Nimrod* lectures, at St. Albans, described him as a 'decidedly entertaining lecturer' and emphasised the simplicity and clearness of his words. 'He sets out the main geographical landmarks, as it were, and links them up with his personal experiences and impressions, and it is because he speaks with sincerity and intimate knowledge that his story becomes so truly graphic.'

Certainly Shackleton did not care to dwell on the hazards and diffi-culties of his journeys. He was more at his ease when he could make facetious comments on the antics of penguins. He kept his audiences interested with homely analogies and illustrations. On one occasion he illustrated the art of sledging to an audience of children by advising them to go home and harness the baby to the coal scuttle and drive round the dining-room.[4] He appealed to the visual sense whenever he could.

In his later years Shackleton came to dislike lecturing, partly because of the emotional strain of recalling in cold blood the events of his second independent expedition. His charm and vitality, his ease of manner, could still be called forth, however, by the right kind of audience. Lecturing at Manchester University, towards the end of his life, 'he happened to say that he thought penguins had a conscience, then the students said "draw it"—he immediately drew it on a blackboard on the wall and put in the conscience ⊙ thus'.[5] He understood very well that a lecture was a dramatic performance which, to be successful, must be at once well-rehearsed and spontaneous; and to be spontaneous he needed only to enjoy himself and to feel in accord with his audience.

At the end of his British tour Shackleton, taking his wife with him, left for three weeks' lecturing on the Continent. He appeared first before the Royal Italian Geographical Society in Rome on 3 January 1910 where he lectured in French. In Berlin, three days later, he spoke in English, and got his points across by a vigorous delivery; but in Vienna on 9 January, speaking before the Imperial Austrian Geograph-ical Society, he launched boldly into German, as the result of many requests that he should do so.

The reporter who wrote that 'his pronunciation was so good that it is hard to believe that he acquainted himself with the language only quite recently' may be taken to be somewhat flattering. As Shackleton did not speak German, all he could do was to have his lecture translated and learn it by heart. His first attempts were not completely successful but he persisted, for he felt that a running translation spoilt the direct communication between speaker and audience. If at first a few points were missed, the general effect of his geniality and toughness was strong, and he worked so hard at the language that by the end of the tour he was even venturing to answer questions in halting German. Charles Mackeller, a family friend, remarked on Shackleton's audacity to Herbert Dorman, saying that he did not realise Shackleton knew enough German to lecture in that language. 'Neither did I' was the reply, 'but if they ask him to lecture in Chinese he'll do it.' Mackeller recalls 'I happened to repeat this to Shackleton. "But I do know some Chinese", he said. "I could lecture in it".'[6]

Undoubtedly Shackleton's boldness in using German for his lectures helped relations between British and German people in the German cities, and he liked to feel that he was representing his country at a time when good relations were important. On the occasion of a second visit to Berlin on 14 January it was noted that 'the loudest applause of the whole evening was evoked when the cinematograph showed Queen Alexandra's flag flying at the farthest south'.[7]

Shackleton visited several of the largest German cities, as well as lecturing in Budapest on 11 January, and on 25 January he appeared before a glittering audience in St. Petersburg. Lady Shackleton had returned to England before he left Germany, and his letters reflect his loneliness, though he was in too much of a rush to write often. He described to her as ingenuously as ever the wonderful reception he had wherever he went.

> 'I went to see the Czar at 1 p.m.' (he wrote[8] on 26 January), 'had lunch at 2 p.m. by myself and then was with him from 2.15 to 3.15. He was greatly interested in everything and talked away then in the evening went (to) the lecture it was run all right and I was given a splendid gold medal given for the 1st time in 66 years. All sorts of grand Dukes and Duchesses there then on to my evening to a party: I lunch with a Grand Duchess today & there is a dinner at the Embassy tonight.'

Behind all the enthusiasm there is a feeling of responsibility. While he was in Germany a rumour had spread that he was going to join with German scientists in an expedition in the near future. There now appeared in *The Field* an article suggesting that he had every right to go for the South Pole at the same time as Scott, if he wished. He was well aware, however, where his obligations lay, and wrote to his wife 'the main thing is to see everything squared up with this show and see that *we* are all right financially before starting again'. The newspapers, however, were determined to make a race of it, and when Shackleton returned to England at the end of January it was to find rumours still circulating. Early in February it was reported that Peary was to organise an American expedition, starting for the Pole at the same time as Scott but attacking it from the Weddell Sea. The *Daily Mail* asked frankly whether Sir Ernest Shackleton would enter for the race. His reply was that he would not, and he supported this by a strong appeal (not the first) for funds for Scott, who was hoping to leave England in July, and who must not be hampered, as Shackleton put it, for lack of money.

It was natural that Shackleton should respond at once to Peary's challenge, even if he could not himself enter the race in opposition to him. The matter was one of national interest, and as such it found space in the national newspapers. The *Eastern Daily Press*, after noting Shackleton's lectures at Norwich on 10 February and at Lowestoft on the next day, took the chance for a short leader[9]:

'The brave man who addressed a great meeting at Norwich
last night on his nearly successful quest for the South Pole is destined
to be very much in the limelight during the next year or two. It is
not thinkable that the sporting spirit of the British people should
fail to respond to the challenge thrown to them from New York.
The American people, who have already annexed the top end of the
world, are bent on being first also at the bottom end; and we, with
our Imperial prestige in southern seas at stake, dare not stand by and
idly see them do it. They have entered Commander—or, as he is now,
Rear-Admiral—Peary for the South Polar Stakes. Congress will almost
certainly vote him funds, and already many firms and private people
are offering to contribute to his equipment. Poor Sir Ernest Shackleton is not yet clear of the financial troubles which he incurred by his
last expedition. But there ought to be no difficulty about drying up
those anxieties and equipping him afresh for another trial, unless the
sporting classes have become infected with that dismal Little
Englandism which some of them are fond of imputing to other
people.'

'Poor Sir Ernest Shackleton' was now in for another race—the race
to earn what money he could from lecturing while the public would still
pay to hear him. Starting in Aberdeen on 31 January, he set out on a
second tour of Britain which lasted until 17 March and which was as
conspicuously successful as the earlier one. Throughout the tour his
vitality and interest in his subject were unflagging, and if he had to use
the same jokes over and over again (the cook picking a sock out of the
hoosh was a favourite one), they seemed to go down very well.

The end of this great tour was marked by a little flurry of newspaper
publicity. One headline read simply '1,176,000 WORDS'; the article
beneath stated that Shackleton might well double this while he was in
America. There were, too, some conclusions—that the penguins were
the most popular feature of the lecture, that afternoon audiences tended
to be unresponsive. 'I have travelled about so continuously,' Shackleton
was reported as having said, 'that in some towns I have awakened and
not known for a moment where I was.'

There were more important matters for the newspapers to take up
than Shackleton's impressions of his tour. The Times,[10] in a long article
on his American plans, announced that if Shackleton did take out
another expedition later, it would be to the Cape Adare–Gaussberg
area. But it will be remembered (pp. 254–58) that at this date discussions
were going forward with Scott and the Royal Geographical Society
about the plans of the two explorers.

On 19 March, when Shackleton and his wife sailed for New York on
the Lusitania, there was a last attempt by reporters to get a story about
his intentions. All he would say was that he hoped his next expedition
would leave in 1911, that it would be on an unprecedentedly large

scale, and that he already had a good deal of financial support (Gerald
Lysaght's name being specifically mentioned). He was quite definite
that so long as Scott was planning to go after the Pole he would not
attempt it, nor would he launch any appeal for funds which might prejudice Scott's own attempts to raise money. With Scott's expedition
now almost prepared, with Peary announcing plans concerning the
South Pole, and with Filchner's appearance in the field (though he had
stated he was not aiming at a high latitude), it was well that Shackleton
had decided to scratch from the race. As *The Times* put it: 'With so
much enthusiasm, so much young blood, so much scientific competence
and organising ability, and so much money available for completing
our knowledge of the world's geography, it would be deplorable if it
were all wasted in making bee lines to the Pole and leaving the great
mass of the continent as unknown as ever.'

Shackleton's plans, in any case, were necessarily uncertain at this
time. He had still much money to earn, and the lectures planned
for America and Canada and later for the Continent would occupy
most of the year. The prospect of more lecturing must have irked him,
although it would be a help that he was going to find fresh audiences.
He had, in fact, made plans for a small expedition on the side to liven
up the tour, to explore the unknown country in Alaska between the
Mackenzie River and Point Barrow. This expedition was referred to as
'scientific' and was to study, for four months, the habits of the Eskimos.
It was typical of Shackleton that he should feel entirely capable of
taking on ethnography and anthropology at short notice. As things turned
out, however, there was no time for this expedition to be carried out.

If it was natural enough that Shackleton should try to provide himself
with an escape from the round of lecturing, there was no need for him
to be bored or discouraged in the United States. From the day of his
arrival in New York on 25 March he was greeted with prolonged applause, and what was more valuable, with genuine and intelligent
appreciation. His first lectures were before impressive audiences. On
26 March he and his wife were entertained at the British Embassy in
Washington and were then received at the White House by President
Taft. That evening Shackleton gave a lecture, under the auspices of
the National Geographic Society, to a large audience, and the President
presented the Society's gold medal to him. The emphatically warm
welcome given to him on this occasion was extended to the following
day when he paid a visit to Miss Jane Wilkes, daughter of the admiral
who gave his name to Wilkes Land, and found that the occasion had
been converted into a party in his honour.

Back in New York, Shackleton was now to be presented to the public
by the American Geographical Society. During the previous year the
explorer's visit had been much discussed in the Society. Some time during

1909 he had arranged that his tour should be organised by the Civic Forum Lecture Agency, whose funds were used to improve cultural relations with other countries. The Agency had guaranteed a large sum to Shackleton, and he hoped to make even more. It was understood that he intended to use the money for his next expedition. An awkward situation arose when the American Geographical Society, very anxious to secure Shackleton for a meeting and to greet him suitably by presenting him with their medal, explained to the lecture agents that on such occasions it was not their custom to charge for admission. A letter[11] exchanged between the American Geographical Society and the Civic Forum during negotiations gives a detached, and so an interesting, view of the public hero.

'As you know, the British government has decided to pay Shackleton's indebtedness of $100,000 incurred for the last expedition. Mr. Massie told me that he is a poor man, dependent upon his pay as a naval officer*, but his wife has rich relatives who advanced the money required for his recent work in the Antarctic. He intends to raise the entire sum needed for his next expedition by his own efforts. He is very popular personally, has proved a great success as a platform speaker, and recently no hall engaged for him has been large enough to hold those applying for tickets.'

Matters were amicably settled, and on the evening of 28 March Shackleton was received at the building of the Engineering Societies, where a select gathering of Fellows and friends watched the President of the Society present him with the Cullum Geographical Medal and listened to a story of exploration which 'was marked both by modesty and by humour'. Now that due honour had been done to him by the two great geographical societies of North America, Shackleton could embark on the lecture tour on which he based such hopes. On 29 March he met the paying public for the first time in the Carnegie Hall, where under the auspices of the Society that had honoured him on the previous day, he gave his lecture once more. Peary presided and many geographical celebrities were present.

Before Shackleton left England he had made it clear that in the dispute between Peary and Cook over the North Pole, he supported the claims of Peary. Now that public opinion had come out on the same side, his cordiality towards Peary was noticed and favourably commented on. The *Scientific American* wrote bluntly[12]:

'The hearty recognition which Shackleton has accorded Peary for the discovery of the North Pole, coming as it does from a man who knows something of the rigors of polar exploration, ought to shame the Congress which refused national honor to Peary without proof

---

* This statement was, of course, incorrect: Shackleton was not a naval officer.

of the North Pole's discovery. The doubt which has been foolishly
cast on Peary's exploit . . . is more than extinguished by the cordial
deference which Shackleton has shown toward Peary on the occasion
of their many public meetings.'

The tone in which Shackleton spoke of Peary and Scott and their
ambitions in the Antarctic pleased the geographical world all the more
because of the jealousies which raged in it and which Shackleton, for
the moment at least, was in a position to forgo.

But it was his personality more than anything else which won the
heart and engaged the attention of the American public. Expecting an
Englishman to be formal and reserved, they noted with surprise and
pleasure his unaffected way of speaking, his breeziness, his jokes, and,
above all, his lack of conceit. The *New York Sun* commented[13] after his
first great lecture:

'It was noticeable from the outset that Sir Ernest has as little use
as possible for the first person singular pronoun. It was readily
obvious, not only from his spoken lecture but from the illustrations
that went with it, that the perils he and his party went through were
real and desperate, but you never heard the Englishman speak of his
own particular danger or of anything he himself had done to save the
lives of others. He never missed a chance to say what fine, splendid
fellows were Adams and Marshall and Wild, who toiled with him
on the last dash, but you would have thought to listen to him that they
dragged him on a sledge with the hard tack, all the way to 88 degrees
23 minutes South.'

The point was reiterated in newspapers all over the continent of
North America as he proceeded on his way.

It was the duty of the reporters, of course, to stress his heroism with
all the stock adjectives; there are plenty of phrases like 'the verve and
dauntless courage of some Viking chief.'[14] But they soon discovered
that the lecturer had other more agreeable attributes. 'Sir Ernest has
a most engaging presence' wrote one in the *Toronto Evening Telegraph*
on 28 April. 'From the platform his appearance is youthful to a degree
of boyishness.' And the impression he made at Winnipeg was pleasantly
described thus[15]:

'Lieutenant Shackleton is pre-eminently an explorer, but as a
lecturer he could not be a greater success. Few persons know better
than he how to tell a story. He does not give out scientific data in a
continuous stream—data which the ordinary man in the street does
not understand and does not trouble his brain about. This ruddy
faced Englishman, a typical Briton in appearance, stockily built and
with a bull-dog chin which denotes stamina, spins his yarn in a
leisurely English fashion and waits patiently for the laugh which
he knows must come. Immaculate in his evening dress, he looks as

far removed from the grizzled eater of pony flesh as one can possibly imagine. Indeed, he himself told a story of one old woman in London, who after hearing him detail his experiences, remarked aloud, "Well, young man, you've done a deal of talking, now are you sure you ever was there?"'

At Winnipeg again, as he was leaving a hall, a member of the audience called for 'Three cheers for the girl he loves', to which he replied at once, 'She's down at the Royal Alexandra, sound asleep.'*

But in this same city he showed that, for all the casualness and humour of his lecturing, he did not feel flippant. His visit had coincided with the annual decoration day, in which veterans of past wars walked in procession to the graves of the heroic dead. Shackleton attended the veterans' banquet, and his speech on that occasion was serious and unaffectedly patriotic. He concluded simply[16]: 'I speak more freely, comrades, than I have ever done in my life, tonight, because I speak to a body of men who have been tried and who know. I thank you for allowing me to talk to you.'

If Shackleton in his later days became less spontaneous in his lecturing, he never became cynical about it. He was a man who always said what he meant and would not be persuaded to say what he did not mean. It is noticeable on this lecture tour that whenever he was called upon to deliver any kind of message, he did the job sincerely and well. In Toronto, for instance, when he visited Upper Canada College and addressed the boys, he made one of his first and most successful appeals to youth. 'Leaning against the lectern to which he held on with both hands, he put himself solid with the boys the moment they heard his first sentence.' Thus a reporter, who went on to quote him[17]:

'You boys in a few years will be grown up, and the destiny of this great country rests in your hands. You have here the carrying out of what your forefathers started years ago. Strong and upright men are needed to make Canada the greatest nation in the world. Some day in the future, you will remember I spoke to you, and don't forget that it rests with you whether you make good or not. Don't look on your masters as enemies, but as friends, and be loyal to them. My men obeyed my orders, and unless you learn at your age to obey you never can command. I don't want to preach, but I was a boy once myself, and experience has taught me a lot of things You may never go to the Antarctic, but the prospects for the youth of this country are wonderful. Remember our flag, our country, and our future.'

* The exuberance and good humour expressed in remarks such as this were greatly appreciated by journalists everywhere. Lee Keedick, the New York lecture agent, told[25] Dr. Mill many years later, 'Reporters would often ask to be allowed to accompany him to the next city, having discovered that he had an abundance of good stories to tell and could furnish columns of interesting material.'

Without any doubt Shackleton relaxed when he was in Canada. The tour in the United States, which had begun in such a heart-warming way, had tailed off badly, and after splendid occasions at Philadelphia and Boston, his lectures in New England had been delivered to small audiences, heralded by poor advertising. Early in April he had broken his American tour to visit Ottawa with his wife, and his American agents, hearing that he was to lecture there, had issued an injunction against him, to restrain him from showing the films, over which they had certain rights. The injunction was quashed, and the lecture delivered. Although Shackleton had to return to America for a further three weeks, to finish the tour, it was undoubtedly a relief when, in the middle of May, he joined his wife once more in Canada. Here he felt himself completely at home, and the stirrings of life in the land affected him very strongly. He wanted to be off doing something. He was excited by the newness of everything, the abounding energy. 'I freely confess', he wrote[18] for a Philadelphia paper, 'that the microbe of Canadian endeavour and Canadian opportunity has entered my blood and it may be my fortune before long to join the ranks of those who cast their lot in our greater land.'

In Ottawa, Toronto, Montreal, Winnipeg and many other towns, his speeches reflect the same enthusiasm, the same desire to be in on the discovery of this vast land. 'Why, you haven't scratched the surface of that vast tract lying to the west of Hudson Bay', he remarked to a reporter on the *Toronto Star*, and he outlined a scheme for geological and mining work. 'I would love to come back and live here', he said, and in Port Arthur, Ontario, he actually bought some town lots as a speculation and so as to have a footing in the country.

The close of the lecture tour saw him nourishing once more the idea of an expedition in Canada, and in Ottawa on 6 June it was reported:

'Sir Ernest Shackleton is expected to accompany Earl Grey on his Excellency's expedition from Winnipeg to Hudson Bay and through the Straits to Quebec. Sir Ernest is in Winnipeg, and is now in communication with the Governor-General. The journey will begin about the middle of August.

There is said to be a possibility that Sir Ernest Shackleton will make his home in Canada and conduct exploration work for the Dominion Government.'

Back in England, in the latter part of June, Shackleton talked often of the scheme for exploring the Mackenzie river district (p. 278). He planned to invite some of his old comrades to go with him. He was confident of raising capital from British business men because, he said, precious minerals might be discovered. His enthusiasm for the opportunities offered in Canada bubbled over in the newspapers and periodicals of Britain. By July both plans had once more been put aside.

Undoubtedly the Press seized too quickly upon the merest hint of a new plan. Thus again at the end of 1910 reporters forced from Shackleton an unguarded admission that he would like to go to Spitsbergen as a relief from working in the City. Shackleton described amusingly to one of his lecture audiences how he saw a placard 'Another British Polar Expedition' and hastened to read about it, only to find that the expedition was his own. In fact he had at one time an idea of going to Spitsbergen, and James Murray was to go with him to work on fresh-water biology. The fact of the matter was that Shackleton was in a cycle of rapid planning, the mood when his abounding energy, caged and confined by lecturing and the search for money, found an outlet wherever it could in large and exciting plans. The merest hint seems to have been enough to start him off: again and again the kite of his ambitions soared into the air, only to be pulled in by the string of his worldly responsibilities.

Schemes for visiting Arctic or Antarctic provided an escape from the grind of earning money, but they were more than this. They represented a strong effort to give himself a status, a design for living. Shackleton had no job to come back to when he returned from the Antarctic. He had cut loose from routine employment in order to take the expedition out. He returned to find more than a year's work ahead of him merely to pay off his debts. This was dead-end employment. When Scott left England in 1901 he left as a naval officer employed by a committee on work which, if it was not routine, was a legitimate development of his regular employment. He was given leave of absence, and when he returned to England his job was open to him. The expedition had interrupted his naval career: it had enhanced it: it had not terminated it. In the same way Douglas Mawson, when he left Australia in 1911 on the Australian Antarctic Expedition, left as a scientist pursuing an adventurous, unorthodox but none the less related line of research. When he returned to Australia he had not lost his status as a scientist. The expedition had enhanced his reputation: it had widened the scope of his knowledge and given him more lines to work on: it had furthered his career.

Not so with Shackleton. He had no job to which to return. The prospect before him was twofold. He must earn money by hard work: but he must earn it by using his position as a public hero, by lecturing and writing about his experiences. Sooner or later, unless he renewed those experiences, his public would have had enough of him. Thus to make money it looked as though he would have to take another expedition south: but to do this he would first have to make money. The solution as he saw it was to make a fortune. He would have a status then, and a job; he could have his cake and eat it, could have an expedition *and* financial security.

But in spite of all his hopes, it did not look as if the British Antarctic Expedition would make a fortune for him. It seemed more likely that at the end of all the lecture tours he would be back where he was in 1906, without a regular income and without regular employment. It is true that there were plenty of people who suggested they could make fortunes for him. Shackleton now had a name which could be useful on a business prospectus, and he was easy to persuade in such matters. With him the word optimism, so often applied to him, had two meanings. When exploration was in question, it connoted a mixture of buoyancy and determination: when money was the issue, it meant rather what we generally mean when we use the word—a somewhat uncritical hopefulness. His confidence in his own business ability was unbounded, and it led him to make many mistakes in his search for that impossible object, a spectacular but safe investment.

So in the years after the great expedition Shackleton toiled to pay off its debts and dreamed of making a fortune. He dreamed, too, of the Antarctic. He knew he must get something to do but he knew also that he was unlikely to find a niche in the civilised world. All through the years of fame, crammed with honours, with new faces and new schemes, the Antarctic kept its hold on him. All through these years he was that most uneasy of characters, a leader without men, an explorer without an expedition.

For the rest of 1910, however, he could forget the emptiness of his working life. After he and his wife got back to England they moved from Edinburgh down to Sheringham in Norfolk, where the family was installed in a furnished house, and after a well-earned summer holiday, Shackleton set out lecturing once more. In August he was on the East Coast, in September in Scotland, in early October in the Potteries, and on 1 November work began in earnest when he left for Germany.

Rumours went with him, for it was announced that he was putting the *Nimrod* up for sale, and to enquiring reporters he said that this did not mean he was abandoning Polar adventure. It was said that he had been approached from Australia with suggestions for what the Press referred to as 'another South Pole expedition'.

But at this particular time Shackleton had temporarily silenced the voice of his Polar ambitions. On 27 September he wrote to his wife, 'I am never again going South and I have thought it all out and my place is at home now I can see it quite clearly. It is too much of a lump out of our lives.' As he had just settled down with his family in the domestic setting which he had so often longed for, it may well be that when he wrote this he really meant it; it is also possible, of course, that he wrote it to silence those very ambitions he described. All we can be sure of is that the planning mood soon came on him again.

Before his second Continental lecture tour, Shackleton had applied himself to the study of German and was reported to have acquired great mastery over the language. 'He was thus able to explain all necessary points', said the *Evening Standard*, reporting a lecture at Wiesbaden on 26 November, 'and evoked much laughter by some of the humorous stories relating to his experience.' The better knowledge of the German tongue was a mixed blessing. He was able to discern an anti-British feeling which disquieted him. At Berlin on 7 November, when he shook hands publicly with Filchner and wished him good luck with his plans, he remarked that 'Science knows no frontiers', but a few days earlier he had written to his wife from Cologne[19]:

'Last night was bad the arrangements were awful and a very poor attendance and they made a worse job of the moving pictures than they did at Buda Pest: it was most unsatisfactory and I was particularly and am particularly anxious to have things right now as I can see a strong anti English feeling in Germany now quite different to when I was here in January: when the picture of the Queen's flag is shown there is a stony silence and altogether it seems different: there are no social arrangements and this may be due to the lack of my lady's gracious presence: If things do not go better soon I will think very seriously of chucking the whole thing and not wear myself out on it and on these unsatisfactory meetings . . . he (i.e. the agent) says that it is due to two causes The Lateness of the summer season so that the proper winter season has not yet come also everything in the concert line is very bad at present but that by next week things will be better: It is a great strain lecturing in German when one does not feel that the people are really with one: I do think that the English people who come might raise a cheer for the flag.'

The situation improved as he continued through Germany, Poland and Switzerland, but he was not happy. There is a note of deep loneliness in his letters, an emptiness and a lack of energy which suggests some dissatisfaction with his life.

His letters are full of schemes for making money. The most attractive was the idea of exploiting certain mining concessions in Hungary, and the old note creeps in—if the scheme comes off, they will be set up for the rest of their lives. This scheme had been discussed before Shackleton left London, and a syndicate had been formed in which he had a prominent position. While he was in Germany he received favourable reports from an engineer he had sent to Hungary. Although experience had at least taught Shackleton to moderate his transports about any new investment, he was obviously hopeful.

Tabard cigarettes, too, were doing well, and so were his shares in a taxi business. His tour gave him opportunities for advertising the cigarettes, and he lost no chance of doing so. From Stuttgart he wrote

buoyantly, on 23 November, that he could rely on these two businesses
to bring in a regular income. 'I got an order for 20,000 for one year here
today; that means £17 profit. If I can devote more time I will get much
more like this and once caught our customers always stay.'

This was a good day: others were less so. He missed his wife very
much during the tour, the more so because she wrote that there was
another baby coming. She was not very confident about the future, and
he set himself to reassure her :[20]

> 'I am wanting to say so much to you and it is hard to write in a
> letter all I want to tell you. One thing is that if we did not care for
> each other the parting and the absence would be of no account, but
> it shows that we do and Sweetheart the greatest thing in all the World
> is Love: of that I am more than ever convinced: and as long as we
> two have each other: whether the days are bright and all is fair: or
> whether the times are dark and cloudy with worries we ought
> to be happy for we have what thousands of rich people have not:
> I am more and more in love with you my wife than I can say and it
> grows all the time and when far away as I am now you can stretch
> out to me and know that I am thinking and caring for you . . . always
> write to me just as you feel for I have strong shoulders to bear all
> your worries and troubles as well as my own and I have been through
> much one way and another and so I can do more. . . . Where would
> my life have led had it not been that for you I wanted to make good
> and the Bad and worrying things will soon be over and we shall rest
> and have good times together. . . .'

The alternations of hope and discouragement continued through the
following year, 1911. He was not yet able to settle down or to reassure
his wife in any practical way about their prospects. The Hungarian
business still seemed attractive but moved very slowly. Shackleton's
frequent journeys to the Continent did not have the definite result he
was led to expect, and while this was the case he could not meet his
wife's wishes. Very much alone at Sheringham, she became depressed
and begged him to take a house for them in London so that they could
be together more often. It was an unsatisfactory life for both of them.
When Shackleton missed his wife, as he often did, it was at moments of
fatigue, at moments when for a short time he was able to pause in the
headlong rush of his engagements. It was then that thoughts of home
and family pressed upon him, and he wrote letters which assuaged his
longing. The next moment he had to be up and doing, and in lecturing,
talking and planning he was able to forget his loneliness once more.
For his wife things were very different, and it was inevitable that she
should gradually turn herself into more of a mother and less of a wife,
finding a consolation in the children while there was less opportunity
of helping her husband. Though she was always ready and eager to

devote herself to him when he came home, there was a change in the passionate relationship they had had in earlier years.

This did not mean that Shackleton had come to depend less on his wife. On the contrary, he needed her more than ever to keep up his interests at home and to refresh him with her loyalty and approval. The heroism of expedition wives has seldom been more thoroughly demonstrated than in her behaviour. Charles Mackeller[6] was of the opinion that 'Shackleton could (never) have essayed or achieved what he did, but that there was Lady Shackleton behind him, never trying to hold him back, but making it easy for him, and taking on herself not only the care of their children and their home, but a very useful devoted and practical share in the affairs of the expeditions when he was gone.'

Mackeller's testimony is important because although to him, as to most people, Shackleton was first and foremost the explorer, he did meet him more often in his home than in public, and from him we have a glimpse of the busy man of affairs relaxing in the domestic atmosphere which he so greatly desired when he was in the south. To Mackeller Shackleton was 'always at his best, and most the real and natural man, in his home life; and when engaged on the work that so called him, and with his comrades. He could then relax and be his natural self.'

The biographer, overwhelmed by information of Shackleton's public doings, finds it difficult to penetrate into the fastnesses of his home, to see him pacing up and down as he outlines his plans to his wife, to listen as she calms him in a moment of exasperation with an inefficient colleague: to see him playing practical jokes on his family, amusing the children, scolding them for their misdemeanours, watching them act nursery plays. There was a side of him here which was as true and as typical as the exploring side, the ambitious side, the competitive side. Often, indeed, Shackleton used his home as a place in which to relax completely; often he was short-tempered; often he felt that nursery discipline was inadequate and set himself to stiffen it. But again there were days of tenderness, of laughter and excitement, days of present-giving and family photographs and games.

There was a good deal of family visiting, especially to the houses of Emily Shackleton's brother and sisters. A niece* of Shackleton's remembers[21] the feeling of excitement in the nursery in her father's house at Sydenham when her Uncle Ernest was coming. Nannies and nursemaids would put on their best aprons and concessions were to be had for the asking. The little girl of four or five, allowed to stay up to dinner on Christmas night, remembers her uncle capping her father's stories and remembers the two servants standing by the serving table with their hands pressed to their mouths, while he told them, 'Now Emma, now Rose, I can see you're laughing, it's no good pretending you're not.'

* Mrs. Pamela Gow, daughter of Herbert Charles Dorman.[21]

His sense of humour was simple and dramatic. He had a tremendous zest for practical jokes and would take considerable trouble over them. On one occasion he had himself made up by Clarkson's in London as an elderly man and, travelling down to Sheringham (where his family were then living), was announced as 'Sir Ernest's uncle' who had come to see Lady Shackleton. As she had never heard of an uncle before, she came down to greet him in some bewilderment and greeted him formally before the twinkle in his eye revealed his identity. Before he removed the costume he went out to the children, who were having a picnic, and astonished them by begging for a kiss for an old man—they were completely deceived.

The unconventional spirit which urged him to explore, which forbade him to accept anything passively, also led him to support his children sometimes in mild acts of rebellion against authority. His daughter remembers a Sunday at Eastbourne when she and her brother went for a walk with their parents in their best clothes. The tide was low, and the children longed to sit on the rocks and let the water wash over them as the tide came in. Their mother, not unnaturally, preferred them to remain dry and tidy. All of a sudden their father gave an artificial cry and let himself fall into the water—after which he swam round saying it was deliciously warm and persuaded her to let them go in too. The return journey along the front in dripping clothes, past the groups of people going home after church, was far more embarrassing for her than it was for the delighted children and their unrepentant father.

This was a Shackleton few people knew—apart from his family, and the expedition comrades who had likewise been caught by some of his tricks. But many people who met him only in public would probably recognise the same element in his conversation as in these anecdotes of the off-duty Shackleton. It was the extraordinary warming power of his presence, his charm if you like, that people remembered. As his niece says now, he could make her feel 'she was the most important of all little girls': it was perhaps the most attractive, if not the greatest, of all Shackleton's gifts.

But in these years between expeditions Shackleton had little enough time to develop his domestic talents. Business called him away frequently. Early in March 1911, from Berlin, he wrote to his wife that he was to go to Budapest to meet certain important financiers; but when he got there on 8 March it was only to find that the general manager of the mining company was away and he would have to wait. This was a nuisance, but he was confident of bringing a signed option away with him.

'Once we get a start in Hungary' (he wrote[22]) 'there is a good chance of much more in the way of woods and forests for timber and all that sort of thing as the grants are in the hands of the Cabinet: I just now want to feel that I am clear of the Expedition and that I have a straight road in front of me: If we live quietly for 2 or 3 years we can then do more I am sure. . . . No darling I don't want to go with Mawson: that time has gone: I want to consolidate our world and make our future lives comfortable and there is much to do: I feel that another Expedition unless it crosses the Continent is not much.'

The reference to crossing the continent is important. It is the first straw that shows the way the wind was blowing, blowing towards the Antarctic, after an interval, as steadily as ever.

The Hungarian business still held fire. After meeting the directors once more and inspecting maps, Shackleton left Budapest with nothing settled; and his money affairs continued in an uncertain state. He was not yet ready to admit defeat. 'Hungary is practically fixed', he wrote to his wife from London on 12 April. 'I don't think anything will stop it now but I only get £1,400 cash at the moment.' Meanwhile he sent her money from time to time as it came in, and they rubbed along.

Life was happier when at last Shackleton decided to move after all to London, where he could see more of his family and cut out a great deal of wearisome and expensive travelling. They saw many houses and examined many leases before they settled on 7 Heathview Gardens, Putney Heath. Before the spring, when they moved in, Shackleton had arranged to use the office of a school-friend, John Quiller Rowett, as a London address. It was certainly with no feeling of self-pity that he wrote to his wife that it was 'a place for me to be'; but this was in fact what it amounted to. Since his return from the Antarctic, where he had so often longed for a little house where he could be with his family, he had in fact seen very little of them. Now, he felt, he and his wife would be able to enjoy the rich and varied social life which was opening out before them.

His letters in this spring of 1911 are filled with the same bustling energy as the letters he wrote to his fiancée when he was interviewing tradesmen in Edinburgh. He will send her samples of wallpaper; he will see to the installing of the stove; he is having a telephone put in; he has chosen a tiled linoleum for the hall, and has matched carpets and wallpapers for some of the rooms; the stair carpets are in good condition, and there are 53 round stair-rods they can take over. No detail is too trivial. 'I think you will like my taste,' he writes on 5 April, rounding off a long list of arrangements. The domestic bustle served to distract him from the worries of the Hungarian concession, which was still delayed. He now had a little time to be a family man, and there was the new baby to get to know—Edward Arthur Alexander, born on 15 July. Shackleton always had a great tenderness for small children and although even now he was never at home for very long, it was one of his happiest periods as a father, watching the development

19

of the children and with no need yet to be anxious about how they would shape for the future.

Except in the domestic sphere, however, this and the following year were far from rewarding for Shackleton. From the very scanty records of this period one can see a life of shifting scenery and of very little purpose. New friends were made, but each new contact had to be viewed with an eye to its practical value. Shackleton was set on another expedition, but as he had no money he could only keep his eyes open for opportunities. His habit of hiring taxis by the day, and keeping them waiting outside any building he wanted to visit was symptomatic of his restless state of mind. It gave the impression that he was desperately pushed and desperately busy, whereas in fact the taxis, a good deal of the time, ticked outside the houses of friends, where he would stop for a time, talk rapidly while pacing up and down, and then hurry off again.

It must have been during this time, too, that he gradually developed a public manner, in which certain of his natural characteristics were as it were fossilised and exaggerated. The bluntness of speech typical of him in moments of emergency became a kind of social defence, and so marked that some people, meeting him for the first time, described him as 'an aggressive fellow'. The aggressiveness was in fact a compound of a dominating character and a recurrent feeling of failure. The expedition that had made him famous had not got him the Pole, any more than it had got him a fortune. Now he could not be content until he had achieved something equally spectacular and important.

These years of waiting on fortune in London must have had a hardening effect on a man whose experience, training and temperament all fitted him for a life of action. Fame had its dangers for him too. Shackleton hated insincerity, and he must often have sensed, and resented, a false note in the admiration so often expressed. At such moments he was at his worst, domineering and not always diplomatic. He was discovering that it was not altogether pleasant to be a public figure. Charles Mackeller[6] detected in him a distaste for the 'inanities' of London society and commented that 'In Town, in public, in crowds, he could not help but be the "famous explorer" and keep up the necessary pose.' No doubt this is an over-simplification. If Shackleton was impatient with his public, he was also capable of enjoying fame. He had an actor's temperament, and he cannot have escaped the actor's desire that his public should remain interested in him.

The old Shackleton, the spontaneous, exuberant talker, was still very much alive, and people who liked him were aware only of this side of him. Philip Gibbs[23] drew a lively portrait of him at this time:

'I think of all the explorers I have met' (Gibbs began) 'Shackleton is the one who belongs most closely to the type which has been pictured for us in old tales and sea romance. Shackleton is one of Captain Marryat's heroes, with a few characteristics borrowed from Clarke Russell, Jules Verne, and Charles Kingsley's "Westward Ho!" He is a living "Midshipman Easy" with additional and admirable qualities not belonging to that delightful soul. When Lieutenant Shackleton comes into a room he brings a breeze with him, and smiles to his company. He has a rollicking air, in spite of his quiet way of speech. When he grips you by the hand—he has the tiniest hands of any man I know—it is a good comradely grip, and his grey-blue eyes fix you with a frank, honest gaze. He has the schoolboy heart, fond of a practical joke, a mad prank with a spice of peril in it, and any kind of lark. Humour bubbles out of him, fresh boyish humour, and he tells the story of his adventures in the South Antarctic with a drollery which is delightful. That expedition to the South Pole was a lark from start to finish except when death came a little too close. Yet in a crisis he was stern and strict in his command, in peril quick and resolute. And underneath all his boyishness there is passion as well as poetry. Poetry, indeed, is one of his passions. He will quote it to you by the yard, and, unlike most seamen, he has the gift of eloquent speech, painting vivid word-pictures of all the ice-fields, the divine beauty of the glaciers and the snow-clad mountains, the mystery and majesty of the Antarctic seas. Lieutenant Shackleton is a very gallant and interesting figure in the history of exploration, and I am glad to have gripped hands with him and to have heard most of his best stories, which are very good.'

This character study brings out one thing very clearly. Shackleton *was* an explorer. When he was dealing with his own subject he spoke sincerely and with authority. In the social circles of London his sense of purpose was occasionally misunderstood. If he sometimes sought acquaintance with men who might be of use to him, he was also prepared to be interested in them as people. To the outside world this could look like cynicism: to Shackleton it was a perfectly natural attitude. He expected people to accept him in a straightforward way, as he accepted them.

His commonsense and intelligence were uppermost when, on 24 May 1911, he attended a meeting at the Mansion House in connection with the Aerial League of the British Empire, a body of which he was a member. Pledging the support of the meeting for the League, he said that in his haste, two years before, he had expressed the opinion that an aeroplane was never likely to be seen at the South Pole, but that now he saw every probability of the event. His speech was firm, patriotic and well-informed. So, too, was his demeanour on another formal occasion, the enquiry into the *Titanic* disaster.[24]

Shackleton's first evidence was given on 18 June 1912, before a distinguished and painstaking committee. He was questioned mainly

by Sir Rufus Isaacs, the Attorney General (leading counsel for the
Board of Trade) and by Sir Robert Finlay (leading counsel for the White
Star line). The Wrecks Commissioner, Lord Mersey, presided. The
questioners put Shackleton on the defensive at once. The Attorney
General, asking him about the difficulty of spotting icebergs, implied
that Shackleton's experience of ice in the North Atlantic was limited
and had been gained when he was a very young sailor. Shackleton, though
he was inclined to speak impatiently, stuck to his firm assertion that
ships in an ice region should drastically reduce their speed. The Commissioner pressed him to define his own experience in the Antarctic.

What was the speed of the boat you were in?—She was only six
knots at full speed. She was 40 years old.

Do you mean to say that you slowed down a vessel of six knots?—
Yes, I always did.

Then what did you get to?—We got very near the South Pole, my
Lord.

What speed did you get down to?—We slowed down to about four
knots. At her best she did six knots.

At her best she did six knots; that was not the ship that you got
near to the South Pole in?—Yes, that is the ship; she was very old;
she was very small.*

Shackleton's remark about the South Pole sounds like an intentional
misunderstanding. He was obviously antagonised by the Court's
questioning of his experience in ice. He pressed his point about slowing
down, and presently got into even more dangerous water. Sir Robert
Finlay, after pressing him to define the 'absolute ice-region' in which
Shackleton had stated it was necessary to slow down, asked him point-
blank if he thought the practice in the North Atlantic had been all
wrong for the last twenty or thirty years. There followed a most interesting discussion. Shackleton's reply was forthright. 'I say a certain
state of things has evolved in the last few years with the great public
desire for speed.' The implication that a competitive spirit could be
dangerous aroused the White Star counsel.

You have been following this case I take it?—I have to a certain
extent.

And you know we have had evidence as to the practice existing
among gentlemen who have been in the trade for 25 years?—Yes; I
think the gentlemen that have been in the trade for 25 years have been
acting under the instructions of their owners.

Have you any ground for saying that?—No more than a general

---

* This and subsequent extracts from the minutes of the enquiry into the
Titanic disaster are quoted with the permission of the Controller of H.M.
Stationery Office.

feeling that I have had, and the feeling I have had that when the owner is on board you *go*.

And supposing the owner is not on board?—I do not want to make surmises and I do not want to lay down any particular rules, but there is a general feeling amongst people at sea that you have to make your passage. If you do not make your passage it is not so good for you. That is only my own personal point of view. I do not know whether I should not refuse to answer this particular question.

The Commissioner: I think not; you are giving us very useful evidence.

Sir Robert Finlay turned to more technical discussion of temperatures and ice, but in a short time the Commissioner returned to the previous matter.

'Supposing it had been the invariable practice to navigate ships of this kind, following the usual track to America, at full speed, notwithstanding ice warnings, in your opinion would a Captain who had been brought up in that trade be justified in following the practice. Now, do not answer that question if you do not like, and I will not ask it, Sir Robert, if you do not want me to ask it. If you have not formed any opinion about it, I will not press you to give me an answer?—We sailors all form opinions, my Lord, like other people, but it opens such a very wide question of relationship between owners and captains that I am not competent to answer it. I think it would be a natural thing for a captain who has been brought up in a line doing the same thing, to continue doing it. But in view of the fact that there is wireless now, I think any accident could be avoided.

Well, yes, that is quite true. If you are right in saying that the better thing would be to reduce the speed to half-speed, about 10 or 11 knots, and if you are right in saying that this berg might be approached practically without any warning to the lookout, it seems to me you would have an accident all the same, 11 knots or 22 knots; you would have to reduce it to 4 knots?—Well, it would be better to do that.'

The awkward point about the behaviour of ships' captains was taken up again by Sir Robert Finlay, on 26 June, when he surveyed the evidence in detail. Shackleton was not present on this occasion. Counsel for the White Star Line, while recognising Shackleton's experience, stressed the difference between ice conditions in the north and south, and the repeated point that Shackleton had served in the North Atlantic only as a boy of seventeen. In his view Shackleton's implication that captains took undue risks as a matter of tradition showed his complete ignorance of the conditions prevailing in the North Atlantic trade. 'He had crossed the Atlantic four or five times as a passenger, and then we have this which is really an echo of what has appeared in some newspaper; it is not a point upon which he can pretend to speak as an expert.' He went on to point out that people would comment, 'Oh, Sir Ernest says there is this terrible competition and racing across the Atlantic and record passages.' He closed his review of the evidence with the strong statement that in his view there was nothing in Shackleton's evidence 'when understood by the light of his experience and the special nature of that experience' to suggest that there had been any negligence on the part of those who managed the *Titanic*.

Shackleton, after reading the minutes, wrote[26] on the following day to Sir Rufus Isaacs, enlarging upon the nature of his experience and his qualifications as a seaman.

'I had been associated with masters and officers of merchant steamers from 1890, and it is common knowledge to us sailors that captains are generally required to make a good passage as far as possible. Should a ship be delayed there is generally something to be said at the office in the home port. Once when I was a navigating officer of a large steamer . . . we had to push to the utmost on a voyage from Shanghai to Rangoon in order to arrive at the latter point by a certain date; otherwise we would have lost our charter. On that particular occasion it devolved upon me to navigate the steamer through a narrow channel in order to save 70 miles, and there was every appearance of a cyclone, which eventually broke.

From the above I think I may claim the right of an opinion as to the feeling that exists among sailors as to their relation towards the owners. . . .

It is to my mind a common sense point of view to take that a captain would not run his ship at full speed and risk disaster unless he had actual instructions or knew the attitude of his owners. . . .'

On this particular point of making a passage, in fact, Shackleton's evidence does not seem to have been entirely relevant, and Sir Robert Finlay's remarks seem to have done away with any suspicion of negligence on the part of the captain of the *Titanic*. However, Shackleton made other points in which the value of his experience was obvious. He asserted that, in watching ice, it was necessary to have a look-out as near to the water as possible, as well as in the crow's nest. He said that he would not himself allow look-out men to use binoculars, but preferred them to keep the freedom of their eyes, as this gave less risk of cutting out a small object from the field of vision. He said, too, that he did not approve of having more than one man on look-out in the crow's nest, since it was only natural that they might begin gossiping and relax their attention. In later years it became the practice to keep only one man on watch in the crow's nest, and the point, as the Commissioner remarked, was a good one.

Indeed, the suggestions Shackleton made *were* good and sensible, and provided a useful background for this part of the enquiry. At the

same time, the biographer cannot help noting the truculence of some of
his answers to criticism or to critical questions. His natural combativeness had increased as he became more important in the world. He was
very quick to react to criticism, and he was apt, when closely questioned,
to put up a smoke-screen of voluble talk. His truculence gave him
confidence for the moment, but it also showed how little his life in
London could satisfy him. Criticism made him examine the achievements of the years since the Great Expedition. They fell far short of
his ambitions, yet he could not afford to doubt himself. Until the moment
came when he could get back to his proper sphere, he must live on his
past achievements. He must remember what he *had been* because
what he *was*, in the slack period, could not be enough for his restless
and striving spirit.

Chapter XVII

DURING 1912 two groups—Scott's British and Mawson's Australian Expeditions—were busy on the Antarctic continent, and there seemed little prospect of Shackleton's sailing in that direction. The climate for Antarctic exploration was not propitious, and John King Davis, visiting London early in 1913 to raise money on Mawson's behalf, found his task a difficult one. Shackleton was still working his tobacco business hard, and a visit to New York in December 1912, where he met a number of useful people, made him feel confident of prosperity. But, as with all his business schemes, the company did not come up to his expectations, and throughout 1913 he continued to search for a way to make big money.* He became more and more restless, especially when Frank Wild returned to London from Mawson's expedition. Wild could think and talk only of the next journey he would make to the Antarctic; he could not imagine life anywhere else; and Shackleton's own desires became stronger than ever.

The South Pole was no longer a legitimate goal. Amundsen and Scott had both reached it in the summer of 1911–12, and Scott's tragic death had associated the place with him in public thought for evermore. Shackleton, taking the chair at the Queen's Hall in June 1913 when Lieutenant Evans† spoke of the expedition, had added his tribute to Scott and his comrades who died on the Barrier.

The more difficult it seemed to Shackleton to find a way back to the south, the more determined he became. We do not know how he put the matter to his wife, but by the autumn of 1913 he was once more sounding the rich men of his acquaintance. For this purpose he had prepared a typed proposal which opened boldly with the statement of his aim—'To cross the South Polar Continent from sea to sea—from the Weddell Sea to the Ross Sea.' His comments on this ambitious idea were, first, that 'from the sentimental point of view, it is the last great Polar journey that can be made', and, secondly, that 'From a

---

* It was possibly during this time that he became friendly with Louis Antoine Neel, one of the first directors of Water Softeners Ltd., a company formed between 1909 and 1914 to exploit a German invention under the trade mark Permutit. There is some evidence that Shackleton was interested in the invention from the business point of view. No doubt it was partly lack of money which made him refuse a pressing invitation from the Liberal-Unionists, in the autumn of 1912, to stand as a candidate once more: but the chief reason was that new plans for exploration left no room for any other ambitions.

† Late Lord Mountevans.

geographical point of view, the complete continental nature of the Antarctic can be absolutely solved by such a journey.'

Shackleton hoped to find a backer who would be prepared to put up all the money for the expedition, holding as security cinematograph and book rights and certain newspaper concessions, and being guaranteed half the receipts of lectures. The ship and the scientific collections would be his. He could name the ship if he chose (although Shackleton suggested the decidedly romantic name 'Golden Vanitee'). He would have the honour of giving his name to the expedition. Shackleton estimated that such an expedition might cost about £50,000. He proposed to try to do the journey with one ship, which would land the party of six who were to make the crossing on the Weddell Sea side, and then go down to the Ross Sea to pick them up at the end of their journey. Should there be any delay in the crossing, 'the ship would leave a fully-equipped unsinkable lifeboat, capable of living in any weather. The party would launch this lifeboat and proceed north to Macquarie Island, where it would be picked up by the ship.'

The idea of a trans-antarctic crossing was not originally Shackleton's, but, in this early stage, was adapted from a plan which W. S. Bruce had put forward as early as 1908.*

But Bruce, a fervent and dedicated scientist, had not been able to rouse enough interest in his scheme, either in the public or in learned societies, to persuade them to support him financially. Shackleton knew and admired Bruce, and the plan changed hands with no loss of good feeling.† By the end of 1913 it was clear that such a journey should be attempted, since the Austrians were after the same thing. Dr. König, supported by the Vienna Geographical Society and by the German explorer Filchner, had published his intention of taking up an old plan of Filchner's and exploring into the Antarctic continent from a base on the Weddell Sea. Shackleton was determined that this sea, in which so many explorers, including Filchner, had been frustrated by ice

* There is a possibility, however, that the idea had been in Shackleton's mind even earlier; a letter he wrote[31] to his wife on 1 January 1908, in the early hours of the day on which the *Nimrod* left Lyttelton for the Antarctic, contains the following inexplicable statement: 'Everything is perfect in food and equipment . . . but we cannot cross the sea [? to the sea] on the other side as the boat "Raymond" never was sent out through some rotten mistake: still darling you can be relieved on that point for it was a very uncertain proposition at the best—the more I think of it, the more I see that we ought to come back from the Pole, the conquest of the Pole ought to be enough for us to do . . .'

There is no evidence in Shackleton's letters or elsewhere to enable us to decide whether this passage does in fact allude to a plan to cross the continent from the Ross Sea to the Weddell Sea by way of the Pole.

† A note by Bruce in *Nature*, 8 January 1914, explains the mutual arrangement between him and Shackleton.

conditions, should yield its secrets only to Britain. As soon as his financial situation allowed, he announced his own plans, on 29 December 1913, in a letter to *The Times*:

> 'Sir,—It has been an open secret for some time past that I have been desirous of leading another expedition to the South Polar regions.
>
> I am glad now to be able to state that, through the generosity of a friend, I can announce that an expedition will start next year with the object of crossing the South Polar continent from sea to sea.
>
> I have taken the liberty of calling the expedition "The Imperial Trans-Antarctic Expedition", because I feel that not only the people of these islands, but our kinsmen in all the lands under the Union Jack will be willing to assist towards the carrying out of the full programme of exploration to which my comrades and myself are pledged.'

A month later König made a protest to Shackleton, stressing that since Filchner had discovered the only known land in the Weddell Sea (on the *Deutschland* expedition of 1911–12, of which König was a member), and since his own proposed expedition was an extension of Filchner's, he had priority in that area and Shackleton should seek a base elsewhere. Shackleton's reply to this challenge, in the *Daily Mail* of 4 March 1914, had a martial ring. It was impossible, he said, for him to alter his plans, and since König was planning a general expedition and not a crossing, it was for him to yield the base. Though Shackleton's letter stated no direct patriotic aim, the newspapers at once seized on the national implications of the dispute between the two explorers.

The Royal Geographical Society approached the matter more cautiously. A memorandum prepared for a Council meeting of 9 March[2] showed that their sympathy on the whole lay with König.

On 2 April Lord Curzon, President of the Society, had an interview with Shackleton in which they discussed the formal protest sent by the Vienna Geographical Society to its sister society in England. Curzon was firm that the British Society should not be called upon to decide upon rights of priority, but that a private conference between the explorers was most desirable. Shackleton agreed to this after some argument,[5] but obviously he did not mean to modify his claims. In a letter to Curzon, dated 17 March, he stated, 'I consider I have as much right to use that Base as Dr. König, even if there were a thousand Expeditions starting from there' and that 'all exploration would be harnessed and stultified' if nations were permitted to stake claims in a land which they happened to have discovered. No doubt it was a matter of relief to him, as it was to the Council*, when war solved this particular

In his Presidential address at the opening of the new session in the Autumn of 1914, Douglas Freshfield said[6]: 'Sir Ernest carries with him our best wishes

problem by putting an end to the Austrian plans. Shackleton had for a
long time felt that the Royal Geographical Society had little sympathy
with his aims. To Bruce he had written frankly,[4] at an early stage in his
plans, 'I cannot look now, and I do not try, for assistance from the
Royal Geographical Society. You know as well as I do that they are
hidebound and narrow and that neither you nor I tend to be particular
pets of theirs.' All the same, in the winter of 1913, before the trouble
with König came to a head, he had submitted his programme (now more
advanced) to the Society, and had asked for help.

Council had voted him a grant of £1,000, the price they were prepared
to pay in token of their respect for his courage and determination. His
vision and imagination they trusted less. They did not wholeheartedly
approve of his plan; nor did Dr. Mill. When he returned from a
journey round the world he was asked by Shackleton to write articles
on his behalf to awaken public interest in the trans-continental journey.
He astonished Shackleton by refusing to do so. He felt the plan was too
dangerous to be successful. He was doubtful whether Shackleton
would find a landing place in the Weddell Sea from which to start his
journey, and he was certain that he had under-estimated the hazards
of the scheme and the time needed to carry it out.[7]

Shackleton appealed[1] to him once more. 'I desperately want to have
one more go. I know you do not believe in tempting Fortune in this
particular sphere too often, but I feel that I would make good.' Always
more frank with Mill than with any other man in geographical circles,
he revealed the very heart of his ambition, the pride which drove him
on: but Mill did not change his opinion.

Shackleton's revised plans were certainly bold: they were also well-
conceived and well-expressed and, in theory at least, they gave splendid
opportunities for scientific research. Indeed, Professor David, to whom
Shackleton had written for advice, replied,[9] 'Certainly one cannot but
be warmly in sympathy with your expedition from the point of view of
science and adventure', and he agreed that it was exceedingly important
from the geographical point of view to prove or disprove the theory
that the great Victoria Land chain of mountains stretched across the
continent and linked up with the Andes. But although Shackleton
hoped to find a mountain range in the interior, he had to admit that this
might in fact prevent him from making the crossing, for he could not
carry enough food to allow for long climbs or detours. Ultimately, what

in his hardy adventure. We trust he may come home to find his country at
leisure to do honour to his exploits: but he will come home to a changed
world. It is, however, an ill wind that blows nobody good: Sir Ernest will
probably have a free hand to land where he likes in the Weddell Sea free from
any risk of interference with the once contemplated Austrian expedition to the
same coast.'

he wanted was the crossing itself—to march slap across Antarctica from the Weddell Sea to the Ross Sea, emerging triumphantly by way of the Beardmore Glacier, and once and for all killing in his own mind the nagging fear that he had failed on his previous expedition.

This was the most compelling reason for the expedition, but his plans extended further than a record journey. Geological observations would be made throughout the crossing, and at one time he certainly intended[8] to take a geologist as one of the party of six that would make it*; continuous magnetic and meteorological observations were also to be made. He proposed to take down to the Weddell Sea as many scientists as he could afford, so that they could be doing valuable work at or near the base while he and his five companions made the crossing. Ideally, he wanted to run two lateral parties of scientists, one to explore Enderby Land (a country then totally unexplored), east of the winter quarters he planned to establish; the other to make scientific surveys in Luitpold Land in the west, while two men would remain at the base. At this stage of his planning he was still working on the assumption that the ship would not winter in the Antarctic, but after landing men and stores and helping to establish a base, would return to South Georgia until the following season.

But there was now an important development. A second ship was to be despatched to the Ross Sea to provide support for the crossing, and to carry a party whose major duty after establishing a base in McMurdo Sound would be to lay depôts on the Beardmore Glacier for the trans-continental party to pick up. They would be permitted to stay for a set time on the glacier, in particular to make geological investigations on Mount Buckley, where Wild had found coal in 1908, and they would then return to their base to carry on with geological, biological and magnetic work and to await Shackleton.

He planned to take 120 trained dogs from Alaska and Siberia as his chief mode of transport. Since his previous expedition he had changed his attitude to dogs, possibly as a result of Amundsen's achievement of

---

* In his earlier and simpler prospectus Shackleton included a section on personnel, in which he named four men who were to cross the continent under his leadership—Frank Wild, George Marston, Bernard Day and Æneas Mackintosh. The fifth was to be 'One of two men who have had experience with me and Scott, but I am not at liberty at the moment to mention either of their names. It is sufficient to say that both of these men are first-class surveyors with a knowledge of geology, and all the others have a good practical knowledge of field scientific work.'

Two of the men mentioned (Wild and Marston) were included in the final version of the Trans-Antarctic party (see p. 342), while Æneas Mackintosh was put in charge of the Ross Sea party as the plan of the expedition expanded (see p. 316). Bernard Day did not in the end join the expedition.

1912 and of conversations with him.* He was also anxious to attempt some form of mechanical transport. He felt that sledges with a conventional motor were useless as 'the amount of work put on the engine when passing over varying surfaces generally causes the motor to break down'; but he was confident that 'in the last three years the aeroplane engine has reached what we may call absolute efficiency'. He therefore proposed to take 'two sledges driven by aeroplane propeller with aeroplane engines' and an aeroplane with clipped wings to taxi over the ice.

Mawson had tried out such a machine on the Australian Antarctic Expedition of 1911–14—a modified aeroplane with its wings removed, and with long sledge-runners fitted with brakes replacing the lower part of the undercarriage. The propellers were expected to increase the speed and steering control of the sledge. This machine had been in the charge of F. H. Bickerton, who went with Mawson as a motor engineer, and in Adélie Land he had made some improvements in its design. When Shackleton came to select the men for his expedition, he engaged Bickerton to do the same work.

Shackleton had been advised that a machine like this would be able to drag 2,000 lb. weight at 5 to 6 miles an hour, and by this means he hoped to get his stores inland for the great journey and spare the dogs for the crucial part of the crossing. Mindful of his own experience and that of Scott, he was determined that the men themselves should not have to pull until the latter part of the journey, and he hoped to reach the Ross Sea base with 26 dogs still alive.

Although Curzon had hailed Shackleton's plan as 'bold and Napoleonic', the explorer could not feel that he had the complete support of the Royal Geographical Society even now. When he spoke at a meeting in February 1914† he was a little on the defensive.[8]

'In my written statement to this Society' (he began) '. . . I said that first and foremost the main object of the expedition is the crossing of the South Polar continent from sea to sea. Some people condemn this object as spectacular and of no particular use, and consider that no expedition should set forth without the one object of being purely scientific. Until the South Pole had been reached, deep in the mind of every explorer who penetrated into the Antarctic was the desire to reach this goal. . . . My desire is to cross the Antarctic continent, and in undertaking this expedition the members of it are the agents of the British nation. If I said differently I would be untrue to my

* Shackleton's views on dogs changed frequently in the years after *Discovery*. As we have seen, an early plan for the 1907–09 journey was based on dogs and not ponies. On the other hand, William Hobbs[10] states that in 1910 Shackleton argued strongly against dogs to him, though before the *Endurance* Expedition he changed his attitude.

† At this meeting Professor David read an important paper on Antarctic problems.

conviction. I have put the crossing of the continent as the great object of this expedition, and there is not one person in this room tonight, and there is not one individual who is under the Union Jack in any part of the Empire, who does not wish the British Flag to be the first national flag ever carried across the frozen waste.'

Shackleton's patriotic feeling must on this occasion have inspired his audience and lulled at any rate for a time any misgivings they may have had. On this occasion, too, he enlarged more on his plans for research, which had developed since his first account of them. He spoke in detail of the lateral expeditions he hoped to organise, and in particular stressed the meteorological work he hoped that two men would accomplish at a base in the Weddell Sea, with the purpose of throwing light on the relations between the rainfall of Chile and the state of the season in the Weddell Sea area. He had now decided to keep the ship in the Weddell Sea after all, to carry out hydrographic work, and he hoped that Captain Davis would accept command of her.*

At the end of this interesting development of his plans, Shackleton once more challenged the audience, insisting that his interest was first and foremost for what sympathetic and unsympathetic alike might call 'a sporting feat'. This sporting aspect disquieted the officers of the Royal Geographical Society, however greatly they may have been stirred by his oration. The confident way he spoke of pushing across the continent made them uneasy. It was too late now to dissuade him; they had tried months ago and had failed completely. On 4 March he was entertained at a conference of members, in order that a special committee might discuss his plans quietly with him and try to discover just how definite they really were.

As might be expected, the conference[11] was not very productive. Shackleton kept his temper, although the cautious queries at times produced from him answers that were evasive or argumentative. He was not, in fact, much more precise than he had been in his public pronouncements. He was, after all, taking out an expedition to explore new land, not to survey land already explored. To questions about the difficulty of landing in the Weddell Sea, he could only reply that it did not matter to him if he had to start his great journey rather far north, and that Bruce's advice had convinced him that shelves of fast ice could be found in the Weddell Sea where a base might be established.

There were questions, too, about when he would attempt the crossing. The geographers knew that the Weddell Sea would present great dangers and difficulties, and they did not think Shackleton could get his

---

* However, Captain Davis was invited, a month later, to take the *Aurora* down to the Ross Sea, and was at first willing to discuss the idea when he came to England. He finally decided not to accept the invitation, since he had been offered a responsible permanent shore job in Australia.

party established early enough to start across the continent in the summer after leaving England. Shackleton asserted that he was prepared for both contingencies—for a quick dash in the summer of 1914–15, or for an extra winter spent in the Weddell Sea, in which case the first summer season would be devoted to laying depôts as far inland as possible.

In questioning whether he could even think of starting from a standing jump, as it were, in the first summer, the geographers revealed a clash of temperaments which is the most interesting element of this conference. They were far from satisfied that Shackleton could carry food enough to get six men across, especially since they might be held up by unsuspected mountain ranges. They suggested that the motor sledges were being taken mainly for publicity purposes and might prove a liability. They were nervous about the arrangements for meeting the Ross Sea party on the other side of the Pole. They enquired, too, about possible accidents. Shackleton's reply was devoid of any cant or foggy thinking.

'If a man broke his leg, or anything like that, and I was on the outward track, I would turn for that man and go back to my winter quarters. If I had got beyond the Pole, I would go on as I could, and it is up to him to do what is right. If I had got just half-way I would turn back to the Weddell Sea. If I had passed that and was nearer to the Ross Sea, I would have to go on.'

He went on to stress the efficiency of his dog transport, and his up-to-date sledging ration. His questioners were more concerned with the distances he would have to cover, and tried to find out whether he had assessed them at all carefully. He could only reply that he was sure to do it, and that, if he came to an insuperable barrier, he would have to 'turn up'. He did not assert (as he might well have done) that a committee could only expect to follow an explorer in his aims up to a certain point, and that planning and caution must ultimately give place to the imagination and drive through which Britain had made her name in the world.

Most revealing of all were the questions and answers sparked off by the question of wireless, a means of communication which, as Mawson had shown in his expedition of 1911–13, had become something to reckon with since Shackleton's earlier journey to the south. Shackleton was asked first whether he would take a wireless receiver during the crossing, such as had been used in recent journeys in Greenland; he replied that the distance was too great. He was also questioned about the possibility of keeping the two ships in wireless communication with each other, to which he replied that he did not feel the system was certain enough and that mountains might interfere with the waves.

Major Darwin put it to him 'You do agree it would add largely to your safety', whereupon Shackleton spoke from his heart:

'I am not going to neglect the safety of the party in any way for any spectacular enterprise. I have thought it out now for three years. The risks I take will be justifiable, and I feel more the risks to my men than to myself.'

How many men who then listened to him must have recalled his words at the end of this incredible expedition: for surely no explorer ever proved his sincerity more emphatically than Shackleton had done then.

Shackleton had more to say, and at the end of the discussion about wireless and communications with the outside world the true man spoke out:

'*Sir T. Holdrich*: Have you any wireless installations at all except those on board ship. Are you not going to have them at the base?

Sir E. Shackleton: They would be very useful. If I had the money I would do that.

Sir T. Holdrich: They could communicate with each other across the Continent?

Sir E. Shackleton: I do not want to communicate with England at all.

Mr. Freshfield: The great uncertain element in your progress is: what is the nature of the ground? You may come across a mountain range?

Sir E. Shackleton: There may be that, but I can always come back.

The President: I suppose you realize that if you found such a range and explored it that it would really be much more interesting than a mere journey straight across?

Sir E. Shackleton: The journey across is the thing that I want to do.

The President: I should not say too much about that. No doubt the public likes it and admires the British spirit, but the scepticism that exists among scientific bodies will be most satisfactorily met by the scientific work you may be able to do, or the geographical discoveries you make.

Sir E. Shackleton: The answer I am going to make you is, with full appreciation of the generous attitude of the Royal Geographical Society, that I must have the public interested—I must have the man in the street interested. The man who gave me £10,000 wanted to see it done so that a British expedition should be first across. The scientific world is very hard to get money out of at all. If I were to go for a purely scientific purpose I should expect them to give me the money.

The President: I was explaining the point of view from which we, as a scientific society, are bound to regard the expedition.

Sir E. Shackleton: I understand that, but I would like to say that everyone being honest with themselves they appreciate the other just as much, and the Geographical Society as an individual and not as a keeper of the conscience of the geographical world.'

The conference ended in a brisk exchange of cordialities, but, for all that, the two parties were no nearer to understanding each other. The Society remembered the occasion as one on which Shackleton threw up a smoke screen of words whenever he was unable to answer a question directly; the Secretary was later to refer[3] to 'the impossibility of getting any clear answers out of Shackleton. He always answered two or three questions together, or one question in two or three different places'. What Shackleton thought is not recorded, but may be deduced from his way of answering the questions. He was challenging the Antarctic. It was a personal matter, a fight which had gone through the first round in 1902, the second in 1909, and was now entering upon the third. While selecting what he wanted from the advice of geographers, he had no intention of allowing his combative spirit to be hampered by the caution of individuals who felt no personal obligation to challenge the unknown. He assessed the situation very fairly. If he succeeded, he knew they would applaud him: if he failed, they would say 'I told you so'.

In fact, this was just what did happen. The President,[12] in his address on 21 May 1917, said:

'Antarctic exploration is for a time at least put aside, but when the day comes for it to be renewed, I trust the experiences of the various expeditions of the last fifteen years will not be forgotten. To my mind they enforce valuable and even essential lessons for future adventurers both in planning and carrying out their explorations. Experience has proved, what some of our council were at pains to point out beforehand to Sir Ernest Shackleton, that the scheme of the late expedition was, in the present state of Antarctic exploration, audacious in the extreme. Proposing to start from an unknown and doubtfully attainable base, it depended for success on the establishment by an independent party of a depôt in the heart of the frozen wastes. It thus obviously involved a struggle against the heaviest odds. It was a challenge to fate which might reasonably be held at least premature even by enthusiasts for Antarctic discovery.'

All this was perfectly true. But the most piercing truth the President uttered was the phrase, 'it was a challenge to fate'. It is the audacity of the plan that is remembered now, not the reasons why the expedition should be risky and dangerous. Contemporary newspaper reports show that it was the audacity that was appreciated then, by the man in the street. The sentiments expressed in *The Field*[13] just after Shackleton's first announcement were echoed many times. 'One thing is certain—that Sir Ernest Shackleton has the courage of his convictions and the ability

20

to do good work, whether or not he carries out his programme in its entirety. If doubts exist on that point, we hope that they will be banished by his complete triumph.'

In the general view, if any man could do it, that man was Shackleton. This was the feeling that led five thousand people to apply to go with him. He could have all the men he wanted. What, it seemed, he could not have for the asking was cash.

In December 1913 he had been offered a Government grant of £10,000 on condition that he found the balance needed from other sources. The money would be voted on two successive years—£5,000 in 1914–15, and £5,000 in 1915–16. As before, the Treasury did not ask for accounts.

At a meeting of the Royal Geographical Society in February 1914 he had spoken [8] candidly about his finances.

'If there is anybody in this hall tonight or in the large audience that will read this tomorrow, who is ready to put up ten, twenty, thirty, or forty thousand pounds to aid the scientific side of the expedition I will take as many geologists as they are ready to provide me with. It has always been the case with Polar expeditions of making bricks without straw, and it really ought not to be any part of the work of the leader of an expedition to have the anxiety of collecting funds; his energy should be entirely devoted, and the energies of his comrades, to the organisation of the expedition.'

This heartfelt and familiar cry had no immediate result. What was worse, a wealthy business man who, in the previous year, had promised him a substantial sum, now changed his mind. This was a blow and an embarrassment to Shackleton, who had, by now, estimated that he would need £50,000 to carry through the simplest version of his plan, and could in fact use far more than this.*

He had gone ahead with securing his transport, the lifeline of the expedition. Mawson had now returned from the south, and Shackleton had arranged to take over from him his ship the *Aurora*, which would be held in Australia for the Ross Sea party. For £14,000 he had bought a Norwegian ship, wooden-built, barquentine-rigged, of about 350 tons. Built for polar work, she was equipped for scientific research, and had some accommodation for passengers. She was larger than the *Nimrod*, but Shackleton, watching her performance in the ice, had moments when he regretted the little ship of earlier years. This Norwegian vessel, named the *Polaris*, he called the *Endurance*, following the family motto, 'By endurance we conquer.' He could not have chosen a more suitable name.

This ship was to be sent to England in June. Meanwhile sledge-dogs were being selected in Northern Canada, and the special motor sledge

* On 10 January 1920, the *Daily Mail* published an estimate of £80,000 as the total cost of the expedition.

with an aeroplane propeller was being designed. Another innovation was a hoop-tent designed by Marston. This igloo-like dwelling had considerable publicity, but nobody seems to have been inclined to finance its manufacture. For the ready money he so badly needed, Shackleton did not want to launch a public appeal. He thought it better to appeal to several hundred wealthy people whom he thought sufficiently interested in his work to be willing to help him to the tune of £50 apiece.

Reactions were various. Many people sent the money at once; many sent at least something. One Irish peer declined to subscribe to a cause which would be, he said, the 301st to which he had subscribed in the first five months of the year. 'Lloyd George should let you have some of the money he wastes : he will have had plenty out of me this year for two sets of Death Duties on the same property.' Many, no doubt, contributed because of their regard for Shackleton and not because the cause was particularly attractive to them. Lord Rosebery,[14] sending a contribution, remarked, 'if things go on as they are going now by the time you return from your horrid Pole you will not find anyone in England with £50 left'.

The largest individual donation to the expedition was promised in June. Shackleton had been invited to go to Dundee to visit Sir James Caird, a jute magnate whose benefactions to that city had been numerous, but who was not, it appeared, especially interested in Polar exploration. Caird made searching enquiries into Shackleton's financial situation, and was told that a large sum had been borrowed against the security of lecture rights and a book on the expedition. He was very much struck with the confidence and determination Shackleton showed in conversation. He promised to give him the £24,000 which would bring him up to his estimate, if he could persuade his other backers to help him likewise without conditions. It was a splendid gesture and the two men, discovering a mutual strength in the face of difficulty, evidently found much to like in each other.

In his search for funds Shackleton had been greatly helped by the editor of the *Daily Chronicle*, and by a member of the staff, Mr. Ernest Perris,* who had suggested many individuals to whom Shackleton might write. Among them was Miss Janet Stancomb-Wills,† a wealthy woman of strong personality. Some years older than Shackleton, of homely appearance, Miss Stancomb-Wills had developed a brusque and some-what forbidding manner as a defence against fortune-hunters. Like Shackleton, she hated flattery and insincerity, and she must have found him refreshing. He had never been good at pretending, and he could now speak his mind and ask for the money he wanted. The two dom-inating personalities took to each other at once. Miss Stancomb-Wills

* Mr. Perris afterwards became editor of the *Daily Chronicle*.
† Afterwards Dame Janet Stancomb-Wills.

was a practical woman, and her wealth and upbringing had given her great wisdom in the affairs of the world. Shackleton quickly fell into the habit of consulting her over the details of the expedition. He visited her often, and wrote freely to her of his hopes and fears. A relationship beginning as something utilitarian on his part soon developed into a genuine friendship.

Thus by judicious enquiry and request, Shackleton collected enough money to float at least the preliminary stages of his expedition. Since the winter of 1913–14 he had been renting an office at 4 New Burlington Street in the West End of London. He had moved his family to Kensington, to a house at 11 Vicarage Gate, and from there he continued to cover London at a great pace in taxicabs, negotiating, planning, making what arrangements he could for the expedition funds that his agents would need after he had left England. He had set himself a stupendous task, but he remained sanguine.

It was not many years since he had trailed all over England, the Continent and America, paying off his debts with lectures which eventually became wearisome to him: but he could cheerfully contemplate having to do the same thing again when he returned from the south in 1916. He did not regard the matter lightly, but the vision before him was strong enough to blind him to any difficulties in his path. He had set his heart on the journey, and nothing must stand in his way. If money was short when he returned, he was willing to go short himself and to work for it, and so compelling was his enthusiasm that he was able to make the men who went with him share his feeling, although they could not be expected to remain calm later when they found their pay curtailed or delayed.

For this expedition, with its striking programme, Shackleton had five thousand applications to consider.* Nor was his task finished then,

---

* One of the most original of these was sent to him on 11 January 1914, and read:

Dear Sir Ernest

We, 'three sporty girls' have decided to write & beg of you, to take us with you on your expedition to the South Pole.

We are three strong, healthy girls, & also gay & bright, & willing to undergo any hardships, that you yourselves undergo.

If our feminine garb is inconvenient, we should just love to don masculine attire.

We have been reading all books & articles that have been written on dangerous expeditions by brave men to the Polar regions, & we do not see why men should have all the glory, & woman none, especially when there are women just as brave & capable as there are men.'

This was perhaps the only time in his life when Shackleton refused a challenge: his reply was terse and diplomatic. He regretted that there were 'no vacancies for the opposite sex on the Expedition.'

for the national crisis in the late summer removed several men of his choice, and others had to be selected to fill their posts.

The manning of the ships presented a problem. In February Shackleton had written[15] to the Admiralty:

> 'I have received many applications from both officers and men wishing to serve and would propose that they are given permission to man one of the two ships entirely from the Navy. This ship will be the Ross Sea ship. The other ship, the Weddell Sea ship, will be manned by the Merchant Service. The Ross Sea ship will have the onerous work of landing a party to proceed South to establish communication with the trans-Continental party and after that will hold a roving commission to chart, sound and survey as much as possible of the Ross Sea quadrant of the Antarctic and the navigable sea between that sea and New Zealand and Australia. For this purpose I would ask for the loan of three executive officers and 15 to 20 men. The ship will not be wintering in the Antarctic and therefore in the event of war these men would not be away from touch with civilization for more than three months and could immediately return to their duties if necessary.'

In making this appeal Shackleton stressed the traditional connection of the Navy with Antarctic exploration which, in his previous expedition, he had rather preferred to forget. Certainly he hoped on this occasion that the Admiralty would not only free men to go with him but would also assist his finances by fitting out one of the ships in an Admiralty dockyard, or, at the least, would give him stores, equipment and clothing and lend him scientific and navigating instruments. Those responsible at the Admiralty were less willing to help than he hoped. His manner of dealing with the help they had given before cannot have made them feel that he was outstandingly business-like. The equipment which had been lent for the *Nimrod* had been returned bit by bit over a long period of time, and at the time when the government grant was made in 1909, the sum of £245 10s. 11d. was still owing. After communicating with the Treasury, the Admiralty had decided to waive this sum, but they required firm guarantees before they lent instruments again.

The Admiralty, it would appear, seconded only one man to Shackleton, Captain T. Orde-Lees of the Royal Marines, who was to join the Weddell Sea party. The *Aurora*, as we shall see, was manned partly in England and partly in Australia. Meanwhile, in London, Shackleton had found a man after his own heart to command the *Endurance*.

Lieutenant Frank Worsley, R.N.R., a man of English parentage but born and brought up in New Zealand, had gone into sail at the same age as Shackleton. His career at sea had toughened a character as adventurous as that of his leader. In his fine book, *Endurance*,[16] Worsley described how he came to join the expedition:

'One night I dreamed that Burlington Street was full of ice blocks, and that I was navigating a ship along it—an absurd dream. Sailors are superstitious, and when I woke up next morning I hurried like mad into my togs, and down Burlington Street I went. I dare say that it was only a coincidence, but as I walked along, reflecting that my dream had certainly been meaningless, and uncomfortable and that it had cost me time that I could have used to better purpose, a sign on a doorpost caught the eye. It bore the words "Imperial Trans-Antarctic Expedition", and no sooner did I see it than I turned into the building with the conviction that it had some special significance for me.

Shackleton was there. He and I only spent a few minutes together, but the moment that I set eyes on him I knew that he was a man with whom I should be proud to work. He quickly divined what I wanted, and presently said to me, "You're engaged. Join your ship until I wire for you." (I was then second officer in the Canadian trade, and had been in command of small vessels.) "I'll let you know all the details as soon as possible. Good morning." He wrung my hand in his hard grasp, and that was that. I was committed to my fate.'

The man thus chosen, apparently on the spur of the moment, was to become a personal friend of Shackleton. That he was a brilliant navigator was of peculiar value. Except for Shackleton, Worsley more than anyone on the expedition made it possible to turn matters from failure to triumph. But apart from his technical skill Worsley had something more important to offer, and something which Shackleton valued more highly. Courageous to a fault, exceptionally strong, he had a spirit as romantic and excitable as Shackleton's. His life was spent in cheerfully running to meet adventure and Shackleton, so quick to assess risk, had to act as a restraining influence more than once. With this temperament it was obvious that Worsley would admire Shackleton. He did more than this. He gave him a complete devotion, a loyalty as unswerving as Wild's. These two were to be associated with him almost continuously until his death.

Two Antarctic veterans, Tom Crean and Alfred Cheetham, were appointed Second and Third Officer of the *Endurance*: they had been with Scott on the *Discovery*, and Cheetham also with Shackleton on the *Nimrod*, and were known to Shackleton as useful men. H. Hudson was taken as Navigating Officer. D. G. Jeffrey was to have gone as Chief Officer, but was called up for active service in August and a substitute had to be found quickly. Lionel Greenstreet, working with the New Zealand Shipping Company, was on leave in Scotland when he had a wire from the Superintendent asking to see him. He told Greenstreet that the ship's captain of the *Endurance* was looking for a Chief Officer and that he would recommend him for his sailing experience. Greenstreet was enthusiastic, and both men wrote to Worsley. In the meantime war was declared and Greenstreet applied for a naval commission. He was told there might be some delay in considering his application. The day before the *Endurance* sailed from Plymouth a wire came from Worsley— 'Come down immediately'. Not dreaming that he would be taken on without an interview, he went down without any kit, only to be told that he was to sail with them at 10.30 the next morning. He collected his gear and joined the ship with half an hour to spare.

L. Rickinson and A. Kerr had been chosen some time before as Chief and Second Engineers, and a crew was made up, chiefly of trawler-hands from Hull, Grimsby and Labrador, ex-naval men most of them and of strong physique and energetic character.

For his shore-party, Shackleton first thought of the old *Nimrod* men, many of whom had applied to join him. Frank Wild had been appointed second in command in the early stages of planning, and had been working with Shackleton all through 1914 on the innumerable details of the expedition. Marston applied after the expedition was announced and was taken on as artist. Frank Hurley, an Australian photographer of repute who had been with Mawson, received a letter from Shackleton while he was making a film of aboriginal life in the Gulf of Carpentaria, inviting him to be official photographer to the expedition, and to take complete responsibility for this important aspect of the expedition. He accepted the invitation in the first instance because it sounded like the kind of adventure he wanted. After meeting Shackleton, he was even more eager to go. Although he found Shackleton different in many respects from Mawson, his previous leader, he recognised[30] that 'Both possessed the fearless, indomitable will of the born leader. Both were strong men, physically and mentally, able organisers, and accustomed to having their own way.'

Both Hurley and Frank Wild are mentioned in a list of names for the shore party in the Weddell Sea, given by Shackleton to *The Times* and published on 17 July 1914. Also on the list are the names of two young scientists whose careers may be said to have been given a powerful push forward by an expedition on which (as it turned out) they were to have few opportunities for research. To get the scientists he wanted, Shackleton applied to Cambridge, where he consulted Raymond Priestley (his geologist in 1907–09 and geologist to Scott in 1910–13) and also other members of Scott's second expedition. James Wordie, who was recommended to him as a geologist and whom he at once appointed, had wanted to travel and to enlarge his experience, and had already considered joining an expedition to Easter Island in 1912. Shackleton's plans offered him an opportunity of examining the land in the Weddell Sea area which he eagerly seized.* The physicist, R. W. James, had read

---

* Another Cambridge geologist, V. Studd of the Camborne School of Mines, also appears in *The Times* list of 16 July, but he did not go with the expedition.

about the expedition and had heard of it from Wordie, but it was almost a matter of chance that he came to apply. Here is his account[17] of how it happened:

'I was about to leave Cambridge and had gone to say goodbye to a friend who was ill in a nursing home, when I was hailed from a window in a street that I had never passed through before in my whole five years at Cambridge, by a fellow research student at the Cavendish Laboratory, with the words, "Hi, James, do you want to go to the Antarctic?" I said, "No, not particularly. Why?" He then told me that Shackleton had not so far got a physicist, and had asked Sir Arthur Shipley, then Master of Christ's, to try to find a man. After a little discussion, I said he might send my name to Shipley, expecting to hear no more about it; but on returning to my rooms in the evening I found a note from Shipley asking me to come and see him after Hall. Shipley was a biologist, and knew little about physics; and plainly all he wanted was to find someone he could send to Shackleton, and he persuaded me to let him send my name forward. After this I heard nothing for about three weeks. Meantime I had got an appointment at Liverpool University. . . . On my way home I visited some relatives in Manchester, and while there received a telegram from Shackleton asking me to see him next morning in London. I did so, and was appointed after an interview of about ten minutes at the outside, probably more nearly five. So far as I remember he asked me if my teeth were good, if I suffered from varicose veins, if I had a good temper, and if I could sing. At this question I probably looked a bit taken aback, for I remember he said, "O, I don't mean any Caruso stuff; but I suppose you can shout a bit with the boys?" He then asked me if my circulation was good. I said it was except for one finger, which frequently went dead in cold weather. He asked me if I would seriously mind losing it. I said I would risk that. He did not ask me about my physics, because Shipley had asked J. J. Thomson, who said that was all right. . . . After this he put out his hand and said "Very well, I'll take you".

This interview was typical of Shackleton. For the scientific qualifications of the men he saw he preferred to rely on the specialists he had consulted. For their personal characters, their powers of endurance, their cheerfulness, he must rely on his own judgment. It was seldom at fault. Now and again he was swayed by a man who talked glibly; but he had an unfailing eye for an optimist.

While he was working through applications Shackleton received a letter from a young man called Hussey, who had graduated from King's College, London, in Anthropology, Physiology and Meteorology. Hussey wrote from the Sudan, where he was just finishing with an expedition, having seen an announcement in an old newspaper about Shackleton's new journey. Shackleton was amused by the idea of anyone going straight from Central Africa to the Antarctic, and when Hussey got back to England he was given an interview.[18]

'He called for me, looked me up and down, walked up and down when he was talking to me, didn't seem to take any notice. Finally he said, "Yes, I like you, I'll take you." He told me afterwards he took me because he thought I looked funny!'

Whatever Shackleton's reasons for choosing Hussey, the choice was emphatically a good one. The young graduate's banjo and his songs, his quick wit and inexhaustible cheerfulness, were to be of incalculable value when things went wrong. Certainly his qualifications, as he admits, were less impressive than those of other applicants. He had gone to the Sudan as anthropologist and had taken on the meteorology almost as a sideline. Shackleton sent him to take some training in meteorology and magnetism; and the apparently casual mode of selection worked out extremely well.

The ship's complement, which was worked out by Shackleton, Worsley and Wild together, was presumably made up largely on qualifications; yet even here Shackleton's personal approach can be seen. Walter How, who had had much experience in sail off the coast of Labrador, applied for a job as A.B. as soon as the expedition was announced. He received the following answer from the expedition office[19]:

'Sir Ernest Shackleton thanks Mr. W. How for his letter of application and appreciates his desire to take part in the expedition but as the personnel of the expedition will not be chosen before June, this letter will not receive more attention until a later date. It is, however, noted as among the lively applications, which are not many.'

When the time came, Mr. How's application was remembered, and he was taken on.

The selection of R. S. Clark as biologist seems to have been made after consultation with Dr. Bruce, who knew him. Clark was an able and experienced scientist, and before he agreed to go, he tried to persuade Shackleton to put him on a salary for a specified period after the expedition, to work up his scientific results. Shackleton, who had made some such arrangement with Murray after his previous expedition, was not willing to adopt it again. He felt strongly that it was enough that he should offer scientists the opportunity to reach unique fields of research. It was not until a short time before the *Endurance* left the Thames that Clark decided to join her. He was to prove an asset to the expedition not so much for his scientific knowledge, which had little opportunity to show itself, as for his strong character and his powers of endurance.

Among the applications were two which Shackleton willingly entertained. Two young Army lieutenants, Courteney Brocklehurst (Sir

Philip Brocklehurst's brother) and Lieutenant Dobbs of the Royal
Dublin Fusiliers, both decided to take the chance of adventure. Sir
Philip Brocklehurst wanted to go, but could not get release from his
military duties. Shackleton appointed the two army officers to take
charge of the dogs, but when war was declared both were immediately
called up, and they were not replaced on the expedition list.

Hussey was to assist when necessary in the medical work of the
expedition. The two official surgeons were not appointed until late in the
year. In *The Times* list of 16 July there appears, in the Ross Sea party,
the name of Dr. Macklin. At the time when he wrote for an interview,
he was working as a House Surgeon at a hospital in Blackburn. He
had been brought up in the Scilly Islands, where his father had a
practice which involved journeying round the islands, and he had grown
up with small boats. Adventurous by nature, he had worked as a deck-
hand on a Mediterranean boat between leaving school and going to the
university. He was immediately attracted by Shackleton's new plan but
had no reply to his letter of application, so one day he called at the
office:[20]

> 'I went in early in the morning, shortly after nine o'clock, but even
> then I was a little too late for him. I met him coming down the stairs
> in a tremendous hurry—he usually was—and I thought "My good-
> ness, is this my chance slipping away?" and I managed to stop him
> and said I wanted to come as his surgeon, blurted that out, and he
> said, "Well, I'm busy just now, but go up and introduce yourself
> to some of the other fellows up there, and just wait for me." I waited
> all that morning, in fact all day, and I think what stood me in good
> stead was that during the time I was waiting for him I got talking to
> the other chaps, including Frank Wild. I went along to lunch with
> them and went back to the office in the afternoon, and Shackleton
> came in in a terrific hurry again, went into an inner room, spent
> about half an hour with Wild, and Wild came out and said, "He'll
> see you in a minute or two," and I said, "Well, will you put in a good
> word for me". Whether he did or not I don't know, but I went in to
> see Shackleton, he looked me up and down, asked me one or two
> questions, and just abruptly, like that, said "All right, I'll take you,"
> without any other reference or requirement of any kind at all. . . .
> One question was "Is your eyesight all right?" I was wearing specs.
> I said it was. He asked "Why are you wearing spectacles?" For want
> of anything better, I said "Many a wise face would look foolish
> without spectacles" and he laughed.'

Shackleton's engaging of his senior surgeon was equally swift. Dr. J.
A. McIlroy had practised medicine in many parts of the world. In the
summer of 1914 he was just back from the Malay States, and it was in
conversation with a friend at the Devonshire Club that the suggestion
was made, 'How would you like to go and get frozen instead of being

burnt up?' Dr. McIlroy enquired further and was told that Shackleton wanted another doctor. He rang up the office and arranged for an interview.[21]

'Shackleton could be a very frightening kind of individual; like Napoleon, he was very stern-looking and fixed you with a steely eye. I wasn't asked to sit down. I stood in front of him, facing the light. . . . He asked me lots of questions. One was "Where have you just come from?" I said the Malay States. He said, "Well, I suppose you know all about malaria and the other fevers they get out there?" I said, "Yes, I'm supposed to know about them." He said, "Well, of course, that's no damned good to me, we won't get anything like that down in the Antarctic! Have you ever had any experience of the cold?" I had to admit I hadn't, apart from the cold one gets in England. However, he said "Well, I'd like you to be examined. You seem to be shaking a lot." I said, "I'm a bit nervous in front of you". As a matter of fact, it was malaria! So I went and saw a physician and he gave me a very good report, and Shackleton was quite content with that.'

One member of the expedition with his own special importance joined after the list was full and the ship on her way south. At Buenos Aires the cook engaged for the Weddell Sea party was discharged and Shackleton instructed Worsley to look out for another. Charles Green, a baker and pastrycook, was on a ship in Buenos Aires when he learned from the butcher that the expedition ship was looking for a cook. Getting leave, he went on board the *Endurance*, and was interviewed. Green had explained in the interview that his experience in cable ships had been hard: he was to cook under the most appalling conditions before his work for the expedition was over, and of all the men who learned endurance with Shackleton, none learned the lesson better or under harder circumstances than Charles Green.*

The party to go to the Ross Sea was entirely separate from the Weddell Sea party, and was not entirely made up by Shackleton. This party altered in size in the course of its forming. Shackleton had originally intended to have only six men in a shore party, to lay a depôt at the foot of the Beardmore Glacier and then to winter at Cape Royds or Cape Evans. This plan was outlined as early as February 1914 to Ernest Joyce, and Shackleton promised that if he was unable to afford to take a second ship, he would find a place for Joyce on the Weddell Sea side.

---

* Shackleton had also engaged a certain Dr. Ross to help with the dogs: it is not clear whether it was intended that he should go into the Weddell Sea with the ship or only to South Georgia. At the last minute his place was taken by Sir Daniel Gooch, a personal friend of Shackleton's, who travelled to Buenos Aires with him to join the *Endurance*, and went with the party to South Georgia, where he gave valuable help in training and caring for the dogs before he returned to England.

As funds came in a little more freely, the Ross Sea party expanded to include more scientists and more sailors.

As leader, Shackleton appointed Æneas Mackintosh, whose promising career on the *Nimrod* had been so tragically interrupted by the accident to his eye. In London, too, Shackleton appointed Ernest Joyce, Ernest Wild (brother of Frank Wild) and V. Hayward, all to work with the dogs and sledges: A. H. Ninnis, to look after the motors: A. P. Spencer-Smith, who went as padre and photographer: A. O. Stevens, as geologist and head of the scientific staff, with J. L. Cope as biologist: and, for the ship, J. R. Stenhouse, as Chief Officer, and A. H. Larkman as Second Engineer. A crew had been engaged in England and went out to Australia on the *Ionic* with the rest of the party, but dissension started among them during the voyage, and several were discharged at Sydney. To fill in gaps there, L. A. Hooke was engaged as wireless operator, Larkman moved up to Chief Engineer, C. A. Donnelly joined as Second Engineer, and at the last moment the Second Officer was also discharged, and replaced by Leslie Thomson, who had been on a Union steamer. Mackintosh also engaged extra deck hands in Sydney.

Shackleton had always intended to add to the Ross Sea party in Sydney, though it seems that Mackintosh made the party even larger than he had been instructed to do. Shackleton had advised him to consult Professor David and the heads of the faculties in Sydney and Melbourne, in the choice of a physicist and a surgeon. During November, while these posts were being advertised in Australia, I. O. Gaze came down to Sydney to see his cousin Spencer-Smith and applied to go on the expedition. He was engaged, primarily as a meteorologist, W. R. Richards as a physicist, and A. Keith Jack to work in the same field. Mackintosh found it impossible to get a surgeon, the war having taken so many from their posts, and finally Cope, who had some medical experience, undertook the duties.

The final party was considerably larger than had been originally intended, and the somewhat confused circumstances of the engagements of both scientists and crew left some feeling of discontent, which was intensified by the frustrating war conditions. Without the status which Shackleton would have had, both Mackintosh and Stevens found it difficult to produce an atmosphere of goodwill in the party. But behind the muddle and improvisation there was a feeling that 'it would all come right on the night', and the feeling was certainly justified. The loyalty which the men gave to Shackleton in his absence, the incredible work they did under difficult and dangerous conditions, were all the more remarkable because of the bad start of the Ross Sea party. As a leader, Shackleton always expected his men to do the impossible; in this case, emphatically, he got what he expected.

The Ross Sea party was to be partly equipped in Australia, but for the *Endurance* party, equipment and provisions were collected at the London office through the summer, under Wild's direction and with Shackleton supervising. Shackleton had always been a good organiser, and now his experience counted for much. His friends, visiting him in his office, were amazed at his calm in the midst of chaos, his patience with the countless callers, and his enjoyment of the eccentric letters and strange gifts he received.

In May he went to Norway to test the air-propelled sledge, and another type of motor-crawler. Captain Orde-Lees had worked on the blueprints of these and the machines were made by the firm of Girling. Orde-Lees accompanied Shackleton to Norway, and the party of nine also included Frank Wild, Courteney Brocklehurst, Bickerton, Dobbs, and a pioneer of ski-ing in Britain. This was Harry Brittain,[*] who recalls[22] the air-sledges as 'odd-looking things, with the propeller standing forward on a raised support, driven by a chain from the engine. They got up a pretty good pace over the snow and ice, and my job (hanging on to a tow-rope behind) was to see how the runners took the hummocks and how the thing behaved generally.'

Shackleton's party camped on a glacier at Finse, near Bergen, and put the new round tents to a severe test, for as well as ice and snow they encountered rain, a hazard which they hardly needed in a rehearsal for Antarctic conditions. 'I do not sleep very well' Shackleton wrote to his wife,[23] 'and the snow is rather crumply and the sleeping bag too hot yet it is cold with one's head out so we are between the devil and the deep sea.' He found, too, that life in London had made him soft, and going on skis tired him. All the same, he felt the test had been useful. The sledges had travelled well but had proved to lack strength, and he had planned to go to Paris to exchange some of the motor parts and get them to Orde-Lees for checking.

On this trip to Norway Shackleton also tried out the sledging ration which had been designed for him. His preoccupation with expedition diet was as strong as ever. Much work had been done on the prevention and causes of scurvy, and on the nature of vitamins, since he took out the *Nimrod*. Indeed, laboratory work was going on as early as 1907,[†] when Holst and Fröhlich began experiments on animals,

---

[*] Now Sir Harry Brittain, K.B.E., C.M.G.

[†] Until the publication of the early papers on vitamins, explorers had to continue to make their decisions empirically in the matter of diet. In his *Polar Exploration*, first published in 1911, Bruce[24] was still assuming that scurvy was 'largely, if not entirely, due to the presence of injurious ptomaines associated with animal food-stuffs, and it has been said by an eminent physiologist that it is simply a form of chronic ptomaine poisoning'. Scott acted on this assumption when provisioning his second expedition of 1910–13, but the experiences of his earlier party, and Shackleton's success in avoiding scurvy

and this work was confirmed and greatly extended at the Lister Institute during the first world war, made urgent by outbreaks of scurvy among British troops in Mesopotamia. The first paper in a long series was published in 1917, and a little earlier Vitamin C had been recognised as a nutritional entity, though it was not named until 1920.

Shackleton's doctors on his new expedition were well aware of this research. Cope[25] wrote an interesting medical report on the Ross Sea party in 1917, in the course of which he stated that scurvy was due to the absence of a substance called a vitamine, which had been found to be present in fresh food and vegetables. Cope did not, however, get the chance to study the disease at first hand on that expedition, although he was evidently well-instructed in current research on the subject. Shackleton had given much thought to the problem of scurvy over the years, and had studied the history of other expeditions very thoroughly from this point of view. In particular, he had been puzzled by the fact that on certain occasions lime juice had been effective in preventing scurvy, while at other times it had failed completely.

In 1914 it was thought that the vitamins in lime juice tended to be destroyed in the process of evaporation or by exposure to air afterwards. Shackleton therefore had lime juice concentrated by evaporation in a vacuum and put up in capsules to prevent exposure to air. These capsules were intended for use on the sledging journeys. Shackleton's knowledge of the whole subject was far ahead of that of most doctors at this time, though in fact this particular theory was only partially correct, as the researches of Harriet Chick were to show later (see p. 35).*

Shackleton was concerned about the sledging ration as a whole, for he realised that the compressed food they had carried on his previous expedition had been inadequate in quality as well as in quantity. He decided to consult an expert, and the War Office put him in touch with Major-General Wilfred Beveridge,† Professor of Hygiene at Millbank, who in 1914 was acting as Director of Hygiene to the War Office in the R.A.M.C.

Major-General Beveridge had been doing chemical research for the Army since the time of the Boer War, and the problems which he had constantly to face, of how to feed armies on the move and in poorly provisioned countries, had made him a most valuable man for Shackleton to consult. When the two men met, the expert indicated that he

on the British Antarctic Expedition, made him insist on the regular serving of fresh food at his base.

    * Dr. Macklin comments,[32] ' I have always regarded as one of the most remarkable traits of this remarkable man his ability to obtain a practical grasp of scientific and technical matters in regard to which he had had no training.'

    † Now Major-General Sir Wilfred Beveridge, K.B.E., C.B., D.S.O. We are indebted to him for a detailed account of his dealings with the Imperial Trans-Antarctic Expedition.

would want to know considerable detail about the amount of energy the men would be using up, their conditions of life and so on. Shackleton agreed to send his second in command for a further consultation about the emergency sledging rations. Shackleton was facing a journey which might be prolonged for as much as four months, during which time the party would be completely dependent on the food they could carry themselves. Major-General Beveridge advised Wild that with the work they would have to do they would need 4,000 calories per man per day, and he worked out a list of essential ingredients which he sent to the Bovril company. They devised composition-cakes, of one pound weight, packed in oblong tin boxes wrapped in parchment paper. This represented a day's ration for one man, to be eaten cold or in hoosh. The calorific value was 2,864, made up as follows: oatmeal 4 oz. (472); icing sugar 1 oz. (116); beef powder 3 oz. (332); lait-proto (casein) 1 oz. (98); oleo 7 oz. (1,846). This block was to be supplemented by nut food (specially prepared in eight-ounce cakes), sugar, Trumilk powder, marmite, tea and salt.*

This ration provided protein, fat and carbo-hydrates, but the question of the vitamins had still to be solved. Major-General Beveridge advised Wild that if they could get a temperature of almost 62° in their tents, they should plant mustard and cress, barley, wheat or any other grain, and grow it to a height of five or six inches. This could be carried on their sledging journey, to provide them with fresh food for the first part of their journey.† They were also advised to collect and carry penguins' eggs on the journey if they got the chance.

The advice was excellent, although, as things turned out, the expedition was to have no chance to grow anything, for the temperatures they had to contend with at the period when they were living in tents were far too low They had to rely on seal and penguin for their fresh food. All the same, their emergency ration, eked out during their hazardous journeying, stood them in very good stead. Good advice and the constant vigilance of Shackleton, his second in command and his doctors, brought the Weddell Sea section of the expedition home without a single case of scurvy: indeed, there had been at no time any sign of it.

As a pendant to this discussion of Shackleton's provisioning, we must quote an interview which a *Daily Mirror* representative[28] had with

* This ration[26] was used by H.M. Exped. Forces in North Russia, and was the same as that recommended for Shackleton's Imperial Trans-Antarctic Expedition.

† Dr. Koettlitz had grown mustard and cress on the skylight of the *Discovery* in 1902, as a direct result of the outbreak of scurvy in the ship,[27] and the sandwiches he gave to the ship's company had proved very popular. This was not done regularly, and there seems to be no record of any other expedition having done this up to 1914.

M. Oddenino of the Imperial Restaurant in London. Oddenino said that he had been asked by Shackleton to give members of the expedition special instruction in cooking. 'Our aim will be to prepare natural dishes', he told the reporter. 'The idea is to provide the expedition with a great variety of really nourishing foods, so as to avoid the illnesses which are brought on largely by eating of similar food every day. We shall teach the explorers to prepare the nourishing soups. Among the eatables which will be novelties in Antarctic regions will be chicken and fish in tins, dry beans, various kinds of peas, potato flour . . . and braised beef.'

If Shackleton thought of this idea, it was a clever piece of publicity, whether the lessons took place or not. In fact, Charles Green, who did nearly all the cooking for the Weddell Sea party, was entirely equal to inventing new dishes and to exploiting the tinned food available at that time, and his fricassees, his cotelettes à la Weddell and his curries continued even after he was cooking under conditions which the most imaginative chef could hardly conceive.

By the end of the summer of 1914 Shackleton could be confident that he had availed himself of every modern idea which could possibly

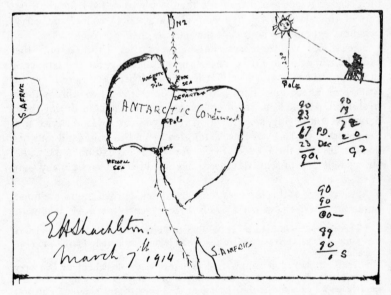

Drawn on the menu card of the 4th annual dinner of the London Devonian Association, held in London on 7 March, 1914.

Big Game Hunting to Cure Heartache. See Pages 8 and 9.

The Daily Mirror

THE MORNING JOURNAL WITH THE SECOND LARGEST NET SALE.

No. 3,178.   Registered at the G.P.O. as a Newspaper   WEDNESDAY, DECEMBER 31, 1913   One Halfpenny.

KNOWN IN LONDON: SHACKLETON PAUSES ON HIS WAY TO THE SOUTH POLE.

a lot of people stopped to look into the shops in Oxford-street yesterday, but it ans, gave a glance of recognition to the great explorer, Sir Ernest Shackleton was standing near the curb—not far from the motor-omnibus danger zone. noticeable that Sir Ernest—perhaps in preparation for his Antarctic experiences

—was not wearing an overcoat. Had Sir Ernest Shackleton been Carpentier or Mlle. Gaby Deslys he would probably have been mobbed. As he was only a great explorer the crowd passed him by—and he seemed supremely indifferent. He was lost in a "brown study," or perhaps a mental study of Antarctic snows.

'UNKNOWN IN LONDON'. 30 December 1913

Trying out the propeller-driven sledge

Shackleton fixing a tent

Both taken during the rehearsal in Norway, May 1908

Left to right: Tom Crean, Mackay, Rickinson, E. H. Shackleton, Queen Alexandra, the Dowager Empress of Russia, Lady Shackleton, Frank Wild, George Marston, Lord Howe, Princess Victoria, Captain Mackintosh. As named by Shackleton

Queen Alexandra's visit to the *Endurance*, 16 July 1914. The handwriting is Queen Alexandra's and is on the back of the photograph presented to Lady Shackleton

...e on board the Endurance by my Sister The Empress Marie of Russia

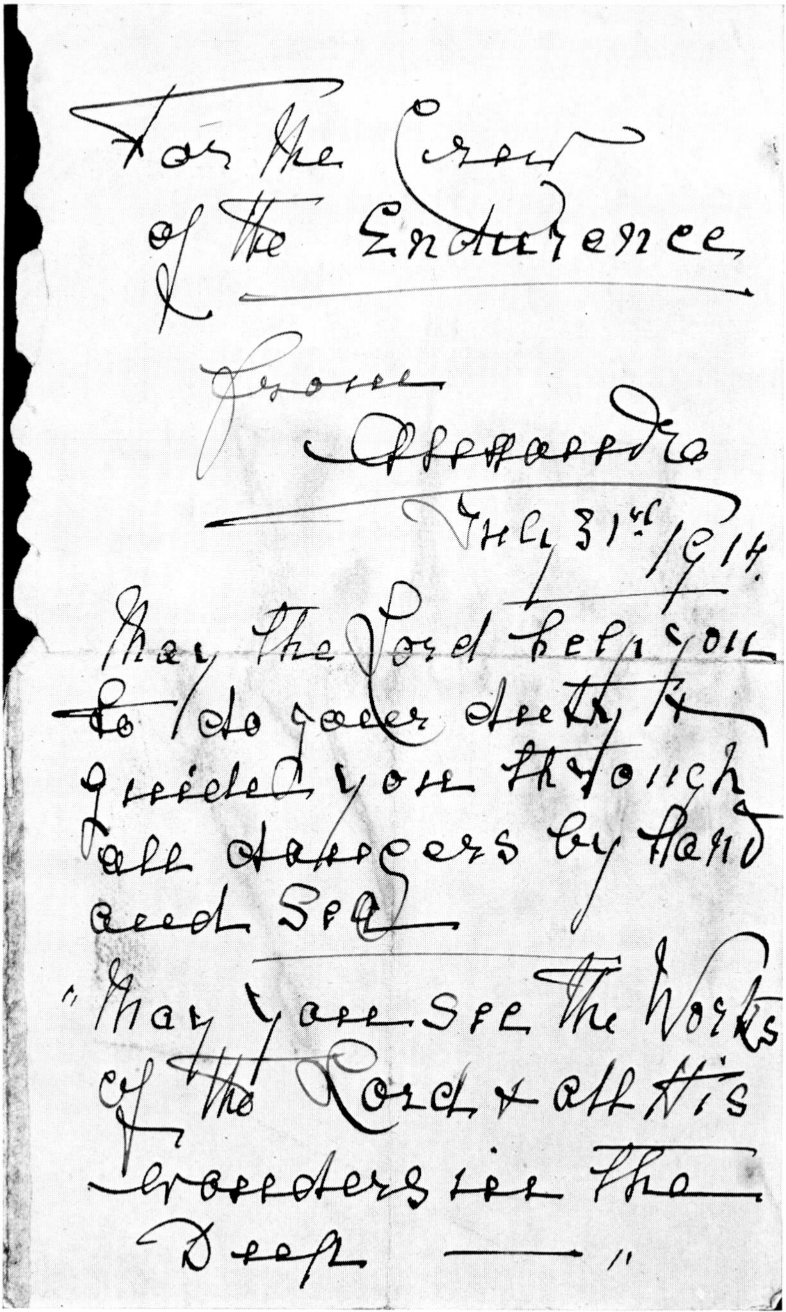

For the Crew
of the Endurance

George

Alexandra

July 31st 1914.

May the Lord help you
to do your duty &
guide you through
all dangers by land
and Sea

"May you see the Works
of the Lord & all His
wonders in the
Deep ——— "

Flyleaf of Bible presented to the *Endurance* by Queen Alexandra and carried
by Shackleton after the loss of the ship (p. 323)

Hurley

The Weddell Sea Party

BAKEWELL
HOLNESS   STEPHENSON   HOWE
                         HUDSON   GREEN
MCNEISH JAMES WILD WORSLEY SIR DANIEL GOOCH RICKINSON HURLEY
CHEETHAM CREAN HUSSEY GREENSTREET SIR ERNEST SHACKLETON   McILROY
                    CLARK   WORDIE   MACKLIN   MARSTON

Hurley

'The Boss', 1915

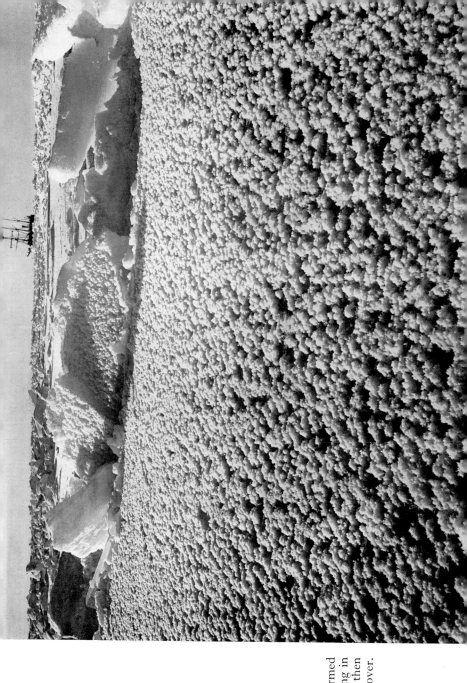

Ice-flowers: formed by a lead opening in the ice and then rapidly freezing over. From *South*

help him. His forward-looking attitude has never been better shown than in preparations for this expedition. And of all his preparations, none provides a more ironic footnote to the expedition now than the article which appeared in *The Times* on 28 July:

'At Lloyd's yesterday the insurance was being effected of the hull and machinery of the Endurance, the vessel on which Sir Ernest Shackleton is making his Antarctic Expedition. The amount of the insurance is £15,000.

An interesting feature in connexion with the business is that the vessel will be covered against risks throughout her voyage. Hitherto the insurance of vessels taking part in Antarctic exploration has ceased at the last port touched, and the Endurance will be the first vessel to be insured in the ice zone.

It is a curious fact that recent records of Antarctic navigation contain no instance of disaster that could be covered by insurance. During the past 16 years some 23 vessels have penetrated the Antarctic and returned safely, the Terra Nova, Captain Scott's vessel, making two successful voyages. The only vessel which failed to return was the Antarctic, but this vessel, which was crushed by the ice, was 30 years old, and her condition was such at the time of her leaving Europe that the Swedish Government refused to grant a subvention for the expedition.'

The *Endurance* set out, then, with generous financial protection. Her hull, machinery and equipment were insured for £10,000, covering a voyage from London to the Weddell Sea via Buenos Aires. £9,000 of this sum was placed at Lloyd's and £1,000 with the Indemnity Marine Assurance Co., Ltd. The premium was £665.*

The concluding paragraph of the article in *The Times* reflects the confidence felt by the members of the expedition:

'The Endurance, which was formerly named Polaris, has been built specially for work in the Polar seas, and although very severe pressure from ice is to be anticipated when the vessel is navigating the ice zone, it must be borne in mind that the vessel has been designed to meet it. Moreover, in an ice-coated sea there can be no turbulent waves which are the causes of so many disasters in warmer zones.'

There were to be turbulent waves, indeed, massed against the ship, waves of ice against which no stout timbers, no insurance, could prevail.

---

* A hundred per cent total loss was settled on 4 June 1916. We would like to thank Lloyd's for putting their time and knowledge at our disposal to provide us with information, and in particular, Mr. Wilfred Hatch, one of Lloyd's underwriters, and Mr. R. A. Williams, of Messrs. Wintle and Co. (Insurance Brokers).

21

Chapter XVIII

THE *Endurance* had been lying in the Thames since June, and Shackleton made use of her for advertisement, for he still needed money.

Thus, on 15 July, he entertained on board a party of members of the Worshipful Company of Shipwrights and their wives. The flat-roofed wooden hut intended for the Weddell Sea base was put up and used as a lunch and tea room. Sir William Dunn, master of the Company, proposing Shackleton's health, pointed out that the caterers, Ring and Brymer, had also supplied the luncheon on board the *Resolute* in which Captain Cook sailed in 1776. The coincidence extended even to the menu, for several similar dishes were served. One of Shackleton's air-propelled sledges was put on a boat in the dock, and the propeller pulled boat and sledge round the dock to demonstrate its efficiency.[1]

On the following day another distinguished party visited the South-West India Dock. The Dowager Queen Alexandra, keenly interested as always in Shackleton's plans*, brought her sister, the Empress Marie Feodorovna of Russia, and the Princess Victoria; the ladies were escorted by Earl Howe and Admiral of the Fleet Lord Fisher. This visit was doubly welcome since the national emergency had prevented King George V from reviewing the ship at Cowes.

Queen Alexandra had arranged to stay for half an hour but her visit became three times as long, for she insisted on being shown all over the ship, commenting favourably on the appointments and posing for numerous photographs. Her royal sister had brought a camera, and copies of some of the groups she took were afterwards sent to Shackleton at Queen Alexandra's request.

Lady Shackleton and her children were present, and Edward, who was then 3 years old, added a human note to the impressive occasion when he declined an invitation to walk round with the Queen, saying

---

* On 30 July she sent a thoughtful and warm-hearted telegram to Shackleton:

I am anxious to tell you how much I am thinking of you and the officers and men of the British Antarctic Expedition (i.e., Imperial Trans-Antarctic Expedition) upon the eve of your departure from England. I know that it must be a sad parting for all of you who are leaving their nearest and dearest but we shall follow you with our thoughts and I pray that the Almighty will have you in his gracious keeping and will guide and guard you through hardships and perils. Wish you from my heart all possible success godspeed and a safe return.

Alexandra.

that he would rather go with his nurse. The Queen presented Shackleton with a silk replica of her own personal standard and a Union Flag, together with two Bibles, one for him and one for the ship ; these she had inscribed on the flyleaf.* She also gave to the ship a medallion in crystal and enamel of St. Christopher. The medallion was not brought back to England, but the inscribed flyleaf of the ship's Bible, and pages from that Bible, survived the incredible journey in Shackleton's pocket.*

This visit was the last piece of heart-warming ceremony the *Endurance* was to know. Impending war had ousted her from her rightful place in the headlines, and had upset some of the arrangements for the expedition. When the ship left the dock on 1 August she lacked certain pieces of scientific apparatus from France and Germany, and several members of the expedition had been called up. Courteney Brocklehurst and Dobbs had reported for active service, Bickerton had gone into the navy, and the biologist, Davis, had also had to resign his post.

* See illustration facing p. 321. The pages were two from the book of Job, with verses particularly appropriate to men alone in an ice-bound land, and the page containing Shackleton's favourite 23rd Psalm.

On 3 August the *Endurance* was lying off Margate. Shackleton went on shore and saw from the newspapers that general mobilisation had been ordered. He returned to the ship and told the assembled company that he had decided to put the resources of the expedition at the disposal of the Admiralty. It was a proper gesture. The Admiralty replied first in a telegram—'Proceed'—sent by the First Lord (Winston Churchill), and then in a letter, explaining that as so much public money had already been spent on the expedition, it was considered better for it to go forward.

It was a situation entirely unsatisfactory to Shackleton. He was genuinely anxious to serve his country, and he could not help realising that if he sailed at such a time he would incur blame from many people who did not understand the circumstances.*

On the following day, 4 August, he left the ship at Eastbourne and went to London, where he was received by the King. 'He was perfectly charming', Shackleton wrote to his wife. 'I stayed 25 minutes and was in my ordinary clothes : he talked a lot and gave me the Union Jack and wished me God Speed and a safe return. This will be in all the papers tomorrow and I told him all about my offer to the Admiralty and he was pleased and said that "Certainly I should go."'

Royal sanction made matters a little better but Shackleton still wanted to get into the fight, and after he had seen the *Endurance* off from Plymouth on 8 August, he continued to canvass the opinions of his friends and backers, and finally, at the end of the month, asked Sir James Caird if he could visit him to discuss the position. News of the war was disquieting, and on the journey up to Scotland he wrote to his wife that he was sure he should recall the ship and go to Kitchener for a job. Sir James Caird's advice steadied him, however, and on 31 August he wrote[2] to his wife that he had been thinking out his problems and had decided that he must go south.

> 'There are hundreds of thousands of young men who could go to the war and there are not any I think who could do my job . . . now I have put myself right with Docker† and Caird I dont care and I feel it is my duty to go:'

---

* No doubt there was criticism at the time, and certainly the situation was recalled two years later, when the question arose of a relief expedition for the *Endurance*. Lady Shackleton answered attacks on her husband in *John Bull* and also in the *Strathspey Herald* of 27 July 1916 : and although the editor of this last paper printed an apology[3], in which he put the blame on the Government for allowing trained men to leave England at such a critical time, the attack made Shackleton all the more anxious to get a war job quickly when he did at last return to England.

† Frank Dudley Docker, father of Sir Bernard Docker, one of the three principal benefactors of the expedition.

Although he had made up his mind, the situation had been a mental strain on him. When he left England, on 27 September 1914, to join the *Endurance* at Buenos Aires, he was tired with the worry and uncertainty of the months before.

There was much to worry him—above all, the lack of money. As on his previous expedition, he had spent everything on preparations and had not been able to do more than hope that something would come in for running expenses. From South Georgia he wrote[7] to Ernest Perris, who had become one of the agents for the expedition and the chief recipient of his confidence, that there would be harbour and coal bills to send back to him, and that most of the men wanted their wages paid over to their families during their absence:

'I have written a letter of thanks to all the people who have subscribed £10 and over and will send you the receipts books so that if you require more money you might easily write to them and say that the expedition has had expenses that cropped up in B.A. and here and ask them would they send a little more I wrote each a nice letter but did not mention that there might be a need for more money, except in one instance and that was to Sir James Caird and I specifically mentioned to him that you would apply to him if it was needed.'

The position was not a happy one but it was the best Shackleton could do; certainly he was less casual about it than was sometimes supposed. When his friend Leonard Tripp took a firm hand in the management of his affairs on a later occasion (p. 419) he was grateful and relieved. Gerald Lysaght, who had given him good advice as well as financial support, wrote[8] to Tripp, 'That was one of Shackleton's greatest setbacks—that he had insufficient capital to run his Expeditions*—and he worried a great deal more than anyone thought over his monetary affairs.' From these two men Shackleton would accept friendly advice; towards other people who were critical he adopted a tone that was determined and sometimes truculent. There was one person, however, from whom he would always accept criticism—his wife.

In 1907 he had left England full of an overwhelming love and loneliness: absence from her made him realise how dependent he was on her. Leaving England now, in 1914, he felt the same surge of feeling, but now it was deeper and more complex. Their married life in the

---

* It may be said to be traditional that British expeditions should disappear leaving representatives to cope as best they could. The British Trans-Antarctic party leaving England in 1957 is no exception despite its unprecedented support from the Government. An article in the *News Chronicle* of 29 October 1956 pointed out that this expedition would be almost £60,000 in debt when they left, and quoted Dr. Vivian Fuchs, the leader, as saying, 'We shall get away all right, but what the expedition headquarters will do when the bills start coming in is another matter.' To the present writers such phrases have a familiar ring.

past year or two had not been easy. Through the earlier years in the
Antarctic he had dreamed of a secure, peaceful life with his family.
But once back in England, the dream had been put aside—sometimes
forgotten in the press of business, sometimes consciously put out of
mind as impossible. In all the years after *Nimrod*, the peaceful home
life had been as distant as the fortune he was seeking. Through those
years he had been, like thousands of other men, a weekend husband,
a weekend father. Constantly absent from home on lecture tours, on
business trips, on visits to possible benefactors, he had never had enough
time to get used to family life. His position as head of the household had
been kept for him by his wife; but he had been a person to be fitted into
the group, not one who had grown naturally into the complex life of
that group.

In spite of his insatiable desire for action and change, Shackleton
was a family man. His tenderness and affection for his children, his deep
love for his wife, were facts that nobody reading his letters could possibly
doubt. At the same time, his temperament made it impossible for him
to remain at peace during the periods he was able to spend with his
family. He was fiercely ambitious for his children and consequently he
was often very critical of them. Time was short, and at home there was
too much to do, too much to say, for him to be able to relax. His wife,
left much to herself, had inevitably turned herself into a mother, and a
mother capable of organising her children and planning for their welfare
and their development. To Shackleton, coming from an executive to a
domestic life, the benevolent and continuous rule of the mother often
seemed less strict than he would wish. Even the day of his final departure
from home in 1914 was marred by a quarrel over the behaviour of one
of the children.

So much was an occupational risk, and one which was to become
more serious in later years, as the children grew older. The lack of
security was a greater trouble. Lady Shackleton, sociable and lively,
had enjoyed the pleasures which her husband's fame had brought: but
gradually the fame had shown itself to be valueless without stability,
without the knowledge that their children were provided for now and
in the future. For years she had had to brace herself for changes in her
husband's plans, to wait upon his innumerable schemes for making
money. She had had to watch the call of the south working upon him, in
spite of his expressed desire to stay at home. She had had to watch him
making friends, men and women, in a set of which she did not approve.

She accepted the situation, for the most part, realistically. But in these
last few months of preparation for his new expedition, she seems to have
protested that she was no longer the centre of his life. Like most men,
Shackleton would put off indefinitely all discussion of the vital but
nebulous atmosphere of his married life. Now, on the way to Buenos

Aires, free for the moment from the burdens of planning and changing plans, he had to stop and think.

It was characteristic of him that he overdid the thinking. He dramatised himself, he half enjoyed writing about his failings and his disappointments. But—and this was of course the important point—he did write. Away from home, he realised that he needed stability as much as his wife did, and the idea that he might be able to change his nature, dear illusion of all human beings, came to him very strongly.

His last farewell from England (27 September) opened the subject: he ended his letter with the phrase 'Life is a puzzle'. Some time later, as he was approaching Vigo, he was able to write more fully.

'My darling I have been having a sort of reaction since I left after the strain of all those last months and could do nothing but sleep and sit down I am better now but am not inclined to write or even read and this is why I am not writing a longer letter: I have your last letter still and have read it many times and I will answer it fully from B.A. I realize all you say and I dont want you to say or think that you have been to blame in the rows that arose: I think I am solely to be blamed: I expect I have a peculiar nature that the years have hardened and yet when . . . you were (upset) just as I was going I found myself just as miserable: I dont want to go away into the South with any misunderstanding between us: I know that if you were married to a more domesticated man you would have been much happier and I also suppose I am just obsessed with my work and all I have to do. . . . one thing stands out quite clearly that I am to blame for all those uncomfortable months: just now my nerves are all on edge and it seemed to me that I could hardly have pulled through those last two months without a breakdown: Now I am better: and will see things in a clearer and calmer light. . . .'[2]

A pause for reflection once again brought Shackleton to realise how rushed his life was, and as on his earlier expedition, he felt the desire to settle down. 'I am going to carry through this work and then there will be an end I expect to my wanderings for any length of time in far places. . . .'

But the remark could hardly ring true in letters which were otherwise full of the zest of planning and the will to succeed. Shackleton's wife must have been at once satisfied and dismayed by these introspective letters. They showed her once and for all that she had her husband's love, but they showed too that—to use her own phrase—he was an eagle who could not be confined in a barnyard. The letter that he wrote her from Buenos Aires told her, once and for all, what she needed to have expressed but what she must already have seen for herself:

'I am just glad to have the worry over and get out to my work and my own life: it seems a hard thing to say but this I know is my

Ishmaelite life and the one thing that I am suited for and in which I yield to no one; I know full well that I am wanting in many ways domestically: that for some time past we have not seen eye to eye and that the fault lies with me that is the trouble and tragedy of life that one never stands still but always moves on one way or the other. I wonder if you know me really: I am not worth much consideration if I were really known and I have shown you that or rather tried to show it to you only you think differently dont you? I hardly know how to write only I dont want you to be all the time I am away worrying about me I am not worth your doing that: I have on the way out done a lot of thinking and all to no purpose I have tried to look at things for (*sic*) your point of view as well as mine and all to no purpose: and I go round and round in a circle You have sometimes asked me to pretend and simulate feelings but I would be worse than I am if I did so; that deep down in your heart you know; and yet I am not without feelings as you know on the day I left London for this voyage I am a curious mixture with something feminine in me as well as being a man, and I had an uncomfortable weak feeling at leaving which according to the plan on which I am supposed by myself to be working out my life: should not exist; anyhow you cannot say that I am not honest and I know that you are fond of me but that at times I upset you: I have a curious nature and I have tried to analyse without much success; I have committed all sorts of crimes in thought if not always in action and dont worry much about it, yet I hate to see a child suffer, or I to be false in any way: I am just good as an explorer and nothing else, I am hard also and damnably persistent when I want anything: altogether a generally unpleasing character: I love the fight and when things easy I hate it though when things are wrong I get worried. I am not going to write more in this strain I am a bit tired tonight and just wandering along . . . now that I am on my own work I will be better and more at peace and I dont think I will ever go on a long expedition again; I will be too old. . . .'[2]

From South Georgia (4 December), preoccupied with his work, Shackleton reiterated his belief that he was a domestic failure and only useful as an explorer. He repeated that he did not want to go on a long journey again, but would 'see the whole family comfortably settled and then coil up my ropes and rest. I think nothing of the world and the public they cheer you one minute and howl you down the next it is what one is oneself and what one makes of one's life that matters: the public are useful in their way they pay their 5/- to hear a lecture and money is the most useful thing one can have:'[2]

The bitterness in these last two letters was only momentary. Shackleton had reached the end of a period of strain, in many ways a very unsatisfactory period. Hope deferred makes the heart sick, and the many disappointments and anxieties he had suffered in preparing for

'Trying to cut a way for the ship through the ice to a lead ahead.' 14 February 1915

Hurley

'The dying sun : the *Endurance* firmly frozen in'

Hussey and a
dog-team,
September 1915

Hurley

'Dogloos' by the
Endurance, when
beset

the expedition had for the time being almost spoiled the moment
when he would launch out on his great journey. He was very tired.
Although his previous letter had ended 'I am tired now but optimistic',
the optimism was having a struggle to outdo the bitterness.

For six years and more Shackleton had been at the top of the tree.
He had moved into a world where the rich, the aristocratic and the
eminent met him with cordial interest and goodwill. He had made for
himself the social niche that he had dreamed of when he was first
married. Yet his position in society was not assured. It depended on
his continuing to shine brightly as a personality; it depended on his
continuing to do spectacular things as an explorer.

He could approach any man as an equal now, but he belonged
nowhere in particular. Geographical circles extended to him a cautious
friendship, fearing his impetuosity and his largeness of vision. For the
rich and the eminent his feelings must always be tainted by the uncomfortable circumstance of his hunt for money. Between him and
certain of his benefactors there sprang up a feeling of warm respect and
regard, but even then (as in the case of James Caird) close friendship
was hardly possible.

There was one exception. Probably even at this date Shackleton's
relationship with Janet Stancomb-Wills was a warm and personal one.
There had always been an element of caution: she was his benefactor
and things must go her way. When she summoned him to visit her
for the weekend to discuss plans for the expedition, he and his wife
realised that he must go. But it is certain that very soon he came to
like her for herself. They had very much in common. Each was possessed
of fierce energy and determination. When Margate was bombed
during the first world war, Miss Stancomb-Wills, whose home stood on
the cliffs, ordered slit trenches to be dug and refused to move. In
local government she was strong-minded and intelligent, and got her
way in something of the manner of Shackleton. She was a woman he
could and did admire, and in doing so he became a close friend, finding
that in this relationship, which was not complicated by personal emotions,
each could give the other much of security and help.

For her part, Miss Stancomb-Wills hid under her blunt and consciously unfeminine exterior a warm feminine heart. Like any other
woman she had to be needed, and she could be sure that Shackleton
needed her. He liked to discuss plans with her as if she were a man, but,
more, to talk about his philosophy, his ideas of life, and to discuss
frankly his men and their potentialities. It was a friendship independent
of the more distracting aspects of sex but all the same depending for
its depth on the fact that she was a woman, ready when he wanted to
talk to her, ready with advice and counsel and admiration. Shackleton's
various employments and interests, and his gregarious temperament,

brought him a host of acquaintances and many friends: yet he gives the impression of having been a lonely man. Certainly he depended more than he knew on the two women who knew and loved him most—the rich woman whose purse was as much open to him as her time and interest,* the wife who perhaps found it less easy to accept him as he was, but who had never swerved in her devotion.

The letters Shackleton wrote on the eve of his departure from civilisation showed, then, the same loneliness, the same feeling of loss and wish for stability as those he had written before the *Nimrod* left him in the south. Always at the moment of casting off and sailing away, he felt most dependent on those he was leaving behind, and now this dependence on his family was greater because his responsibility was greater.

The strain of the past months had intensified these feelings. He had not been altogether well. A letter he wrote to Perris admitted that shortly after leaving Buenos Aires he had had an attack of what he called 'suppressed influenza'. Possibly this phrase was then, as it became later, an evasive one, hiding trouble with his heart.

Although the expedition had officially started when he joined the *Endurance* at Buenos Aires, on 16 October, there were still problems to solve. There had been some trouble with the crew. Worsley had had to discharge four men who had proved unsatisfactory, including the cook. He took on two new men. One of them, Charles Green, baker and pastrycook, has already been mentioned (p. 315). William Bakewell had been wandering round the docks looking for a ship when he spied the *Endurance*; as he says, he fell in love with her at first sight.[4] He signed on at £8 a month as an Able Seaman, and was to become one of the staunchest and hardest working members of the expedition. The *Endurance* thus left Buenos Aires two men short: but the gap was soon to be partially filled. At Buenos Aires another British seaman, a boy of nineteen, had begged for a job, but Shackleton and Worsley had considered him too young. They now had nine forecastle hands and eight officers, together with the nine scientists and specialists who would help on the ship according to the terms of their agreement; and they were satisfied that the *Endurance* was adequately manned.

---

* On his return from the Imperial Trans-Antarctic Expedition, Shackleton received a poem from Dame Janet on his achievements. He liked it, he told her[10], because 'you do realize that in spite of this dusty workaday life I have ideals and far away in my own White South I open my arms to the Romance of it all and it abides with me now; I feel more than ever since you sent me those words that you and I understand each other: there is strength in what you write. I feel in you the sense of reliance that I did with one or two of my men and yet it does not take away from the woman side and that quick sympathy that we men lack so much. I write very openly because I know you understand. I have hammered through life made but few friends and it is good to know you.'

The young seaman, Percy Blackborrow, thought otherwise. Worsley[5] described later how 'After we had been out a couple of days . . . one of the seamen had come to me in some concern when I was on the bridge, and had rapped out, "If you would come to the locker where the oilskins are kept, sir, I wonder whether you'd see what I think I see." I had followed the seaman and looked at the oilskins, which hung about eight inches from the deck. And what I saw against the wall was a pair of legs. I put my hand in under the oilskins, and pulled, and out came young Blackborrow, the boy we had turned away. He had been there for a couple of days, with scarcely any food and nothing whatever to drink.' The stowaway was taken to Shackleton who at first spoke fiercely to him* and then got Worsley to sign him on as one of the crew. As Worsley truly said, they never regretted it.

Shackleton left Buenos Aires still wishing that his ship could have been taken over for war service, but full of renewed energy. He wrote[6] in his diary, on the evening of 26 October:

'It is wonderful how after all we have got everything on board and our 69 dogs are safely bound in kennels on the upper deck. All the work of preparation is now over; all the strain is finished and there now comes the actual work itself. As I stood tonight at nine and looked over the calm sea and upwards to the great stars blazing in velvet sky my mind flew forward to the unknown ways and the lonely trails as yet awaiting the feet of men and I wondered how our little party now playing mouth organs, banjos and mandolines would work and fare in the long dark days to come; the fight will be good.'

He can almost be seen recharging his energy in a poetic view of the situation.

They reached South Georgia at the beginning of November. Here Shackleton was able to get first-hand information from returning whalers about the state of the ice in the Weddell Sea. Here he took on extra stores and clothing, and some coal which brought his total up to 160 tons; this was accommodated by building a deck right along both sides of the ward-room. He had written to his wife about the ship from Buenos Aires:

'You will have heard by the time that this reaches you that I have decided to winter the ship:† I cannot risk her running up and down

* Mr. Theodore Savory[9] was told once that Shackleton's final words to Black-borrow were 'And if anyone has to be eaten, you will be the first.' This piece of gossip has the true ring of Shackleton humour.

† Shackleton had originally intended to land the shore party and send the ship back to South Georgia in the autumn of 1915. His change of plan was announced in a cable sent from Buenos Aires to the *New York World* on 28 October. In this he stated that he had changed his plan so as to have more coal 'to make rapid progress to the South' and that if he could get far enough south

. . . this ship is not as strong as the Nimrod constructionally this I
have seen from her way of behaving when in a gale pressing against
the dock wall here though there is nothing to be scared of as I think
she will go through the ice all right only I would exchange her for the
old Nimrod any day now except for comfort: I have stopped the leak
but have not dared load her down too much with all these dogs on
board and now am going to South Georgia to exercise the dogs and
pick up coal before finally trying my luck in the ice. It seems to be a
very bad ice season after all and I think the wisest thing is to winter
her.'[2]

His letter[7] to Ernest Perris gives the final version of his plans.

'I see no chance of our getting through this season by the ice
report it is bad so you will look for us about the beginning of March

early in the season, he might continue his journey overland. However, at almost
the same date he cabled to the *Daily Chronicle* that it 'would hardly be possible'
to reach his intended base in time to start the journey in the summer of 1914–15:
and the letter to Perris quoted above suggests that by the end of November he
was thinking in terms of the following summer. The effect of these changes of
plan on the Ross Sea party are discussed on page 400fn.

1916 from New Zealand the Endurance will return to South Georgia also about that time and do some work scientifically and then go to B.A. but when I shall send(ing) cable from New Zealand I shall include in it all the work done by the whole expedition up to the time that we leave for the cross country journey so the cable from the ship will only deal with the summer work . . . What I expect will happen is this we ought to sail from here about the 2nd or 3rd of December that will give a chance for the ice to be breaking up in the South and we ought with luck to get a landing about the end of the month, if the ice had been up North we would have landed about the beginning of December, we will at once investigate the road to the South and if Filchners landing place* proves to be any sort of harbour suitable for the ship I will put both anchors down and wait for her to freeze in, then I will know that the ship will be handy to take if [off] the remainder of the shore party about the 1st February 1916 I am not going to risk them later, the ship will go North then to South Georgia, as we are short of coal during the winter the hands will be employed in skinning seals and taking the blubber which will be put in empty boxes and this will be used to stoke the boilers on the way up. The cross country party will have their depots laid out and be ready to start about the 1st of November 1915 and they ought to cross in 4 months, and be met on the other side so far for my hopes. What God may arrange I cannot say. . . . '

Even with this press of work, with the constant need to change and improve his plans, with the prospect ahead of the biggest thing he had ever attempted, Shackleton still could not suppress his treasure-hunting instincts. To Perris he confided the latest of his schemes to make big money: when he returned he would form a whaling company. He believed that 'on a capital of £50,000 one can make for certain 50 to 100 thousand pounds a year net profit it is a gold mine only very few people know of it. This is a British island and the Norwegians and the Argentine people take over £500,000 profit a year from it and its vicinity.'[7]

It was unfortunate that Shackleton did not follow up his better ideas for making money. If he had formed a whaling company, he might have made the fortune he was still dreaming of when he died.†

---

* At the south-eastern corner of the Weddell Sea, at Vahsel Bay, the area of 'Shackleton Base' of the operations of forty years on.

† In March 1914 Shackleton had been contemplating a big business deal which would not bring him in money at once but which had considerable promise, as he thought, for the future. At this time the Colonial Office was looking for someone to take up a lease of the Falkland Island Sealeries, and on 6 March Shackleton wrote[11] to the Governor, W. L. Allardyce, applying for a twenty-one-year lease, on the expectation of being able to form a company to use it. An agreement[12] was drawn up on 20 March 1914, which laid down that the Falkland Island Fur Seal Company Ltd. (which was to be British) should be formed with

But now at last the time had come to leave. They had delayed to hear the latest ice reports, but these had now come in, and loading was finished. They had hoped to get war news from a friendly source before they sailed, but had only heard stories from a pro-German ship that came in to the whaling station at Grytviken the day before they left. The station ship, which carried mails for them, came in two hours after the *Endurance* had sailed towards the ice on 5 December 1914.

a nominal capital of at least £25,000, within a year of taking up the option on the lease.

For an annual rent of £150, Shackleton's company was to lease about 4560 acres of the Falkland Islands, comprising (with adjacent islets) the islands of South Jason, Flat Jason, Elephant Jason, North Fur Island, South Fur Island, Beauchène Island, Bird Island and Volunteer Rocks. Under the agreement he would have the right to take fur seal for the whole period of 21 years, under certain conditions, which included accepting the control of a Government Inspector in regard to numbers, and providing enough vessels and men to be able to prevent illicit sealing.

In fact Shackleton was not able to form a company before he left England, and the option lapsed in May 1915, when he was on the *Endurance*.

"ENDURANCE."

Chapter XIX

THE *Endurance* was not three days out from South Georgia when she met a belt of heavy pack ice at latitude 57° S., much further north than Shackleton had expected to find it. He gave orders to push south into the pack, hoping to reach open water, but the ship was soon surrounded, and it was 9 December by the time they got clear by moving north-east.

This was the first of many skirmishes with the ice. The ship dodged about, pursuing a course due south whenever it was possible, steaming through what leads could be found, and ramming hard against the young ice to force a passage. Worsley, enjoying the excitement of ramming, directed operations from forward or from the crows' nest, signalling by semaphore to the man on the bridge. A platform was rigged under the jib-boom for Hurley but for much of the time he was clambering into even more precarious positions to get film shots of the ship's progress.

Shackleton's own description[1] of the ice and its movements helps to give a vivid picture of the conditions they were contending with as they tacked and dodged day after day, moving in a field of ice which gave them a foretaste of the far worse conditions they were to encounter:

'Pack-ice might be described as a gigantic and interminable jigsaw-puzzle devised by nature. The parts of the puzzle in loose pack have floated slightly apart and become disarranged; at numerous places they have pressed together again; as the pack gets closer the congested areas grow larger and the parts are jammed harder till finally it becomes "close pack", when the whole of the jigsaw-puzzle becomes jammed to such an extent that with care and labour it can be traversed in every direction on foot. Where the parts do not fit closely there is, of course, open water, which freezes over in a few hours after giving off volumes of "frost-smoke". In obedience to renewed pressure this young ice "rafts", so forming double thicknesses of a toffee-like consistency. Again the opposing edges of heavy floes rear up in slow and almost silent conflict, till high "hedgerows" are formed round each part of the puzzle. At the junction of several floes chaotic areas of piled-up blocks and masses of ice are formed. Sometimes 5-ft. to 6-ft. piles of evenly-shaped blocks of ice are seen so neatly laid that it seems impossible for them to be Nature's work. Again, a winding canyon may be traversed between icy walls 6 ft. to 10 ft. high, or a dome may be formed that under renewed pressure bursts upward like a volcano. All through the winter the drifting pack changes—grows by freezing, thickens by

335

rafting, and corrugates by pressure. If, finally, in its drift it impinges on a coast, such as the western shore of the Weddell Sea, terrific pressure is set up and an inferno of ice-blocks, ridges, and hedgerow results, extending possibly for 150 or 200 miles off shore.'

On the morning of 18 December, the ship being between large floes formed by thin ice, and heavy continuous pack-ice, Shackleton decided to put out an ice-anchor and wait for a break. It was clear that in order to find a base on the coast of Luitpold Land, as he hoped, he would probably have to sail almost in a half-circle east and then south, and he was anxious about his coal-supply. In planning from day to day he had to weigh the need for caution in handling the ship and using coal with the need to reach a suitable base before the winter. It was the first demand on him for patience.

To the men at this time he seemed always to be on deck. He was vigilant in the matter of the ship's course, and he was also observing those under his leadership who were having their first experience of pack-ice. At this early stage of the adventure everyone was in high spirits, and the system of using the specialists as sailors was working well.

If Shackleton had already got the measure of his men, they had likewise come to know him. They realised that he expected efficiency from them all and that he was intolerant of bad work. Probably the scientists realised already that he half expected them to be absent-minded and unpractical, and that he was watching them keenly for any sign of weakness. They must have known now that the quickest way to win his approval was to make themselves as proficient in ship's chores as they were in handling scientific instruments.

By now, Shackleton had established some kind of personal relation with each of his men. The warming effect of his charm was especially felt by the younger men. There was a particular flattery in being invited to discuss Browning with the Boss, even when he did most of the talking. Shackleton's conversation, apparently random, could settle a man and make him feel important in the general scheme of the expedition.

Macklin, who was only 24 when he sailed on the *Endurance*, felt this very strongly.[2] 'When he came across you by yourself', he remembers, 'he would get into conversation and talk to you in an intimate sort of way, asking you little things about yourself—how you were getting on, how you liked it, what particular side of the work you were enjoying most—all that sort of thing. Sometimes when you felt he'd been perhaps a bit ruthless, pushing you round a bit hard, he seemed to have the knack of undoing any bad effect he'd had with these little intimate talks; he immediately put you back on a feeling of rightness with him. . . . He'd be mostly talking about books and poetry. One found it rather flattering at the time, to have him discussing Thackeray,

The 'Rampart Berg'

Hurley

Frank Hurley's most famous photograph of the *Endurance* beset;
flashlight in the winter of 1915. From *South*

for instance, or asking you if you'd ever read Browning. I never had, and he would tell me what I was missing.' This communicativeness in Shackleton was one of the things his men most valued in him: it was also, of course, a most effective way of establishing good relations with a very mixed company.

Certainly Shackleton must have had definite thoughts about morale, even if he allowed his impulsive nature to take over the planning in this matter. There was also the whole question of diet to be watched. As before, he aimed at establishing from the start a high standard of fitness, by a varied diet and by plenty of fresh food. As they pushed through or alongside the pack, he stopped to kill seal when they were near enough to the ship. He had already arranged that although, for reasons of space, officers and scientists should have a separate mess-room from the men, there should be no difference in the food served there. At the same time, he knew that among some of the hands there existed a prejudice against eating the seal meat which was to be had free and which was therefore to be presumed inferior to the tinned or frozen varieties of meat.

On 12 December the first seal was shot by Wild and hauled on board. Sir James Wordie is fond of telling the story[3] of Shackleton's next move. 'When he came up on deck Shackleton said at once, I think deliberately, "There's only enough for the ward-room. The mess-deck will have to wait for the next one." Very shortly a deputation from the men came to say that they would like to have their share of the fresh meat, and having once got it like that, they never looked back.' It was a simple solution typical of Shackleton.

Gales and low temperatures were now the rule, and the ship was able to move only slowly and in bursts. By Christmas Eve their position was 64° S., 32' E., and Christmas Day brought a series of stops and starts as the strong wind packed the ice round the ship. Shackleton did not let the opportunity for a celebration go by. Worsley described[4] that Christmas Day in his diary:

'Today was kept up by jovial greetings & grogoh at midnight, to all on deck & again at breakfast where Lees had decorated the wardroom 'most tastefully' with flags & had a little Xmas present for each of us, wrapped & addressed & in our plates. Had a splendid dinner Turtle soup, whitebait, jugged hare, Xmas puddg. fired with brandy in approved style, mince pies, dates, figs, crystallised fruit &c. rum & stout for drinks. Hussey has made a splendid little 1 string violin, on which he discoursed quite painlessly. Party & singsong in evening!'

The celebration helped to keep up the spirits of the party, who might well be wearying of the game of 'Up and Down' as Worsley called it: but surviving diaries show a constant cheerfulness. Even when the

22

ship was held in the pack she was drifting a good deal of the time, and in the late evening of 30 December she crossed the Antarctic Circle.

The following day came the first taste of real danger, when the *Endurance* was jammed between two floes drifting to the northward, and heeled over six degrees. An ice-anchor was put out, and by hauling on the chain the men were able to remove her from the area of pressure, where just afterwards they saw huge slabs of ice being forced at an angle, ten or twelve feet up on one of the floes.

The New Year came in with a mood of sober hopefulness. There were handshakings and greetings once more. The carpenter, a Scot, wrote in his diary that he hoped to spend the next Hogmanay at home. It was hoped that another day's steaming would bring land in sight. Shackleton and Worsley were well pleased with the performance of the ship through 480 miles of ice-work (see map pp. 376–377).

But conditions became more difficult, the pack-ice grew thicker and closer, and on 5 January Shackleton moored once more to a floe. The men took the chance of a game of football, and on the following day, as the weather was clear and calm, the dogs were taken on the ice for exercise. The next morning they were able to move once more, and on 8 January they reached open water, which gave them a clear run southward for a hundred miles. The sight of whales spouting and a clear way ahead cheered them for two days, when they once more encountered loose pack.

At 5 o'clock on the afternoon of 10 January they sighted Coats Land, a gentle snow-slope rising high to the southward. For three days they cruised, with occasional setbacks, along a barrier edge, past the coast charted by Bruce and along new land, which was afterwards named after the chief benefactor of the expedition, Sir James Caird.

Although he was watching all the time for possible landing-places, Shackleton still hoped to reach Vahsel Bay, where Filchner had touched land, and this decided him to push on when, on 15 January, the ship reached a good bay. He and his men were afterwards to regret that they had not made a base here at Glacier Bay, as Shackleton called it, by the end of Dawson-Lambton Glacier, more than 100 miles short of Vahsel Bay. 'It looked as though it would afford an ideal track to the interior of the Continent', wrote Worsley[10], and added, 'Shackleton afterwards regretted that he had not landed here instead of endeavouring to go a hundred miles further south. He mentioned this to me next day, but it is easy to be wise after the event.'

Shackleton[1] 'had reason later to remember it [Glacier Bay] with regret'. As things turned out, the expedition had lost its only chance of landing on the Antarctic Continent. Not for fifteen months did its members reach land—and without their ship.

Still skirting the coast, between the barrier and the pack, under sail

for much of the time, the *Endurance* reached 76° S. before being brought
to a halt. It was not a good rule to leave the coast, but the *Endurance*
was compelled to do so by grounded bergs. It was exceptionally bad
luck that just at that time an east-north-easterly gale piled up the pack-
ice behind and around her. The temperature dropped suddenly. The
wind persisted. Signs of pressure appeared in the pack-ice. After some
days Shackleton had to admit that the ship was beset.

It was on 27 January that he gave orders that the boiler fires should
be let out, for the stock of coal must now be husbanded. The ship,
held firmly in the ice, drifted slowly in a more or less westerly direction.
There was still plenty of work for everyone to do. The state of the ice
was not so settled that vigilance was not required. Sea-watches were
still kept. There was ice to be brought on board for melting into water,
seal to be hunted, the routine of ship management to be carried on.
The carpenter was set to make furniture for the Boss's cabin, and
for the hut which was to be erected at the base. Whenever the chance
arose the hand-dredge was put over the side, and geologist and biologist
eagerly seized on the contents. James, and Hudson, the navigator, rigged
the wireless receiving set in the hope of getting a message from the
Falkland Islands. Hussey kept continuous meteorological observations.

Shackleton took the chance to try out the motor-crawler, a vehicle
with some resemblance to a tank, designed to carry a sledge. On 30
January this was taken out of the main hatch and on to the ice, where
Orde-Lees got it running 'to the accompaniment of delighted yells
from the dogs. Before this Marston takes charge of the machine & in
his inimitable style dispenses imaginary ice creams to the crowd &
bystanders, some of whom give very creditable representations of small
Cockney boys.'[4]

It may be imagined that Shackleton enjoyed the horse-play as much
as anyone, but his responsibility was heavy, all the more so because
many of his decisions were forced on him by circumstances. One of the
most striking features of this expedition was to be the constant, pressing
need for improvisation. This is made particularly clear in Worsley's
diary, where every change in routine was carefully noted. Through this
diary is reflected that characteristic of Shackleton's which had already
been marked in his previous expedition—his extraordinary power of
flexible planning. Once again the speed of his decisions was noticeable—
a speed based on observation of outside conditions, on reading and on
constant thought.

From the very outset of the expedition Shackleton had been thinking
ahead. Planning his attack on the Antarctic continent was one thing
while he was still in London or on the steamer going to Buenos Aires.
Once on the *Endurance*, emergency after emergency was to arise in
which he must act promptly and decisively, always keeping a jump

ahead of danger. He was not once found wanting. Confident of success, he yet prepared for failure, and in this lay his strength. He was, above all, an *intelligent* explorer.

At the beginning of February Shackleton still hoped that the ship would float free again. Whenever a crack opened in the floe some attempt was made to break through. The men worked hard with chisels and ice-picks but all their efforts failed to do more than edge the ship forward a little through the young ice, and they had to give up. Shackleton accepted the possibility that the ship might remain beset all through the winter. No doubt most of his men guessed at the situation, but the company was a cheerful one. On 8 February Worsley commented in his diary:[4]

'We are now 6 months out from England, & during the whole of this time we have all pulled well together & with an almost utter absence of friction. A more agreeable set of gentlemen & good fellows one could not wish for shipmates. Any & every duty is undertaken cheerfully & willingly & no complaint or whining is ever heard no matter what hardship or inconvenience may be encountered. The principal credit of this is due to the tact & leadership of the Head of the Expedition & the cheery happiness & bonhomie of Wild They both command respect confidence & affection.'

Leadership, rather than tact, was needed at this particular moment. On 22 February the *Endurance* had drifted to the 77th parallel—her furthest south, as it turned out—and with very low temperatures, the pack was freezing harder than ever round her. Shackleton made it clear to his men that they must prepare for a winter in the ice. They were caught a mere 25 miles from their objective. 'It was more than tantalizing', Macklin commented,[5] 'it was maddening. Shackleton at this time showed one of his sparks of real greatness. He did not rage at all, or show outwardly the slightest sign of disappointment; he told us simply and calmly that we must winter in the Pack; explained its dangers and possibilities; never lost his optimism and prepared for winter.'* Worsley wrote[4] that the leader 'laughs & jokes as tho' he'd never a care in the world.'

Shackleton's behaviour was not achieved without a struggle. He was too quick in his emotions for equanimity to come easily to him, and yet he must show equanimity. He set himself to be calm, and his men imitated his example.

So the month of February saw the last of the *Endurance* as a sea-going establishment. On 24 February ship's routine was discontinued

---

* This and other extracts up to 27 October 1915 are taken from a continuous narrative written by Macklin soon after his return to England after the expedition, to replace the day-to-day diary of the first year, which was lost when the ship was abandoned.

and she became a winter station. There were no more watches, but all
hands worked by day and slept by night, each man taking his turn in
rotation as night-watchman.

Now that there was no heat in the engine-room, the cabins proved
far too cold to live in. It was decided to house the officers and scientists
in the forehold, the stores being transferred to the empty coal bunkers
and to the engine-room. In the excellent space thus cleared (and renamed The Ritz) the carpenter built cubicles, which were quickly
christened and adapted to the personality of their owners. Wild,
Worsley, Marston and Crean took up quarters in the deck-house, and
Shackleton kept his own cabin. The sailors in the forecastle, with a
good stove, also made themselves comfortable.

CHIPPY & HIS MATE

There emerged, as the winter dark began to close in, a curious polity
in which freedom of speech and a certain disregard of class-distinction
existed side by side with a sharp consciousness of difference in rank
and function. It is clear from the diary of Harry McNeish the carpenter
that he stood slightly apart from the other sailors as a master craftsman,
just as McLeod, by far the oldest of the sailors, stood apart by virtue of
seniority in service. McNeish evidently regarded himself as superior
to his mess-mates, and although he addressed officers and scientists
as Sir, it is clear that he respected them for their skill rather than for
their status. Inevitably, as the time in the ice wore on, the two com-
munities drew apart a little. The mental resources of the officers differed
somewhat from those of the men, and subjects worthy of complaint
likewise differed in character in each group. But in practical matters

and in the vital matter of morale, the group remained on the whole remarkably close-knit.

Shackleton made sure that each man should still have his own work to do. The scientists could still exercise their proper functions, even if it were only in identifying stones from the stomachs of penguins or in studying the reactions of these odd birds to their first sight of human beings. Marston painted the scene round him, and took time off to mend shoes with some skill. For him, as for Hurley the photographer, there were endless changes of sky and ice to record in pictures. Crean took charge of sledges and sledging gear, and Cheetham continued to be directly responsible for the men.

Shackleton had chosen the trans-continental party before he reached South Georgia, and from there he had sent the list of names back to Perris—Wild, Crean, Macklin, Hurley, Marston and himself. After the *Endurance* had left South Georgia these men had been told of their good fortune, and Shackleton did not let altered circumstances shake him in his resolve to attempt the journey if possible the following summer. At this time the situation presented itself to him as one of delay rather than of danger. When they were able to free the ship from the pack, which he hoped would be in spring or early summer, they would return to South Georgia, refit, and set out once more to find a base and start the great journey. He was not going to be beaten.

Accordingly, he set aside stores and clothing for the trans-continental party, and worked out a routine for the dogs to fit them for the journey when it could be attempted. Each of the men chosen was put in charge of a team of seven dogs, McIlroy taking the team which Shackleton would use. It was the duty of each man to get on terms with his animals, to feed and tend them, choose a leader, collect and organise the harness, exercise the dogs whenever conditions allowed, and produce a workable team. On the comparatively flat ice round the ship the landmarks were soon designated by nostalgic names, and down the Embankment, up Northumberland Avenue and into Trafalgar Square the teams made their way, surprising the penguins and occasionally shooting ballast-passengers into the loose snow.

Shackleton had learned on his previous expedition how important the organised training of dogs could be. Unfortunately, soon after they entered the ice the animals had begun to fall off in health. One or two gave way to the rigorous conditions, and many died during a disastrous epidemic of worms, in which it was discovered that the necessary powders had been left in England. Enough dogs remained, however, to make six teams, which after months of steady hard work became highly efficient.

As soon as the ship had been declared a shore station, the dogs had been moved on to the ice, and here all hands set to work to build 'dogloos', on which they lavished much ingenuity and thought, shaping turrets and pinnacles of snow into wonderful edifices in which the animals could shelter from wind and weather. Shackleton encouraged rivalry over the dogs, as a way of keeping up the spirits of the party, which remained marooned in a sea of ice for the ensuing eight months.

This long period had its peculiar dangers, of which perhaps the worst was familiarity. Once the party had accepted the fact that they could not expect to move during the winter, they set to work to make themselves as comfortable as they could. Secure in the shelter of the ship, they could easily become over-confident. One of Shackleton's chief problems was to keep them alert and lively at a time when hours of daylight were becoming shorter and there was a temptation to hole up and become soft. Work must be kept interesting and must be made to seem important, no matter how temporary it might be in its effects.

McNeish's diary[6] makes it clear that one reason, perhaps the chief reason, why Shackleton succeeded in keeping morale so high during these months was the way in which he saw to it that everyone participated in the expedition. Every change of plan could be, and was, freely discussed and commented on, and although Shackleton had the final decision at all times, he was known to be approachable. All hands could go to him with suggestions, and all hands were made to feel that they were important in the general scheme. The fact that no changes or dangers were hidden from them, and that Shackleton never gave anyone false hope, was of incalculable importance. Not only this, but it meant that Shackleton was liked by his men, because he took the trouble to keep a living human relationship with each one of them. William Bakewell,[7] who went as an A.B., recalls how, when he returned books to the 'Library' which Shackleton looked after, they would discuss the books; he recalls conversations in which Shackleton talked to him about Canada and the opportunities there, and how on one occasion he explained the different devices on his coat of arms.

In the Ritz, Shackleton joined in absurd guessing games, and in interminable arguments. There were competitions to find the worst singer, in which he won the palm from Worsley and Macklin. With Worsley he discussed, as a contrast to their existing circumstances, an extended tour round the Pacific islands. On one occasion (on 20 May 1915) he joined in a ceremonial hair-cutting, which Worsley described[4] in lively fashion:

'After some pressure Rickinson gives in & agrees to let Sir E. cut his hair, on condition that he (R) cuts Sir E's first. Sir E. agrees R. gloatingly seizes the clippers & plies them till not a vestige of hair longer than a bristle is left, & his victim looks like one of the Roman Emperors. But it is when the roles are reversed, that we all clipped to a man & looking like a group of convicts get our fun. The amateur barber seizes his victim with the air of a man about to do a mighty deed. He brandishes the clippers aloft, they descend & a yell of protest rises from the unfortunate object of his attentions. Anon things settle down somewhat, but it is a study to see the look of determination with which he gets his own back on the rash Engineer. Meantime Hurley on the other side of the table is being operated on, & each as he looks across at his neighbour goes off into fits of laughter. All now look so irresistibly quaint, comical or criminal that the camera is called in to perpetuate this evening & to cure us, where necessary, of conceit of our personal appearance.'

The forecastle hands joined in this useful scene, which was reflected in McNeish's diary,[6] where he described how 'we all had our hair cut to the scalp & then had our fotograph taken after in the Ritz we do look a lot of convicts & we are not much short of that life at present but still hoping to get to civilisation some day.'

There was always plenty of entertainment when work was done. On several occasions Hurley and Worsley gave slide lectures on Australia, New Zealand and the Far East, which were very popular. For some time there was a craze for mock trials in the Ritz. Worsley described one when he was tried for 'Robbing a Presbyterian Church of a trouser button out of the Offertory bag & having turned the same to base & ignoble use'. Wild acted as Judge, and Shackleton as Clerk of the Court, 'egged on the Jury to find Worsley guilty'. It is small wonder that he should write[4] that Shackleton's spirits were 'wonderfully irrepressible considering the heartbreaking reverses he has to put up with, & the frustration of all his hopes for this year at least. One would think he had never a care in his mind & he is the life & soul of half the skylarking & fooling in the ship.'

It is easy to imagine Shackleton being tempted out of his cabin by the sound of laughter, as he had been in the hut at Cape Royds. But, for all that, the months on the ship were anxious months for him. He had put thoughts of the cross-country journey aside for the time being, and his chief preoccupation was the comfort and safety of his men. While encouraging them to get out and walk on the ice whenever it was possible, he issued strict warnings against opening cracks, and early in the winter he gave orders that a wire should be run round the ship and across the surrounding ice, supported on posts and ice-pillars, as a guiding line to anyone who might miss his way back to the ship in the dark. As an additional help, Hurley, who was an experienced electrician, fixed lights on twenty-five foot poles at the starboard and port sides of the ship, which lighted a good deal of the floe. Lights were also installed all over the ship, and it would now be possible, if the ice should break up in the dark of winter, to get the dogs on board and everything shipshape.

The pack in fact was never entirely stationary during the winter. At the beginning of April the young ice round the ship began to raft, and all hands were busy picking and shovelling the loose snow and rubbish from round her, to give her free play if she were caught in the pressure. Early in June, too, there was much pressure near the ship, and Worsley, walking out to look at it, recorded[4] his impressions:

'The noise was very loud like an enormous train with squeaky axles being shunted with much bumping & clattering. Mingled with this were the sound of steamers whistles starting to blow, cocks crowing, & underfoot moans & groans of damned souls in torment. A constant undertone as of a heavy distant surf is heard whenever the louder noises decrease or cease for a moment. Approaching very cautiously, the motion is found not to be nearly as dangerous as it sounds. It is impressive to stand on the blocks of heavy rafting ice & feel the irresistible forces of Nature working under your very feet as the Weddell Sea North current exerts its slow but mighty force.'

A certain amount of pressure was heard all through the month of June, but the ice near the ship remained firm, and the men were still able to get out for exercise during daylight. The suggestion of a Dog Derby was taken up enthusiastically by Shackleton, for the drivers now had their teams in splendid order. On 14 June everyone was busy laying bets. The race-track lay along the pylon track from a distant gap known as the Khyber Pass, where Shackleton acted as starter. Hurley[8] later described the scene—the holiday crowd gathered, bets being taken in chocolate and cigarettes, some of the sailors getting themselves up as bookmakers, the short, dim twilight in which the eager dogs raced down the Pylon Way. Wild's team covered the distance in two minutes sixteen seconds, and Hurley, whose team was second, challenged him to another race, with passenger up, on the following day. This he won on a protest, since Wild's passenger, the Boss, was pitched off the sledge during the run.

It was not long before another occasion for festivity arose—Midwinter Day. Orde-Lees, who as official store-keeper was strict in his dispensing, was persuaded to give out to the cook the materials for three good meals —fried sausages and onions for breakfast, Bovril, cheese, Lax, bread and a cup of tea for lunch, tea and cake as an extra at four o'clock, and a grand dinner of roast pork, peas, stewed apples, plum pudding and cocoa. The Ritz was decorated with flags and Shackleton, as Chairman, made a bombastic speech praising his own accomplishments and deploring the entertainment he was about to see. Orde-Lees as the Reverend Bubblinglove replied in a humorous speech: Rickinson and McIlroy acted as women with great success: there were numerous songs, Marston (dressed as a yokel) being particularly effective with Widdicombe Fair. James got himself up as an elderly German professor and gave a dissertation on the Calorie: and at midnight a collation of fried bread and onions was served.

For the moment nobody had any thoughts of the future. They could not see the next Midwinter Day, which most of them were to spend in a dark and dirty hut, feasting on fish from inside a sea-elephant, sheathbills caught with a cotton snare, and a pudding made of mouldy nut-food and sledging biscuits, and roaring out topical songs which they had composed in the long dark days.

The light-hearted evening may be said to have marked another division in the weary passage of time. Up to Midwinter Day, although the men could frequently observe the work of pressure ice on their sledging runs, the ship had been left alone. From July onwards the ice was increasingly disturbed, and Shackleton, who must always have faced the possibility of losing the ship, was now forced to a greater vigilance.

He had all along taken his turn as night-watchman, but it was observed by his men that if anything unusual happened he was always there at any time of day or night. On one occasion (25 July) the carpenter recorded that he had orders to report *every half hour* to Shackleton while he was on watch. As they had wondered at Cape Royds, so they now wondered when their leader ever slept.

On 22 July the pressure had come to within 300 yards of the port bow, where huge blocks of ice were piled in confusion, some of them very good imitations of Stonehenge in ice. In the same quarter a large crack running S.W. to N.E. had decided Shackleton to get the sledges on board and to disengage the dogs' chains from the ice in case they had to be brought on board. Worsley wrote of a night on watch with Shackleton and Wild, a night divided between tea bibbings and excursions on to the ice to see if any dogs had fallen into the water or if the ship was menaced by any moving ice. Shackleton was delegating no responsibility now.

It was the beginning of a series of hopes and fears, as for three months the ice cracked and heaved all round the *Endurance*, and preparations were made time and time again for the longed-for moment of her freeing. One of the most decisive movements took place on 1 August when pressure forced the ship over to port and roughly along with the ice, which was in a state of strong movement after a gale. The dogloos were completely wrecked, and the dogs were brought on board. But although boats were cleared for lowering, stores prepared and the men told to be ready to get out and start a journey, the ship settled down once more in the ice, and the squeezing she had received appeared to have done no damage to her hull, though the rudder had been violently forced out of position.

Everyone could now interpret the signs of the next two months, the

ice piling ever in new shapes, the constant groaning and creaking. The
ship was drifting in the pack all the time, and was approaching the
westerly corner of the Weddell Sea, where pressure would probably be
at its worst. There was, too, some anxiety about their food supply.
Seals and penguins seemed to have deserted the floe completely; it
was now four months since a seal had been killed; and even when a rare
quarry was sighted, Shackleton had to decide whether it was safe to
go out for it over the troubled ice.

The surface remained smooth enough, however, for the dog teams
to be exercised, and in the increasing daylight the men made up games
of hockey and football whenever they could. In one hockey match
McCarty stopped a ball with his face and had to have his lip stitched.
Worsley commented,[4] 'This happens not to be seen by Sir E. who
invariably raises hell if anyone gets injured in any way, unnecessarily.'

Day after day, as the pressure moved ever closer to the ship, Shackleton had to be watching and planning. He remained completely calm,
acting when necessary, planning in the seclusion of his cabin, and showing a confident demeanour in public. He and Worsley discussed the
performance of the ship, who was acting up to her name and resisting
every squeeze and heave of the ice; it was clear that she would soon
be finally put to the test.

On the last day of September the pressure once more moved up to
her and they watched her with special anxiety as a floe pressed down
upon her; but it cracked in time to allow her to recover her upright
position. Cracks and leads were frequently to be seen in the next month,
but never large enough or near enough to float the ship. All the same,
Shackleton still hoped that he might have a chance to get her into open
water. On 11 October he moved the afterguard from the Ritz back
to their old cabins on the main deck, and had all put in readiness for
working ship. The carpenter built a wheel house for shelter in heavy
weather, and Hussey's meteorological screen, which had been set up
here, was moved to the motor boat. The move up from the depths
of the hold, and the increased daylight, had a cheering effect on the
men who had so splendidly worked and joked their way through a
rigorous winter.

Ice persecuted the ship without intermission. On 18 October severe
pressure threw her over to port on a thirty-degree list, in which awkward
position she was firmly held by the floe on the starboard side. The lee
boats were now almost resting on the floe, the midships dog kennels
broke away and crashed down on the lee side, and the dogs added
their howls of fright to the sounds of the ice. All hands set to work to
fasten everything movable, and while things were put to rights, Hurley
got to work with his camera and made a record of this new blow to the
Endurance.

In the ward-room, the men sat to their food on the deck, with their
feet braced against a batten and a plate on their knees, while those
opposite them were partly sitting on the wall. The situation was received with humour, but it was clear that something decisive must soon
happen. The next day the fires were lighted in the engine-room and
steam was got up very slowly. Ship's watches were set, and the scientists
and forward hands were put on watch and watch under the officers,
four hours on deck and four below, but with orders to be ready to turn
out at a moment's notice. Shackleton, as Worsley commented, retained
'the privilege of being up all the time'.

The engines stood up to the pressure and the fires remained alight,
being fed with the smallest possible amount of coal eked out with
wood, ashes and blubber.

Seal had now begun to appear more frequently, and on 22 October
a party brought in three, which would usefully provide fresh livers and
hearts for the men, food for the dogs and fuel for the fires.

Pressure on the ship continued, and on 24 October she began to
leak. All hands manned the pumps and the carpenter built a coffer dam
which was caulked with blankets and which kept the water abaft of the
engines. On the following day the leak was kept under control but the
ship was continually bending and straining, and on 26 October

Shackleton ordered boats, gear, provisions and sledges on to the floe. A thrill of superstitious fear was felt by some of the men when a little band of eight Emperor penguins came and stood near the ship while she was undergoing a severe squeezing, singing what sounded like a dirge for

her. McLeod was heard to remark, 'do you hear that, we'll none of us get back to our homes again', and Macklin noticed that Shackleton seemed impressed by the incident.

At seven o'clock in the evening the pressure slackened and all hands returned to the ship to pump and to take some rest. The next day the piling of the ice had intensified, and it was evident that she would not get safely out. Shackleton, facing the greatest loss a sailor could suffer, was planning ahead, checking stores and equipment, setting himself the task of getting his men safely to land.

The events of 27 October, a landmark in the history of Antarctic exploration, were vividly described[8] by Hurley:

'We have just finished lunch and the ice-mill is in motion again. Closer and closer the pressure-wave approaches. Immense slabs are rafted, balance a moment, then topple down and are overridden by a chaos of crunched fragments. Irresistibly this stupendous power marches onward, grinding through the five-foot ice-floe surrounding us. Now it is within a few yards of the vessel. We are the embodiment of helpless futility and can only look impotently on. I am quickly down on the moving ice with the cinema, expecting every minute to see the sides, which are springing and buckling, stave in. The line of pressure now assaults the ship, and she is heaved to the crest of the ridge like a toy. Immense fragments are forced under the counter and wrench away the stern-post. Sir Ernest and Captain Worsley are surveying the ship's position from the floe when the carpenter announces that the water is gaining rapidly on the pumps. All hands are ordered to stand by to discharge equipment and stores on to the ice. The pumps work faster and faster and someone is actually singing a chanty to their beat. The dogs are rapidly passed down a canvas chute and secured on the floe, followed by cases of concentrated sledging rations, sledges and equipment. The ship is doomed.'

By eight o'clock that evening all essential gear had been moved from the ship, but the men returned to her for a last meal, which was eaten to the accompaniment of groaning of timbers and crunching of ice. As they left the ward-room after their meal the clock was ticking on the wall and the water was swirling through the holds. Tongues of ice could be seen protruding from the ship's side. Shackleton hoisted the blue ensign and the flag was cheered. Last of all his men, he left the ship and joined the group of men who must now make a home on the ice.

Camping on the floe, they observed a last portent. 'We had a long arm with an electric cluster, over where the dogs were,' Commander Greenstreet[9] remembered. 'Something set that off, and you could hear the ship being crushed up, the ice being ground into her, and you almost felt your own ribs were being crushed, and suddenly a light went on for a moment and then went out. It seemed the end of everything.'

Chapter XX

'I PRAY God I can manage to get the whole party to civilization and then this part of the Expedition will be over.' When Shackleton wrote these words in his diary[1], two days after abandoning ship, he was facing a situation of danger. The sea-ice which was crushing the *Endurance* before his eyes was in a state of constant movement, and it seemed to him that he must try to reach land as soon as possible.

His present plan was to organise sledges and make for Paulet Island, 346 miles from their present position. There was a hut there built by the Swedish expedition of 1902, and stores left there for the men of the *Antarctic* by the Argentine relief expedition of 1903, which Shackleton himself had helped to equip (p. 78). This seemed to him the nearest point of land worth making for, since if they camped on the barrier they would be further from open water and from sources of food.

After they had left the *Endurance* on 27 October, all hands were set to make camp on a floe a hundred yards from the ship; but before long pressure began to break it up, and they had to move. By 8.0 that evening the five tents were pitched, and the party divided between them. By an intelligent arrangement, Shackleton ensured so far as he could that such cliques as might form now that the men had left the ship would be comparatively harmless, and that each group should have a good chance of settling down in harmony.*

When the tents had been pitched for the second time, Shackleton called the men round him and explained the position simply and openly. He put to them his plan of marching to Paulet Island. Thanking them for their steadiness in the crisis, he said that he was sure that if they would all work hard and trust him, they could reach safety.

All the men now living who were in that party remember his words as impressive above all because of their simplicity. Shackleton had, as a rule, an excellent sense of timing. When the occasion seemed to demand dramatics (the ceremonial raising of a flag) or relaxing humour (a comic act in costume) he was ready to provide the necessary atmosphere. The situation now was as bad as it could be, and heroics would be out of

---

* The arrangement in the tents was as follows: No. 1 Tent (small pole-tent) Shackleton, Hudson, James, Hurley; No. 2 Tent (small hoop tent) Wild, Wordie, McNeish, McIlroy; No. 3 Tent (large hoop tent) How, Bakewell, Stevenson, Holness, McCarty, McLeod, Vincent, Green; No. 4 Tent (small hoop tent) Crean, Cheetham, Hussey, Marston; No. 5 Tent (pole tent) Worsley, Greenstreet, Orde-Lees, Clark, Kerr, Rickinson, Macklin, Blackborrow.

place. The calm and confident way he spoke, the complete openness with which he discussed their plight, set a tone which was reassuring as well as bracing.

None of the men can have slept much that night but Shackleton, it seems, did not sleep at all. After they had settled down for the second time, he continued to patrol the floe in the darkness, and at midnight he saw a crack open right across it through the camp. He blew the alarm whistle, and tents and stores were moved to the larger portion of the divided floe. For the rest of the night he continued to pace up and down, while his own tent, which had been taken down, remained on the ground, and his tent-mates found shelter elsewhere. With others of his men, he saw, in the early morning, the light flicker on near the ship and suddenly go out.

At daybreak, with Wild and Hurley, he went to the wrecked ship to get petrol. The three men built a fireplace from the water-tank of the lifeboat, boiled milk and took it round the tents. There was some joking, and Wild was heard to remark 'If any of you gentlemen would like your boots cleaned just put them outside.' This convention of badinage continued throughout the expedition, a useful defence against depression in their precarious situation.*

There was, indeed, much need for humour. In the cold morning the camp had to be moved once more, and Dump Camp was established about two hundred yards from the ship's starboard bow. After the cook had prepared a breakfast of biscuit and hoosh, the men were ordered to sort their property and to equip themselves as well as they could for a journey over the ice. The sledges were already packed with

---

* When Shackleton described[2] this incident in *South* he wrote:

'Then we three ministering angels went round the tents with the life-giving drink, and were surprised and a trifle chagrined at the matter-of-fact manner in which some of the men accepted this contribution to their comfort. They did not quite understand what work we had done for them in the early dawn, and I heard Wild say, "If any of you gentlemen would like your boots cleaned just put them outside!" This was his gentle way of reminding them that a little thanks will go a long way on such occasions.'

Wild's remark was apparently sparked off by such comments as 'I like my tea strong'. Dr. Macklin's recollection[3] is that everybody was well aware of the position they were in and the efforts that were being made on behalf of the party: he feels that these and other such remarks fell into the pattern of badinage which was one way in which the men kept up their spirits. In his book, *Endurance*, Worsley afterwards quoted the shoe-cleaning remark, and commented,[17] 'That made us laugh at a time when we really didn't think that we could smile.' Macklin believes that Shackleton in his anxiety that morale should remain high was occasionally apt to misunderstand the typical reactions of some of the men. It is possible, of course, that this particular passage, and another of a similar kind,[2] may be due to Edward Saunders' interpretation of the incident. Shackleton did not see his draft of the whole book until 1918, when time had inevitably changed his memory and his attitude to such small incidents.

The *Endurance* squeezed between two floes

Wild beside the *Endurance* during her final break-up

emergency sledging and boat rations. A complete new set of Burberrys, underclothing and socks was issued to each man, and fur and woollen sleeping bags were distributed.

They slept a little to the sound of grinding ice, and the next day they got the boats on to the sledges—the aero-sledge being used for the cutter, and the whaler being mounted on the motor-crawler, with sledges under the front part. Ten more working sledges were to be pulled with equipment and stores. The young dogs born in the ice were formed into an extra team, and Greenstreet was given charge of this.

On 30 October Shackleton went with Wild to prospect, and found a route which seemed possible for the sledges. The men were ordered to restrict their personal gear to two pounds apiece. Of the treasures then kept, Macklin regarded his sheath knife and carborundum stone as of prime importance; Hussey was instructed to take his banjo, in spite of its weight; Shackleton threw away sovereigns and a gold watch, and tore pages from the ship's Bible which are still treasured in his family (see illustration facing p. 321).

The same afternoon Shackleton started out with Wordie, Hussey and Hudson to make a road with pick and shovel through the pressure-ridges, and the hauling parties followed. Worsley, with fifteen men, organised the boats, taking one forward for half a mile and then returning for the other, and the dogs relayed the other sledges. This policy was dictated by caution. Shackleton was determined to keep the party together as far as possible, for fear the ice on their route should split up. Safety was more important than speed. In fact they made only one mile forward, though covering much more by relaying, before they camped on some young flat ice, each man taking an hour's watch.

The next day was damp and snowy, and they remained in camp until the afternoon, when the dogs successfully took a turn in pulling the larger boat. A struggle over six miles of heavy ground brought them one mile nearer their objective before they camped for the night. Shackleton[1] was watching his men closely. 'Many look on this as spree it is better so. Hurley splendid, in fact all,* Wild always same.'

Snow continued on the next day, 1 November, and the leader decided they must stay where they were for the present. They were on a large thick floe, apparently at least two years old, and he thought they would be safe from pressure here, for a time at least. They established their camp (which they named Ocean Camp) in the centre of this floe. It was obvious to the men that they might never reach Paulet Island under existing conditions, and they were all cheerful enough to accept another delay.

They were now only a mile and a half from the *Endurance*, and a

---

* A comma has been inserted here by the writers, since it is essential if Shackleton's meaning is to be clear.

party returned to Dump Camp to bring on anything useful they could find. Five men, including the carpenter, returned to the ship and cut away some of the tangle of masts and lines on the deck so that salvaging could go forward as long as it was safe. For the next few days most of the men visited the ship, some of them taking considerable risks to get at the precious objects below the water-line. Operations were organised in a systematic way. Macklin[4] wrote in his diary that 'one party was on the ship enlarging the holes in the deck (difficult work for the deck was 3–4 ft. under water), and spearing cases with a boat hook and guiding them up through the holes. When the cases reached the surface they were hoisted up and received by the dog drivers, who carried them to their sledges and lashed them on.'*

Shackleton, keeping the sledging stores intact, had a separate dump made of all eatables that were discovered. His diary,[1] always laconic, gives a vivid picture of one of these salvaging trips:

'Fine & fortunate day. broke into Billabong. rescued stores. 1st float barrel of nuts. next case sugar loud cheers. next soda crystals groans. then jam. 2nd Break in flour comes up. . . . Wild, got $3\frac{1}{2}$ tons of stores essential. 100 cases wood floors to tents. hoosh in binnacle as stove. 23rd Psalm. fine weather.'

As well as valuable stores and equipment, all manner of odd things were retrieved which were later turned to good use. They saved a quantity of wood, including the binnacle mentioned by Shackleton, which was used as the basis of a cooking stove, and a party set to work to pull the nails out of every available plank, to set them aside for the carpenter. Some of the cabins were still within reach, though Wordie and Clark had lost all the specimens they had so carefully collected, and many diaries and private treasures sank for ever in the ice. Worsley's full dress uniform was dredged up and 'Sir E. amuses us by donning my cocked hat, boat cloak & sword belt with a shovel dragging behind for a sword.'[5]

Most important of all, Hurley's photographs were saved, those magnificent pictures of the *Endurance* at every stage of her winter drift. These had been sealed in tin boxes and placed in the strong-room. The carpenter made a hole in the side of the hold and How and McCarty went in and fished in the water to find the tins. Shackleton and Hurley then settled on the ice and went through the photographs to cut them down to what could be contained in one tin. Hurley recalls the agony of choice; as a picture was rejected, he smashed it so that there could be no second thoughts.

On 6 November, the eleventh night since the ship was abandoned,

---

* This and subsequent quotations are from the original diary which Macklin started on 28 October 1915 and which is in his possession.

Shackleton held a council of war in his tent with Wild, Worsley and Hurley. Three possible eventualities were discussed. First, if the pack drifted north-east without giving them a free passage for the boats, they might have to spend another winter on the ice. Secondly, they might drift near enough to Graham Land or the South Orkneys to be able to reach them by the end of summer and so be nearer to civilisation. Thirdly, they could, at the end of January, make a dash to the east on a small punt which the carpenter had made, hauling it over the ice and ferrying over what leads they found.

This last procedure was preferable to the appalling risks of another winter on the floe, but all agreed that their best chance lay in the boats. As for food, with the stores they had been able to rescue from the ship, and the seal and penguin meat they could be confident of getting, they could afford to go on full rations for the time being. Shackleton's policy showed an intelligent blend of optimism and caution. He saw no point in weakening the health of his men for the sake of the problematical future. Rather, he would feed them well now, while he could, so that they would be physically capable of standing up to greater hardships if such should come.

Although Orde-Lees acted as store-keeper while they were on the ice, Shackleton supervised the issue of food throughout this period, and he marked special occasions still by some small luxury for everybody. An extra couple of sardines, the King's flag flying on a pole, a hot drink, a schoolboy joke—these were his weapons against despondency and fear.

'Everyone is happy & contented & hopeful, if not confident, of the future', Worsley wrote[5] on 7 November. 'Speaking for myself while looking ahead & planning to meet all possible dangers I do not worry about those dangers which will probably be very great but live comfortably & happy in the present. . . . Someone has said that man when warm & fed is happy. I quite agree & if you can add health & freedom from worry then his happiness is perfect. Responsibility is a heavy weight but Sir E. on whom practically the whole of it falls carries it splendidly no man could carry it better under any conditions.'

During those early days in Ocean Camp Shackleton and Hurley had been busy improving conditions for the cook. Green had cooked his first meals on a stove made from an oil-drum mounted on three boat-hooks. This had been precarious and only moderately efficient, and not many days after they left the ship it had cost them a luxury meal. Mr. Green remembers :[19]

'We had been back to the ship and we'd rescued 28 tins of Irish stew in a case. Well, Shackleton gave us a pound tin each—everybody had to share—and after that he said, "If you give them to the chef,

he'll hot them up for you." I put them into the ash-bucket, got some
wood, blubber, petrol, and made a good fire on the ice, with a tin
can underneath, and just as I shouted out "Hoosh-O", the bottom
fell out and we lost our Irish stew. It fell on to the cinders, you see.
They started kicking it about right and left and as it went off the
cinders it froze and of course they started eating charred wood and
fat and everything. We went back to raw meat then for a day or two,
then we made another kind of stove.'

This was a more substantial one made out of the ship's ash-shoot, and
Shackleton was very proud of it:[2]

'Two large holes were punched, with much labour and few tools,
opposite one another at the wider or top end of the shoot. Into one
of these an oil-drum was fixed, to be used as the fire place, the other
hole serving to hold our saucepan. Alongside this another hole was
punched to enable two saucepans to be boiled at a time; and further
along still a chimney made from biscuit-tins completed a very efficient,
if not a very elegant, stove.'

The wheel-house had been removed bodily from the ship, and this
was now put up, together with sails and tarpaulins stretched on spars,
to form a galley and storehouse. This ramshackle but effective building,
and a look-out made from planking, spars and the binnacle, formed
the two focal points of the camp. The untidy settlement, looking, as
Worsley said, like a huddle of Indian wigwams, had nevertheless its
own order and method.

Method, order, routine—these were natural extensions of Shackleton's
matter-of-fact acceptance of the situation. His first task had been to plan
for emergencies. He had worked out in meticulous detail what each
man was to do if they had to strike camp in a hurry. A copy of these
orders was pinned to each tent, and in addition, on 15 November, the
leader read them out to the assembled party, warning his men that he
might at any time give a false alarm to test them in their parts.

This done, he set himself next to produce an atmosphere of security.
Although he encouraged the men to believe that they would soon be
able to move on from Ocean Camp, he did not want them to suffer the
discomforts of a casually-organised perching place. He felt it was worth
taking trouble to make an efficient kitchen, to establish a sensible
routine, even if the kitchen were carried away on a floe, the routine
altered at a moment's notice. It was worth taking trouble to make
Ocean Camp homelike and comfortable within the limits of their resources, however temporary its comfort might be.

Expeditions such as this one, which survive dangers and stress over a
long period, can be written up in a very melodramatic style. But the
heroics usually come afterwards. Not one of the extant diaries of the
Imperial Trans-Antarctic Expedition is preoccupied with heroism or

even with danger.* Certainly Shackleton did not put on an artificially heroic manner. He did not bring all his men safely out of the ice because he struck attitudes and made speeches. His qualities as a leader were qualities of character that showed not obtrusively but continuously through the two years of hazard and hardship. Intelligence guided him to make and remake plans a hundred times over. Endurance carried him through fatigue of body and weariness of mind. Self-control enabled him, a hasty, impatient, excessively active man, to remain calm and confident through a long period of inaction.

On one occasion he ended an entry in his diary, 'Put footstep of courage into stirrup of patience.' On another, he wrote by themselves, in a firm and deliberate hand, the words Waiting Waiting Waiting, and on another day Patience Patience Patience. This was the nearest he ever got to expressing his own feelings: most of the time, he was too busy thinking about those of his men. Shackleton's courage was innate and unthinking: the bravest and most difficult thing he ever did was to force himself to be patient.

Some of his men may have taken his behaviour for granted: it may be supposed that most of them appreciated it, and those who knew him well were well aware of what it cost him. Worsley, always pre-occupied with the course of daily life, wrote:[5]

'The blasting of our Leaders hopes & plans—at all events for this year—must be bitterly hard on him, but he, as ever, bears up wonderfully against misfortune & comes, almost blithely, thro' any adversity. No matter what turns up, he is always ready to alter his plans & make fresh ones, & in the meantime laughs, jokes, & enjoys a joke with anyone, & in this way keeps everyone's spirits up. Not that we need cheering up—all are almost without exception, hopeful. Most of us are optimists—I am for one—& I don't think we have a genuine pessimist amongst us. Certainly a good deal of our cheerfulness is due to the order & routine which Sir E. establishes wherever he settles down. The regular daily task & matter of fact groove into which everything settles inspires confidence in itself & the Leader's state of mind is naturally reflected in the whole party.'

Shackleton was to need all his equanimity, for no chance presented itself for a move from Ocean Camp until the end of December 1915. The ice was slowly drifting, but not always in the northerly direction they hoped for. Everyone waited anxiously for the moment when they should cross the Antarctic Circle once more. Worsley and James, who took

---

* Dr. Hussey,[6] looking back on the past, remembers telling himself what an adventure it all was: he does not remember ever worrying about being in danger. Dr. Macklin[7] finds it 'interesting to recall incidents of what must have been a very great adventure, though we did not think much about it at the time. Man is a very adaptable creature!'

regular sun-sights and occultations of the stars, were eagerly questioned. So was Hussey, who made observations at the meteorological screen which had been fitted up on a post. The discomfort of a howling blizzard was welcomed because it increased the rate of the drift.

Paulet Island was still their goal, but they might also get into a position from which they could make for Snow Hill, and thence to Wilhelmina Bay, where whalers sometimes called. Accordingly, the expert cobblers Hurley and Marston set to work to put screws into the soles of the Burberry boots, so that if they reached Snow Hill they would be able to negotiate the mountains between that point and Wilhelmina Bay.

This planning was wholesome and consoling for everyone, and so was the daily round. There were the dogs to look after and exercise, whenever the surface allowed. Each man took his turn of acting 'peggy' and fetching the rations for his tent from the galley at mealtimes. In the shelter of the galley was the 'library', and a workroom where Hurley worked on his various useful contraptions and Marston at his cobbling. There were the tents to keep shipshape; they had to be constantly mended and patched, and pathways were made round them in the snow. The carpenter needed assistance; there was hunting to be done; and in the evening cards or reading or talk or songs passed the time.

On 21 November the pack momentarily loosened and the men saw the last of their ship. Worsley[5] described her sinking:

'At 4.50 P.M. Sir Ernest on the floe sees her funnel moving downwards & hails me in No. 5 Tent. Without hearing what he said, I somehow knew she was going, rushed out & up the lookout, where we watched the death of the ship that had carried us so far & so well & then put up the bravest fight that ever ship had fought before yielding crushed by the remorseless Pack. Nothing is now visible of her but 20 feet of her stern pointing pitifully up to Heaven. She remains like this a few minutes & then slowly slips down beneath her icy shroud & is seen no more. A slight gap shows in the pack but this soon closes up & no one could tell that a gallant ship had floated there. At 5 P.M. we saw her end.'

Shackleton chronicled[1] the event very briefly. 'I cannot write about it', he finished—but the end of the day's entry shows his magnificent powers of recovery. He wrote 'good hooshes: all cheerful cut a ventilator in galley it was so hot. Perhaps 10 days in the boats may put us safe ashore'.

Just after the first disaster to the ship, when the men were sorting themselves out in Ocean Camp, the carpenter had suggested to Shackleton that he should build a sloop, out of the wreck, which would carry the whole party once it could be launched. Shackleton vetoed the idea. He felt it was very likely that they would have to manœuvre whatever craft they had for some time on the ice, perhaps for a long journey. A sloop such as McNeish planned could not be dragged as the smaller boats could. Moreover, it could not be pulled up on to an ice-floe, and Shackleton foresaw that if they were able to launch any craft, they would have to steer it through loose ice and find what anchorages they could for the night, perhaps in stormy water. His judgment proved to be good.

Accordingly, the carpenter had been set to improving and strengthening the whaler and the second cutter from the *Endurance*. High thwarts and bulwarks were added to the whaler, and the boats were caulked with cotton threadwick, oakum and worsted unravelled from somebody's muffler: the seams were paid with Marston's oil colours, which made an effective substitute for putty. On 26 November the work on the two boats was completed, and Shackleton formally named all three, after the principal benefactors of the expedition—James Caird, Dudley Docker, Stancomb-Wills.

At this time he was not sure of being able to haul the third boat, the *Stancomb-Wills*, but the carpenter was now ordered to repair it. Shackleton drew up alternative lists for boat stations, based on the use of two and three boats respectively. His final decision would depend on the state of the ice when the time came to move. All three boats were rigged with such sails as could be contrived. The same evening Shackleton cheerfully discussed an expedition to Alaska when this one was finished. As Worsley remarked,[5] 'We look up all the maps & books on the subject that we can lay our hands on, & are enthusiastic about our next trip before we can definitely settle how the devil we are going to get out of this one.'

During December the ice loosened and preparations went on for the next move. Some of the sailors made bags to carry the flour (now packed in tins) and the spare clothing. The ice was firm enough for hunting parties to go out, assisted by the dogs, and several loads were fetched from Dump Camp. Shackleton encouraged private enterprise up to a point, but he was more strict than ever in his precautions. Macklin recorded[4] on 24 November how he and Greenstreet went out looking for seal and for diversion 'got on a small piece of ice, and shoved out into the lead, paddling ourselves along with ski sticks. We were just like a couple of schoolboys doing a stupid thing just for devilment. Sir E. saw us, and I personally had the feeling of a schoolboy caught stealing apples or something of the sort.' The same afternoon Macklin went with Wild and Hurley to the place where the ship had sunk. The ice was rotten and broken in places, and on the way back they found themselves with a broad lead between them and the camp. 'Sir E., who had been watching us,' Macklin wrote, 'came to our assistance and we finally got across by flinging him the traces of the sledge and putting the sledge and ourselves on a small floe, thus being ferried over.'

Towards the end of the month the need for vigilance became greater. The ice was breaking up fast now, and Shackleton knew that the time at Ocean Camp was nearly at an end. On 21 December he went with Wild, Crean and Hurley, taking two dog teams and camping equipment, to explore to the westward. They found good going for at least six miles to the north. It was arranged that the next day would be celebrated as Christmas Day, and after that they would break camp. Once the sledges were loaded the remaining stores were free to all, and the menu for that day included ham and sausages, tinned milk, jam, biscuits, coffee, cocoa, pickles, jugged hare, peaches, parsnips and baked beans.

On 22 December, at 3 a.m., all hands were called to move the *James Caird* and the *Dudley Docker* on to safe ice, and then the tents and the remainder of the sledges were fetched. The temperatures being high by day, and the surface slushy, Shackleton had decided to travel largely by night, and sleep in the afternoon. That day they progressed only just over a mile, and on 23 December they soon found their way barred by an open lead. Shackleton and Wild went ahead and marked the route with small flags or pieces of wood. The boats had to be relayed, and going was very hard. Christmas Day found them sitting on the ice eating stale bannocks and drinking cocoa, very cheerful at having made a move at last.

They continued their laborious and difficult progress for some days. Their rations were small now, and the strain of pulling heavy loads told on them after the comparative inactivity at Ocean Camp. There was also, one may guess, some secret fear of the unknown beneath the excitement of the move.

Shackleton can hardly have been satisfied by the infinitely slow progress over the ice. On 27 December, after a short early morning march, he and Hurley went forward to pioneer a road. They succeeded in marking one for two and a half miles, which was little enough, and returned to find a crisis in the ranks. Harry McNeish the carpenter had resented an order from Worsley and had abused him. At any other time the incident might have been glossed over; now, when everyone was tired and when it was essential that discipline should be firm, it was more than unfortunate. Only Shackleton himself had the status to laugh off the incident, and possibly if it had happened to him he would have done so, for the carpenter habitually had a dour, independent way of speaking and Shackleton would have understood his feelings. But as it had happened to Worsley, who was acting as his deputy, he had to take action. That evening, after camp had been made, all hands were mustered, and Shackleton appeared with a copy of the ship's articles, which he read aloud.

He explained that he himself had signed on as master at Buenos

Aires, Worsley being then called Sailing Master, and that the crew
had signed an agreement[8] which contained the following proviso. . . .
'All members of the crew without exception to have interchangeable
duties and to perform any duty on board in the boats or on the shore as
directed by the master or owner.' They were therefore in fact still
under the orders of the ship's officers, as Shackleton's deputies, the ice
floe being equivalent to land.

The corollary of this was that the men were technically still in Shackleton's pay. 'Although there has been no trouble or questioning from the
hands', Worsley wrote,[9] '& Sir E. never having had any intention of
availing himself of ordinary Merchant Service usage which is that
crews' pay ceases from day of loss of ship, he has informed them as
above that there may be no doubt in their minds about their pay.'

This dramatic reading of the articles received a bare mention only
in Shackleton's diary[1] for that day, but on 28 December, tired and
dispirited after having to admit temporary defeat, he allowed himself to
brood over the incident, and what he might earlier have smoothed over
with a word and a joke he interpreted as an act of disloyalty.

'Turned out at 8.15 breakfast 8.30 pm. under way just after nine
pm. had bad work crossing leads but got on to big floe camped I
am this morning for lunch then on to edge of old floe at 3. H. & self
went on to pioneer passed some heavy pressure and bad country
then got on to thin ice showing diatomaceous for 2 miles. then from
the top of a height saw disintegrating ice: returned to camp 7 am:
turned in but did not sleep. thought the whole matter over & decided
to retreat to more secure ice: it is the only safe thing to do. 24 hours
sleep now: am anxious: for so big a party & 2 boats in bad conditions
we could do nothing: I do not like retreating but prudence demands
this course: Everyone working well except the carpenter: I shall
never forget him in this time of strain & stress. . . . Wild always same.'

The reference to Wild gives the key to Shackleton's attitude, just
as the whole entry, with its tale of disappointment and self-control,
gives the background. When the party returned to England, Shackleton
would not recommend McNeish for the Polar Medal,* although he had a
good word to say for his splendid work in the second year of hardship.

Shackleton's conception of leadership was never as impersonal as it
was with some explorers, and the loyalty which he rated so highly had
a complex and particular meaning for him. It meant devotion, no less.
This had been so on his previous expedition. Now, when his energies

---

* The Polar Medal was also withheld from three of the other sailors. There
is nothing that can help us to discover Shackleton's reason for this. It may be
said in general that he felt that to give the Medal when he did not feel it was
deserved was to detract from its value to those who had truly earned it. Letters
he wrote after the expedition make it clear how highly he valued the co-operation
of his men, and he would certainly want their reward to be a real one.

were bent towards saving a more ambitious venture from ruin, it was more than ever so. For him, at this moment, McNeish became as much the pattern of disloyalty as Wild was the pattern of loyalty.

So it was with a heavy heart that Shackleton directed a movement on to a strong old floe, where a camp was established, and named, appropriately, Patience Camp. But he could not afford to show his feelings to everyone, for he knew the men were as disappointed at this new setback as he was.

Fortunately there was plenty to do. Once the camp was organised, he had to review his food supplies. Besides the reserve sledging rations there remained 110 pounds of pemmican (for dogs and men) and 300 pounds of flour, besides tea, sugar, dried vegetables and suet. Hurley and Macklin were sent to Ocean Camp, and returned with a few useful items. It was obvious that rations would now be low and that it was vital to get some fresh meat. It was obvious, too, that the dogs would have to go. They had worked magnificently but they could no longer be useful. Worsley and one or two others wanted to make one last attempt to reach Paulet Island, but Shackleton was unwilling to take the risk. The ice was seamed with leads, the surface soft and treacherous, and he had put aside any idea of travelling on it. They must now put their faith in the boats, and they would no longer need dog teams. Moreover, seal were far less plentiful and would probably disappear entirely in the winter, and they could no longer afford to feed the dogs on meat that was needed for the men.

On 14 January four teams of dogs were shot. Macklin's and Hurley's, and the strong team of young dogs, were left for the time being, for sledging stores from Ocean Camp as long as this was practicable.

New Year's Day saw the party still cheerful, although infinitely less comfortable than they had expected to be on this day, lying in tents which were soaked through by the wet snow beneath. The previous day James had written[10] in his diary of that ceremonial occasion, New Year's Eve, 'Few people are having a stranger one but we are very cheery expecting a move before long.' 'This time last year', Macklin recalled,[4] 'we prophesied that just now we would be well across the Continent.' McNeish[11] put the matter in its simplest form:

'Saturday Jan 1st New Years Day which we celebrate in Scotland with cake & wine while we are celebrating it here afloat on the Antarctic ice floes not knowing what way we will drift next or be frozen in for another winter I am thinking on the tucker so many at Home are having today while we had for Breakfast a seal steak & a cup of tea dinner 1 pancake made from flour & water fried in seal blubber supper stewed seal meat & cocoa then we turn into our sleeping bags on the snow & dream of the Loved Ones at *Home* & Happy Days to come. . . .'

Shackleton[1] also marked the passing of a strenuous year with a rare personal comment. 'The last day of the old year: May the new one bring us good fortune a safe deliverance from this anxious time & all good things to those we love so far away . . . Reading Babylon & Assyria out of E.B.* Ice seems to be rotting away. Thinking much makes one not desirous of writing much.', and on the next day, 'I long for some rest free from thought. but thank God all are well & fit & safe.'

The next three months passed slowly and wearily. The surface of the ice was atrocious, and nobody could do more than crawl when they went outside. On the rare occasions when a wind dried the snow a little, there was general rejoicing. Clothes and sleeping bags would be hung up to dry, and the men, once more able to walk upright, revived 'a nearly forgotten sensation'. But for most of the time they could barely struggle to the galley to fetch their unsatisfying meals. There were few luxuries now, but Shackleton administered these with brilliance. On suitable occasions he produced an extra bannock, a little Virol, an extra drink—as for instance on 21 January, when at last they drifted across the Antarctic Circle. On Leap Year Day there were notable meals—seal steak and onions for breakfast, a fine bannock of flour and dog pemmican fried in blubber for lunch, and for supper penguins' kidneys and tinned Irish stew: thus they celebrated 'the escape of some of our bachelors from the Fair Sex', as Worsley chivalrously put it.

Thereafter the hooshes grew thinner and thinner, and as blubber was short, the hot drinks were cut down to one a day. Shackleton sometimes went round to the tents extolling the food value of a certain drink of dried milk or a certain supper mixture: the men were not deceived but they realised that he was trying to make their burdens seem lighter.

During this period of treacherous ice, Worsley and Macklin pressed Shackleton to send for the third boat, and on several occasions the leader did order a party to get it, only to cancel the journey for fear it might lead to disaster. It was not until 2 February that 18 men under Wild were sent off with the boat sledge, with strict instructions about the length of time they were to be away. They got off at one o'clock in the morning, using the best time of day for travelling, and by eleven o'clock they were to be seen coming back. Shackleton and Hussey went out to meet them with two large hoosh pots full of hot tea, and by 12.30 the *Stancomb-Wills* was safe in camp.

Shackleton's anxiety while trips such as this were in progress was evident to those who knew him well. Colonel Macklin, looking back,[7] sees in perspective a caution which at the time seemed rather a nuisance. 'I have to admit that behind a screen of pressure ridges we did all sorts

* They had taken one volume of the *Encyclopaedia Britannica* with them on their march over the ice.

of things he did not like and which in some cases had been expressly forbidden—ferrying our teams on small bits of ice across open leads, racing them over rubble from floe to floe (sometimes in the process putting sledges, dogs and ourselves into the sea!). He was not however blind to the fact that we did these things—I remember one or two embarrassing occasions when we were "caught" and got the rough edge of his tongue—and quite a number of seals which could have been brought in were left alone because he thought the risks which we light-heartedly took in this way outweighed the immediate needs of the moment.'

Deprived of exercise, accepting the imminence of danger, Shackleton suffered more at Patience Camp than during any other period of the expedition. Hurley remembers how sometimes at night the leader would call out in the grip of nightmare, and when he was woken, would describe some accident which his tired mind had too vividly foreseen. But once awake (and this was entirely characteristic of him) he would set himself there and then to think of a plan to circumvent the imagined danger: only then would he sleep again. He was always a planner, and his diary has lists on every spare page—lists of boat parties or emergency orders. Yet to very few others was his anxiety at all apparent. 'He was always cheerful', Mr. Bakewell[12] remembers, 'and gave everyone confidence that we would get out', and Mr. How[13] put into words what all the forecastle hands felt about him when he said, 'He was a tower of strength and endurance, and he never panicked in any emergency.'

If Shackleton was occasionally seen with a somewhat gloomy countenance (especially at times when he could not follow his usual custom of pacing up and down the ice), he battened down his quick temper. Whatever he felt about his men in his heart (and he watched their behaviour very closely), his manner to them was one of solicitude and care. The observable quickness of his planning, as well as his calm manner, reassured them. Professor James sums up[14] this quality as 'a wonderful power of inspiring confidence and an uncanny flair for the right thing to do. He kept his plans elastic, and did not hesitate to change them completely with changing circumstances. We did not always think his judgement right at the time, but it always turned out to be so. I do not think there is any doubt that we all owe our lives to his leadership and his power of making a loyal and coherent party out of rather diverse elements.'

Most of all his men trusted him because they knew his first thought was for them. It was by now clear to all of them that he would not seek any of the privileges which a leader could so easily reserve for himself. He shared the semi-starvation, the discomfort, the danger, equally with everyone. 'If he had half a pipe of tobacco', Mr. How said, 'he'd give you half of it, if there was no other to share out'.

Now, if ever, it was necessary for Shackleton to know his men. The second enforced period of waiting, so much more depressing and uncomfortable than the first, might well have its effect on them. Nobody could go on feeling patient for ever, and for the active patience as they waited for a chance of a dash for land was substituted, in some cases, a dangerous apathy. Even the lively Worsley could write[5] in his diary, 'It is to be hoped we can soon be "up & doing" something however little to aid our escape from this white interminable prison where the minds energies & abilities of all of us are atrophying & where we are rusting & wasting our lives away, while the whole world is at War & we know nothing of how it goes.'

The carpenter had a caustic comment to make on the men who had temporarily lost the power to act. On 14 March he wrote[11]:

'There is a Blizzard on at present from SE. so everything is closed up again. But we expect. It will open up after this. More than it has before. We have not been outside the tents & everything is wet. So it is not very comfortable. & still we have some here that dont wish to get in the boats. They want to drift ashore. Which we cant do. But I notice Those are the ones who have never don a days work in this world & dont intend to as long as they can act the Pharasite on some body else They know themselves to be useless & I expect They wont be much more use in a boat.'

All that Shackleton could do at this time was to watch and wait. Often he would go round the tents and enquire about the comfort of the inmates. He had his own resources. He enjoyed a tune from Hussey's banjo. He played interminable games of bridge, and instructed others in the game. He and Hurley played four hands of poker every afternoon, and at the end of ten weeks Hurley[15] had become 'the possessor of an imaginary shaving-glass, several top hats, enough walking-canes to equip a regiment, several sets of sleeve-links, and a library of books.' He had dined at Shackleton's expense at Claridge's and had occupied a box at the opera, while Shackleton in his turn had been Hurley's guest at the Savoy and visited most of the theatres in London at his expense, besides acquiring 'scores of fine linen handkerchiefs, silk umbrellas, a mirror and a coveted collector's copy of Paradise Regained. . . .'[18]

Most of the men remember Shackleton reciting poetry at great length or arguing with zest on some subject very remote from their lives at that moment. James recorded in his diary a dispute between Shackleton and Hudson about the difference between the Greek Orthodox and Roman Catholic churches which became quite heated. Shackleton's favourite relaxation, however, was the discussion of buried treasure and plans for getting rich.

In his diary, lists of inventions and undiscovered hoards bear witness to this preoccupation. There was the treasure of Alaric the Goth, said to have been hidden in a dry water-course into which a stream was then diverted; Shackleton discussed with Worsley the possibility of turning the stream back again. There was King John's treasure, perennial lure for the adventurous. There was a scheme for pearl fishing in the South Seas. Other notes mention copper mining in Cyprus, tin in Paraguay, cotton-picking machinery, an improved electric tin opener, and, mysteriously, the Southern Arabian Desert and the excavations at Endum. The idea of getting rich was appealing, but in their predicament on the ice, the idea of free adventure was probably even more so.

Towards the end of March the ice round Patience Camp broke up and the floe they were on was gradually whittled down. From this time Shackleton always had two men on watch, and the party was divided into two, each to be in readiness for a call when on duty. The state of the ice made it impossible to go anywhere on foot, and they had to watch various desirable points go by, as their floe moved more swiftly with the pack. On 17 March they were a mere 60 miles from Paulet Island. Joinville Island was sighted on 23 March and for three days they drifted past the tip of Graham Land, until at last the peak of Mount Haddington on James Ross Island disappeared from view.

It was not out of the question that they might drift to Deception Island, to the west, where there were stores for shipwrecked sailors, and a small church where timber could be had for building a substantial boat. There were also, to the north, Clarence and Elephant Islands, which were sighted on 7 April. If they could not reach one of these places, by drift or by boat, they would be left to the mercy of the Atlantic, with South Georgia far distant and difficult to reach in the prevailing conditions of wind and currents.

Shackleton was now pinning his faith to the three boats. On 30 March the last of the dogs had been shot. The sledges were abandoned, but one set of runners was stowed in a boat, in case they should be able to reach any part of Graham Land and have to travel overland.

On 8 April a crack opened under the *James Caird*, splitting the camp in two. Shackleton had already organised the loading of the boats and arranged the division of the men, giving himself command of the *James Caird*, and Worsley and Hudson that of the *Dudley Docker* and *Stancomb-Wills* respectively.

On 9 April, after a hasty breakfast, tents were struck and everything was prepared for launching the boats as soon as open water could be reached. In the middle of the morning the floe cracked across, but the crack knit almost at once. Shackleton ordered lunch of seal meat for all hands. At 1 o'clock several channels were seen. The boats were quickly launched and rowed out through jostling ice into a largish open pool. The departure was recorded,[4] telegraphically and graphically, by Macklin:

'Under way at last: large amount of bird life flew all round—annoyance of dropped excreta—whales blowing all round us—difficult rowing through the ice—thick and fouled the oars—bumping into lumps—rowing cold to fingers. Dudley Docker packed with food cases—stove—meat bag—sleeping bags under canvas in bow—paraffin—tent—clothing bags. Seats too low for rowing—sat on packing-cases—not a satisfactory arrangement. Four oars and 2 spare ones—one mast & small lug sail. Caird main and mizzen and foresail. Wills lug and small foresail. Wills & Caird also packed with provisions, tents etc. Docker started towing sledge—fouled ice and so cut adrift. Water breaker thrown over from Caird, floated away and we wondered at its destination. Sudden tide movement of ice floe. High flat berg—good headway—skilful ice navigation by Sir E. . . .'

After the first few hours of rowing, when dark began to come on, they pulled the boats up on to a thick floe of old ice and camped for the night. About 11 o'clock something roused Shackleton to go out and look round the improvised camp. It was just at this moment that the ice cracked through the centre of the big dome tent where the forecastle hands were resting. Mr. How remembers[13] the incident vividly:

'We were all in our sleeping bags when it happened to break just where Holness was lying. He couldn't help himself—it dropped him into the drink. Shackleton he came on the run—"Who's missing"—and could see this bag floating about and there was this chap in the bag. Shackleton luffed him out. "You all right, Holness?" "Yes, Boss, only thing I'm thinking about is my 'baccy I'd left in the bag". That was his greatest anxiety, his tobacco! We kept him on the run all night long, because we had no clothes to change to give him, kept him up and down, and every movement he made with his legs and arms, there was a crackle of icy clothes. Well, he got over it.'

Cold and apprehensive, the men did not try to sleep again. Shackleton ordered hot milk and nut food to be served, and they huddled round the portable blubber stove (like hobgoblins, Macklin thought) till dawn.

But this was by no means their most uncomfortable night. On 10 April the floe they camped on was solid enough, but on the next day the ice they chose was in such a state of movement that they had to stay in the boats, fending off obstacles and watching whales blowing very near. The night after was as hard, as they lay in the boats, with the temperature four degrees below zero and their clothes freezing as they huddled together.

This dreadful night proved to be their last chance of rest, for the next day they were out in the open ocean, and until they reached Elephant Island two days later they had to remain as alert and alive in the boats as they could, suffering agonies of thirst and cold far beyond any pangs of hunger, some rowing, some baling, the boats now tied together, now separated, now moving with a set distance between them to avoid ramming.

Every man now has his own particular memory of the worst part of that gruelling journey. To Mr. Green and Mr. How it is the nights spent in the boats, lashed together with a painter, hearing the whales moving in the darkness. To Dr. Macklin it was not the whales that made the worst night of lying-to (11 April) so dreadful but the combination of freezing seas covering the boat and its inmates, sea-sickness, and diarrhœa from the uncooked dog pemmican they had been eating. The physical conditions appalled the doctor and he scarcely noticed the dangers round them. To both Hurley and Greenstreet the worst moment came just before they drew into the open ocean. Commander Greenstreet, recalling[16] the day forty years later, found himself living it all over again.

'We'd cleared the pack and were all set for Elephant Island. Then when we woke in the morning we found all the pack closed round us, a howling gale was blowing and a terrific sea running. One moment we were right away up on the tremendous crest of a swell, you could see right away to the horizon, nothing but sea and ice, and then down you'd drop in the hollow and would see a great big roller coming up with a huge block of ice, crash against the side and a piece would break off, and the floe got smaller and smaller, we had a big lump on one end which we used as a look out and we'd climb up to see what was happening. Our only chance was to get into one of these big pools of water. You'd see one coming along, and you'd shout down to the others "Stand by, boys, here comes a pool", but it would pass half a mile to the right or half a mile to the left. Then a crack started—it looked like a crack right through the very centre of the floe we were on—we thought this is the end of everything, the whole thing's going to break up in a few minutes and we'll all be struggling in the water and that's finish. And we were all of us on the point of shaking hands and saying Well, cheerio lad, this is the end of everything, when a pool of water we hadn't seen coming

Hurley

Ocean Camp: Shackleton and Wild in foreground

Hurley

Relaying the *James Caird*. Frank Wild directing operations

Hurley and Shackleton at Patience Camp

towards us—it was some trick of the current coming up against the big floe and the backwash sent the ice off a bit, so it formed a big pool round us, and we found we were in a pool of water. "All right, launch the boats, chuck in the stores anyhow, get in the centre of this patch of water"—and we did that, and then got things stowed properly and worked through a narrow neck of brash ice into another big pool and then another one, down a long lead and there was the open sea before us. I think it was the most marvellous thing that's ever happened.'

It was in such conditions that Shackleton got his men to land once more—got twenty-eight cold and suffering but cheerful people out of the ice, helped by the imperturbable Wild, by the brilliant navigation of Worsley, by the dogged endurance of every man of the company—helped, above all, by his unflinching determination not to be beaten. From the vantage point of the *James Caird* he gave his orders, saw to it that the men had what food there was to have (though for the last day or two they were too parched to eat), called to the other boats to know how they fared, was never unwary, never at a loss, never, it seemed, slept or relaxed for a moment.

The description in Shackleton's book *South*, long and detailed as it is, hardly does justice to Shackleton's own part in this incredible journey, though he is at pains to mention every individual who distinguished himself in any way. For his own achievement one must turn to the books of Worsley[17] and Hussey[18] and Hurley,[15] to the diaries which bear witness to his thoughtfulness and skill, to the memories of those men still living who remember the journey as the most remarkable of Shackleton's achievements.

'You felt that if he led you everything was going to be all right'—so Greenstreet. 'We put such absolute faith in the Boss that we knew that if anybody could get us through he'd get us through, and we just did as he told us. We didn't worry about anything else'—so Hussey. 'I always found him rising to his best and inspiring confidence when things were at their blackest'—so Hurley. 'He made the best of any predicament. He was quite undefeatable'—so Orde-Lees. And Macklin summed up decisively, 'I think his taking of those overloaded boats through the ice, with seventeen hours of darkness in the twenty-four, breaking up and grinding of floes, and the whole set of conditions of the seven days we were in the boats, constituted a truly remarkable piece of leadership.'

It was indeed a remarkable feat. Once out of the dangerous embrace of the pack, they faced conditions of weather from which the ice had shielded them. On 12 April a sun sight showed that they had been swept by a current to the south east of Clarence and Elephant Islands, and though they later got back on to course again, hard winds and heavy

24

seas made it difficult to work at the oars. Everything became iced over, but on 14 April their weary spirits were cheered by a sight of Clarence Island ahead, and later that day Elephant Island appeared. Shackleton hoped to make shelter by nightfall but darkness found them still cruising close to the steep and inhospitable cliffs of Elephant Island. The *Dudley Docker* had become separated from the other two boats just after dark, and the hazards of their position were intensified as each man wondered what had become of his comrades.

It seemed almost too good to be true when on the morning of 15 April the three boat-loads came together in a sheltered bay on Elephant Island. Shackleton proposed for Blackborrow, the youngest of the party, the honour of being the first to set foot on the island, but the boy had badly frostbitten feet, and when he was helped over the side he collapsed and sat in the surf. James wrote in his diary shortly afterwards, 'Most people were I think in a semi-hysterical condition and hardly knew whether to laugh or cry. We did not know, until it was released, what a strain the last few days had been. We took childish joy in looking at the black rocks and picking up the stones for we had stepped on no land since Dec. 5 1914.'

Weary and worn as they were, the men raised enough energy to pull the boats up on the beach and land the stores they had been able to preserve. The next twenty-four hours were spent in feasting and sleeping, and none will ever forget how the cook produced meal after meal from the seal killed on the barren beach.

But there was little rest for Shackleton. He realised at once that this was no safe place for a camp. On the day after their landing he sent Wild with a boat-load to search westwards along the coast for a better place, while he and Hurley prospected on foot. They were not able to get far, but in the evening Wild returned to report that he had found a long sandy spit which would serve them well enough. Next morning (17 April) the three boats were rowed, with great effort and difficulty, to the place christened Cape Wild, where the tents were set up.

Conditions on Elephant Island were rigorous in the extreme. The wind blew savagely, there were snow-storms, the ground was sodden and uncomfortable; one tent had been blown to ribbons, and the *Dudley Docker* was providing a temporary shelter for its inmates. The abundance of fresh food was consoling; they were able to kill seal, sea-elephants and penguins in those early days. Indeed, their new camp was hard by a rookery of ringed* penguins, and they imagined they were provided with a regular supply of food, but on the day after their arrival the ringed penguins migrated, and from that time they had to rely on the gentoos which now and then came ashore and which were quickly despatched.

*The ringed penguin is often known as the chinstrap penguin nowadays.

In spite of their worn-out state, the men were soon working hard to improve their domestic circumstances—digging a hole for the galley, finding various supports for the tents, making the boats safe. There were serious limits, however, to what could be done, and Shackleton knew that relief must be sought.

Elephant Island, one of the largest of the South Shetland Islands, lies in lat. 61° 05′ S., long. 55° 10′ W. It is about 23 miles long (E.–W.) and about 13 miles at its widest. From the point where the *Endurance* was first beset it is a little over a thousand sea-miles. The island was right off the track of whalers and sealers, and nobody was likely to look for them there. Port Stanley in the Falkland Islands was the nearest haven, about 550 miles away; but it lay in the teeth of the prevailing north-westerlies. Shackleton decided that a boat must go 800 miles across the sea to South Georgia and from there arrange for a relief ship: he decided that the boat must go under his leadership.

Any sensible person with a knowledge of exploration and its problems would have found it perfectly reasonable that Shackleton should have gone in the *James Caird* to seek help for his men. To them his decision was as wise as it was obvious. They saw his journey as one into danger, for to take a small boat into the sub-Antarctic ocean, manned by six men weakened by exposure and hardship, seemed indeed an act of courage. They believed, and rightly, that Shackleton was taking the risk himself and leaving them in comparative safety. They were sure they could survive a winter on Elephant Island. Wild was designated leader in Shackleton's absence, and he had orders to take a boat's crew, if no relief came, and try to reach Deception Island when the ice went out in the spring. That was a journey infinitely less dangerous than a crossing to South Georgia.

Besides, in time of war it was not going to be easy to get help for the marooned men. They could have no better ambassador than Shackleton. Wild, a splendid leader in straightforward circumstances, did not possess Shackleton's gifts for diplomacy, his powers of persuasion, which stood him in good stead in the neutral countries of South America, where careful dealings were essential.

All this was to become apparent in the future. At the time, everyone on Elephant Island accepted the decision simply and without question. When Shackleton called for volunteers for the *James Caird* almost every man offered to go. He chose to take with him Worsley, as navigator, Crean, Vincent, McCarty and McNeish.

The carpenter at once set to work to deck the boat in at the forecastle end, making a frame of sledge runners and box lids covered with canvas; equipment and provisions were selected and packed in the scanty shelter thus provided.

It was at mid-day on 24 April that the *James Caird** left Elephant Island. She had been loaded with some difficulty from the *Stancomb-Wills* and McNeish and Vincent had got soaked through in the process; but How and Bakewell exchanged clothes with them, and it was in this spirit of goodwill and hope that the journey began.

Left on the island, the men had now to dig themselves in properly for the winter. Wild modelled himself very closely on Shackleton as a leader. Like Shackleton, he believed in routine and method, and although there was little enough 'work' to do, he arranged the domestic chores in a definite order and set each man his tasks. Like Shackleton, he insisted on optimism. He took the lead in organising parties and sing-songs. He settled disputes and grumbles with a direct approach. He refused to contemplate any failure in Shackleton's plans. Every morning he roused all hands with 'Lash up and stow, boys, the Boss may come today.' He would not build up a stock of food for more than their immediate needs, for he felt this would indicate a pessimistic view of the future. No man ever forgot what he owed to Frank Wild for his direction of the party in those long months: Shackleton, certainly, never forgot.

It was obvious that the party on the island must find some alternative shelter to the tents, which were far too worn and flimsy to stand up to the tremendous force of the wind. The men first tried literally to hole up, by digging an ice-cave in the cliff against which they were camped; but melting ice dripped from the inside walls and made the place uninhabitable. They decided to build a hut, with walls of stone and with a roof made of the two boats.

The long, low building (it was only just over five feet high) was covered with tent material bound and strengthened with pieces of sea-boot; this formed a valance hanging to the ground at the back. Two overlapping blankets made a door—but this was afterwards altered to a sack-mouth shape which was more effective in keeping out the wind. A layer of pebbles served as a floor to the hut, and over the pebbles they spread the rest of the tent material. The chinks in the walls, soon picked out by the gales, were stuffed with snow. After they had been living here for a time more or less in darkness, they contrived two minute windows, one (eight inches across) made from the glass cover of a chronometer stitched into the canvas, the other made from a small square of celluloid that had covered a photograph.

In this hut, measuring ten by eighteen feet, twenty-two men were to live for four months. Twelve of them found spaces to sleep on the floor, the remainder took up quarters in the boats, on boards and hammocks stretched over the thwarts. The cook had done his work

---

* It is worth noting that the dimensions of the boat in which this hazardous journey was to be carried out were 22 feet 6 inches in length, with 6-foot beam.

outside at first, but it proved impossible to contrive enough shelter for him, so the cooking stove was rigged inside the hut. Everyone felt it was fortunate that the cooking was done in twilight gloom, for the hooshes often had strange ingredients in them, fallen from above. The atmosphere of soot, smoke and the fumes of improvised tobacco defied description; but they all got used to it, and to the encroaching black on their faces.

The hut was, for good or ill, their home, and they were relieved to be all together in shelter. A routine was quickly established. Food was equitably distributed, and the few luxuries were doled out by Wild at regular intervals. The word luxury indeed took on a new meaning;

to the men on Elephant Island a mouldy bar of nut-food was rarer than caviare, and there was a certain amount of bargaining with small units of food. To augment the seal and penguin they killed, several of the party became expert in snaring skuas and sheathbills with thread. Otherwise, the meat diet and the rigorous conditions outside made them disinclined to move outside the hut.

There were three invalids among them. Blackborrow's feet had never recovered from the journey in the boats, and on 15 June the doctors amputated the toes of his left foot. The operation, performed under almost impossibly uncomfortable conditions, with the minimum of equipment, was a complete success, and the courage of the patient was only equalled by the skill and coolness, and the subsequent attentiveness, of the doctors. Hudson had suffered some kind of collapse while they were in the boats, and he had to lie up; and Rickinson had strained his heart and could not move about. These three men were given the warmest and most comfortable positions on the floor of the hut.

With these exceptions, the party remained healthy. The increasing privations on the ice and in the boats may have had a certain weakening effect on them, and the meat diet caused considerable flabbiness, but they had adapted themselves well to their marginal existence. Food which in any other circumstances would have been nauseating was now welcome. At the camps on the ice they had developed the habit of chewing fried blubber as if it were bacon. Now, all prejudices forgotten, they ate the rich fat raw when they could not afford to use the stove, and 'half a cup of penguin oil could be quaffed like a draught of mellow vintage'. Thus there was not a single case of scurvy nor any suspicion of it, and the minor physical defects of their life were quickly corrected after their rescue.

Thanks to Wild's vigilance, their own energies and the blessings of Providence on which they frequently commented, they were never actually starving, though they came near to it. In the last weeks of their sojourn on the island their diet was low indeed. From meat and milk they had come down to boiled seaweed, and had even begun to seek out the bones thrown out earlier on, to boil down for any juice that might remain in them. Wild was convinced that they would not have to remain on the island for another summer, but relief came only just in time.

The morning of 30 August was spent like any other morning. Some of the men dug away the snowdrifts from against the hut, others collected limpets for the supper hoosh, plunging their arms deep in the freezing water to prize them off the rocks. Hussey afterwards described[18] what happened then:

'It was just before lunch-time that Marston who was standing just outside the hut saw a ship emerging from the mist that hung over the sea. . . . At first when Marston yelled "Ship O!" we took no notice, mistaking it for the much more customary call of "Lunch O!". It was not long, however, before he came running up towards the hut, breathless and excited. In a state of great excitement, he gasped out to Wild, "There's a ship! Hadn't we better light a flare?" As one man we made a dive through the narrow door of the hut. It was a scrum. We were so excited and thrilled by the news that some of us tore down the canvas walls so as to get out and see the great sight. Our lunch—precious limpets and seaweed, I remember—waiting for distribution in a pot was knocked over. Who cared? It was a much better tonic to see approaching us a small ship flying the Chilean flag.

We tried to cheer, but excitement had gripped our vocal chords. Macklin had made a rush for the flag-staff, previously placed on the most conspicuous position on the ice-slope. The running-gear would not work, and the flag was frozen into a solid, compact mass; so he tied his jersey to the top of the pole for a signal.

Wild put a pick through our last remaining tin of petrol, and soaking coats, mitts, and socks with it, carried them to the top of Penguin Hill at the end of our spit, and soon they were ablaze.

. . . Then . . . the ship stopped. A boat was lowered. And we were able to recognize Shackleton as he got into her. Again we gave a cheer, with more feelings from the heart than I could express in words. We said to each other, "Thank God the Boss is safe." We were more concerned about his safety even than our own.

The boat came towards us, and when it was within calling reach, Shackleton stood up in its bows, crying out to Wild, "Are you all well?" To which Wild answered, "All safe, all well", and we could almost feel the joy this answer must have given the Boss.'

So the leader and his men were together once more, and soon on their way to face the exhausting receptions accorded to shipwrecked sailors, to face the rigours of a country at war. In that long hoped for moment, when they watched the boat coming towards the shore, there can be no doubt that, as Hussey recalls, their first feeling was one of thankfulness that Shackleton was safe. They had gone through the best part of two years with him and they would never forget him. They would remember him as a stern taskmaster, a leader who expected work to be done properly and one who did not spare his words if he found a man careless or lazy. They would remember him as a man who could delegate responsibility, who did not nag while they were doing a job. Above all, they would remember him as a man whose conception of leadership was to share—to share work, to share hardship, to share food, to share laughter.

In the whole history of the expedition Shackleton's personal authority had never been directly questioned. He had kept the power in his hands and had never had to grasp for it. There could be only one reason for this, and everyone knew it. Shackleton was their leader, but he was also, and most of all, their comrade.

JAMES CAIRD

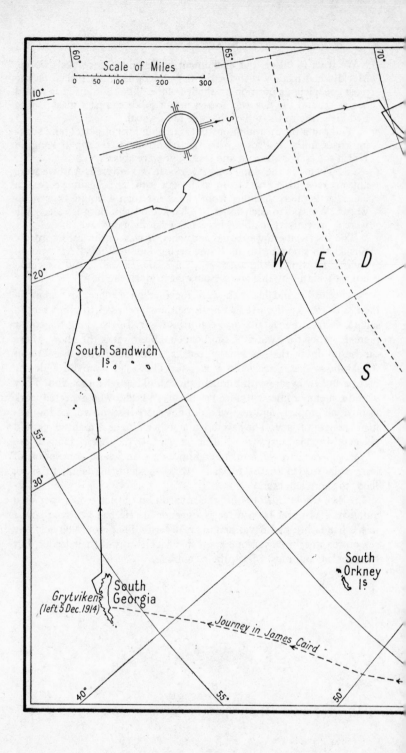

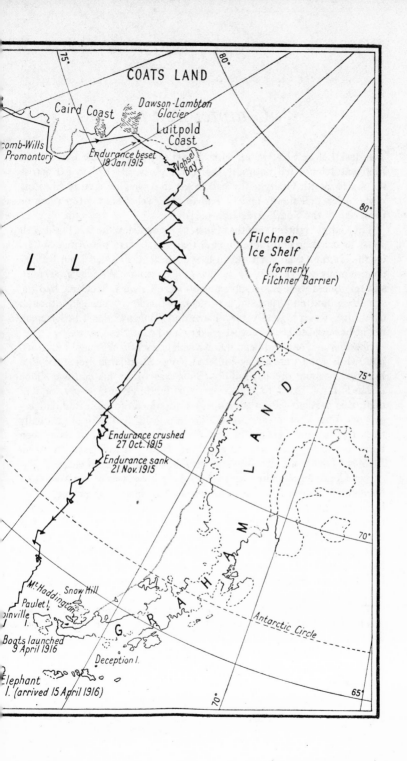

Chapter XXI

THE task before Shackleton, when he set out in the *James Caird* from Elephant Island, fell naturally into three parts. He had to get across the sea to South Georgia: he had to get to a whaling station from his place of landfall there: and he had to get a relief ship, from there or from one of the South American ports.

Thus, after eighteen months of increasing hardship, he was faced with a task as exacting and more difficult than any he had performed so far. Of the six men who went out in the small boat, five had been leading continuously active lives as sailors or fishermen. Worsley's strength and toughness were remarkable and so were Crean's, McCarty had the steadiness and endurance of a professional sailor, McNeish, although over fifty, was physically very hard, and Vincent, as a trawler man, might be supposed to be accustomed to hard conditions at sea.

Shackleton alone had been living a sedentary life. Worsley[1] described how while they were being buffeted along Shackleton remarked that he knew nothing of boat-sailing. 'This was where his courage shone most. For me, used to boat-work, surf-landings, and every kind of craft, this passage was an adventure—a too uncomfortable and dangerous one—but still an adventure. To him, who had drifted gradually from the sea and become mainly a land explorer, it must have been more menacing, perhaps even appalling. He could well have stayed on Elephant Island but . . . always for him the forward post of danger.'

Shackleton's power of enduring physical stress was as remarkable as his mental strength. He was not noticeably affected by the change from life in London to life on an ice-floe. Except for an attack of sciatica while they were at Ocean Camp, he had suffered no ill-health at all. In fact his men, and particularly his doctors, remember him as one of the healthiest members of the party. He quickly adapted himself to the hard life in wind and weather; more remarkable was the resilience of his mind, the speed with which even when he was tired and anxious he could collect his energies for a new effort.

The journey that lay ahead of him might have daunted anybody. He was taking a small boat into one of the stormiest seas in the world. There were, it is true, certain advantages in their position compared with that of the boats on the way to Elephant Island. The prevailing wind was north-west, and could be at least some help to them. The *James Caird*, carrying fewer passengers than before, had been so far improved that there was, theoretically at least, some shelter under her deck, and her sides had been usefully raised to give her a depth of 7 feet 7 inches. They were as well equipped as their resources allowed. A pump had been contrived from part of the ship's compass, and the mast and sail from the *Stancomb-Wills* had been cut down and fitted as a mizzen mast. They carried, among their meagre stores, a small medicine chest and a Primus.

These advantages were worth little in the appalling seas they were to meet. After the first four days, when they were running north before the wind, they set a course east, for South Georgia. On their third day a north-westerly gale shifted the supports of the 'deck' so that the canvas sagged and held pools of icy water which found their way into the boat. There was soon not a dry inch anywhere except immediately under the bows, where the biscuits were stowed, and they had to bale almost all the time.

Shackleton had divided his men into two watches, to operate for four hours on and four off. On watch, one man held the tiller, the second watched the sail, the third baled. The three men off watch were permitted to rest, but this meant lying in soaking, moulting sleeping-bags, plagued with cold and disturbed by the plunging of the boat. The boulders which had been put in as ballast shifted continuously, and each man got to know their contours from painful experience. They were too cramped to move very much, and in any event it was too dark, for during the night they used their scanty store of candles only when they had to, and during the day there was little enough light under the decks. 'When a watch turned out', Shackleton[2] wrote afterwards, 'it was necessary for me to direct each man by name when and where to move, since if all hands had crawled about at the same time the result would have been dire confusion and many bruises'.

True to his principle of creating a feeling of security where security there was none, Shackleton insisted on regular meals. Exposure was as great a danger as that of capsizing. Chilled, wet and chafed, the men could have lost their lives if he had relaxed his vigilance in this matter. In the morning three men set to work to prepare Bovril hoosh for eight o'clock breakfast; with this went two biscuits, nutfood and sugar. The simple routine was described by Worsley[1]:

'Crean pricked and lit the "Primus" and put his back against one side of the boat while I put mine against the other. We extended our legs towards each other till we could jam the "Primus" between our feet. Any deficiency in the length of my legs was made up for by Crean's excess. In this way we held the "Primus" firm on its base. . . . My unworthy hands held the aluminium cooker that was to receive the sacred HOOSH, and my duty as scullion was swiftly, but reverently, to raise it on high whenever the boat gave a madder leap than usual, and so save the precious contents from spilling in the bilges or on the "Primus" flame. At the bidding of Crean, the High Priest of Cookery, and tender of the Sacred Flame, Macarty broke in the lumps of ice. When melted, Crean himself broke up and stirred in the ration—half a pound a man. All eyes, save the helmsman's, were glued on the cooker; hoosh-pots and spoons were ready. As soon as it boiled Crean shouted "Hoosh" and blew out the "Primus". The pots shot forward, Crean rapidly, but carefully, filling them in turn. We swallowed it scaldingly hot, having gradually trained mouths, throats and stomachs to a pained acquiescence. So we felt the glorious heat going right through our chilled, numbed bodies and limbs, putting new life into us. The first to finish his hoosh jumped outside and relieved the helmsman so that he might take his while it was still hot.'

At lunch-time they ate sledging ration raw, and each man had a pannikin of hot milk; tea was the same; and in the night they made another hot drink.

Shackleton's account of this gruelling journey, vivid though it is, says little about himself. Those who were with him were warmed not only by the hot drinks but by the impulse behind them. Worsley[1] noticed 'a touch of woman' about the leader's solicitude. 'If a man shivered more than usual, he would plunge his hands into the heart of the spare clothes bag for the least sodden pair of socks for him. . . . If he noted one with signs of the strain telling on him, he would order hot milk. . . . At all times he inspired men with a feeling, often illogical, that, even if things got worse, he would devise some means of easing their hardships.'

Certainly Shackleton's indomitable front in the face of danger helped his men to endure the discomfort and strain, but they could not all keep up through the journey. At the end of the first week Vincent's strength ebbed, and McNeish began to flag, although his determination remained high. The rest kept going. Worsley remarked on McCarty's cheerful optimism and his habit of handing over the helm with 'It's a fine day, sorr', and Shackleton[2] recalled with feeling the comforting sound of Crean at the tiller, singing a tuneless song nobody ever identified and 'as monotonous as the chanting of a Buddhist monk at his prayers; yet somehow it was cheerful! In moments of inspiration Crean would attempt "The Wearing of the Green".'

So they wallowed on through the first week. Soon ice had settled so thickly on the boat that she was riding sluggishly, and to the dangers they knew already was added the new one of chopping ice, clinging precariously with one hand and wielding the axe with the other, while the boat bucked like a mad mule. The second week saw them advancing slowly towards their goal, but on the eleventh day a north-westerly gale brought up a tremendous cross-sea. That night almost finished them. Shackleton[2] described it:

'At midnight I was at the tiller and suddenly noticed a line of clear sky between the south and south-west. I called to the other men that the sky was clearing, and then a moment later I realized that what I had seen was not a rift in the clouds but the white crest of an enormous wave. During twenty-six years' experience of the ocean in all its moods I had not encountered a wave so gigantic. It was a mighty upheaval of the ocean, a thing quite apart from the big white-capped seas that had been our tireless enemies for many days. I shouted, "For God's sake, hold on! It's got us!" Then came a moment of suspense that seemed drawn out into hours. White surged the foam of the breaking sea around us. We felt our boat lifted and flung forward like a cork in breaking surf. We were in a seething chaos of tortured water; but somehow the boat lived through it, half-full of water, sagging to the dead weight and shuddering under the blow. We baled with the energy of men fighting for life, flinging the water over the sides with every receptacle that came to our hands, and after ten minutes of uncertainty we felt the boat renew her life beneath us. She floated again and ceased to lurch drunkenly as though dazed by the attack of the sea. Earnestly we hoped that never again would we encounter such a wave.'

Everything was now soaked. The cooking stove had been floating in the bottom of the boat and it was more than two hours before they could get it to light. The peculiarly thorough soaking caused great pain to the men in joints and chafed thighs, but on 6 May they were cheered by a brief appearance of the sun. Worsley took a sight and found they were not more than a hundred miles from the north-west corner of South Georgia.

The situation was critical enough. The water supply was running short, and each man could have only a bare half pint a day, besides the hot milk drink at night which Shackleton considered essential. One of the water-breakers had been knocked at the launching and sea-water had got in; intense thirst made the following two days a nightmare.

On 8 May, a stormy morning with squalls from the north-west, they passed a piece of kelp and later a larger mass with two shags perched on it, and at 12.30 p.m. McCarty sighted the cliffs of South Georgia.

They had been out in the boat for fourteen days and their physical strength was almost exhausted. The set of wind and water kept them from attempting a landing that day. In the early hours of the next morning, as they lay hove-to off the craggy island, a hurricane blew up which drove them towards the shore and the sheer, perilous rocks. All day they edged down the island, wondering desperately if they would find a landing-place before they were smashed to pieces. Then their attention was drawn to one of those pieces of luck which Shackleton, with his innate superstition, never forgot. The gale eased, and at that moment the pin that locked the mast to the thwart fell out: if it had gone during the hurricane, nothing could have saved them.

The tenth of May began with a cross-sea running but with the wind abated. They could now see a part of the coast which Shackleton took to be King Haakon Bay, and he decided to seek a landing there. Glaciers running into the sea, jagged reefs of black rock, made this look impossible, but with the help of the oars they steered in through the kelp to a small cove.

Shackleton was first ashore and directed operations as the boat was made secure. A small stream almost at their feet gloriously solved the problem of thirst. Before they could rest, however, they had to unload the boat and pull it further up the beach, which was considerably exposed to the weather. Somehow they struggled through the unloading, constantly falling over, their feet numbed and their bodies cramped.

As they ran into the cove Shackleton had noticed a small cave in the rocks, and here they took their sleeping bags and enjoyed a hot meal. The men turned in, and Shackleton took the first watch, from eight to one. This was no easy task. The boat had to be eased on the rope as the sea advanced and receded. He stuck to his job in the cold and dark until he could keep awake no longer, and then arranged watches—one-hourly—before he turned in.

The following morning the sea had calmed a little and they were able to get the boat above the high-water mark. They surveyed their haven, a tiny patch of tussocked land backed by mountain ranges. Shackleton saw that they would have to sail to the head of the bay before they could attempt to get into the interior and from there to the inhabited parts of the island. In their cave, small as it was, they had shelter, and dry ground to lie on. They could use tussock grass for bedding, and there was plenty of water. The matter of food was soon settled. On a headland overlooking the sound, Crean and Shackleton found a colony of albatrosses, with chicks in the nest. They made a fire of driftwood and Crean made a stew with four of the young birds and a thickening of Bovril ration. The dish roused Worsley to a height of poetical description, and he recalled that after the feast, smoking cigarettes made of scrapings of tobacco out of the boat, he and Shackleton discussed 'making enough money to start another expedition by taking some hundreds of baby albatross and selling them to the epicures, gourmets, gourmands, gluttons, and whatnots of Europe and New York at £50 apiece, quite ignoring the fact that there is a regulation forbidding the killing of these chicks, which we were then transgressing under the sterner law of necessity. We were then a law unto ourselves, and looked it.'

The next four days were days of recuperation. McNeish[3] described the routine, in which all but Vincent (who was suffering badly from exposure) quickly recovered their strength:

'Friday May 12th. I am still busy at the boat. Whilst the skipper does the Nimrod and bring home the food Vincent lays down by the fire & smokes some times coming out for more wood while the Boss & Crean looks after the cooking & McCarthy is my assistant We had four young birds for lunch then we think of hard times.'

It had been obvious to Shackleton, from the moment of their landing, that they could not think of sailing the *James Caird* round to Stromness whaling station, some 150 miles away by sea. McNeish and Vincent were unfit for further exertions. The only chance was to cross the island inland.

It probably never occurred to Shackleton to doubt that he could make the crossing. His one thought was for the men who were confidently waiting on Elephant Island for him to fetch them. Accordingly, as soon as the bay was free from ice, on 15 May, he launched the boat to move up the bay and find better shelter for the invalids. Two days before this, another minor miracle had occurred. The rudder, which had been unshipped in the seas outside the cove, was washed back almost to their feet.

They had to take the boat into the open sea to reach the main bay, and soon after mid-day they found a good landing-place on a shelving beach, sheltered by cliffs and housing numbers of sea-elephants. Here they turned the boat upside down, turfing it over with tussocks and raising it on stones to provide an entrance. In this shelter, which they called Peggoty Camp, McNeish and Vincent were to recruit their strength with McCarty to look after them. The three others must find a way round a glacier to the east of their camp, up a snow-slope and on to what they hoped might be a pass in the Allardyce Range leading to the rolling mountain country beyond; from there they must work eastward to Stromness Bay.

On 17 May Shackleton and Worsley prospected as far as the snow-slope and found a reasonable route for a sledge; a rough one had been made from driftwood by McNeish and McCarty and food was packed on this for the first part of the journey. For the real climb, the travellers took Bovril ration and biscuit packed in socks, the Primus filled with oil, the small cooker, the carpenter's adze (as an ice-axe), and fifty feet of alpine rope: a box of 48 matches completed their equipment.

On 19 May, at one o'clock in the morning, the three men had a meal and started off, speeded on their way by the carpenter. A hard tramp brought them to the snow-slope, and at daybreak they were 3,000 feet up, hoping to see their way ahead. They found that they had got across to the top of Possession Bay, which was uninhabited. From their chart, which they now saw to be inaccurate, they could see more bays than they had expected in the coast before Stromness, and, getting their course as accurately as they could, they returned to the glacier and made for a ridge between two peaks. At 11 a.m., after some climbing on ice, they looked down a sheer precipice: this was not their way. They had to turn down the slope which had taken three hours to climb, and after hoosh they climbed once more to the crest of a mountain—only to see another precipice before them. Another descent, another climb to another ridge. With no sleeping bags and with tattered clothes, they must reach the valley below them before nightfall. Worsley describes later[1] how they tried to see through the foggy darkness if there was a way down, and how Shackleton decided to try it. After cutting steps down for about 200 yards, he halted the party on a little ledge. 'In the darkness it was impossible to see whether the slope steepened to a precipice or eased out on to the level that seemed so dim and far below. It looked like the latter, so again [Shackleton] said: "We'll try it." Each coiling our share of the rope beneath us for chafing gear, I straddled behind Sir Ernest, holding his shoulder. Crean did the same for me, and so, locked together, we let go. I was never more scared in my life than for the first thirty seconds. The speed was terrific. I think we all gasped at that hair-raising shoot into darkness. Crean had hard work to prevent the short-handled adze coming round and cutting us. Then, to our joy, the slope curved out, and we shot into a bank of soft snow. We estimated we had shot down a mile in two or three minutes, and had lowered our altitude by two or three thousand feet. We stood up and shook hands—very pleased with ourselves—until we inspected our trousers!'

They now had to make eastward on a snowy upland between two great patches of crevassed ice, and after a meal, at 6.0 p.m., they set out in the night up a gradual upward slope. The moon shone brilliantly, and helped to show up the crevasses as they plodded on their way, finding themselves at midnight at the edge of a snowfield. Here they were deceived by a north-easterly slope and came down some distance before they realised that their route was taking them to Fortuna Glacier, and not to Stromness Bay. They turned upwards again and made for a jagged line of peaks through which a gap on the ridge led to safety. On this mountainside they took a rest in the shelter of a rock. Shackleton let his companions sleep for five minutes, then woke them and told them they had slept for half an hour.

They went through the gap early in the morning of 20 May, and ahead of them they saw Husvik Harbour. Though twelve miles of difficult country still lay before them, this seemed as nothing beside the incredible fact that they had hit the right route, and they gazed joyfully at the water far below, the ripples on the beach, 'the penguins strutting

The landing on Elephant Island : the *Stancomb-Wills*

'The first drink and no food for three and a half days'

Elephant Island: left to right: ORDE-LEES, WORDIE, CLARK, RICKINSON, GREENSTREET, HOW, SHACKLETON, BAKEWELL, KERR and WILD

Hurle

'In sight of our Goal'

The *James Caird* nearing South Georgia, drawn from material supplied by the Boat Party

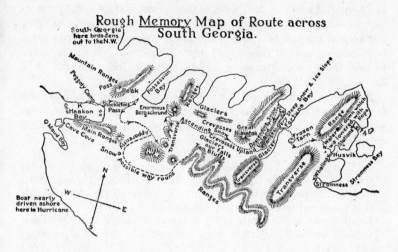

SHACKLETON'S OWN SKETCH-MAP OF THE CROSSING OF SOUTH GEORGIA

to and fro, and dark objects that looked like seals lolling lazily on the sand'.[2]

Shackleton set Crean and Worsley to prepare breakfast and as he walked off to reconnoitre he thought he heard the sound of a steam-whistle. He could still scarcely believe that safety lay ahead, and the three of them waited anxiously until the chronometer pointed to seven o'clock, the hours when a working whistle should blow in the whaling station. 'Right to the minute', Shackleton[2] remembered, 'the steam-whistle came to us, borne clearly on the wind across the intervening miles of rock and snow. Never had any of us heard sweeter music. It was the first sound created by outside human agency that had come to our ears since we left Stromness Bay in December 1914.'

There were still many dangers to pass—first a steep snow slope which clogged their steps, then a piece of blue ice down which Shackleton cut steps and which they had to negotiate with the rope; then a plateau where they nearly sank into a lake hidden under the snow-crust. At last, at 1.30 p.m., they rounded a last ridge and there came into their view first a small steamer entering the bay, then the masts of a sailing ship lying at a wharf, then men moving about and the sheds of the whaling factory.

They solemnly shook hands. Then they found a difficult way down the last mountain side, at one moment lowering each other through a waterfall. It was their last obstacle. Their way lay clear ahead to safety

25

and help, and now they took stock of themselves, worn out and presenting an astonishingly filthy and uncivilised appearance. As they
approached the station, none of them was surprised to see two small
boys running away at the sight of them. An old man, whom they asked
to take them to the manager, looked as if he had seen the devil
himself.

Shackleton's dramatic entry into the manager's office has never been
forgotten in South Georgia. Years later Mansell, who was in the manager's office on that day and who became factory manager in his turn,
enlarged upon the scene to an English visitor:[4]

'Everybody at Stromness knew Shackleton well, and we very
sorry he is lost in ice with all hands. But we not know three terrible-
looking bearded men who walk into the office off the mountainside
that morning. Manager say: "Who the *hell* are you" and terrible
bearded man in the centre of the three say very quietly: "My name
is Shackleton." Me—I turn away and weep. I think manager weep,
too.'

There followed news of the war, food, hot water to wash in, fresh
clothes; and the travellers relaxed in the knowledge that they had
achieved the impossible. Shackleton,[2] when he recalled this day
afterwards, set down his idea of what the journey had meant to him.*

* What the journey meant to a later explorer, who trod some of the same
ground in October 1955, is well expressed by Duncan Carse:[22]

'A man may travel on foot from the head of King Haakon Bay to the
whaling station of Stromness, keeping either high or low. The high-level route
is circuitous, a gradual rise and fall *via* the spacious crest of the Kohl-Larsen
Plateau. The low-level route is direct, a saw-tooth thrust through the tortured
upheaval of mountain and glacier that falls in chaos to the northern sea. In
distance, they are nowhere more than 10 miles apart; in difficulty, they are
hardly comparable.

'We to-day are travelling easily and unhurriedly. We are fit men, with our
sledges and tents and ample food and time. We break new ground, but with
leisure and opportunity to probe ahead. We pick and choose our hazards,
accepting only the calculated risk. No lives depend upon our success—except
our own. We take the high road.

'They—Shackleton, Worsley and Crean—were desperate castaways with
sick companions and their only asset a boat that would never sail again. They
travelled under headlong duress, reduced by long privation to exhausted
starvelings destitute of all but their worn out clothing—no sledges, no tents,
little food, and less time. They broke new ground in a race against failing
reserves of strength. Their only safety lay in speed and the short cut regardless
of danger; they dared not fail because "22 men were waiting for the relief
that we alone could secure for them." They took the low road.

'I do not know how they did it, except that they had to—three men of the
heroic age of Antarctic exploration with 50 feet of rope between them—and
a carpenter's adze.'

'Wehad pierced the veneer of outside things. We had "suffered, starved, and triumphed, grovelled down yet grasped at glory, grown bigger in the bigness of the whole." We had seen God in his splendours, heard the text that Nature renders. We had reached the naked soul of man.'[2]

But to him there was something more to be expressed, and the expression of it gave rise afterwards to many speculations about his character and his beliefs. This is how he ended the chapter on the crossing of South Georgia, in *South*,[2] the epic of the Imperial Trans-Antarctic Expedition:

'When I look back on those days I have no doubt that Providence guided us, not only across those snowfields, but across the storm-white sea that separated Elephant Island from our landing-place on South Georgia. I know that during that long and racking march of thirty-six hours over the unnamed mountains and glaciers of South Georgia it seemed to me often that we were four, not three. I said nothing to my companions on the point, but afterwards Worsley said to me, "Boss, I had a curious feeling on the march that there was another person with us." Crean confessed to the same idea. One feels "the dearth of human words, the roughness of mortal speech" in trying to describe things intangible, but a record of our journeys would be incomplete without a reference to a subject very near to our hearts.'

On this seemingly simple passage, very many sermons have since been based; it has been the inspiration of many people who require their heroes to have a basic religious belief; conversely, the passage has been read by some as an attempt on Shackleton's part to court publicity, at a time of national emotion, by producing his own 'Angel of Mons'. One or two points suggest that it may in fact have been some time before he spoke of the experience to anyone. Mrs. Worsley remembers[5] a lecture in the Isle of Wight, some time after the expedition, in which he spoke of four men crossing South Georgia. 'I said afterwards, "Do you know, you said there was four," and he said, "Whatever will they think of me, I can't get it out of my mind." ' At this time she had not heard any such story before, either from Shackleton or from Worsley. It must also be noticed that this passage did not appear in the account of the South Georgia crossing which was worked on by Shackleton and Edward Saunders in Australia in 1917; it could be supposed that Shackleton wrote the paragraph himself after he had received Saunders' first version of the book or that it was written in 1917, cancelled, and later restored to the book.*

The truth may be very simple. Shackleton had never bent himself to the outward expression of Christian feeling. He had always, for instance, taken the tired breadwinner's privilege of staying away from

* See Appendix, pp. 503–511.

church. To his intimate friends he would say that he did not think it right to pray to God for help in times of danger when he did not pray to Him in times of security. 'God helps those who help themselves' had always been his working principle.

But Shackleton was a sailor, and though his life took him far from the sea, it seems he never lost the instinctive belief of the sailor in what was by old custom known as Providence, or, familiarly, as Provy. Phrases like *Thank God* or *With the help of Providence* were not formalities as Shackleton wrote them: neither were they fervent expressions of faith, but a compound of superstition, wishful thinking, and that emotion summed up in the majestic word awe. Providence meant something to Frank Wild, to Ernest Joyce, to Shackleton when they used the word in their diaries: this is not to say that they ever tried to examine what they meant by it.*

Nothing is more likely than that Shackleton had had, during that crossing of South Georgia, an access of a mysterious feeling of another presence, which he had not tried to define until afterwards. It is also possible, of course, that the feeling was crystallised for him by something said by one of his companions. Certainly he must have regretted later that he ever allowed the feeling to be made public because of the many interpretations which people put on it. On occasions he would speak of it lightly, or with embarrassment. At whatever stage he decided, or was persuaded, to use the story in his book we cannot discover; but we believe it had its beginning in an emotion so tenuous, so instinctive and so entirely personal that it could hardly escape distortion.

But we must return to the narrative of events, to that twentieth of May 1916 when Shackleton was thinking of his men and how to reach them on Elephant Island.

---

* In a letter to his wife written on 23 October 1916, from the *Imperial*, Shackleton made one of his rare statements about his belief in a life after death. It should be noticed that, like the impression of the 'fourth man', it belongs to that period of his life when his deepest emotions were most fully engaged, the time when he was most at unity with himself: and it may be taken as an additional proof that he was sincere in his story of the South Georgia crossing. While he was in the Falkland Islands, Shackleton had heard from his wife of the sudden death of her younger sister Daisy Dorman, who had lived with the Shackletons for many years and for whom Shackleton had a deep affection. He told his wife, 'I cannot write about poor little Daedles it was and is still such an awful shock. You must if you believe in the future at all realize that you will see her again I have no doubt at all about the future and I have been very near it lots of times.' On 21 August 1920, writing to his wife after his father's funeral, he told her he had visited the graves of other members of the family and found them all beautifully kept. 'These flowers are from Daedles' grave: It looked so bright and I am sure that life does not end with Death: I somehow seemed to see her more than any of the others.'

While he and his companions were recovering from their journey, a whaling ship was being prepared, and Worsley went with it to King Haakon Bay. He was amused when his three comrades in Peggoty Camp failed to recognise him in his tidy state. The party was back in Stromness Bay on 22 May.

Meanwhile, Shackleton had arranged for messages to be taken to Grytviken Harbour and for letters to be sought there. He and Crean had gone round to Husvik, and here they found a large whaler, the *Southern Sky*, lying up for the winter. The nearest wireless communications were at Port Stanley, in the Falkland Islands, and there was no time therefore to get in touch with the English company that owned the ship. Shackleton made arrangements with the manager at Husvik to take over complete responsibility for her. An old friend, Captain Thom, agreed to command her in an attempt to reach Elephant Island, and there was no difficulty in making up a volunteer crew.

On Monday night there was a gathering on Captain Thom's ship, the *Orwell*. Shackleton makes little of this in his book, but it is clear from Worsley's[1] account that it was a celebration of a rare and moving kind:

'In the evening the manager told Sir Ernest that a number of old captains and sailors wished to speak to and shake hands with him and us. We went into a large, low room, full of captains and mates and sailors, and hazy with tobacco smoke. Three or four white-haired veterans of the sea came forward; one spoke in Norse, and the manager translated. He said he had been at sea over forty years; that he knew this stormy Southern Ocean intimately, from South Georgia to Cape Horn, from Elephant Island to the South Orkneys, and that never had he heard of such a wonderful feat of daring seamanship as bringing the 22-ft. open boat from Elephant Island to South Georgia, and then, to crown it, tramping across the ice and snow and rocky heights of the interior, and that he felt it an honour to meet and shake hands with Sir Ernest and his comrades. He finished with a dramatic gesture:

"These are men!"

All the seamen present then came forward and solemnly shook hands with us in turn. Coming from brother seamen, men of our own cloth and members of a great seafaring race like the Norwegians, that was a wonderful tribute, and one of which we all felt proud.'

On 23 May, the first rescue party sailed towards Elephant Island. The *Southern Sky* was steel-built and Shackleton knew that he could only succeed if the sea was clear. This unfortunately was not so, and after three days they found themselves being gradually surrounded by pancake ice. Dodging, advancing and retreating, they came within 70 miles of the island but could find no passage through the pack. The

ship was small and carried coal only for ten days. Shackleton decided
to make for the Falkland Islands, where he could get messages to the
outside world.

On 31 May they reached Port Stanley, and Shackleton sent numerous
cables. To his wife he gave[6] the bare bones of the story and elaborated
a little later in a hasty letter of 3 June:

'My darling

I can only write a line as the mail is coming in and I am rushed to
death with cables and arrangements for the relief of our people: I
have had a year and a half of hell: and am older of course but so no lives
have been lost, though we have been through what no other Polar
Expedition has done. It was Nature against us the whole time the
cable but barely describes a little of what it was. Wild and Crean were
splendid throughout discipline was always good: but towards the end
about 10 of the party were off their heads'.

This letter, and the long one[7] written to Ernest Perris at the same
time and containing comments on the men individually, must be read
with the knowledge that they were written when Shackleton was in a
state of nervous excitement and when he was taking the opportunity, for
the first time since the expedition started, of letting himself go. The use
of the phrase 'off their heads' is not to be taken completely literally. It is
Shackleton's way of expressing his own fear of emotional expression, of
behaviour, the reverse of his own iron self-control through the whole
adventure. To Perris he says that some of the men wept and wished to
die, in the boats and after the landing on South Georgia. This may be
true, though it must be stated that three of the most level-headed of the
men who were there (Sir James Wordie, Dr. Macklin and Mr. How) are
emphatic that only two individuals lost their heads and that morale was
in fact astonishingly high at these crises in the expedition. It may be
supposed that the truth lies somewhere in the middle of two extremes.
If time has wiped out the memory of any breakdown, it is equally clear
that such breakdowns need only have been temporary, but that Shackleton, with his aversion to emotional excess and instability, would have
taken them very seriously. He was watching his men with a searching,
an anxious feeling all through those last terrible stages of the journey,
and (as had happened on his previous expedition) he may well have
interpreted as mental breakdown what was an impulsive and momentary
expression of fear. Most of the men must have been afraid in the boats
and it would be surprising if some of them had not shown it, but the
recollections of those who were there suggest that if a few wept, they
also continued to row and to bale. It must also be stated that Shackleton
all along underestimated his own power of reassurance. Because of his
own outward confidence and determination, the expressions of fear *were*

only momentary, the men trusted him to bring them through, but he himself could not be sure of this, and in his account of the expedition he made no allowance for this, the most important single fact in the whole story.

To the Admiralty Shackleton cabled[22] thus:

'Found impossible reach Elephant my definite conclusion unless radical change in ice occurs is that wooden steam whaler or the Discovery or sea going ice breaker only suitable vessels: Urge that you obtain if possible immediate dispatch of ice breaker or Discovery: Breakers operating in White Sea either Russian or Canadian should now be free failing this how long would it take sending Discovery Falklands. Can I meanwhile negotiate ask Uruguay Government authorize trawler to proceed immediately Punta Arenas to dry dock and then we can make a second attempt as she will steam ten knots and we will have a moon also. Propose to dispatch trawler tomorrow evening cable at once Uruguay Government agreement this plan. Shackleton.'

At the same time he cabled to the South American republics asking what they could manage. The first offer of help came from Montevideo, where the British Minister cabled that a trawler, the *Instituto de Pesca No. I*, would be fitted out at the expense of the Uruguayan Government and sent down to Port Stanley with all speed. Shackleton eagerly accepted the offer, and on 10 June he set out once more for Elephant Island. According to contemporary newspaper reports, the British auxiliary cruiser *Macedonia*, then in Uruguay, was stationed halfway to the island to maintain wireless communications, and an officer off the cruiser was on board the *Instituto de Pesca No. I*.

Elephant Island was sighted on the third day out, but the pack barred the way once more and when they tried to push through the ice the ship was badly battered. Shackleton was thankful that fog hung over the island, so that the marooned men could not have been given any false hope by a sight of the trawler.

Back at Port Stanley, he reported to the Uruguayan Government, and received an offer for a second loan of the ship. He decided, however, that the necessary repairs to the engine, and the docking which the trawler had been awaiting when she was lent to him, would take too long.

From Port Stanley he took a mail boat to Punta Arenas, in Chile, accompanied by Worsley and Crean. The three men were warmly welcomed by the British Association of Magellanes, and a group of men raised £1,500 and equipped a wooden schooner, the *Emma*, for him. A small steamer, the *Yelcho*, was lent by the Chilean Government as a tug, though as she was steel-built she could not go into the ice.

On 12 July the third rescue party set out, in gale weather. The *Yelcho* battled with her tow as long as she could, but conditions were impossible, and on 14 July she had to turn back. The *Emma*, lightly built and with only a small auxiliary engine, could not stand up against the ice they encountered a few days later. The ship became encased in ice, the engine failed repeatedly in the cold, and once more Shackleton had to turn back. He reached Port Stanley on 8 August, where he found reports waiting for him on the progress made by the Admiralty. He wrote[6] to his wife that he intended to try again before the *Discovery* came out; he commented that the Admiralty had been 'a devil of a time.' He was tired, and longed to get home and rest, but clearly had no intention of waiting upon events.

In fact, many people had been active on his behalf in England, although wartime conditions made it very difficult to get him the help he asked for. Since early in 1916 there had been grave anxiety about his safety. On 25 or 26 March news came from New Zealand that the *Aurora* was clear of the ice and on her way there after her own particular adventure (pp. 401–04). As this ship had not been able to wait in the Ross Sea according to plan, it was hoped that Shackleton had not been able to make his journey across but that he had been spending the time in the safety of the *Endurance*. The *Times*[8] expressed the general hope that 'they have provisions enough to carry them through another winter'.

News of Shackleton had been expected at least by the end of March, and when no news came his representatives, who met in London on 28 March to discuss the situation of the Ross Sea party, expressed grave anxiety about the fate of the Weddell Sea party also. The Ross Sea side was best dealt with from Australia and New Zealand, and in those countries plans began to go forward, which were discussed with the British committee. The situation in the Weddell Sea, more difficult because more uncertain, was to be handled from England.

Captain Davis, who was in England at this time, had a private interview with Admiral Perry at the Admiralty, and (on 10 April) with the President and Secretary of the Royal Geographical Society (Douglas W. Freshfield and A. R. Hinks). Captain Davis had been asked by Shackleton's relatives and representatives whether he would take charge of an expedition to the Weddell Sea to search for the missing *Endurance* party, and he sought to discover exactly what this would mean.

The conversation[9] was frank and forceful. Each man exercised the privilege of saying 'I told you so', and each man, conscious of Britain's needs in time of war, spoke in a tone of acerbity about the new burden which Shackleton had brought upon them. 'The great disadvantage of these Antarctic expeditions', the President remarked, 'is that as a rule they do entail relief, but I do not think you can avoid sending it.'

Captain Davis found much to criticise in Shackleton's original plans for this expedition. He felt that its personnel included too many amateur explorers and not enough professional sailors or men with experience of ice-work. He thought it lamentable that Shackleton had not taken a wireless transmitting set on the *Endurance* (he seems to have attributed this failure entirely to Shackleton's wish to be independent, and not to lack of money). He was willing to lead a relief expedition, however, provided he was given a free hand in planning his search with due regard to the safety of his ship and his men.

He was doubtful how the money could be raised. The Royal Geographical Society could not make itself responsible for anything but technical advice. All three men felt it should be a Government responsibility. 'In my opinion', the President said, 'they ought never to have let the expedition start off when war began'; to which Captain Davis replied, 'That is what everybody realises and that is why there is very little patience.' This conversation was taking place at the very moment when Shackleton, his small boats launched from the ice, was beginning to make his dangerous way towards Elephant Island.

Certainly the officers of the Royal Geographical Society were not surprised that Shackleton had got himself into trouble, and they recalled conversations in which he had insisted on minimising the risks he proposed to take. They now set to work to prepare statements of the situation and to communicate with the Admiralty.

An unofficial group of experts, including Captain England, Commander Evans (*later* Lord Mountevans) of Scott's second expedition, Apsley Cherry-Garrard, and Commander Adams (Shackleton's comrade of the *Nimrod*), were in consultation with the Royal Geographical Society. On 17 April a Council meeting resolved that a relief expedition was necessary, and on 8 May the President announced that a Government Commission had been set up to consider what could be done. This committee, as finally formed, was under the chairmanship of Admiral Sir Lewis Beaumont, and serving on it were Captain J. F. Parry (Hydrographer to the Navy), R. S. Meiklejohn (representing the Treasury), a representative of the Board of Trade, Major Leonard Darwin (representing the Royal Geographical Society), Sir Douglas Mawson, Dr. Bruce, and Alfred Hutchison and Ernest Perris as Shackleton's representatives.

The committee worked out a complete plan for searching the Weddell Sea, recommending that the *Discovery* or the *Terra Nova* should be obtained for the relief expedition. It was suggested that Captain Davis should command it but that a shore party under a scientist, with a doctor as one member, should possibly be landed to winter in a hut and continue a land search.

At the May meeting of the Royal Geographical Society, Dr. Mill spoke of the possible situation of Shackleton and his men to an anxious audience. Many of Shackleton's old comrades had offered to join the relief expedition if they were released from their wartime duties. Nansen cabled to the Royal Geographical Society offering to lend the *Fram*.

The time of waiting was soon to end. On 31 May Shackleton's cable from the Falkland Islands reached Britain, and the news that his men were still alive was rushed into the newspapers. Now that it was clearer what had to be done, everyone took up the work more cheerfully.

At an afternoon meeting at the Royal Geographical Society on 15 June, while Shackleton was at sea in the *Instituto de Pesca No. I*, R. G. Mossman read a paper on *The Physical Conditions of the Weddell Sea*. This had originally been prepared for the guidance of the Admiralty relief committee and had now been adapted to the situation of the men on Elephant Island. Dr. Mill[10], opening the discussion after the paper had been read, remarked dryly, 'The special importance of this paper has been taken out of it by the happy perversity with which Sir Ernest Shackleton emerged just at that moment when we were planning how we could best try to find him.' He made it clear, however, that the paper would be of great value to those planning relief in England, if the Uruguayan ship failed: for by now the Admiralty Commission had been adapted to this end.

Rudmose Brown,[10] who had been with Bruce on the *Scotia* when that ship was held in the ice near Laurie Island, in 1903, cheerfully predicted that the men would not only find seal and penguin on Elephant Island but that they might find 'whaler's huts' there 'left by Argentine and Chilean whalers who may have visited the island' and that there was even a 'bare possibility of finding a lowly form of coal, which if mixed with blubber makes an uncommonly good fire.' His remarks, logical though they may have seemed in the comfortable surroundings of the lecture room, would have brought a wry smile to the grimy faces of the men in the improvised hut on the bleak island.

The Admiralty had requested Bruce to go to Dundee and examine a possible ship, the *Balaena*, but time went on and no suitable captain had been found. Bruce, clearly imagining the plight of the men on the island, became impatient. It was finally decided to send the *Discovery*, now the property of the Hudson Bay Company. She was in dock at this time, but it was arranged that repairs should be speeded up and that she should be held in readiness until Shackleton had made his third attempt at rescue, in the *Emma*. Meanwhile the Committee advised him to settle down in Port Stanley and take what rest he could. Shackleton's reply was forceful. The only path where he could pace up and down, he said (he did not trouble to mention the idea of resting), was between the slaughter-house and the graveyard: he could not guarantee to follow this depressing path for two months or so.

Hastily summoned, the *Yelcho* came over and towed him in the *Emma*, to reach Punta Arenas on 14 August. He determined to try once more, and asked the Chilean Government to put the *Yelcho* itself at his disposal for another attempt, undertaking not to take her into the ice. His luck held. Leaving Punta Arenas on 25 August, he slipped through the ice on the only possible day, and on 30 August he was welcomed by his men on Elephant Island.

We take up the story of this party once more at the time of their rescue.

The four-day run back to Punta Arenas gave the castaways a chance to get used to normal rations, but although they ate and slept as they pleased, they were requested to keep their hair and beards long for publicity purposes. It was not until after photographs had been taken on shore that they were permitted to remove the tangible signs of their months on Elephant Island.

They reached Punta Arenas on 3 September, and Shackleton sent a characteristic message[6] to his wife:

My darling
I have done it. damn the Admiralty: I wonder who is responsible for their attitude to me. not a life lost and we have been through Hell: Soon will I be home and then I will rest: this is just a line as I have only arrived today and the steamer sails at once: Give my love and kisses to the children

Your tired "Micky".

A reception awaited him and his men which demanded all their restored strength. The Chileans, proud of their growing navy, had much praise for Captain Pardo, who had taken the *Yelcho* down, but their applause for Shackleton and his men was unstinted. Shackleton's radiogram to the Chilean Admiral, Munoz Hurtado, sent on the day of his return, received the following reply[11]: 'Please accept our sincere congratulations for the happy outcome of endeavour due entirely to your perseverance and enterprise. The Chilean Navy has received the news of the rescue of the English sailors as if they were its own people.' Macklin described in his diary[12] their entrance into the city:

'The harbour was full of ships (a large number of them German, hung up on account of the War), and as we steamed with flags flying (the Union Jack and the Chilean Flag the most predominant) all the ships hoisted their flags and blew their sirens. The noise was deafening. Flags flew on all the public buildings of the town.

As we got nearer we saw that all the wharves were crowded with people, and as we came to anchor two launches came off with all the most prominent people of Punta Arenas, amongst them Admiral Lopez and the Consuls of the various countries, Chilean officers etc. etc. We had done our best to make ourselves clean and respectable, but in spite of all our efforts we were dirty and grimy compared with the immaculate people who came to see us. . . .

We wasted no time in getting into one of the launches, and were taken to the pier, which was so crowded that we could barely make our way along it. I was astonished at the feeling shewn by the people. the men shouted and shook our hands : there were women, many of whom were weeping copiously. . . . Firemen and military were drawn up along our route, and the police had to form a barrier to keep back the crowds : it seemed incredible that folk could take so much interest in us.'

After this astonishing return to civilisation, the men were taken off by members of the British Colony, and for the next twelve days they all enjoyed the lavish hospitality and comforts of the Chilean port.*

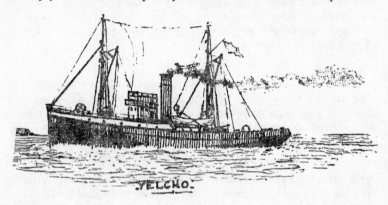

YELCHO.

On 15 September the party boarded the *Yelcho* once more and cruised up to Valparaiso. Captain Pardo, who had brought them from Elephant Island, was again in command, and Macklin commented on his insouciant attitude to dangerous reefs and faulty charts. At Valparaiso, on 27 September, a reception awaited them as heartening and suffocating as that at Punta Arenas. Macklin recalled that it took them over half

* In Punta Arenas Shackleton was the guest of Senor Francisco Campos Torreblanca, then Spanish Consul in Chile. Now that he could relax after the long strain, there was time to admit to his mind the poetry and emotion which had lately been crowded out by more practical affairs. In Senora Campos's visitors' book he inscribed the following lines by St. John Lucas :

> We were the fools who could not rest
> In the dull earth we left behind,
> And burned with passion for the south,
> And drank strange frenzy from its wind.
> The world where wise men sit at ease
> Fades from our unregretful eyes,
> And thus across uncharted seas,
> We stagger on our enterprise.

an hour to cover the fifty yards from the ship to the Naval Club. The following day Shackleton lectured in Santiago, for the British Red Cross and a Chilean naval charity. His men were presented to the President, and he was given a Chilean order.

On the following day the party was sent by special train across the Andes to Buenos Aires. Here, and on a brief visit to Montevideo, Shackleton was able to give his personal thanks to the people who had been so unstinting in their help.

It was time now for the comrades to split up. Several of the men worked their way home on tugboats which had been waiting to be taken to England, others were sent home by steamer. They were all eager to get into the war, but Shackleton had to wait a long time yet. Reports of the fate of the *Aurora* had reached him very quickly. At the time of his arrival at South Georgia rumours had been circulating about her drift, and at Port Stanley he had been able to discover all that was known. There were still men under his command who were suffering hardship, perhaps worse, and he resolved to rescue them. He and Worsley, when their duty calls in Buenos Aires were done, hurried north to Panama to take ship for New Zealand.

The situation of the Ross Sea party must now be explained.* This side of the expedition had been organised partly by Shackleton, partly by its leader, Æneas Mackintosh; the divided responsibility had brought its own troubles, particularly in the matter of finance and public relations.

Shackleton had made arrangements for taking over the *Aurora* early in 1914. She was then in Australia, and since she had been altered for Mawson's expedition, Shackleton hoped that she would not need very much refitting. In the preface to *South*[2] he stated that sledges, equipment and most of the stores were sent from England to Australia for the Ross Sea party, but he added (as he had long before told Mackintosh) that he depended 'somewhat on the sympathy and help of Australia and New Zealand for coal and certain other necessities, knowing that previously these two countries had always generously supported the exploration of what one might call their hinterland.' It would appear that the phrase 'certain other necessities' was an under-statement.

---

* The scope of this book does not allow of an adequate treatment of this side of the expedition, which produced extremes of danger and endurance no less striking than those experienced by Shackleton and his men in the Weddell Sea. Ernest Joyce's book,[13] *The South Polar Trail*, published in 1929, recorded briefly and forcibly from his diaries the events of those astonishing years: but there is still the need for a further book in which the attitudes and recollections of other members of the party could be expressed. The whole of the Ross Sea adventure, its inception, the mixture of personalities, the endless battle to contrive something out of nothing, the politics and complexities of the relief arrangements—all these are material for an interesting addition to the literature of Antarctic exploration.

On 18 September Shackleton[14] had written his final instructions to Mackintosh, the latter part of which read thus:

'5. I am remitting £1000 to you through Lloyds Bank to our agents. This money, I trust, will be sufficient for you to get the ship out of dry dock with the minimum of repairs compatible with safety.

6. You will economise in every possible way, as the Expedition, owing to extra expenses incurred by this war, has only limited funds.

7. You will do your utmost to get whatever you can free as gifts: this especially refers to the coal. You might be able to get sufficient coal to carry you down and back, as a gift.

8. You will seek the services of Professor David and Professor Masson and ask them to do everything they can to assist the Expedition, explaining to them the need for economy.'

Mackintosh arrived in Sydney in November 1914, to find that in fact no money had been sent out from England. He had no written authority to raise money himself. He realised that expenses would be far heavier than had been expected. He cabled to the London office of the expedition that he must have the £2,000 he had originally been promised. He was told that the fund could only run to £1,000 and that he must mortgage the ship. This he could not do, as he had no power of attorney: an interview with Professor David and with a firm of solicitors confirmed this. In any case it was now discovered that Shackleton's title to the ship had never been correctly established, and the Registrar of Shipping at Liverpool had the ship still registered in the name of Sir Douglas Mawson, who had to be pursued by post to Australia by way of the United States to provide evidence of the transfer of the ship to Shackleton. Finally a committee was formed with Professor David as a principal member, and a mortgage was finally raised by this committee, bringing in £700.*

Mackintosh was granted an interview with the Prime Minister of Australia, who agreed that a certain proportion of the work on the *Aurora* should be done at Government expense: it turned out that plenty needed to be done.

This docking in fact caused some displeasure to the Australian Government, as a more extensive overhaul was ordered than had been authorised. Overtime, and a strike of shipwrights, also added to the cost. Nobody connected with the Government or public services could fail to be shocked and dismayed at the lack of order in the financial arrangements of the expedition, and this fact had some importance later, when the question of a relief ship for the Ross Sea party arose.

* The mortgage was finally signed on 15 December 1916, being taken out in the names of Thomas Forster Know and Alfred George Nilsom of Sydney, executed by Messrs. Creagh.

Stevens* wrote in his report that during their stay in Sydney 'an unpleasant feeling with regard to the Expedition grew and became strong. The Government expenditure on the *Aurora* was freely discussed, and frequently strong opinions were expressed. There were numerous minor contributory causes. The representatives of the press were not well treated, and appointments in general were badly kept. A suggestion of a civic reception to Sydney was received very ungraciously. There was confusion in the soliciting and receiving presents. Unfortunately the feeling seemed to be much directed against headquarters, and to have a counterpart in sympathy for the Ross Sea party.'

The next difficulty arose over the stores. When Mackintosh checked these, he found them far short of the original inventory. Among the goods not fully stocked were boots, sledges, ski, flour, sugar, tea, chocolate, milk and butter; some of these goods had been lost or diverted or left behind at various stages of the journey out. Some of the finneskoe had been damaged by moths and rats on the steamer, and these could not of course be replaced.* War-time conditions made it difficult and expensive to fill in the gaps, and indeed, it was hard to get anyone interested in the plight of the expedition, although not long before the ship left Sydney there was some quickening of public enthusiasm and, among other things, the wireless Mawson had used was subscribed for and fitted on the ship.

The scientific equipment, which was also inadequate, was supplemented by gifts of photographic gear, a solar radiation thermometer and some meteorological instruments, and a small sum was put together at the last moment for medical comforts. Mackintosh had to put the matter frankly to the members of the scientific staff who arrived to take up their posts expecting to have their travelling expenses paid and who found instead that they would have to use their own money to supplement the scientific equipment if they wanted to do their work properly.

There was, too, the matter of wages. Enough money was raised, with loans and with £700 which was eventually sent out from England, to pay the ship's crew and leave money on deposit for their dependants. Again, there was an atmosphere of improvisation, of last-minute contrivance, which was not good for the expedition. The *Aurora* left behind her an impression of muddle which was inevitable but unfortunate; and the anxiety which had pressed upon Mackintosh and the other members of the shore party during the weeks before sailing left them in no very good frame of mind about the expedition.

It was on Christmas Eve that the *Aurora* left Hobart, six weeks later than Shackleton had planned. After a call at Macquarie Island, she

* These and subsequent details are taken from the report by A. O. Stevens written for Shackleton in 1917.[15]

made her way down to McMurdo Sound. On 16 January 1915 she reached Cape Evans and the men landed a depôt of coal and oil, then made a difficult way up the sound to within nine miles of Hut Point.

Mackintosh had been instructed to prepare for a possible dash over the continent by Shackleton as soon as he reached the Weddell Sea. He was to try to lay some depôts, at least one at latitude 80°, in the summer and autumn of his party's arrival. Although the *Aurora* was so late in reaching Hut Point, Mackintosh decided that this plan must be carried out.* Sledging equipment was prepared and three parties left the ship at the end of January, on successive days, and made for the *Discovery* hut, with stores which they would afterwards sledge out on to the Barrier. The first two parties took dogs and the third the motor tractor. Here, at the outset of their work, misfortune began.

Ernest Joyce was in charge of the dogs, as he had been on the *Nimrod*. His experience then had taught him that it was worth putting in some time on training before the sledging work began. He had counted on at least a week or so to get the dogs running in harness and the men accustomed to driving. Besides, he knew that after the long confinement on the ship the animals would be out of condition and should be exercised gradually into fitness.

However, no preliminary work was possible. The journey from the ship to the *Discovery* hut, in soft snow, was a gruelling start to extraordinarily hard work, which was pushed on, in spite of bad weather. Mackintosh and Joyce converged on Minna Bluff on 11 February, and were able to discuss the situation. Mackintosh had lost one dog and some of the others were suffering from physical strain. Joyce urged that the 80° depôt should be laid by man-hauling, but Mackintosh was anxious about time and decided that he would push on with a dog team, taking Joyce and Ernest Wild with him.

They reached the desired latitude on 20 February, and on the following day they built the depôt and a line of cairns running eastwards. Then began a dreadful journey back. The Barrier produced its cruellest

---

* We have already said that Shackleton felt it doubtful, even before he reached South Georgia, that he would be able to start across the continent in the summer of 1914–15 and that he had sent messages to England to this effect. Dr. Mill[16] states that this was a definite decision and that it 'was sent home in time to reach the *Aurora* before she sailed for the Ross Sea'. This does not square with Mackintosh's acute anxiety about laying the depôts to 80°S. in the first summer, nor with Joyce's remark[13] in an entry from his diary dated 11 February 1915: 'I tried to persuade him (i.e. Mackintosh) not to take the dogs further south, as they were feeling the effects of the hard sledging. However, he decided otherwise. I quite see his point of view, that Shackleton may get across this year, and expect to find the depôt laid at 80°S.'

'All safe! All Well!' 30 August 1916

Hurley

ackleton at the end of the First World War

With Cecily and Edward

The *Quest* in London, August 1921

The Avro float-plane assembled in St. Katharine's Dock

driving winds. The men were all shockingly frost-bitten, their food was desperately short, and the dogs collapsed one by one, so that when they reached the *Discovery* hut on 25 March they were entirely dependent on their own efforts.

They found three men there, the rest having been picked up by the *Aurora* early in March. They took stock of their circumstances. Joyce[13] recorded that Ernest Wild might have to lose one toe from frost-bite, and that he himself parted with the top of one ear; he and Mackintosh were very badly blistered, and they were all glad of Cope's medical attentions.

They settled down to make the best of things. The hut had never been designed as more than an emergency shelter; they lived there for the next nine weeks, with no furniture except discarded provision cases, no fuel except blubber when they could get it, no light but a blubber lamp, no food but the seal they could kill and a scanty store of tins in the hut. The ice in McMurdo Sound had gone out while they were on the Barrier, and they could not get down to Cape Evans, where they learned that the rest of the party had gone, until it had formed again. Prudence forbade any attempt to reach the more northerly hut by a land-route across the glaciated south-west slopes of Mount Erebus.

Before he had left the hut in January, Mackintosh had written a note for Stenhouse, who had taken over the command of the ship, telling him to leave stores in the *Discovery* hut when he came to pick up the subsidiary sledging party, in case the depôt-laying party should be delayed. This had not been done, and the three men already at the hut knew nothing about the ship's movements.

Stenhouse had, in fact, encountered as many difficulties as Mackintosh, and while his leader was sitting in the dim and dirty hut speculating about him, he was trying in vain to carry out his orders to find a safe wintering place for the ship.

Shackleton had originally intended that the *Aurora* should wait in the south only long enough to unload stores and help to establish a winter base centred round one of the old expedition huts; he had intended, in fact, to use the plan he had used for the *Nimrod*. When he had later decided to winter the ship in McMurdo Sound, he had regarded it as of primary importance that she should be free to take all hands back to New Zealand in 1916, assuming that the trans-continental party got over to the Ross Sea. Accordingly, he had given strict orders to Mackintosh that the ship was not to be taken further south than Glacier Tongue, nine or ten miles from the *Discovery* hut; the safe anchorage at Hut Point was consequently out of bounds.

Mackintosh had been confident that the ship would find an anchorage clear of moving ice near Glacier Tongue, and had told Stenhouse that he wanted the ship used as a main base, with a small party at the Cape

26

Evans hut to carry out scientific work.* Unfortunately things were not
so easy. All the way from Hut Point to Cape Evans the ice was in a
constant state of movement and Stenhouse could find no shelter from
the tearing winds and the frequent blizzards. In this situation, which
in many respects resembled that of Captain England in 1908 and
Captain Evans in 1909, on the *Nimrod*, he was obliged to use far more
coal than could really be spared. The diary[18] of the then Second Officer,
Leslie Thomson, gives a detailed picture of this harrowing time.
Thomson did not think Cape Evans a good place to winter the ship, as
it was completely open to the north-west, and icebergs were driven
into the bays, but he thought it 'as good a place as there is at present
offering and beggars can't be choosers'; he felt they were wasting coal
to no effect and he hoped they would have enough to take them back
to New Zealand, as the sails were 'nothing to boast of'.

They continued to search for an anchorage until the beginning of
March, when Stenhouse decided to stay off Cape Evans. Weather and
ice still seemed disposed to argue the point. Time and again ice-anchors
were firmly embedded, only to be wrenched out by a high sea; or, on
other occasions, the ice went out, the *Aurora* perforce steaming before
it. If she was able now and then to hold her own floe against the shore,
she was in danger from drifting ice all round her.

On 23 March Stenhouse had put Stevens, Gaze, Spencer-Smith and
Richards on shore, to establish themselves at the hut and begin winter
work with the meteorological and magnetic instruments. There was
much coming and going between ship and shore, but very little was
landed in the way of provisions or equipment except what was needed
for the scientific work. This was partly because of the state of emergency
on the ship, partly because it was assumed that once safely anchored,
she would remain off Cape Evans through the winter.†

So the men worked on as best they could until the month of May
came in with driving blizzards and low temperatures. Stenhouse had
begun to convert the ship into a winter station. One funnel had been
blocked in, to make the sleeping and living quarters warmer, and one
of the masts had been taken down and was in the process of being
re-erected as a wireless mast. The fires were out, the boilers empty, and
only one boxful of fresh ice, for water, was on board.

---

* Stenhouse explained this and other details in a letter[17] to Shackleton
accounting for the drifting of the *Aurora* and asserting that in fact ice conditions made all orders useless.

† In Stenhouse's letter to Shackleton, already mentioned,[17] he wrote that
Captain Mackintosh 'in his instructions written and verbal (he) did not mention
landing stores or clothing other than the stores to be placed at Hut Point for
sledging parties' but that Stenhouse 'had intended to do so at the first opportunity, but was prevented from doing so by the ship breaking adrift', and he
added that 'All sledging stores were put on shore at Cape Evans'.

After many moves in and out of the ice, the *Aurora* had been anchored, apparently very firmly, off Cape Evans. Two anchors had been embedded in the gravel near the hut, and to these the ship was moored by five wire hawsers over the stern; in addition, she had two anchors out forward. To the shore anchors the ship was constantly being adjusted, and although Stenhouse continued to feel anxious, the moorings held during some very strong gales.

On 6 May the Second Officer wrote[18]:

'At 9.35 p.m. or thereabouts I had just been turned in when the after moorings began to strain and the decks to groan and then I knew the ice had again started to go out of North Bay C. Evans. This was a very dangerous thing as the ice was so thick. I did not turn out immediately but it got so bad that Hooke woke me to come out and I was thinking it was about time I was making a move. As the strain was so great that something had to go either the decks with the bits or the wires. I soon found out which it was as the two wires parted with reports like the report of guns and then I hear several other snaps and by the time I was dressed fit to go on deck I could see we had carried away all our moorings and we were going out into the Sound with our bow anchors down. We called all hands and put tackles upon our cables to relieve our windlass of the strain when we dragged our anchors. The Engineroom were set to work to get everything ready for steam. I was let go and turn in after midnight by the Chief Officer but there was mighty little sleep to be had as the ship got out from under the shelter of the land. The wind was blowing fiercely and it was so thick that one could only see a few yards from the ship and when the floe we were stuck fast in began to break up and we got amongst the loose pack, the pounding this ship got would have sent almost any steel ship to the bottom but this old ship stood it wonderfully well. So ended the most eventful night of the trip up to the present.

The *Aurora* now had to take her chance with the pack. The shore party was continually in the minds of Stenhouse and his companions, for they realised how important it was that the stores still on the ship, and the equipment so necessary for sledging the depôts, should be landed. However, although they tried more than once to get the ship back to the south, it was useless, and they failed to make contact with the receiving wireless set at Cape Evans. The *Aurora* remained held in the pack and drifting northward until 12 February 1916, and for much of that time she was in almost as great a danger from ice-pressure as her sister ship, the *Endurance*, who by a tragic coincidence was, until October 1915, carrying on the same battle on the opposite side of the Antarctic continent.

It was natural that after the adventure was over, many people should blame Stenhouse for the drifting of the ship, and it was equally natural that Shackleton should be criticised for denying to his ship's captain the known safety of Cape Armitage and Hut Point. The proportions of ill-luck and blame cannot now be decided. What is important is the skill and patience with which Stenhouse and his men kept the ship safe and brought her safely out of the ice on 13 February 1916. It was a battered but a safe ship which reached Port Chalmers, in the south of New Zealand, on 3 April.*

On 6 May 1915 some of the shore party had visited the ship, which was moored not far from the hut. About 3 a.m. in the morning of 7 May, Richards went to take outside readings at the meteorological screen, and realised she had gone—and realised, too, that she must have been forced out and therefore might not be able to get back. Under the direction of Stevens, who was in command of the party until Mackintosh returned, they took stock of their position. Stevens' report written later shows what stores they had. The sledging stores (Bovril ration, dog pemmican, nut food and dried milk) already landed were stacked in a safe place. They had small quantities of milk, fruit and tea which had been landed for their current requirements; enough flour and biscuit for ten men for two years, and plenty of vegetables and jam were found in the hut, but they were very short of tea, coffee, butter and potatoes, and had very little tinned meat.

Some bags of coal had been landed from the ship, but these were lost. There were also nine bags left in the hut by Scott. They proceeded at once to ration the food, and to procure blubber for burning in the hut.

Of the shortages revealed by their examination, by far the most serious was that of sledging equipment. The rest of the winter saw an extensive make do and mend in which every available object was pressed into service. There were some old clothes at Hut Point and at Cape Evans, but nothing in good condition. The Burberrys they got together, in particular, were poor stuff for the start of a strenuous sledging season, and they had only three tents—a new one brought down by the expedition and two old ones left by Scott. The Primus lamps, also Scott's, gave Joyce much anxiety. Old sleeping bags were cut up to make finneskoe, and to mend the best of the sleeping bags that could be found. Discarded socks, canvas parts of pony rugs, leather—they made use of a whole collection of oddments which Joyce[13] described as 'a very poor line for Petticoat Lane.'

* Stenhouse made many attempts to send wireless messages during the drift of the *Aurora*. On 1 June he tried to call Macquarie Island, but the staff there had been recalled to Australia as a war economy, and the wireless station had been moved to a safer place. On 25 March, when an aerial had been rigged, he got signals from stations in Tasmania and New Zealand and sent out details of the expedition. The message was sent 900 miles with an apparatus normally suitable for a radius of about 200 miles. A newspaper report commented that the news 'eclipsed for a day at least the interest in the great world war'.

In this contriving the skill of Joyce and Ernest Wild was particularly valuable. Together with the rest of the men from Hut Point, they had reached Cape Evans on 2 June, and the wintering party was now under one roof.

Mackintosh arranged the daily work so that the scientists could carry on regular observations and at the same time the necessary preparations for the summer's work need not be held up. It may be deduced from his diary that although morale was high, the party was not entirely harmonious. In essentials it was no more ill-assorted than the party waiting in the ice with Shackleton or the party which he had more or less successfully welded into unity at Cape Royds eight years before. The important difference was that Shackleton was not personally in command at Cape Evans now. Instead of one leader, who could be praised or blamed but whose word would be law, the winter of 1915 in Scott's old hut saw a group containing three strong characters, each with his own right to make decisions.

Mackintosh, appointed leader, tried to model himself on Shackleton, to plan for a busy, and so for a cheerful, winter. But he was not sure of himself. This is evident not only in his diary, and in Stevens' report, but also in a letter which Mackintosh[19] wrote to Stevens from Hut Point on 26 October 1915, just before he started on the long task of depôt laying. He warned Stevens that he intended to have 'quite a new system of routine' during the next winter, and that he wanted him to take absolute charge of the scientific staff. 'There is to be no each individual choosing his own work, but you as chief of the Scientific Staff, must direct the work, and give each member what you consider necessary towards the good name of the Expedition in that direction.' Cooking arrangements, he said, would be made more definite, and everything would be more strictly planned.

A letter written[20] at Cape Evans on 29 August 1915, and left for Stenhouse, has a revealing paragraph:

'Whatever you do, keep the discipline that existed before the sledging commenced, and which I expect you still maintain vigorously. And don't get familiar more than you can help. You will find it far harder to manage now, as living ashore the discipline has been nil to all extents. I mention this, for a lot depends on the safety of the ship.'

In short, Mackintosh, brought up in the discipline of a ship's company, had not been able to achieve the more flexible rule which Shackleton had established at Cape Royds. Although he bore the name of leader, Mackintosh in fact had not a stronger character than had Joyce, whose experience of Antarctic travel gave him the right to be dogmatic in some spheres. The two men did not always agree over method, though generally Mackintosh took Joyce's advice. There was also Stevens, who as head of the scientific staff had to try to work out an adequate programme and who, while submitting to the discipline of the leader, did not always regard the conduct of the party as being effective.

There was a certain amount of jockeying for position at Cape Evans during the winter. But beyond this there lay a common cause to which each man was devoted. As remarkable as the ill-luck that dogged the Ross Sea party was the staunchness with which each man set himself to do the impossible in order to carry out Shackleton's instructions. They were determined that the depôts should be laid for the trans-continental party. No lack of equipment, no contrary weather, no inexperience, no consideration of any kind was to be allowed to interfere with that.

The leader of the Ross Sea party was not, in fact, Æneas Mackintosh the officer, not Joyce the tough sailor, not Stevens the scientist, but the spirit of Shackleton reaching out from the other side of the continent. What was he doing? When would he come? How many men would be with him, and where would they camp? All these and many other questions ran through the minds of Mackintosh and his party as they set to work to muster every ounce of food, every inch of material, every item of equipment, to make the depôt-laying a success.

Their transport was as inadequate as their stores and clothing. They had not been able to repair the motor tractor, which had been damaged in the landing at Hut Point at the beginning of the year. They now brought it to Cape Evans, and Richards and Gaze began to work on it. Stevens reported that 'It was got to run eventually, but found unreliable. Rivets and bolts would not hold in face of the vibration, and even the tractor wheel began to break up.'

The five remaining dogs were worked whenever possible, for seal hunting and, late in the winter, for fetching stores from Cape Royds. Joyce intended to use them on the last leg of the depôt journey, between Minna Bluff and the Beardmore Glacier. But most of the work would have to be done by man-hauling, and each man would have to be prepared to pull up to 200 pounds in weight.

Joyce[13] afterwards commented, 'Under ordinary circumstances, with so poor an equipment, one would not consider for a second such a journey, the Bluff depôt would be the limit of our mileage.' But the work had to be done.

An exceptionally early date was fixed for the beginning of sledging; on 1 September they would start taking loads from Cape Evans to Hut Point. This early date was to be of great importance in the history of this party. During the winter they had eaten seal meat in great quantities (they killed about 500 seals that year), but neither Mackintosh nor Spencer-Smith liked it, and they had taken more tinned meat. Once sledging began, the men had very little chance to recruit their strength with fresh food, except when one or other of the parties briefly rested at Hut Point. The result was that they began sledging with less reserve of good health than they might have had, and they lost rather more than a month of fresh food by starting early; while their sledging ration was insufficient in quality and in quantity.

The party was divided into three units of three for sledging, Stevens remaining alone at Cape Evans to carry on the scientific work. Mackintosh's plans were carried out: by 9 October they had taken all the stores for depôts and for their own use south to Hut Point and the depôt journeys now began.

In spite of the improvised equipment and a difficult surface on the Barrier, the men worked with such determination that by 28 December the depôt at Minna Bluff had been well stocked. From the start Mackintosh had thought only of carrying out his leader's instructions, and early in October Joyce had to argue with him about the excessive loads, which were eventually reduced from 200 to 150 pounds per man. The two men disagreed also about the dogs, which had been used for some of the sledging between Hut Point and the Bluff. Mackintosh wanted to send them back to Hut Point now and rely on man-hauling for the rest of the job: Joyce believed they would make all the difference to the success or failure of the mission in its last stage, and was insistent enough to overrule Mackintosh. In fact, from the Bluff onwards the leadership was gradually passing from Mackintosh to Joyce.

It had become necessary to make a drastic alteration in sledging arrangements, for on 3 January one of the Primuses gave out, and three men had to return to the base. The remaining six continued on their way, Joyce with Hayward and Richards, Mackintosh with Ernest Wild and Spencer-Smith.

On 8 January Mackintosh asked Joyce to act as leader to both parties. The following day he complained of a sprained knee, and Spencer-Smith was observed to be feeling the strain of hauling. He explained his stiffness by saying the wind had got through his torn Burberrys: but it soon became clear that both men were losing strength. Joyce tried to persuade Mackintosh to turn back, but he emphatically refused. Dogs and men struggled on until 22 January, when Spencer-Smith (whose heart was now known to be slightly weak) had to be left behind; he was made comfortable in one of the tents, with stores for a fortnight.

On 24 January the sledging parties were held up by a blizzard, and Joyce took the opportunity of examining Mackintosh's knee, which had been giving him trouble. He commented,[13] 'it is blue; cannot understand how a sprain should remain so long; of course, it requires rest. Massaged it which made it much easier. What a pity he did not take advantage and lay up with the Padre!'

But the matter was not so simple. For the moment the chief

consideration was laying the most distant depôt for Shackleton, but once Mount Hope had been reached and a depôt left on 26 January, at the foot of the Beardmore Glacier, there was more time to investigate their circumstances.

They were starting the long journey back in a parlous state. Joyce was suffering from snow-blindness; Mackintosh's legs were terribly swollen; and the gums of all the party were turning black. The word scurvy was first used by Joyce in his diary on 28 January. On the following day they reached the tent where they had left Spencer-Smith, and the signs in him were unmistakable also. Joyce put his faith in the dogs. Smith was wrapped up on the rear sledge, and they pressed on. Mackintosh refused to give in, though his swollen ankles made it desperately hard for him to walk, and Hayward's symptoms were also becoming acute.

The month of February was appalling for the sledgers. They continued to move slowly towards Hut Point, hindered by exceptionally severe weather and bad surfaces. Spencer-Smith was pulled on the sledge all the time, Ernest Wild nursing him as well as he could. Mackintosh refused to be pulled, or even to be tied to the sledge. By the last week in February food was desperately short, and Joyce, estimating that there was one meal left and that they were ten or eleven miles from the nearest depôt, made the inevitable comparison with the fate of Scott's party in 1912.

On 23 February weakness and cold made it impossible for them to pull the invalid any further. It was decided that he and Mackintosh must be left, with Wild to look after them, while the other three tried to reach the depôt. 'If a mortal soul were to meet us,' Joyce wrote in his diary on 25 February, 'without a doubt, they would receive a shock, three men staggering on with four weak dogs, fair wind, and sledge practically empty, clothing in tatters and finneskoes worn through and tied with provision bags.'

They reached the Bluff depôt a day later. Hayward was now in a state of collapse. Joyce and Richards, triumphing over their weakness, struggled with agonising slowness to make camp and prepare food. They gave themselves the minimum of time to recover strength before they forced the unwilling dogs southward again. They reached their comrades on 29 February and gave them what food they had been able to carry. The first day of March saw three men striking out for the north, pulling with the dogs, while Mackintosh, Spencer-Smith and Hayward were lashed on the sledges. It was a fantastic order of march which could not long continue. The three men still on their feet were now affected by scurvy, Wild only mildly compared with the others. They tied pieces of bamboo to the backs of their knees to keep them straight, for they feared that if they allowed them to bend at night, they would never straighten them to walk again.

On 7 March it was decided that one man must be left behind for a time, and Mackintosh volunteered to stay. Two days later Spencer-Smith died early in the morning while they were lying in the tent. Hayward collapsed completely; the other three plodded grimly on until on 11 March they reached Hut Point. With difficulty they hoisted Hayward through the window, the door being blocked by falling snow, and set to work to prepare food. Richards and Wild killed two seals in the bay, and the regimen of fresh food was started to combat the scurvy.

Two days later they started back for Mackintosh, reaching him on 16 March. They found him outside the tent, and soon had him on the sledge and moving northwards. 18 March saw the party back in the hut, where Mackintosh with deep emotion thanked his comrades for their loyalty and determination. It had been one of the most remarkable, and apparently impossible, feats of endurance in the history of polar travel. From the start of the depôt work they had done 1,561 miles, out of reach of fresh food, with poor equipment, tattered clothing and starvation rations. But they had carried out their leader's orders.

At Hut Point the three who were least affected by scurvy ministered to the sick men, and a useful, easy routine was soon established. Joyce wrote,[13]* 'Patients recovering rapidly. It is miraculous how they have progressed. The enormous amount of seal meat they eat and the exercise "weather permitting", have brought them through.† Richy has spent many hours in massaging them. This relieved their hard-bound muscles. Richards and Wild are still doing good work, sealing. They have brought in 10 since we have been back. . . . Everything is going along fine.'

They could not yet get over to Cape Evans, for the ice was still disturbed northwards in McMurdo Sound. Joyce did not allow impatience to affect his judgment. It was Mackintosh who suffered from his desire to get down to the others and to learn whether there were any news of the ship. On 7 May he and Hayward made a short journey northwards to test the newly-formed sea ice, and found it about four inches thick, bearable but unsuitable for sledging.

On that day and on the following morning Joyce and his companions did all they could to dissuade Mackintosh and Hayward from making the attempt. The weather seemed to be getting worse and they could not understand the driving impatience and anxiety which carried Mackintosh for the moment beyond reason. The best that could be

---

* Under date-heading 'Wednesday, March 22nd to April 5th'.

† R. W. Richards writes[23]: 'The only diet we had from then until we left was seal meat—nothing else—and I mean nothing—no flour or biscuits, nothing but fried seal meat all the time from March till May—not even salt which we had to obtain by evaporating sea water. But this restricted diet had marvellous anti-scorbutic properties and our recovery with it was magical.'

extracted from him was a promise that he would turn back if conditions seemed to be deteriorating.

About 1 p.m. on 8 May Mackintosh and Hayward left the hut, and were last seen about a mile away, close to the shore but apparently making for Cape Evans. By 3.0 a blizzard had come up, and the men at Hut Point were intensely anxious. They could not get out until 10 May, when they walked northwards to see if they could find any indication of what had happened to their comrades. 'Their footmarks were seen clearly enough raised up on the ice, and these we followed for about 2 miles in a direction leading to Cape Evans. Here they ended abruptly, and in the dim light a wide stretch of open water very lightly covered with ice was seen, as far as the eye could see, no doubt one night's freezing. It was at once evident that part of the ice over which they had travelled had gone out to sea.'[21]

It was some time still before they could be certain that the two men had perished, for the weather and ice continued to hold them at Hut Point. It was not until 15 July that Joyce judged it safe to sledge down to Cape Evans, and here they confirmed their fears.

Joyce, now in command, heard reports of the scientific work and took an inventory of the stores. He concluded that they could, if need be, last for eighteen months on what they had, augmented by fresh food, but that sledging was quite out of the question. Scientific work would continue through the winter, and he himself would collect as many zoological specimens as he could. Late in September he went with Ernest Wild and Gaze to Cape Royds, where they stayed until December, collecting, skinning, and observing the Adélie penguins at the rookery close to the hut. For the latter part of the time Joyce was alone there. Life continued peacefully at Cape Evans, and the men remained in good health, except for Richards, who had collapsed with a strained heart soon after their return from Hut Point and who had to lie up through the rest of the winter. They waited for relief, using their time as usefully as they could. They did not know whether Shackleton would come from the south, overland, or from the north by sea: but they were all confident that he would come.

EMMA.

Chapter XXII

WRITING to his wife from the steamship *Imperial*, on which he was hastening to Panama, Shackleton[1] told her he had been entertained in Chile 'as if I had made a triumph instead of the Expedition having failed.'

Looked at literally, the expedition had indeed failed. He had not made his journey across the continent: he had not even been able to start it. His scientific results had been very different from what he had hoped. The geological and biological collections had been lost; the observations on winds, ice-drift and other such conditions had been snatched, as it were, out of the teeth of misfortune.* He had lost one ship, and the other had barely escaped from the ice. Some of his men were still marooned in McMurdo Sound. Yet, although he was not satisfied, he must have felt some pride in the outcome of his long, hard fight against the forces of Nature, a fight which had drawn upon every ounce of energy and courage and endurance that he possessed, and besides, every ounce of sympathy and tolerance and patience. When he was opposed to a human rival, Shackleton's courage sometimes became aggressiveness, his energy ruthlessness, his patience a grim obstinacy. As he grew older, he showed a hard relentlessness to those who opposed him. But fighting against a simple adversary, fighting to beat the Antarctic, he demonstrated, more clearly than anyone else in this sphere, the power of man's unconquerable mind.

The months that followed his triumphant return to South America, the months during which he fought and plotted and argued his way to the Ross Sea to rescue his men, show both sides of his character—the ruthlessness against men, the determination against Nature.

Shackleton took it for granted that he would be organising the relief of his men in McMurdo Sound. In South America, however, he had received news by cable that, while he was still missing, relief plans had been drawn up by committees in England, Australia and New Zealand, and that these plans were still going forward. The *Aurora* was to go south again, this time under the command of Captain John King Davis, who had been proposed by the Australian relief committee.

Shackleton received the news of the rescue committees and their activities in a blaze of wrath. 'I am dead tired and very lonely,' he wrote[2] to Ernest Perris, 'but all my fighting blood and spirit of endurance is

---

* See Appendix C, pp. 512–517, 'The Scientific Results of the Shackleton Expeditions' by J. M. Wordie and B. B. Roberts.

411

alive at this last damned impertinence from Australia and the cheek of
Davis and that bloody old fool Kinsey.' A letter evidently written in
some anxiety by his wife called forth the impatient reply, 'I *will* be
tactful in Australia but I am very sore about it all.'[1] He can hardly be
blamed for his outbursts or for the fury of intolerance that swept through
him when he learned that committees (the very word was hateful) were
arranging to rescue *his* men.

But the situation was not simple, and he began to understand it
somewhat better when he received, before he left South America, a
long explanatory letter from his friend Leonard Tripp[3] of Wellington.
Tripp explained that the existing relief plans had been at a fairly mature
stage by the time Shackleton had announced his arrival in the Falkland
Islands, and that it would be impossible to change them now without
much waste of time and money. Certainly there were many people in
New Zealand who would have sent Stenhouse down again in command,
but since the Commonwealth of Australia had put up by far the greater
proportion of money for the relief expedition, that Government must
be allowed to choose the commander. All this was logical enough and so
was Tripp's theory that the root of the trouble was money, that the
Australian Government were annoyed that the expedition which had
cost them so much in 1914 should again be appealing for funds; as
Tripp put it, 'they are inclined to run their own show with regard to
the relief, so that they can have control of the finances, and their servant
can dictate what is to be done.' The Australian committee, Tripp said,
had refused to allow Captain Davis to resign in Shackleton's favour,
as he had offered to do, and there seemed nothing to do but to accept
the situation.

In fact, Tripp repeatedly counselled Shackleton to be prudent
and patient, when all that Shackleton wanted to do was to get to New
Zealand and fight for his rights. His strongest anger was felt on behalf
of Stenhouse. He held him responsible for the drifting of the *Aurora*,
since he had been in command at the time, but equally he still regarded
him as the rightful captain, after Mackintosh's death. He could well
imagine Stenhouse's feelings when he heard that he was not to take the
ship down again to McMurdo Sound.

It was in a mood of angry loyalty to the officer he had appointed that
he cabled to Stenhouse telling him to take legal advice, to hold to his
command, and to do nothing and say nothing to any offers until Shackleton reached New Zealand, where the *Aurora* was awaiting the time of
departure. This order was natural but unfortunate. It cut right across
the temperate advice given by Tripp to Stenhouse, which was to meet
Captain Davis privately and offer to go down as Second Officer. It
meant that Stenhouse, who had been told to treat Shackleton's orders as
confidential, had to refuse Davis's offer to him of the Second Officer's

post with scant explanations. Goodwill between the two captains became impossible. The ship's papers had been handed over to Kinsey as expedition agent when the *Aurora* reached New Zealand, and Kinsey had been obliged to hand these to the Australian Government's representatives. Thus the awkward situation came about that a captain had been appointed without Shackleton's consent or approval on a ship which was legally Shackleton's own property.

When Shackleton arrived in Wellington, at the beginning of December, this point must have seemed to him a very cogent one. It was not one, however, which he could press in his own favour, as Tripp repeatedly pointed out to him. In time of war it was unthinkable that there should be a legal dispute between a loyal Britisher and his Government. If Shackleton exercised his legal rights over the ship (which the Solicitor General of New Zealand, among others, had assured him were firm), there would be an outcry against Britain in the New Zealand papers. The point could only be used in negotiations with Australia.

The feeling against Shackleton in that country must be separated into two aspects. The feeling of disapproval and criticism of Shackleton's financial affairs was lifted out of the sphere of intrigue into the sphere of Government affairs. The personal hostility to him is far more difficult to describe or to assess. He and his supporters in New Zealand were convinced that certain individuals were out to humble him. No names were ever mentioned in writing, nor were any private motives ever suggested for this attitude. Shackleton himself had thought at one time that Kinsey had been disloyal to him, but he discovered later, and freely admitted, that he had been mistaken. The biographer, lacking any evidence other than the references in letters to people working against Shackleton, can only record that some personal hostility did exist. It seems likely that the situation between Shackleton and Captain England in 1909 was recalled. Certainly that situation had strengthened Captain Davis's feeling (which he had expressed to the Royal Geographical Society when a relief expedition was discussed in 1914*), that a ship's captain *must* be free to direct the use of his ship.

The tangle of emotions behind the minutes of committee meetings will probably never be straightened out. It is important to stress, all the same, that there *was* a tangle—that Shackleton, when he reached New Zealand, was plunged into an atmosphere of intrigue, of telegraphing, of dramatic scenes and dramatic conversations. He arrived in the middle of a fight which his supporters had been carrying on in a highly dignified manner, and to which he now added his own characteristic energy and frankness.

The long strain had told on him. Though some of his men were safe,

* See pp. 392–93.

he was not sure about the others. He had seen the Elephant Island group dispersing to fight for their country, and he must have considered the possibility that some of those lives for which he had so strenuously fought might soon be lost in a bigger fight.

There were other anxieties, too, in connection with those men. Shackleton had told them, when the *Endurance* was abandoned, that he would continue their pay until they got back to England, although he was not technically obliged to do so. When he reached the Falkland Islands, however, he had to reconsider this promise in the light of reason. Cabling to Perris, he instructed him to pay wages over to dependents only up to the date of their first taking to the ice.

It is clear from a letter written to Perris in the autumn of 1916 that he still felt his promise was morally binding; but the expedition had no money then, and was not likely to get any so long as the war continued. In 1917, Shackleton could only guarantee to pay what was legally due, and he was not even sure where that was coming from.

To Perris he sent a detailed analysis of the character of each man in the expedition,[2] and in the course of this analysis he advised him which of the men must be paid in full up to his return and which of them could be asked to wait for some back pay.

The division is an interesting one. The scientists were to be asked to defer their salaries, and Frank Wild and Worsley had already offered to do this. Naturally Shackleton wanted the crew paid so far as was possible, since they would need the money: but certain men of whom he could not give a good report were to be paid only up to the abandoning of the ship. Two of the ship's company, who had been particularly staunch and loyal, fell into a special category. They were to be told that they would be paid in full only when the money could be found; that is, no promises were to be made to them which might not be fulfilled, but they were to be asked straight out to help their leader out of a difficulty. The men to whom this compliment was paid (and compliment it certainly was) were Tom Crean and Walter How.*

The whole of this document shows Shackleton's state of mind as well as his general criterion of human conduct. The men he criticised were those whom he had felt were either disloyal or cowardly: the men, that is, who had tried to undermine his authority, or who, by allowing their fear to be expressed in public, had endangered the morale of the party. '. . . after two years' experience of them under every circumstance known to man,' he told Perris, 'I *know these men's hearts*'. He had missed very little that went on, and he had exaggerated surprisingly little also,

---

* When Wild sent his report from Elephant Island to *The Times*[4] he wrote, 'I wish to place on record the good *moral* of the entire party, and especially the energy and ability of How, Hussey, Hurley, Macklin, McIlroy, Kerr, and Rickinson'. How alone is mentioned among the sailors.

when we consider the heightened state of mind in which he watched his men.

All these things—recollections of danger, anxiety about money, reflections about individual behaviour—crowded into his mind just at the moment when events seemed to be shaping against him and demanding his complete attention.

Finally, he was dreadfully tired. Tired in body, tired of intrigue, tired of criticism, tired of delays and frustrations. The old desire for domestic peace, which his wife always regarded as a sign that he was not himself, was expressed over and over again in his letters to her. 'I don't suppose for a moment that the Antarctic will ever see me again', he wrote[1] on 6 December from Wellington. 'I must settle down and I want to: I have seen nothing of you or our children really for years and it does not matter how small the house we can see that the children will be educated and started in life properly and I still feel certain that when this is all over there will be money enough to make things comfortable. . . .'

In spite of all these hampering circumstances, Shackleton turned with energy to the fight. In New Zealand he had many sympathisers. In particular the New Zealand Minister for Marine, Robert McNab, fell under his spell. He was convinced that Shackleton's anger was not selfish, that he was expressing his loyalty to his men when he protested that Stenhouse should command the ship. He understood Shackleton's overwhelming desire to go down to the Ross Sea himself, to finish the job he had started; and he believed from the beginning that it should be perfectly possible for Shackleton to go down, as leader of the shore party but not in command at sea.

The complicated negotiations between Australia and New Zealand regarding the relief expedition were passing through McNab's hands, and it was to him that the Australian Government sent the proviso that they would accept Shackleton's presence on the expedition if he would sign on under Captain Davis: he was not to go as a passenger on the *Aurora* but as a subordinate. McNab regarded this as a slight, directly intended to hurt Shackleton: Shackleton himself was not interested in pride or vanity or dignity at this moment. Matters had been simplified for him by the decision of Worsley and Stenhouse not to ask for places in the ship. This sacrifice Shackleton accepted as an expression of loyalty which he valued highly but which did not surprise him. Now he could treat the situation in the only possible way, the practical. It did not matter to him whether he went south as a civilian, a leader or a ship's steward, so long as he went: and he told the Minister of Marine that he would sign on as a supernumerary officer on the *Aurora*.

But before he accepted Captain Davis's command, he must be

sure how he stood as regards his ship. He must be assured that none of
the three governments who had spent money on refitting the *Aurora*
and paying her crew would make this a reason for exerting any claim
on her, in respect of this money. The New Zealand government agreed
at once to waive any claim, and because there was some delay in receiving agreement from Britain and Australia, New Zealand expressed her
confidence in Shackleton by announcing that if the British government
should make any claim afterwards, she would help Shackleton to appeal
against it.

By this time the Australian committee had sent an impatient telegram
to Kinsey :[5]

> 'Our government will not be party to any arrangement with
> Shackleton other than that defined in our ministers letter to him of
> fifteenth November Davis must have supreme & undivided command
> of whole expedition. If shore party prove necessary Davis may if he
> approves appoint Shackleton to lead it giving him written instructions.
> an absolute first condition is that Shackleton before sailing signs
> undertaking of loyal service under Davis. on thus finally insisting our
> Government is acting strictly in accordance with previous decisions
> of three governments as ratified at London conference. if New
> Zealand now sanctions any departure from these conditions it does
> so without Australias consent or support & must be prepared to
> financial responsibility for the expedition. our govt cabling officially.
> Aurora Committee.'

Kinsey sent this cable on to Shackleton, having tried several drafts of a
warning telegram to accompany it : his final version was, 'Have you
agreed otherwise looks rather like evasion.'

No doubt Shackleton did put off answering Australia's challenge as
long as he could, but there could have been no doubt in his mind about
his reply. He drafted this reply[6] in a tense, excited mood, but in the
end he accepted the terms of the Australian Committee simply and
without argument.*

He looked at the matter in a wholly practical light. He knew that

---

* The draft, which was afterwards sent to McNab, said originally that he
would reserve his right to 'complain of the commandeering of the vessel'. This
was deleted, and the message finally stated that 'under the circumstances I will
proceed with the "Aurora", sailing under the command of Capt. Davis.

I desire to acknowledge my sense of the courtesy and fairness with which the
New Zealand Government and yourself have dealt with me in the unexpected
and somewhat unpleasant conditions which have arisen.

I will of course reserve all my rights as owner to or in connection with the
"Aurora". '

Leonard Tripp described[32] to Dr. Mill one occasion when Shackleton was
spoiling for a fight and he was advising him to be calm : 'Shackleton commented,
"You are saying to me: Here is a piece of bread and jam, eat it and be a good
boy." '

Charles Green, the cook, with Shackleton on the *Quest*

MACKLIN	GREEN		MCILROY	JEFFREY		MARR	CARR			F. L. Horton
	Visitor		SHACKLETON	WILD				WORSLEY	Visitor
				KERR					

On board the *Quest*

CARR, JEFFREY, DELL, KERR, SHACKLETON

Gossip on the *Quest* in the tropics between Madeira and Rio

A. H. M.

Shackleton and Wild on the *Quest*. The last photograph of Shackleton,
taken between Rio and South Georgia

further delay might be dangerous for his men. He was prepared to sacrifice his pride when necessary; and on this occasion it could only hinder him.*

Even now there were anxious moments. In the middle of December a telegram from Dunedin had been printed in many New Zealand papers, announcing that the *Aurora* would sail on the 15th. Knowing that Shackleton's own plans were incomplete, Tripp could only interpret this as an attempt to get the ship away before Shackleton could make the journey from Wellington in the North Island to Dunedin in the South. It may or may not be true that there was a plot to leave without Shackleton. At any rate, the Minister for Marine acted promptly, and an order was sent that the ship was not to sail.

In the end Shackleton was escorted to Dunedin by McNab, taken out to the ship, then lying in the harbour, and seen safely on board. It is still believed in some quarters that Shackleton leapt on a motor launch and jumped the ship just as she was casting off. This is the kind of apocryphal story which was apt to attach itself to the name of Shackleton: but behind the ceremonial send-off by a Cabinet Minister there lay who can say how much annoyance, frustration, jealousy and relief. Shackleton had, in fact, kept remarkably calm, at least in public, during these vexed weeks: but the impression of violent, combative action was created none the less, wherever he went.

The *Aurora* left Port Chalmers, Dunedin, on 20 December, and reached McMurdo Sound on New Year's Day, 1917, and Cape Royds on 10 January. Shackleton described his first sight of his men thus[7]:

'This morning in beautifully clear weather we entered McMurdo Sound and brought up alongside the ice foot fast ice alongside Cape Royds. No sign of life at my old hut. We fired a distress signal no sign of life at Cape Evans hut. I went alone to our hut and found there a note unsigned dated Dec. 15. 1915 stating that the party was housed at Cape Evans. there was no statement as to the safety of all hands

---

* Robert McNab and Leonard Tripp both admired Shackleton greatly for the way he faced this difficulty and the way he solved it. Dr. Mill went somewhat beyond admiration in his biography, when he said,[8] after describing how Shackleton agreed to sign on under Captain Davis, 'He knew himself that this was as big a thing as he had ever done, one of the greatest triumphs of the spirit which animated his great-great-grandfather, the friend of Burke.' Leonard Tripp wrote[9] to Lady Shackleton in criticism of the tone of this passage, 'Ernest knew that he had done the right thing in insisting on signing on under Davis. He knew it was a big thing for him to do but that was all. He discussed the matter freely with me and when he came back he was so proud of his discharge. . . . All he really cared about was relieving his men. He knew that it might be vital for him to be present at the relief of his men. . . . I personally would much sooner that Dr. Mill would state that it was in his (Dr. Mill's) opinion the biggest thing that Ernest had ever done in his life not that Ernest thought so because I honestly do not believe that he did.'

27

but the very absence of this augured well especially as on looking round I noticed Wilds name and Jacks in paint that was still wet. As the two men were on the Barrier party they were the ones we were most anxious about. I returned to ship. saw Party coming out.'

His uncompleted account may be filled in by Joyce's narrative.[10] He and his men had sledged out from the Cape Evans hut, after a dramatic intimation of Shackleton's arrival. 'On January 10th, after breakfast, Richy went out of the hut. Shortly afterwards, he walked in quietly and whispered in my ear, "Joycey, the b—— ship." I replied, "Let us make certain." True enough, there she lay alongside the ice in the bay. We exclaimed "Ship ho!" Our shouts brought the inmates of the hut out with a wild rush. We shook each other by the hand, all worries and troubles passed overboard.'

As leader of the shore party, Shackleton now organised a series of searches for the bodies of Mackintosh and Hayward : he found no trace of them. In his official report[11] he stated, 'I consider that all places at all likely to hold the bodies of Lieutenant Mackintosh and Mr. Hayward have now been searched and there is no doubt in my mind that they met their deaths on the breaking of the thin ice when the blizzard came on May the 8th 1916.'

While Shackleton was searching, Wild and Jack had built a cross to the memory of the three men who lost their lives on this expedition, and among the fragmentary entries in Shackleton's diary there appears a page in which he tried to arrange a suitable inscription to go on the cross, deciding ultimately on some splendid lines from Browning full of the fearless optimism which he so deeply admired.*

On 17 January the *Aurora* turned northwards again. During Shackleton's absence in the south, Leonard Tripp had been active on his behalf.

---

* The verses were the splendid lines from *Prospice*:
'I was ever a fighter, so—one fight more,
   The best and the last!
I would hate that death bandaged my eyes, and forebore,
   And bade me creep past.
No! let me taste the whole of it, fare like my peers
   The heroes of old,
Bear the brunt, in a minute pay glad life's arrears
   Of pain, darkness and cold.
For sudden the worst turns the best of the brave,
   The black minute's at end,
And the elements rage, the fiend-voices that rave,
   Shall dwindle, shall blend . . .'

Shackleton placed these verses, together with the names of the three men, into a copper tube which was presumably buried near the cross. On 28 February 1947, Rear-Admiral Cruzen, commanding the United States naval task force 68, engaged in Operation Deepfreeze, discovered this tube in the snow near the Cape Evans hut. It was later presented to the Admiralty.

He knew that the men who were returning had money due to them, and he felt that public sympathy and interest might be turned to account. More than this, he believed Shackleton's work was of great value to the Empire, and that the British Government should help him further in the matter of his debts.*

This argument he put to Shackleton when he returned to Wellington on 9 February, but Shackleton insisted that the expedition was very small beer compared with the war, and that he preferred to manage his affairs himself, as best he could. The *Aurora* was officially declared his property and her sale was put in hand. But this could not be done in a hurry, and meanwhile he had to find cash to pay his men. Mr. Tripp engaged the sympathy of a number of businessmen and landowners, chiefly in and around Wellington, and from this group the sum of £5,000 was raised.

The money went to Tripp's office, where accounts and lists of names were carefully kept. A letter of acknowledgement was drafted, and Shackleton signed copies of it before he left New Zealand. Soon after he left for Sydney, in the middle of March, £8,000 was available from the sale of the ship and her effects. As he had arranged with Shackleton, Leonard Tripp returned the money advanced by his friends, plus an agreed interest.

The effect of this efficiency was what might have been expected. Most of the men concerned returned the interest, some returned the whole amount of the loan, and one or two added donations. One letter out of many may be quoted: the writer returned the interest and sent a further sum of money as 'a little help to a brave man who has had cruel bad luck and has set us all a bright example.'[12]

Leonard Tripp had in fact taken upon himself the duties of a confidential secretary, and in doing so had shown how much Shackleton's mistakes over money matters were due to lack of time and method. Even after Shackleton had reached England, his friend continued to give him useful advice on public relations. He advised him to let his first public lecture in England be for the New Zealand and Australian soldiers, and gave him names of people who could help him to arrange this. He knew very well that much criticism of Shackleton was based on hearsay reports of his character and that a meeting with him could

---

* In fact the British Government had spent on the Imperial Trans-Antarctic Expedition the total sum of £19,265 7s. 4d. Provision was taken in a Supplementary Estimate (Scientific Investigations, etc. Vote) in the summer of 1916 for a sum of £20,000. In the Estimate for 1917–18, £15,000 was revoted. According to the Civil Appropriation Accounts, £8,569 2s. 6d. was spent in 1916–17, and £10,696 4s. 10d. in 1917–18. Almost the whole of the second amount was in respect of the Ross Sea expedition despatched by the Governments of Australia and New Zealand. (We owe this information to Mr. D. J. D. Clark of the Information Division of the Treasury.)

count for much. 'I am anxious to hear how you get on in Melbourne,' he wrote[3] soon after Shackleton had sailed from New Zealand.[6] I only hope that you will have more than one day there because then you will get the people with you.'

Shackleton bowed to Leonard Tripp's knowledge of the world. In fact, the short period in New Zealand after his dash to the Ross Sea was better managed than most other public occasions in his lifetime. Shackleton was extraordinarily inconsistent in the way he dealt with his obligations. He treated his expeditions like campaigns, planning and adapting his plans with endless patience. With people, on the contrary, he acted on impulse. Personal contact stimulated him; he was less efficient at planning contacts or dealings with people who were not actually present.

He was a man to whom the complexities of human relationships did not as a rule matter very much. His few close relationships were straightforward ones—with Miss Stancomb-Wills, with Wild and Worsley, with one or two of his theatrical friends. He fought shy of self-analysis as a rule, and preferred his dealings with people to be short and to the point.

All the same, it was people he needed. Now that he had organised and led two expeditions, he could not be anything but a leader if he was to be himself. To his wife he wrote[1] from Wellington, where he was tying up loose ends and waiting for a ship to Australia, that he did not think he would ever venture far from the homeside again, but on the same page he told her, 'I have battled against great odds and extraordinary conditions for now more than 3 years and it is true that I should have a rest from it all. I would not alter or have changed one bit of the work and all its trials for there is a feeling of power that I like but at times I have grown very weary and lonely.'

His wife must have deduced from this candid outburst that she could not even now be sure of having her husband by her side for long. Leonard Tripp, who had been working with the tired and worried Shackleton during these weeks, had different views, and later in the year he wrote to Shackleton begging him to settle down.[3] He felt it would be years before the public would put up any more money for exploration, and that Shackleton would then be too old to enter upon another expedition (he was just 43). He advised him to keep in touch with the Australian and New Zealand people he met in England, for he felt sure a diplomatic job would suit him. He was to return to this idea later; but although Shackleton's vision of the unknown south was misted over at this time, it was not yet completely obscured.

Certainly it was not in a spirit of diplomacy that he went to meet the Australian relief committee, but in this instance, his directness and determination settled the matter in the best possible way. Edward

Saunders, who went with him as a friend and a secretary, wrote an account of the meeting afterwards :[13]*

'Sir Ernest told the members of the Board very plainly and bluntly that they had treated him unfairly. He said that he had received immediate and generous support from South American Governments in the rescue of the Weddell Sea party. Ships and men had been placed at his disposal without hesitation or stint. But when he came to New Zealand to undertake the relief of the Ross Sea party in his own ship, he had found hostile influences arrayed against him. He had gone south as a member of the crew of his own ship, under Captain Davis, because he felt that the prompt relief of the party was the matter of prime importance. He wished to tell the members of the Board now that they had not played the game.

A general discussion followed. I received the impression that some members of the Board had been strongly prejudiced against Shackleton and that personal contact was forcing them to revise their estimate of the man. A member suggested that Shackleton had virtually thrown the responsibility for the relief voyage upon the Governments (British, Australian and New Zealand), which were justified in taking full control. Shackleton denied warmly that he had parted with any of his responsibility. He stated that he had come round the world to rescue his own men and that he could have resumed command of his ship with the concurrence of the New Zealand Government if he had chosen to exercise the rights that were his.

Finally Shackleton said that, having stated his opinion, he did not wish to carry the argument any further. He intended to regard the incident as closed. Admiral Cresswell, the chairman of the Board, said that he and his colleagues would like to bury the hatchet. He would not deny that they might have been misled. Admiral Cresswell virtually apologised to Shackleton, and said he hoped that all the trouble would be forgotten. Other members of the Board, I think all of them, expressed regret that there should have been any misunderstanding. They all shook hands with Shackleton. Admiral Cresswell said smilingly that it was long since he had listened to such a reprimand.

Later that day Admiral Cresswell met Shackleton again and said that he would like to take the chair at the Melbourne lecture. He did take the chair and he spoke of Shackleton in warmly admiring terms before a Melbourne audience.

After this meeting Shackleton telegraphed Leonard Tripp,[29] 'have had committee on carpet for very frank talk now feel better and buried hatchet.'†

* This account was sent by Edward Saunders to Leonard Tripp, to be forwarded to Dr. Mill for use in his biography of Shackleton. 'I did not take any notes', he wrote, 'since it was his wish that the interview should be informal and should close the incident'; but Saunders was satisfied that his memory of the meeting was vivid and true.

† Shackleton's vigorous behaviour in Australia greatly impressed R. W.

Thus Shackleton rounded off the complexities of the Ross Sea rescue, and turned to what he thought more important now—the war. He did not underrate his achievements. He knew that at this moment he was a figure of national importance, and he meant to use this position to help Britain. In Sydney on 20 March he spoke to 11,000 people about their duty to the Mother Country. His speech, afterwards printed by the Australian Government as a recruiting pamphlet, was exactly suited to the occasion. The opening paragraphs have been quoted many times but they must be quoted again.[14]

'To you men and women of Australia I have something to say. I come from a land where there are no politics and no clashing of personal interest. For nearly two years I heard nothing and knew nothing of what was happening in the civilised lands. Then I came back to a world darkened by desperate strife, and as people told me of what had happened during those two years I realised one great thing, and that was this:

To take your part in this war is not a matter merely of patriotism, not a matter merely of duty or of expediency; it is a matter of the saving of a man's soul and of a man's own opinion of himself.

We lived long dark days in the South. The danger of the moment is a thing easy to meet, and the courage of the moment is in every man at some time. But I want to say to you that we lived through slow dead days of toil, of struggle, dark striving and anxiety; days that called not for heroism in the bright light of day, but simply for dogged persistent endeavour to do what the soul said was right. It is in that same spirit that we men of the British race have to face this war. What does the war mean to Australia? Everything. It means as much to you as though the enemy was actually beating down your gate. This summons to fight is a call imperative to the manhood within you.

. . . Death is a very little thing—the smallest thing in the world. I can tell you that, for I have been face to face with death during long months. I know that death scarcely weighs in the scale against a man's appointed task. Perhaps in the quiet hours of night, when you think over what I have said, you will feel the little snakes of doubt twisting in your heart. I have known them. Put them aside. If we have to die, we will die in the pride of manhood, our eyes on the goal and our hearts beating time to the instinct within us.

For this call to fight means to men more than ease, more than money, more than love of woman, more even than duty; it means the chance to prove ourselves the captains of our own soul.'

Richards, of the Ross Sea party, who writes[30]: 'I saw him in action immediately on his arrival in Melbourne. His first words were "Where is Jensen" (then Minister for Navy). He would definitely face his critics and my money would be on him. He was chock full of personality and a born leader—in my opinion the outstanding personality in all Antarctic exploration. He had his faults. Some say he was unscrupulous. If so, it was probably due to his overriding passion for his task.'

It was a magnificent piece of rhetoric, of the simple rhetoric with which Shackleton could express his thoughts when he was deeply moved. It may be taken not only as a direct appeal to men to risk their lives for their country, but also as an unconscious statement of what that magnificent failure, the Imperial Trans-Antarctic Expedition, had meant to Shackleton. It was the justification, if such were needed, of his use of the adjective Imperial in the title of that expedition. It was as true a description of the spirit of his men as that other day-to-day truth of fear and occasional breakdown, of grumbling and boredom and impatience.

Patriotism was now Shackleton's guiding principle. He refused offers of a lucrative lecture tour in America because he was determined to get home to help in the war. In New Zealand, in Christchurch and other towns, he had lectured on the expedition, giving the proceeds of his lectures to the New Zealand Red Cross and to Mrs. Mackintosh, for whom he felt a strong responsibility. He had done the same thing in Australia. He had created a trust fund for Mrs. Mackintosh, which he confided to the care of Leonard Tripp, and in the following year he helped to find her a post at the Admiralty. He would take no money for himself in New Zealand because that country had helped him so generously.

Early in April he left Sydney for San Francisco, where he was greeted by a heart-warming reception. The Bohemian Club gave him a dinner on 9 April, during which poems were recited and songs sung which had been composed especially in his honour; and a lecture he delivered there on 19 April was packed out.

He treated this month in the United States as a period of duty, and tried in his lectures to put across his views about the war and to impress on the Americans what it meant to be an ally. Tired as he was, it was an effort to him to lecture, and the arrangements made for him were not always very efficient. His sense of humour was pricked into life by a visit to Tacoma, where he addressed a small audience. He wrote to Leonard Tripp[16]:

'The only sign of advertising that I could see was when I arrived— a boozy looking old man carrying a banner, evidently from some fancy dress performance they had once, covered with white cotton wool to represent snow and the words taken from my telegram, "All well all saved." He was leaning up against a lamp post covered with the cotton wool. Result of the lecture very poor. I was guaranteed five hundred dollars but as it was a woman running this and as she had staked my filling the hall, I cut my guarantee down so that she would not lose on it. It was not her fault. I don't believe the last trump will affect the Tacoma people. There has been a mistake in the name TACOMA.—the T and A should come off and it should read "Coma".'

At the box office he overheard a man asking the clerk in an aggressive voice whether the entertainment was fit for a lady. Shackleton enquired whether his wife was very particular, and advised him 'that the most risqué thing is the sight of two small penguins making love to one another.' The good man decided to take his wife.

There were not many such diverting moments. But if Shackleton found it painful to dwell publicly on the dangers he had survived, his audiences for the most part were carried away by the tale. At the end of April he gave several important lectures under the auspices of the American Geographical Society and the American Museum of Natural History, starting by addressing a packed audience at the Carnegie Hall, New York, on 29 April 1917, and repeating the performance in Philadelphia, Chicago, and again in New York in the Aeolian Hall on 2 May.

At the Carnegie Hall, in particular, his personality made a powerful impression. He spoke as an unofficial ambassador for Britain, for a country whose stock was low in America at that time; what he said and how he said it were of enormous importance. Among the large audience was Sir Shane Leslie, who has described[28] the occasion as one of overwhelming excitement and emotion. The hall was crammed as for a first night, long before the lecture was due to start. The audience were prepared to accept this as one of the greatest lectures in New York history:

'Then came the flaw. The chairman, an elderly member of council, had never chaired a meeting before. What I presume had happened was that he had conferred with Shackleton, who had unfortunately given him all his points. The chairman got up. Every time he mentioned Shackleton, who was alone, sitting back, the whole audience gave a rousing cheer. The chairman was encouraged and proceeded to give Shackleton's lecture. He spoke for 40 minutes before he could be pulled down. It was agony. The audience tried to shout him down with cheers, which of course only encouraged him more. Sometimes the cheering went on for several minutes. Shackleton was going about like a lion, up and down, and the whole audience shouting for him. He was really worked up. Finally they got the chairman down and Shackleton repeated what had been said—but it was Shackleton. He did it magnificently, and the emotion between him and his audience was such as you very seldom feel. The only other time I've felt it was between Winston and his audience. And that I say perfectly deliberately, because I've heard great speakers and great occasions all my life; but I've never felt the audience played on like an organ by a man talking, except by Winston and Shackleton, and on both occasions it hardly mattered what they said.'

Shackleton got home late in May. His impatience had been matched by that of his wife, but she could not help having misgivings about how he would fit into her customary world, after the past two years. During his absence she had left the Kensington house and settled in Eastbourne, where the children would be safer and healthier and where she could live more economically. She had worked to make a secure life for them, and she must have wondered what changes he would wish to make. Some of her thoughts were confided to Leonard Tripp, to whom she wrote[15] while she was waiting for her husband to come from America:

'This is quite a small house—and I know it would bore Ernest to be here for any length of time—but the children have been very happy here . . . & I dont bother about the future—if only Ernest comes safely back. Things looked very black a year ago & I have been so thankful ever since the news came from S. Georgia—that nothing else seemed to matter much. I only hope he will get something to do—that will interest him— as he could never be happy in a quiet domestic life. I have always realized that, though I should not mind having a little more of him myself!'

Once he was at home, there was so much to do that Shackleton had no time to get bored with domestic life, as his wife had feared. He began at once meeting as many people who might help him to get a war job as he could. There were the outstanding affairs of the expedition also to be settled. The photographs had reached England long before, and Ernest Perris had arranged for Hurley to go back to South Georgia in the summer of 1917 to get some more pictures. They hoped he would be able to get into the mountains and get film material of Shackleton's astonishing journey; but although the party was well-equipped, they were not able to do this.

The film material of the *Endurance* was magnificent on its own, and it was perhaps from an advance on expectations from this material that Shackleton paid off his men, for in a postscript to a letter Lady Shackleton wrote to Leonard Tripp in July, he wrote,[16] 'The whole Expedition is now paid off and clear and there are no liabilities.'* Most of the men had been satisfied with their treatment. One or two demanded more money, and one claimed that his health had suffered from the expedition. Shackleton dealt with him summarily, pointing out that he had gone at his own risk, but the situation preyed on his mind and he spoke of it more than once to James Dell during the last days of his life.

As to his own financial affairs, no information is available of how he kept his family during this period. He could not yet realise any money for himself, either out of a film or out of the book of the expedition,

---

* On 10 January 1920 the *Daily Mail*, reporting on Shackleton's lectures with the *Endurance* film, stated that there were still heavy liabilities to pay off for the expedition. We cannot explain the discrepancy, unless it be that part of the money earned by lecturing was put to wages and salaries which had been deferred by the consent of the men.

which Edward Saunders was working on in New Zealand. He would not lecture for his own profit while the war was on and the first job he was given was an honorary one.

The long wait for this job had sorely tried his patience. Shackleton revealed his state of mind to Dame Janet Stancomb-Wills, when he told her,[17] 'I am a little vicious that after people saying why did I ever go south when the great war was on, should have to chase from pillar to post in order to get a job and the F.O. is so hidebound that they resent me thinking I might not be tactful.' He had many ideas about what he should do. During the summer of 1917 he worked out a plan for a Russian winter invasion of Germany and Hungary. Some time before, Leonard Tripp had suggested to the High Commissioner for New Zealand in London that Shackleton's special knowledge of polar conditions should be used[18] to help in improving the food supplies to the army and their equipment: and to Shackleton it seemed equally obvious that the lessons of his last expedition should not be wasted. 'I am trying to get to Russia,' he wrote[16] to Tripp, 'there is more scope there even though times are troublous out there. I have applied to get the transport work especially the winter work it is right in my line.'

It was almost arranged that he should go out to Russia to join the American railway and transport commission, but difficulties arose and the Foreign Office decided against sending him. The Russian Commission in England later asked for his services, but negotiations dragged on and nothing was arranged.

Late in the summer he wrote[1] to his wife that it had been suggested to him that he should 'organise and carry out a scheme for the Co-ordination of the food supplies for the Allied Nations: it is very important but it means sticking in England at Grosvenor House and working day and night and of course I don't like that . . . I would have my own staff and secretaries and about £1,000 a year: but it is what one would call departmental work: I am not deciding one way or the other until I . . . have talked it all over with you: I know there are many who would jump at it but the question is whether it might in some quarters be thought that I was avoiding the active side of the war.'

This plan, too, was dropped, perhaps by Shackleton himself. Meanwhile, he spent much of his waiting time visiting people from the Dominions to thank them for help received. To show his appreciation he gave lectures at one or two hospitals, and one New Zealander was heard to say afterwards, 'He left a lot out [i.e., about his hardships] and I shan't mind going over the parapet now.' Shackleton's comment on being told this was typical. 'Of course,' he said to his wife, 'after sitting through my lecture, the poor chap wouldn't mind anything.'[15]

The job, when it came, had nothing to do with polar conditions, but it linked up none the less with the expedition. Before Shackleton returned to England, Leonard Tripp had written to Ernest Perris in these terms[19]:

'I was talking a few days ago to a man who was in South America when Shackleton was there, and he told me that Shackleton's work and his personality appealed very much to the people there. He said that the ordinary Englishman is so reserved, but Shackleton is different. He is admired for his work and he has got a personality besides. I have been wondering whether, seeing the name he has now got, some important job could not be found for him as a sort of visiting consul. Supposing he was given a good salary and a roving commission, that is to say, a commission to go to America and other places, especially South America, it being understood that he was to be allowed to give a certain number of lectures in each place. . . . In that way he would get hold over the people and would be able to do good work for the Empire.'

It seems probable that a word was dropped in the right quarter. In any event it was to South America that Shackleton was directed in September, to work under Sir Edward Carson, head of the Department of Information. The neutral countries of South America were of great importance to Britain, more especially those like Chile which were permeated with German influence. Shackleton's instructions were expressed in very general terms: he was to examine the existing propagandist agencies and to assist in spreading British propaganda, and he was to suggest to the Department any changes or extensions of policy and method in these countries which he thought desirable.

It may be guessed from his letters that he often found the work irksome, but it called upon certain qualities which he probably underestimated in himself—his power to get on with people, his frankness and impatience with protocol, his toughness. Moreover, he was an imperialist. Although he would have preferred to fight at the front, he interpreted his travelling and office work in South America as a fight against the Germans, and within the limits of diplomatic relations, this was how he carried it out.

When the time came for him to leave England he regretted the fresh break with his family. The reunion with his children, whose acquaintance he had had to make all over again, had been intensely interesting— sometimes satisfying, sometimes provoking. As in former years, he found it difficult to accept the particular form of discipline which had grown up in his absence. Like most fathers, his affection was expressed most easily in efforts on his children's behalf, and these efforts included what he considered suitable organising. He was occasionally shocked at the free and easy way they spoke to their mother, and there were inevitably disagreements about parental method.

'I am sorry I went off this morning in a fluster', he had written to his wife[1] on one occasion, 'but I am just now very anxious about the future and I suppose the continual questioning and having to keep saying No to the children gets a bit on my nerves. You know they ought to obey at once and not be told two or three times. . . . I dont like to interfere for I am so little at home.'

Indeed, he was very little at home during the summer of 1917. He and his wife occasionally took a flat in Queen Anne's Mansions where they could be together for part of the week. His multifarious interests in London did nothing to alter the fact that he was still deeply dependent on her and on the family life which still had to be conducted to a great extent by post. The letters which came to Eastbourne from South America showed once more the familiar pattern of loneliness and longing for peace, which started as soon as his ship had sailed. From the *Vestris* he wrote:[1]

'I miss you more than ever I have done before Sweeteyes Your photo and the childrens is up in my cabin and I long to be back in the dearest little house I have ever been in : I was happy really happy this time when all was right between us, and now I do not feel far away though I am missing you : I think darling that you are wonderful in many ways and the more I think about you the more I see what a wonderful wife you have been to me : I suppose darling that I am a funny curious sort of wanderer but take this me I have been far happier at home these last few months than ever before : and the work I am doing is I hope going to be of permanent help to the country. I think our children are just sweet in all their ways and I am proud of them of each in some particular way : from B.A. I can write more fully for my letter will go in the bag and that may not be done here. You see darling, I find it difficult to say anything in the way of news I can only tell you that I love you and that is stale news but there it is : God bless you darling and keep you safe and well and free from all harm. . . .'

Letters like this demonstrate the bond which no outside attachments could break between Shackleton and his wife. The heavier his responsibilities grew, the stronger his need became for his family, although he half knew that once he settled down with them again, that need would soon be supplanted by the old urge to wander.

He did his delicate work very well. Such fragmentary reports as survive among his papers indicate that he saw matters very clearly and that he was capable of making useful deductions from the many interviews and casual conversations he had as he went up and down the country. With his headquarters at Buenos Aires, he travelled widely, and a visit to Chile gave him particularly valuable information. He was quick to note, and to advise, that British methods in propaganda and diplomacy were too slow. He was quick, too, to see how much of the

German influence in the South American countries was ultimately valueless because it had been crudely superimposed upon ideals which were temperamentally closer to those of Britain. In Chilean commerce, in the Chilean Navy, in the Argentine's idealistic attitude to political freedom, he found matter for hope, and gave succinct and clear reasons for his optimism.

His mission ended in mid-March 1918, and he returned home by way of North America, arriving at the end of April. In June he submitted his reports to the Department of Information. In addition to providing concrete information and advice on the situation in South America, Shackleton gave his general views on the methods of the Ministry as a whole. His views and suggestions were forceful, and after he had given evidence at a commission, Lord Beaverbrook sent him a neatly-worded note of congratulation:[20]

> 'Immediately after you left the room I was called on to give evidence. . . . It became abundantly clear that so powerful had been the testimony of the last witness that there was no doubt in the mind of the committee about the organisation of the Department. In fact so fixed was the opinion of the audience that I think it may safely be said that the last witness had left on their minds an impression which will never fade!'

Unfortunately this success did not at once lead to further employment. For much of the summer of 1918 Shackleton had to hang about in London in the old discouraging search. To Dame Janet Stancomb-Wills he wrote[17] that he gathered 'they are afraid of too much activity on my part out of the ordinary routine: they say I am a very difficult person to place; and also that they supposed I could not be content with a small regular post: I said "give me the work and I will look after it and if my ideas are not sound you can always reject them" I am being as tactful as I can but bitterly restless now and hear the guns booming on the other side and also see this great German advance. My place is out in the war:'

At last, in August, the War Office appointed him to take charge of winter equipment for the North Russian expedition. The post was, as that of the South American mission, very much what he could make it. Before he went out to North Russia he tried to fit in a visit to Spitsbergen, on behalf of the Northern Exploration Company. This syndicate, which had had money in Spitsbergen since 1904, had already sent a Trinity House pilot, Captain David Thomson, on the S.S. *Repertor*, to report on the possibilities of the country and particularly on the available harbours. In 1918 the Company commissioned Captain Thomson to find a suitable ship and equip an expedition which would prospect for coal, iron and gold, and which would re-establish the land claims which had been jumped by the Germans.

Shackleton had invested some money in the company, and had agreed to lead the expedition, for which he had collected Wild and McIlroy (the latter invalided from the army).

The Company's ship, the *Ella*, left London on 21 July, and proceeded in a convoy, which was attacked more than once by German submarines off the North Coast. At Aberdeen Shackleton joined the party, and they sailed for Norway on 2 August. Freed from the necessity for caution and diplomacy, bound for the kind of climate (physical and psychological) which best suited him, he threw off his cares and became once more the high-spirited leader.

A fascinating glimpse of him at that time comes from an acquaintance of Shackleton's, who acted as storekeeper to the expedition as far as Tromsö (where an accident obliged him to return to England). Mr. M. P. Fisher recalled[21] in letters to his wife the ebullient way Shackleton spoke of his ambitions and his ideas of what wonderful things could come out of Spitsbergen. He described how Shackleton got round the difficulties of war-time transport and how a word from him could smooth away all difficulties. The storekeeper, who had been a chiropodist when Shackleton persuaded him out of his quiet life, was greatly impressed by his first glimpse of Shackleton and of an exploring group in full tongue. He wrote to his wife of the devotion he saw between Shackleton and his men, and his care for them. He described a sing-song, with 'the boss just like a grown up kid . . . always full of boyish fun'; with Wild singing a sailor's song and Shackleton pulling the leg of 'the rope-way surveyor a very nice quiet young man'; and last of all 'the boss reciting one (of) his pieces of poetry relating to some former arctic exploit. It was splendid.'

From Tromsö Shackleton was recalled by the War Office, and the rest of the party carried on under the leadership of Salisbury-Jones, Chairman of the Northern Exploration Company, and under the care of Captain Thomson, who took his ship safely to Spitsbergen. Frank Wild took charge of the prospecting party, and the winter was usefully spent: but the Company did not produce the spectacular results Shackleton had hoped for, and this became yet another enterprise from which he failed to make a fortune.

Although Shackleton was relieved from a great mental strain when the War Office gave him a staff job, this was not going to bring in big money, and he had not given up his hopes of that. In fact, allowing for the hampering circumstances of war time, and for his resolve not to lecture for money, he seems to have been casting round for a lead in business affairs, very much as he had done in the years between *Nimrod* and *Endurance*. For instance, in the autumn of 1918 he had been put in touch with Mr. George Constantinescu, a Rumanian engineer who had been working on a new science of transmitting power by vibrations in columns of water. Shackleton first went to see him on 27 September and was much interested in Mr. Constantinescu's ideas (he called his invention Sonics). In particular a special device for firing machine guns through aeroplane propellers (which was adopted in the Air Force) impressed Shackleton. Mr. Constantinescu was at this time unable to raise money to pursue his researches and he warned Shackleton that there could be no money in the scheme for him; but Shackleton had faith in the idea and wanted to join with him after the war. In a letter dated 27 October, from North Russia, he wrote,[22] 'I have been thinking that after the war if there is any chance of my coming into your business I would be very glad to do so and would like you to consider it for I have the greatest faith in it all and would like to be associated with you if you think I could be of any use. . . . I want to get into something good and progressive and your sonic power seems to be the thing of the immediate future and especially the propeller idea.'*

After he reached London, at the end of August, Shackleton worked with furious haste to get the equipment together for the North Russian Front. He was bound for the port of Murmansk, near the Norwegian frontier of Russia, where a small British expeditionary force had been uncomfortably encamped since June. Murmansk and nearby Pechenga were threatened by the Germans, who wanted both ports for submarine bases. German forces were pressing through Finland and menacing North Russia by means of two single-track railways, from Petrograd to Murmansk and from Petrograd to Archangel. Local and Finnish troops were fighting alongside the British. They had as enemies not only the Germans but also Bolshevik forces, the Soviet Government having by this time declared against Britain.

From the summer onwards the very limited British force tried to establish itself with some degree of comfort and efficiency in Murmansk, a town consisting of log-built sheds and houses set on an untidy fore-shore, with mountains towering behind, and with a very assorted population. Major-General C. M. Maynard, in command, was confronted with a problem which had for many years been familiar to Shackleton. Inadequately equipped, inadequately housed, inadequately staffed, he had no money to put things right: he could not even pay the regular wages of workmen and railway employees, let alone the increases they demanded. His requests for more men from Britain, America and France were not fulfilled, and the independent command at Archangel, under Major-General W. E. Ironside, was in the same uneasy position.

* Mr. Constantinescu has kindly allowed us to quote from a letter in his possession, and has supplied us with information concerning Shackleton's connection with Sonics. Shackleton entertained the idea for some time but the money was never forthcoming for developing the scheme.

In the autumn of 1918, however, 150 Canadians were sent to Murmansk. They had been trained in Arctic techniques. At the same time another specialist was sent out, from Britain, with sledges, dogs, skis and polar equipment ready for a winter campaign against the Bolsheviks. This specialist was Ernest Shackleton, now a Major in the British Army.

Shackleton set out for Murmansk in a buoyant mood. For the past few weeks he had been doing his own kind of work, an inspired mixture of storekeeping and imaginative planning. He set out as for an expedition, and the fact that he managed to have four of his own men transferred strengthened this impression. Hussey and Macklin had already been transferred to the North Russian front from other spheres in the Army, and Shackleton had managed to get the Navy to lend Worsley and Stenhouse. Worsley wrote excitedly to Leonard Tripp[23] that they were all 'happy as sandboys' and going everywhere together. 'I'm sorry I cant say anything of what we are going to do', he wrote, 'but what I'd like would be for us to finish up each driving a dog-team over the snow into Berlin, what time the victorious British, New Zealanders, Yanks & French troops burst in from the Western Front.'

General Maynard was not as sanguine as Shackleton and his comrades about the success of the new appointment. He made no secret of the fact that he did not want Shackleton on his staff. The reputation had preceded Shackleton of being difficult to lead, impatient under restraint, headstrong and opinionated: some at least of these reports seem to have emanated from a member of one of Scott's expeditions who had also been sent to North Russia as an expert in polar affairs. Be that as it may, Maynard was afraid that Shackleton's value as a consultant would be outweighed by his reputed intractability.

These fears of Maynard's were soon allayed. 'The impression I had gathered from hearsay,' he afterwards wrote,[33]

'was that he was somewhat dictatorial if not overbearing; and that, though doubtless a fine leader of men, he was unlikely to accept gladly a subordinate position. Events soon proved, however, that my fears on this score were totally unfounded, for from the moment of his arrival to the time of his departure in the spring of 1919, he gave me of his very best, and his loyalty from start to finish was absolute. He fitted at once into the niche awaiting him, and both he and his friends of past Antarctic expeditions who were working with him laid themselves out unreservedly to further the interests of my Force.'

Macklin, who had reached Murmansk some time before Shackleton, was well aware of this undercurrent, and as it turned out he was able to warn Shackleton that the situation would demand tact.

Shackleton succeeded in subordinating himself successfully to Maynard's command, but this did not prevent him from commenting on matters which he thought needed improvement. One of his first actions was to have the hutments cleared from the water-front, so as to free the way to the piers. He quickly put himself on good terms with the officers and men whom he had to deal with, and showed the same solicitude for their welfare as he had always shown to the men on his expeditions. He was popular with the troops because of his friendly, unconventional manner towards everyone,* and because he was so obviously tackling his job with all his energy. To the best of his ability he diverted the attention of press photographers and journalists from himself, as Macklin well remembers, but his name was now too well-known for him to be able to escape altogether the jealousy and close criticism which attach to anyone in the public eye.

Shackleton's letters home[1] were, as he said to his wife, like Cecily's from school, 'asking for all sorts of things, but you see, I will be away from this place at various times perhaps for a month and then back again so this is my permanent address and I may (as well) be as comfortable as I can during the times I am here and on the march I will be just the same as the men.' From his hut looking out on virgin woods and also on a 'plentiful supply of frozen mud', he pressed on with his work, which is adequately described in his official title—Director of Equipment, Clothing, Rations and Transport of the Mobile Columns and Director of Clothing for the Syren Force.† He was disappointed when time went on and he was not sent on any raids: he was sorry, too, when Worsley was sent down to Archangel to command a force there. But, working in close contact with Hussey and Stenhouse, and with Macklin when he was in Murmansk, he settled down comfortably enough.

At the end of November he accompanied Maynard to London on H.M.S. *Dublin*, and spent a short time helping his leader to get their equipment and allowances increased.‡ A Lieutenant in the R.N.R., in that ship, was enthralled by his stories in the ward-room, many of them told against himself. He thought Shackleton an amazing personality, and has never forgotten him.§ In particular he remembers Shackleton telling the story of his feeling that a fourth man accompanied

---

* Mr. B. C. Howells,[31] who was Cipher Officer to General Maynard at the time, remembers how Shackleton used to look in at his office after a game of bridge with the general, with the words, 'Put that work away and draw me some funny pictures'. Mr. G. E. Wilson recalls[34] the 'wonderful service' he did to the Elope Squadron in planning equipment.

† The code name for the force at Murmansk.

‡ Shackleton spoke bitterly to Mr. Constantinescu about the lack of adequate provision for the men in North Russia, and said he was determined to get from the Government what General Maynard wanted for those who were in his charge.

§ Mr. Reginald Greenhough has sent us this interesting reminiscence[24] of his meeting with Shackleton in 1918.

28

him on his journey over South Georgia. He attempted no explanation, but simply said, 'In religion I am what I am.'

General Maynard[25] recalled later the cheerful atmosphere of that journey home with Shackleton and a second staff officer, all three feeling like 'schoolboys starting home for the holidays'; all enjoying the goodwill and hospitality of the ship, the sunshine in Scotland as they landed, and the games of cut-throat bridge with which they whiled away the long journey from Thurso to London.

On Christmas Day, 1918, they embarked at Invergordon on the S.S. *Asturian* for the return journey. An Army officer returning from leave, Captain A. F. Birch-Jones, remembered how Shackleton as he came aboard 'smilingly approached the master, shook his hand, and said, "I'm Shackleton. I'm a sailor really. I'm only dressed up like a soldier." '*

After he had got back to Murmansk, Captain Birch-Jones was detailed (as Assistant Base Commander) among other things to get up a concert party, and he recalls that Shackleton and his doings made excellent material for topical songs and that Hussey with his banjo was a welcome guest artist. The 'Shackleton boot', a modification of the finnesko, had been issued to the troops ; it was excellent for their purpose but unfortunately it had been given hard hide soles which made it difficult to walk in. There are many anecdotes and poems centreing round the Shackleton boot, among them Birch-Jones' skit on a popular song, which ended :

> 'But always remember, from January to December,
> Your Shackleton boots you can praise.
> For they have taught you to stumble,
> To skid and to tumble,
> Three hundred and sixty-five ways.'

The leader of the concert party, early in 1919, applied to Shackleton for instruction in skiing, although he was not attached to any of the mobile columns. Shackleton, he remembers, at first 'growled' at him, but when he realised that the young officer wanted to learn, he took him out himself once or twice a week. Mr. Birch-Jones remembers :[26]

'No one could call these excursions sociable. For the most part he might just as well have been alone. He kept about 25 yards ahead. I slithered behind in silence. Occasionally he would halt and gaze over what to me was the abomination of monotony—a murky, grudging

---

* We are indebted to Mr. A. F. Birch-Jones for many interesting reminiscences[26] of Shackleton in North Russia, and in particular for giving us much valuable information about Shackleton's negotiations with Russia in the matter of timber concessions (pp. 437-9).

light; vast expanses of snow; in the distance the gun-metal glimmer
of the Kola Inlet stretching northwards to Alexandrov—an appropriate place for exile, which was what it was used for in Tsarist days!;
across the water, semi-frozen, stunted trees in the steep slope. For
a full minute Shackleton would look at it, taking stock of it all, as
though he wished to imprint it on his memory.

He liked it—actually liked this stark, cold desolation.'

On one of these runs Shackleton, leaning on his ski-sticks, began to
declaim poetry. His companion had been reading English Literature at
the university when he was called up; he identified the poem. Shackleton's comment was, 'First man in that uniform I've met who'd even
heard of Browning.' Some days later he recited something his companion did not recognise, and he asked where the lines came from.

'Well, Shackleton said it' was the answer.

'That explorer man?' I asked. 'He must be a man of parts. I never
knew he was a poet.'

'Then why the devil did you think he became an explorer.'

It was a masterly and a characteristic answer.

If Shackleton enjoyed the scenery of snow and fir-trees, his work did
not really give him what he wanted. The nearest he got to action was the
hustle of a campaign early in January, when Maynard was ordered to
move an infantry battalion and a company of machine gunners at speed
to relieve Ironside, who was suffering a Bolshevik attack at Archangel.
One hundred and fifty miles of desolate country had to be covered by
soldiers not yet fully trained in Arctic conditions. Shackleton and his
colleagues worked at high pressure to organise transport, pack sledges
with emergency rations, and give last-minute instructions. The work
was well done and the troop movement successfully accomplished, but
Shackleton stayed at the base as before.

His letters home were lonely. He urged his wife to write often, and
complained of the irregular mails. He had not had his fill of domesticity
since his return to England. He wanted to know more about Ray at
Harrow, about Cecily at Roedean, about 'the little chap'. He wrote
notes, sometimes illustrated, to the children, making jokes about
mermen and sirens, asking questions about lessons and marks in the
time-honoured way of fathers. His letters to his wife tried to express his
gratitude for her patience with his wanderings, and with the financial
situation at home, which was still not sound. He had made what
provision he could for his family before he left for the Northern Front.
Presumably he had been able to make some allotment of his pay;
certainly he had arranged to realise some money from his shares in the
Spitsbergen company, which money was to be transferred to his wife;
but unfortunately this plan did not work out. Lady Shackleton accepted
the situation as she had always done. She knew her husband was

restless and that he was not satisfied with the course his life had taken.

'Sometimes I think I am no good at anything', he wrote to her[1] in one revealing letter, 'but being away in the wilds just with men and sometimes I grow restless and feel any part of youth is slipping away from me and that nothing matters: I want to upset everybodys calm and peace of mind when I meet calm and contented people. I feel I am no use to anyone unless I am outfacing the storm in wild lands. . . . I think you are a wonderful girl and woman to have stood my erratic ways all these years: I think you understand me more than all the people I know put together.'

All men live their lives in a spirit of search, some more actively, some more consciously than others. Shackleton's search was passionate and manifold. Sometimes it was for domestic felicity, sometimes for a point on the globe, sometimes for a true understanding of himself. He was not satisfied with his life. 'I *will* make good' is a phrase which he repeated in his letters towards the end of his life.

His dissatisfaction was very obvious during his life time and perhaps became more obvious to people after his death. One reviewer of Mill's Life,[27] for instance, felt it to be a tragedy 'that he was dissatisfied with his own accomplishments, that he laboured in a sense under unfulfilled ambitions, and that he had never shown all that was best in him to the world at large'.

But satisfaction with his life would have been, for a man like Shackleton, nothing less than a living death. It was because he did not feel he had made good, as an explorer or as a family man, that he made so strong an attack on circumstances. It was because he was never satisfied that he remained to the end of his days a man of action, a man of impulse, a man of power.

He did not, like most of us, begin to lose interest in life as he grew older. In all his forty-eight years he never grew middle-aged, although he often said he felt old. He kept the freshness of a boy in typical, often amusing ways: to the end he enjoyed practical jokes, and the warm facetious atmosphere of a ward-room. And to the end he remained young in this too, that he never stopped trying to discover the purpose of his life.

Chapter XXIII

BRITISH forces remained in North Russia until October 1919, but Shackleton resigned his commission in February of that year, judging that his particular job was finished. He believed the time had now come when he could go ahead with a plan which would at once solve his financial difficulties, provide him with an interesting sphere of action and help his country. He hoped to obtain from the White Russian government a commercial concession on a large scale, and to set up a company to develop the resources of part of North Russia. He knew at first-hand the country he wanted to work, and he had observed the conditions and circumstances of the people who lived there.

Shackleton's scheme, like most schemes which he devised, was bold and simple and had behind it the impulse of his superb confidence. How far he had already sounded his business friends we do not know, but he was sure he could find enough backers to raise a capital of from one to two million pounds sterling to float a company.

The money would be used first 'to alleviate existing hardships and in the future to develop British interests'.[1] The population in North Russia was suffering greatly as a result of war, in a land which could at no time provide its inhabitants with a good living. Shackleton's bargaining point with the Russian government, as he explained[1] to the Assistant Governor-General at Murmansk, was that he was prepared, as soon as he was granted the concession, to despatch to the area 'sufficient supplies (over and above the existing allowance), in the form of clothes, tobacco, furniture, etc., which will relieve the straitened circumstances of the population, and at the same time put a stop to the stealing of goods belonging to the Allied governments, and the selling of them at exorbitant prices'.

In return he was to be allowed to establish British interests in the area of his winter campaign. If he prospered, Britain would prosper. He therefore applied to the Russian government for a ninety-nine year lease of some land in Murmansk, including a portion of the central business section of the town, and part of the sea-front for the building of docks and warehouses. He stipulated that if the Russian government decided to develop Murmansk commercially, his company should be given the opportunity of acquiring any land released from military use. He asked for 'the right of exploring the entire area which forms part of the Alexandrovsky and Kemsky regions'. This right was to be conceded for not less than five years and, while he could not ask for a monopoly,

437

he wished to make it a condition 'that my company be allowed to occupy and secure any mineral beds discovered by it, or any known mineral beds which are not occupied at the time of my company's declaration'.

In his occasional journeys around Murmansk, in his discussions with the people he worked with, Shackleton had used his eyes and ears to good purpose. He saw the picture clearly and was able to foresee certain contingencies. He wished to secure certain rights over the local rivers and bridges, for transport, and the right to bid for the Murmansk-Sorosky railway, should the government ever decide to sell it. He wanted rights in any fishing that might be commercially useful. He insisted on the right to run ships to and from the White Sea ports. All these provisos, set out in detail in letters to the Russian and British governments, show both vision and organising ability.

The scheme owed its impetus not to a purely disinterested desire to make money for Britain, not only to a desire to make money for himself, but most of all to that desire, which was always present, to give himself the special security of a congenial occupation. He was still looking for the perfect job, which would fully employ his abundant energies, which would be regular in its payment but varied and changeable in its scope. This scheme for the development of the Murmansk area may have represented Shackleton's most serious attempt to regulate and regularise his life, and if the Russian government had not failed, it is possible that his last years might have seen the stabilising of that personality which had so far been only fitfully expressed.

Negotiations had reached an advanced stage before the victory of the Soviet forces in Russia rendered them useless. On 7 June 1919 the Brigadier-General of the General Staff at Archangel had communicated a document[2] from Shackleton to Lieutenant-General Miller, Governor-General at Murmansk:

'Please notify General Miller and M. Yermolov that I have formed the proposed company, which represents large British interests, on the lines approved by Miller. Goods and other articles of prime necessity will be dispatched in the near future, and I am coming to Murmansk, bringing with me the experts required for all the branches of the undertaking. I shall hold the post of Managing Director in Russia. The Company will operate in accordance with your wishes, and will supply articles of prime necessity at a small profit. The Company leaves me freedom of action to arrange matters in any way which shall meet with your approval, and fully recognises the necessity of submitting to military emergencies.'

Shackleton had returned to England at the end of March, and it was from England that, throughout the summer, he developed the details of his enterprise. In Murmansk it was occasionally overlooked that the scheme should be of advantage to Britain. This may be partly because it was still a diplomatic secret, and known only in a general way outside headquarters. There were men in the army in Murmansk who thought he was using his military position in time of war* for his own ends. They ignored the fact that he had done no more than formulate his plans until he had resigned his commission, and that he had obtained the approval of the army authorities in North Russia† and of the War Office at home for a scheme which might well benefit both countries.

A very familiar pattern now emerges. Here is Shackleton, optimistic, happy to be dealing in large issues, not yet ready to be precise about their financial side. Here are colleagues and acquaintances, jealous of his ideas and of his prominence, to whom his enterprise is simply a bit of adventuring. Certainly Shackleton wanted to make money: equally certainly, nobody but Shackleton had thought of making money out of the depressing, cold northern town where he saw hidden treasure and where everyone else saw darkness and discomfort. To each man what he deserves. Shackleton at this moment deserved to have his chance of success. At the same time it may be guessed that if the company had been formed he would somehow have come out of it badly, as he had come badly out of all the business enterprises he had undertaken.

There is of course more than one way of looking at Shackleton's unguarded optimism in money matters. If it involved other people in trouble, it was also one facet of a generous and aspiring nature, the kind of nature which can be worthy of intense admiration and at the same time can be, the world being as it is, extremely troublesome. Each man who was involved with Shackleton in a financial transaction necessarily judged him by that transaction: the world at large took a more general view. A reviewer of Mill's biography of Shackleton wrote,[3] 'it is a fair question whether a more prudent man would have possessed the curious and poetical courage that enabled Shackleton to make the opportunities that brought him so little material reward'.

All this time Shackleton was virtually without money of his own. Most of the outstanding debts of his last expedition had been paid: so far he had made no money out of it for himself and his family. During the summer of 1919 he lectured round Britain, earning money in a way which kept him for long periods away from his home. He was also working on the proofs of *South*, the story of the Imperial Trans-Antarctic Expedition, which was published in November and which was greeted at once with public acclaim. Book and lectures were

* The North Russian front was still involved in the contest between White Russia and the Soviet.

† General Maynard was evidently helpful, for Shackleton wrote to his wife[1] on 29 January 1919, 'What I am doing to do is a thing that if he did not trust me in he would not have cabled the W.O. as he did.'

complementary, and when Shackleton managed to get the *Endurance* film ready for exhibition, there was a large audience waiting to see it.

But the book was not profitable to Shackleton. When he had returned to England after the expedition, he had found many claims outstanding for money he had borrowed. One such claim came from the executors of a benefactor who, had he lived, would certainly have turned his loan into a gift in recognition of Shackleton's glorious failure. The executors had no choice but to ask for the return of the loan, and Shackleton hastily turned over the rights in *South* to them, so that no money from the book could ever reach his family, even when the amount of the original debt had been repaid.

The film material brought him more profit. Before he left on the expedition he had formed a company to exploit this material, the I.T.A. Film Syndicate Ltd. On 2 May 1918 the British copyright was sold[5] to Jury's Imperial Pictures Ltd.* for £5,000 plus a fifty-per-cent royalty, leaving Shackleton with rights to use still pictures for illustrating books and articles, and to use the film (which had now been put together and entitled *South*) for lecturing. The transaction was later complicated by the fact that Shackleton had assigned certain rights to lecture with the film to Ernest Joyce, who after the expedition had claimed that money was owing to him.

The exact position between Joyce and Shackleton is not clear, but Shackleton's opinion of the claim was clear enough. As he saw it, he had given the men who went with him an unique opportunity. When they returned to civilisation, he fulfilled his obligations to them as best he could and when he could. Any attempt to hurry him or to make him pay more than he thought he could afford, or (as sometimes happened) to claim more than was due, drove him to a bitter hostility. It seemed to him an act of disloyalty on the part of his comrades that they should demand more than he was prepared to give.

Those who were devoted to him preferred him to remain in their debt, or to wait until he remembered that he owed them money (when

* On 13 October 1926 Jury's Imperial Pictures Ltd, which had gone into voluntary liquidation, signed over all rights[5] in the *Endurance* material to Sir William Jury, in consideration of the sum of £40. In 1932 Jury also acquired the film material of Shackleton's last expedition (see page 459 et seq.). In the following year the W. and F. Film Service (afterwards Gaumont-British) arranged with Jury[5] that they should make a first feature film with added sound, a composite of the *Endurance* material and some material from the *Quest*. Frank Worsley was engaged to deliver a lecture to be used in the sound track. This film, entitled *Endurance*, was shown to the public early in 1933. On 10 January 1955 negotiations were completed[5] by which the British Film Institute acquired all the film material which Jury had left in the hands of his executors, including a number of slides. This material comprises *South* (the original *Endurance* film), *Gateway to the South* (material from the *Quest*) and *Endurance* (the composite film mentioned above).

he was quite likely to pay them double). To those who demanded what they believed to be their rights (whether they were justified or not), he often acted impetuously in presenting them with assignments of money in excess of what was due to them; this could, and sometimes did, make an unfortunate impression.

At this time, more than ever, it was essential for Shackleton to be sensible, for he needed money for his family. He was empowered to lecture with the *Endurance* film for his own profit, and late in December he began a season at the Philharmonic Hall in Great Portland Street. The film had already been shown in the Albert Hall on 19 December in aid of the Middlesex Hospital; here a large audience was able to inspect the battered boat, the *James Caird*, outside.*

Shackleton lectured at the Philharmonic twice a day, six days a week, for five months. The material for the lecture was superb and the audiences were responsive, but Shackleton seems to have been oppressed by fatigue and distress. It upset him to recall the events of that harrowing time; he feared the access of emotion and feared also that he might become mechanical. Many of those who heard him, especially young people, were inspired to search further in the world for better things: those who knew him felt that he was tired and that his lectures were less spontaneous than they had been in the past.

It was a relief to him when the lectures finished, in May 1920. During the season he had been escaping from the present by planning action for the future. Late in 1919 he talked to Macklin in London about a new venture in the Arctic. Here a great area challenged him, what was then the last completely unknown part of the Arctic, the Beaufort Sea. Shackleton told his old comrade that he intended to operate in the Zone of Inaccessibility but that he might also try to reach the North Pole.

As in 1913, so now, Shackleton was able to forget the obverse side of exploring. He had not even finished the task of paying for his previous expedition, but the captivating prospect of a new plan, with the romantic appeal of an unknown sea, was enough to make him forget the fatigue and distaste of repeated public appearances.

---

* The *James Caird* was subsequently on view in the Middlesex Hospital Garden for some days, and the sixpences went to the hospital's appeal fund. At some time this same year the boat was also on view at Selfridges. Shackleton's sister, Miss Eleanor Shackleton, remembers[4] being told by the commissionaire that an elderly man, insisting on being allowed to get into the boat, explained that he greatly admired Shackleton, to whose parents he had been supplying fish for 28 years: he had come up from Sydenham to see the boat. When Shackleton's affairs were wound up after his death the *James Caird* became the property of the late John Quiller Rowett, and was taken to his house in Sussex. On 11 April 1924 he presented it to Dulwich College (his and Shackleton's old school), where it is now,

At the end of February 1920 he wrote to the Royal Geographical Society about his Arctic plan and received a general approval of it, the Council advising[6] that he should consult the Canadian Government at once. By the summer Shackleton was able to say that the Government was interested in the plan, though no definite promises had been made. In the spring he also conferred with the explorer Stefansson, who had wide experience of the Arctic, and received cordial offers of help from him.[7] The *Daily Mail* and the *Times* agreed to enter into an arrangement for handling his news before and after the expedition. He felt justified in launching into a new sphere.

All these offers of help were enumerated in a printed prospectus similar to his previous proposals, which he drew up,[8] perhaps in the late summer or autumn of 1920, to attract the attention of possible backers. Mindful of the dangers of the piecemeal method of collecting money, he hoped to find one or two men who would put up all the money he needed and save him from nagging anxiety.

His plan was taking a familiar shape. There was one main object, clear-cut and bearing the hall-mark of a romantic mind; there were subsidiary objects logically derived from this. The Beaufort Sea, west of the Canadian Arctic Archipelago, had seen the crushing of many vessels which had tried to penetrate its ice-guarded stretches. Shackleton proposed[8] to leave his ship in winter quarters at the last point of land (on Parry Island) and to launch out with a sledge party 'to proceed over the ocean ice to the heart of the sea'. Records of tides and currents in this area of sea ice, compiled by former expeditions, convinced him (wrongly) 'that the centre of this area consists of a land mass larger than the whole of the United Kingdom or else a cluster of islands of the same dimensions'. As he pointed out, the discovery of such a land mass would be of 'the greatest scientific interest to the World, apart from the possible economic value'. The rainbow Shackleton saw in his mind's eye always had a crock of gold at the end of it.

He believed that two sciences in particular could be greatly advanced in this area—magnetism and anthropology. There was evidence, he said, that there might be Eskimo tribes hitherto unknown, which could be studied. He proposed to carry experts to study every other scientific problem that might present itself.

About the North Pole he wrote more guardedly. He believed (again wrongly) that there might be land in its vicinity, and he hoped to take over the plan which Amundsen had temporarily abandoned, and try to clear up once and for all the great Cook-Peary controversy about the Pole of Inaccessibility.

'I feel absolutely certain', he wrote in his prospectus, 'as far as energy and ability on the part of my staff and myself count for anything that we could, by leaving our ship, carry out the programme I propose in a speedy and efficient manner and set at rest once and for all the mystery of the North Pole and fill in this great blank now called the Beaufort Sea.'

In his search for a backer he was more fortunate in 1920 than he had been in 1907 or in 1912. The prospectus had not been long printed when he chanced to meet his old school-friend John Quiller Rowett, whom he had not seen since he had borrowed his office to work on early plans for the Imperial Trans-Antarctic Expedition. Rowett was interested in his plans and agreed, as Sir James Caird had done, to advance Shackleton a sum substantial enough to form a nucleus and to enable him to begin making plans in earnest.

Shackleton now approached the British Government. At the end of the year he wrote[9] to the Admiralty asking whether the ship he chose for his expedition could be fitted out and conditioned in a naval dockyard. He had already submitted his plans to the Treasury and said that he had reason to believe that the Canadian Government, the Hudson Bay Company, the Canadian Pacific Railway and many private individuals would help him. He estimated the probable cost of his expedition at the moderate sum of £50,000, and was able to state that £20,000 was already guaranteed privately. He had in mind a two-masted schooner, the *Goshawk*, which was then available; he estimated that she could be reconstructed for £9,800. Later he gave a lower estimate of £5,000 based on another vessel. The Admiralty was unable to accede to his request for help with his expedition ship, but Mr. Frederick Becker came forward with an offer of help, and it was announced at the end of January 1921 that Shackleton, who had visited Norway earlier that month, had bought a ship from the Norwegian Whaling Fleet, the *Foca I*, a wooden vessel of 204 tons, built in 1917, fitted with an auxiliary motor and with what reports described as 'a large and spacious deck'.

The *Times* of 11 February carried details of Shackleton's plans. The expedition, which was expected to last for two years, would begin in May or June, when Shackleton would take out a dozen men ('chiefly those who accompanied him on former expeditions') to Hudson Bay. Here 150 huskies would be taken on board and the expedition would proceed by way of Baffin Bay, through Lancaster Sound to Axel Heiberg Island, and explore the islands westward to Parry Island and the Beaufort Sea. It was reported that Shackleton hoped to obtain much of his equipment from the war surplus of the North Russian campaign.

The news story ended, 'Sir Ernest Shackleton has told an acquaintance in Christiania [presumably in the first half of January] that he had given up the idea of exploring the South Polar regions, and in future will devote himself to the Arctic'. This was still so in

March, when Shackleton returned from Canada assured of support from the Government.

He began in earnest to study the ground for his new expedition. Macklin, who had agreed to join him at the very outset of his planning, was now required to go through books, maps and papers, selecting useful information, from which Shackleton took what he wanted to prepare his ground. He studied thoroughly the history of earlier sledge parties, noted weather conditions and ice movements, and worked out what he thought he would need in the way of equipment.

Now for the first time he wrote[10] to Dr. Mill, asking for his advice on this new idea and suggesting he should draw up a scientific programme for him in return for a fee. He was able to give Mill details of his ship, which had now been renamed the *Quest*, on his wife's suggestion, and he told Mill, too, that he would take 'a party of 15 all told, no sailors or firemen, the staff to work the ship'.

While Mill was working on the Beaufort Sea plan Shackleton visited Canada again, returning on 19 April. On 28 April Macklin started across the Atlantic, also for Canada, to collect the hundred sledge dogs for which Shackleton had been negotiating. It was on 12 May that Macklin (in Winnipeg) heard from the editor of a Montreal paper that the Canadian Government had changed and with it the policy on the matter of expeditions. Shortly afterwards he received a cable[11] from Shackleton announcing a drastic change of plan. 'Government postpones their project until next year. return at once. quest will carry out Antarctic coast survey and Southern islands exploration. elected Royal Yacht Squadron.* should you require funds call on Lee Keedick four three seven Fifth Avenue New York. Shackleton.'

The last sentence was sanguine. Lee Keedick proved to be away, and the second man Shackleton had advised Macklin to approach put him through a complicated test before he was satisfied of his identity. Macklin had just satisfactorily arranged about the money he needed when he received 400 dollars cabled from Shackleton, who asked if he needed any more. Dr. Macklin comments,[12] 'The only money I had when I set off for Canada was my own, and then he threw it at me in bucket loads. He certainly had a most unbusiness-like mind.'

A change of government in Canada, marked by a strict economy drive, had put an end to Shackleton's hopes in the immediate present of exploring the Beaufort Sea. He was not prepared to wait and try his luck with the new Government in the following year. He was now in a spiral of action and there was no question of his getting out of it. The

---

* Shackleton was elected a member of the Royal Yacht Squadron on 12 May 1921. He was proposed by the then Vice-Commodore, Sir Richard Williams-Bulkeley, Bt., R.N.R., C.B., and seconded by Major Philip Hunloke, C.V.O.

ship must be used, the men standing by must be given the work for which they had been engaged, the stores already accumulating must not be wasted. Above all, the impulse to search and find could not be checked. Shackleton had planned one more move out of the humdrum, frustrating, bewildering world and he could not forgo it now. The *Quest* must sail.

Chapter XXIV

SHACKLETON'S alternative programme had no one striking object like the discovery of the South Pole or the crossing of the Antarctic continent. It was a diffuse programme and far too comprehensive for one small body of men to tackle in two years. It almost seemed as though he had gathered under headings every idea he had ever had about the Antarctic. At the same time, the plan had a spaciousness that appealed to the public. Early in 1920 Shackleton was written up[1] as the World Celebrity of the Week in a daily paper: the eulogistic summary of his aims and character ended: 'Though his age is forty-six his friends declare that only now is he beginning life. What will he do next? Put a girdle round the earth from Pole to Pole.' If the circumnavigation Shackleton now proposed had not quite this extent, it was ambitious enough.

At some date* Shackleton had drawn up a printed prospectus[2] for what he called an oceanographic and sub-antarctic-expedition. The prospectus was designed to attract the attention of a backer, who, according to Shackleton's estimate, would have to find about £100,000 as a 'capital expenditure without looking for any return'. The scheme, in fact, was larger in scope than the scheme for exploring the Beaufort Sea. The backer, in return for carrying the show financially, would be invited to lend his name to it. It was only right, Shackleton wrote, 'that a man who is public-spirited enough to advance the prestige of our country should allow his name to be intimately associated with the

---

* This prospectus, like all his others, is undated, and it is difficult to assign a date to it. Internal evidence suggests that it might have been drawn up early in 1920, before Shackleton became completely absorbed in the Arctic plan. The fact that it is designed to attract a backer suggests that it was drawn up before Rowett made his first offer of help in the summer of 1920. The mention of the *Research* as a name for the ship suggests a date before the naming of the *Quest* (which was in March 1921). Mill, in his biography of Shackleton, says[27] that in March 1920 Shackleton was contemplating two schemes, Arctic and Antarctic, and gives details of the schemes now under discussion.

However, this is not consistent with the letter which Shackleton wrote[28] to Mill on 24 June 1921, in which he announces 'a surprise' and tells his friend about the sub-antarctic plan quite as though Mill had never heard of it before. Dr. Macklin remembers[29] hearing Shackleton and Mill discussing the plan at this time as though it was a completely new idea: it was obvious from their conversation that there had been no detailed planning as there had been for the northern venture.

The date of the prospectus, which is in itself extremely interesting, must therefore be left in doubt.

object he finances; not so much for the present time but because of the
historical value in future days'.

He was also offered more substantial inducements. Shackleton
regarded the sub-antarctic regions as most promising from the economic
point of view. He suggested that reports of wolfram (natural ferrous
tungstate) and tungsten in that area ought to be investigated, that there
might be valuable deposits of guano to be exploited, that there were
possibilities in phosphates, coal, oil, nickel, pearl fisheries, whaling
and sealing. He believed that there were opportunities for trade with
some of the South Pacific islands, as well as considerable scope for
ethnological research; and he believed a useful preliminary survey
could be made of native customs, physiology and physiognomy, and
medical practice.

At this stage of his planning he thought of calling his ship the
Research. There were many branches of science which he wished to
represent. Geographical research came first. He proposed to comb the
South Atlantic waters for doubtful or badly located islands and reefs,
in particular for Dougherty Island and the Haymet Rocks and the
lost island of Tunaki, which he thought he might locate in a shoal some
200 miles south-east of Rarotonga. 'If the shoal turns out to be the lost
island', he wrote, 'it would be one of the most interesting geographical
and geological discoveries of modern days.'

There was also much to be done in mapping the coastline of the
Antarctic continent, particularly Enderby Land. He hoped in two
summer seasons to fill in 2,000 miles of the coast, and this in itself was
a big enough programme.

He wanted, too, to improve existing charts by observations in all
quarters: to investigate possible sites for wireless and meteorological
stations, and for coaling and whaling plants: to study glaciation and
volcanic activity: and to take extensive meteorological observations,
which might ultimately be of great value to shipping and to farming in
the Southern Hemisphere. While it was at sea, his ship would also be
available for marine biological dredging, the taking of salinities, the
observations of currents and sea temperatures, and would make him
free to extend the scope of his study of any one particular island.

His prospectus makes it clear that he had given much thought to the
question of technique. His value as an innovator was seen most plainly
in a section of his prospectus headed 'Aerial Work'. He spoke mainly
of the potential value of aeroplanes in spotting islands and reefs and
acting as a pathfinder, but he evidently regarded this new form of
transport as having infinite possibilities.* At some date after the printing
of his prospectus he evidently submitted it to the Air Ministry, for a

* An article or memorandum exists among Shackleton's papers which would
seem to date from this time, in which he discusses the possibility of flying to

questionnaire is in existence[3] in which the Ministry instructs him to report on all the islands he visits, on their geological and meteorological conditions, on possible sites for aerodromes, seaplane stations or airship mooring-masts, on existing wireless stations and lighthouses, and on anything else which might be relevant to the development of air power.

As will be seen (p. 452), Shackleton took an aeroplane on the *Quest*. In his last message before he left England he referred[4] to it as 'a pioneer ship, laying the lines for the future development of aerial services'. As things turned out (p. 452, n.), the honour of pioneering in this field fell instead to one of the men who accompanied him and whose lifelong desire to explore received new and strong encouragement from Shackleton.

It is possible that the terms of Shackleton's prospectus, so adventurous and wide, might have frightened a great number of rich men who preferred their risks to be less spectacular : but there was much to appeal to a man of Shackleton's own spirit. Shackleton made it clear that he wanted his backer to accept results without interference, except that he could appoint his own auditor for accounts. The concluding paragraphs made it clear that he was to run the expedition 'as a lone hand with an absolute veto on everything concerned with it, but with a definite contract as to my obligations. I am opposed as a matter of principle root and branch, with the interference of Committees ; and though at a later stage, I think it might be advisable to have an advisory committee of the Royal Society and of the Royal Geographical Society, the function of this advisory body must be purely advisory'.

Rowett had been deeply interested in the Arctic scheme and had been disappointed when it had to be given up : but when Shackleton put forward his Antarctic plan, his friend changed his earlier offer in a spectacular fashion by offering to take over the whole of the remaining financial responsibility for the expedition. He would treat this as an investment, and Shackleton bound himself to pay off a certain proportion of the money after his return, from the proceeds of a book, lecturing and film material.

Rowett's fine gesture freed Shackleton at once from the shackles of financial anxiety and of personal argument ; he offered Shackleton help, counsel and a listening ear, but no interference.

Thus Shackleton was able to recover quickly from his disappointment over the Beaufort Sea plan. He did not have to lose momentum but could go straight on with arrangements for the new expedition. He had

the South Pole, and the necessity for laying depôts along the route. The article ends with a characteristic remark : 'The man is short-sighted indeed who predicts that anything is unattainable because at the present moment it is impracticable.'

his ship, he had his money, and a wise and experienced geographer was advising him.

It was in June that Shackleton asked Mill to draw up a scheme for exploring the Enderby Quadrant, having paid him £100 for the details he had supplied about the Beaufort Sea. Mill must have felt, as many people did, that Shackleton was trying to do too much. Indeed, in a letter which he sent to him after he had sailed on his venture, he advised him[5] to 'let the oceanic islands take care of themselves till you get back from the ice'. He could not but admire Shackleton's breadth of vision, but he felt it to be in this instance too broad.

He felt, too, that Shackleton was asking too much of his ship. When he first saw the *Quest* he had been disappointed by her small size, and disquieted[6] by the exuberance with which Shackleton was 'cramming her with new devices and elaborate gear that (I felt) could not be worked effectively in the confined space of the tiny craft'.

If it were possible to draw a distinct dividing line between what has been called the Heroic Age of Antarctic exploration and the Mechanical Age, the Shackleton-Rowett expedition might make as good a point as any at which to draw such a line. Always interested in mechanical inventions, Shackleton took full advantage of his subsidy to equip not only his expedition but also his ship with the most up-to-date appliances. The crow's-nest was electrically heated, and there were heated overalls for the look-out: the newest wireless installations were provided: he obtained one of the only three examples made at that time of the Odograph, an electrically-worked recording instrument which could automatically trace the ship's route and record her speed on a chart.

Newspaper men, who had been taking an active interest in Shackleton since he announced his new expedition at the end of June, were greatly impressed by his mechanical aids. One of them described,[7] under the heading 'Shackleton's Box of Tricks', how 'a journalist with an engineering mind said, with ecstasy in both eyes and his ears dithering with excitement as he roamed her deck, "Gadgets! Gadgets! Gadgets everywhere! I could stay here for weeks!"' It was this kind of publicity, and the many articles stressing too unctuously the romantic personality of the Boss, which made some of Shackleton's friends feel the expedition was less serious than his others. But Shackleton could not afford to neglect his public, which would help him to earn money to pay back his supporters. As things turned out he was never able to prove that each of his elaborate preparations was justified.

He was, in fact, as well-off for publicity now as he was for funds. The months of preparation in the late summer and autumn were signalised by a persistent succession of news stories; the public wanted to know all about Shackleton and in particular his reasons for being an explorer.

29

His answer could have been provided readily by anyone who knew him. If he was enjoying the modern machinery and the prospects of economic advantage, he was enjoying most of all the prospect of an adventure. The *Daily Graphic* reported[8] him as saying, 'Why do I do these things? . . . I go exploring because I like it and because it's my job. One goes once, and then one gets the fever and can't stop going. So I return to the wild again and again, until, I suppose, in the end the wild will win. There is the fascination of striving after the almost impossible —of attempting something hard to accomplish'; and on another occasion he said[9] that in his case 'and it is the same with most of the men with whom I have been in contact during the last twenty years in the work of exploration—the adventure is the main-spring of the effort, and the fact that it is adventure appeals not only to those who go but also to those who stay behind'.

Certainly he was justified in speaking for his men on this point. Many of his old comrades saw behind the diffuse programme the prospect of a true quest, and arranged their lives so that they could go with him. Frank Worsley, for instance, who had something of Shackleton's uneasiness in civilisation, had held himself free as soon as he had heard of the proposed expedition. Wild and McIlroy, who had gone cotton-planting in Africa after their period in Spitsbergen (p. 430), answered a cable from Shackleton by taking the next convenient ship for England. Wild was to go as First Officer, with Worsley as Captain and Lieutenant-Commander D. G. Jeffrey, R.N.R. (who had been prevented by the war from going south on the *Endurance*) as navigating officer.

Dr. McIlroy planned at first to go only as far as Madeira with the *Quest*, but once he was on the ship the adventure claimed him completely. Macklin, too, was immediately interested when Shackleton told him he was going on a new expedition, and when the invitation was repeated in a more definite form, in March 1920, he agreed to help with preparations.[10] The collapse of the Canadian plan was a blow to him, but he decided to carry on with the new programme, and was put in charge of stores and general equipment.

Hussey had been in close touch with Shackleton since the Spitsbergen expedition and had been working for him for a time on the proofs of *South*. He had become a medical student after the war, and had not qualified at the time when Shackleton was planning his new Antarctic expedition, but he put the case to the authorities at King's and was given leave of absence.

There were others who wanted to repeat the experience of being led by Shackleton. Green, the cook, had never lost his ambition to go again. He remembers[11] a day in 1915, when the company had left the *Endurance* and were camped on the ice, and he was cooking on his improvised stove, snow and ice melting all round him and a high wind bringing tears to his eyes. 'Well, the Boss turned up, and asked me how I was getting on. "All right," I said. He said, "What are you going to do with all the money when you get home?" I said, "I'm coming on another expedition with you if I can." He turned to Worsley and said, "Would you believe it!"' Green's ambition, when he heard of the Arctic plan, was to be the only cook who had been across both the Arctic and Antarctic Circles; when Shackleton invited him to go he accepted at once, and needed no persuasion to stay with the expedition as it was reconstituted.

Another *Endurance* man, Walter How,[12] was in a Merchant Service job ashore when he went down to see the *Quest* in St. Catherine's Dock one afternoon. Wild and Worsley suggested that he should sign on and he enthusiastically agreed; had it not been for his father's death, which occurred not long before the *Quest* sailed from Plymouth, he would undoubtedly have gone with her.*

The London docks lost another workman to the *Quest*. James Dell, who had been in hospital when the *Endurance* left England, took advantage of a happy accident to join her successor. He was held up in his work by a coal strike and went round to see Shackleton's new ship. There he ran into the Boss and talked to him about his job. 'He said, "You'd better come away with us. I want a wireless operator." I said, "I'm not a wireless operator. I could look after your business for you but I'm no operator." He said, "That's all right" and he turned round to old Frank and he said, "You put Jimmy right and get him signed on." It was all done within a few hours.'[13] In exactly the same way Shackleton caught McLeod (who had been on the *Endurance*), out of his ordinary life. He went to see the *Quest* out of curiosity, having a perfectly good job at the time, and paid a longer visit than he had expected; for he sent for his luggage and signed on as a stoker.

It was a good day for Shackleton when he took two such experienced sailors as Dell and McLeod with him. He had held to his resolve not to take any professional sailors on his new expedition, not wanting to take the responsibility for men whose reactions he could not easily predict. He felt that for this expedition a small company of officers and specialists would be easier to handle and would settle down harmoniously together. But although the scientists willingly bent themselves to ships' chores, as Shackleton's men had always done, they were able to do more of their own work, and incidentally to learn their second job more easily and thoroughly, because of the old hands.†

---

* He recalls that Shackleton was very helpful to him in his time of trouble and insisted on making sure he was all right for money before he left the ship.

† On 1 January Shackleton entered an extra clause in Dell's agreement,[30] stating that he was raising his salary 'in view of the efficiency of the member and the growing importance of his work'.

Shackleton had arranged that Hussey (with McIlroy to help so long as he was with the ship) should manage the meteorological work of the expedition. As biologist he appointed Hubert Wilkins, an experienced naturalist and collector who had been on Stefansson's expedition to the Canadian Arctic between 1913 and 1917. He had met Shackleton in 1912 and had talked to him then of his wish to do polar work. In 1921 he was in New York, waiting to start on an Antarctic expedition of his own; this was to be a pioneering venture in flying, and he had two German planes ready for his use. Shackleton invited him to join the *Quest* and offered him a British plane to fly. He also indicated that he would accept him 'as an apprentice in the leadership of expeditions because he felt the Quest Expedition would be his last and he would like someone else prepared to carry on with the work in the Antarctic'.[14]*

As pilot, Shackleton engaged Roderick Carr, a New Zealander in the Royal Air Force. Carr had come in contact with Shackleton in North Russia, where, as a Major, he was flying the only fighter in the British squadron. He had subsequently become chief of the Lithuanian Air Staff and was planning to leave this post and go into business when he was invited by Shackleton to go to the Antarctic. Carr knew the staff of A. V. Roe and Company, and he and Wilkins were able to work with Hawker's chief designer on a modified single-seater Fairey-type monoplane. An 80-h.p. Le Rhône engine was put in, floats and a second seat were added, and the machine was equipped for photography and for navigation over ice. Like most of the men who worked with Shackleton, Carr was struck by the freedom he was given to develop his own ideas in his own particular sphere.[15]†

The geologist for the expedition was engaged before the *Quest* became an Antarctic vessel. G. Vibert Douglas was a graduate of McGill University at the time when Shackleton was in Canada, early in 1921. In the course of a lecture there Shackleton said he wanted men to go north with him; Douglas was introduced to him by his urgent wish, looked over, asked if he was fit, and sent to Alfred Cook, Shackleton's secretary, to make arrangements for joining Shackleton's staff.

When the Canadian expedition was cancelled, Douglas took a geological job in Alberta, and it was while he was in Edmonton that he had a cable from Shackleton inviting him to go to the Antarctic. He sailed for England at once, and like Wilkins, was told to make his own

---

* After the *Quest* expedition Wilkins continued to develop a distinguished career in the world of polar exploration. In 1928 and 1929 he made, with Carl Ben Eilson, the first flights over the Antarctic, surveying part of Graham Land from the air.

† The aeroplane was never used during the expedition, since certain parts had been sent on to Cape Town and the ship was unable to collect them. Carr therefore took on part of the meteorological work.

arrangements for his work. Shackleton particularly requested him to interview various people who might be interested in guano, for he had hopes of pursuing Sir John Murray's exploitation of this commodity during the *Challenger* voyage.[16]*

The roll of the expedition was completed with the engagement of Kerr, who had been Second Engineer on the *Endurance* and who now became Chief Engineer of the *Quest*: of C. R. Smith as second engineer and telegraphist and H. Watts as wireless operator; of a Norwegian, Eriksen, as harpoon expert; and of Bee Mason as photographer. Shackleton also included his friend Gerald Lysaght, an ardent and skilled amateur yachtsman who signed on as helmsman for part of the outward journey.

The two youngest members to be appointed were in a sense the most important. At an early stage of his preparations Shackleton had hit on the idea of taking a Boy Scout to the Antarctic. The idea was set in motion by the *Daily Mail*, which paper had acquired first rights in the news of the expedition, and was turned into a publicity stunt. It is easy to exaggerate this aspect of the plan, however. Shackleton and his wife had both followed the progress of the Scout and Guide movement keenly and approved of its aims, both practical and idealistic.† Mrs.

* Douglas did in fact send samples of guano from Nightingale Island to Rowett and he had them examined. The report stated that the nitrates had been washed out and that the guano was not suitable for exploiting.

† It was partly at his wife's instigation that Shackleton decided to take a Scout on the *Quest*. Lady Shackleton had been working for the Guide movement since 1917, when Baden-Powell himself invited her to take over the Eastbourne District as District Commissioner. In four years she had increased the Guide Companies from 4 to 24, and the District was promoted to the status of a Division, with Lady Shackleton still as its head. When she resigned in 1927 the Division had grown conspicuously once more, and warm tributes were paid to her enthusiasm and efficiency, and, still more, to the friendly and sympathetic way she spoke, whether privately or from the lecture-platform.

Besides working for the Guides, Lady Shackleton took a deep interest in the many Scout companies which were named after her husband. There was the 9th South West Leeds (Shackleton) Group, formed by Rev. H. A. Gates in 1923 and still flourishing. There were the troops bearing Shackleton's name which Mr. Alfred Berry formed in New Zealand, from 1922 up to the present time, in and around Auckland. Lady Shackleton was patron of the Mount Eden company, and it was at her suggestion that they adopted the Shackleton family motto, Fortitudine Vincimus; after her death, her daughter, Miss Cecily Shackleton, continued to act as patron to Mr. Berry's troops at St. Helier's Bay, at Thames, and at New Plymouth. Mr. Berry writes,[31] 'Here we are in 1957 going strong with a full membership of 36 good boys and a waiting list, still trying to live up to the ideals Sir Ernest Shackleton set before us, and ever remembering his motto which we have used in every Group under my control for 35 years.'

The same story is told from the Shackleton Lodge in South Africa, from houses in many English schools for boys and girls, and from Barry, Glamorgan, where Mrs. Henrietta Lomas formed a Sea Ranger Company of Guides in

Rowett[17], who saw a great deal of Shackleton during the summer and
autumn of 1921, was struck by his feeling of responsibility towards the
young people of Britain. There are very many men and women living
who can trace their first unselfish impulse of patriotism to the words of
Shackleton—sometimes to his written words but far more often to
something they heard him say in a lecture, in the breezy but genuine
manner which made him so popular.

Certainly Shackleton was well aware that his decision to take a Scout
would make excellent publicity for the expedition, but this was not his
only motive. He had learned to serve his country under conditions of
hardship and hard work, starting in his youth. It would be a fine example
and encouragement to the movement if a Scout proved the value of
the precepts he had been taught in the hardest of all environments.

The *Daily Mail* advertisement for a Scout to accompany Shackleton
received something like 1,700 replies. These were sorted out and
considered by Baden Powell and the Boy Scouts' Association until a
short list of ten was reached. On the afternoon of 18 August the ten
boys were interviewed by Shackleton at the Scouts' Headquarters in
London, and on the following morning it was announced that he had
been quite unable to choose between two outstanding candidates, and
had decided to take them both. To the parents of the remaining eight
he sent a telegram—'Shackleton selecting Marr and Mooney, but
wanted to take the lot.'

Norman Mooney came from Orkney: J. W. S. Marr, a hefty
young man of 17, was a native of Aberdeen and was at this time a
biology student at the university there. He recalls[18] that in his interview
with Shackleton he was asked the inevitable question, Why do you
want to go? and gave the inevitable answer, Because I want to do
something. He remembers also being pleased to find Shackleton was
human; for when he enquired about the Royal Humane Society's
medal and the Scouts' Silver Cross, which the Scout was wearing, and
was told briefly that they were for 'pulling a girl out of the water',* he
repeated this definition with a delighted smile.

Once the two Scouts were selected, they became the target for
reporters, and they continued to receive attention from the press
intermittently through the *Quest*'s voyages and after her return.

The ship herself was on view to the public in St. Catherine's Dock
for two months before she sailed. They could not go on board

1920 with the name Quest. The log book of the company (which Mrs. Lomas
still leads) shows how closely its members followed the fortunes of Shackleton's
last expedition, and shows, too, how they, like all the other young people who
worked and learned under Shackleton's name, found inspiration in his striving
and his achievement.

* The medals commemorated the scout's prompt and brave action in an
unpleasant accident on the Banffshire coast.

because of the many expensive electrical installations and also because she was too small to accommodate anyone except those who were frantically working to get her provisioned and equipped. They could file past her, and did in great numbers, scrutinising with interest the important features which were clearly labelled for them. Shackleton followed his usual practice in putting their money towards the funds of the London Hospital and the Docks Hospital.

The *Daily Mail* meanwhile kept up a running commentary on the gifts received by the expedition. These were multifarious, and included two kittens and a young Alsatian. The newspaper also ran a competition for Scouts, for the best essay in 250 words on 'Why I should like to go with Shackleton.' There were money prizes, and the first fifty were to visit the *Quest*, being given £1 and their return tickets and left to make their journeys unaided. There were news stories and pictures about every incident of the preparations. Shackleton's romantic feelings about lost islands were translated into chatty paragraphs,* and the phrase 'gallant little *Quest*' was permanently attached to his ship. He remained patient and good-humoured with the reporters who beset him, and one in particular who visited him from the *Daily Mail* remembers his courtesy and lack of affectation, his straightforward, deliberate way of answering questions, and the fact that he never once used the word 'I'. He remembers too that Shackleton was very emphatic that this was a fight that had to be won, something big in which he was going to succeed.

The publicity Shackleton received did not entirely commend itself to the learned societies with whom his relations had always been slightly uneasy, and the Admiralty may well have also had reservations. However, the Royal Geographical Society had helped him with some of his preliminary work, and the Admiralty lent him instruments and charts, as well as supplying experts to advise over the installation of wireless sets and other special instruments. They made one condition. Shackleton was to pay the sum of £213. 7s. 6d. owing for instruments lost when the *Endurance* sank. He settled this debt, in the same way as he had settled the debt owing from the *Nimrod* just before he sailed on the *Endurance*.

The Admiralty, in fact, was concerned with much of Shackleton's programme, since it was to be predominantly oceanographical. It is true that he was planning to take sledges and sledge dogs, and that he had had sledging rations put up of a type similar to those he had taken on the *Endurance*. But sledging would form a very small part of the programme. Those who knew him well felt that this was in truth to be Shackleton's last expedition and that he was planning it to show that he was not yet an old man; yet they felt he knew that he could no longer carry out a

---

* Incidentally, in an interview with a *Times* reporter[19], Shackleton struck off an excellent definition of the fascination of island-seeking. 'There is something compact and personal about an island,' he said, 'no matter how desolate it may be.'

sustained effort as he had on the *Endurance*. When Macklin was discussing the Beaufort Sea plan with him in 1920 he felt sure that Shackleton did not intend to join in the sledging part of the expedition himself. The same subject was raised with Hussey, when Shackleton consulted him about severe pains in his feet, not long before the ship sailed. Hussey remembers[21] taking him to the chief consultant at King's, who diagnosed bad flat feet and advised that he should wear a support with his sledging boots. Shackleton remarked to Hussey, 'When we get on the ice, if my feet are bad I'll be able to get on the sledge and you can drive me along and you fellows can run alongside.' It was a joke with an undertone of seriousness in it.

This particular examination (though it was not of course an exhaustive one) showed nothing wrong with Shackleton's health. He was tired, certainly, and he had put on weight since his return from Russia. He was not in the best trim for hard physical work. But there was no obvious reason to suspect ill-health, and Shackleton would not admit any such idea. Dr. McIlroy afterwards suspected him of having had a slight heart attack while they were together on the way to Spitsbergen, but Shackleton had refused to allow him then to get out his stethoscope; and though, at his wife's request, he had visited a specialist before he sailed on the *Quest*, he had, in Dr. McIlroy's words,[20] 'examined the specialist instead of the specialist examining him!'. The pains in his shoulders and chest from which Shackleton had suffered intermittently for some time he described as rheumatism or indigestion. It was enough for him that he had to endure the feeling that he was growing old: he had no intention of allowing himself to be ill.

This was the background of the Shackleton-Rowett expedition, which one of his men described as his 'long but not entirely selfish joy-ride'. It was Shackleton's challenge to encroaching time, his last chance to make good, to show what he could do in his own environment, to lead an expedition which should be an unqualified success. It was a quest in the poetic sense, in that he was once more looking into the unknown, beyond the confines of the world he had to live in. It was his last and greatest treasure-hunt.* It was, more than all this, a fight against everything that had frustrated and trammelled him in his life.

---

* Shackleton had one concrete plan for discovering buried treasure. On his journey to the ice he planned to stop at the island of South Trinidad, off the coast of South America. Here there was said to be a vast treasure hidden by pirates, gold and silver plate taken from the great cathedrals of Spanish South America; a marked map given by the only surviving member of the pirate band to a sailing ship captain who had befriended him, early in the nineteenth century, was reputed to be still in existence. During that century there were several expeditions in search of the treasure, culminating in that of E. F. Knight on the *Alerte* in 1889–90. Knight did some extensive and well-organised digging (in vain) and afterwards wrote a book[22] about his expedition. Shackleton had a copy of this book (now in the possession of Mrs. Rowett),

Not that Shackleton stopped to analyse his motives for taking out another expedition. He was pressed for time, he was determined nothing should stand in his way, and his emotions, as always, were released in hard work. To his family the new expedition was treated as a professional matter. 'I have to keep reminding myself that he is a sailor, and this is his "job" as he calls it', his wife wrote[23] to Dame Janet Stancomb-Wills, while preparations were going on. She was glad that her husband had a programme 'so scientific and at the same time so romantic'. She knew that she must control her own feeling of dismay at losing him so soon, and she had the private satisfaction of his promise that this would really be his last expedition.

For the general public the romantic aspect of the expedition dominated. Numerous poems in the press, addressed to Shackleton or to his ship, stressed this side of it. Newspaper reports spoke of the 'search for the unknown'. According to the *Star*[24] the *Quest* was a 'casket in which is shut up the essence of England. She sails forth to take up once again on behalf of the English the gage flung down by Nature before men of daring and endurance. Proud mission! High fate, whatever it may be!' The *Observer* commented very pertinently[25] that 'The health of civilisation depends upon incessant challenge to the unknown and the undone.' The innumerable people who applied to Shackleton for a place on the expedition* were looking for a ticket to

and while he was fitting out the *Quest* he evidently read it thoroughly, for it is systematically annotated, with one symbol for details of the island itself, measurements, condition of soil, presence of rock and so on, another for details of currents, reefs and weather. Knight had planned his expedition with a mixture of practical sense and romantic optimism which was very much like the spirit of Shackleton in action, and many ideas were common to both men. For instance, Knight decided to avoid any danger of mutiny by taking, instead of a ship's crew, a band of 'gentleman adventurers' who would contribute financially to the expedition and would thus have a good reason for being loyal and energetic.

It is small wonder that Shackleton was attracted to this detailed account of a treasure hunt, and it is interesting to note that Worsley had also been fascinated by the treasure of South Trinidad from his early years in sailing ships.

* As on his previous expedition, there were some charming oddities among Shackleton's letters. Mrs. Rowett has in her possession one written in pencil and addressed to 'H.M. the King'.

Dear Sir

Will you pleas try and persuade Sir E. Shackleton the explorer to take me to the South pole with him. My parents are agreable. If I don't go my life will be wrecked. Oh please do your best. If you succeed please send word quickly. I will live in the coal place if I can only go. I am not joking when I say that.

Yours truly,

V. HAMBLING

This ingenuous letter was sent to Buckingham Palace in July, and sent on from there to Rowett, with the endorsement 'This letter has *not* been acknowledged.'

adventure, a commodity which the world was beginning to miss and to regret.

The last word was said in a leader in the *Times*[26] under the heading 'A Great Adventure':

> 'The bare catalogue of the hopes of the Shackleton-Rowett Expedition may well tempt high-spirited boys into running away to sea, and may turn old men into wistful youths. For what are scholarship examinations, or the counting-house, or even a comfortable armchair that they should not be as dust and ashes compared with the quests for petrified forests, lost islands, and submerged continents? Are not whales and fur seals, unknown birds, the mystery of the Antarctic ice, and lone rocks to serve as wireless relays, better than the dull duties of home? But SIR ERNEST has no vacancies; his old and tried companions have turned to his call. There is nothing for us but to wish him good luck and to look forward to the joy of reading his stories.'

Chapter XXV

THE *Quest* had her first farewell ceremony on 17 September, when she left London on her way to Gravesend and then to Plymouth. To Scout Marr[1] it seemed as though 'all London had conspired together to bid us a heartening farewell. Crowds and bigger crowds massed on the quays and the banks of the Thames. Both the Tower Bridge and London Bridge were packed with cheering people who clustered like flies. The bigger shipping in the river roared welcome and farewell to the little *Quest*—every siren was bellowing at its fullest blast, and our ineffective whistle was hard-set to make even a decent showing in reply.'

Shackleton left the ship at Gravesend, for there was still outstanding business to attend to. On 23 September he returned to her in Plymouth harbour.

The last evening was a cheerful one. Rowett gave a dinner for the expedition; there was a reunion of Scouts to do honour to the youngest members. Shackleton had sent off a last message to the public who were watching him so closely; this was reproduced in holograph in the centre of the *Daily Mail*'s account[2] of his sailing on the following day:

'The lines are now cast off, and over the horizon lies the goal of our endeavour. As our bows point south we send farewell to our island home, secure in the belief that we will be followed with true interest, and conscious that the responsibility of making good rests with us under the guidance of Providence.'

Conventional and correct as this message is, it expressed as much Shackleton's own feelings as the feelings which he well knew were expected of him. He was sailing in a mood of high hopes, in a mood of determination to make good, and his sense of occasion led him to express his feelings in resounding words. Equally, he enjoyed the ceremony of leavetaking, over which the spirit of Drake presided, the spirit which the Mayor of Plymouth invoked in his speech. Indeed, many who were present to see the *Quest* sail compared Shackleton with that most impressive of Elizabethans.

Shackleton's own description[3] of the departure on 24 September is very characteristic of him, a long passage mingling poetic musing and an effortless, simple account of fact:

'At last we are off. The last of the cheering crowded boats have turned the syrens of shore and sea are still and in the calm hazy gathering dusk on a glassy sea we move on the long Quest. Providence is with us even now: At this time of Equinoctial gales not a catspaw of wind is apparent: I turn from the glooming mystic immensity of the sea and looking at the decks of the Quest am roused from dreams of what may be in the future to the needs of the moment for in no way are we shipshape or fitted to ignore even the mildest storm: Deep in the water decks littered with stores our very lifeboats receptacles for sliced bacon green vegetables for sea stock: steel ropes and hempen brothers jostle each other: mysterious gadgets connected with the wireless on which the Admiralty officials were working up to the sailing hour are scattered about; but our 21 willing hands will soon snug her down.'

After this set-piece, his diary turns to a more relaxed reporting of daily events. For the first three or four days there is a note of contentment in the entries which is very different from the youthful egotism of the *Discovery* diary or the clipped, factual reports from the *Nimrod* and the *Endurance*. It is the diary of a man at ease with himself and with his environment. Crowded into Wild's cabin (for Gerald Lysaght had his own), watching the men to see how they would settle down, not yet rested after the three months of hurried preparation, Shackleton was still able to be easy and happy in the one rôle that really suited him—the rôle of the Boss, the man who liked to feel that people relied on him, who liked to plan for them, to watch their well-being and their response to him.

On shore, Shackleton's strong character had sometimes led him off his proper path in his search for power and fulfilment. At sea, he did not think about his power, he exercised it and enjoyed it, just as he enjoyed the sunshine and the jokes of Green the cook and the feel of his ship rolling along 'like an old time ship' and the ludicrous grimy faces of 'a gang of the boys' with whom he was photographed after they had been trimming coal.

It was 'a black and dusty job', he wrote in his diary,[3] 'but they were quite happy'. Nearly all his men felt that the *Quest* was a happy ship. As for Shackleton, his happiness was as undeniable as it was brief. On 27 September he wrote: 'How far away already we seem (to) have (left) ordinary life. I stopped the wireless operator from taking in the news last night it is of no importance to us now in a little world of our own.'

Yet on this same day a warning note had been sounded. 'The "Quest" does not steam very fast 5½ being our best so far' he had written. She had been reported as capable of eight knots. This difference in speed forced him to reconsider his plans. He had also to take into account the date of their sailing, which had been later than he had planned, since a strike at Thorneycroft's had held up work on the ship's engine.

He had intended to visit most of the main islands in the South Atlantic, including Gough and Tristan da Cunha, on the outward journey, and then to proceed to Cape Town, where he would collect the equipment he had sent there to save space on the *Quest*. From Cape Town he intended to visit Marion, Crozet and Heard Islands and then enter the ice, exploring the coast of Enderby Land and trying to link it with Coats Land, using the aeroplane for reconnaissance. When the summer was over he would visit South Georgia, refit at Cape Town and then cruise among the islands of the South Pacific.

This plan now had to be revised in the light of the new situation, which he described clearly in an entry in his diary on 28 September.[3]

'The ship is more than lively and makes but little way she evidently must be treated as a five knot vessel dependent mainly on fair winds and all this is giving me much food for thought. for I am tied to time for the ice: I was relieved that she made fairly good weathers [*sic*] of it but I can see that our decks need to be absolutely clear when we are in the roaring forties Her foremast also gives me anxiety: she is not to [*sic*] well stayed and I think that the topsail yard is a bit too much: The main thing is that I may have to curtail our island programme in order to get to the Cape in time: Everyone is cheerful which is a blessing all singing and enjoying themselves though pretty well wet: several are a bit sick ... I can see also that we must be cut down in crew to the absolutely efficient and only needful for the Southern voyage: Douglas is now stoking and doing well. It will of course take time to square things up and for everyone to find themselves: she is so small It is only by constant thought and care that the leader can lead: There is a delightful sense of freedom for [*sic*] responsibility in all others, and it should be so; These are just random thoughts: but borne in on one as it all being so different from the other strain of preparation: it is a blessing that this time I have not the financial worry or strain to add to the care of the active Expedition. Lysaght is doing very well and so is the scout Marr.'

This was to be the last entry in Shackleton's diary for some weeks. On this particular day the engine was stopped for adjustment and on 2 October it developed a bad knock. The Chief Engineer was emphatic that it must be overhauled, and Shackleton decided to turn in to Lisbon and have this done.

The *Quest* had by now shown herself to be a vessel with a character of her own. She had engaged successfully with some rough weather and Shackleton praised the way she rose to high seas like a duck bobbing about in the water. The comparison might have been used by other members of the party in a different spirit. Almost everyone suffered from sea-sickness in the Bay of Biscay, and Bee Mason and Norman Mooney became really ill.

To Marr the early days of the voyage were a nightmare. In a state of acute seasickness he forced himself through the duties of steward, stoker and A.B. in turn. He did not come across Shackleton for a day or two. Then he was sent to the bridge as a helmsman, where Shackleton advised him, 'Remember a ship is a live thing. You'll feel her and she'll be alive under you.' This was interesting but not interesting enough to stop him from feeling ill. The Scout was still not fully recovered when one day, with a gale blowing and the cook off duty, he was trying to wash up the breakfast crocks. All at once a heavy sea crashed over the ship and sent the cook's mate and all his gear on to the deck. Marr can still remember his fury:[4]

'I was a filthy mess of porridge from all these pots and pans and I lost my temper. The cook had packed up and I felt to hell with this. Although I was a Boy Scout I was no prude. I burst into a stream of the filthiest obscenity and abuse and profanity, as I was trying to collect all the pots and pans and put them back in the galley to wash and they were all scurrying up and down in the waist of the ship. I was really giving a very good exhibition, one a sailor would have been proud of if he'd been listening—and indeed somebody was, for Shackleton poked his head out of his cabin to see what the noise was and saw the Boy Scout. I remember I just glanced round, and he smiled and went back in his cabin.'

A day or two later Marr was cleaning out Shackleton's cabin when he came in and offered the boy an extra pound a week, to help him, as he said, with his fees in the Granite City. He told Marr he was shaping well, and Marr felt sure that the exhibition of his fluency had helped to form Shackleton's opinion of him. Certainly one of the most attractive aspects of this voyage was Shackleton's attentiveness to his young apprentice. He was not conspicuously sympathetic. He intended to make sure that the boy was capable of being useful and of taking hard knocks. He was watching him carefully during those first days. But it is noticeable that he was also advising him—now teaching him a certain knot, now warning him not to be too venturesome on the yards, now showing him how to fit in his work with the work of his shipmates. The Boss obviously enjoyed the moments when he tossed educational asides to the Scout in the midst of high winds and tearing seas.

Shackleton impressed Marr as a man of great wisdom and patience. On the other men he made varying impressions. Carr[5] admired the way he handled his men, and was interested by the way the scientists, under their leader's influence, settled down as ship's crew. He found Shackleton congenial and entertaining to talk to. Douglas, too,[6] enjoyed Shackleton's robust sense of humour and was struck by his evident enjoyment of being on a ship again.

To Wilkins,[7] however, Shackleton was not so much a jolly sailor as a man of formidable and conscious ambition. Shackleton seems to have spoken very freely to him of the difficulties that beset an explorer when he returns to civilisation—the obstacles to his aims, the consciousness of being in the public eye, the insidious effects of the publicity so greatly needed, the hard grind and the indignity of trying to raise funds. All these practical necessities seemed to Wilkins to have interfered with Shackleton's strong poetic urge towards the unknown. Meeting him at a time of transition between civilian and exploring life, Wilkins was struck particularly by the contrasts in his temperament, contrasts which he felt were rather uneasily resolved by Shackleton's charm and his lively response to people.

This response, of course, varied with the reaction of other people to it. There were those who felt that Shackleton used his personality to influence people and bend them to his will; and this was particularly so towards the end of his life. There were others who had no wish to investigate the sources or the reasons for the warm interest which they felt coming from the Boss. Those who knew him well liked his personal approach (anecdotes, explosions of impatience, reciting and all) and thought that it was perhaps his most important asset as a leader. For Shackleton's way with people, whether he employed them or met them socially, was always direct and warm. Sir Hubert Wilkins[7] believed that 'Shackleton, more than any other man I know, realised the influence of the spoken word'. His public relations were brilliantly managed, for the most part, because they were managed as personal matters and not in a spirit of detached calculation. He needed approval and admiration, as any man does who is in the public eye, and he felt so deeply the opinion of other people that he regarded everybody he met as potentially important to him.

His judgment of men being, then, emotional rather than reasoned, he did at times make mistakes and let himself be swayed by someone who was self-confident and showy. As a rule he looked for men who were ready to be influenced, in civilian life and for his expeditions. He regarded leadership, rightly, as a lonely and single state, and for his purpose the kind of man he wanted on an expedition was a man who had it in him to make his mark, but who had not yet made it. He wanted youth—keen, energetic, with the spark of greatness in it, with the will to endure for the sake of adventure. The teacher in him as much as the leader distinguished in men their innate capacities and sought to develop them. This was yet another reason why he was at his best when he was leading an expedition. In ordinary life he instinctively sought the company of those he could dominate, and if he found himself opposed, he attacked at once to put himself in a position of advantage. Towards the end of his life he appeared to many who met him casually to be aggressive as well as fascinating. On an expedition, when to be a leader was his duty and not his ambition, the whole man was seen in action, superbly controlled and superbly presented.

It might be said that a man becomes a leader not only because he has the strong and courageous personality of a leader but also because he needs to be one. This was entirely so with Shackleton. His virtues—his energy, his strong will, his vision, his warm heart, his simplicity of mind, his practical competence—all pointed in this direction; so did his faults—his obstinacy, his combativeness, the ruthlessness which he occasionally showed. Perhaps more than any other explorer of his time he needed the particularly delicate balance of command and dedication and emotional dependence which leadership implies.

To the men who were now getting to know Shackleton on the *Quest* his methods of running an expedition were of primary interest. To his old comrades, who were his men for life, the important thing was his comfort and well-being. James Dell, who had last served with Shackleton on the *Discovery*, found the atmosphere of the *Quest* very agreeable. He was in a position where his technical knowledge was valuable and where he could use his experience of ship work to help the expedition; and he was feeling for the first time the characteristic atmosphere of a Shackleton expedition, the feeling that every man had an equal importance in the general scheme. It was clear to Dell that Shackleton had found his proper sphere since the old days.

To Macklin and McIlroy, Shackleton's health was the chief preoccupation. They both knew he was not as fit as he should have been, and in these early days, when things began to go wrong, they were more anxious about the effect on him than on the expedition. They were watching him closely during the week they spent at Lisbon, and afterwards on the journey from there to Madeira, which they reached on 16 October. Shackleton was still jovial and apparently happy, still enjoying being with the boys. He wrote to his wife,[8] 'the old guard are going strong'. But a postscript to another letter from Lisbon was equally significant. 'Your pillow is deliciously soft but I have not had much chance of using it.' Weather conditions still continued to be bad, and the doctors were aware that Shackleton was overtaxing his strength.

At Madeira two of the company left the ship. Shackleton had decided that Bee Mason and the Scout Mooney were not well enough to proceed with the expedition, but he saw to it that no disgrace was attached to their return. His distinguished passenger, Gerald Lysaght, was persuaded to stay with the *Quest* until 28 October, when they put in to St. Vincent, in the Cape Verde islands, for coal. Here they held a farewell dinner to Lysaght reminiscent of the dinner to George Buckley on the *Nimrod* so many years before. Healths were drunk, and a poem was presented to Lysaght which Shackleton had written for the occasion.

The leader threw himself into the spirit of the party but it cannot have been easy to seem light-hearted. Even at Lisbon he had been in some anxiety about the *Quest*. A report[9] sent from there to his secretary, Alfred Cook, said that storms had strained the rigging of the *Quest*, and that the crankshaft of the engine had been bent out of alignment. He explained that he might have to give up the visits to the islands, except for landing mails at Tristan, and make straight for Cape Town in order to be in time to go into the ice, during the working summer. He did not want to try his ship too hard, though she had behaved creditably throughout the bad weather. In moments of relaxation he could let the poetry of the sea in all its moods sweep over him. In the poem he wrote as a farewell for Lysaght he predicts[3] that back in his peaceful home in Somerset he will be 'shaking the bars of the prison of comfort and ease': and four splendid lines in the same poem show how well the sea's violence fitted with his own nature. He reminds his friend:

'You have seen the force of the gale fierce as a thresher's flail
Beat the sea white.
You have watched our reeling spars sweep past the steady stars
In the storm wracked night.'

Shackleton responded ardently to the challenge of the storm; it was only because of his responsibility for the ship's company that he felt perturbed by it.

At Madeira he had to give his plans further consideration, and he wrote[8] to his wife from there that he had been anxious about the engines, which were still not as they should be: 'before I go into the ice they must be put right and if this takes too long I must do the islands only this year and early next year and hope that I may get sufficient results to justify the Expedition without having to go for any time into the ice.'

Here in this letter is the old loneliness and weariness, but this time at the outset and not at the end of an expedition. 'Darling I did so love your letters; all the little gossip is so interesting after the stress and strain of the sea: This is a lonely life after all: I said to John [Rowett] did he think it was in any way possible for Ellie and he and you to make a trip to the Cape so that I could see you if we did not go into the ice.' And the letter ends, 'I miss you more than I put into words. Your old Micky but not so bad after all and I love you.'

After St. Vincent the engines ran more smoothly for a time, but Shackleton had decided even before reaching the Cape Verdes that something drastic must be done. On 25 October Macklin wrote in his diary,[10] 'Boss came along & told us of arrangements to put into Rio de Janeiro to get the ship fitted finally for good & all. It is becoming more

30

& more apparent that the work done by the British workman at home is not the best in these times.'

Although the islands had to be given up, the ship paid a brief call at St. Paul's Rocks on the way to Rio. This visit was a godsend to the scientists, and particularly to Wilkins and Douglas, who had up to now been chiefly in demand as stokers and stevedores. When Shackleton decided to make for Rio, he had thought of sending these two men to Graham Land to prospect while the ship was laid up. Meanwhile, they were landed at St. Paul's Rocks on 8 November, with Marr and Dell to assist them, while Hussey and Carr were to do balloon and meteorological work. The boat party put in an interesting day fishing and observing the crabs, while the scientists surveyed the island as thoroughly as they could before they were recalled to the ship in the late afternoon.

The *Quest* now turned towards Rio. Calm, hot weather put everyone in a good humour, although the very restricted space on the ship made it difficult for the men to enjoy their leisure hours. Coaling at high temperatures became distressing, but Macklin commented[10] that he did not 'altogether object to a good hard day's trimming, especially as the Boss, who is very appreciative of workers, gives the rest of the day as holiday till the dog watches commence, which gives one a chance for a bit of washing, cleaning up etc.' For Macklin there was also the job of organising stores (a very considerable one when so much was stowed in the hold) and a share of the painting of the ship, which Shackleton decided to change from white and yellow to a serviceable grey and black.

It was a smart ship that approached Rio on the evening of 21 November. There was a beautiful sunset and the party sat on deck listening to Hussey's banjo while Shackleton and Macklin had a competition to guess the tunes (the other members of the party listening to them with some derision).

The next morning they steamed into the harbour where they were to stay for nearly a month, while the ship was docked for a thorough overhaul. The party was dispersed, most of the men being entertained on shore. Douglas and Wilkins went down the coast on the mail steamer *Orcoma* to Montevideo, and then sailed on the *Woodville* on 28 November for South Georgia, where they were to carry on scientific work until the *Quest* arrived there. At Rio the *Quest* was put in the hands of Messrs. Wilson. They were not only to take down the engines but also to examine and overhaul the rigging and to build additions to the deck-house so as to provide a ward-room. Wilson's chief engineer gave a report on the engines that was far from satisfactory; they would stand the work if they were run at a reasonable speed and if the strain on them was not varied. Shackleton knew that if he took the ship into the ice these conditions could not be fulfilled, but he could not face a complete reversal of his plans, or what was left of them.

He decided to make for South Georgia as soon as the ship was ready, sacrificing the equipment and stores that were waiting at Cape Town and relying on being able to get sledges, dogs and winter clothing in South Georgia. It is not hard to imagine his thoughts as he waited in Rio through the heat for his ship to be ready. As Wild said,[11] 'the Boss might well have thrown in his hand and retired from the unequal struggle. But nothing could have been more foreign to his mind—each obstacle but strengthened his resolve to carry on, and we who served with him never for one moment felt distrust or doubt that under his leadership all would go well.'

The Quest

It was not until 17 December that the *Quest* could leave Wilson's wharf, and by that time further changes had been made in the ship's company. Eriksen the harpoonist had left and three new men had been taken on. The announcement that Shackleton was looking for men had caused a stir in Rio. Among those who hopefully applied was Sir Michael Bruce, who was then working on a Latin-American newspaper there. Long afterwards he recalled[12] how he was taken on board the *Quest* for a test in seamanship (in which he was not found wanting). Unfortunately, although Shackleton wanted to take him the British Consul-General informed Shackleton that he had a war-wound pension and would not be able to go. Bruce's memory of Shackleton and his talk has never faded. 'He talked of the British character, and (how) he prayed that the spirits of Drake and Hawkins would live on through generations of British boys. He spoke so simply, so sincerely, that I felt a boy again.' He never forgot the Boss's idealistic way of talking, his companionable way with his men, and he never quite got over his disappointment at missing the chance of adventure with him.

Shackleton had made up his mind to fill the three places on the *Quest* with strong and effective workmen. The voyage had been more exacting than he had expected, and the days of severe weather had not only found out the *Quest*'s weak spots and shown her difficult to handle, but had also shown that the scientists must not give so much time to ship work if they were to do any research. In the letter he sent to Cook[9] from Lisbon he said he was hoping to get Stenhouse to meet him at Cape Town 'for I can see it will require everyone to be a sailor to handle this ship'. Accordingly, from the many men who flocked to the *Quest* to offer their services, he engaged C. S. Young, a casual, vigorous South African, and H. A. Argles, a Canadian who had been a lieutenant in the R.F.C., both as stokers.

The third man who joined, Christopher Naisbitt, was a native of Cheshire who had worked for many years in Portugal and who at the time of the *Quest*'s arrival in Rio was on a three-year contract with the New York shipping company of W. R. Grace. Naisbitt was a member of the British Club at Rio and attended the reception given to Shackleton and his comrades. On that evening he and the 'ninety-nine other Englishmen' who volunteered to join were told that the places would not be filled, but he was determined to go, and eventually persuaded the secretary of the Club to take him to Wilson's yard and introduce him to Shackleton. He remembers:[13]

'When I was introduced Shackleton cast a fleeting glance at me (I was dressed in a Palm Beach suit and wore a Panama hat) and he said to the secretary, "So this is Mr. Naisbitt". He asked if I had ever done a day's hard work in my life. I said I had served in the Navy four years and that I was fond of sport: this remark, for what it was worth, did not displease him. He asked if I realised I might have to carry meals from the galley to the forward mess, the little ship rolling and pitching in heavy seas and the decks awash most of the time. I told him I was sure I could do the job. He asked me what I was doing in Rio and I told him. Then he seemed to hesitate and endeavoured to discourage me: thinking no doubt that I was throwing away my commercial career, but he saw I was keen. He turned and said to Worsley, "What do you say?" Commander Worsley turned the scale in my favour, agreeing that a willing man was sometimes as good as one of experience.'

Shackleton offered Naisbitt a day's trial on the day the ship was moved from the harbour, and a hard day it was. At the end of it he asked Naisbitt to come back the next day with a reference. Afterwards Naisbitt learned that he had said to Green, whose assistant the new man was to be,* 'You won't see him again.' He is proud to have been the cause of what he calls 'the only mistake Shackleton ever made, as far as I know'.

As for Naisbitt, he had made no mistake, in his view, in leaving his shore job and launching himself on the sea of adventure with Shackleton. Although his acquaintance with the leader was very short, he had already been strongly impressed with him when he had met him on shore, and a day or two on the ship confirmed him in his belief that he was a remarkable man. He sums up[13] the Shackleton he knew on the *Quest* as 'talented, clear-sighted, decisive, sure of himself in everything he was doing or about to do, thoughtful for others, a good judge of what could be expected of his men and how he was to get it, a man who could look you straight in the eyes and tell you to go to hell if you stood in his path—in one word, he was formidable'.

Others who met Shackleton at this time felt also that he was a formidable person. He was less cheerful and talkative than usual.† In Rio, amid the entertainments lavished on his company, he often sat aloof and thoughtful. There were good reasons for this. First, he was worried about the ship and about the future of the expedition, upon which he had staked his reputation and his friend had staked his money and his faith. More important even than this, he must have been worried about his health.

At St. Vincent Shackleton had posted a letter to his wife[8] in which he admitted, 'I am not very well but I think in a couple of days will be my old self.' There was little in his situation to improve his health. By the time the ship reached Rio he had tried his physical as well as his emotional strength very hard. Captain Sharpus, a member of the staff of Wilson's, saw this very clearly as he worked with Shackleton, and he wrote afterwards:[14]

'Poor Sir Ernest. He had a hell of a time here. Everything in the engine-room of that ship seemed to be wrong. He smiled to everyone, and to a certain extent made light of what was the matter. But I knew he was worried almost to death. I dreaded his meeting Crashley, the ship's chief engineer,‡ or Howard our engineer, who was in charge of the repairs, for fear they'd tell him some new trouble.

I could see by his face it hurt him so. All his hopes and ambitions seemed centred in that little ship, and she seemed to let him down so

* Naisbitt signed on as Ship's Clerk, and as well as working with the cook, he did considerable clerical work for Shackleton and for the expedition as a whole.

† Mr. F. L. Horton[31], who as a young man met Shackleton in Rio (at dinner in the Leopoldina Railway Company's mess at Nictheray), remembers his fine physique, his weather-tanned features, and his quiet, reserved, apparently preoccupied manner.

‡ A mistake for Krasski, which was Kerr's nickname among his shipmates.

much that I got to hate the damned boat. I was always glad when he came away from it. Often, when we left, if we were alone, he'd sit in the launch gazing at nothing, and hardly say a word on the half-hour run from the ship to the city.'

As always, Shackleton was finding the torrid atmosphere very trying, and on the eve of departure from Rio he wrote to his wife in a weary mood[8]:

My darling This cannot be a long letter for I am just tired and hot: I wrote to you 5 days ago: I have been in a whirl and strain ever since we came in: Everything seemed to go wrong twice the engines had to be altered then I had trouble with some of the new men and I have dismissed Erikson and altogether it has been hell. now it is 110° in the shade and the blasted mosquitoes are biting me. Cook will give all the official details I only just write this to say that you must not worry about me and that my health is really all right only I am feeling the strain of the delays especially with the eyes of the world on us, I am going to take no risks in the ice so dont worry: I cannot understand only getting one letter from you I heard from Ray & Cecily such sweet letter(s) and a little letter a dear letter from Eddie. I am thankful he is all right again: I expect John is worried about the Expedition I cannot help it: I am doing my best. I could just love to be in the little house now darling but here I am away I shall be always thing [*sic*] and please God I come out of the work and can run home for even a month or two next May. Kiss the children for me: I know are thinking God keep you

Your loving

"MICKY"

P.S. Darling I am a little tired but all right you seem always young:
P.P.S. You are rather wonderful.

The bold front he put on things probably did not deceive his wife, who could read his state more clearly in the letter than he intended. To his friend Janet Stancomb-Wills he wrote somewhat more openly about his troubles[15]:

My Dear Dame Janet

It has been day and night work with me since I came: things were terribly wrong with the ship as Cook can show you when you get from him the statement. I have been working in the sweltering heat without rest and in daily anxiety but now all is done: and now we make another start: You(r) help (h)as been as usual tremendous for I was able to do things right off with(out) fear or favour: I had some trouble with the staff not my own tried men but it is all right now: This is a very trying place and difficult in many ways, but the visit of the Quest has done a great deal to keep up the British prestige which was marred

a little time ago by a certain rudeness of a British man 'o war. I am very
late starting but in 14 days will not be far off the ice and into the work:
The ship is small but strong: I have not been well only I am just telling
you that: it was I suppose largely due to worry: the years are mounting
up but I can do it all right, don't think I am not cheerful but I do hate
the heat: You are and always have been a wonderful friend to me; I have
asked to send copies of some recent photos; the temperature at this
moment is over 110°: so you can guess how I am feeling. I would
rather all the bad things happened at the outset than later: a week ago
the ship looked like a wreck now she is all right: our trial trip to sea
was a success and with the new propellor we are doing well. I just loved
your letters so fresh and keen and just you: I have been lucky in
hearing from you like this for several letters are missing I don't know
what happens to the mail now-a-days: It may in fact it must be the heat,
but I find it difficult when I come away from the ship to sit down and
write We are tucked away about 9 miles from Rio on an island baking
hot with mosquitoes and clanging hammers all day. then at night I
have to dress and attend some long drawn out function and all the time
I am mad to get away: If I knew you less well I would not write all this
but I want to open up: from South Georgia we go into the ice into the
life that is mine and I do pray that we will make good: it will be my
last time I want to write your good name high on the map: and however
erratic I may seem always remember this: that I go to work secure in the
trust of a few who know me and you my friend not least among them:
The work you are doing for the country is perhaps more in its way than
mine but more or less our motives and thoughts are the same: Christmas
will be over before you get this but let me tell you all on board will
have on Christmas day raised their glasses to you and all you have done
for us.

I am ever more and more gratefully
ERNEST SHACKLETON

On the *Quest*, anchored in a bay on the Nictheray side of the harbour,
on this 17 December, Shackleton and Sharpus were working in
Shackleton's cabin on accounts and messages for the English papers,
while some of the men went ashore to dine on this last night at Rio.
But Shackleton was too ill to work, and at ten o'clock, when the launch
came for Sharpus, Shackleton asked him to take him ashore where he
could get some cool air. He was taken to the mess of Wilson's company
and the next morning claimed that he felt better, but the growing heat
of the day soon affected him again. Sharpus sent the launch for
Macklin, who was told that Shackleton had had a heart attack. The Boss
received Macklin cheerfully, refused to be examined, and said that he
had quite got over what had been merely a fainting fit. He insisted that

Macklin was to speak of his attack as being of no great significance. Macklin, for his part, realised then that Shackleton must have had such attacks before, and both he and McIlroy watched their leader more closely than ever when, on 18 December, the *Quest* set out on her journey to South Georgia.

Their advice to him was, naturally, that he should rest. They did not expect him to take it, but Macklin in particular was surprised that he listened in what was, for him, an unusually docile and subdued manner. He was disquieted too by an indecision in Shackleton which he had never expected to find. The Boss seemed unusually ready to talk, and one night when they were on watch together he questioned him about the future[10]:

> 'The Boss says now quite frankly that he does not know what he will do after S. Georgia, & gives several alternative propositions, one of which is that he will go direct to Cape Town delivering the mails at Tristan da Cunha, & then put it to the supporters at home that he should return at once to England &, instead of coming back here again, go up Dana Straits into the Arctic, when as he said "It is not too long a journey to reach land if the ship does get crushed". He also proposed wintering in the Antarctic ice, & I pointed out that we had no sledges, unsuitable tents, & practically no winter clothing. He replies however that we will get them & also sledge dogs at S. Georgia. I have very sincere doubts as to the latter. I do not quite understand his enigmatical attitude—I wonder what we really shall do. Being in charge of equipment & stores, this uncertainty is very worrying.'

Indeed, Shackleton's 'enigmatical attitude' and the fact that at least he did not cut the doctors short when they proffered advice, were infinitely disquieting to them. To all but a searching eye, however, Shackleton seemed to be his usual brisk and cheerful self, though everyone knew he was doing too much. For instance, on the day of sailing Jeffrey injured his leg and was ordered to bed for two or three weeks: Shackleton decided to keep his watch for him. As always, he had his eye on everybody and everything. Naisbitt, who as steward was having a hard time of it in the rough weather which attacked them soon after sailing, found Shackleton's methods of leadership novel and striking, and two entries in his diary[16] are especially vivid:

> '(19 December) We experienced rough weather this morning and at about 3 a.m. when "all hands" were called I leaped out of my bunk and went on deck to see what was taking place. The Boss was in the Port alley way with several hands trying to secure barrels, drums, boxes & such which had taken charge during the heavy rolling. The water was pouring in over the gunwales as we rolled and at times the alley way was flooded waist deep. I gave a hand with

the rest and within an hour everything had been again made secure.

. . . at 11.30 p.m. all hands were again called, the engines were stopped for repairs and I turned out and took a turn at the hand pump to help clear the bilges. About midnight the Boss told me to turn in—he said he did not expect me to come up with "All hands" at night—my work was day work & he only required those working watches. I took the tip and returned to my bunk.

(23 December) . . . In the afternoon an Albatross hovered over & followed the ship—this is the first Albatross I have ever seen. . . . The Boss was on deck at the time—he shewed as much interest as anyone else—it was the first albatross of the trip and he took an opportunity of describing the characteristics of the Albatross to those around—relating episodes of the last expedition intermittently.

When I have, during these first days of my participation in the expedition, listened to the Boss expounding on various subjects—I have observed that readiness to answer any intelligent enquiry & welcome the interest shewn by anyone is noticeably one of his great features. And it is easy to draw him into an informative mood when & where he seems so much at home. He may be a man of moods. I can imagine he is—and this is perhaps his best mood—for he is a born and inspired lecturer at all times.'

This was perhaps the last leisure moment Shackleton had. He certainly did not allow himself many, and in order to be able to go on managing his ship in the only way he knew, by participating in everything, he deviated from a principle which he had always held to strongly. Some cases of champagne had been presented to the ship in England and now on most mornings during the run to South Georgia, Shackleton had a bottle opened and took a glass, offering it also to the officers and surgeons. He had never previously allowed liquor at sea except on rare and special occasions, and, ashore as well as at sea, was noted for his abstemious habits in eating and drinking. This deviation from his own rule was a sign that he was feeling the strain in a way which he had never done on previous expeditions.

Undoubtedly, too, he was trying to deaden the pain from which he was suffering from time to time; but he did not mention this to anyone and did not encourage any enquiries about his health. Macklin ventured one night, when he and the Boss were on watch, to suggest that Wild and Worsley could take over more of the routine responsibility, as they were well able to do, thus saving Shackleton from constant overwork and lack of sleep. He got no very satisfactory answer, although he did persuade Shackleton to hear him out.

It was expected that Christmas Day at least would bring everyone some rest. Christmas Eve was fine and clear, and 'in spite of sundry croakings from Hussey, our weather prophet', as Wild put it[11], 'we anticipated a cheery Christmas dinner'. But the next day a full gale was blowing, the crockery was flying about on the breakfast table, and Shackleton decided to postpone opening the boxes of delicacies provided by his wife* and by Mr. and Mrs. Rowett. Green, the cook, was ordered to serve out thick bully beef sandwiches and cocoa for lunch. This collation was served at the galley door and Naisbitt wrote in his diary[16] that 'despite the conditions a spirit of good cheer prevailed, & wit and rich philosophy dominated the conversation as in turn we ate, loitered and relieved each other on the old "Downton" pump'. In the evening the company was regaled on stew, washed down with a tot of rum or whisky.

The storm did not die down until 26 December. On that day Shackleton had a fresh anxiety to bear, for the large forward water tank was found to have leaked dry. As the after-tank was nearly exhausted, orders had to be given for rigid economy of water.

The next day the bad weather returned, and by 28 December a furious westerly gale was pushing the *Quest* along at a great speed. Early that morning Shackleton gave orders to heave to, and during the day they made good use of oil bags. To the men he said that he had never himself experienced a more severe storm. Everyone was exhausted by the time the weather had moderated on the following day.

Now came the worst blow. Kerr reported to Shackleton that he had found a leak in the furnace. The ship must steam at reduced speed until she reached South Georgia; only then could it be ascertained how serious this new accident was. It might even stop the expedition altogether.

This news came upon Shackleton at the worst possible time. He had been on the bridge almost continuously during the storm, and had been taking what sleep he could on a bunk in the ward-room, his own cabin having been flooded out. It was not surprising that he became, for a short time, depressed and irritable. Those who knew him well had met him in this mood before and welcomed it as they knew it would give him some relief. To Naisbitt it seemed far more momentous, in contrast to the calm, confident leader he had first seen; and on 26 December he wrote a description in his diary[16] which shows much of what Shackleton

---

* Among the tributes printed in the *Times*[17] after Shackleton's death was the following from Mr. F. Hatter, managing director of Buszard's:

'A fortnight before the *Quest* sailed . . . Sir Ernest and Lady Shackleton called on me and said they wanted to give a little surprise to the crew of that vessel either on Christmas or New Year's Day, when Sir Ernest expected to be well away among the ice of the Antarctic seas. They accordingly asked me to have a large almond-iced cake made, with a seasonable inscription, which Sir Ernest directed to be taken aboard in an ordinary case, not bearing the maker's name, as ship's stores. We accordingly made the case and had it smuggled aboard as desired.'

must have been feeling as well as showing the effect his mood could have on others:

'We are about ten days out of South Georgia yet—fortunately the weather is becoming cooler. When the Boss is annoyed about something it seems to upset him altogether—nothing is right. At meal times there is something to complain about—the plates have not been warmed for the hot dishes—his macaroni-cheese is not sufficiently crisp—or something else is wrong. One can easily observe those about him doing their best to humour him. Conversation at table is chosen for such days—someone tries to recall some pleasing reminiscence. Capt. Hussey seems to be a very useful man in this direction—being rather resourceful and possessing a goodly share of wit—he generally administers the right dope for a boisterous Irish spirit and after a while you find Dr. Jekyll climbing out of Mr. Hyde.'

The steward's outburst probably relieved his momentary pique* more surely than Shackleton's outburst relieved him. Nothing but the rest which he could not get or would not take could have calmed him during these difficult days. On 30 December the steward wrote[16]:

'Sir Ernest has been suffering somewhat from neuralgic pains in the back but despite this he has spent a great deal of time on the bridge & about the decks—looking very anxious many times when the storm was at its worst—but always calm and collected. One can easily see his great strength of character, his masterful personality, and resourcefulness when things are at their worst. He has great consideration for everyone and seems to know just how much any one man can endure and yet, it would seem, sacrificing himself. He will go long hours at a stretch without rest and all the entreaties—however skilfully submitted—would not budge him. Aggressive in the face of opposition, defiant in the time of adversity I think that would just about sum him up.'

The stormy weather now abated, and Shackleton, certain that the *Quest* would reach South Georgia safely, if slowly, fell into a calm and reminiscent mood, in which the romantic note of the expedition could be heard again. On New Year's Day he began writing his diary once more, and his mood is faithfully reflected in the first entry[3]:

'Rest and calm after the storm: The year has begun kindly for us: it is curious how a certain date becomes a factor and milestone in ones

* Charles Green remembers the incident well.[18] 'Naisbitt used to serve the dinners and he served a nice centre piece of macaroni cheese on a plate. The Boss came out of the dining-room straight to the galley. He said "Green, where's this from?" and he threw the whole thing in the scupper. Of course Naisbitt was upset, he didn't know what he'd done. I said, "You've done wrong. You have to scrape it all off the side. That's Shackleton's bit, that is."' The story sounds through the years like an anecdote of a loved and eccentric schoolmaster told by one of his pupils.

life: Christmas Day in the raging gale seemed out of place I dared not venture to hope that today would be as it was: Anxiety has been probing deeply into me: for until the very end of the year things have gone awry: Engines unreliable: furnace cracked, water short: heavy gales: all that physically can go wrong but the spirit of all on board sound & good:

"There are two points in the adventures of the diver" one when a beggar, he prepares to plunge

one when a prince he rises with his pearl.'*

On the next day they sighted their first iceberg. To Shackleton it brought associations which, now that he could relax, he could admit into his mind. He reflected, 'Ah me: the years that have gone since in the pride of young manhood I first went forth to the fight I grow old and tired but must always lead on.' Crossed with this mood was the mood of anxiety, softer but not altogether stilled, the mood in which he was, as he said, 'on the qui vive'. On 3 January he wrote 'Another beautiful day, fortune seems to attend us this New year. but so anxious have I been, when things are going well I wonder what internal difficulty will be sprung on me.'

On 4 January they sighted South Georgia and moved down the coast. Shackleton, in high spirits, spent most of the day on the bridge with Wild and Worsley, picking out the familiar spots through binoculars and telling those who were new to the place the story of his boat journey from Elephant Island and the crossing of South Georgia.

Late in the morning the *Quest* let fall her anchor in Grytviken harbour, in the anchorage which the *Endurance* had used. The manager of the whaling factory came aboard and soon afterwards took Shackleton ashore. The visit to his old haunts warmed and refreshed him. He returned to the ship in a happy frame of mind. He told the men to turn in early and get some sleep and pleased them by promising them the next day ashore to make up for their hard work. Wild recalled[11] how as he said goodnight he told him, 'Tomorrow we'll keep Christmas.'

When most of the men had turned in, Shackleton played some hands of Double-decker with McIlroy and then said he felt tired and would follow them. As he was going to his cabin he met Dell[19] going aft to his bunk. They were in the passage they called the Rubicon, and each of them remembered the stormy days behind them when the water had been running through it and Shackleton had had difficulty in getting to his cabin. The Boss said jocularly, 'Seaboots we shall not require, Jimmy; carpet slippers we must have', and passed on into his cabin.

* This passage is printed exactly as Shackleton wrote it in his diary, although his inconsistent use of inverted commas makes it somewhat confusing. These lines from Browning were often quoted by him, and it is easy to understand why, for all through Shackleton's life the planning of an enterprise was as rewarding and important as the result of it.

It may have been now that he wrote the quietly emotional entry in his diary[2]:

'At last after 16 days of turmoil and anxiety: on a peaceful sunshiny day we came to an anchor in Gry(t)viken. How familiar the coast seemed as we passed down: we saw with full interest the places we struggled over after the boat journey. Now we must speed all we can but the prospect is not too bright for labour is scarce The old smell of dead whale permeates everything: It is a strange and curious place. Douglas & Wilkins are at different ends of the island. A wonderful evening.

"In the darkening twilight I saw a lone star hover, gem like above the bay."'

In the night McIlroy, going off anchor watch, heard him snoring gently as he passed his cabin and was relieved that he was getting some good sleep. Macklin now took over the watch, and some time after 2 a.m. he was summoned by whistle to Shackleton's cabin. He found him in a quiet mood and evidently wanting to talk, and they had some conversation about the ship and her future before Shackleton said he would try to get to sleep again. Macklin resumed his patrolling of the ship. A little later he heard another whistle and went at once to Shackleton's cabin[10]:

'I was taking the 2–3 am anchor watch when I was attracted by a whistle from the Boss cabin. He told me that he was suffering from pains in the back & bad facial neuralgia. He wished for some drug that would produce immediate relief. He said he had taken 3 tablets of aspirin & that they had done him no good. I noticed that he was covered by only one blanket & as the night was cold I said "You should be more warmly covered. I will get you my blanket" which I did & tucked it all round him. He was impatient however for some drug to immediately relieve him of pain & to give him sleep. I left him & went to the medicine cupboard & got 10 minims of Chlorodyne, which I gave him in water. He did not take it at once but said "put it down there while I talk to you". He then said I do not believe that aspirin is any good it takes too long to act, will that stuff of yours act quickly". I told him "yes". He asked "what is the cause of this trouble of mine" & I told him, as I had told him many times before, that he had been overdoing things, & that it was no good expecting any single dose of medicine to put him right, but that it was much more important to try & lead a more regular life, get sleep regularly, have a good daily motion of the bowels & have a regular simple diet. He replied "You're always wanting me to give up things, what is it I ought to give up". I replied "chiefly alcohol* Boss I don't think it agrees with you". He then said "I can feel the pain coming again give me the medicine quickly". He swallowed it but immediately

* I.e., the use of alcohol as a medicine.

had a very severe paroxysm during which he died. I stopped by him till I saw that all was hopeless & then went to McIlroy, for it flashed through my mind that his death would cause a sensation & that there might be an enquiry & said "Mick come at once & see the Boss he is dying. He came but on entering the room said as soon as he saw him "Yes! he's gone". Naturally it staggered us & for a few moments we said & did nothing. Then we woke up Wild & told him, & later Worsley. On my way to McIlroy I also woke Hussey & told him to get a hypodermic injection of ether ready at once, but I did not give it as it would have been quite useless. Death is a terrible thing to witness, & I can never get used to it, but this was much more so, as can easily be understood. The cause of death is, I feel perfectly sure, angina pectoris.* I laid him out & fixed things up, turned out the lamp, which was burning, & shut the door. We all retired to think things over, & nothing further will be done till 6.0 am, when I will notify the magistrate who is also coroner. I will notify of exactly what happened & then give a certificate of death from angina pectoris. Heart failure. Mick agrees about this.

I have written this, one hour later, so that I may have an account of it while fresh in my mind, to refer to at a later date, in case of enquiries which people are bound to make.'

That night of 4–5 January several people were disturbed by unusual noises. Marr was surprised at being sent back to bed when he got up for an early watch. The cook and Naisbitt were told by Wild to announce and serve breakfast quietly, as the Boss was not very well. Mr. Green remembers[18] 'just as we were going to breakfast Wild said, "I want you all on the poop". We all mustered on the poop and there was a lot of chattering among us, we thought the expedition had gone broke, all sorts of funny things. Wild came up and he said, "Boys, I've got some sad news for you. The Boss died suddenly at three o'clock this morning. The expedition will carry on".'

The men, dismayed and shocked, dispersed to their work. For them it was as if the bottom had fallen out of the adventure. Whatever they

---

* The death certificate read:

I, the undersigned, do hereby certify that I attended Sir Ernest Shackleton during his last illness and that, to the best of my knowledge and belief, the cause of his death was Atheroma of the Coronary arteries and Heart failure, and that, previous to his death, he was in no way exposed to infections or contagious disease.

Signed:
A. H. MACKLIN, M.D. (Vict.)

January 10, 1922

The post-mortem showed atheromatous plaques which the doctors thought might have been the result of Shackleton's Southern Journey of 1902–03. The cause of death would, in modern medical terms, be called a coronary thrombosis.

had noticed of weariness in the Boss, they had all of them, really, believed him to be indestructible.

Wild, Macklin and McIlroy went ashore in the morning to report the death to the magistrate and to arrange about the death certificate. They also visited Jacobsen, the manager of the whaling factory, to arrange about the temporary care of the body while suitable arrangements were being made. They could get no message to the outside world, since their own transmitting set on the *Quest* had failed and could not be repaired, and there was none on South Georgia. It was arranged that Wild should go to Leith where the *Albuera* was lying and arrange for her to transmit the news as soon as she got within range of a receiving station.

Meanwhile they decided the body must be embalmed and eventually sent back to England. Macklin and Dell sewed the body in canvas and it was taken ashore and laid in the hospital in Grytviken, covered with the white ensign.* On 7 January the doctors, helped by the Grytviken medical staff, injected the body with formalin and prepared to transfer it to the *Professor Gruvel*, a steamer which was due to return to Montevideo. Hussey had decided that he ought to return to England and work for his finals, now almost due; the expedition had lost its savour for him with the Boss's death. Wild agreed, and entrusted the body of his leader to him.

There was little time for mourning, for Wild (now in command) and every other man in the expedition knew that Shackleton would have wanted them to carry on. They were all determined to execute his plan as far as they possibly could. Wild and Macklin set out for Leith and Husvik to seek equipment, clothing and stores for the journey into the ice, which must be started as soon as possible. On 18 January Douglas and Wilkins returned to the *Quest*. They had received the news nine days before, and it was a sad homecoming for them.

On 19 January the *Professor Gruvel* sailed for Montevideo, arriving there ten days later. Here Shackleton was given the full honours due to a Minister of State. A hundred marines conveyed the coffin, covered with the British flag, to the military hospital, where it was guarded day and night by privates of the Uruguayan army. On the coffin the Matron and nurses of the hospital kept fresh red and white roses from the garden. In these practical and immediate ways the Uruguayan people and the British residents in that country expressed their appreciation of Shackleton as an unofficial ambassador from Britain.

The news had reached Lady Shackleton by now, and, putting her private wishes aside, she decided that her husband would have wanted to be buried in South Georgia. The President of Uruguay, Baltasar

* As a member of the Royal Yacht Squadron, Shackleton had the privilege of flying this ensign.

Brum, when he was informed of this decision, decided that the re-embarkation of the coffin should be carried out with full military honours, and in his presidential decree he[20] paid Shackleton a striking tribute :

'Sir Ernest Shackleton synthesised every splendid quality: courage, always quiet and modest; invincible energy; limitless abnegation; fine tenacity, . . . all applied to the conquest of universal science, with a life-long devotion. Explorer of unknown regions, a famous geographer, interested in everything that tends to give a man a full knowledge of the planet on which he lives, Shackleton is not only one of the great glories of England, but is also a magnificent type of humanity. In a material age he felt the supreme inquietude of knowledge unsatisfied; in an age of warlike heroism he was the hero, calm and strong, who left behind him neither death nor grief.

Uruguay, which on another occasion lent the intrepid navigator sincere and affectionate aid, now has the honour of guarding his ashes and placing them beneath the Flag which formerly guided his audacious steps.'

On 14 February the coffin was taken to Holy Trinity Church, and on the following day a memorial service was taken by the chaplain, assisted by the Chaplain of the Missions to Seamen in Buenos Aires, who had been a personal friend of Shackleton. The President of the Republic arrived at the church before the service and paid his personal tribute to Shackleton by remaining by the coffin in the chancel for a few moments. The congregation was representative of everyone from officers of the Uruguayan forces and diplomatic officials to members of the community, British and Uruguayan, who had been impressed by Shackleton's personality on his previous visit to the country.

The British Chargé d'Affaires, Edward Hope Vere, sent to Lord Curzon at the Foreign Office a moving description[21] of the procession after the service :

'After the benediction had been pronounced and during the playing of the "Dead March in Saul", twenty members of the Ex-Service Clubs of Montevideo and Buenos Aires, many of whom held His Majesty's Commission during the war, shouldered the coffin, which was draped in the folds of the Uruguayan flag and the Union Jack and crowned with the wreath placed upon it . . . on behalf of His Majesty the King and His Majesty's Government.

At the door of the Church the coffin was placed upon the gun-carriage, while a squadron of the famous Uruguayan Cavalry Regiment, . . . known as the "Blandengues de Artigas", presented arms and then formed up in double file as a Guard of Honour on both sides of the gun-carriage and funeral procession, and the fortress of Montevideo fired minute guns. The Uruguayan wreath and those of Shackleton's family were then placed upon and around the coffin,

Grytviken
Whaling Station,
South Georgia

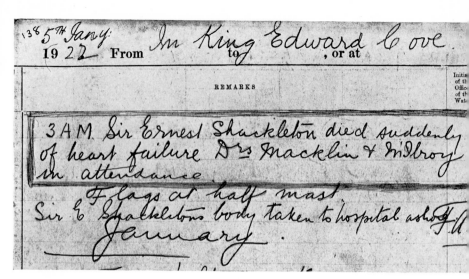

138 5th Jany: 19 22 From In King Edward Cove to , or at .

REMARKS

3 A.M. Sir Ernest Shackleton died suddenly of heart failure Drs Macklin & MᶜIlroy in attendance.
Flags at half mast
Sir E Shackleton's body taken to hospital ashor[e]
January .

Deck-log of the *Quest*; Worsley's entry

Shackleton's coffin leaves the English Church at Montevideo, 1922

With the cross made by his men of the *Quest*. Shackleton's grave at Grytviken, South Georgia

Shackleton's grave with the headstone put up in 1928

Bust of Ernest Shackle
ton, made by J. A
Stevenson, shortly afte
his return from th
Antarctic in 1909

Statue of Ernes
Shackleton designed b
Sir Edwin Lutyen
and executed by Charle
Jagger

the other being borne in the procession by ex-Officers in His Majesty's Army.

Opposite the English Club, Doctor Buero, the Uruguayan Minister for Foreign Affairs, accompanied by General Sebastian Buquet, the Uruguayan Minister of War and Marine, and General da Costa, Chief of the Uruguayan General Staff, joined the procession, the streets being lined on both sides by troops with reversed arms and all flags half-masted in sign of mourning. Doctor Buero drew my attention to the sympathetic attitude of the large crowd of spectators and to the fact that eighteen hundred troops had been paraded to do honour to Shackleton and as a demonstration of sympathy with Great Britain.

At the landing stage His Excellency formally handed over the remains to me in an eloquent speech. . . .

Shackleton's coffin was then carried on board the British steamer "Woodville", which left this morning at six a.m. for South Georgia, being escorted to the limit of Uruguayan territorial waters by the cruiser "Uruguay", which then returned to this port after firing a salute.'

On 5 March Shackleton was buried in the cemetery at Grytviken, after a service in the Lutheran church at which Mr. Binnie, the English magistrate, officiated. No congregation of uniformed dignitaries and ministers of state here, but sailors and whaling captains: no military escort, but a company of hard-working, hard-handed men walking over the tussocks after a coffin carried by ex-service men from the Shetlands who were working in Leith Harbour. On the grave was a wreath of flowers made by Mrs. Aarberg, the only woman on the island: it kept company with the bronze wreaths from the British and Uruguayan governments, which Hussey had brought from Montevideo, hanging on the simple wooden cross which had been made in Grytviken. Hussey represented his shipmates of the *Quest* at the funeral, for the ship had already steamed off towards the ice.

The memorial service for Shackleton in Montevideo had been splendid indeed. His sense of occasion would have responded to the glitter and pomp of the procession, and he would have felt proud that he was thus honoured as a British subject. He had always been deeply conscious of being responsible for the good name of Britain when he was in a foreign country; and, indeed, few men have been as well fitted, by personality and achievement, to represent her. But if the majesty of the occasion at Montevideo would have touched his emotions, the simple ceremony at Grytviken would have gone nearer to his heart.

Nobody ever doubted that South Georgia was the one place where he should be buried, and a dignified leader in the *Times*[22] expressed this feeling particularly well:

31

'. . . we believe that the present decision will commend itself to the nation more than any that might have been taken for his funeral at home. His name is already so indissolubly linked with the Antarctic, that nothing could be more appropriate than his burial in that region. South Georgia, besides being the place of his death, has other strong claims to be the receptacle of his mortal remains. It was by his landing there, in circumstances of immense difficulty, that he was able to save not only those companions that were with him six years ago, but also those others whom he had been forced to leave marooned on the still more forbidding shores of Elephant Island. It cannot be said, therefore, when we remember so critical an episode in his career, that South Georgia was ever inhospitable to Shackleton. On the contrary, its scenery must have been associated in his mind with some of his most grateful memories. Though not actually so far south as the Antarctic circle, its peaks and glaciers are of such grandeur as to leave nothing, from the imaginative point of view, wanting in his place of burial. In the performance of the last rites over the body of every great man there ought, unless we are so resigned to discourage the imagination as invariably to subordinate it to convention, to be a kind of poetic justice; and in the remote scene which is soon to be enacted in the English Church at Grytviken, we may be sure that it will be fittingly done to Shackleton.'

On 6 April the *Quest* returned to South Georgia after a voyage into the ice, to refit before she went on to Cape Town. Shackleton's men used their last days on the island to put up a memorial to their leader. Douglas suggested a site on the lower slopes of Duse Fell, on a headland overlooking the entrance to Grytviken Harbour. They climbed high on the hillside with sledges to drill and blast stone for a cairn,* which was built with great difficulty and as a labour of love.

On 4 May Macklin wrote in his diary[10]:

'After lunch Wild took the cross which Dell had made & which Kerr and Smith had secured into a drum, & erected it in the cairn. The cairn with the cross forms a conspicuous mark. I think this is as "the Boss" would have had it himself, standing lonely in an island far from civilisation, surrounded by stormy tempestuous seas, & in the vicinity of one of his greatest exploits. It is likely to be seen by few, but the few who see it are men who themselves lead hard lives, & who are able to appreciate better than those at home, the work which he accomplished.'

The cairn was completed on the next day, and a block was cemented in, bearing a plate inscribed 'roughly, but as well as we could do it',

---

* The cairn was designed by Douglas, who sent his sketch to Lady Shackleton. A visitor to South Georgia in 1927 noted[23]: 'The cairn, though built by Shackleton's own comrades and in their own words "solid and will stand the ravages of frost and blizzards for many years to come", was in 1927 torn down and rebuilt very neatly, and the cross painted white.'

Sir Ernest Shackleton Explorer. Died here January 5th 1922 Erected by his comrades. On 6 May, just before the *Quest* sailed, Wild and those who had been with Shackleton on his last two expeditions went over the bay to his grave and said their last farewell to their leader before they continued an expedition which, curtailed as it proved to be, represented their attempt to carry out what they could of his wishes.*

In England the most striking of many public tributes was paid to Shackleton in a memorial service held at St. Paul's Cathedral on 2 March, conducted by Dean Inge. At this simple, impressive service each member of the royal family was independently represented, and there stood side by side men and women of many countries and circumstances who, as they listened to the hymn 'Eternal Father, strong to save', to Shackleton's favourite 23rd Psalm, to the Last Post sounded by the boys of H.M.S. *Worcester*, felt the pressure of Shackleton's personality as each had felt it in his lifetime.

Shackleton had become the property of the nation. The hundreds of letters which reached Lady Shackleton came from people of all kinds and from all stations. Shackleton had accepted the social hierarchy of his day and the idea of anything different would not have commended itself to him; but within this framework he had made his own freedom. It was in no spirit of condescension that he talked about Browning to a forecastle hand, at a period when such a thing was well outside convention, or gossiped with taxi-drivers at an all-night coffee stall. When he liked people he could meet them on equal terms without losing the sense of his own position. One of the truest tributes came from Hussey, who cabled[24] to Lady Shackleton from Montevideo: 'Sincerest sympathies from all the boys we feel with you that we have lost the best friend that we ever had.' Some years after his death a heart-warming letter came to her from a London taxi-driver[25]:

'You have mentioned that we were his distinguished friends. And I am very pleased to say that the friendship was entirely reciprocal. We admired him for this Philosophy as he imparted to us a knowledge that it would have been impossible to gain from any other source. He was our ideal of a worldly man and of the many notabilities we

---

* Leaving South Georgia on 18 January, the *Quest* set out towards Coats Land, passing Zavodovskii Island, and entering the pack in latitude 65° 7′ S. and 15° 21′ E. They remained in the ice, taking soundings and making observations, until 21 March. They returned to South Georgia by way of Elephant Island, where they landed twice, but were unfortunately not able to land on the beach where the *Endurance* party had wintered, because of bad weather. Leaving South Georgia in May, Wild took the ship to Tristan, Gough Island, and so to Cape Town, allowing the scientists what time he thought suitable for observations ashore. At Cape Town he received orders from Mr. Rowett to return to England, which journey was made by St. Helena and St. Vincent, and so home on 16 September.

came into contact with, he was to us the man of men. My lady as you are aware we have a personal letter from him which we highly treasure and his name to us will remain immortal.'

There were many who wished to make his name immortal and who spoke out strongly in the months that followed his death. Most striking of the tributes to Shackleton was the long, passionate, sustained eulogy[26] by his brother-in-law, Charles Sarolea, published in the *Contemporary Review* in March. It is a brilliant summary of the main points of Shackleton's character. Sarolea saw him first and foremost as the *conqueror* of the Antarctic, and it is as an example of courage, endurance and determination that he holds him up to the nation.

Sarolea's article is a sonorous mingling of lofty sentiments and vivid reminiscence. Of the straightforward obituaries, none put into words the particular flavour of Shackleton's personality better than James Wordie[30], who summed up:

> ' Caution and shrewdness were combined, however, with invincible optimism ; this made him a trying partner at card games, and was also responsible for a continual hankering after and belief in hidden treasure. The latter feature was but another instance of his romantic nature. It was perhaps this which first suggested to his intimates a likeness to Raleigh. Then his friends found that he was a Raleigh in many ways—courtier, poet, explorer, and lover of his country. In an age which is producing modern-Elizabethans Shackleton will surely be reckoned as most true to type.'

Hugh Robert Mill had not been silent among those who hastened to pay their tribute to Shackleton, but he let some time pass before he asked Lady Shackleton's permission to write a life of her husband. It was to be his memorial to his friend, and, besides, a very practical help to the widow and her children, for he proposed that all the profits from the book should go to her. *The Life of Sir Ernest Shackleton* was published in April 1923, a compendious, scholarly volume on which any future writer on Shackleton must depend in great measure. If it is of first importance as a factual document (it was written with the direct help of Lady Shackleton), Mill's *Life* also represents a striking effort to draw together the multifarious threads of a complex character. To Mill Shackleton was an idealist whose destiny had been followed out amid the wastes of the Antarctic, a man who steered by a star, and that star the poetic vision of life.

Though he had developed this definite theme in his biography, Mill's letters at this time make it clear that he was well aware of the unpredictable, the indefinable element in Shackleton's nature. He knew well the strange combination of combativeness and imagination which could not easily be described. It occurred to many people, during

Shackleton's lifetime as well as after his death, to try to describe it through a comparison with the explorers of the Elizabethan age. It was a good comparison. The world could more readily remember and appreciate Shackleton's turbulent energy, his quick emotions, his formidable determination, his lively imagination, his habit of being unconventional within a convention, when the associations of the adjective Elizabethan were there as a guide. The people of England, then and now, readily accepted Shackleton as the lineal descendant of Drake and Raleigh.

Mill's biography was to be a practical attempt to help the explorer's family, as well as a tribute to his memory, for Mill and many others knew that Shackleton, in spite of his years of effort, had been unable to leave his family with the material provision he had so much desired to make. In May 1922 a committee was formed to raise and administer a Shackleton Memorial Fund. The committee included Lord Curzon, Lord Invernairn, Frederick Becker, Gerald Lysaght, J. Q. Rowett, Shackleton's brother-in-law Charles Sarolea, Dame Janet Stancomb-Wills, and, of his old comrades, Sir Philip Brocklehurst, Frank Wild and James Wordie (who acted as secretary to the committee).

For many years Shackleton had helped his parents and after his father's death in 1920 he had been almost entirely responsible for his mother and two of his elder sisters* who lived with her. It was first decided that the two chief objects of the memorial fund would be to help with the education of his children and the support of his mother, but Lady Shackleton expressed the wish that the greater part of the income from the fund should be devoted to Shackleton's mother.

During the years that followed after Shackleton's death, the investments made by Charles Dorman for the benefit of his children gradually came to maturity and Lady Shackleton was able to enjoy the considerable income which was her share of her father's estate, and the privilege of residing in a grace-and-favour apartment at Hampton Court Palace, which was granted to her by Royal Warrant in 1929.

When Shackleton's mother died in 1929, it was decided that the remaining capital of the fund could now be devoted to the erection in this country of a permanent memorial.

Already in 1928 a granite headstone and kerb had been made and taken to South Georgia for Shackleton's grave. It was a fine monument, bearing on it the nine-pointed star which had been very particularly Shackleton's own symbol in his lifetime,† and an appropriate quotation

---

* These sisters are no longer living.

† Shackleton had a strong streak of superstition in him. He noted that the figure 9 recurred strangely in his life. He had become engaged on the 9th of the month, married on 9 April 1904, and on 9 January 1909 turned north again after his struggle towards the South Pole. He adopted the nine-pointed star as

from Browning, 'I hold that a man should strive to the uttermost for his life's set prize.' The lines were peculiarly appropriate, for they had been often quoted by Shackleton and they had become a goal and an encouragement to his wife on the many occasions when she was tempted to ask him to stay at home. In 1907 she had had these same lines engraved on a miniature case, in which she sent photographs of herself and the two young children, Ray and Cecily, to be given to her husband on his birthday. The whole conception of the headstone reflected the striving, thrusting character of the man just as strongly as the cairn his comrades had built for him reflected their conception of him as the strong, simple leader.

The stone was unveiled on 26 February by the governor of the Falkland Islands after a service in the church which was attended by the Governor's personal staff, the magistrate of Grytviken and other Government officials, and the whalers of South Georgia, who had come from every side of the island to show their admiration for Shackleton the sailor.

On 17 December 1932 the Very Reverend Harold E. Lumsdale, Dean of Stanley, Falkland Islands, visited South Georgia in a trawler. This visit he described some time later to Lady Shackleton in a letter[28]:

'. . . knowing that your noble husband had only been buried by a Layman I decided to hold a Service at his grave. I said the Office of the Dead and added the words of Committal so that I could give his remains all that it was possible for the Church to give. It was a beautiful afternoon as the summer sun shone down at 5.0 pm upon those huge snow-capped mountains nested in which was the cemetery and the outstanding grave, as was seemly, that of Sir Ernest. The Captn (Commander Cary) and officers and crew of the RRS. Discovery II, the Manager of Pesca Whaling station and all his staff and many employees, the government officials all were there.'

In January of this same year, at the Royal Geographical Society, the Marquess of Zetland unveiled a fine statue of Shackleton designed by Sir Edwin Lutyens and executed by Charles Jagger. The world's opinion of the explorer was reaffirmed by the President of the Society, Admiral Sir William Goodenough,[27] when he said in concluding the speeches, that the statue would remind everyone 'of a man who had he lived in the gold age would have been a Drake or a Raleigh; of one among those men whose names encircle this hall as they themselves encircled the world; of one to whom adventure was an inspiration, death an incentive'.

his particular emblem, and he had a silver figure 9 made which was fastened to the door of his cabin on the *Quest*. By a strange coincidence Lady Shackleton, after many months of serious illness, died on the morning of the ninth of June 1936.

The statue stands in a niche on the Royal Geographical Society's building*, looking over Exhibition Road, a strong, formalised representation of Shackleton as so many had seen him in the Antarctic—muffled in sledging clothes, on his face a keen, challenging expression, an expression full of the will to conquer. It is a representation of the man who could always inspire less purposeful men by the strength of his purpose.†

Beside Jagger's statue may be set something more fluid and living—the picture of Shackleton as he appears in the film shots taken of him on the *Quest*. There are only a few glimpses of him in these scenes of snow and ships. Once he appears for a moment pursuing or tending a dog. It is difficult to see which: it is only clear that he is exasperated by the whole procedure. But there is one sequence in which the man suddenly comes to life—leaning over the binnacle, absorbed, concentrating, untidy, and then suddenly allowing his almost scowling expression to change, as he lifts his head, to a schoolboy grin, the whole face expressing an unwilling pleasure in being made the centre of the picture. For want of a better word, we must say that the picture shows Shackleton's charm. It is a word that, at its most superficial, can mean blarney—and Shackleton could use blarney when he needed to. At its best, it connotes a special warmth of personality which can distinguish one man from a thousand others, so that he will be notable not because of what he does or what he is going to do but because of what he is, because of a magnetism which draws people to listen to him and follow him.

* The statue was in fact designed to stand on a plinth: it was later felt that with the rapid growth of London, a statue in the street would possibly have to be moved, and the offer of the Royal Geographical Society to provide a niche for it was gratefully accepted.

† Ernest Shackleton's inspiration to men of action is, in another way, celebrated by sea and air. In 1937 a 245-foot Fleet Minesweeper of 1260 tons was completed in the Royal Dockyard, Devonport. As H.M.S. *Sharpshooter* she served through World War II, at the end of which she was converted to a surveying-ship for service with the Royal Naval Surveying Service. In 1953, after she had for some years been surveying in British Home Waters, her name was changed to *Shackleton*: the other two Home Surveying Ships at that time being *Franklin* (now in reserve) and *Scott* (still, like *Shackleton*, on active work). In 1955 the Falkland Islands Dependencies purchased a two-hundred-foot motor-ship, built in 1954 as the *Arendal*.[32] Her name changed to *Shackleton*, this surveying-vessel of 1102 tons gross (274 net) now crosses Ernest Shackleton's Antarctic trail many times every year.

On 9 March 1949 the first prototype of a powerful maritime reconnaissance bomber, developed from the *Lincoln* class, flew as a *Shackleton* aircraft. The *Avro Shackleton M.R.*3, to give it its full title, was still in production in 1955.[33]

Sir Ernest Shackleton is the name of a Vickers Viscount V701 propeller-turbine aircraft, G-AMNY, in service with British European Airways since early 1953. It was the third such aircraft to enter their passenger fleet.

Shackleton's personality was of this order, and it is for this reason that he has never been formalised—not in words, not in stone, not in the memories of those who knew him. There is among his admirers, inevitably, some hero-worship. Stories which might have been told against him have been pointed in another direction. Modifying and explanatory phrases have been found to explain the failings which his friends recognised in him. But even allowing for all this, his friends, his comrades and his family do not speak of him with bated breath. They do not regard him as a figure enshrined in formal memory, the general figure of a hero, but as a man whom they cannot forget.

Shackleton's reputation has remained to an exceptional degree a *living* one, the reputation of a man who can still dominate those who speak of him. Mill wrote, in a moving obituary,[29] 'Shackleton lived like a mighty rushing wind, and the very strength of his nature made him enemies as well as friends'. The wind has not yet died down. Men still speak of Shackleton with conviction. Some speak of him jealously, critically, even abusively: some with devotion, with enthusiasm, with understanding. They all speak of him as a man who still lives in their memory, and so strong is their impression of him after thirty and forty and fifty years that they are able to pass it on to those who never met him.

While one man remains alive who knew Ernest Shackleton, there can be no standard interpretation of him, for each and every man who knew him has his own idea of what he was like, and each man would defend his conception against any other. Shackleton has not yet taken to himself the trappings of a hero, the accepted 'character' of the great man who has passed into the company of the historic great and left behind him a version of his true self. Perhaps this smoothing process will never come to him. The letters he left behind him, the diaries of his men, the anecdotes written down by those who met him seldom but could not forget him—these things hold his personality to an extraordinary degree. Those who knew him did not want to present him to the world as a hero, but as the most interesting, the most bewildering, the most impressive person they ever knew. Shackleton was no textbook hero, but 'the elements so mix'd in him that Nature might stand up and say to all the world, "This was a man!"'

APPENDIX A
Shackleton's Men

A FULL and accurate list of all the men who went to sea, or trod southern lands, under Shackleton's leadership has been beyond our power. Shackleton did not spell all the names of his men consistently in his books, or give them the correct initials; he listed all those who were destined for shore-parties, but not always all those who were of his ships' complements.

ADAMS, Commander Sir Jameson Boyd, K.C.V.O., C.B.E., D.S.O., R.N.R. (retd.). Born 1880. Second-in-command of *Nimrod* shore-party 1907–09; member of Furthest South Party. Afterwards entered Civil Service, served with distinction in the two World Wars, and now leads active life in London as Hon. Appeals Secretary, King Edward VII's Hospital.

AITKEN (or ATKIN). Served as A.B. on *Aurora*, 1914–16.

ANSELL. Served as steward on *Nimrod*, voyages of 1907–08 and 1908–09.

ARGLES, H. J. Served as trimmer on *Quest*, 1921–22, joining in Rio.

ARMYTAGE, Bertram. Born 1869. Served with distinction in S. African War. *Nimrod* shore-party 1907–09. Died in 1943.

BAKEWELL, William L. Served as A.B. on *Endurance*, 1914–16. Now farming in Michigan, U.S.A.

BLACKBORROW, A. Joined *Endurance* as stowaway, Buenos Aires, signed on as steward 1914–16. Died in 1949.

BROCKLEHURST, Lieutenant-Colonel Sir Philip Lee, Bart. Born 1887. *Nimrod* shore-party 1907–09. Served with distinction in the two World Wars. Now leads active life on his Staffordshire estate.

BUCKLEY, Lieutenant-Colonel George A. McLean. Joined *Nimrod*'s outward voyage 1907–08, returned on *Koonya*. Died in 1935.

CARR, Air Marshal Sir Charles Roderick, K.B.E., C.B., D.F.C., A.F.C. Born 1891. Served on *Quest* as aviator 1921–22. Served with distinction in the two World Wars, becoming Deputy Chief of Staff (Air) S.H.A.E.F., 1945. Now leads active life in Oxfordshire.

CHEETHAM, Alfred B., whom Shackleton called 'the veteran of the Antarctic'. Served on *Morning*, 1902–04, *Nimrod*, 1907–09, as third officer and boatswain, *Terra Nova*, 1910–13, as boatswain, *Endurance*, 1914–16, as third officer. Torpedoed and drowned on active service in 1918.

CLARK, Dr. Robert Selbie, M.A., D.Sc. Born 1882. Biologist on *Endurance*, 1914–16. Served in the first World War, afterwards rose in his profession to become Director of the Marine Research Laboratory, Torry, Aberdeen. Retired in 1948, died in 1950.

COPE, J. L. Biologist and surgeon *Aurora* shore-party, 1914–17. Leader of the abortive British Imperial Expedition to Graham Land, 1920–21.

COTTON, Professor Leo Arthur, M.A., D.Sc. Born 1883. Sailed on *Nimrod* to McMurdo Sound and back in 1907–08. Became Professor of Geology in the University of Sydney in 1925; Emeritus Professor since 1949; lives near Sydney, Australia.

CREAN, Thomas. A.B. on *Discovery*, 1901–04, petty officer on *Terra Nova*, 1910–13, second officer on *Endurance*, 1914–16—member of *James Caird* boat-party. Died in 1938.

D'ANGLADE, E. Steward on *Aurora*, 1914–16.

DAVID, Professor Sir Tannatt William Edgeworth, F.R.S. Born 1858. Chief scientist on *Nimrod*, 1907–09, reached South Magnetic Pole at age of 50. Australia's greatest geologist and geographer. Died in 1934.

DAVIS, Captain John King. Born 1884. First officer *Nimrod*, 1907–09, and captain homeward voyage, 1909. Captain *Aurora* on Mawson's Expedition, 1911–14, and again for Ross Sea relief voyage, 1916–17. Second-in-command Mawson's *Discovery* expedition, 1929–30, and captain of ship. Later Director of Navigation for the Commonwealth of Australia; lives in Melbourne.

DAY, Bernard C. Born 1884. Motor engineer on *Nimrod*, 1907–09, and *Terra Nova*, 1910–13.

DELL, James William. Bosun's yeoman on *Discovery*, 1901–04. Electrician and boatswain on *Quest*, 1921–22. Lives in retirement in Somerset.

DONNELLY, C. A. Second engineer on *Aurora*, 1914–16.

DOUGLAS, Professor G. Vibert, M.C., M.Sc. Geologist on *Quest*, 1921–22. Geological expeditions in Newfoundland Labrador, 1946–48. Until 1957 Professor of Geology, Dalhousie University, Halifax, Nova Scotia. Now working in Toronto as a consulting geologist.

DOWNING, A. A.B. on *Aurora*, 1914–16.

DUNLOP, H. J. L. Chief engineer on *Nimrod*, 1907–09.

ELLIS. Steward on *Nimrod*, 1908–09.

ENGLAND, Lieutenant-Commander Rupert G., R.N.R. (retd.). First officer on *Morning*, 1902–04. Captain on *Nimrod*, 1907–08. President of the Antarctic Club, 1933–34. Died in 1942.

ERIKSEN. A Norwegian harpoon expert who accompanied *Quest* as far as Rio in 1921.

EVANS, F. P. Captain of *Koonya*, 1907–08, and of *Nimrod*, 1908–09.

GAZE, I. O. Scientific staff on *Aurora*, 1914–17, shore-party. Now farming in Western Victoria, Australia.

GLIDDEN, C. Ordinary seaman on *Aurora*, 1914–16.

GOOCH, Sir Daniel Fulthorpe, Bart. Born 1869. Accompanied *Endurance* as far as South Georgia in 1914. Died in 1926.

GRADY, S. Fireman on *Aurora*, 1914–16.

GREEN, C. J. Cook on *Endurance*, 1914–16, and on *Quest*, 1921–22. Now living in retirement in Kingston-upon-Hull.

GREENSTREET, Commander Lionel, R.N.R. (retd.). First officer of *Endurance*, 1914–16. Served in the two World Wars. Now living in retirement in Devon.

HANDCOCK. Steward on *Nimrod*, 1907–08.

HARBORD, Commander A. E., R.N. (retd.). Second officer on *Nimrod*, 1907–09. Now living in retirement in Worcestershire.

HAYWARD, V. Dog-driver on *Aurora*, 1914–16. Lost when crossing sea-ice on about 8 May 1916.

HOLNESS, A. Fireman on *Endurance*, 1914–16.

HOOKE, Sir Leslie A. Wireless operator on *Aurora*, 1914–16. Now Managing Director of a business in Sydney.

HOW, W. E. A.B. on *Endurance*, 1914–16. Now living in London.

HUDSON, Commodore Hubert T., R.D., R.N.R. Born 1886. Navigating officer on *Endurance*, 1914–16. Served as Captain in Merchant Navy between two World Wars. Killed in action, 1942.

HURLEY, Captain James Francis (Frank), O.B.E. Born 1890. Photographer on *Aurora* (Mawson), 1911–14, *Endurance*, 1914–16, *Discovery* (Mawson), 1929–31. Official war photographer in both World Wars. Lives in Sydney, Australia.

HUSSEY, Dr. L. D. A., O.B.E. Meteorologist on *Endurance*, 1914–16, meteorologist and assistant surgeon on *Quest*, 1921–22. Served in the two World Wars. Now in medical practice in Hertfordshire.

JACK, A. Keith. Physicist on *Aurora*, 1914–17; shore-party. In first World War, worked as chemist in Australian Department of Defence. Important work in connection with munitions in second World War. Until retirement in 1950, Secretary of Operational Safety Committee of Department of Munitions Supply in Australia.

JAMES, Professor Reginald William, F.R.S. Born 1891. Physicist on *Endurance*, 1914–16. Served in first World War, after which lecturer, then reader in physics at Manchester University. Became Professor of Physics in the University of Cape Town, S.A., in 1937; Vice-Chancellor and Acting Principal in 1956. Lives in retirement in Cape Town.

JEFFREY, Lieutenant-Commander D. G., R.N.R. Navigator of *Quest*, 1921–22.

JOYCE, Ernest Mills. Born 1875. A.B. on *Discovery*, 1902–04. Left Navy (P.O.) by purchase to join *Nimrod*, 1907–09. In 1910 chose dogs for Mawson's *Aurora* expedition in Copenhagen and took them to Tasmania. Dog-driver on *Aurora* shore-party, 1914–16, succeeding to leadership, 1916–17, after death of Mackintosh. Albert Medal. Died in 1940.

KAVENAGH, W. A.B. on *Aurora*, 1914–16.

KERR, A. J. Second engineer of *Endurance*, 1914–16; chief engineer of *Quest*, 1921–22. Lives in retirement from Merchant Service in Essex.

LARKMAN, A. H. Chief engineer of *Aurora*, 1914–16.

LYSAGHT, Gerald. Friend and supporter of Shackleton, who accompanied *Quest* as helmsman as far as Madeira in 1921.

McCARTY (or McCARTHY), T. A.B. on *Endurance*, 1914–16; member of *James Caird* boat-party. Killed at his gun in the Channel, 1917.

McGILLAN (or McGILLON), Thomas. Crew on *Nimrod*, 1908–09. Fireman on *Terra Nova*, 1910–13.

McILROY, Dr. J. A., M.R.C.S., L.R.C.P. Surgeon on *Endurance*, 1914–16. Served in first World War (badly wounded at Ypres). Surgeon and meteorologist on *Quest*, 1921–22. Still leads active life as ship's surgeon at time of writing.

MACKAY, Alistair Forbes. Born 1878. Biologist and surgeon on *Nimrod*, 1907–09. Lost in February 1914, on Vilhjalmur Stefansson's Canadian Arctic Expedition.

MACKINTOSH, Æneas Lionel Acton. Born 1881. *Nimrod*, 1907–09. Leader and captain of *Aurora*, 1914–15, and leader shore-party, 1915–16. Lost when crossing sea-ice on about 8 May 1916.

MACKLIN, Dr. A. H., O.B.E., M.C., M.D., R.A.M.C. Surgeon on *Endurance*, 1914–16. Served with distinction in first World War, partly with Shackleton in N. Russia. Surgeon, and in charge of stores and equipment, on *Quest*, 1921–22. President of Antarctic Club, 1939–45. Now Head of Student Health Service, University of Aberdeen.

McLEOD, Thomas F. A.B. on *Terra Nova*, 1910–13. Fireman on *Endurance*, 1914–16. A.B. on *Quest*, 1921–22.

McNEISH, W. Carpenter on *Endurance*, 1914–16, member of *James Caird* boat-party.

MARR, Lieutenant-Commander James William Slesser, M.A., B.Sc., R.N.V.R. Born 1902. Boy (Scout) on *Quest*, 1921–22. Zoologist *William Scoresby*, 1927–29, *Discovery I* (Mawson), 1929–30, *Discovery II*, 1931–33 and 1935–37. Whaling Inspector in Antarctic, 1939–40. Served in second World War. Commanded advance F.I.D.S. parties in Graham Land region, 1943–45. Marine biologist to *Discovery*'s Investigations.

MARSHALL, Dr. Eric Stewart, C.B.E., M.C., M.R.C.S., L.R.C.P. Born 1879. Surgeon and cartographer on *Nimrod*, 1907–09, member of Furthest South party. British Expedition to Dutch New Guinea, 1909–11. Served with distinction in the first World War. Now lives in retirement in the Isle of Wight.

MARSTON, George Edward. Born 1882. Artist on *Nimrod*, 1907–09, and on *Endurance*, 1914–16. Art teacher and Director of the Rural Industries Bureau. Died in 1940.

MASON, Bee. Appointed photographer and cinematographer on *Quest*, 1921; but returned home from Madeira on outward voyage.

MAUGER, C. C. Carpenter on *Aurora*, 1914–16. Badly wounded in first World War.

MAWSON, Professor Sir Douglas, O.B.E., D.Sc., B.Eng., F.R.S. Born 1882. Geological Investigation of New Hebrides, 1903. Scientific staff of *Nimrod*, 1907–09, leader on *Aurora*, 1911–14, *Discovery I*, 1929–31. Has been Professor in Geology and Mineralogy in the University, Adelaide, since 1920.

MICHELL, Dr. W. A. R. Surgeon on *Nimrod*, 1907–08.

MONTAGUE. Cook on *Nimrod*, 1907–08.

MOONEY, Norman E. Appointed Boy (Scout) on *Quest*, 1921; but returned home from Madeira on outward voyage.

MUGRIDGE, W. Fireman on *Aurora*, 1914–16.

MURRAY, James. Born 1865. Biologist to *Nimrod*, 1907–09. Lost in February 1914, on Vilhjalmur Stefansson's Canadian Arctic Expedition.

NAISBITT, Christopher. Ship's clerk on *Quest*, 1921–22 (joined in Rio). Lives in retirement in London.

NINNIS, A. H. Motor engineer on *Aurora*, 1914–16.

ORDE-LEES, Lieutenant-Colonel T., S.R.M. Motor expert on *Endurance*, 1914–16. Now lives in retirement in New Zealand.

PATON, James. Member of crew of *Nimrod*, 1908–09. A.B. on *Terra Nova*, 1910–13, boatswain of *Aurora*, 1914–16.

PRIESTLEY, Sir Raymond Edward, K.B.E., M.C., M.A., D.Sc., LL.D., D.Litt. Born 1886. Geologist on *Nimrod*, 1907–09, and *Terra Nova*, 1910–13. Served in first World War. Cambridge University, 1923. Vice-Chancellor Melbourne University, 1935. Principal and Vice-Chancellor Birmingham University, 1938. President of the British Association for the Advancement of Science, 1956. Directs Falkland Islands Scientific Bureau and leads active life in London and Gloucestershire.

RICHARDS, R. W. Scientific staff on *Aurora*, 1914–17, shore-party. Now Principal of School of Mines and Industries, Ballarat, Victoria, Australia.

RICHES. Member of crew of *Nimrod*, 1908–09.

RICKINSON, Engineer-Commander Louis, R.N. (retd.). Chief engineer on *Endurance*, 1914–16. Served in first World War. Since 1920 naval architect and consulting engineer. Died in 1945.

ROBERTS, William. Born 1872. Cook and assistant zoologist on *Nimrod*, 1907–09.

ROSS, G. H. Fireman on *Quest*, 1921–22.

SHAW, H. Fireman on *Aurora*, 1914–16.

SMITH, C. E. Second engineer on *Quest*, 1921–22.

SPENCER-SMITH, Rev. A. P. Photographer on *Aurora*, 1914–16; died on shore-party, 9 March 1916.

STENHOUSE, Commander J. R., D.S.O., D.S.C, R.N.R. Born 1887. Chief officer of *Aurora*, 1914–15, captain, 1915–16. Served with distinction in first World War. Captain of *Discovery I*, 1925–27. Served with distinction in World War II; died on active service in 1941.

STEVENS, Professor A. O. Chief of scientific staff on *Aurora*, 1914–17, shore-party. Now at Glasgow University.

STEVENSON (or STEPHENSON), H. Fireman on *Endurance*, 1914–16.

THOMSON, Leslie James F. Second officer on *Aurora*, 1914–15, first officer, 1915–16. Died in Australia.

VINCENT, J. A.B. on *Endurance*, 1914–16, member of the *James Caird* boat-party.

WARREN, A. A.B. on *Aurora*, 1914–16.

WATTS, Harold. Wireless operator on *Quest*, 1921–22.

WILD, Ernest (brother of Frank Wild). Stores and dogs on *Aurora*, 1914–17, shore-party. Killed in first World War when mine-sweeping in Mediterranean.

WILD, Commander Frank, C.B.E. Born 1874. Rating on *Discovery*, 1901–04. Sledger on *Nimrod*, 1907–09, member of Furthest South party. Leader of Queen Mary Land wintering station on *Aurora* (Mawson), 1911–14. Second-in-command of *Endurance*, 1914–16. Led expedition to Spitsbergen in 1918–19, when Shackleton recalled. To Nyasaland as farmer, 1920. Second-in-command of *Quest*, 1921–22, in command of expedition, 1922. To Swaziland, 1922, thence to Johannesburg, where died in 1939.

WILKINS, Sir George Hubert, M.C. Born 1888. Second-in-command, Vilhjalmur Stefansson's party, Canadian Arctic Expedition, 1913–17. Served with distinction in first World War. Second-in-command abortive Graham Land expedition, 1920–21. Naturalist on *Quest*, 1921–22. Leader Australia and Island Expedition, 1923–25. Commander of Detroit Arctic Expeditions, 1926–28. Commander of Wilkins-Hearst Antarctic Expedition, 1928–29. Commander of *Nautilus* Arctic Submarine Expedition, 1931. Manager of Lincoln Ellsworth Antarctic flights (*Wyatt Earp*), 1933–39, and Operation Snow Cornice (arctic), 1948. Lives in Massachusetts, U.S.A.

WISE, E. Cook on *Aurora*, 1914–16.

WORDIE, Sir James Mann, C.B.E., M.A. Born 1889. Geologist on *Endurance*, 1914–16. Served in first World War, when badly wounded at Armentières. Arctic expeditions, 1919, 1920, 1921, 1923, 1926, 1929, 1934, 1937. Antarctic cruise of F.I.D.S., 1946–47. Master of St. John's College, Cambridge; has been associated with Scott Polar Research Institute, principally as Chairman, since its foundation. President of the Royal Geographical Society, 1952–53.

WORSLEY, Commander Frank A., D.S.O., O.B.E., R.D., R.N.R. Born 1872. Captain of *Endurance*, 1914–16. Served with distinction in P and Q ships in first World War. Hydrographer and sailing-master on *Quest*, 1921–22. British Arctic Expedition, with Grettir Algarsson on *Island*, 1925. Treasure hunt to Cocos Island, 1935. In trading vessels to 1939; President Antarctic Club, 1938. Served in second World War; died in 1943. The navigator of the *James Caird* boat-journey.

YOUNG, S. S. Fireman on *Quest*, 1921–22, joined in Rio.

Shackleton's Writing

I. POETRY

After Shackleton's death there were one or two proposals that his poems should be printed. Dr. Mill commented[1] that although there were excellent lines in them and some were good as a whole, he did not feel they were of such an order of excellence that a collection of them would much enhance his reputation. 'They gave expression to his feelings at the time,' he said, 'but his literary genius shone in his extempore addresses rather than in his written verse.'

Certainly Shackleton's poems, few and varied as they are, would not have made a volume, nor would he have wanted them to be so presented to the world. Most of them were 'occasional' poems, written for a particular purpose or a particular scheme, while one or two were personal and written to relieve a great pressure of feeling. Such feelings were more often expressed through quotations from the poetry of others. Shackleton's friends were well accustomed to his habit of crystallising a mood, emphasising a point or expressing a strong emotion in lines from his favourite poets. This habit of quotation, which had developed in his boyhood, had increased during the years when he was courting Emily Dorman. They kept a joint commonplace book into which each copied favourite lines. In this book by far the greater number of quotations come from Browning, and, after him, from Tennyson and Swinburne.

There was never any ostentation in the way Shackleton quoted poetry. With him it was a natural form of expression—as natural as the breezy humour of his lectures or the simplicity of his diaries. Quotation was one of the many outlets which he found for his superabundant energy, a quick way of compressing much thought or feeling into a meaningful form.

It is not surprising that Browning should have been the poet to whom he turned most often for a spokesman. Browning's poems have two predominant moods which agreed well with Shackleton's temperament. The poems of love—vital, deeply urgent in feeling, sanguine and dominant—expressed what Shackleton felt about Emily Dorman in their courtship and after their marriage—so much so that such poems, and particularly *Prospice*, became an enduring symbol for them.

But Browning had also an active, convincing, optimistic philosophy of life which, because of its very simplicity, must make a strong appeal to a man of action. It was a philosophy very close to Shackleton's own, and he liked to be able to find himself so closely represented in the compact, quotable phrases of this poet.

Shackleton's own poetry did not as a rule come easily, if we can judge from the one or two drafts which survive. He wrote in a derivative style for the most part, the influence of Swinburne and Tennyson being predominant. He liked to build his poems round a generalisation; to paint a romantic picture of a place (usually the Antarctic) and combine this with a general message. The poems, indeed, served to crystallise his thoughts and feelings rather as quotation did. He himself probably valued them simply as this, as an expression of his mood.

After his first independent expedition, he gave a lecture to the Poetry Society in London (on 28 October 1911), his subject being 'Poetry in Active Life'. He spoke, in fact, almost exclusively about men at sea, and in particular about the men of the expeditions he had been on. He believed, he said, that most of them had been helped to bear the solitude and majesty of the Antarctic by reference to the great poets, but he observed that quite a number of them had been moved by their surroundings to make poetry of their own. Shackleton himself depended on this same inspiration.

His poems, then, must be seen as being of the same nature as his conversation—vital, varied and romantic, and springing from the great poetic drive of his nature that led him to conceive plans more ambitious and more imaginative than those of most explorers; a drive which, even in the stress of translating conception into fact, he never lost.

But though the poems are as it were incidental to his life, great interest attaches to them as a particular manifestation of his complex character. It has therefore seemed desirable, as well as convenient, to collect the best of them together, and to give brief notes on the circumstances in which they were written.

1. A Tale of the Sea

(A copy of this poem in Shackleton's handwriting survives among the Shackleton family papers, with the date February 1895. It is superscribed Emily M. Dorman 15th March 1899. In 1895 Shackleton was scarcely twenty-one years of age and serving as Third Officer on the *Monmouthshire* in the Far East (see page 10). We here reproduce the poem from Shackleton's copy, with his own characteristic punctuation.)

> I slept and dreamt of the ocean:
> Of tarry sailors joys:
> Of the tales which they loved to fashion
> Of days when they were boys:
> And I laughed aloud in my sleep:
> "In those days they said they were men:
> Is there one who has a record
> Of worth: for a poets pen"?
>
> The dream soon faded and left me:
> But it returned again

And I smelt the Galleys odour
Heard curses of sailor men.
Heard moaning of bitter salt winds:
Shrieking of gathering gales:
Wings of wild sea birds rising,
Beat the waves like threshers flails.

Then I saw a great long line
Of ghostly ships from the North;
Come churning the seas to foam
Splashing their bows with froth.
Dipping now into the hollows:
Now on the top they rise;
Pointing their booms to the oceans bed
And anon to the wind swept skies.

They in the foremost ships,
With tattered sails, and torn,
Thus spoke from the high poop aft:
Where the deck with their tread was worn:
Where nailed to the rotting flagstaffs:
The old white Ensigns flew
Badge of our English freedom
Over all waters blue.

"We fell for our countrys glory
And not for the yellow gold:
No: not as reward for greed:
Has the Arctic o'er us rolled:
We fell for the light of science,
To make clear the hidden paths
When the iceberg crunches our timbers,
As though they were only laths."

Then they told me a wondrous tale
And I strove to write it down
But my pen refused its duty:
And I lost my chance for renown
But since that vision left me:
I have looked on those sailor men
As worthy the brightest idyll.
That poet could ever pen.

Oh! the deepest blue of the sky:
Oh! the greenest sward on the lea:
To me seems dull and paltry,
Since I dreamt of that tossing sea,

For now I know it is peopled
With wandering souls of the past:
Blown to & fro on its surface
At the mercy of every blast.

2. FANNING ISLE

(This was a favourite poem of Lady Shackleton's. The verses were given to a friend from South Australia shortly after Shackleton's arrival in London in 1903, and may therefore be presumed to have been written during his voyage across the Pacific on the *Oratava* on his way to San Francisco, in February 1903. The sub-title of the poem is 'A Link in the All-British Cable'.)

Surf-bound, lonely islet,
Set in a summer sea,
Work of a tiny insect,
A lesson I learn from thee.
For to your foam-white shores
The deep sea cables come.
Through slippery ooze, by feathery palms,
Flies by the busy hum
Of the nations linked together,
The young, with the older lands,
A moment's space, and the Northern tale
Is placed in Southern hands.
So, green isle small and lonely,
I find as I think it o'er
That your place in the scheme of nations
Shows to me more and more
That every deed of Nature
Helps to the finished plan,
That starts with the lowly worm
And will end in the perfect man:
That the smallest leads to the greatest,
And your worth may now be seen
As the pulsing heart of the ocean
Goes by your island green.

3. TWO WAYS

(We have found this poem only in the *Sunday Express* of 5 February 1922, with no note of how it came to the paper or why it is not to be found among the other poems preserved by his wife. The poem was printed as a facsimile from a manuscript, inscribed at the end 'E. H. Shackleton, S.S. India, 12.11.07'.)

You may love the calm and peaceful days,
And the glorious tropic nights
When the roof of the Earth with broad stars blaze
And the Moon's long path of light

Steals in a shining silver streak,
From the far horizon line
And on the brink of the ocean's rim
Still greater planets shine.
But all the delight of summer seas,
And the sun's westing gold
Are nought to me for I know a sea
With a glamour and glory untold.
The gloom and cold of the long stern night
The work with its strain and stress
Hold sterling worth and sheer delight,
And these soft bright times hold less.
For all is new on our ice bound shore
Where white peaks dare the stars
There strong endeavour and steady hand
Alone can unloose the bars.
Then by faith unswerving we may attain
To the oft wished for distant goal,
And at last to our country's gain
Hold with our flag the Southern Pole.

4. TO THE GREAT BARRIER

(This long romantic poem, with its echoes of Swinburne and Tennyson,
was written for the *South Polar Times*, the magazine of Scott's
expeditions, and was included in the August number of 1902, over the
signature NEMO.)

Mother of mighty icebergs, these Kings of the Southern Seas,
Mystery, yet unfathomed, though we've paid in full our fees,
Eyes strained by ceaseless watching, when the low grey fog doth screen
Your walls from our aching vision, and the great grim giants you wean
Away from your broad white bosom, where for aeons untold is laid
Each yearly tribute of fallen snows, that this wonderful plain has made.
We have felt, more than seen, the danger, close ahead of our long jib
    boom,
But a turn of the icy wheel has made for us more sea room.
We have sailed from your farthest West, that is bounded by fire and
    snow,
We have pierced to your farthest East, till stopped by the hard, set floe.
We have steamed by your wave worn caverns; dim, blue, mysterious
    halls,
We have risen above your surface, we have sounded along your walls.
And above that rolling surface we have strained our eyes to see
But league upon league of whiteness was all that there seemed to be.
Ah, what is the secret you're keeping, to the Southward beyond our
    ken?
This year shall your icy fastness resound with the voices of men?

Shall we learn that you come from the mountains? Shall we call you
a frozen sea?
Shall we sail to the Northward and leave you, still a Secret for ever
to be?

5. L'ENVOI

(This poem represents Shackleton's most ambitious attempt to sum up
the feelings which the Antarctic had called forth in him. It was also
written for the *South Polar Times* over the signature NEMO, and was
included after the end-piece of the last number produced on Scott's
first expedition (August 1903), after Shackleton had been invalided
home to England.)

Slowly, though touched with glamour, the winter night went by,
  And we longed to see the sunlight sweep up in the Northern sky.
Still we wait in this icy fastness till the good sun sets us free,
  When no longer the tumbling billow is chained to a frozen sea.
Then shall our hardened bows dip gladly once more to the foam
  Of the Southward driving roller as the good ship strives for home.
Brothers, we then shall be parted in a world that is greater far
  Than this weird and wondrous region shut in with an icy bar.
We shall read then in other pages words fashioned with easier pen,
  Each day with its list of changes in a world of busy men.
But our hearts will still be faithful to this Southern land of ours,
  Though we wander in English meadows 'mid the scent of English
    flowers,
When the soft southerly breeze shakes the blossom away from the
    thorn,
  And flings from the wild rose cup, the shining gift of the morn;
And when the scarlet poppies peep through the golden wheat,
  As the stronger winds of Autumn march in with heavier feet;
And when the fields are snow clad, trees hard in a frosty rime,
  Our thoughts will wander Southward, we shall think of the grey old
    time;
Again in dreams go back to our fight with the icy foe;
  The crash of the steel clad bows; the sob of the tilted floe;
The tearing, rending asunder; the crack in the frozen field;
  The grating beneath the keel of the piece that sunk sooner than yield,
Our run through the ice free ocean till the snowy peaks appeared,
  Crowned by the gold of the morning, shod with the glaciers weird.
Then our joy at the furthest East where never yet man had been;
  When through the curtain of falling snow the bare, black rocks were
    seen;
We shall dream of the ever increasing gales, the birds in their Northward
    flight;
  The magic of twilight colours, the gloom of the long, long night.

We shall dream of those months of sledging through soft and yielding
   snow;
   The chafe of the strap on the shoulder; the whine of the dogs as they go.
Our rest in the tent after marching; our sleep in the biting cold;
   The Heavens now grey with the snow cloud, anon to be burnished
   gold;
The threshing drift on the tent side exposed to the blizzard's might;
   The wind-blown furrows and snow drifts; the crystal's play in the
   light;
And when, in the fading firelight, we turn these pages o'er,
   We shall think of the times we wrote therein by that far off Southern
   shore.
With regret we shall close the story, yet ever in thought go back,
   And success for each comrade will pray for on Life's still unbeaten
   track;
And the love of men for each other that was born in that naked land,
   Constant through life's great changes will be held by our little band.
Though the grip of the frost may be cruel, and relentless its icy hold,
   Yet it knit our hearts together in that darkness stern and cold.

6. MIDWINTER NIGHT

(This is the only example that survives of Shackleton's light verse. The
poem was contributed to *Aurora Australis*, the magazine of Shackleton's British Antarctic Expedition of 1907–09. It is signed 'Veritas' but
appears in the contents list under 'Nemo', the pseudonym Shackleton
had used in the *South Polar Times*. On 17 June 1908 Marshall wrote in
his diary, 'Sh. composing poetry. Rather good on night watchman.'
The poem was illustrated by a drawing by Marston.)

        The acetylene splutters and flickers,
        The night comes into its own.
        Outside Ambrose and Terror
        And snarling over a bone.

        And this is the tale the watchman,
        Awake in the dead of night,
        Tells of the fourteen sleepers
        Whose snoring gives him the blight.

        The revels of Eros and Bacchus
        Are mingled in some of their dreams,
        For the songs they gustily gurgle
        Are allied to bibulous themes.

        And subjects re barmaids and bottles,
        Whisky and barrels of beer,
        Are mixed with amorous pleadings
        That sound decidedly queer.

Darling you really love me?
Stutters one dreaming swain;
The watchman whispers "Never",
And the dreamer writhes in pain.

From the corner cabin a mutter,
The listener knows not what;
It sounds like "yon pale moon",
Or some other poetic rot.

Murder is done in another's dream
And falls from shuddering heights;
Erebus rises to dance on the sea
And the dreamer flees south in tights.

Another sails north on the broken ice
Just dressed in Nature's clothes,
Whilst seals and penguins grin in delight
And the frost plays hell with his toes.

And some see tailors they knew of yore,
Stalk in with their mile-long bills;
And everyone when morning broke
Made a rush for calomel pills.

7. Erebus

(This, probably Shackleton's best and most satisfying poem, was also contributed to *Aurora Australis* over the signature 'Nemo'.)

Keeper of the Southern Gateway, grim, rugged, gloomy, and grand;
Warden of these wastes uncharted, as the years sweep on, you stand.
At your head the swinging smoke-cloud; at your feet the grinding floes;
Racked and seared by the inner fires, gripped close by the outer snows.
Proud, unconquered, and unyielding, whilst the untold aeons passed,
Inviolate through the ages, your ramparts spurning the blast,
Till men impelled by a strong desire, broke through your icy bars;
Fierce was the fight to gain that height where your stern peak dares
    the stars.
You called your vassals to aid you, and the leaping blizzard rose,
Driving in furious eddies, blinding, stifling, cruel snows.
The grasp of the numbing frost clutched hard at their hands and faces,
And the weird gloom made darker still dim seen perilous places.
They, weary, wayworn, and sleepless, through the long withering night,
Grimly clung to your iron sides till with laggard Dawn came the light;
Both heart and brain upheld them, till the long-drawn strain was o'er,
Victors then on your crown they stood, and gazed at the Western shore,

The distant glory of that land in broad splendour lay unrolled,
With icefield, cape, and mountain height, flame rose in a sea of gold.
Oh! Herald of returning suns to the waiting lands below;
Beacon to their home-seeking feet, far across the Southern snow;
In the Northland, in the years to be, pale Winters first white sign
Will turn again their thoughts to thee, and the glamour that is thine.

II. PROSE

Shackleton wrote in many styles and for many purposes. The two books, *The Heart of the Antarctic* and *South*, which tell of two of his expeditions, were written in collaboration and must be discussed by themselves. Besides these, he contributed several articles to the *Geographical Journal*, either summarising his plans or giving some account of the results of his expeditions. These articles, and the account of Scott's first expedition which he wrote for the *Illustrated London News* in 1903, are written in the neutral style proper to such factual pieces. Of a similar kind is the very compressed account of his own expedition of 1907–09, which was published in *Pearson's Magazine* in three instalments, in the autumn of 1909, under the general title 'Nearest the South Pole'. A more general article in the August number of 1914, 'The Making of an Explorer', gave him more scope. It is a well-planned discussion of the qualities of optimism, patience, physical endurance and courage, the qualities which Shackleton felt were essential to an explorer. He uses a terse, unaffected style, and illustrates his points neatly with anecdotes from his experience.

All these journalistic writings are straightforward, with no frills and no false notes; they are not especially characteristic of Shackleton. He had command of a very wide and rich vocabulary, but this he reserved very largely for his conversation. There can be no doubt that the reason why he was always able to hold people from their work when he chose to talk was because of his flowing, lively sentences, his delight in words and the use his rich voice made of them, even more than the intrinsic interest of his subject.

This easy, lively varied way of talking can occasionally be found in his writings, notably in his diaries, where he mixes poetic language and simple vivid narrative just as he pleases. One or two of the reflective entries in the *Discovery* diary are of this kind, and so is the sustained passage from his *Quest* diary already quoted (see pp. 459–60). But it is seen perhaps most clearly in the editorials he wrote for the first five numbers of the *South Polar Times*. The first is beautifully keyed to the tone of the magazine, the easy, friendly, accomplished tone which the editor did so much to maintain. Two drafts of this editorial among the Shackleton papers show that he took great trouble to strike the right note; but the final effect is one of ease and naturalness.

'This the twenty-third day of April marks the disappearance of the Sun for many long months; and as we can expect no light from without, we look for light from within. So in the hope that this idea may even in a small way be realized, the first number of the *South Polar Times* appears.

A pioneer of the antarctic Press must necessarily differ in many respects from the papers of our Homeland, and the world in general. I might stand at the door, and look in vain for the row of boys, each with his red-rimmed bicycle, ready to fly to the street corner with his bundle, the moment the paper leaves the printer's hands, in vain I might look for the flaunting flag, and plastered sides, of that terror to nervous ladies, and mild old gentlemen, the high cart with its six foot wheels, which in half an hour spreads the news of the world from one end of the city to the other. I know we have not here as in England, the early train, which draws up at the many stations of Suburbia, to deposit with the milk, bundles of still damp sheets, rolled off by the press in hours when all the rest of the world was asleep; sheets that in due time will be read propped up against the coffee pot or loaf; and the latest rumour from the Far East, or the tragedy of last night, commences the conversation of the day.

No; the surroundings are far different where this small paper starts its career. I look out of the door, and see a wide white world of snow, and ice, with black volcanic peaks rising above the drift, and far in the snowy distance I see a great column of smoke from a chimney of no mans building, but from the great volcano Erebus, at whose foot our little colony dwells. Instead of the hum of busy streets, the only sounds that mingle with the whistling winds, are the squawking of a few belated penguins going Northward, the blowing of the seals as they come up to breathe, the sighing and crunching of the ice moved up and down by ever changing tides. A few red beams, dying quickly away, and the Sun has gone to warm the Northlands, where our hearts turn ever.

One thing is essential for the success of this paper, the co-operation of all its readers as contributors; and any new ideas or suggestions will be warmly welcomed, so that when the coming hundred days of darkness are over, we may look back upon them as having been not only tolerable but happy, and whatever may through the medium of this little paper help to bind us in still closer comradeship, and give pleasure to all, will be very gladly accepted.

Now freighted with goodwill and in hopeful anticipation of winning the approval of its little public, the first Antarctic paper goes forth.'

Shackleton's editorial for June 1902 shows an even more characteristic mixture of poetic and prosaic; it is a good piece of journalism, varied and neat, and very much of its period.

'Midwinter has come and gone. "What was it like?" is a question we are sure to be asked some day. I record it here.

A calm clear day; a golden moon, almost at its full, was sailing low down over the far South Western Mountains, which stood out sharp and white in the clear atmosphere. High above us swung the

Southern Cross, in a sky studded with scintillating points of light, watch fires of countless stars. Jupiter, like the boss of a golden shield, and the smaller planets, like beacons, shone.

To the Northward, lowdown on the horizon, was a broad band of reddish light, above which the dark blue sky began; a sign that the sun, though absent, was not so very far away. In the calm frosty air arose the steam and smoke from the ship, and all round the Colony activity prevailed.

Such was Midwinter Day with us. Everything and every one was bright and cheerful; the dark demon of Depression finds no home here; "Depression" can be taken out of our Polar Dictionary, and the phrase "white silence" will not suit a place where the hills re-echo the voices of busy men.

It is not hard to be like those men of old, "who ever with a frolic welcome took the storm and sunshine". True, there are many storms at this time, but in a few months we will have our share of the sunshine.

I need say no more; The energy of the contributors and artists has again filled the columns of the paper; the doings of the month are in its pages.'

It is evident from those of Shackleton's writings that are available that he was very well able to handle the accounts of his expeditions. But because he could not spare enough time to carry through the writing of a long book, he took the traditional privilege of the man of action and sought for a collaborator. His choice was an excellent one.

In 1901, when the *Discovery* docked at Lyttelton, many people were entertained on board—among them a young man of 19 who was just beginning his career as a reporter on the *Lyttelton Times*. The young man, Edward Saunders, was the son of Samuel Saunders, who edited this paper between 1891 and 1914. His grandfather, Alfred Saunders, one of the first party of settlers in Nelson, had written an excellent history of those days; his maternal relatives were descended from a Captain Cargill who led the first body of settlers in Otago. Thus the young man had inherited a keen feeling of responsibility for the young New Zealand nation, a desire to develop his literary talents in the service of his country. Indeed, his record was one of the finest in the history of journalism in the Dominion.

Edward Saunders probably did not meet Shackleton on the *Discovery*, but it seems that he was one of the reporters who interviewed him in Lyttelton in 1907 before he set out on the *Nimrod*. When Shackleton returned to Lyttelton in 1909 he consulted Sir Joseph Ward (then Prime Minister of New Zealand) about a secretary to help him with the documentation of the expedition. He may already have had Edward Saunders in mind, for he had thought well of the reports of the expedition in the *Lyttelton Times*. The two young men now struck up a warm friendship, and Shackleton offered Saunders the post of confidential secretary for four calendar months, starting on 15 April

1909, at a generous salary of £10 a week and expenses, including a return fare to New Zealand.

Shackleton and Saunders tackled the writing of *The Heart of the Antarctic* with energy and intelligence. Although the first months in England were very full ones for Shackleton, he succeeded in finding long hours to work at the book with his secretary. Some of it he had almost certainly drafted during the winter at Cape Royds. A good deal was written at Hinton Charterhouse, where his brother-in-law Arthur Dorman was vicar, and considerably more in a hut at Newhaven Court, Cromer, which was lent to him by Mrs. Locker-Lampson.

The two men worked in intimate partnership on the book, and Shackleton's conversation and descriptions were so vivid that Saunders was able to get a clear picture of the Antarctic scene. Shackleton, being very much occupied with outside affairs, must have had on many occasions to leave the book for Saunders to work on, with notes and dictated passages as a basis for his writing. The book was particularly well suited to this kind of collaborative treatment, because the central part of it, the account of the great Southern Journey, is in fact a slightly expanded version of Shackleton's diary. At rare moments in his diary Shackleton had let himself go and had written with real feeling and with full expression. Such a moment came when he described how the party of four men came upon the gateway to the Pole[2]:

'After travelling for ½ mile we reached the base of mountain or hill we hoped to climb to gain a view of the surround(ing) country. this hill is composed of granite the red appearance no doubt due to the iron: At 1 pm we had a couple of biscuits and some water and then started to climb the precipitous rock face. This was the most difficult part of the whole climb for the granite was weathered and split in every direction and some of the largest pieces seemed just to be nicely balanced on some of the smaller pieces so that one could almost push them over by the mere touch. With great difficulty we clambered up this rock face then ascended a gentle snow slope to another rocky bit but not so difficult to climb and from the top of this ridge there burst upon our vision an open road to the South for there stretched a great glacier running almost South and North between the great mountain ranges. And as far as we could see the glacier except towards the mouth appeared to be smooth yet this was not certainly for the distance was so great. Eagerly we clambered up the remaining ridges and over a snow slope and found ourselves on top at a height of 3350 feet by aneroid and hypsometer: From the summit we could see the glacier stretching away inland till at last it seemed to merge into inland ice. Where the glacier fell into the Barrier at about an N E bearing the pressure waves were enormous and for miles the surface of the Barrier was broken up.'

There are few sustained passages of this kind; for the most part the diary tells its tale simply, and briefly, and the two men, when they were writing the narrative that surrounds the diary, let the story tell itself in the same way, vividly and simply. Saunders collected material partly by asking Shackleton numerous questions, and undoubtedly this helped also to solve one of the major problems in a book of this kind, the selecting of information so that the general reader may get a clear picture of scenes which are new to him.

Two portions of the book survive, outside the diary section, which offer interesting evidence of a most successful collaboration. Among the Shackleton family papers there is a block of typescript, the pages numbered 1–128, which correspond very closely to pages 39–137 of the first volume of *The Heart of the Antarctic*. The typescript begins with the *Nimrod* leaving Lyttelton, and ends in the middle of a description of the hut at Cape Royds. The typescript is heavily corrected by both Shackleton and Saunders, Saunders' corrections being made in black and later in green ink, Shackleton's in pencil (a few in red pencil). There are a number of pencilled deletions, some of long passages, which were presumably made by Shackleton. In a few passages the two men can be seen trying to work out together a simple, clear version of a sentence. Very occasionally Shackleton has made an alteration which could only have been made by an eye-witness, and which makes for greater vividness: for instance, the phrase 'upheaval' applied to ice becomes 'breaking away'. On the whole, however, the corrections are extraordinarily similar. Behind them can be sensed hours of conversation between two men who understood each other very well.

There is a second portion of the book, written in Shackleton's hand and with corrections by him and also by Saunders, among the papers of Dr. Mill at the Scott Polar Research Institute in Cambridge. These sheets correspond with pages 53–105 of the book.

The book as a whole is workmanlike and the style is easy and interesting. Saunders, who had returned to New Zealand in the winter, had news in due course of the good reception that was given to it when it was published. On 6 December Shackleton cabled to Kinsey,[3] 'Please communicate this to Saunders senior—Many thanks for your letter. Before your son returns wish to say he was indispensable. The success of the book largely due to him. I can not speak too highly of him in every way. This is not only my own feeling but my publishers and all he came in contact with.'

It was not surprising that he should ask for the help of Edward Saunders again over the book of his next expedition. Saunders had stayed with the *Lyttelton Times*, to become Associate Editor in 1914, and had then moved to Wellington, working first on the *New Zealand Times* and then, in 1917, on the *Dominion*. When Shackleton reached Wellington in 1917 after his journey down to the Ross Sea, he was joined by his friend. Saunders worked with Shackleton in Wellington for a few days and then travelled to Sydney with him, where they spent three weeks together. During that time, on boats and trains, at odd hours in the intervals of Shackleton's many engagements, Saunders learned the important parts of Shackleton's new story. He took full notes of their conversation, and Shackleton dictated certain passages to him, besides leaving with him one or two diaries kept by members of the expedition. The most important of these was the very full, descriptive diary of Frank Worsley, much of which was incorporated in the book. It will be remembered that Shackleton was returning to England with the intention of getting a war job at the earliest possible moment: he would not be able to undertake any writing, and he gladly gave Saunders complete responsibility for putting the material together, confident that his friend knew him well enough to write it as he wanted it to be written.

Some years later Saunders wrote to Mill[4]:

'Shackleton's method was to tell me the story, often under conditions that made even the roughest notes difficult. Sometimes he would dictate passages, where his interest was keenly stirred. But he liked questions and suggestions. I find, for example, that the account of the crossing of South Georgia increased in length by about one-third between the first draft and the final draft. Worsley told me some part of that story. I had to leave a gap somewhere between the loss of the ship and the start of the boat journey because I found that I had no record at all covering the period—Shackleton filled that gap after he received the manuscript.'

The particular part of the book mentioned by Saunders above survives in manuscript in his family, and Mr. L. B. Quartermain, who has had an opportunity to examine it, has kindly written the following account of it:

MSS. of Shackleton's 'South'
In papers in possession of family of Edward Saunders

This 230-page budget corresponds almost exactly with *South*, pp. 117–55 ('Escape from the Ice'), 197–212 ('Across South Georgia' and a few extra pages). The first 23 pages and two or three others are typewritten; the rest are in Edward Saunders' characteristic hand. Saunders always carried a typewriter with him, and he did so when he accompanied Shackleton to Australia in 1917. He evidently had time before Shackleton left for England and the war to type only those few pages of this part of the MS.

Saunders himself has revised this draft considerably. There are many verbal emendations and occasionally a paragraph or more has been erased and a different version written, e.g. on the back of the sheet. This then is clearly the original MS. written by Saunders partly from the several diaries in his possession, partly from his discussions with Shackleton and partly from his shorthand notes of Shackleton's own account of some of the most moving episodes.

It would appear that these are the papers from which Saunders' sisters typed the version which was sent to England for Shackleton's final revision. With very few exceptions they correspond exactly with the printed form. The main exceptions are a few places where Saunders had to be content with notes, or where he left out a word or two to be supplied by Shackleton.

The Alexander Turnbull Library in Wellington, New Zealand, has much of the same material, donated by Mr. Leonard H. Tripp of Wellington, all typescript. This appears to be a carbon copy of the version typed by the Saunders sisters and sent to Shackleton in England. Mr. Tripp noted on this typescript that part of it had been dictated to Saunders by Shackleton in his presence.

The first 23 pages, typescript, in the Saunders family papers are of special interest. These pages have a considerable number of pencilled alterations in what appears to be Shackleton's hand. Some are verbal changes of a 'stylistic' nature. For example, 'it is liable at any time now to break up and deposit us and our belongings in the ocean' (MS.) becomes '. . . fling us into the unplumbed sea' (final version and book). The search for the right word is apparent on p. 19 of the type-script: originally 'our road was across the open sea', 'road' has been crossed out and 'course' substituted: then 'course' itself is deleted and the word 'way' written in, the word which appears in *South*, p. 126, l. 17. All these alterations are in pencil and evidently made by Shackle-ton before he and Saunders parted. Once or twice Saunders overrules Shackleton: 'They were in need of a night's rest' is pencil-altered to 'All hands were in need of a night's rest', but this again is changed, by Saunders, to 'Everyone was in need of rest', and this is what appears in *South*, p. 126, ll. 32–3.

If the handwriting left us in any doubt that Shackleton had made the pencilled emendations, the nature of some of them would alone suggest that Shackleton must be responsible for them. For instance, the sailor corrects the journalist: 'We could see that the piece of ice we occupied had turned', wrote Saunders: 'slewed' has been written in in pencil. Similarly, 'goods' has been altered to 'gear'.

More striking still, there are cases where the eye-witness corrects the reporter. 'It was a fine big berg', wrote Saunders: after the pencil has been at work this becomes 'a fine big blue berg'. And who but Shackle-ton himself would, could, have made this alteration? Saunders had written, of the occasion when 'a sleeping-bag with a man inside' had fallen through an ice-crack, 'I saw a dark object floating in the water.' Shackleton—who else?—altered this to 'a whitish object'.

Several times, when the pencilled emendation is not very clearly written, it has been written over or re-written in ink in Saunders' hand, presumably to ensure that the sister-typist made no mistake.

There is one rather puzzling omission. The final paragraph in Chapter 10 of *South*, in which Shackleton speaks of the 'fourth person' they felt to be with them during the crossing of South Georgia, does not appear in the MS., which goes on without interruption with what appears as the opening of Chapter 11 in the book. This small section does occur in the 'Tripp' typescript, on a separate sheet headed 'NOTE'.

It is possible that this passage, which Leonard Tripp remembers hearing dictated, was withheld by Shackleton and restored by him after he received the draft of the book from Saunders in 1918.

L. B. QUARTERMAIN.

Saunders worked on *South* for a year, and Shackleton was delighted with the result. It was indeed a notable achievement. Saunders, who was now a man of more mature character than when he helped Shackleton with his earlier book, might well have obtruded his personality into the narrative. Instead, he responded so intuitively to his friend's descriptions and appreciated his feelings so deeply that he was able to write a first-person account of this remarkable expedition in which the character of Shackleton shines brightly in its many facets.

Indeed, it is obvious that Saunders, like so many people before him, had fallen under the spell of Shackleton's words, and was able to see many aspects of those two years in the ice as Shackleton would have seen them. His own comment on the collaboration,[5] to Leonard Tripp, showed that he had worked as a friend rather than as an employee:

' If I said that either book, or any chapter, was simply my transcription of notes taken from Shackleton's dictation, I should be telling an untruth. If I said that any chapter was entirely mine, I should be telling an untruth. My work was complementary to his. I could say that Shackleton had remarkable gifts of literary suggestion and selection and that, when his interest was stirred at critical portions of his narrative, he had a command of vivid, forceful English. But he needs no commendation of that kind, and my own feeling is that the books should stand without any attempt being made to explain just how they were produced.'

Shackleton in fact wanted Saunders to take more credit for his work than he was ever willing to take. He always acknowledged Saunders' share in the writing, and proposed, in 1917, that Saunders' name should be placed in the preface of *South* as editor of the book. Saunders, however, refused to take any public credit for his work, and requested Dr. Mill, who wrote to him for information about the work, not to draw attention to it in his biography. Shackleton's gratitude, and the knowledge that the work had been well done, was all the reward he wanted. Shackleton for his part was anxious that he should be suitably rewarded, and enlisted Tripp's help in selling certain equipment from the *Aurora* so that he could leave a substantial advance with Saunders, before he left for England. He asked him if he would later work with him on an autobiography. But for both of them the knowledge of their comradeship was more important than payment or further work. *South*, that epic of man's endurance, with its dramatic start in South Georgia, its revelation of the greatest moments in Shackleton's life and the greatest flowering of his personality, bore witness to a friendship which Shackleton valued no less because it had to be conducted very largely by letter, but which continued unfaded until Shackleton's last days.*

* Edward Saunders died suddenly on 14 December in the same year as Shackleton.

Like a brilliant accompanist, Saunders had extended all his power and skill to present Shackleton's story for him, weaving into a continuous pattern Shackleton's own words, his perceptions of Shackleton's moods, and the reflections of some of his comrades. The result is a great book and one which will continue to inspire men and women for generations to come.

References to Appendix on Shackleton's Writings

[1] H. R. Mill to L. O. H. Tripp, 1 September 1922. MS. letter, Tripp papers, Alexander Turnbull Library, Wellington, N.Z.

[2] Ernest Shackleton. MS. *Nimrod* diary, S.F.P. Entry covering 3 and 4 December 1908.

[3] Ernest Shackleton to J. J. Kinsey, 6 December 1909. Cable, copy among Saunders family papers.

[4] Edward Saunders to H. R. Mill, 5 August 1922. Copy letter in Saunders family papers.

[5] Edward Saunders to L. O. H. Tripp, 10 August 1922. Copy letter in Saunders family papers.

APPENDIX C

The Scientific Results of the Shackleton Antarctic Expeditions

by J. M. WORDIE and B. B. ROBERTS

[reprinted from *Polar Record* (1943). Vol. 4, No. 26, pp. 72–6, with minor additions]

FREQUENT letters reach the Scott Polar Research Institute asking for the whereabouts of scientific collections from various expeditions and enquiring if the material has been worked over and published. One of the difficulties of many expeditions when they return home is the publication of results. In the case of national expeditions on a very large scale a separate series is at times arranged, as in the case of Scott's *Discovery* and *Terra Nova* expeditions, Bruce's *Scotia*, and Rymill's British Graham Land Expedition. One of the disadvantages of this method is the small circulation of a new and generally expensive series. Many research workers would prefer to see publication in a well-known periodical dealing with the science in question, which would not only ensure a wide circulation, but would also be more certain to reach the specialist reader. One disadvantage of this method, however, is the lack of any listing of the results as a whole. The Institute has had this difficulty under consideration, and proposes in future, when expedition results have been published in this widespread manner, to sum them up as opportunity offers.

The Shackleton results have recently been summarised with some difficulty, and are listed below. Three expeditions are dealt with, and between them they show the advantages and disadvantages which attach to any method of publication, by series or otherwise. An attempt was made after Shackleton's *Nimrod* expedition to publish a series; but Government support was lacking, and the idea was finally abandoned. The *Endurance* and *Aurora* results were published by the authors, acting independently, in different publications. The *Quest* results were dealt with by the British Museum (Natural History) in a single volume. In the case of all three expeditions, however, some of the best work takes the form of appendices to popular volumes, and additional publications of value kept appearing spasmodically for several years.

British Antarctic Expedition, 1907–09 (*Nimrod*)

The main scientific results of the expedition were published in a special series of reports published by Messrs. William Heinemann, 21 Bedford Street, London, under the title *British Antarctic Expedition* 1907–09, *under the Command of Sir E. H. Shackleton, C.V.O., Reports on the Scientific Investigations.*

Biology. Vol. I:

Part 1. 'On collecting at Cape Royds', by James Murray, pp. 1–15.

Part 2. 'On microscopic Life at Cape Royds', by James Murray, pp. 16–40.

Part 3. 'Antarctic Rotifera', by James Murray, pp. 41–76.

Part 4. 'Musci', by Jules Cardot, pp. 77–9.

Part 5. 'Tardigrada', by James Murray, pp. 83–202.

Part 6. 'Rhizopodes d'eau douce', by Eugène Penard, pp. 203–62.

Part 7. 'Fresh-water Algae', by W. West and G. S. West, pp. 263–98.

(Parts 1–5 published in 1910; Parts 6–7 in 1911.)

Biology. Vol. II:

Part 1. 'Mollusca', by Charles Hedley, pp. 1–10.

Part 2. 'Antarctic Fishes', by E. R. Waite, pp. 11–18.

Part 3. 'Mallophages', by L. G. N. Neumann, pp. 19–24.

Part 4. 'Astéries, Ophiures et Echinoides', by R. Koehler, pp. 25–66.

(Parts 1–4 published in 1911. No further parts issued.)

Geology. Vol. I. 'Glaciology, Physiography, Stratigraphy and Tectonic Geology of South Victoria Land', by T. W. Edgeworth David and Raymond Priestley; with short notes on Palaeontology by T. Griffith Taylor and E. J. Goddard (319 pp., with 95 Plates and 67 Text-Figures), 1914.

Geology. Vol. II. 'Contributions to the Palaeontology and Petrology of South Victoria Land' (270 pp., with 38 Plates and 18 Text-Figures), 1916.

Part 1. 'A contribution to the study of Ice Structures', by D. Mawson, pp. 1–24.

Part 2. 'Report on the Foraminifera and Ostracoda from elevated deposits on the shores of the Ross Sea', by Frederick Chapman, pp. 25–53.

Part 3. 'Report on the Foraminifera and Ostracoda out of Marine Muds from soundings in the Ross Sea', by Frederick Chapman, pp. 54–80.

Part 4. 'Report on a probable Calcareous Alga from the Cambrian Limestone Breccia found in Antarctica at 85° S.', by Frederick Chapman, pp. 81–4.

Part 5. 'Report on Mollusca from Elevated Marine Beds, "Raised Beaches", of McMurdo Sound', by Charles Hedley, pp. 85–8.

Part 6. 'Report on Antarctic Soils', by H. I. Jensen, pp. 89–92.

Part 7. 'Report of the Petrology of the Alkaline Rocks of Mount Erebus, Antarctica', by H. I. Jensen, pp. 93–128.

Part 8. 'Report on the Inclusions of the Volcanic Rocks of the Ross Archipelago', by J. Allan Thomson, pp. 129–52.

Part 9. 'Report on the Petrology of the Dolerites collected by the British Antarctic Expedition, 1907–09', by W. N. Benson, pp. 153–60.

Part 10. 'Report on the Pyroxene Granulites collected by the British Antarctic Expedition, 1907–09', by A. B. Walkom, pp. 161–8.

Part 11. 'Petrological notes on some of the erratics collected at Cape Royds', by W. G. Woolnough, pp. 169–88.

Part 12. 'Report on the Petrology of some Limestones from the Antarctic', by Ernest W. Skeats, pp. 189–200.

Part 13. 'Petrology of Rock Collections from the Mainland of South Victoria Land', by D. Mawson, pp. 201–37.

Index to Vols. I and II, pp. 239–70.

[We are informed by Messrs. Heinemann (April 1943) that *Geology*, Vol. I is now out of print; stocks of the other reports are still available.]

The following papers were also published separately or in scientific periodicals:

Baschin, Otto. 'Die Geographischen Resultate von Shackletons Südpolar Expedition', *Zeitschrift der Gesellschaft für Erdkunde zu Berlin*, 1910, No. 4, pp. 245–60.

Darbyshire, O. V. 'Cryptogams from the Antarctic'. *Journ. Botany*, Vol. 61, 1923, pp. 105–7. [Descriptions of collections made during 1907–09 and 1914–17 Expeditions.]

Darwin, George. 'The Tidal Observations of the British Antarctic Expedition, 1907–09', *Proc. Roy. Soc. Lond.*, Series A, Vol. 84, No. A 572, 1910, pp. 403–22.

David, T. W. E. 'Antarctica and some of its Problems', *Geog. Journ.*, Vol. 43, No. 6, 1914, pp. 605–30.

Davis, J. K. 'Voyage of the S.Y. "Nimrod", Sydney to Montevideo via Macquarie Island, May 8–June 7, 1909', *Geog. Journ.*, Vol. 36, No. 6, 1910, pp. 696–703.

Kidson, Edward. *Meteorology. British Antarctic Expedition, 1907–09. Report on the Scientific Investigations.* Government Printer, Melbourne, Council for Scientific and Industrial Research, [1930]. 188 pp.

Mawson, D. 'Auroral Observations at Cape Royds Station, Antarctica. British Antarctic Expedition, 1908', *Trans. and Proc. Roy. Soc. South Australia*, Vol. 40, 1916, pp. 151–212.

Mirrlees, S. T. A. 'Meteorological Log in the Antarctic, November 1908 to February 1909', *Quart. Journ. Roy. Met. Soc.*, Vol. 57, No. 239, pp. 201–16.

Murray, James. 'Rotifera collected by the expedition in Australia, New Zealand, Fiji, Hawaii, Canada and South Africa'. *British Antarctic Expedition, 1907–09, under the command of Sir E. H. Shackleton, C.V.O.* London, published for the expedition by William Heinemann, 1911, 111 pp. [Reprinted from *Journ. Roy. Microscop. Soc.*, 1911, pp. 164–74, 285–97, 429–35, 573–87; with index to species.]

Priestley, R. E., and David, T. W. E. 'Geological Notes of the British Antarctic Expedition, 1907–09', *Compte Rendu du XIe Congrès Géologique Internationale*, Stockholm, 1910, pp. 767–811.

Ritchie, James, 'The Hyroid Zoophytes collected by the British Antarctic Expedition of Sir Ernest Shackleton, 1908', *Proc. Roy. Soc. Edinburgh*, Session 1912–13, Vol. 33, Part I, No. 2, 1913, pp. 9–34.

Shackleton, E. H. 'Some results of the British Antarctic Expedition, 1907–09', *Geog. Journ.*, Vol. 34, No. 5, 1909, pp. 481–500 (Maps, p. 592).

Seven Appendices on the scientific work of the expedition were included in Sir Ernest Shackleton's *Heart of the Antarctic*, Vol. II (London, 1909):

I. 'Biology', by James Murray, pp. 233–67.

II. 'Geological Observations . . .', by T. W. Edgeworth David and Raymond Priestley, pp. 268–307.
'Notes in Regard to Mount Erebus', by T. W. Edgeworth David and Raymond Priestley, pp. 308–10.
'Additional Notes on Eruptions', by James Murray, pp. 310–14.

III. 'Scientific Results of the Western Journey', by Raymond Priestley, pp. 315–33.
Section 1. 'Geological and Geographical', pp. 315–22.
Section 2. 'Descriptions of the Stranded Moraines and Dry Valley, with special reference to the recent elevation of the land bordering McMurdo Sound', pp. 322–30.
Section 3. 'Effect of the Summer sun on different varieties of Ice and Snow', pp. 331–3.

IV. 'Notes on Physics, Chemistry, and Mineralogy: Ice and Snow', by Douglas Mawson, pp. 334–8.
'Additional Notes' [ice and snow], by James Murray, pp. 339–43.
'Mineralogy and Chemistry', by Douglas Mawson, p. 344.
'Meteorological Optics', by Douglas Mawson, pp. 345–7.
'Additional Notes' [meteorological optics], by James Murray, pp. 347–57.
'Magnetic Observations. The Magnetic Pole and the Aurora', by Douglas Mawson, pp. 358–61.
'Notes on the Aurora Australis', by James Murray, pp. 361–7.
'Tides and Currents', by James Murray, pp. 367–75.

V. 'Meteorology. A Summary of Results', by T. W. Edgeworth David and J. B. Adams, pp. 376–83.
'Additional Notes' [meteorology], by James Murray, pp. 385–8.
'Note on Thermometers for Polar Work', by James Murray, pp. 389–90.
'Cloud Forms', by James Murray, pp. 390–6.

VI. 'Report on the Health of the Expedition', by Eric Marshall, pp. 397–9.

VII. 'Southern Journey Distances', pp. 400–4.

British Imperial Trans-Antarctic Expedition, 1914–17
(Endurance and Aurora)

Darbyshire, O. V. (see under 1907–09 Expedition).

[Davis, J. K.] *Aurora Relief Expedition. Report of Voyage by Commander* [J. K. Davis], 20 December 1916 to 9 February 1917. Melbourne, 1918. 14 pp., 2 maps.

James, R. W. 'Antarctic Pack-ice and the fate of the "Endurance"', *Discovery*, Vol. 4, No. 46, October 1923, pp. 260–5.

James, R. W. 'Some Problems Relating to Antarctic Sea-ice', *Memoirs and Proceedings Manchester Literary and Philosophical Society*, Vol. 68, Part I, No. 7, 1924, pp. 81–90.

Mossman, R. C. 'Meteorological Results of the Shackleton Antarctic Expedition, 1914–17 (Weddell Sea Party): Preliminary Notice', *Quart. Journ. Roy. Met. Soc.*, Vol. 47, January 1921, No. 197, pp. 63–70.

Wordie, J. M. 'The Drift of the "Endurance"', *Geog. Journ.*, Vol. 51, April 1918, pp. 216–37.

Wordie, J. M. 'Ross Sea Drift of the "Aurora" in 1915–17', *Geog. Journ.*, Vol. 58, September 1921, pp. 219–24.

Wordie, J. M. 'Shackleton Antarctic Expedition, 1914–17: Geological Observations in the Weddell Sea Area', *Trans. Roy. Soc. Edinburgh*, Vol. 53, Part I, No. 2, 1921, pp. 17–27.

Wordie, J. M. 'Shackleton Antarctic Expedition, 1914–17: Depths and Deposits of the Weddell Sea', *Trans. Roy. Soc. Edinburgh*, Vol. 52, Part IV, No. 30, 1921, pp. 781–93.

Wordie, J. M. 'Shackleton Antarctic Expedition, 1914–17: The Natural History of Pack-ice as observed in the Weddell Sea', *Trans. Roy. Soc. Edinburgh*, Vol. 52, Part IV, No. 31, 1921, pp. 795–829.

In addition to these papers, the following Appendices were included in Sir Ernest Shackleton's *South* (London, 1919):

'Scientific Work', by J. M. Wordie, pp. 343–4.
'Sea-ice Nomenclature', by J. M. Wordie, pp. 344–7.
'Meteorology', by L. D. A. Hussey, pp. 247–51.
'Physics', by R. W. James, pp. 351–5.
'South Atlantic Whales and Whaling', by Robert S. Clark, pp. 256–64.

Shackleton-Rowett Expedition, 1921–22 (Quest)

Campbell Smith, W. (Ed.). *Report on the Geological Collections made during the Voyage of the 'Quest' on the Shackleton-Rowett Expedition to the South Atlantic and Weddell Sea in 1921–22.* London: British Museum (Natural History), 1930, 161 pp. [A collection of thirteen papers dealing with the geology and petrology of South Georgia, Elephant Island, Zavodovskii Island, Weddell Sea (dredgings), Tristan da Cunha, Gough Island, St. Helena, Ascension Island, Cape Verde Islands and St. Paul's Rocks.]

Douglas, G. V. 'The Geological Results of the Shackleton-Rowett (Quest), Expedition', *Quart. Journ. Geol. Soc.*, Vol. 79, 1923, Proceedings, pp. x–xiii.

Hamilton, J. E. 'A Rare Porpoise of the South Atlantic, *Phocaena dioptrica* (Lahille, 1912)', *Discovery Reports*, Vol. 21, pp. 227–34. Cambridge, 1941.

Lowe, P. R. 'Notes on some Land Birds of the Tristan da Cunha Group collected by the "Quest" Expedition', *Ibis*, Eleventh Series, Vol. 5, 1923, pp. 511–28.

Wilkins, G. H. 'Account of the Voyage of the "Quest"'. *Bull. British Ornithologists' Club*, Vol. 43, 1922, pp. 2–5.

Wilkins, G. H. 'Report on the Birds collected during the voyage of the "Quest" to the South Atlantic', *Ibis*, Eleventh Series, Vol. 5, 1923, pp. 474–511.

Wilkins, G. H. 'Gough Island', *Journ. of Botany*, Vol. 63, 1925, pp. 65–70.

Wild, Frank. 'The Voyage of the "Quest"'. *Geog. Journ.*, Vol. 61, No. 2, 1923, pp. 73–108. [Includes an Appendix on the Hydrographic work by F. A. Worsley, pp. 97–103, and on the Geological work by G. V. Douglas, pp. 103–05.]

In addition to these papers the following Appendices were included in Frank Wild's *Shackleton's Last Voyage: The Story of the Quest* (London, 1923):

I. 'Geological Observations', by G. V. Douglas, pp. 314–28. [Contains petrological report by W. Campbell Smith.]

II. 'Natural History', by G. H. Wilkins, pp. 328–40.

III. 'Meteorology', by J. A. McIlroy, pp. 340–3.

IV. 'Hydrographic Work', by F. A. Worsley, pp. 343–51.

V. 'Medical', by A. H. Macklin, pp. 352–65.

APPENDIX D

A Shackleton Chronology

1874

Feb. 15. Ernest Henry Shackleton born at Kilkea House, near Athy, Co. Kildare: son of Henry Shackleton and Henrietta Letitia Sophia, *née* Gavan.

1880

Father left his small property to study medicine at Trinity College, Dublin. Family moved to 35 Marlborough Road, Dublin.

1884

Dec. Family moved to South Croydon.

1885

June. Family moved to Aberdeen House, 12 West Hill, Sydenham. Ernest entered Fir Lodge Preparatory School, Sydenham, under Miss Higgins.

1887

Passed into Dulwich College as a day boarder.

1890

Left school to join North-Western Shipping Company as a Boy on probation, with some of the privileges of an Apprentice.
Apr. 30. Sailed on *Hoghton Tower* from Liverpool for Valparaiso.

1891

Apr. *H.T.* returned to Liverpool. Formally indentured as Apprentice.
June 25. Left Cardiff on *Hoghton Tower* for Iquique.

1892

May 15. *H.T.* returned to Mersey.
June 27. Left on *Hoghton Tower* for Madras–Mauritius–Australia–Chile (long voyage, through 1893).

1894

July 3. Returned home.
Oct. 4. Passed Board of Trade Exam. for Second Mate.
Nov. 15. Third Mate of *Monmouthshire* (Welsh Shire Line) to Far East.

1895

July, late. Returned home.
Aug. To sea again in *Monmouthshire*.

1896

Apr. 19. Returned home.
May (about). Passed Board of Trade Exam. for First Mate.
June 19. Sailed in *Flintshire* as Second Mate, China–Japan–San Francisco–S. America.

1897

Jan. 27. Returned home.
Feb. 26. To sea again in *Flintshire*, to Saigon.
June 29. Returned home.
July. First met Emily Dorman.
July 17. To sea in *Flintshire*, Japan–Canada.

1898

Feb. 20. Returned home.
Mar. 11. To sea in *Flintshire*.
Apr. 28. Passed Exam. for Master at Naval Court in Singapore.
June 29. Returned home.
July 27. To sea in *Flintshire*.
Dec. 5. Returned home.
Dec. 25. To sea in *Flintshire* (coastal voyage).

1899

Jan. 7. Discharged. Resigned from W.S.L., joined Union Castle Line.
Mar., end. To sea as Fourth Officer on *Tantallon Castle*, to Cape-town. Three voyages in this ship, this year.
Dec. 14. To sea as Third Officer on *Tintagel Castle*, carrying troops from Southampton to S. Africa.

1900

Feb. 25. Returned home.
Mar. 8. To S.A. again in *Tintagel Castle*.
May 31. Returned home.
July. *O.H.M.S.* (with Dr. McLean) published by subscription.
Oct. 4. Joined *Gaika* as Third Officer, to Cape.
Dec. 16. Returned home.
Dec. 27. Signed on *Gaika*.
Dec. 29. Discharged.

1901

Jan. 5. To sea as Third Officer of *Carisbrooke Castle*, to Cape.
Mar. 13. Returned home.
Mar. 21. *Discovery* launched at Dundee.
June 4. Gazetted Sub-Lieutenant, R.N.R.
Aug. 6. Left the Solent for the Antarctic on *Discovery*.
Dec. 24. *Discovery* left Port Chalmers, N.Z.

1902

Jan. 5. Reached pack-ice.
Feb. 9. *Discovery* became 'shore-station' in McMurdo Sound.
Feb. 19–22. First Antarctic sledge-journey, with Wilson and Ferrar.
June 13. Chosen by Scott for Southern journey.
Nov. 2. Set out on Southern journey with Scott and Wilson.
Dec. 30. Reached Furthest South at 82° 15′ S.

1903

Feb. 3. Reached *Discovery*.
Feb. 28. Embarked on *Morning*.
Mar. 1 or 2. *Morning* sailed for N.Z.
May 9. Sailed from N.Z. on *Orotava via* San Francisco and New
    York to England.
June 15. Reached home.
Sep. Became sub-editor of *Royal Magazine*.
Dec. 6. Selected as Secretary/Treasurer of Royal Scottish Geo-
    graphical Society.

1904

Jan. 11. Took up appointment at R.S.G.S.
Feb. 18. Last entry in Navy List as Sub-Lieut., R.N.R.
Apr. 9. Married Emily Mary Dorman at Christ Church, Westminster.
Apr. 11. Settled at 14 South Learmonth Gardens, Edinburgh.
Sep. 16. To London to greet *Discovery*.

1905

Jan. 16. Offered resignation to R.S.G.S. on adoption as Liberal-
    Unionist candidate for Dundee.
Feb. 2. Son Raymond born.
July. Resignation R.S.G.S. took effect; took house St. Andrews for
    summer.
Dec. 4. Govt. resigned. Began canvassing.

1906

Jan. 16. Polling Day. Unsuccessful.
Feb. Plan for transporting Russian troops from Vladivostock to the
    Baltic fell through.
Became Secretary of technical committee at Beardmore's engineering
    works, Parkhead, Glasgow.
Dec. 23. Daughter Cecily born.

1907

Feb. 11. Outlined plans for own Antarctic Expedition at Kosmos
    Dining Club of Royal Geographical Society.
Feb.–May. Involved correspondence and negotiations with Scott and
    friends of both.
Apr. To Norway to buy sledges, etc.

June 15. *Nimrod* arrived in Thames.
July 30. *Nimrod* left Thames.
Aug. 7. *Nimrod* left Torquay for N.Z.
Oct. 31. Left England for Australia.
Dec. Lecturing in Australia; joined *Nimrod* in N.Z.

1908
Jan. 1. *Nimrod* left Lyttelton Harbour, towed by *Koonya*.
Jan. 14. Reached Antarctic Circle.
Jan. 15. *Koonya* returned to N.Z.
Jan. 23. Great Ice Barrier sighted.
Jan. 26. Decided to establish base McMurdo Sound.
Feb. 3. Chose Cape Royds as base.
Feb. 22. *Nimrod* returned to N.Z.
Mar. 5–11. Party climbed Mt. Erebus.
Aug. 12–22. First sledge-trip, with David and Armytage.
Sep. 22–Oct. 14. Adams, Marshall, Joyce, Wild and Marston lay
    main depôt.
Oct. 29. Began South Polar journey, with Adams, Marshall and Wild.
Nov. 7. Supporting party started back to base.
Nov. 26. Passed furthest south point of 1902.
Dec. 3. Climbed Mt. Hope, saw and named Beardmore Glacier.
Dec. 7. Pony 'Socks' lost in crevasse.
Dec. 25. Christmas Day feast on scratch rations, 85° 51' at 9500 feet.

1909
Jan. 1. Passed 87°—furthest south or north.
Jan. 6. 113 geogr. miles from Pole, 88° 7' S.
Jan. 7. Decided to turn back, but caught in blizzard.
Jan. 8. Confined to tents.
Jan. 9. Blizzard eased; travelled light and fast to 88° 23' S., 97
    geogr. miles from Pole. Raised Union Flag at Furthest South and
    annexed plateau.
Jan. 20. Picked up depôt E on Beardmore Glacier, 85° S.
Jan. 26. Fasting.
Jan. 28. Lower Glacier depôt (D) reached.
Feb. 2. Depôt C reached.
Feb. 4. Confined to tent with dysentery.
Feb. 13. Depôt B reached.
Feb. 20. Depôt A reached.
Feb. 23. Joyce's Bluff depôt sighted.
Feb. 24. Marshall ill; confined to tents in blizzard.
Feb. 27. Forced march with Wild to Hut Point, leaving Marshall
    with Adams.
Feb. 28. Reached *Discovery* hut—empty.
Mar. 1. Reached *Nimrod*; returned with relief party.
Mar. 2. Reached Marshall and Adams.
Mar. 3. All rejoined *Nimrod* at Hut Point.

Mar. 4. *Nimrod* passed Cape Royds.
Mar. 9. *Nimrod* left ice of Ross Sea.
Mar. 22. *Nimrod* anchored off Stewart Island.
Mar. 25. *Nimrod* reached Lyttelton Harbour.
Apr. 14. Farewell lunch Wellington.
June 12. Landed at Dover from France.
June 14. Homecoming at Charing Cross.
June 28. R.G.S. Albert Hall meeting.
July 12. Invested by King with Royal Victorian Order.
Aug. 27. *Nimrod* reached Torbay.
Sep. *Nimrod* open to public on Thames, Antarctic Exhibition.
Sep. 27. Lectured to King at Balmoral.
Oct. Lecture tour on Continent.
Nov.–Dec. Lecture tour in United Kingdom.
Nov. 4. Publication of *The Heart of the Antarctic*.
Nov. 9. Knighthood announced in Birthday Honours.
Dec. 14. Invested with Knighthood.

1910

Jan. Lecture tour on Continent.
Feb.–Mar. Lecture tour in U.K.
Mar. 19. Left for New York and lecture tour in U.S. and Canada.
June 10. Left Quebec for England.
July. Moved family from Edinburgh to Sheringham.
Aug. Lectured on East Coast.
Sep. Lectured in Scotland.
Oct. Lectured in England.
Nov. Lectured on Continent, mainly in Germany.

1911

Mar. Lectured on Continent.
Apr. Moved family to 7 Heathview Gardens, Putney Heath, London.
June 18. Gave evidence before *Titanic* Commission.
July 15. Son Edward born.
July. Business trip to Hungary.

1912

Dec. Visit to New York.

1913

Dec. 29. First public announcement of Imperial Trans-Antarctic
Expedition.

1914

May. To Norway to test sledges.
June. *Endurance* arrived in Thames.
July 16. *Endurance* visited in S.W. India Dock by Queen Alexandra
and her party.

Aug. 1. *Endurance* left London.
Aug. 8. *Endurance* left Plymouth.
Sep. 25. Left Liverpool for Buenos Aires to join *Endurance*.
Oct. 16. Joined *Endurance*.
Oct. 26. *Endurance* left B.A.
Nov. *Endurance* reached South Georgia.
Dec. 5. *Endurance* left S.G.
Dec. 30. Crossed Antarctic Circle.

1915
Jan. 10. Sighted Coats Land.
Jan. 15. Glacier projection and bay sighted on new-found Caird Coast.
Jan. 19. *Endurance* caught in ice, 76° 34′ S.
Feb. 22. Drifted furthest south, 77° S. off Luitpold Land.
Feb. 24. Ship treated as winter station.
July 22. Bad ice-pressure began.
Oct. 18. 30-degree list.
Oct. 24. *Endurance* began to leak.
Oct. 27. *Endurance* abandoned.
Nov. 1. Ocean Camp.
Nov. 21. *Endurance* sank.
Dec. 22. Attempt to march over ice.
Dec. 29. Attempt abandoned, Patience Camp formed.

1916
Jan. 14. Four dog-teams shot.
Mar. 23. Joinville Island sighted.
Apr. 7. Clarence and Elephant Islands sighted.
Apr. 9. Boats launched.
Apr. 12. Boats in open, heavy sea.
Apr. 15. Boats beached on Elephant Island.
Apr. 17. Party moved to Cape Wild.
Apr. 24. Left for South Georgia in *James Caird* with Crean, McNeish, McCarty, Vincent and Worsley.
May 8. Sighted mountains of S.G.
May 10. Beached on S.G.
May 15. Moved up inlet to Peggotty Camp.
May 19. Started journey across mountains with Crean and Worsley.
May 20. Reached Stromness Whaling Station.
May 22. Worsley brought the rest back from Peggotty Camp.
May 23. Sailed in *Southern Sky* for Elephant Island, with Worsley and Crean.
May 26. *S.S.* turned back—pack-ice.
May 28. *S.S.* tried again, no good.
May 31. *S.S.* entered Port Stanley, Falkland Islands.
June 10. *Instituto de Pesca No.* 1 reached P.S., sailed same day for E.I.

June 13. *I. de P.* driven back by pack 20 miles from E.I.
June 16. *I. de P.* back in P.S.
June. Crossed from P.S. to Punta Arenas.
July 12. *Yelcho* started from P.A., towing *Emma.*
July 14. *Yelcho* gave up tow.
July 21. *Emma* stopped by ice 100 miles from E.I.
Aug. 8. *Emma* reached P.S. *Yelcho* summoned to P.S. for tow.
Aug. 14. *Yelcho* towed *Emma* into P.A.
Aug. 25. *Yelcho* left P.A., alone.
Aug. 30. *Yelcho* embarked party from E.I.
Sep. 3. *Yelcho* reached P.A.
Sep. 15. To Valparaiso in *Yelcho.*
Sep. 27. *Yelcho* reached Valparaiso.
Sep. 29. To Buenos Aires by train.
Oct. To New Zealand *via* Panama and San Francisco.
Dec. Arrived Wellington, N.Z.
Dec. 20. Left in *Aurora* for Ross Sea, under Captain Davis.

1917

Jan. 1. *Aurora* reached McMurdo Sound.
Jan. 10. *Aurora* reached Cape Royds.
Jan. 17. *Aurora* left McMurdo Sound with survivors of Ross Sea party.
Feb. 9. *Aurora* reached Wellington.
Mar. In Australia.
Apr. In San Francisco and New York.
May. Reached London.
June–Sep. With family, based on Eastbourne.
Oct. 17. Sailed from Liverpool for New York.
Nov. 3. Sailed from New York for South America.

1918

Mar. (mid). From Buenos Aires *via* Valparaiso, Panama, New Orleans and Washington to New York.
Apr. (end). To England.
May–July. In London.
Aug. 2. Sailed from Aberdeen to Norway.
Aug. (end). In London.
Sep. In London.
Oct. 8. Sailed for Norway, thence North Russia (commission as Major—staff).
Nov. (end). Returned to London.
Dec. 25 Sailed from Invergordon back to Murmansk, N. Russia.

1919

Jan.–Mar. In Murmansk.
Feb. 9. Resigned Army Commission.
Apr.–Dec. With family at Eastbourne.

June 7. Formed Russian Company (abortive).
Dec. 19. First exhibition of *Endurance* film, Albert Hall.

1920

Jan.–end May. *Endurance* lectures in London.
Feb. (end). R.G.S. approved Arctic plan.
June–Dec. With family at Eastbourne.

1921

Jan. (early). Visit to Norway, bought *Foca I*, renamed *Quest*.
Jan. 18. In London.
Jan. (end)–early Mar. Visit to Canada.
Mar. 10–23 in London (Dulwich).
Mar. 24. Sailed for Canada again.
Apr. 19. Returned from Canada.
Apr.–Aug. Based on Eastbourne. Spent much time in London, planning *Quest* expedition, now switched to Antarctic.
Sep. 18. *Quest* left Thames.
Sep. 24. *Quest* left Plymouth.
Oct. 4. *Quest* put into Lisbon for repairs.
Oct. 26. *Quest* at St. Vincent, Madeira.
Nov. 8. *Quest* at St. Paul's Rocks.
Nov. 22. *Quest* reached Rio de Janeiro.
Dec. 18. *Quest* left Rio.

1922

Jan. 2. *Quest* sighted first iceberg.
Jan. 4. *Quest* reached Grytviken, South Georgia.
Jan. 5. Ernest Henry Shackleton died in his cabin on *Quest*, of coronary thrombosis, at 3.30 a.m.

APPENDIX E
References

CHAPTER I

[1] Ernest Shackleton to Emily Dorman, 20 April 1901. Letter, S.F.P.
[2] Begbie (1922).

CHAPTER II

[1] Mill (1923), p. 31.
[2] *Ibid.*, p. 33.
[3] McLean and Shackleton (1900), p. 31.
[4] *Ibid.*, p. 47.
[5] Thomas Peers. Recorded conversation with J.F., 19 May 1957.
[6] Emily Shackleton to H. R. Mill, 1923. MS. letter, S.P.R.I.
[7] Ernest Shackleton to Emily Dorman, 12 August 1898. MS. letter, S.F.P.

CHAPTER III

[1] *Sphere*, Vol. 4, p. 326 (1901).
[2] *Geogr. J.*, Vol. 9, pp. 594-5 (1897).
[3] *Ibid.*, Vol. 13, p. 10 (1899).
[4] *Ibid.*, Vol. 13, pp. 425-6 (1899).
[5] *Ibid.*, Vol. 13, p. 53 (1899).
[6] Scott (1907).
[7] Albert B. Armitage to Hugh Robert Mill, 20 May, answered 24 May 1922. Memo in Mill Bequest, S.P.R.I.
[8] *Geogr. J.*, Vol. 19, p. 448 (1902).
[9] Edward A. Wilson. MS. diary of *Discovery* expedition in S.P.R.I.
[10] G. Murray (1902), *Geogr. J.*, Vol. 19, p. 443.
[11] *Sphere*, Vol. 6, pp. 129, 249 (1901).
[12] Bernacchi (1938), pp. 221-2.
[13] Mill (1923), p. 61.
[14] R. F. Scott to H. R. Mill, 6 November 1901. Mill bequest, S.P.R.I.

CHAPTER IV

[1] Edward A. Wilson. MS. diary of *Discovery* expedition in S.P.R.I.
[2] Harris (1953).
[3] Ernest Shackleton. M.S. diary of *Discovery* expedition in S.F.P.
[4] Scott (1905).
[5] Scott (1907).
[6] Bernacchi (1938), p. 63.
[7] Robert Falcon Scott to Ernest Shackleton, 17 February 1902. MS. instruction, S.F.P.

[8] Ernest Shackleton and Edward A. Wilson to Robert Falcon Scott. MS. report, S.P.R.I. MS. Coll., *Discovery* exped.

[9] Reginald W. Skelton. MS. diary of *Discovery* expedition in S.P.R.I.

[10] Armitage (1905), pp. 90–1.

[11] Frank Plumley, blacksmith on *Discovery*. Letter to M. F., November 1955.

[12] Charles Hare to M. F., December 1955. Letter and memorandum.

[13] James Dell. Recorded conversation with J. F., 10 October 1955.

[14] Charles Ford to M. F., 12 January 1956. Letter in answer to questions.

[15] Michael Barne. Recorded conversation with J. F., 16 October 1955.

[16] Mountevans (1946), pp. 77–8.

CHAPTER V

[1] Edward A. Wilson. MS. diary of *Discovery* expedition in S.P.R.I.

[2] Ernest Shackleton to Emily Dorman, 1 November 1902. Letter, S.F.P.

[3] Ernest Shackleton. MS. diary of *Discovery* expedition in S.F.P.

[4] Scott (1905).

[5] Scott (1907).

[6] Begbie (1922), p. 26.

CHAPTER VI

[1] *Field*, Vol. 102, p. 150 (1903).

[2] Robert Falcon Scott to Reginald Koettlitz, 19 February 1903. MS. instruction (and reply) S.P.R.I. MS. Coll., *Discovery* exped.

[3] Edward A. Wilson: MS. diary of *Discovery* expedition in S.P.R.I.

[4] Armitage (1905).

[5] Armitage (1925).

[6] Albert B. Armitage to Hugh Robert Mill, received 24 May 1922. Memo in Mill Bequest, S.P.R.I.

[7] Mill (1923).

[8] Ernest Shackleton. MS. diary of *Discovery* expedition in S.F.P.

[9] Clements R. Markham to Ernest Shackleton, 4 June 1903. Letter, Mill Bequest, S.P.R.I.

[10] Ernest Shackleton to Emily Dorman, 2 December 1903. Letter, S.F.P.

[11] Ernest Shackleton to Hugh Robert Mill, 15 December 1903. Letter, Mill Bequest, S.P.R.I.

[12] E. S. to E. D., 11 January 1904. Letter, S.F.P.

[13] *Ditto*, 3 February.

[14] E. S. to H. R. M., 3 and 26 February 1904. Letters, Mill Bequest, S.P.R.I.

[15] Clements R. Markham to Emily Shackleton, 16 November 1904. Letter, S.F.P.

[16] E. S. to Emily Shackleton, 15 May and postmark 15 October 1904. Letters, S.F.P.

[17] E. S. to H. R. M., 22 November 1904. Letter, Mill Bequest, S.P.R.I.

[18] Minutes of Council, Royal Scottish Geographical Society's Archives.
[19] Ernest Shackleton to Robert Falcon Scott, 21 January 1905. Letter, S.P.R.I. MS. Coll.
[20] E. S. to Emily S., postmark 4 April 1905. Letter, S.F.P.
[21] *Ditto*, undated January 1906.
[22] Brodrick (1947), p. 275.
[23] E. S. to Emily S., undated and 9 February 1906. Letters, S.F.P.
[24] *Ditto*, 14 February 1906.
[25] *Ditto*, 25 February 1906.
[26] A. B. Macduff. Recorded conversation with J. F., 15 June 1956.
[27] *Pearson's Weekly*, week ending 8 April 1909.
[28] H. R. Mill to Ernest Shackleton, 30 November 1903. MS. letter, S.F.P.
[29] William Huggins and Clements R. Markham to Lords Commissioners of the Admiralty, 28 June 1903. Copy letter, R.G.S.
[30] Qualifications and Testimonials of Ernest Henry Shackleton. Printed document, S.F.P.

CHAPTER VII

[1] Mill (1930).
[2] Ernest Shackleton to Emily Shackleton, 12 February 1907. MS. letter, S.F.P.
[3] H. R. Mill (1909), *Geogr. J.*, Vol. 33, p. 570 (1909).
[4] Kathleen Shackleton. Recorded conversation with J. F., 27 November 1955.
[5] Ernest Shackleton to Robert Falcon Scott, 28 February 1907. Letter, S.P.R.I.
[6] Mill (1909).
[7] *Times*, 12 February 1907.
[8] *Geogr. J.*, Vol. 29, p. 330 (1907).
[9] Charles W. R. Royds. MS. diary of *Discovery* expedition, lent by his daughter, Mrs. Richard Eyre.
[10] E. S. to Emily S., 14 August 1907. MS. letter, S.F.P.
[11] George Mulock to Ernest Shackleton, 19 February 1907. MS. letter, S.F.P.
[12] Hugh Robert Mill to Emily Shackleton, 22 June 1908. MS. letter, S.F.P.
[13] Edward A. Wilson to Ernest Shackleton, 15 February 1907. MS. letter, S.F.P.
[14] E. S. to E. A. W., 17 or 27 February 1907. MS. copy letter, S.F.P.
[15] Ernest Shackleton to Robert Falcon Scott, 28 February 1907. Copy letter, S.F.P.
[16] E. A. W. to E. S., 28 February 1907. MS. letter, S.F.P.
[17] E. S. to R. F. S., 4 March 1907. Copy cable, S.F.P.
[18] E. S. to R. F. S., 7 March 1907. Copy letter, S.F.P.
[19] Ernest Shackleton to J. Scott Keltie, March 1907, copy cable and letters, S.P.R.I. and S.F.P.
[20] J. S. K. to E. S., 6 March 1907. MS. letter, S.F.P.

21 Ernest Shackleton to Michael Barne. 28 March 1907. Copy letter, S.F.P.
22 Clements R. Markham to Ernest Shackleton, 26 February 1907. MS. letter, S.F.P.
23 Ernest Shackleton to William Beardmore, 8 March 1907. Copy letter in possession of A. B. MacDuff.
24 E. A. W. to E. S., 8 March 1907. MS. letter, S.F.P.
25 E. S. to E. A. W., 11 March 1907. Copy letter, S.F.P.
26 E. S. to R. F. S., 23 March 1907. Copy letter, S.F.P.
27 E. S. to R. F. S., 17 May 1907. Copy letter, S.F.P. The S.P.R.I. copy has some small differences.
28 Shackleton (1909b), Vol. 1, p. 16.
29 Ibid., Vol. 1, p. 5.
30 Taylor (1916), p. 7.
31 Cherry-Garrard (1922), p. 548.
32 Bernacchi (1938), p. 15.
33 Hayes (1928).
34 Times, 16 October 1907.
35 Raymond Priestley, MS. diary of Nimrod expedition, lent by the diarist.
36 Sphere, Vol. 33, p. 122 (1908).

Chapter VIII

1 Charles Mackeller to Emily Shackleton, April 1908. MS. letter, S.F.P.
2 Jameson Boyd Adams. Recorded conversation with J. F., 5 October 1955.
3 Mill (1909), p. 4.
4 Raymond Edward Priestley. Recorded conversation with J. F., 5 October 1955.
5 Shackleton (1914), p. 142.
6 Mill in Joyce (1929), p. 22.
7 Times, 5 August 1907.
8 E. H. Shackleton (1907). Geogr. J., Vol. 30, pp. 336–7.
9 Field, Vol. 118, p. 1171 (1911).
10 Byrd (1931), p. 4.
11 Scholes (1911), p. 14.
12 Ernest Shackleton to Emily Shackleton, 31 October 1907, 5 and 16 November, etc. MS. letters, S.F.P.
13 Gerald Lysaght (1908). Spectator, 1 January.
14 T. W. Edgeworth David to Emily Shackleton, 7 December 1907. Cable, S.F.P.
15 T. W. Edgeworth David to the Prime Minister of Australia. Letter of 10 December 1907; printed by Govt. Order on 13 December 1907 as 1907 (Second Session) The Parliament of the Commonwealth of Australia, Code No. 140-F 15964.
16 M. E. David (1937), pp. 117–18.
17 E. S. to Emily S., 1 and c. 14 January 1908. MS. letters, S.F.P.
18 Polar Record, Vol. 6, pp. 45–79 (1951).

Chapter IX

[1] Raymond Edward Priestley to his father, J. E. Priestley. Diary-letter sent back on *Nimrod*, in the possession of the diarist.

[2] T. W. Edgeworth David (1908). An excellent series of dispatches sent back to the *Sydney Daily Telegraph*, and printed therein in fourteen instalments.

[3] Shackleton (1909b), Vol. 1, p. 41.

[4] The messages are recorded in the *Nimrod*'s log. This and later extracts are made from a microfilm of the fair copy of this log, which is in the Alexander Turnbull Library, Wellington, N.Z. Edward Shackleton possesses what is clearly the deck copy of certain portions of the log for 1907–08.

[5] Ernest Shackleton to Emily Shackleton, 10 and *c*. 14 January 1908. MS. letters, S.F.P.

[6] George Buckley. Special report to Christchurch papers, 22 January 1908.

[7] A. E. Harbord. MS. diary of *Nimrod* voyage, lent by the diarist.

[8] Raymond Edward Priestley. Recorded conversation with J. F., 11 September 1955.

[9] E. S. to Emily S. Undated (1908) cable, S.F.P.

[10] *Geogr. J.*, Vol. 31, p. 448 (1908).

[11] E. S. to Emily S., 26 January 1908. MS. letter, S.F.P.

[12] Mill (1923).

[13] Rupert G. England to Jessie Turner, February 1908. A long letter sent from New Zealand, from which Captain England's widow has kindly allowed us to quote.

[14] A. E. Harbord. Recorded conversation with J. F., 9 June 1956.

Chapter X

[1] Shackleton (1909b), Vol. 1, pp. 84–5, 89, 115.

[2] Eric Marshall. MS. diary of *Nimrod* expedition, studied from a microfilm in S.P.R.I., with the permission of the diarist.

[3] A. E. Harbord. MS. diary of *Nimrod* voyage, lent by the diarist.

[4] *Nimrod* log, see citation 4, ch. IX.

[5] Rupert G. England, see citation 13, ch. IX.

[6] Æneas L. Mackintosh to Emily Shackleton, 22 March 1908. MS. letter, S.F.P.

[7] H. J. L. Dunlop to J. D. Morrison, 3 June 1908. Copy letter, S.F.P.

[8] A. E. Harbord. Recorded conversation with J. F., 9 June 1956.

[9] Rupert G. England to Emily Shackleton, 23 April 1908. MS. letter, S.F.P.

[10] Rupert G. England to J. J. Kinsey, 20 March 1908. Copy letter in possession of Mrs. Rupert England, from which she has kindly allowed us to quote.

[11] *Times*, 10 March 1908.

[12] *Daily Mail*, 11 March 1908.

[13] Ernest Shackleton to Emily Shackleton, *c*. 14 January and 22 February 1908. MS. letters, S.F.P.

[14] *Lyttelton Times*, 24 and 25 April 1908.
[15] William Coull, quoted in *Lyttelton Times*, 21 March 1908.
[16] John King Davis and others to Emily Shackleton, 23 April 1908. MS. letter with numerous signatures, and MS. letters, S.F.P.
[17] Debenham (1948).

CHAPTER XI

[1] Ernest Shackleton to Emily Shackleton, 18 February 1908. Letter, S.F.P.
[2] Raymond Edward Priestley. Diary of *Nimrod* expedition, lent by the diarist.
[3] Shackleton (1909b), Vol. 1, pp. 131–50, 229, 240.
[4] [Raymond Edward Priestley] 'A Messman' (1908). 'Trials of a messman', *Aurora Australis* ('published' in Antarctic).
[5] Mill (1923), p. 128.
[6] Giæver (1954), p. 92.
[7] T. W. Edgeworth David (1908). 'The ascent of Mount Erebus', *Aurora Australis*.
[8] Hydrographic Department, Admiralty (1956).
[9] Raymond Edward Priestley. Recorded conversation with J. F., 11 September 1955.
[10] Philip Lee Brocklehurst. Recorded conversation with J. F., 16 December 1955.
[11] C.T.V.M. in Byrd (1937), p. 188.
[12] Shackleton (1909b), Vol. 3.
[13] Marston and Murray (1913), pp. 104–5.
[14] Eric Stewart Marshall. MS. diary of *Nimrod* expedition, studied from a microfilm in S.P.R.I., with the permission of the diarist.
[15] E. H. Shackleton (1907). *Geogr. J.*, Vol. 29, pp. 329–32.
[16] Ernest Shackleton. Letters and orders to members of *Nimrod* expedition, S.F.P.
[17] Ernest Shackleton to Emily Shackleton. Letter to be delivered in the case of his death on the *Nimrod* expedition, and final note, S.F.P.
[18] Ernest Shackleton. MS. diary of *Nimrod* expedition in S.F.P.
[19] Jameson Boyd Adams to J. F., 17 June 1957. Memorandum.

CHAPTER XII

[1] Ernest Shackleton. MS. diary of *Nimrod* expedition in S.F.P.
[2] Marshall (1943).
[3] Frank Wild. Diary of *Nimrod* expedition. Copy in S.F.P.
[4] Jameson Boyd Adams. Recorded conversation with J. F., 5 October 1955.
[5] Armitage (1925), p. 200.
[6] *Sphere*, Vol. 37, p. 260 (1909), and other reports.
[7] Owen (1948), pp. 175–6.
[8] Hayes (1932), p. 55.

Chapter XIII

[1] Eric Stewart Marshall. MS. diary of *Nimrod* expedition, studied from a microfilm in S.P.R.I., with the permission of the diarist.

[2] Ernest Shackleton. MS. diary of *Nimrod* expedition in S.F.P.

[3] Frank Wild. Diary of *Nimrod* expedition. Copy in S.F.P.

[4] Jameson Boyd Adams. Recorded conversation with J. F., 5 October 1955.

[5] Kearns and Britton (1955), p. 106.

[6] Jameson Boyd Adams to Mrs. Edmund Phipps, 10 March 1909. Copy letter kindly lent by the writer.

[7] Shackleton (1909b), Vol. 2, pp. 73–222 (David), 404.

[8] Owen (1948), pp. 175–6.

[9] *Nimrod* log, see citation 4, ch. IX.

[10] Mrs. Valerie Gould to M. F., November 1955. Memorandum.

[11] Raymond Edward Priestley. Diary of *Nimrod* expedition, lent by the diarist.

[12] Alistair Forbes Mackay. MS. diary of part of *Nimrod* expedition, in S.F.P.

[13] Ernest Shackleton to F. P. Evans, 27 March 1909. Letter among Tripp papers in Alexander Turnbull Library, Wellington, N.Z.

[14] James Murray to Emily Shackleton, 25 February 1913. Letter, S.F.P.

[15] Herbert Dorman to Emily Shackleton, 10 March 1909. Letter, S.F.P.

[16] Ernest Shackleton to Emily Shackleton, 8 April 1909. Letter, S.F.P.

[17] *The Winning Post*, 3 April 1909, p. 3.

[18] E. S. to Emily S., 25 April 1909. Letter, S.F.P.

[19] Michael J. N. Foster. Recorded conversation with J. F., 6 November 1956.

Chapter XIV

[1] Fridtjof Nansen to Emily Shackleton, from Lysaker, 8 April 1909. Letter, S.F.P.

[2] Fridtjof Nansen to Royal Geographical Society (J. Scott Keltie), early April 1909. Letter, R.G.S.

[3] Nils Adolf Erik, Baron Nordenskjöld to R.G.S. (J. S. K.), from Göteborg, 10 April 1909. Letter, R.G.S.

[4] Roald Amundsen to R.G.S. (J. S. K.), from Christiania, 25 March 1909. Letter, R.G.S.

[5] Mill (1930), p. 174.

[6] J. Scott Keltie (R.G.S.) to Ernest Shackleton, 1 April 1909. Copy letter, R.G.S.

[7] *Geogr. J.*, Vol. 33, pp. 485–8 (1909).

[8] H. R. Mill (1909), *Geogr. J.*, Vol. 33, pp. 570–73, (1909).

[9] Ernest Shackleton to Hugh Robert Mill, from Melbourne, 5 May 1909. Letter, S.P.R.I.

[10] Clements R. Markham to Emily Shackleton, 26 May 1908. Letter, S.F.P.

[11] Clements R. Markham to R.G.S. (J. S. K.), from Broussaka, 27 March 1909. Letter, R.G.S.

[12] Clements R. Markham to Leonard Darwin, April and 5 September 1909. Copy letters, Mill Bequest, S.P.R.I.

[13] Shackleton (1909a), p. 491.

[14] Jameson Boyd Adams. Recorded conversation with J. F., 5 October 1955.

[15] Eric Stewart Marshall, MS. diary of *Nimrod* expedition studied from a microfilm in S.P.R.I., with the permission of the diarist.

[16] Markham (1913).

[17] Markham (1921).

[18] Leonard Darwin (1909). *Geogr. J.*, Vol. 34, p. 122.

[19] Royal Geographical Society (J. Scott Keltie) to Cuthbert Bayes, 19 April, 11 and 21 May. Copy letters R.G.S.

[20] Frank Debenham. Recorded conversation with J. F., 5 October 1956.

[21] Philip Lee Brocklehurst. Recorded conversation with J. F., 16 December 1955.

[22] *Review of Reviews* (1923), May.

[23] Robert Falcon Scott to Leonard Darwin, 26 March 1909. Copy letter, Mill Bequest, S.P.R.I.

[24] Lewis Beaumont to Leonard Darwin, 19 June 1909. Copy letter, Mill Bequest, S.P.R.I.

[25] R. F. S. to L. D., 27 June 1909. Copy letter, S.P.R.I.

[26] R. F. S. to E. S., 1 July 1909. Copy letter, S.P.R.I.

[27] E. S. to R. F. S., 6 July 1909. Copy letter, S.P.R.I.

[28] L. D. to E. S., undated 1909. Copy letter, S.P.R.I.

[29] E. S. to R. F. S., 1 February 1910. Copy letter, S.P.R.I.

[30] Mawson (1915), p. x.

[31] R. F. S. to E. S., 25 February 1910. Copy letter, S.P.R.I.

[32] R. F. S. to L. D., 29 March 1910. Copy letter, S.P.R.I.

[33] Frank Wild. Diary of *Nimrod* expedition. Copy in S.F.P.

Chapter XV

[1] *Lyttelton Times*, March 1909.

[2] Archbishop Julius (1909). Quoted from a New Zealand paper, 29 March.

[3] *Daily Telegraph*, 15 June 1909.

[4] *Sphere* Vol. 37, p. 14 (1909), 3 April.

[5] Christchurch Press, 1909.

[6] Unidentified press report, S.F.P.

[7] Trinity House to Ernest Shackleton, 17 June 1909. Letter, S.F.P.

[8] Shackleton (1909b), Vol. 2, p. 414.

[9] Herbert Dorman to Emily Shackleton, 2 June 1908 and 14 January 1909. Letters, S.F.P.

[10] Unidentified press cuttings, S.F.P.

[11] Herbert Henry Asquith to Ernest Shackleton, 19 August 1909. Letter, S.F.P.

[12] D. J. D. Clark to M. F., 24 July 1956. Letter.

[13] Ernest Shackleton to Emily Shackleton, August 1909. Letter, S.F.P.
[14] E. S. to Emily S., 25 September 1909. Letter, S.F.P.
[15] *Daily Mail*, 20 August 1909.

Chapter XVI

[1] Shackleton (1909b).
[2] *Evening Standard*, 4 November 1909.
[3] *Herts. Advertiser*, 3 June 1911.
[4] Mill (1923), p. 90.
[5] Mrs. Henrietta Lomas to M. F., 29 January 1957. Letter.
[6] Charles Mackeller to Hugh Robert Mill, 1922 or 1923. Memo, S.F.P.
[7] Unidentified press report, S.F.P.
[8] Ernest Shackleton to Emily Shackleton, 26 January 1910. Letter, S.F.P.
[9] *Eastern Daily Press*, Norwich, 11 February 1910.
[10] *Times*, 1 March 1910.
[11] Chandler Robbins, secretary of the American Geographical Society, to Civic Forum, September 1909. Copy letter, S.F.P.
[12] *Scientific American*, New York, 9 April 1910.
[13] *New York Sun*, 30 March 1910.
[14] *Toronto News*, 28 April 1910.
[15] *Free Press Evening News Bulletin*, Winnipeg, 23 May 1910.
[16] Unidentified Winnipeg paper. Cutting in S.F.P.
[17] *Evening Telegraph*, Toronto, 27 April 1910.
[18] *The News*, Philadelphia, 23 April 1910.
[19] E. S. to Emily S., 3 November 1910. Letter, S.F.P.
[20] E. S. to Emily S., from Stuttgart, 23 November 1910. Letter, S.F.P.
[21] Pamela Gow. Recorded conversation with J. F., 1 April 1957.
[22] E. S. to Emily S., from Budapest, 8 March 1911. Letter, S.F.P.
[23] Philip Gibbs (1911). *Dublin Daily Express*. February.
[24] *Proceedings on a formal investigation ordered by the Board of Trade into the loss of the S.S. "Titanic"*. London, June 1912. Extracts kindly provided by Percy Faulkner, C.B., and quoted by permission of Her Majesty's Stationery Office.
[25] Lee Keedick. Notes sent to Dr. Mill in 1922. Mill Bequest, S.P.R.I.
[26] Ernest Shackleton to Rufus Isaacs, 27 June 1912. Copy letter, S.F.P.

Chapter XVII

[1] Ernest Shackleton to H. R. Mill, 13 August 1913. Mill Bequest, S.P.R.I.
[2] Lewis Beaumont to Royal Geographical Society, 1914. Copy memorandum in S.P.R.I.
[3] A. R. Hinks to Douglas W. Freshfield, 1 May 1916. Copy letter, R.G.S.
[4] Ernest Shackleton to W. S. Bruce, 20 August 1913. Letter, S.P.R.I.
[5] Royal Geographical Society, Minutes of Council, 6 April 1914. Copy of memo by President, Earl Curzon of Kedleston, S.P.R.I.
[6] Douglas Freshfield (1914), *Geogr. J.*, Vol. 44, p. 525.

[7] Mill (1945), p. 120.

[8] E. Shackleton (1914), *Geogr. J.*, Vol. 43, pp. 318–21.

[9] T. W. Edgeworth David to Ernest Shackleton, 4 November 1913. Typed letter, S.F.P.

[10] Hobbs (1941), fn. p. 88.

[11] Royal Geographical Society. Report of a conference of a committee of the Society with Sir Ernest Shackleton, 4 March 1914. S.F.P.

[12] D. W. Freshfield (1917), *Geogr. J.*, Vol. 50, pp. 1–2.

[13] *Field*, Vol. 123, p. 45 (1914).

[14] Lord Rosebery to Ernest Shackleton, 16 October 1912 and 18 May 1914. Letters, S.F.P.

[15] Ernest Shackleton to the Lords Commissioners of the Admiralty, 2 February 1914. Letter, Admiralty.

[16] Worsley (1931), pp. 12–13.

[17] R. W. James to M. F., October 1955. Letter in answer to questions.

[18] Leonard D. A. Hussey. Recorded conversation with J. F., 12 October 1955.

[19] Walter E. How. Recorded conversation with J. F., 1 September 1955.

[20] A. H. Macklin. Recorded conversation with J. F., 12 and 13 March 1956.

[21] J. A. McIlroy. Recorded conversation with J. F., 26 August 1955.

[22] Brittain (n.d.), p. 197.

[23] Ernest Shackleton to Emily Shackleton, dated 'Friday, on the Glacier', S.F.P.

[24] Bruce (1911), p. 107.

[25] J. L. Cope. MS. report on Ross Sea Party, 1917, in S.F.P.

[26] W. G. Macpherson and others (1923).

[27] Scott (1905).

[28] *Daily Mirror*. Undated cutting in S.P.R.I.

[29] R. T. Pemberton, Managing Director of the Permutit Company Ltd., to M. F., 11 April 1957. Letter in answer to questions.

[30] Hurley (1948), pp. 3–4.

[31] Ernest Shackleton to Emily Shackleton, 1 January 1908, MS. letter, S.F.P.

[32] A. H. Macklin to M. F., 21 May 1957. Letter in answer to questions.

CHAPTER XVIII

[1] *Daily Mail*, 16 July 1914.

[2] Ernest Shackleton to Emily Shackleton, 31 August, 27 September, 26 October and 4 December 1914 (and two undated letters). MS. letters, S.F.P.

[3] *Strathspey Herald*, 27 July 1914.

[4] William Bakewell to M. F., letter 16 April 1956.

[5] Worsley (1931), p. 5.

[6] Ernest Shackleton, *Endurance* diary. (Isolated extracts from this in typescript in S.F.P.)

[7] Ernest Shackleton to Ernest Perris, letter 30 November 1914, from South Georgia. Copy in S.F.P.

[8] Gerald Lysaght to Leonard Tripp, 29 November 1922, MS. letter in Tripp papers, Alexander Turnbull Library, N.Z.

[9] Theodore Savory. Miscellaneous notes, kindly given to the writers in 1955.

[10] Ernest Shackleton to Janet Stancomb-Wills, 17 July 1917. MS. letter, S.F.P.

[11] Ernest Shackleton to W. L. Allardyce, 6 March 1914. Public Record Office, Minute Falklands 8807. Quoted with permission.

[12] Public Record Office, Falklands 10397, 20 March 1914. Quoted with permission.

Chapter XIX

[1] Shackleton (1919), p. 11.

[2] A. H. Macklin. Recorded conversation with J. F., 12 and 13 March 1956.

[3] Sir James Wordie. Recorded conversation with J. F., 31 July 1955.

[4] Frank Worsley. MS. diary of *Endurance* expedition. From microfilm copy made for the writers from the original in S.P.R.I.

[5] A. H. Macklin. Typescript account (substituted for lost diary) of *Endurance* expedition up to 28 October 1915, kindly lent by the diarist.

[6] Harry McNeish. MS. diary of *Endurance* expedition. From microfilm of original in Alexander Turnbull Library, Wellington, N.Z.

[7] William Bakewell to M. F. Letter, 16 April 1956.

[8] Hurley (1948), pp. 44, 62–5.

[9] Lionel Greenstreet. Recorded conversation with J. F., 11 October 1955.

[10] Worsley (1931), p. 39.

Chapter XX

[1] Ernest Shackleton. MS. diary *Endurance* expedition. S.F.P.

[2] Shackleton (1919), pp. 78, 80, 87–8.

[3] A. H. Macklin. Recorded conversations with J. F., 12 and 13 March 1956.

[4] A. H. Macklin. MS. diary *Endurance* expedition (from 28 October 1915 onwards), kindly lent by the diarist.

[5] Frank Worsley. MS. diary of *Endurance* expedition. From microfilm copy made for the writers from the original in S.P.R.I.

[6] L. D. A. Hussey. Recorded conversations with J. F., 12 October and 12 November 1955.

[7] A. H. Macklin to M. F. Letter of 12 June 1956.

[8] Ernest Shackleton and the members of the *Endurance* expedition. Copy of formal Agreement in S.F.P.

[9] See citation (5) above; but extra entry not under date heading.

[10] R. W. James. TS. transcript of diary *Endurance* expedition in S.F.P.

[11] Harry McNeish. MS. diary *Endurance* expedition. From microfilm of original in Alexander Turnbull Library, Wellington, N.Z.

[12] William Bakewell to M. F. Letter of 16 April 1956.

[13] Walter How. Recorded conversation with J. F., 1 September 1955.
[14] R. W. James to M. F. Letter of October 1955.
[15] Hurley (1948), pp. 80–2.
[16] Lionel Greenstreet. Recorded conversation with J. F., 11 October 1955.
[17] Worsley (1931) and (1940).
[18] Hussey (1949), pp. 152–4.
[19] Charles Green. Recorded conversation with J. F., 5 September 1955.

CHAPTER XXI

[1] Worsley (1940), pp. 79, 93, 134, 140–1, 165–6, 185–6.
[2] Shackleton (1919), pp. 167, 174–5, 202, 205, 209.
[3] Harry McNeish. MS. diary *Endurance* expedition. From microfilm of original in Alexander Turnbull Library, Wellington, N.Z.
[4] Robertson (1956), p. 59.
[5] Jean Worsley (Mrs. Frank Worsley). Recorded conversation with J. F., 12 October 1956.
[6] Ernest Shackleton to Emily Shackleton, MS. letters of 3 June, 22 August, 3 September 1916. S.F.P.
[7] Ernest Shackleton to Ernest Perris. MS. letter of 3 June 1916. S.F.P.
[8] *Times* (London), 25 March 1916.
[9] Royal Geographical Society and John King Davis. Shorthand notes of conversation on 10 April 1916, and *verbatim* extracts from it, preserved in the *Endurance* file of the Society, with whose kind permission they have been consulted.
[10] *Geogr. J.* (1916), Vol. 48, pp. 498–50.
[11] A quotation from Pinochet de la Barra (1948), p. 31, kindly translated and sent to us by José Miguel Barros, Second Secretary of the Chilean Embassy in Washington, on 18 August 1955.
[12] A. H. Macklin. MS. diary *Endurance* expedition (from 28 October 1915 onwards), lent by the diarist.
[13] Joyce (1929), particularly pp. 73, 80, 87, 135, 185.
[14] Ernest Shackleton to Æneas Mackintosh, 18 September 1914. MS. (copy) letter, S.F.P.
[15] A. O. Stevens. TS. report on Ross Sea party, in S.F.P.
[16] Mill (1923), p. 204.
[17] J. R. Stenhouse to Ernest Shackleton, 15 February 1917. MS. letter, S.F.P.
[18] Leslie J. F. Thomson. TS. copy diary *Aurora* expedition, kindly lent by his widow, Mrs. V. Thomson, owner of the original (particularly entries for 7 and 8 February and 6 May 1915).
[19] Æneas Mackintosh to A. O. Stevens, 26 October 1915. MS. letter, S.F.P.
[20] Æneas Mackintosh to J. R. Stenhouse, 29 August 1915. MS. letter S.F.P.
[21] R. W. Richards. Summary MS. accounts of events in McMurdo Sound, preserved in S.F.P.; these accounts were used in Ernest

Joyce's MS. report, 'Circumstances concerning the loss of Captain Mackintosh and V. G. Hayward, 1916', also in S.F.P.

[22] Ernest Shackleton to Lords Commissioners of the Admiralty. Draft cable, S.F.P.

[23] R. W. Richards to M. F., 28 March 1957. Letter in answer to questions.

CHAPTER XXII

[1] Ernest Shackleton to Emily Shackleton. MS. letters of 23 October, 10 November and 6 December 1916; 27 February, 20 and 28 August, and 9 November 1917: 1 November 1918: 29 January 1919. S.F.P.

[2] Ernest Shackleton to Ernest Perris. Copy letter, 23 October 1916. S.F.P.

[3] Leonard Tripp to Ernest Shackleton. Copy letters 8 November 1916 and 14 March and 25 April 1917. From microfilm of Tripp papers in Alexander Turnbull Library, Wellington, N.Z.

[4] *Times* (London), 5 September 1916.

[5] Aurora Committee in Australia to J. J. Kinsey. Cablegram (and appended drafts of reply) of 15 December 1916. From microfilm of Kinsey papers, Alexander Turnbull Library.

[6] Ernest Shackleton to Aurora Committee in Australia, sent via Robert McNab. Holograph undated, presumably of cable. From microfilm of Tripp papers. Alexander Turnbull Library.

[7] Ernest Shackleton. MS. diary *Aurora* relief expedition 1916. S.F.P.

[8] Mill (1923), pp. 242, 261.

[9] Leonard Tripp to Emily Shackleton. Copy letter of 14 March 1923. From microfilm of Tripp papers, Alexander Turnbull Library.

[10] Joyce (1929), p. 202.

[11] E. H. Shackleton. Report on search for bodies of Mackintosh and Hayward, in J. K. Davis (1917).

[12] G. Moore to Leonard Tripp. MS. letter of 14 March 1917. From microfilm of Tripp papers, Alexander Turnbull Library.

[13] Edward Saunders to Leonard Tripp. Copy letter of 24 June 1917. From microfilm of Tripp papers, Alexander Turnbull Library.

[14] Shackleton (1917).

[15] Emily Shackleton to Leonard Tripp. MS. letters of 3 May and 13 or 18 July 1917. From microfilm of Tripp papers.

[16] Ernest Shackleton to Leonard Tripp. Postscript to MS. letter from Emily Shackleton of July 1917, and MS. letters of 21 April and 20 July 1917. From microfilm of Tripp papers.

[17] Ernest Shackleton to Dame Janet Stancomb-Wills. Copy letter of 4 September 1917, in Mill Bequest at S.P.R.I.: and MS. letter of 31 May 1918, in S.F.P.

[18] Leonard Tripp to Sir Thomas Mackenzie. Copy letter of 1 March 1917. From microfilm of Tripp papers.

[19] Leonard Tripp to Ernest Perris. Copy letter of 20 March 1917. From microfilm of Tripp papers.

[20] Lord Beaverbrook to Ernest Shackleton. MS. letter of 20 June 1918 from Ministry of Information, S.F.P.

[21] M. P. Fisher to Mrs. Fisher. MS. letters of 11 and 15 August 1918, in possession of Mrs. Freda Fee (daughter of the late Mr. M. P. Fisher) who has kindly allowed us to use them.

[22] Ernest Shackleton to George Constantinescu, 27 October 1918. From photostat copy of MS. letter in the possession of Mr. Constantinescu, and kindly given to the writers by him.

[23] Frank Worsley to Leonard Tripp. MS. letter of 26 October 1918. Microfilm of Tripp papers.

[24] Reginald Greenhough to M. F. Letter of 9 October 1956.

[25] Maynard (1928), p. 156.

[26] A. F. Birch-Jones to M. F. Letter of 14 November 1956.

[27] *Westminster Gazette*, 12 May 1923, under heading 'The General Reader'.

[28] Sir Shane Leslie. Recorded conversation with J. F., 17 November 1955.

[29] Ernest Shackleton to Leonard Tripp, 17 March 1917. MS. letter, Tripp papers, Alexander Turnbull Library, Wellington, N.Z.

[30] R. W. Richards to M. F., 28 March 1957. Letter in answer to questions.

[31] B. C. Howells to M. F., 30 May 1957. Letter in answer to questions.

[32] Leonard Tripp to H. R. Mill, 1922. Statement for use in biography. Mill Bequest, S.P.R.I.

[33] Mill (1923), pp. 261–62.

[34] G. E. Wilson to M.F., 9 May 1957. Letter in answer to questions.

CHAPTER XXIII

[1] Ernest Shackleton to Assistant Governor-General Murmansk, April 1919. Included in C. E. Vulliamy (1929), pp. 313–17.

[2] Ernest Shackleton to Lieutenant-General Miller, Governor-General at Murmansk, 7 June 1919. In C. E. Vulliamy (1929), p. 318.

[3] *Daily Mirror*, 12 May 1923.

[4] Eleanor Shackleton to M. F., 23 January 1956.

[5] Documents, National Film Archive.

[6] Arthur R. Hinks (Secretary, R.G.S.) to Ernest Shackleton, 1 March 1920. Reprinted in prospectus (see citation 8).

[7] V. Stefansson to Ernest Shackleton, 15 April 1920. Reprinted in prospectus (see citation 8).

[8] *Plans for a North Polar Expedition*. Printed prospectus drawn up by Shackleton supposedly in 1920. Copy in possession of Dr. A. H. Macklin, who kindly lent it to the writers.

[9] Ernest Shackleton to Admiral Field, 23 December 1920 (and reply 27 December 1920). Admiralty File. Quoted with permission.

[10] Ernest Shackleton to H. R. Mill, 15 March 1921. MS. letter in Mill Bequest, S.P.R.I.

[11] Ernest Shackleton to A. H. Macklin, 16 May 1921. Cable in possession of Dr. Macklin, with whose permission it is quoted.

[12] Dr. A. H. Macklin to M. F., 17 April 1956. Letter with answers to questions.

CHAPTER XXIV

[1] Unidentified newspaper, 3 April 1920; World Celebrity of the Week, No. 59. Cutting in collection presented by Mrs. George Pitcairn to S.P.R.I.

[2] *Plans for an Oceanographical and Sub-Antarctic Expedition.* Printed prospectus drawn up by Shackleton, supposedly in 1920. Copy in possession of Dr. A. H. Macklin, who kindly lent it to the writers.

[3] The Shackleton (1921) Expedition. Air Ministry Questionnaire. TS. document in possession of Dr. A. H. Macklin, who kindly lent it to the writers.

[4] *Times,* 26 September 1921. Interview with Shackleton.

[5] H. R. Mill to Ernest Shackleton, 5 November 1921. Copy letter in Mill Bequest, S.P.R.I.

[6] H. R. Mill (1945), p. 122.

[7] *Evening News,* 15 September 1921 (W. McCartney).

[8] *Daily Graphic,* interview in summer 1921, repeated in notice of Shackleton's death, 30 January 1922.

[9] *Daily Mail,* 26 September 1921. Interview with Shackleton.

[10] A. H. Macklin. Recorded conversations with J. F., 12 and 13 March 1956.

[11] Charles J. Green. Recorded conversation with J. F., 23 August 1955.

[12] W. E. How. Recorded conversation with J. F., 1 September 1955.

[13] J. W. Dell. Recorded conversation with J. F., 10 October 1955.

[14] Sir Hubert Wilkins to M. F., 27 June 1956. Letter with answers to questions.

[15] Sir Roderick Carr. Recorded conversation with J. F., 11 December 1955.

[16] Professor G. Vibert Douglas to M. F., 29 November 1955. Letter with answers to questions.

[17] Mrs. John Quiller Rowett. Recorded conversation with J. F., 29 November 1955.

[18] J. W. S. Marr. Recorded conversation with J. F., 20 November 1955.

[19] *Times,* 30 June 1921.

[20] J. A. McIlroy. Recorded conversation with J. F., 26 August 1955.

[21] L. D. A. Hussey. Recorded conversations with J. F., 12 October and 12 November 1955.

[22] E. F. Knight (n.d.).

[23] Emily Shackleton to Dame Janet Stancomb-Wills, 6 July 1921. MS. letter, S.F.P.

[24] *Star,* 17 September 1921.

[25] *Observer,* 18 September 1921.

[26] *Times,* 4th Leader, 29 June 1921.

[27] Mill (1923), p. 268.

[28] Ernest Shackleton to H. R. Mill, 24 June 1921. Mill Bequest, S.P.R.I.

[29] A. H. Macklin to M. F., 24 May 1957. Letter in answer to questions.

30 Agreement between J. W. Dell and Ernest Shackleton, 16 September 1921. In possession of J. W. Dell and used with his permission.
31 Alfred Berry to M. F., 11 March 1957. Letter in answer to questions.

CHAPTER XXV

1 Marr (1923), pp. 6–7.
2 *Daily Mail*, 24 September 1921.
3 Ernest Shackleton. MS. *Quest* diary, S.F.P.
4 J. W. S. Marr. Recorded conversation with J. F., 28 November 1955.
5 Sir Roderick Carr. Recorded conversation with J. F., 11 December 1955.
6 Professor G. Vibert Douglas to M. F., 29 November 1955. Letter in answer to questions.
7 Sir Hubert Wilkins to M. F., 27 June 1956. Letter in answer to questions.
8 Ernest Shackleton to Emily Shackleton, 18 October, 27 October and 17 December 1921. MS. letters, S.F.P.
9 Ernest Shackleton to Alfred Cook, 5 October 1921. Copy report in form of letter, S.F.P.
10 A. H. Macklin. MS. *Quest* diary, lent by the diarist.
11 Wild (1923a), pp. 47–8.
12 M. Bruce (1954), pp. 102–3.
13 Christopher Naisbitt to M. F., October 1956. Memorandum on Shackleton.
14 Captain A. D. P. Sharpus to his father. Letter reprinted in newspaper (unknown name and date) 1922.
15 Ernest Shackleton to Janet Stancomb-Wills, 17 December 1921. MS. letter, S.F.P.
16 Christopher Naisbitt. MS. *Quest* diary. In possession of the diarist, who has given the writers permission to use it.
17 *Times*, 31 January 1922.
18 Charles Green. Recorded conversation with J. F., 23 August 1955.
19 J. W. Dell. Recorded conversation with J. F., 10 October 1955.
20 Baltasar Brum and J. A. Buero. Presidential Decree of January 1922. Copy of translation sent to Foreign Office by Edward Hope-Vere, 9 February 1922, in S.F.P.
21 Admiralty Dispatch No. 30 of 17 February 1922. Quoted with permission.
22 *Times*, 3 February 1922. Fourth leader, 'Farthest South'.
23 Matthews (1931), p. 148.
24 L. D. A. Hussey to Lady Shackleton, 30 January 1922. Cablegram in S.F.P.
25 C. Powell to Lady Shackleton, 11 January 1932. MS. letter in S.F.P.
26 *Contemporary Review*, Vol. 121, pp. 321–8.
27 *Geogr. J.*, Vol. 79, p. 167. Speeches at the unveiling of the Shackleton Memorial.

[28] Harold E. Lumsdale to Emily Shackleton, 24 February 1933. MS. letter, S.F.P.

[29] *Nature*, Vol. 109, pp. 143–5.

[30] *Geogr. J.*, Vol. 59, pp. 228–30.

[31] F. L. Horton to M.F., 16 May 1957. Letter in answer to questions.

[32] Lloyd's Registry of Shipping, inquiry, July 1957.

[33] Green and Pollinger (1956), p. 53.

APPENDIX F
Bibliography

There are many bibliographies of the Antarctic and its exploration; and this one does not attempt to be a complete one, even of the period in which Ernest Shackleton explored the south. It contains the principal references cited in the text of this book, and some other citations of general interest. It excludes most of the citations of the published scientific results of the Shackleton Expedition (which are the subject of the Appendix (p. 512) kindly provided by Sir James Wordie and Dr. Brian Roberts, reprinted, with minor additions, from their paper published in 1943), and minor notes cited in the References (p. 526).

AMUNDSEN, Roald (1912). *The South Pole . . . Norwegian Antarctic Expedition in the* Fram, *1910–12*. London, Murray, 2 vols.

ANON. (1908). 'Stamps for the South Pole!', *London Philatelist*, Vol. 17 (195), pp. 53–4.

ARMITAGE, A. B. (1905). *Two Years in the Antarctic; being a narrative of the British National Antarctic Expedition*. London.

ARMITAGE, A. B. (1925). *From Cadet to Commodore*. London.

BAGSHAWE, Richard W., and GOLDUP, John (1951). 'The postal history of the Antarctic, 1904–49', *Polar Rec.*, Vol. 6 (41), pp. 45–79.

BEGBIE, Harold (1922). *Shackleton a Memory*. London, Mills and Boon.

BERNACCHI, L. C. (1938). *The Saga of the Discovery*. London, Blackie.

BRITTAIN, Sir Harry (n.d.). *Happy Pilgrimage*. London, Hutchinson.

BRODRICK, Alan Houghton (1947). 'Shackleton, 1874–1922', *in* André LEROI-GOURHAN (ed.), *Les Explorateurs célèbres*. Paris and Geneva, Mazenod.

BROWN, R. N. Rudmose (1923). *A Naturalist at the Poles. The life, work and voyages of Dr. W. S. Bruce the polar explorer*. London, Seeley Service.

BRUCE, Sir Michael (1954). *Tramp Royal*. London, Elek.

BRUCE, W. S. (1911). *Polar Exploration*. London, Williams and Norgate.

BYRD, Richard Evelyn (1931). *Little America*. London, G. P. Putnam's Sons.

BYRD, Richard Evelyn (1937). *Exploring with Byrd . . .* New York, G. P. Putnam's Sons.

CARSE, Duncan (1956). 'In Shackleton's Tracks', *Times*, 16 Mar.

CHERRY-GARRARD, Apsley (1922). *The Worst Journey in the World . . .* London, Constable, 2 Vols.

CRESSWELL, M. (1938). 'Sir Ernest Shackleton', *Marine Observer*, Vol. 15, pp. 11–17, 57–60.

DAVID, M. Edgeworth (1937). *The Life of Sir T. W. Edgeworth David*, *K.B.E.*, *F.R.S.* London, Edward Arnold.

[DAVIS, John King] (1918). *Aurora Relief Expedition. Report of voyage by Commander, 20 December 1916 to 9 February 1917*. Melbourne, Govt. of Australia.

DAVIS, John King (1919). *With the* Aurora *in the Antarctic*. London, Melrose.

DEBENHAM, Frank (1948). 'The problem of the great Ross Barrier', *Geogr. J.*, Vol. 112, pp. 196–218.

GIÆVER, John (1954). *The White Desert; the official account of the Norwegian-British-Swedish Antarctic Expedition; . . .* London, Chatto and Windus.

GREEN, William, and POLLINGER, Gerald (1956). *The World's Fighting Planes*. London, Macdonald, 2nd ed.

HARRIS, Leslie J. (1953). 'Scurvy in retrospect', *Nature*, Vol. 172, pp. 50–2.

HAYES, J. Gordon (1928). *Antarctica: a treatise on the Southern Continent*. London, Richards Press.

HAYES, J. Gordon (1932). *The Conquest of the South Pole: Antarctic exploration 1906–1931*. London, Thornton Butterworth.

HOBBS, W. H. (1941). *Explorers of the Antarctic*. New York, Field.

HURLEY, Frank (1925). *Argonauts of the South*. New York, G. P. Putnam's Sons.

HURLEY, Frank (1948). *Shackleton's Argonauts. A saga of the Antarctic ice-packs . . .* Sydney and London, Angus and Robertson.

HUSSEY, L. D. A. (1949). *South with Shackleton*. London, Sampson Low.

HYDROGRAPHIC DEPARTMENT, ADMIRALTY (1956). *Antarctic Pilot*. London, Admiralty, 2nd ed. of 1948 with revisions to supplement No. 4.

IRONSIDE, Edmund (1953). *Archangel 1918–1919*. London, Constable.

JOYCE, Ernest E. Mills (1929). *The South Polar Trail . . .* London, Duckworth.

KEARNS, William H., Jr., and BRITTON, Beverley (1955). *The Silent Continent*. London, Gollancz.

KENDALL, E. J. C. (1955). 'Scurvy during some British Polar Expeditions, 1875–1917', *Polar Rec.*, Vol. 7 (51), pp. 467–85.

KNIGHT, E. F. (n.d.), *The Cruise of the 'Alerte'*. London, Nelson.

McLEAN, W., and SHACKLETON, Ernest Henry (1900). "*O.H.M.S.*" *an illustrated record of the voyage of S.S. "Tintagel Castle" conveying twelve hundred soldiers from Southampton to Cape Town March 1900*. London, Simpkin Marshall, Hamilton, Kent & Co., Ltd.

MACPHERSON, W. G., and others (1923). 'Medical services: hygiene of the war', London, H.M.S.O., Vol. 2. Part of *History of the Great War based on official documents*.

MARKHAM, Clements R. (1913). 'On the exploration of the Antarctic Continent', *Rep. Brit. Ass. Dundee, 1912.*

MARKHAM, Sir Clements R. (1921). *The Lands of Silence: a history of Arctic and Antarctic exploration.* Cambridge, University Press.

MARR, [J. W. S.] (1923). *Into the Frozen South.* London, Cassell.

MARSHALL, Eric Stewart (1943). 'An Antarctic episode', *Medical Press and Circular, London,* for 8 Dec., pp. 359–62.

MARSTON, George Edward and MURRAY, James (1913). *Antarctic Days.* London, Melrose.

MATTHEWS, Leo Harrison (1931). *South Georgia, the British Empire's sub-Antarctic outpost.* London, Simpkin Marshall, and Bristol, John Wright and Sons.

MAWSON, Douglas (1915). *The Home of the Blizzard being the story of the Australasian Antarctic Expedition, 1911–1914.* London, Hodder and Stoughton, 2 vols.

MAYNARD, Sir Charles Clarkson Martin (1928). *The Murmansk Venture.* London.

MILL, Hugh Robert (1909). 'Ernest Henry Shackleton, M.V.O.', *Travel and Exploration,* Vol. 2, pp. 1–10.

MILL, Hugh Robert (1923). *The Life of Sir Ernest Shackleton.* London, Heinemann. The new edition of 1924 has some alterations.

MILL, Hugh Robert (1930). *The Record of the Royal Geographical Society, 1830–1930.* London, Roy. Geogr. Soc.

MILL, Hugh Robert (1945). 'Life Interests of a Geographer, 1861–1944; an experiment in biography'. A mimeographed document privately issued by the author.

MILL, Hugh Robert (1951). *An Autobiography.* London and New York, Longmans, Green.

MOUNTEVANS, Lord (1946). *An Adventurous Life.* London and New York, Hutchinson.

ORDE-LEES, T. (1955). 'The "Endurance" story', *Antarctic News Bull.,* No. 19, pp. 13–15.

OWEN, Russell (1948). *The Antarctic Ocean.* London, Museum Press.

PINOCHET DE LA BARRA, Oscar (1948). *La Antarctica chilena. Estudio de nuestros derechos.* Santiago de Chile, Editorial del Pacifico S.A.

PIRIE, J. H. Harvey (1948). *Antarctic Posts and Stamps.* London, Stamp Collecting Ltd.

PRIESTLEY, Raymond Edward (1938). 'Sir Edgeworth David', *Australian Quarterly,* June.

ROBERTSON, R. B. (1956). *Of Whales and Men.* London.

SAROLEA, Charles (1922). 'Sir Ernest Shackleton, a study in personality', *Contemporary Review,* Vol. 121, pp. 321–8.

SCHOLES, Arthur (1951). *Fourteen Men; the story of the Australian Antarctic Expedition to Heard Island.* London, George Allen and Unwin. (First publ. 1949, Melbourne, F. W. Cheshire.)

SCOTT, Robert Falcon (1905). *The Voyage of the 'Discovery'.* London, Smith Elder & Co., 2 vols.

SCOTT, Robert Falcon, *ed.* (1907). *The South Polar Times.* London, Smith Elder & Co.

SEAVER, George (1933). *Edward Wilson of the Antarctic* . . . London, John Murray.

SEFI, Alexander J. (1912). *King Edward VII Land.*

SHACKLETON, Ernest Henry (1909). 'Life in the Antarctic', *Pearson's Mag.*, pp. 308–22.

SHACKLETON, Ernest Henry (1909a). 'Some Results of the British Antarctic Expedition, 1907–09', *Geogr. J.*, Vol. 34, pp. 481–500 (maps p. 592).

SHACKLETON, Ernest Henry (1909b). *The Heart of the Antarctic.* London, Heinemann, 3 vols., the third being 'The Antarctic book, winter quarters, 1907–09', in a limited ed. of 300 copies.

SHACKLETON, Sir Ernest Henry (1914). 'The Making of an Explorer', *Pearson's Mag.*, pp. 138–42.

SHACKLETON, Sir Ernest Henry (1917). *Sir Ernest Shackleton's Stirring Appeal for Men for the A.I.F.* Issued by the New South Wales Recruiting Committee. Sydney, W. A. Gullick, Govt. Printer.

SHACKLETON, Sir Ernest Henry (1919). *South: the story of Shackleton's last expedition 1914–1917.* London, Heinemann.

TAYLOR, Griffith (1916). *With Scott—the Silver Lining.* London, Smith Elder.

VULLIAMY, C. E. *ed.* (1929). *The Red Archives, Russian state papers and other documents relating to the years 1915–1918.* London, Bles.

WILD, Frank (1923). 'The voyage of the "Quest"', *Geogr. J.*, Vol. 61, pp. 73–108.

WILD, Frank (1923a). *Shackleton's Last Voyage; the story of the Quest.* London, Cassell.

W[ORDIE], James Mann, and R[OBERTS], Brian B. (1943). 'The Scientific Results of the Shackleton Antarctic Expeditions', *Polar Rec.*, Vol. 4 (26), pp. 72–6.

WORSLEY, Frank A. (1924). 'Shackleton's boat journey', *Blue Peter*, Vol. 4, pp. 47–54, 110, 141–8, 223–9, 242–7, 318–24.

WORSLEY, Frank A. (1931). *Endurance, an Epic of Polar Adventure.* London, Philip Allan.

WORSLEY, Frank A. (1940). *Shackleton's Boat Journey.* London, Hodder and Stoughton, Black Jacket Series.

INDEX